THE AWAKENING OF CHINA
1793–1949

ROGER PELISSIER

THE AWAKENING OF CHINA

1793-1949

EDITED AND TRANSLATED BY
MARTIN KIEFFER

G. P. PUTNAM'S SONS
NEW YORK

TO ALL WHO HAVE REPORTED ON CHINA

CONTENTS

	EDITOR'S PREFACE	11
	CHRONOLOGICAL TABLE	17
I	THE WESTERN "BARBARIANS" AT THE DOORS OF CHINA	27
II	THE OPIUM WAR, *1839–42*	54
III	THE T'AI P'ING REBELLION, *1851–64*	88
IV	THE ANGLO-FRENCH EXPEDITIONS, *1856–64*	122
V	THE ERA OF VICEROYS, *1860–94*	159
VI	THE PARTITION OF CHINA, *1894–1905*	193
VII	THE END OF THE CHINESE EMPIRE, *1906–16*	230
VIII	BETWEEN ANARCHY AND RECONQUEST, *1917–28*	261
IX	VICTORIES OF THE KUOMINTANG, *1928–35*	311
X	FROM MANCHUKUO TO THE "UNITED FRONT," *1931–37*	342
XI	THE SINO-JAPANESE WAR, *1937–45*	367
XII	RED CHINA, *1935–45*	413
XIII	THE COLLAPSE OF THE KUOMINTANG, *1945–49*	457
	SOURCES	505
	ACKNOWLEDGMENTS	519
	INDEXES	523

Illustrations appear after pages 160 and 384.

MAPS

GENERAL MAP OF CHINA 24–25

SPHERES OF INFLUENCE OF THE GREAT POWERS IN
CHINA, c.1900 195

ROUTES OF THE LONG MARCH 339

AREAS OF COMMUNIST DOMINATION, 1944–45 474

PREFACE

FROM ANCIENT times to the present day, the Chinese have called their country *Chong Kuo*, or "Land of the Middle". This name, besides being considerably older than that of any Western country, is also a very proud one. Until well into the nineteenth century, its full meaning was best illustrated by Chinese maps of the world. In the middle of four seas a massive expanse of land, larger than all other countries put together, represented China. Scattered about this land mass and looking insignificant by comparison were a number of islands called England, Africa, Spain, Portugal, India, Russia, Holland, France, America, and so on. In the opinion of her scholars, China lay in the "middle" of the world and for all practical purposes *was* the world, the beginning and end of all creation. Sprawling mightily across the surface of the earth and faithfully devoted to a rigid pattern of ancestral traditions, China lived in peaceful isolation behind the forbidding natural barriers—mountain ranges, deserts and oceans—that enabled her to shut out the rest of the world during the greater part of her long history.

Traditionally, the Chinese kept to themselves and preserved their conservative ways. So much, in fact, did they cling to their indigenous habits that conservatism passed into the very marrow of the people and became a striking racial characteristic. On the other hand, the Chinese were convinced that their "Celestial Empire"—so called because its ruler bore the title "Son of Heaven"—had no equal on earth. To them, China was not only the largest and most populated, but also the most civilized of all nations. In the middle of the world she stood unique, self-sufficient and unchanging, the living symbol and embodiment of strength, greatness and stability. The Chinese knew little about the small "island" nations scattered throughout the seas, and yet their sailors traveled far and wide before the seafaring Westerners began roaming the oceans. Moslem chroniclers report Chinese ships on the

Euphrates in the seventh century, and during the golden age of the large oceangoing junks—the twelfth through the fifteenth centuries —China's remarkably well-built vessels sailed to India, Arabia, and the east coast of Africa (where Chinese coins are still dug up occasionally). The bluff and sturdy junks were seaworthy enough to circumnavigate Africa, and, had they chosen to do so, the Chinese could certainly have "discovered" Europe, instead of waiting for the more curious and enterprising Europeans to come to the Far East.

But the "Celestials" were not really interested in getting closely acquainted with humankind at large. Nor did they desire to conquer overseas territories like Europe. China never built a colonial empire, and before the nineteenth century few of her people settled permanently abroad. Why should they? Other countries were so much smaller, and therefore poorer, than their own. China's civilization had flourished for thousands of years, and, as far as the Chinese knew, their way of life lacked nothing to stir envy of other nations. Also, why concern oneself with other peoples' business? In order to live happily and undisturbed, a nation had better mind her own affairs, which she alone understood.

In the long run, this aloofness and lack of regular intercourse with other cultural groups bred in the "black-haired race", as the Chinese call themselves, an intense feeling of superiority and contempt. For many centuries, they had known no other people with a civilization equal to their own and as a result looked upon the rest of mankind as "barbarians" who had nothing to teach the Celestial Empire. By the same token, the educated Chinese was supremely proud of his country's amazing social immobility, the persistence of manners, customs, rites and institutions which in a vast territory had welded hundreds of millions of individuals into one human family sharing the Confucian ethics of charity toward others and loyalty toward one's kin. In his eyes, China owed her stability and relative happiness first and foremost to her enduring civilization. And he was right: traditional China was, and to some extent probably still is, a civilization rather than a nation.

As for the Europeans, they owed their first reliable information about China to the famed Venetian traveler Marco Polo. In 1298, three years after his return from a quarter-century-long sojourn in Asia, Polo dictated his memoirs to a friend. Within a short time the original manuscript of the *Travels* had been copied and reproduced often enough to become a sort of "best seller" that passed through the hands of practically every well-read man in Europe. Polo's amazing adventures in the Far East, and more particularly his life at the sumptuous court of Kublai Khan, at once fired the imagination of princes, artists, scholars and merchants. Western explorers set out to find a sea route to China, or Cathay as they called her, but it was another two centuries before Vasco da Gama ventured beyond the Cape of Good Hope and thus showed the way to the lands of spices and silk. Only a few years earlier, Columbus had sailed westward in the hope of reaching India and Cathay. Subsequently, the Portuguese and Dutch were the first Westerners to trade with China and to bring to Europe, together with her products, the magic of her colorful and strange civilization.

Also during the second half of the thirteenth century, Western missionaries, Franciscans for the most part, began preaching the gospel in China. Like Marco Polo, they trudged and trekked their way along the old caravan road, or "silk road", that linked Sinkiang Province (where China exploded her first A-bomb) to the southwestern plains of Siberia. Giovanni de Montecorvino, despatched in 1288 by Pope Nicholas IV, became the first successful promoter of the Christian faith in China. He baptized some 5,000 converts and in 1307 was named Archbishop of Peking by the Pope. Toward the end of the fourteenth century, however, the Mongol conqueror Timur (Tamerlane) ordered the massacre of all Christians throughout his vast domains, after which missionary activities in Asia came to a near standstill for several generations. Not until the later part of the sixteenth century did Catholic missionaries resume their preaching and teaching in the Land of the Middle. This time, the leading role fell to the Jesuits, and they used the latest European mathematical and geographical knowledge as their calling card. The most outstanding figure of that period was Father Matteo Ricci, a distinguished linguist and mathematician who rose to a prominent position at the Court of Peking. Among the hundreds of volumes which the Jesuits wrote about China, many are still of great historical value today, but they were not published until the nineteenth century and therefore failed to enlighten Europe at a time when accurate information was most needed there.

Trade and religion actually were the main forces that lured Europe, and subsequently America, to the Far East. In both fields, the Westerners soon realized the enormous opportunities offered them by China and did their best to increase their volume of trade on the one hand and the number of proselytes on the other. As a rule, however, the Chinese proved unreceptive to the goods or convictions which the foreigners endeavored to bring into their lives. Only toward the middle of the nineteenth century did Western trade begin to expand substantially, but the methods employed by many Westerners were all too often incompatible with the teachings of their missionaries. The latter, whether Catholic or Protestant, had to admit that China was arid ground for sowing the gospel. Not that the Chinese were hostile —they proved frequently more tolerant and broad-minded than Westerners—but it was quite difficult to overcome their fundamental skepticism which bordered on irreligion. The overall results of the contacts between East and West thus fell far short of the high expectations harbored by the Western intruders. Many of the latter's ambitious projects never materialized, but this was hardly surprising. For their failures in China, the Westerners could indeed blame their greed and arrogance at least as much as the unreceptive mood of the Chinese who, after all, wished only to be left alone.

The pioneering Portuguese reached the shores of China in the early sixteenth century, yet it took Europe nearly four more centuries, and repeated use of superior force, to break China's determined refusal to have intercourse with "foreign devils". Time and again, she proclaimed her proud and unapproachable supremacy and systematically rejected the pretensions of other nations to be considered as her equal. To growing Western commercial pressure, increased still further by military demonstrations, she opposed the manifold resources of Oriental shrewdness and resilience in her futile struggle against foreign encroachments. Only at the end of the nineteenth century, after the Boxer debacle, did she grudgingly agree to establish normal diplomatic relations with the West. By that time, a series of humiliating defeats, including two occupations of Peking, had more or less forced her to her knees. Also, her leaders had come to realize that China was a giant with clay feet, one that could in no way match the military might of the Western powers. The Chinese government now decided, somewhat belatedly, on a national policy of "self-strengthening", or reorganization and modernization of the country along Western lines.

China's unrelenting opposition to the presence of foreigners on her soil was fully understandable, and so was her suspicion of Western motives. For one thing, the Westerners rarely represented the *élite* of their respective countries. Many Europeans (and Americans) who sought their fortune in China were little better than bandits. On the other hand, the all too obvious and almost exclusive purpose of the nations trading in China was to increase their own wealth and prestige. They were rarely, if ever, entirely disinterested in their dealings with the natives. Indeed, the satisfaction of their many appetites almost always took precedence over their desire to have China benefit from the achievements of Western civilization.

Probably the most important consequence of this continued opposition between Chinese resistance and Western aggressiveness was that East and West practically never met on a footing of equality. With few exceptions, neither the Chinese nor the foreign "barbarians" tried very hard to understand and respect each other. The Europeans, in particular, displayed from the very beginning a kind of master complex which they never quite lost in the course of time. Already in the sixteenth century, the overbearing and often brutal Portuguese, soon imitated by the Dutch, antagonized the peace-loving and easygoing Chinese. Before long, the latter were convinced that little good would come from their association with the greedy foreigners. More than anything else, the European gunboat and land-grabbing policy of the nineteenth century confirmed the Celestials in their belief that all Westerners were barbarians indeed, since they relied on intimidation and force much more than on wisdom and forbearance, as was the traditional Chinese custom. After centuries of more or less regular contacts, the Far Eastern and the Western civilizations still were, and remained, far apart from one another.

Naturally, not all Westerners who went to China behaved in a selfish and domineering manner. A great many men and women among them were ambassadors of goodwill, who generously gave their time and talents in order to help the Chinese live better. Thousands of missionaries, teachers or technicians spent most of their lives in China. They spoke and wrote the difficult Chinese tongue fluently, they loved China and the Chinese, and in turn were loved and respected by the natives. Unfortunately, as is usually the case when a nation looks back upon her relationship with other nations, the negative memories prevail over the good ones. What the Chinese remember best at the present time is the nineteenth century, when their country was a helpless quarry exploited by Western imperialism. They have not forgotten, or forgiven, the military humiliations, the economic exploitation and the "unequal treaties" forced upon them by Western might and appetite.

Today, Red China is in many ways still the "Land of the Middle", at least in the opinion of her leaders. Besides being the third-largest nation in the world, she is by far the most populous, and probably also the most ambitious. She aims at becoming the world's leading power, and the leader of world Communism as well. As in the past, her ultimate goal is to depend as little as possible on the outside world, and once more to become self-sufficient in order to follow her own inspiration whether other nations like it or not. Together with the grudges she still bears the West, the renewed confidence gained from the spectacular progress she has recently achieved in many fields help us understand not only her frequently angry and touchy mood in the realm of international relations, but also her increasingly dogmatic attitude in the current ideological dispute with Moscow. More than ever before, the China of Mao Tse-tung seems to be determined to go her own way, and the least one can say at this time is that she means business, and that she *is* incomparably stronger and more dangerous to her neighbors than ever before in her long history.

Finally, it must be stressed that our information about China, or that of China about the world around her, remains, as before, woefully inadequate. Modern technology has overcome the problems of distance, but man has replaced nature's barriers by even more formidable political obstacles. The little we know about Red China, however, should convince us that she has a number of surprises in store for the not too distant future. Let us hope that her traditional ethics of kindness and patience will not be altogether overlooked in her vast designs!

MARTIN KIEFFER

CHRONOLOGICAL TABLE*

1516   Arrival of first European (Portuguese) caravel in Canton.

1582   Father Matteo Ricci landed in Macao.

1622   The Dutch settled in the Pescadores and on Formosa.

1684   The British *EAST INDIA COMPANY* established a trading center in Macao.

1685   China's ports opened to Western trade by imperial edict.

1692   Catholicism officially tolerated in China, but forbidden in 1717.

1757   Western trade confined to the port of Canton.

1784   Arrival of first American ship in China (Canton).

1793   Unsuccessful mission of Lord Macartney to Peking.

1795   Equally futile mission sent by the *Dutch* East India Company.

1802   First U.S. consular agent appointed to Canton.

1816   New, but still vain, British mission to Peking, under Lord Amherst.

1819   Promulgation of *EIGHT TRADE REGULATIONS* by China.

1833   Expiration of monopoly of trade of the British East India Company, chief importer of Indian *OPIUM* to China.

1834   Fruitless commercial mission of Lord Napier.

1839   Imperial Commissioner Lin Tse-hsü forced surrender of opium in Canton.
Outbreak of the *OPIUM WAR.*

* Main events, places and characters are mentioned in italic type.

1842   The *TREATY OF NANKING* opened five Chinese ports to Western trade.

1844   The Treaty of Wanghsia, signed by Caleb Cushing for the United States, placed American (and ultimately all foreign) residents under extraterritorial jurisdiction.
The French treaty of Whampoa secured toleration of Roman Catholicism, was extended (1845) to Protestantism.

1851   Outbreak of the *T'AI P'ING REBELLION* under Hung Hsiu-ch'üan, mystic founder of the *Heavenly Kingdom of Great Peace*.

1854   Yung Wing first Chinese to graduate from an American University (Yale).

1856   Lorcha *ARROW INCIDENT* at Canton, precipitating *ANGLO-FRENCH EXPEDITIONS*.

1858   The *TREATIES OF TIENTSIN* opened more Chinese ports to Western trade, and permitted legations at Peking.
The Treaty of Aigun ceded the north bank of the Amur to Russia.

1860   Occupation of Peking and *LOOTING OF THE SUMMER PALACE* by the Anglo-French expeditionary forces.
Treaties of Peking, confirming those of Tientsin.
Foundation of *VLADIVOSTOK* ("Master of the East") by Russia.

1861   Creation of the *TSUNGLI YAMEN* to handle foreign affairs.
Empress Dowager *TZU HSI* became *de facto* ruler of China.

1861–4 Decisive role of *TSENG KUO-FAN* and of the *EVER-VICTORIOUS ARMY* (especially under C. G. "Chinese" Gordon) in crushing the waning *T'AI P'ING* rebellion.
Study of the West begun for the purpose of "*SELF-STRENGTHENING*".
(Sir) Robert Hart built up the Chinese Maritime Customs Service as mainstay of government revenue.

1868–70 The American diplomat Anson Burlingame and two Chinese associates were sent on a goodwill mission to Europe and the United States.

1870   The *TIENTSIN MASSACRE* of French missionaries.

1872–81 Hundreds of Chinese students sent to the United States, England and France for technical training.

1876–79 Dreadful *FAMINE* killed millions in northern China.

1877 First Chinese railroad destroyed in Shanghai.

1877–79 Chinese diplomatic missions established in Western capitals and Tokyo.

1885 Second Treaty of Tientsin, by which China recognized the French protectorate in Annam and Tonkin.
The Cantonese scholar *K'ANG YU-WEI* began publishing books that roused China's desire for reform.

1894 Dr. *SUN YAT-SEN* (Sun Wen) organized at Canton the first of his secret (anti-Manchu) societies.

1894–5 The *SINO-JAPANESE WAR* led to the *TREATY OF SHIMONOSEKI*.

1896 Secret Russian-Chinese Treaty, by which China allowed Russia to extend the Trans-Siberian railway across northern Manchuria to Vladivostok.

1897 Germany occupied Kiachow Bay with *TSINGTAO*.

1898 *SCRAMBLE FOR CONCESSIONS*, involving most European Powers.
The *HUNDRED DAYS OF REFORM*, under the guidance of K'ang Yu-wei, ended in failure.

1899 John Hay, American Secretary of State, secured *OPEN DOOR* Policy from the great Powers.

1900 The *BOXER REVOLT*. General attack upon foreigners in Peking and Tientsin. Murder of German Minister, Baron von Ketteler, and siege of foreign legations in Peking. Flight of Tzu Hsi before an international expedition.

1901 The Boxer Protocol provided for punishment of main culprits, and payment over forty years of a heavy indemnity.

1902 Tzu Hsi and her court returned to Peking *by rail*.
The Empress Dowager sponsored sweeping reforms.

1904–5   The *RUSSO-JAPANESE WAR*. Stunning Japanese victories, both on land and at sea. President Roosevelt the mediator.

1905   Creation of a Chinese *MINISTRY OF EDUCATION*. Thousands of Chinese students swarmed to Western-trained Japan.
Dr. Sun Yat-sen organized the *Sworn Chinese Brotherhood Society* in Japan, and became official leader of China's (exiled) revolutionary movements.

1908   Death of *TZU HSI* and of the Emperor.

1911   Outbreak of the *CHINESE REVOLUTION* on the "Double Tenth". General *YUAN SHIH-K'AI*, a pioneer of China's modern army, elected Premier by the National Assembly.

1912   Abdication of the boy Emperor P'u-I (born 1906).
Dr. Sun Yat-sen resigned as President of the Chinese Republic. His party, the *KUOMINTANG*, championed parliamentary government in opposition to strongman Yuan Shih-k'ai.

1913   Sun Yat-sen's "Second Revolution" failed in southern provinces. Yuan Shih-K'ai elected President of the Republic of China, dissolved the National Assembly.

1914   China declared herself neutral in the European conflict. Japan declared war on Germany, captured Tsingtao.

1915   Japan presented her *TWENTY-ONE DEMANDS* to China.

1916   Death of General Yuan Shih-K'ai, followed by period of *ANARCHY* and *CIVIL STRIFE*.
Schism between the governments of Peking and Canton.

1917   *CHINA* (Peking) *DECLARED WAR ON GERMANY AND AUSTRIA-HUNGARY*, with Sun Yat-sen (established in Canton) dissenting.

1918   Foundation of the "*SOCIETY FOR THE STUDY OF MARXISM*" in Peking.

1919   *CHINA REFUSED TO SIGN THE TREATY OF VERSAILLES*. Students of Peking University led the *MAY FOURTH MOVEMENT* ("National Shame Day").

1920   Frightful *FAMINE* once more killed millions in northern China.

1920–6   *CIVIL WAR* between local military dictators, or war lords. Numerous anti-foreign strikes in Chinese harbors, culminating in *SHANGHAI INCIDENT* (May, 1925).

1921   The *CHINESE COMMUNIST PARTY* ("Kungch'antang") founded in Shanghai and in . . . Paris.

1922   The *WASHINGTON CONFERENCE* guaranteed China's sovereignty, and temporarily halted the Japanese expansion.

1923   Sun-Joffe Declaration inaugurating short-lived cooperation between the Kuomintang Party and Communism.
Soviet advisers in China help reorganize the Kuomintang.

1924   First National Congress of the Kuomintang in Canton. Communists admitted to its ranks.
CHIANG KAI-SHEK at the head of the new Whampoa Military Academy, assisted by Russian and German instructors. *CHOU EN-LAI* political director.

1925   *DEATH OF DR. SUN YAT-SEN*, "Father of the Country".

1926   Chiang Kai-shek's victorious "*MARCH TO THE NORTH*" at the head of the "People's Revolutionary Army".

1927   Conservative Kuomintang (or "Nationalist") government established at Nanking, and dominated by the "*SOONG CLAN*".
The Communists, hunted out of large cities by the Nationalists, retreated to *HUNAN* and *KIANGSI* provinces, and set up a *SOVIET REPUBLIC OF THE LANDLESS* under *MAO TSE-TUNG* and *CHU TEH*.

1928   *SECOND NORTHERN CAMPAIGN* of Chiang Kai-shek. Peking occupied, and renamed *Peiping*.

1929–32 Persistent *FAMINE* in northwest China killed several million people.

1930–5 Chiang Kai-shek's "*ANNIHILATION CAMPAIGNS*" against the "Red bandits" led to the Communists' year-long "*LONG MARCH*" to Shensi Province.

1931–2 *JAPANESE OCCUPATION OF MANCHURIA*, following assassination of Captain Nakamura.

1932   Japan proclaimed the *INDEPENDENCE OF MAN-CHUKUO*, installed Henry P'u-I (boy Emperor who abdicated in 1912) as Regent, later (1934) promoted him Emperor. Japanese occupation of *SHANGHAI* in order to break the Chinese boycott.
The *LYTTON REPORT* to the League of Nations condemned Japan's aggression, whereupon Japan quit the League.

1936   "Young Marshal" Chang Hsueh-liang kidnapped Chiang Kai-shek at Sian, in order to force him to declare war on Japan.

1937   Lengthy negotiations between Nationalists and Communists led to the formation of a *"UNITED FRONT"* against Japan.
The Shensi Soviet Republic was declared an "Autonomous Border Region", and the Communist forces became the *"EIGHTH ROUTE ARMY"*.
THE SHANGHAI CAMPAIGN (following the Lukouchiao incident near Peking) opened the long *SINO-JAPANESE WAR* that ended with Japan's surrender in 1945.
Merciless bombing of Chinese cities shocked world opinion. Conclusion of a nonaggression treaty between China and Russia.
FALL OF NANKING, and horrible Japanese atrocities. *CHUNKING* became wartime capital.

1938   *CANTON* and *HANKOW* fell to the Japanese, who began sponsoring "autonomous" Chinese governments.

1939   The *BURMA ROAD* was terminated.

1940   The puppet government of *WANG CHING-WEI* (former favorite disciple of Sun Yat-sen) installed in Nanking.

1941   The grave *ANHWEI INCIDENT*, in which Nationalist forces nearly wiped out the Communist *"NEW FOURTH ARMY"*.
The *NATIONALIST BLOCKADE OF SHENSI* did not prevent the Chinese Reds from scoring increasingly important victories over the Japanese.

1942   General "Vinegar Joe" *STILWELL* arrived in China, but the Burma Road fell to the Japanese. It was replaced by the "Hump" (airlift) of General Chennault's "Flying Tigers."

1943   The war's worst famine, in Honan Province.

1944   Series of uninterrupted defeats sustained by rapidly deteriorating Nationalist armies: Southern China cut in two by *JAPAN'S LAST MAJOR CAMPAIGN* of the war.
General *WEDEMEYER* replaced General Stilwell.

1945   *VICTORY IN BURMA* (exploits of "Merrill's Marauders" along the new Ledo—or Stilwell—Road).
CAPITULATION OF JAPANESE FORCES in China.
Race for control of ex-occupied China between the fast-moving Red columns and the American-supported Nationalist troops.
General Chu Teh's refusal to comply with Chiang Kai-shek's orders started the *CIVIL WAR BETWEEN THE "TWO CHINAS"*, or Red and White China.

1945–6   General Marshall's fruitless mission of conciliation.

1946   Spectacular Nationalist victories in Northern China, but the Reds held the countryside, denying final victory to the Kuomintang.

1947   The great *COMMUNIST COUNTEROFFENSIVE* forced the Nationalists into the defensive. Increasing popular support for the Reds, and growing defeatist attitude of both Nationalist leaders and troops.

1948   Decisive battles of the civil war, and turning of the tide in favor of the Reds against a background of economic chaos. Anti-Americanism spread in "liberated" areas.

1949   (January) *CHIANG KAI-SHEK FLEW INTO* (temporary) *RETIREMENT*.
PEKING FELL TO THE REDS.
(June) *THE REDS ENTERED NANKING*, reached the vicinity of Hong Kong in October.
China had "turned over" into the Red camp.

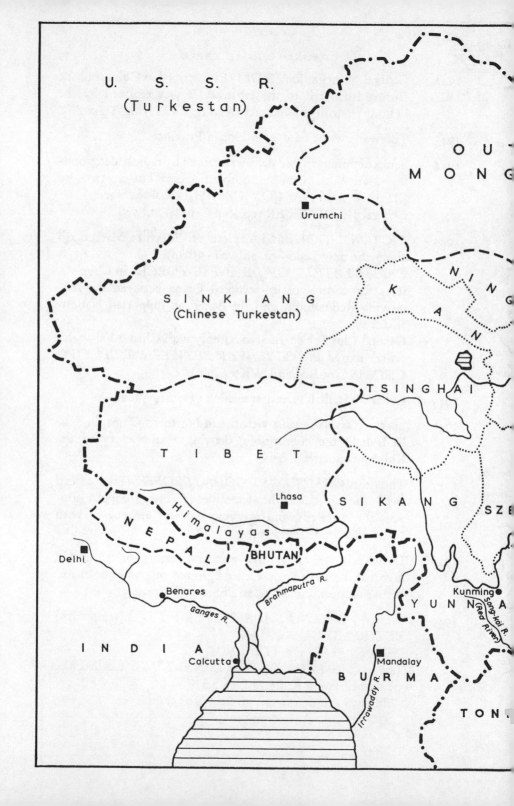

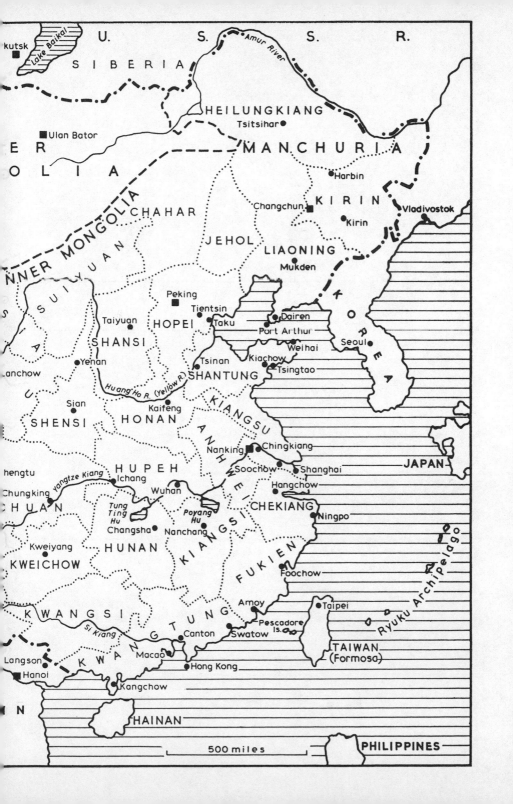

CHAPTER I

THE WESTERN "BARBARIANS" AT THE DOORS OF CHINA

EVER SINCE the early Middle Ages, trade between Mediterranean countries and the Far East had been largely monopolized by the Arabs. At the beginning of the sixteenth century, however, and as a result of Vasco da Gama's voyage around the Cape of Good Hope, the Indian Ocean became the realm of the Portuguese. Their trading fleets went regularly to India, and within a matter of years much of southern Asia's coasts fell under their control. Goa became capital of their possessions in 1510. Malacca, center of the East Indian spice trade, was occupied in 1511, and from there the enterprising Portuguese established communication with Siam, the Moluccas (or Spice Islands), and China.

It was in 1516 that the first Portuguese—and Western—caravel entered the harbor of Canton. Other southern and eastern Chinese harbor cities were also visited by the Portuguese, but their piratical conduct soon raised the natives in revolt against them. They were driven from Canton in 1521, and nothing was finally left them but the island of Macao, where they firmly established themselves in 1557—and are still there today.

At about the same time, the Spaniards occupied the Philippines, discovered by Magellan in 1521, and in turn endeavored to gain a foothold in China. Trading concessions were granted them in Amoy, and Spanish missionaries preached the Christian gospel in that area. Spain's influence, however, remained very limited in both time and space, and was religious rather than commercial.

The Dutch, arch-rivals of Portuguese and Spaniards alike, entered Chinese waters in 1622. They settled in the Pescadores and on the west coast of Formosa, but were expelled by the Chinese some forty years later. Their colonizing efforts thereafter centered upon the Indonesian islands: the thriving *empire which they built there—the Dutch East Indies—remained in their hands until the middle of the twentieth century.*

As for the English, who subsequently played a major role in China's history, they were latecomers of sorts because they spent much of the seventeenth century wresting India from the Portuguese. The latter in turn succeeded in keeping their powerful rivals out of China until 1684, when they reluctantly agreed to let the British East India Company open its own trading center in Macao. The official Chinese mood was favorable at the time: in 1685, indeed, an imperial edict opened all of China's ports to the Western trade. In 1757, however, a new edict confined that trade to the harbor of Canton, where it was carried on under severe restrictions. Foreigners were not allowed to reside within the city wall, and outside that wall they were only permitted to rent ground on which to build their "factories", or trade establishments. No foreign women were allowed on the premises.

For nearly a century, the Celestial Empire maintained an attitude of haughty contempt toward the "Fan Kwae", or "foreign demons"* whom it regarded as barbarians having but worthless products to sell. In the opinion of the Chinese, Europe was a group of small islands inhabited by a few merchants speaking different tongues and maintaining themselves chiefly by their trade with China. The overbearing and often brutal behavior of most Europeans, on the other hand, strengthened the Chinese in their belief that their ancient civilization was vastly superior to that of the Western nations. The Emperor of China, whose official title "Son of Heaven" supposedly placed him above all other monarchs, considered the latter politically tributary to him and expected them to render him homage. China and Europe, in short, were not drawn closer to one another by what little intercourse they had so far, and did little to understand each other better.

Undaunted by past failures (and errors), the stubborn Europeans endeavored anew, toward the end of the eighteenth century, to obtain broader trade concessions on China's mainland. In 1793, a British mission led by Lord Macartney went all the way to Peking, only to be told that the Empire of the Middle was in no need of foreign goods—or visitors. The reception granted the embassy at the Emperor's summer residence was gracious enough though, and has been described by Lord Macartney through the pen of one of his assistants, John Barrow:

On the 14th September . . . we alighted at the park gate, from

---

* Also spelled "Fan Qui" by various authors, and sometimes translated as "foreign ghosts", "outlandish demons", or "barbarian wanderers".

whence we walked to the Imperial encampment, and were conducted to a large handsome tent prepared for us, on one side of the Emperor's. After waiting there about an hour, his approach was announced by drums and music, on which we quitted our tent and came forward upon the green carpet. He was seated in an open Palankeen, carried by sixteen bearers, attended by numbers of officers bearing flags, standards, and umbrellas; and as he passed we paid him our compliments, by kneeling on one knee, whilst all the Chinese made their usual prostrations. As soon as he had ascended his throne I came to the entrance of his tent, and holding in both my hands a large gold box, enriched with diamonds, in which was enclosed the King's letter, I walked deliberately up and, ascending the steps of the throne, delivered it into the Emperor's own hands, who, having received it, passed it to the Minister by whom it was placed on the cushion. He then gave me, as the first present from him to His Majesty,* the *En-shee*,† or symbol of peace and prosperity, and expressed his hope that my Sovereign and he should always live in good correspondence and amity. . . . Other presents were sent, at the same time, to all the gentlemen of my train. We then descended from the steps of the throne, and sat down upon cushions at one of the tables on the Emperor's left hand. And at other tables, according to their ranks, the chief Tartar princes and the Mandarins of the Court at the same time took their places; all dressed in the proper robes of their respective ranks. These tables were then uncovered and exhibited a sumptuous banquet..The Emperor sent us several dishes from his own table, together with some liquors, which the Chinese call wine; not, however, pressed from the grape, but distilled or extracted from rice, herbs, and honey.

In about half an hour he sent for Sir George Staunton‡ and me to come to him and gave to each of us, with his own hands, a cup of warm wine, which we immediately drank in his presence, and found it very pleasant and comfortable, the morning being cold and raw. Among other things he asked me the age of my sovereign and, being informed of it, said he hoped he might live as many years as himself which were then eighty-three. His manner was dignified, but affable and condescending, and his reception of us was very gracious and satisfactory.

* King George III.
† Whitish, agate-looking stone about a foot and a half long, highly prized by the Chinese.
‡ Minister Plenipotentiary in the absence of the British Ambassador.

The order and regularity in serving and removing the dinner was wonderfully exact, and every function of the ceremony performed with such silence and solemnity as in some measure to resemble the celebration of a religious mystery.[1]

Two years later, in 1795, the Dutch East Indies Company sent an official delegation to Peking. It was equally well received, achieved just as little, and departed with a flowery and condescending letter intended for the King of Holland. This typical specimen of official Chinese composition has been preserved by John Barrow:

. . . I have received from Heaven the sceptre of this vast Empire. I have reigned for fifty years with glory and happiness; and have established the most profound peace upon . . . this said Empire, to the benefit of the nations bordering on it. The fame of my majesty and proofs of my magnificence have found their way into every part of the world, and they constitute the pride and the pleasure of my vast domains.

I consider my own happy Empire, and other Kingdoms, as one and the same family; the princes and the people are, in my eye, the same men. I condescend to shed my blessings over all, strangers as well as natives; and there is no country, however distant, that has not received instances of my benevolence. Thus, all nations send to do me homage, and to congratulate me incessantly. . . . I feel a lively joy in observing the anxiety with which they flock together from every quarter to contemplate and admire the wise administration of my government. . . . I applaud therefore your government which, although separated from mine by an immense ocean, has not failed to send me congratulatory letters, accompanied by tributary offerings.

Having perused your letters, I observe that they contain nothing but what I consider as authentic testimonies of your great veneration for me, from whence I conclude that you admire my mode of governing. In fact, you have great reason to applaud me. Since you have carried on your trade at Canton (and it is now many years), strangers have always been well treated in my Empire; and they have individually been the objects of my love and affection. . . .

Your Ambassador being about to return to the presence of his Sovereign, I have directed him to present to this Prince pieces of silk and other valuable articles to which I have added some antique vases.

May your King receive my present. May he govern his people with
wisdom; and give his sole attention to this grand object, acting always
with an upright and sincere heart: and, lastly, may he always cherish
the recollection of my beneficence! May this King attentively watch
over the affairs of his Kingdom. I recommend it to him strongly and
earnestly. . . .[2]

*The explanation for this "superiority complex" displayed by the Chinese
emperors, and the fact that the Chinese as a nation likewise looked down
upon the rest of the world, resulted from their traditionally willful ignorance
of that world and its inhabitants. Traveling in China in the middle of the
nineteenth century, the American doctor and missionary Charles Taylor found
Chinese geographical (and ethnological) knowledge still unchanged:*

The ridiculous self-conceit of the Chinese, in regarding themselves
as the only civilized people on earth and occupying the "Central
Flowery Land", while all others are designated as "outside barbarians",
has suppressed all desire to learn anything of the history or geography of
other countries. These subjects, consequently, form no part of their
school instruction. Maps of "The World" are met with, in five
separate scrolls, to be hung side by side, forming when thus placed
together, a surface of about five feet square. It is almost entirely filled
up with the "Middle Kingdom" while a few insignificant islands in
the corners are severally called America, England, France, Germany,
Russia, Italy, Spain, Africa, and so on. Peking is, in their estimation,
the center of the universe, and they have a chart which represents
mankind as not only being less and less civilized, in proportion to their
distance from that capital, but also as actually found lacking or changed
in some of the natural features of a human being, taking their own type
as the standard. I saw on this chart a specimen of a tribe, supposed to
dwell some thousands of miles from Peking, portrayed as having but
one eye, and that in the middle of the forehead! Another, at a still
longer distance, had a hole through the middle of his body, through
which a pole was thrust, and instead of requiring a sedan, he was borne
along by this means, on the shoulders of two others! My old teacher
remarked that it must be a very convenient mode of locomotion, and
gravely asked me if such a people existed! He told me that during the
war with Great Britain in 1842, he himself read official proclamations
that were posted up about the city of Shanghai, exhorting the people to

a courageous resistance to the "red-haired devils", *i.e.* the British, who had no joints at the knees, and who, when once they fell down, could not rise again to their feet, and would then become an easy prey! Therefore all possible obstructions must be placed in their path, so as to throw them down![3]

During the first fifteen years of the nineteenth century, the "weak-kneed" English had their hands full fighting Napoleon I. Hardly was he defeated, however, than a new British mission, conducted by Lord Amherst, journeyed to Peking. Its main purpose, of course, was to find new overseas markets on which England depended more and more in the course of that century.

Ceremonial formalities prevented Lord Amherst from attaining his ends. The Chinese kept insisting that the Britons do homage to their emperor by going through the customary procedures required of all envoys of "tributary" nations, namely three genuflections and nine prostrations. As a true son of Britain—herself second to none in the whole world—Lord Amherst adamantly refused to impose such humbling exertions on his stiff Western spine. After protracted and inconclusive negotiations between his party and the Chinese officials, or Mandarins, the Britons reached the vicinity of Peking at the end of August, 1816. The inland journey over scores of miles of bad roads contributed to their impatience and fatigue. Lord Amherst's secretary, Henry Ellis, has recorded the "mixed" reception experienced at the Celestial Court on that occasion:

Three miles from the halting place we entered the large suburb, which continues to the gate of Peking: the crowd was immense, but, as usual, orderly. I remarked that the soldiers were more decisive in asserting their authority as we approached the capital. Most of the spectators carried a paper lantern, to prevent their curiosity being disappointed by the darkness of the night: the carriage, as might have been expected, was the great object of attraction, and notwithstanding the badness of the road, of the cattle, and the hurry under which it had been put together, performed its part very well. Our eyes were dazzled by the splendid decorations of the shops; the gilded carved work is really handsome; and it is extraordinary, that the profits of trade should allow of such an unproductive expenditure. We reached the gate by which Lord Macartney entered Peking about midnight, and having been informed that the Emperor, in his special favour, had ordered the gates to be kept open, contrary to the usual practice, were place but the residence assigned to him; adding, that he was so over-come with fatigue and bodily illness, as absolutely to require repose. Lord Amherst further pointed out the gross insult he had already received, in having been exposed to the intrusion and indecent curio-sity of crowds, who appeared to view him rather as a wild beast than the representative of a powerful sovereign. . . .

A message soon arrived . . . to say that the Emperor dispensed with the Ambassador's attendance; that he had further been pleased to direct his physician to afford his Excellency every medical assistance that his illness might require. The Koong-yay himself soon followed, and his Excellency proceeded to the carriage. . . . Soon afterwards the Man-darins announced that the Emperor, incensed by the Ambassador's refusal to attend him according to his commands, had given orders for our immediate departure. The order was so peremptory that no alteration was proposed: in vain was the fatigue of every individual of the embassy pleaded; no consideration was allowed to weigh against the positive commands of the Emperor. . . .

The officer of government . . . into whose hand it would seem the execution of the Emperor's orders had been put entered upon the question of the ceremony, using, as might be expected, the most absurd language; asserting that the Emperor's claim to it from his superiority of rank over all monarchs, and the consequent impro-priety of our conduct in pertinaciously refusing. . . .

The only act of civility we experienced during the day was a hand-some breakfast sent by the Emperor, which was most acceptable, as many of the party had tasted nothing since the preceding day. At four Lord Amherst got into his chair; and thus to all outward appearances has the embassy terminated.[4]

In the teeming southern harbor of Canton, meanwhile, business went on as usual; that is, the European traders who had been granted concessions on the city's waterfront took whatever advantage they could from the cramped facilities which Chinese authorities had grudgingly leased to them. The chief exports were tea, silks, fine cottons and china, while imports were mainly limited to opium and specie.

By far the more numerous "barbarians" were the English. In 1836, they outnumbered the Portuguese 162 to 28; between these two nationalities, in terms of numbers, was a group of "flowery-flag devils", as the Chinese called the Americans, exactly forty-four of them. They had sent their first ship to

WESTERN "BARBARIANS" AT THE DOORS OF CHINA 33

not a little disappointed at finding the cavalcade defiling by the wall. Our eyes anxiously looked for the next gate, only to be again disappointed, when it clearly appeared that we were to be taken round the walls to our destination.

29th of August.—Daylight found us at the village of Hai-teen, near which the house of Sung-ta-jin, one of the principal ministers, intended to be our quarters, is situated; here, however, we did not remain, but were carried directly to Yuen-min-yuen, where the Emperor is at present. The carriage stopped under some trees, and we ourselves were conducted to a small apartment belonging to a range of buildings in a square; Mandarins of all buttons* were in waiting; several Princes of the blood, distinguished by clear ruby buttons and round flowered badges, were among them: the silence, and a certain air of regularity, marked the immediate presence of the sovereign. The small apartment, much out of repair, into which we were huddled, now witnessed a scene I believe unparalleled in the history of diplomacy. Lord Amherst had scarcely taken his seat, when Chang† delivered a message . . . informing him that the Emperor wished to see the Ambassador, his Son, and the Commissioners, immediately. Much surprise was naturally expressed; the previous arrangement for the eighth of the Chinese month . . . and the utter impossibility of his Excellency appearing in his present state of fatigue, inanition, and deficiency of every necessary equipment, was strongly urged. . . . During this time the room had filled with spectators of all ages and ranks, who rudely pressed upon us to gratify their brutal curiosity, for such it may be called, as they seemed to regard us rather as wild beasts than mere strangers of the same species with themselves. . . . Lord Amherst having alleged bodily illness as one of the reasons for declining the audience . . . this produced a visit from the Koong-yay‡ who, too much interested and agitated to heed ceremony, stood by Lord Amherst, and used every argument to induce him to obey the Emperor's command. . . . All proving ineffectual, with some roughness, but under pretext of friendly violence, he laid hands upon Lord Amherst, to take him from the room; another Mandarin followed his example. His lordship, with great firmness and dignity of manner, shook them off, declaring that nothing but the extremest violence should induce him to quit that room for any other

* Marks of ranks, according to the buttons' colors.   † A Mandarin.
‡ High official close to the Emperor.

China in 1784, and during the next few decades their trade increased to fairly large proportions. The American flag was first hoisted at Canton in 1802 when a consular agent was appointed from among the American merchants residing there.

On the Chinese side, the monopoly of foreign trade was in the hands of a group of twelve government-appointed traders, the Hong merchants, associated into a corporate body called the Co-Hong and directly responsible for all exports and imports to an imperial official, the Hoppo.

J. F. Davis, Chief Superintendent of the British East India Company (which monopolized all English trade in the Far East at the time) has described the Canton "factories" at some length:

It may, perhaps, seem incredible that the whole frontage of the buildings, in which foreigners of all nations are shut up together, for the prosecution of their trading business at Canton, does not exceed between seven and eight hundred feet. Each front, of which there are about thirteen, extends backwards about a hundred and thirty yards into a long narrow lane or thoroughfare, on each side of which, as well as over arches that cross it, are the confined abodes of the English, French, Dutch, Americans, Parsees, and others. Many of these spend a large portion, if not the whole, of their lives here in the worship of Mammon, without the sight of a female face, and with no recreation but the jingling of dollars, as they are perpetually being weighed or examined by the Chinese money-changers, in receipts or payments! Many years back, a considerable number of flags, as the Danish, Swedish, and Austrian, were hoisted in front of the factories, besides the English, Dutch, and American; but for the last quarter of a century these three, with the French tricouleur, which was erected soon after the revolution of 1830, have been the only foreign ensigns seen there.

The European factories are called by the Chinese "the thirteen Hongs"; the word Hong being always used by them to denote a commercial establishment or warehouse. According to their custom, each factory is distinguished either by some appellation denoting wealth and prosperity, or by its flag. Thus the Austrian or imperial factory was called the "Twin-eagle Hong", a name which it retains to this day; the Danish, the "Yellow flag Hong"; the Company's, "the Hong that ensures tranquillity"; the American, "the Hong of extensive fountains"; and so on. To the east of all there is a narrow inlet from the river—a fetid ditch, which serves to surround a portion of the city wall, as well as to drain that part of the town. This is crossed with a single arch, by a narrow street at the back of the factories, that leads to the warehouses of the several Hong merchants, all of them communicating with the river by wooden or stone stairs, from which the tea and other merchandise is shipped.

The space occupied by the foreign factories is crossed by two well-known thoroughfares, one of them named China Street, and the other very appropriately dignified with the descriptive title of Hog Lane. The former is rather broader than the generality of Chinese streets, and contains the shops of the small dealers in carved and lacquered ware, silks, and other articles in common demand by strangers. These are attracted to the several shops by inscriptions in the European character, which sometimes promise more than they perform; as when the dauber of truculent likeness calls himself a "handsome-face painter", etc. The shops, instead of being set out with the showy and sometimes expensive front of an English or French boutique, are closed in by gloomy black shutters, and very ill lit by a small skylight, or rather a hole in the roof. The inmates, instead of showing the civility and alacrity of shopkeepers in London or Paris, and anticipating the demands of their customers in the display of their goods, slowly, and sometimes sullenly, produce the articles from their cases and cupboards as they may be asked for; so that shopping at Canton is far from being an agreeable pastime.[5]

In this very special atmosphere, Hog Lane epitomized the frequently brutal contacts between Chinese traders and European sailors; the narrator is again Chief Superintendent Davis:

The alley called Hog Lane is not easy to describe by any standard of comparison, as we believe that nothing so narrow or so filthy exists in a European town. The hovels by which it is lined are occupied by abandoned Chinese, who supply the poor ignorant sailors with spirits, medicated to their taste with stimulating or stupefying drugs; and when the wretched men have been reduced to a bestial state by these poisonous liquors, they are frequently set up by their wily seducers, and robbed as well as beaten; until those sent in search of the sailors arrive, and carry them to their boat in this disgraceful condition. It was here that the affrays, which many years since so frequently led to homicides and discussions with the government, in general originated;

until the Company's authorities invested the senior commander of the fleet with the complete regulation and control of all boats, with their crews, at Canton. . . .

Those who anciently witnessed the fearful tumults generated in Hog Lane described them as something quite remarkable. A few straggling sailors, fresh from their ship, in passing a spirit shop would be greeted by some Chinese with "How you do, Jack?" which would be immediately followed by a general exchange of similar brief and familiar appellatives, as Tom, Bill, and Ned, be the person addressed Christian or Pagan. A pipe and repeated glasses of grog (all on the sailor's side) would immediately follow— with what might be called their ulterior consequences; for when the Chinese at length made their singularly unreasonable demand for payment, as, perhaps, a few *dollars* for what might be worth a few *pence*, Jack would have just sufficient reason left to discern the extent of the enormity, without being at all in a condition to meet the case by a logical *reductio ad absurdum*. The place of reason would therefore be supplied by the fist, or by any thing still harder that chanced to be grasped within it. The Chinese, not unprepared for the emergency, and in full possession of their wits, would discomfit by dint of numbers, and drive the sailors down the lane; but these would presently return with strong reinforcements; and so the tumult would grow, with successive charges and recharges, and wounds deep and broad, until several individuals on either side were maimed or killed.[6]

In order to keep the "redheaded devils"* well under control at the gates of Canton, the Chinese authorities in 1760 issued eight regulations that were confirmed by an imperial edict in 1819. Their English translation, recorded by the American trader W. C. Hunter, reads as follows:

1. All vessels of war are prohibited from entering the Bogue.† Vessels of war acting as convoy to merchantmen must anchor outside at SEA till their merchant ships are ready to depart, and then sail away with them.

2. Neither women, guns, spears, nor arms of any kind can be brought to the Factories.

* Name first given to the Dutch, later commonly applied to Europeans.
† Narrow passage leading to the inner harbor.

3. All river pilots and ships' Compradores* must be registered at the office of the "Tung-Che"† at Macao. That officer will also furnish each one of them with a license, or badge, which must be worn around the waist. He must produce it whenever called for. All other boatmen and people must not have communication with foreigners, unless under the immediate control of the ships' Compradores; and should smuggling take place, the Compradore of the ship engaged in it will be punished.

4. Each Factory is restricted for its service to 8 Chinese (irrespective of the number of its occupants), say 2 porters, 4 water-carriers, 1 person to take care of goods, and 1 ma-chen [merchant].

5. Foreigners are not allowed to row about the river in their own boats for "pleasure". On the 8th, 18th, and 28th days of the moon they may "take the air" . . . these foreign barbarians may visit the Flower Gardens and the Honam Joss-house,‡ but not in *droves* of over ten at a time. When they have "refreshed" they must return to the Factories, not be allowed to pass the night "out", or collect together to carouse. Should they do so, then, when the next "holiday" comes, they shall not be permitted to go. If the ten should presume to enter villages, public places, or bazaars, punishment will be inflicted upon the *Linguist* [official interpreter] who accompanies them.

6. Foreigners are not allowed to present petitions. If they have anything to represent, it must be done through the Hong merchants.

7. Hong merchants are not to owe debts to foreigners. Smuggling goods to and from the city is prohibited.

8. Foreign ships arriving with merchandise must not loiter about outside the river; they must come direct to Whampoa.§ They must not rove about the bays at pleasure and sell to rascally natives goods subject to duty, that these may smuggle them, and thereby defraud His Celestial Majesty's revenue.[7]

Strict as they were, the "Eight Regulations" could not altogether prevent the foreigners from letting off some steam by breaking out of their crowded precincts in order to go and "carouse" in the Chinese town. Local authorities did not generally interfere in such cases, but when in 1830 some impatient European

* From the Portuguese *comprar*, to buy; Chinese assistants of the Hong merchants.

† Chinese magistrate, a sort of Customs officer.   ‡ Buddhist temple.

§ Anchorage south of Canton, where Chinese pilots came on board.

women residing in Macao went to visit their husbands, it was quite a different story, as told here by a French traveler:

Chinese policy is definitely opposed to the coming of European women to Canton. The government thinks, not without reason, that if Europeans are allowed to settle their families in the factories, violence would be required to get them out again, but such idea is altogether repugnant to the administration of the Celestial Empire.

Some years ago, a few ladies living in Macao grew tired of their prolonged widowhood and, desirous of getting closer to their husbands, decided to test Chinese tolerance. Five or six of them boldly contravened the Viceroy's instructions and on a fine morning popped up in front of the factories. The Viceroy became highly indignant. To have the woman arrested and thrown out of Canton was rather dangerous, as all foreigners were armed and very much decided to defend their wives to the utmost, but as I have said before, the Chinese carefully avoid getting involved in a conflict with Europeans that might lead to bloodshed. Yet these women were somehow expected to leave Canton and return to that center of impurity called Macao. Besides, how could the Court ever be informed that European women had successfully flouted the authorities' rigid vigilance?

The Chinese first appealed to the women's feelings and pride: on the door of every factory they posted a decree of the Viceroy enjoining the barbarian women to stop defiling the Chinese city with their presence. His Excellency in fact used words that would make me blush if I tried to repeat them, and would make the women blush too, if any one were bold enough to translate them properly. This method, however, remained ineffectual, for the ladies from Macao did not heed the Viceroy's request. The customary supreme means was therefore resorted to: an official decree suspended trade, dismissed all Chinese employees from the factories, and starved out their inhabitants.

For some days, patience prevailed among Europeans, and conjugal love enabled them to endure many a hardship. Before long, however, they realized their foolishness in staying on in China without making any money, and starving on top of it. Their only choice lay between their own departure and submission to the unfair demands of the Chinese government. A few ladies, braver than the rest, endeavored to hold out, but their resistance soon became useless. They too eventually bade a tearful farewell and then departed, cursing the Chinese and their complete lack of courtesy. Ever since, the Europeans established at Canton have renounced the hope of indulging in the joys of conjugal life. Whenever they get tired of their loneliness, they have no other choice but go and spend a few days in Macao.[8]

In the opinion of the well-known French missionary Father M. Huc (who traveled widely throughout the Chinese empire in the first half of the nineteenth century, and probably was the first European ever to visit the forbidden city of Lhasa), the Chinese have traditionally been born traders gifted with patience, shrewdness, and practical wisdom:

The Chinese, par excellence, is a man installed behind the counter of a shop, waiting for his customers with patience and resignation, and in the intervals of their arrival pondering in his head, and casting up on his little arithmetical machine the means of increasing his fortune. Whatever may be the nature and importance of his business, he never neglects the smallest profit; the least gain is always welcome, and he accepts it eagerly. Greatest of all is his enjoyment, when in the evening, having well closed and barricaded his shop, he can retire into a corner, and there count religiously the number of his sapeks,* and reckon the earnings of the day.

The Chinese is born with this taste for trade, which grows with his growth, and becomes stronger with his strength. The first thing a child longs for is a sapek; the first use that it makes of its speech and intelligence is to learn to articulate the names of coins; when his little fingers are strong enough to hold the pencil, he amuses himself by drawing figures, and as soon as the tiny creature can speak and walk, he is capable of buying or selling. In China you need never fear sending a child to make a purchase; you may rely on it, he will not allow himself to be cheated. Even the games that are popular among the little Chinese reveal this mercantile spirit; they play at keeping shop, and opening little pawnbroking establishments, and familiarize themselves with the jargon, the tricks, and the frauds of merchants. Their knowledge in all that relates to commerce is so clear and precocious, that you need not hesitate to entrust them with the most important affairs, and to give them serious business to manage at an age when other children are mostly occupied with their toys.[9]

* Chinese common coin.

The Chinese merchants' resourcefulness and adaptability were revealed, among others, in the way they overcame the language barrier: "pidgin English", of which a few samples have been noted by the American doctor and missionary Charles Taylor, is their invention:

At Canton an abominable jargon has sprung up from the efforts of some of the natives to learn our language. It is called "pidgin English" —"pidgin" being their pronunciation of the word "business." It is in general use at all the ports; but so uncouth and barbarous is it, that to learn to use it readily is almost as difficult as to acquire the true dialect itself. To give a few examples: on our arrival at Hong Kong, having occasion to call at the residence of one of our countrymen, I asked the native servant who came to the door if Mr. ——— was at home. "Yes sir, top side have got." Not understanding his reply, I repeated the question. "Yes, sir—yes, sir," said he, "top side have got"; at the same time pointing upward. I then understood that he meant upstairs. Nearly all the native boats and junks have large eyes painted on their bows. I inquired of one who professed to speak English what was the design. Said he: "S'pose no have catchee eye, how fashion can see, wanchee walkee water?" That is, suppose it has no eyes, how can it see to walk on the water? On asking one when a certain ship would sail, he said: "I tink two three piece day dat ship can walkee." When he would tell you that he does not understand any particular matter or business, it will be, "Me no savee* dat pidjin.". . .

They are remarkably fond of having articles in pairs. Seeing one wearing two watches, one in each breast pocket, on the outside of his coat, with the chains dangling, I asked why he wore more than one. His answer was: "S'posee one piece catchee sickee, no can talkee, dat udder piece can talkee." One, announcing the birth of a female infant, and not knowing the proper term in English, said: "My one piece wifo have catchee one piece number one pretty cow-chilo."[10]

Canton harbor was teeming with life by day and by night. Foreign visitors were invariably struck by the thousands of vessels of all sizes crowding its facilities, but also by the impressive numbers of Cantonese—almost exclusively lower-class people—who spent practically all of their life on the water. Such was the case of the British doctor, C. Toogood Downing:

* Corruption of the French *savoir*, to know.

Nothing strikes the stranger with more astonishment on his first visit to China than the almost endless variety of craft which is seen upon the river. The ingenuity displayed in this single instance will always be sufficient to prove that the Chinese, as a nation, are endowed with great originality.... Here custom appears to be the result of unbounded experience, and the great degree of excellence attained is the work of ages of continual, though sluggish improvement. ...

Among the great variety of large junks, floating houses, chops, and small craft, which are seen constantly moving about on the river, or passing up and down with the tide, you are able to distinguish two classes—those with an eye, and those without one. All the river craft need, it seems, no such organ; but those junks which are intended to go out to the sea are all ornamented with a large eye painted on either side of the bows. Whether it is considered that the sea vessels are more liable to run against obstacles, which this large eye, that cannot be closed night or day, may enable them to evade, when the human one is closed in sleep, it is impossible to decide. It may be a piece of super-stition founded upon almost primitive simplicity; for if you ask a Chinaman what it is for, he answers very gravely, "Have eye, can see; can see, can saavee. No have eye, no can see; no can see, no can saavee". —as if he believed that this painted eye could *bona fide* perceive objects, discriminate between them, and avoid dangers. ...

It makes one fancy that these people are amphibious, when we see a mother sitting at needlework in a boat, quietly looking on, while a child of five or six years of age is swimming around it, and another not able to walk is scrambling on all fours about the little deck, liable at every turn to fall overboard. This is, however, not so awful a catastrophe as might be expected, for a precaution is adopted against accidents of this nature. A light, wooden affair, some-times a gourd as large as a bladder, made airtight, and painted with rings of green and red, is fastened with a tape at the back of the shoulders of the newborn infant, which the child wears until it is able to take care of itself. If it should crawl too far and fall into the stream, as frequently happens, the mother has nothing to do but fish it out of the water and put it back to its place again. ...

Great numbers of the lowest orders of Chinese live upon what they pick up upon the water. Their boats are fastened astern of the ships for this purpose, and whatever refuse is cast overboard is picked up by them with great expertness. I have sometimes, for the purpose of trying their quickness, watched a boat until every one on board of it was hidden, and apparently asleep, as not the slightest noise or motion was perceptible; and then dropped a piece of crumpled paper from the poop, noiselessly into the water. Before the current . . . had carried it the short distance from the place where it fell to the side of the boat, it was perceived, and two or three hands stretched over the gunwale to receive it as it passed. . . .

No description I should think can convey to the reader a distinct idea of this wonderful place, unequalled in singularity by any other spot on the surface of the globe. The crowd of boats of all sizes, shapes, and colours, passing in every direction, with the hubbub and clamour of ten thousand different sounds coming from every quarter and with every variety of intonation, make an impression almost similar to that of awe upon the first visit of the stranger. Upon myself, the excitement produced was so great that I can even now recollect it. . . . I may appear rather enthusiastic, but I verily believe that the coldest nature must have been roused at first by the sight.[11]

The Europeans and Americans had much to criticize about the Chinese way of life, judging it generally inferior to their own. But the Chinese were just as critical of the "foreign devils", especially of their physical features and their ridiculously tight clothes. The French missionary, Father Huc, who spoke their language well, often listened to their sarcastic comments:

The Chinese from the inner provinces whom business takes to Canton or Macao are always most eager to go and watch the Europeans taking their walk. It is a very entertaining sight for them. They squat in rows along the sides of the quays, light their pipes and open their fans, after which they observe with an amused and ironical eye the English and Americans promenading back and forth, all the while keeping time with admirable precision.

Europeans arriving in China are most likely to consider the inhabitants of the Celestial Empire very odd and ridiculous. The Chinese visiting Canton and Macao behave in exactly the same manner toward us. You should hear them poking fun at the appearance of the western devils, and expressing utter amazement at the sight of their tight-fitting garments, their narrow trousers, their huge stovepipe hats, their shirt collars likely to cut off one's ears yet gracefully framing their grotesque faces, with long noses* and blue eyes, without beard or mustache, but wearing reddish and curly whiskers instead. Above all, they are puzzled by the shape of our overcoat.

They try hard, yet unsuccessfully, to understand this strange attire of ours, calling it half-garment, because it is impossible to make it meet over the breast, and also because of the complete absence of coattails in front. They admire our judgment and exquisite taste in sewing large, coin-shaped buttons on our back where, they say, they stay forever without having anything to button. How much handsomer they think themselves with their narrow, oblique black eyes, high cheekbones, and little round noses, their shaven crowns and magnificent pigtails hanging almost to their heels. Add to all these natural graces a conical hat, covered with red fringes, an ample tunic with large sleeves and black satin boots with a very thick white sole, and it must be evident to all that a European cannot compare in appearance with a Chinese.[12]

How unhappy the Chinese could be when special circumstances forced them to wear Western clothes is shown in the following letter, which the scholar Hwuy-Ung wrote home to his brother from Melbourne (where he lived as a political self-exile at the end of the nineteenth century, at the home of a cousin shopkeeper):

Just as their language has the sameness of the desert of Gobi, so is their appearance. They all look alike, though differing in height, some being very tall. They remind me of the water buffaloes I have often seen in our rice fields, and could never distinguish one from the other. . . .

Their garments are tight-fitting, and very uncomfortable in hot weather; in the dignity and grace of our flowing drapery they are wanting. . . . Though I have difficulty in bending my knees, they seem to have overcome that, for they lift their feet like prancing Manchu ponies: so different from our smooth gliding over the ground! Truly a wonderful people: they do everything in a manner contrary to us. . . .

Around the neck they wear a hard band which took me a long time to endure; it is most unpleasant in this hot weather, for it is like a small

* The Chinese have always been struck (and still are) by the size of European noses. *Ta-pi-tze* ("big nose") was a common nickname.

cangue.* Other articles worn round the wrists like manacles are also of linen, hardened with gum, and very shiny. Why they should punish themselves with wearing these things I do not know, unless it may be as a penance for their sins, as is the practice among some of our Buddhist monks.

These remarkable people, contrary to us, like clothes that imprison them. Their thick coats fit tightly around their arms and body, narrow trousers restrict the movements of their knees, tough leather pinches their feet, and hats unyielding in shape grip their heads. Their movements, nevertheless, are quick and abrupt; what they would do without the restraint of their garments, I do not fancy; perhaps, these cramping clothes are a necessary check to their fury, instituted by their sages.

They have a great number of slits in their clothes leading into small bags, a most curious device for retaining objects such as coins, a cloth for the nose, a watch, papers, tobacco, pipe, matches, and many other things.† I counted as many as five in my jacket, four in my little undercoat, and three in my trousers, making twelve in all! Surely if they put an object in one of them they may have to hunt among all of them to find it. This really happened to the man that is clerk to my cousin. When he was required to give up his ticket after a journey with the steam-horse, he could find it nowhere; and remained plunging his fingers into all the openings in his clothes many times, in great trouble. After an hour he was compelled to pay again for his journey, which was a great loss. Five months later, in exploring one of the less used slits—there was the ticket. But he did not receive his money back. . . .

Now, when I am fully prepared in these different garments of the West for entering the street—it is a long preparation—I walk about like a criminal in chains and cangued, unhappy; but when I am back in the house, with relief I cast off the tight clothes, again put on the national garb, and feel once more reasonable and at ease.[13]

"So different from our smooth gliding over the ground": the scholar's remark about the individual Chinese would have been equally true of the crowds. In their traditionally narrow streets, the Chinese cities were packed and throbbing with life, and just as in the country's busy harbors thousands of

---

* Portable pillory commonly worn by Chinese criminals.

† Pockets were all but unknown in the traditional Chinese apparel, and small objects were usually carried in the broad sleeves.

vessels were constantly plying back and forth without hardly ever colliding, so the streets' human flow would steadily keep moving on. The contrast between the smoothness of this regular stream with its crosscurrents, and the hustling and jostling often encountered in European or American crowds, has struck many a Western observer, such as the Reverend Macgowan of the London Missionary Society:

The scene before us is a thoroughly Oriental one and in some respects a very picturesque one. The narrow street only six feet wide, packed as it were with human life, is a splendid place from which to view the various items of which the life of the city is composed. Here is a scholar in his long gown, threadbare and showing signs of decay. Amidst the crowd of passers-by we should never mistake him for anything but what he is. His face has that keen intellectual look that the students of this Empire usually have. Though poor, he has a proud and haughty air, as though he felt himself higher than any of the crowd that brushes up against him. Coming close behind him is a farmer, rough and unsophisticated, with the sun burnt into his face, and with the air of a man who never opened a book in his life except the ancient book of nature which he has studied to such a purpose that he can read her secrets and can extract such crops from her as make his fields laugh with gladness. Following on is a countryman whose home lies at the foot of the hills in the near distance. He is carrying a huge load of brushwood balanced on the ends of a bamboo pole slung across his shoulders, which he is carrying to the market to be sold as firewood. He occupies more than half the roadway, and when he swings his burden from one tired shoulder to the other, the width of the street is only just enough to contain it. He passes along, however, at a steady trot as though the town belonged to him. His loud cries, "Clear the way", "Get to the side", "I'll bump against you", are uttered with an air of authority as though some royal edict has given him the authority to take possession of the road in this masterful manner.

It is amusing to watch the good-natured way in which the ebbing and flowing crowds yield to this man from the hills. Everyone gets out of his way, and even the scholar, with pride and contempt in his heart for the unlearned masses, stands meekly at the side of the road and crushes himself up against a counter to let the imperious seller of firewood pass by. No thanks are given and none are asked, and as the tide of men close up behind him, we can hear coming down the air, "I'll bump you", "I'll bump you," "Go to the side", "Fly, fly", until the sounds so masterfully given and so meekly obeyed are lost in the distance.

In looking at this moving panorama there is one thing that is strikingly conspicuous, and that is the good-natured, easy, tolerant way with which they treat each other on the street. It would seem as though every man, the moment he got on it, had determined that forbearance shall be the word that shall guide his conduct in his treatment of everyone that he meets. Just think of it: a roadway of five or six feet wide, along which constant cross currents of people, of all kinds and conditions, are travelling, and yet no collisions, or at least so rarely that they are not enough to be quoted. Businessmen, clerks, coolies, opium smokers, thieves and vagabonds, country bumpkins and elegant and refined scholars, all with an instinctive sense of the rights of others, yield to the necessities of the road, and bear with infinite good nature whatever inconveniences may arise, and treat each other with patience and courtesy.[14]

Every now and then, however, this pleasant "panorama" would abruptly change and freeze into a scene of typically Oriental submission: preceded by the age-old sounds of gongs, a Mandarin would pass on his way to some official business. The same narrator describes an altogether different crowd, epitomized in its new attitude by a street vendor who, behind his portable kitchen, had been doing a roaring business:

All at once there is a sudden and mysterious change in his attitude. Instead of standing with a benevolent look upon the group sitting on their haunches round his eating house, he becomes agitated, and hastily bidding his customers to hurry up, he begins to make preparations for an immediate move. The men gulp down their rice, the bowls are hurriedly piled up on the dresser, and before one can hardly realize what is taking place the kitchen has been shouldered, and he has disappeared at a jog trot amidst a stream of people that have engulfed him and his belongings.

While we were wondering what it is that caused this sudden panic and collapse in a business that was so prosperous, we hear the clang of the slow and measured beatings of gongs. Higher, too, than the voices around us there comes trailing in the air, as though unwilling to leave the locality from which it started, the sound of the word I-O in a crescendo note, but which finally dies away in a slowly decreasing volume till it finally vanishes in silence. There is now an agitated movement amongst the crowds in the street before us. Some seem full of hesitation, as though undecided what to do; others assume a perplexed air and look about for some opening into which they may escape. . . .

The beating of the gongs, and the prolonged wailing sound I-O, in the meanwhile advance rapidly in our direction, when all at once, all indecision on the part of the passers-by vanishes, and every man flattens himself up against the outstanding shop counters, drops his queue that has been twisted round his head, lets fall his hands by his side and assumes a look of humility and respect. The centre of the street is in a moment deserted, and there bursts into view a Mandarin with his retinue.

The first members of it who come swaggering down the empty lane are the men that fill the air with the sound of I-O, in order to warn the crowds ahead of the coming of the great man. They are a most villainous-looking set of men, and seem as though they might have been picked up out of the slums and gutters for the special duty of today. . . . In their hands they carry long rattans, which they wield menacingly as though waiting for a chance to let them fall heavily on the shoulders of some unwary one who is transgressing the rules of the road and thus showing disrespect to his Excellency. They have a truculent look as they furtively glance over the silent walls of human beings that line the roadway, and a discontented, sullen frown overcasts their faces as they find no chance to use their despotic power on the person of any unfortunate one.

Immediately behind them comes another set of men, quite as evil-looking, with chains in their hands. These have a proud and haughty mien, as though the supreme authority of the town rested in their hands. Should any one be unwise enough to dispute that for a moment, he would find himself instantly bound and shackled, and bundled off to prison, where ample time would be given him to review his temerity.

Coming close behind these scamps, the luxurious chair of the Mandarin, carried by eight bearers, fills the vacant space in the street. He is the mayor of the town, and for all practical purposes the supreme power in it. He is an ideal-looking official, for he is large and massive in appearance, whilst he has that stern and uncompromising look that is supposed to be necessary in any magistrate who would hope to keep his subjects in order. He has a stern and forbidding aspect, as though he were on his way to the execution ground to have some criminal decapitated. This is the kind of air the Mandarins put on when they appear in public. In the course of many years' experience, I have never seen any one of them, from the highest to the lowest, with a smile on his face or a look of sympathy for the people whilst he was being carried officially through the streets. In a few seconds the procession has passed and the human stream again flows along its ancient channel, and the life of the street is once more resumed.[15]

Foreigners in China came into direct contact with Mandarins whenever a matter of some importance had to be settled. They discovered that behind their formidable appearance, the Mandarins had their weak sides too, like any human being. The widely traveled French missionary, Father Huc, has expertly analyzed and illustrated their supple mentality:

We have observed elsewhere that the Chinese, and especially the Mandarins, are strong against the weak and weak against the strong. To domineer over, and crush all around them, is the object they constantly have in view, and to attain it they have an inexhaustible resource in their native cunning and pliability of character. Once allow them to get the upper hand, and it is all over with you; but if you can only succeed in mastering them, you will find them ever after as docile and manageable as children. You may turn them and twist them any way you wish; but beware of showing yourself weak with them for a moment, for they must be ruled with an iron hand. The Chinese Mandarins are pretty much like their own bamboos. If one can but manage to get hold of them in the right way, they are easily bent double and kept so; but if for a second you let go, they are up again in a moment as straight as ever.

It was on a constant struggle therefore, that we were about to enter . . . from Ta-tsien-lou to Canton. There was no middle course: we must either submit to their will or make them submit to ours; and we were determined to adopt the latter manner of proceeding. . . . We cast aside our Tibet custom . . . and we got a skillful tailor to make us some beautiful sky-blue robes in the newest fashion of Peking. We provided ourselves with magnificent black satin boots, adorned with soles of dazzling whiteness. So far the Tribunal of Rites had no objection; but when we proceeded to gird our loins with red sashes, and cover our heads with embroidered yellow caps, we caused a universal shudder among all onlookers, and the emotion ran through the town like an electric current, till it reached the civil and military authorities. They cried aloud that the red sash and the yellow cap were the attributes of Imperial Majesty, allowable only to the family of the Emperor, and forbidden to the people under pain of perpetual banishment. On this point the Tribunal of Rites would be inflexible, and we must reform our costume accordingly. We, on our side, alleged that being strangers, traveling as such and by authority, we were not bound to conform to the ritual of the Empire, but had the right of following the fashion of our country, which allowed every one to choose the form and color of his garments, according to his own fancy. They insisted, they became angry, they flew into a violent rage; we remained calm and impassive, but vowing that we would never part with our red sashes and yellow caps. Our obstinacy was not to be overcome, and the Mandarins submitted—as they ought to do.[16]

The dreaded Mandarins were particularly "cunning and pliable" when money was involved. It was an open secret that most of them used their exalted position to fill their pockets by a complex system of bribery, corruption, and extortions of all kinds.

In Canton, the prosperous Hong merchants constituted a favorite prey; the Mandarins squeezed large sums out of them on as many occasions as possible: birthday of the Emperor, demands from the Imperial Revenue, repeated gifts to the Hoppo (who was not paid by the government from which he bought his highly lucrative office). The annual minimum thus handed over by the Co-Hong, or corporate body of Hong merchants, amounted to hundreds of thousands of dollars (at least 140,000 pounds sterling).

Yet the Hong merchants were able to build enormous fortunes for themselves. The duties they charged on foreign trade were highly flexible, varying as they did according to the needs of the moment. Their main source of profit came from the opium trade, whose volume increased enormously during the first half of the nineteenth century. In 1834 the wealthiest of Hong merchants, Houqua, estimated his fortune at no less than six million pounds!

Like rich people anywhere else at any time, these merchants indulged in the construction of palatial mansions and had them enhanced with all the means of oriental splendor and refinement. On April 11, 1860, the Gazette de France (of Canton) published the following letter in which a Frenchman relates his visit to one such mansion:

I lately visited the estate of a Chinese merchant of Canton, named *Portingus*, and on which he spends three million francs a year—an immense sum in a country where labor is to be had almost for nothing. The property is larger than a king's domain. This Chinaman made his fortune in the opium trade, and is said to possess more than ten million francs. He has fifty wives and eighty domestics, without counting thirty gardeners, laborers, etc., and owns in the north of China a still finer estate. He has a great liking for the French, and receives them well. When I went with two friends to visit his mansion he had just left, but I was received by a steward, who conducted us over the house and grounds. In front of the house is a vast garden in which are the rarest flowers, and a wide alley leads to the principal entrance. The apartments are vast, the floors being in marble; they are ornamented with mother-of-pearl, gold, silver, and precious stones. Splendid mirrors of a prodigious height, furniture in precious wood covered with Japan lacquer, and magnificent carpets of velvet and silk, decorate the rooms. The apartments are separated from each other by movable partitions of cypress and sandalwood, which are ornamented with charming designs cut right through the wood, so as to enable one room to be seen from the other. From the ceilings are suspended chandeliers ornamented with precious stones. There are more than thirty piles of building in the whole edifice, which are united by covered galleries with columns and pavements in marble. The lodgings of the women are decorated with more than Eastern splendor. An entire army might be lodged in the house and grounds. Watercourses, on which are gilded junks, traverse them in all directions, and at intervals are vast basins, in which are swans, ibises, and an infinite variety of birds. There are also pagodas nine stories high, which are very remarkable; some are in marble, others in sandalwood carved with great art. . . .

In front of the women's apartments is a theatre in which a hundred actors can perform, and so placed that people in the apartments can see without difficulty. Near the outer door is a printing office, in which M. *Portingus* is having the memoirs of his family prepared for posterity.[17]

The Hong merchants, various Mandarins, and an increasing number of opium smugglers were about the only Chinese to benefit from the activities of European (and some American) traders on the "Celestial" shores. Few among these Chinese or among Western intruders, unfortunately, endeavored to transcend business ventures in order to understand the opposite party's culture and way of life, or its deeper needs. Thus, after three centuries of sporadic intercourse, East and West remained worlds apart: on the one hand, there was self-isolated, self-complacent and self-sufficient China, very much set in her ancient traditions but minding her own business; on the other, the slowly growing swarm of adventurous, aggressive and profit-seeking "foreign devils" bent on imposing their presence, their commerce—and possibly their Christian faith—on an ever larger scale. Between the proud Empire of the Middle unwilling to open its doors to outside "barbarians" and the latter's amounting impatience to force these doors wide open, a conflict was inevitable.

During the first half of the nineteenth century, European pressure for broader trading concessions in China increased steadily. This was largely due to the march of the Industrial Revolution through Western Europe: the factories were soon producing more manufactured goods than could be absorbed by local demand, and new foreign markets were sought, as well as new sources of raw material. The accumulation of capital greatly increased the Western nations' purchasing power, and made them more eager to buy the products of other continents. Their ships, sailors and merchants appeared ever more numerous—and insistent—before the gates of Old China.

England was the first nation that experienced the Industrial Revolution, and quite naturally became China's leading tormentor, so to speak. Already at the time of Lord Amherst's unsuccessful mission to Peking, in 1816, she stood out as the chief European power in India and the Far East. She dominated the foreign trade of China throughout all of the nineteenth century, and most of the time was also that country's outstanding influence in foreign affairs.

As mentioned earlier, British trade with China developed under the monopoly of the East India Company. By the end of the eighteenth century the principal British export to China was opium, mainly opium cultivated in Bengal. Fast sailing vessels, called opium clippers, brought it into Chinese waters before Canton, whence it was smuggled to the mainland. Before long, substantial numbers of Chinese had taken to opium smoking despite official decrees prohibiting its use. This growing fondness of the Chinese for the forbidden article in turn led to ever larger imports from India, and, of course, resulted in growing profits for all those—"barbarians" or Chinese—who were engaged in the illegal traffic.

The spectacular increase in opium trade during the first half of the nineteenth century is best illustrated by plain figures*: in the year 1817, a total of 3,210 chests (containing some 150 pounds each) of Indian opium was imported;

* Quoted by a well-informed and reliable author, C. Toogood Downing.

ten years later, the figure had risen to 9,969 chests; in 1833, nearly 24,000 chests were sold, and four years later no less than 34,000 chests found their way to China. But the record was yet to come, in 1860, when 85,000 chests were disposed of!

It was largely over the opium question that the long-pending (and irritating) problem of broader trade concessions came to an issue. China's determined effort to put an end to the pernicious traffic, and England's stubborn resolve to keep the Chinese doors open, led to the first bloody clash between the two countries. The celebrated Opium War proved that nineteenth-century China was no match for Western military might.

CHAPTER II

THE OPIUM WAR, 1839-1842

OPINIONS ABOUT the origins of the Opium War have long been (and to a large extent still are) divided, according to whether they stem from Chinese, British, or other sources. The mounting tension that characterized East-West relations in the eighteen-thirties in the Canton area was undoubtedly over-shadowed by the annoying opium question. But several other, and sometimes deeper, factors were also involved.

Chinese authorities, of course, had been increasingly alarmed by their people's growing fondness of opium. Its widespread consumption* entailed a considerable outflow of silver.† Its moral and physical effects on opium smokers, on the other hand, could not leave them indifferent. The Throne was alerted, and imperial edicts frequently fulminated from Peking against the import of "foreign mud", as the drug was often called in official language. Various Chinese officials denounced its dangers. The well-known French Sinologist Georges Maspero has summed up some of their most typical complaints:

As early as 1838, a censor sent the following petition before the Throne: "Everywhere transactions are slow, and the revenue does not come in, because money is expensive and bullion depreciated. Now money is expensive because it is leaving the country in large quantities, being drained by the opium trade. This trade is the work of the English. This people, not having enough to live on at home,‡ tries

---

* Although it is quite impossible to quote precise figures (no statistics were ever kept), it can safely be assumed that the number of opium smokers ran into the millions, and probably exceeded 10 million toward the middle of the nine-teenth century.

† Value of the imports in 1837: about $20,000,000.

‡ Common Chinese belief regarding Europeans.

to bring other countries into subjection by first weakening their inhabitants. . . . Now they have come to China, and brought us a disease which will dry up our bones, a worm that gnaws at our hearts, a ruin to our families and our persons. Since the Empire first existed it has run no such danger. It is worse than a world deluge, than an invasion of wild beasts. I demand that the smuggling of opium be inscribed in the Code among the crimes punishable by death."

At the same time, the Governor of Hu-Kuang, Lin Tse-hsü, declared that "unless this trade is stopped, before ten years have passed there would not be a man left fit to make a soldier".[1]

As a result of such and similar complaints, increasingly severe decrees were promulgated with a view to frightening the Chinese away from the "foreign mud".* While opium smokers were liable to flogging and the pillory,† people engaged in smuggling or selling opium were threatened with imprisonment and even the death penalty by strangulation. But the temptation was too strong for the smokers, and the profits too high for all those—Chinese or foreigners—involved in the business; opium imports kept rising year after year.

In striking contrast to the stern tone of the anti-opium decrees, there were the half hearted measures to crush the illegal traffic; and, most of all, there was the venality of the Cantonese authorities, that thwarted attempts at restriction and actually permitted the rise of imports. The American trader, W. C. Hunter, who knew the inside story well, characterized and illustrated the goings-on prevailing in Cantonese waters:

Needless to say, the opium trade was prohibited by Imperial edicts as well as by proclamations of the Canton authorities. The Chinese who dealt in "foreign mud" were threatened even with capital punishment, but so perfect a system of bribery existed (with which foreigners had nothing whatever to do) that business was carried on with ease and regularity. Temporary interruptions occurred, as, for instance, on the installation of newly arrived magistrates. Then the question of fees arose; but was soon settled, unless the newcomer was exorbitant in his demands. . . . In good time, however, all would be arranged satisfactorily, the brokers reappeared with beaming faces, and "peace" and immunity reigned in the land.

* The poppy flower, source of opium, was but little known in China, being cultivated on a small scale only, and mainly for medical purposes.

† Traditional punishment for common offenders.

Opium was never found for sale in Chinese shops at Canton; nor were there any signs by which one could judge where it was prepared for sale or for smoking, it being used in no other form.[2]

Much of this "peace" and immunity was due to the relative ease with which local Mandarins could be bought off: forty dollars per chest was their price. The opium dealers, meanwhile, contributed to a "corruption chest" that paid out some 100,000 dollars annually.

As Hunter recorded, each deal invariably called for a definite pattern of formalities:

We owned at the time a Boston clipper schooner called the *Rose*, which, in 1837, was about leaving for that anchorage with a quantity of opium sold at Canton for delivery there, and an additional number of chests to try the market. The whole cargo consisted of nearly 300 chests, of the Canton value of about $300,000. I joined the vessel at Capsyhuymun from Macao with an English gentleman, my guest there, whom I invited to accompany me. The *Rose* was soon ready for sea; we made sail and started with a moderate southwest monsoon. . . . We kept an eye upon the barometer, it being the typhoon season, and a sharp lookout upon the fleet of "fishing boats" which covered the waters, and the crews of which were peaceable fishermen or cutthroat pirates according to circumstances.

We anchored on the inside of the island of Namao on the third day, close by two English brigs, the *Omega* and the *Governor Findlay*. Inshore of us were riding at anchor two men-of-war junks, with much bunting displayed; one bore the flag of a "Foo-Tseang", or Commodore. Knowing the formalities to be gone through with the Mandarins, we expected a visit from one, and until it was made no Chinese boat would come alongside, nor would a junk, nor even a bumboat. We had no sooner furled sails and made everything shipshape, when "his Excellency" approached in his "gig", a sort of *scow* as broad as she was long. Besides the oarsmen, there were official and personal attendants, in grass cloth with conical rattan hats and flowing red silk cord surrounding them to the brim. He himself sat majestically in an arm-chair smoking quietly. A large embroidered silk umbrella was held over his head, while servants protected him from the attacks of flies and mosquitoes.

He was received at the gangway by Captain Foster. His manner and bearing were easy and dignified. When cheroots and a glass of wine had been offered, the "Commodore" inquired the cause of our anchoring at Namao. The Captain gave him to understand that the vessel, being on her way from Singapore to Canton, had been compelled through contrary winds and currents, to run from Namao to replenish her wood and water. Having listened attentively, the great man said that "any supplies might be obtained, but when they are on board, not a moment must be lost in sailing for Whampoa, as the Emperor did not permit vessels from afar to visit any other port". He then gravely pulled from his boot a long red document and handed it to his secretary, that we might be informed of its purport. It was as follows:

AN IMPERIAL EDICT

As the port of Canton is the only one at which outside barbarians are allowed to trade, on no account can they be permitted to wander about to other places in the Middle Kingdom. The Son of Heaven, however, whose compassion is as boundless as the ocean, cannot deny to those who are in distress from want of food, through adverse seas and currents, the necessary means of continuing their voyage. When supplied they must no longer loiter, but depart at once. Respect this.

Tao-Kuang, 17th year, 6th moon, 4th sun.*

This "Imperial Edict" having been replaced in its envelope and slipped inside of his boot (for service on the chance of another foreign vessel "in distress"), his Excellency arose from his seat, which was a signal for all his attendants to return to the boat except his secretary. The two were then invited to the cabin to refresh, which being done, we proceeded to business. The Mandarin opened by the direct question, "How many chests have you on board? Are they all for Namao? Do you go further up the coast?" intimating at the same time that *there* the officers were uncommonly strict, and were obliged to carry out the will of the "Emperor of the Universe", etc.; but our answers were equally as clear and prompt, that the vessel was not going north of Namao, that her cargo consisted of about 200 chests. Then came the question of "Cumsha",† and that was settled on the good old Chinese principle of "all same custom".

* Instead of months, the Chinese counted in moon cycles, or revolutions (around the earth). On the other hand, the Chinese character which represents "day" is literally "sun".

† Cantonese word meaning "golden sand", i.e., the percentage (or bribe) paid to the officials.

Everything being thus comfortably arranged, wine drunk and cheroots smoked, his Excellency said "Kaou-tsze" ("I announce my departure"). We escorted him to the side, over which he clambered with the aid of his secretary; we saw him safely deposited under his brilliant silken canopy, and in a short time rejoin his junk.

Chinese buyers came on board freely the moment they saw the "official" visit had been made . . . and in a surprisingly short time received from the *Rose* in their own boats the opium, which had been sold at Canton, and there paid for, deliverable at this anchorage.[3]

The British East India Company, principal carrier of the drug from India to the coast of China, had discovered the Chinese as an immensely profitable market for opium and was earning handsome dividends for its investors. In 1833, opium constituted about one-half of the total value of British imports to China.* Yet, because of largely hostile public opinion at home, the company exercised some restraint in the traffic.

In 1833, however, the company's monopoly over British trade expired, and was not renewed by Parliament. The latter was then under pressure from independent merchants, advocates of "free trade", stressing that the rapidly expanding British commerce could no longer brook the restrictions imposed by Chinese authorities. In 1834, Lord Napier arrived at Canton at the head of a royal commission that was to open negotiations directly with the Chinese government (and not with the Hong merchants, as in the past), in order to obtain broader trading concessions. His fruitless efforts to communicate with the Viceroy marked the opening of a period of friction which gradually ripened into war.

Opium sales, meanwhile, leaped with the arrival of free-trading British shippers, who were soon joined by a few Yankee skippers who had also succumbed to the temptation of rapid profits. Dent, Jardine, Matheson and Russel were the trade's outstanding names at the time. From its original center at Macao, the trade had moved to the nearby island of Lintin, and in 1837 it was driven to the coast of Fukien, farther to the east. The opium clippers delivered it to the Chinese smugglers by written orders from agents at Canton. Swift river boats called "fast crabs" or "scrambling dragons" took full advantage of the intricate system of Cantonese waterways to elude official surveillance and bring the drug to its ultimate destination, the opium dens. These, of course, did not advertise their existence yet had an appearance all of their

---

* The amount of opium brought in by British ships exceeded the amount of tea (main Chinese export) that was taken out by them.

own. *A British missionary strolling through the streets of Canton with some friends after the city had been opened to foreigners (as a result of the Opium War) took a close look at one such den and "life" within its walls:*

While we have been sauntering around, we have noticed one particular kind of building that differs from all the others about it. It is not a private dwelling house, and yet it has none of the signs that it is a shop, where goods of some special description may be purchased. Its front is not open like those next door to it so that the public can see what is going on inside. Its aim, indeed, seems to be to conceal from the passers-by the movements of the people within, whilst at the same time intimating that anyone that likes to enter may do so freely.

Every window is closed up so that one can get no glimpse of what is going on behind them. The door, indeed, stands wide open, but hanging about two feet in front of it is a bamboo screen that effectually guards the secrets of the house. Any attempt to peer inside will be ineffectual, for the utmost that can be seen beyond the sentinel screen is the posts of the door that are but the outer works of the fortress beyond.

As we stand speculating why this house and others that we have seen of a similar character during our stroll should be so different from the rest, a man approaches in a furtive manner, with head cast down as though he were ashamed, and glides in a ghostlike manner into the opening behind the screen and vanishes into the dark interior. We caught but a glimpse of him, but what we did see did not favourably impress us. His clothes were greasy and dilapidated-looking, and his face wore a leaden hue as though his blood had been transmuted by some chemical process into a colour that nature would never recognize as a product of her own. . . . Hardly has he disappeared when a man still in the prime of life, with slightly stooping shoulders and the same dull colour in his cheeks and on his lips, advances quickly to the screen, dives behind it, and except for a momentary shadow that falls upon the doorway, disappears at once from sight.

We begin to speculate as to what kind of place this is that pretends to have a huge secret from the public, and what is the nature of the goods that it supplies to men that have one characteristic at least that seems common to them all. . . .

While these thoughts run through our own mind, a young fellow of about twenty hurries up with an impetuous rush as though he were racing to catch a train, and after a quick glance up and down the street he plunges behind the screen and is gone.

Our curiosity is excited. This man differs from the two that preceded him in that he has no leaden hue, but the evident desire to avoid being seen going into the place is just as strong as it was in the case of the others that came before him. We feel we must investigate, and so we cautiously get within the screen and peer into a dimly lighted room that lies right in front of us. No sooner have we got to the doorway than a sickening, oppressive odour at once reveals to us the secret of the place. It is an opium den.

We advance into the room and the fumes are so dense that we feel inclined to retreat, but we are inquisitive, and we should like to have a glimpse at what at the present moment may be called the curse of China. We find the owner seated in front of a little desk where he keeps the opium all ready for the use of his customers. . . . His face is thin and emaciated and his Mongolian high cheekbones jut out like rugged cliffs that have been beaten bare by the storms. . . . His fingers are long and attenuated and stained with the dye that the opium has put into them, and they are deftly measuring out into tiny little cups, in antici- pation of coming customers, the various amounts that he knows by experience each man may need.

With a ghastly smile that would have suited a corpse he invited us to be seated, for he knew at a glance that we were no opium smokers, but had wandered in simply out of curiosity. . . . We noticed that the three men had already curled up, each one on his own particular bench, busily manipulating the opium and with infinite pains thrusting it with a knitting-like needle into the narrow opening in the bowl of his pipe. He then held it close to the flame of a small lamp, and as it gradually melted, he drew a long breath, and the essence of the opium traveled in a cloud to his brain, while at the same moment he expelled the smoke from his mouth.

"You do not seem to be particularly busy just now," we remarked, as we noticed a considerable number of empty benches in the room, all set out and ready for immediate use.

"No," he replied, "this is our slack time, as it is still early in the afternoon. We shall have to wait till night falls before our regular customers will begin to drop in, and then we shall be busy until the small hours of the morning. You know," he continued, "that the ideal time for the opium smoker is the nighttime, when the duties of the day are over, and when, free from care or anxiety of any kind, he may dream and while away the hours under the soothing influence of the pipe. . . .

"Opium," he continued as he fixed his lacklustre eyes upon me, "is an imperious master and treats its subjects like slaves. It first of all comes with gentle touch as though it were full of the tenderest love for man. Then in a few weeks, when it has got its grip upon the man, it shows itself to be the cruellest taskmaster that ever drove man to a lingering death. It knows that no one in the world can allay the intolerable craving that comes over a man's life but itself, and as though it were playing with a man's soul, it demands that before relief is given the dose must be increased. It has no pity or remorse. It will see the home wretched and the girls sold into slavery, and the boys calling another man father, and the wife in the home of a stranger, rather than remit a single pain or give one hour's release from the agony with which the opium tortures both body and soul.

"By the way," he added suddenly, "is it not true that opium was brought to China by you English? How cruel of you people," he said with a passionate flash in his eyes, "to bring such wretchedness upon a nation that never did them any wrong!"[4]

To a large extent, the Chinese was right: his country had done no harm to England. But for the trading community established in the cramped quarters of the Canton factories, life became increasingly difficult during the eighteen-thirties. Official corruption and arbitrariness in arranging import or export duties according to the whims of the moment, as well as the arrogance with which foreigners were often treated, were in themselves irritating enough. The restrictions on personal freedom, and denial of appeal to the central government, were at least as annoying. Finally, a number of conflicts arose over Chinese versus foreign demands—or refusals—to judge criminal cases under local or foreign laws. Such and similar limitations were highly resented by the Western traders, especially the British opium traders, who constituted their most aggressive element.

After Lord Napier's failure to assert diplomatic equality in 1834, his successors followed a moderate policy. In 1836, Chinese proposals to legalize the importation of opium, and anxiety over the mounting drain of silver to pay for it, led to heated discussions among the Emperor's councilors at Peking: some recommended legalization of the trade, while others advocated its total prohibition. The latter prevailed, and toward the end of the year 1837, a series of imperial edicts advised foreign ships to leave the coast, and foreign merchants to repair from Canton to Macao. A year later, it became known that an Imperial Commissioner was about to come to Canton to "investigate port affairs", i.e. to discover means of suppressing the opium trade.

This piece of news frightened the otherwise lax Mandarins into their excessive severity which led to the initial incidents from which actual hostilities ensued. The American trader W. C. Hunter witnessed the first anti-foreign outbreak:

The appointment and approaching arrival of the Imperial Envoy became known at Canton in the latter months of 1838. The local Mandarins therefore began a system of harshness towards dealers in order to appear vigilant and active in the carrying out of old decrees. This led to much cruel punishment, to the execution of one man in the Square in front of the Factories, in December 1838 (by way of casting obloquy upon the foreigners), and an attempt to strangle another one in February 1839. This latter caused an unprecedented riot, led to an attack upon all foreigners who happened to be out of their residences, several of them being injured, and to the Factories being besieged by many thousands of vagabonds, who kept an incessant attack on windows and gates with stones and brickbats.

They tore down and used as "battering rams" the heavy posts of which the small enclosures in front of each Factory were constructed, yelling and shrieking like so many wild animals. . . . The Mandarins had brought an "opium dealer" to the Square about noon, in order to strangle him there. The cross* was already driven in the ground, and in a few minutes it would have been all over, when an unusual hubbub of something extraordinary being about to take place attracted the attention of some foreigners who were on the Square at the time. Instantly the news flew from Factory to Factory, when all we could muster, perhaps seventy to eighty, rushed up to stop the proceeding. I acted as spokesman on behalf of all present, and protested against the Square being turned into an execution ground. The Mandarin in charge said that the orders he had received must be carried out, that the Square was a portion of his Majesty's Celestial Empire. He was told that might be, but it was leased to us as a recreation ground, and

---

* The prisoner's neck and outstretched arms were fastened to it. It was a more ignominious death than beheading, the other form of capital punishment.

that we *would not permit* its desecration by a public execution! This
was a bold thing to say. During this short interval the scene was a most
extraordinary one. There was the cross, and close to it the victim
with a chain about his neck held by two jailers, all looking on with a
quiet curiosity. The servants of the Mandarin were supplying him with
constantly renewed pipes; his attendants, a few soldiers, and his chair-
bearers, seemed more amused than anything else. There is no telling
what might not have taken place had it not been for a boat's crew who
happened to come from Whampoa that morning. They belonged to
the old East India Company's ship *Orwell*, Captain "Tommy" Larkins,
a well-known and general favorite in our community. These sailors
had been wandering about the Square, but gradually approached the
spot and looked on. Seeing the drift things were taking, suddenly they
seized the cross, smashed it to pieces, and began to lay them over the
heads and shoulders of the executioners and any Chinaman within
reach. The jailers dragged the prisoner away. Jack* tore down a
tent that had been pitched for the Mandarin, capsized the chairs, the
table, with the teapots and cups, and would next have attacked the
Mandarin himself had we not interfered to protect him. We were
much relieved when his Excellency and his aides were carried away
and no harm done to them, and we found ourselves in possession of the
ground. Then cried out one of the sailors to another, "I say, Bill, we
don't get such a lark as this every day!"

The siege of the Factories by the mob was continued throughout
the afternoon, the guards at the corners of the American Factory
were obliged to retreat after ineffectual efforts to clear the ground of
our assailants, and things looked very serious. In the "Imperial"
Factory, Captain Ste. Croix, of the *Alexander Baring*, had collected all
the inmates, armed with such weapons as they had amongst them,
revolvers and fowling pieces, and proposed a rush out, but happily no
demonstration was made. There were without doubt eight or ten
thousand of the vilest of the population seemingly bent on the destruction of the "foreign devils.". . . It looked as if the Mandarins had left
us at the mercy of the mob.[5]

*At this critical juncture, Hunter and a friend were fortunately able, by
climbing over some rooftops, to reach the leading Hong merchant, the
wealthy (and very influential) Houqua:*

* Common nickname of British sailors.

He at once dispatched a messenger to the "Kwang-Chow-Foo", the chief magistrate of the city, and we returned the way we had come. About half-past six o'clock, to our great relief we heard the approaching sound of the gong, denoting the coming of the officers, and witnessed from our veranda the immediate dispersion with whips of the rabble. No one was spared, the sight of the numerous soldiers in attendance on the Mandarin caused a rush toward every outlet from the Square, and even to the river, where several were drowned, not a boatman offering them the least assistance. Wide open flew the Factory gates, and in an instant their imprisoned occupants appeared with looks of relief indescribable. The Mandarins passed the night on the ground, chairs were procured for them, official lanterns were lighted, and, conscious of the entire safety which we now enjoyed, and without being disturbed by the hourly beating on gongs of the different watches of the night, we all turned in. The next day everything reassumed its normal state of comfort and safety. . . . Approaching the Mandarins in the morning to thank them for their timely assistance (rather a "cool" thing to do, as someone remarked, seeing we had taken the law in our own hands and had driven away the officer of justice the day before!), they received us very courteously, and assured us we had "nothing to fear"!

This was the most serious of many provocations inflicted by foreigners upon the authorities. We treated their "chops", their prohibitions, warnings, and threats, as a rule, very cavalierly. We often spoke of their forbearance and wondered at the aid and protection they extended to us; in fact, they considered us more as unruly children, people who had never had an opportunity of becoming acquainted with "Taou-Le", or "reason".[6]

This very frank admission by a foreigner who knew local conditions well, shows that the Chinese were by no means solely responsible for the rapidly deteriorating situation. Events now moved fast.

The man empowered by Peking to act as Governor of Kwangtung (Canton) and adjacent provinces in order to take whatever coercive measures were required to stop the opium trade, was Lin Tse-hsü, former Governor of the Hu-Kuang Province, a Mandarin of high reputation and an able administrator. Lin was determined to act swiftly and uncompromisingly.

His arrival at Canton, in early March 1839, took place in an atmosphere

of tense expectation. The American trader W. C. Hunter once more was among the curious onlookers:

The appointment of a "Kin-Chae", or Imperial Envoy, to Canton for the express purpose of putting a stop to the opium trade, had now become known. This appointment—only made on an occasion calling for extreme measures—was conferred upon Lin Tse-hsü, and involved control not only over all the Canton authorities, but those of the southern and southeastern provinces. His Excellency "Lin" was the son of an independent gentleman of Tseuen-Chow in the province of Fukien who lived on the revenues of a porcelain manufactory, in which he himself had worked as a day laborer it was said.

The "Kin-Chae" at length arrived in Canton on Sunday morning, at half-past eight o'clock of March 10 [1839]. Two gentlemen and myself went on board of a small schooner lying off the Factories to witness his arrival. He was seated on board of a large official boat, with a few red- and blue-button Mandarins standing a little to the rear so that we had an excellent view of him personally. He had a dignified air, rather a harsh or firm expression, was a large, corpulent man, with heavy black mustache and long beard, and appeared to be about sixty years of age. His own boat was followed by a great many others, on the sides of which, on a black ground, were painted in gold letters the ranks of the principal occupants, while flags of various colors were displayed abaft. The crews were neatly dressed in new uniforms and red trimmed with white, and conical rattan hats of the same colors. These boats contained the principal officers of the city, civil and military, from the Viceroy to the Superintendent of the Salt Department.

The walls of the "Red Fort", nearly opposite the Factories on the Honam shore, were lined with soldiers, as were those of the "Dutch Folly",* arrayed in bright new uniforms. Both shores of the river, every door and window, and every spot of standing ground, were thick with people. Everyone was observing the novel scene quietly and as curiously as ourselves. No one boat of any description was moving about; all were lying close to the shores, and a universal silence prevailed. Besides my companion and myself, not a "foreign barbarian" was to be seen in the vast gathering.[7]

A week later, in the account of W. C. Hunter, Lin summoned the
* Old Chinese fort east of the Factories.

frightened Hong merchants, charged them with having connived at the pernicious opium trade, and threatened to have some of them strangled if they did not stop the traffic at once.

At the same time, Lin issued an edict ordering the surrender of all the drug then held in stock by the foreign merchants, and directing the latter to sign bonds to discontinue the trade, "under penalty of death".

Some 20,000 chests of opium, valued at 12 million dollars, were stored in a score of foreign vessels then anchored in Cantonese waters. In view of the enormous losses they were about to sustain, the foreign and Chinese merchants tried to arrange a compromise, by offering the surrender of a thousand chests. Lin would have none of it; he surrounded the factories with troops, and ordered all Chinese subjects out of them:

On March 23, every Chinaman in the Factories, from the Compradore to the cook, left by order of the "Kin-Chae", and were threatened with decapitation if they dared to return. The day before, Mr. Lancelot Dent, chief of Messrs. Dent and Co., had been *invited* to enter the city and meet his Excellency, which he declined to do. Other but ineffectual attempts by the authorities to induce him to go were also made, when on the 24th, Captain Charles Elliot, Her Majesty's Superintendent of Trade, arrived from Macao and immediately assumed charge, on behalf of the English residents, of the perplexing question of the "total surrender" of the opium. The street in rear of the Factory was now filled with soldiers, a strong guard was also placed in the "Square", and a triple cordon of boats drawn up from the Creek to the Danish Factory. The whole community were thus prisoners in the hands of the Chinese. Provisions were not allowed to be brought in, no one was permitted to go to the "Square", and matters assumed a decidedly serious aspect.[8]

In their factories, according to Hunter, the besieged foreigners faced the now "serious" situation as best they could:

The night of March 24 was one of unusual brilliance in its cloudless sky and full moon. The Factories, forcibly abandoned by several hundred Chinese [estimated at eight hundred] at a moment's notice, resembled somewhat places of the dead! Their foreign occupants were thus left literally in a state of destitution as regards service of any kind, not even a scullion being allowed to remain. The consequence was that

they were compelled, in order to *live*, to try their own skill in cooking, to make up their own rooms, sweep the floors, lay the table, wash plates and dishes! It may be supposed that it produced discontent, complaints, and impatience. Not at all; we in the Suy-Hong—and it was the same with our fellow prisoners in the other Factories, with few exceptions—made light of it, and laughed rather than groaned over the efforts to roast a capon, to boil an egg or a potato. We could all clean knives, sweep the floors, and even manage to fill the lamps. But there were mysteries which we could not divine; our chef, Mr. Green, after a vain attempt to boil rice—which, when prepared, resembled a tough mass of glue—proved a most wretched cook, and took to polishing the silver, but abandoned that and finally swept the floor! . . . The rest of us, from modesty or a feeling of sheer incapacity, did no more than was absolutely necessary. . . .

Thus, by hook or by crook, we managed to sustain life of which the "bread" was nightly supplied to us by Houqua's coolies. They also brought (made up in bags, as if "personal effects" or "blankets to keep off the dew", thus passing the guards) edibles of all sorts.[9]

A determined opponent of foreign trade, particularly in opium, Lin was firmly resolved to bring its traffic to an end. The following entries from his diary give an idea of his frame of mind:

March 27 [1839]. At the Hour of the Snake [9 A.M.] I received through the guild merchants* a note from the English Consul Elliot asking in obedience to my instructions to hand over the opium. I shall have to discuss my reply with the Governor General and Governor. One must know what quantity they are surrendering. At midday ate at the Governor's place. Today it has been very hot, and many of the people were working naked. Got back to my lodging at dusk.

March 28. At the Hour of the Snake the guild merchants brought a note from Elliot saying that the English would surrender 20,283 chests of opium and were awaiting instructions about the checking of its reception. So I went to the Governor General's office . . . to arrange about the day and hour for reception, and circulated urgent dispatches giving the necessary orders. I also sent to the foreigners a present of beef, mutton and other food.

March 29. Elliot is now inventing reasons for delaying the surrender

* Or Hong merchants.

of opium, insisting that liberty of movement must first be restored to the foreigners in the factories.[10]

Elliot's delaying tactics proved of no avail. Over a period of some two months, all of the opium stored in foreign ships was surrendered for destruction. On May 13, Lin wrote in his diary that he inspected "the trenches that are being made to drain off the opium when it is destroyed." About a thousand chests remained to be delivered at that time.

It seemed as though matters would slowly settle down, at least temporarily. From Macao where he had taken refuge, the British Superintendent Elliot demanded that the value of the destroyed opium be refunded as an indemnity, but Lin would not hear of such a solution.

Still, negotiations were kept open, when an untoward incident definitely compromised the chances of a peaceful settlement. In early July, a party of intoxicated English and American sailors started a quarrel with Chinese farmers, one of whom died from his wounds.

This affair at once raised the long-standing dispute over extra territoriality.* Lin demanded that the culprit be handed over, in order to be tried according to Chinese law. Elliot replied that it had proved impossible to discover which of the sailors had dealt the fatal blow, that he had "no proofs", whereupon Lin decided to occupy Macao. The British colony hurriedly embarked for Hong Kong, which the Chinese began to blockade with their war junks.

Lin's "occupation" of Macao did not materialize. Instead, he himself set out for the Portuguese stronghold and there had a rather friendly meeting with the Portuguese governor. His diary shows that he was not a little surprised at the foreigners' manners and habits:

To the foreign officials I gave coloured silks, folding fans, tea and sugar candy; to the foreign soldiers, beer, mutton, wine, flour and four hundred pieces of silver from abroad. . . . The foreigners build their houses with one room on top of another, sometimes as many as three stories. The carved doors and green lattices shine from afar like burnished gold. Today the men and women alike were all leaning out of the windows or thronging the side of the streets to see me pass. Unfortunately foreign clothes are no match for foreign houses. The bodies of the men are tightly encased from head to toe by short jackets

---

* Western Powers were unwilling to submit the lives and property of their nationals to the operation of Chinese laws.

and long close-fitting trousers, so that they look like actors playing the parts of foxes, hares and other such animals on the stage. Their hats are round and long . . . and even at the height of summer are made of felt, velvet or other such heavy material, so that to catch their sweat they have to carry several kerchiefs inside their hats. When they meet a superior they salute him by raising their hats. . . . Their hair is very curly, but they keep it short, not leaving more than an inch or two of curl. They have heavy beards, much of which they shave, leaving one curly tuft, which at first sight creates a surprising effect. Indeed, they do really look like devils; and when the people of these parts call them "devils" it is no mere empty term of abuse.

They also have devil-slaves, called black devils, who come from the country of the Moors and are used by the foreigners to wait upon them. They are blacker than lacquer, and were this colour from the time of their birth. The foreign women part their hair in the middle. . . . Their dresses are cut low, exposing their chests, and they wear a double layer of skirt. Marriages are arranged by the young people themselves, not by their families, and people with the same surname are free to marry one another, which is indeed a barbarous custom.[11]

On his way back from Macao, at the beginning of September, Lin learned of the first naval action which was a prelude to the Opium War. British vessels had dispersed a number of Chinese war junks which, near Kowloon, were preventing native villagers from supplying British merchantmen with food. Her Majesty's Navy had entered the scene, too. The war's actual beginning is usually traced to the so-called "battle" of Chuen-pi, fortress town at the entrance of the Bogue, where on November 3 two British frigates sank several war junks.

News of the worsening crisis in China caused considerable emotion in England (which it reached with a delay of about four months). In her Address from the Throne at the State Opening of Parliament on January 16, 1840, Queen Victoria expressed concern over China's recent decision to cease all trade with English "barbarians", and pledged her ministers' full attention to a problem directly affecting "the interests of my subjects and the dignity of my Crown".

Lord Palmerston, Foreign Secretary in the second Peel Cabinet, was at the time under considerable commercial pressure to take a tough stand.* But

---

* British opium dealers in Canton had turned to their government to obtain from China an indemnity for the opium seized by Lin.

strenuous Tory opposition in Parliament, led by Lord Stanhope and fiery young William Gladstone, who stressed the illegal and immoral aspects of opium trade,* at first prevented him from throwing the government's weight behind British mercantilism in China.

An Anti-Opium League aroused British public opinion, and included Members of the Parliament. One of them was Sir George Staunton, who had been in Peking with Lord Amherst in 1816, and who in 1847 was appointed to the parliamentary committee inquiring into the state of British commercial relations with China. He subsequently published a booklet quoting typical anti-opium interventions in the British Parliament, including his own. This is what he told the House of Commons:

With respect to the immorality and impolicy of this traffic, I yield to no Member of the House in detestation of it; and in the anxiety for the adoption of measures for effectually putting it down altogether. . . . I feel very strongly on this subject . . . I entirely disapprove of all the evils and enormities which have occurred in the prosecution of the opium traffic, down to the present crisis of the total interruption of all trade and intercourse between Great Britain and China. . . .

I think the cultivation of opium, in India, for the supply of the China market, ought gradually to have been discontinued, and the trade proportionally discouraged. I think a better system might have been introduced gradually; that the best lands in India might be safely devoted to produce beneficial to man, instead of that which exercises the most baneful influence, and tempts him to his destruction. I quite agree with the opinion expressed by Captain Elliot, even before the late crisis, that it cannot be good that the conduct of a great trade should be so dependent upon the steady continuance of a vast prohibited traffic in an article of vicious luxury, high in price, and liable to frequent and prodigious fluctuations. . . . I think with him that "the fact that such an article should have grown to be by far the most important part of our import trade, is of itself a source of painful reflection". And I think, lastly, that there are many cogent reasons for regretting the extent to which the Indian income is dependent on such a source of revenue.[12]

---

* Gladstone had called it "infamous and atrocious". And in 1843, Lord Ashley told the Parliament that the opium traffic was "utterly inconsistent with the honors and duty of a Christian kingdom".

Another parliamentary gesture made in the same spirit, at the height of the Opium War, was the intervention of Henry St. George Tucker, former Chairman of the East India Company, whom Sir George Staunton called "the most distinguished authority" on the subject of opium:

I have steadily and uniformly opposed the encouragement given to the extension of the manufacture of opium; but of late years we have pushed it to the utmost height, and disproportionate prices were given for the article in Malwa.* We contracted burdensome treaties with the Rajput States† to introduce and extend the cultivation of the poppy. We introduced the article into our own districts, where it had not been cultivated before, or where the cultivation had been abandoned; and we gave our Revenue Officers an interest in extending the cultivation in preference to other produce much more valuable and deserving of encouragement. Finally, we established retail shops, which brought it home to every man's door.

How different was the policy of Lord . . .‡ who circumscribed the produce within the narrowest limits, confining the cultivation of the poppy to two of our Provinces, and actually eradicating it from districts where it had been previously cultivated! How fatal have been the consequences of a departure from this wise and humane policy! Is there any man still so blind as not to perceive that it has had a most injurious effect upon our national reputation? Can any man be found so hardy or perverse as to deny that it has led to the total derangement of our trade with China, which was heretofore the source of wealth and prosperity, both to India and the mother country?

If a revenue cannot be drawn from such an article otherwise than by quadrupling the supply, by promoting the general use of the drug, and by placing it within the reach of the lower classes of the people, no fiscal consideration can justify our inflicting upon the Malays and Chinese so grievous an evil.[13]

Lord Palmerston eventually threw his authority on the side of those who insisted that the importation of opium was essential to maintaining the balance of trade with China, and that its discontinuation would be disastrous to the

* Area in northeastern India.

† States ruled by Hindu princes, the Rajputs, claiming descent from a famed ancient warrior caste.

‡ Here follow the names of several high officials in India.

finances of India. After weeks of lively debates, he obtained a majority of nine votes in the Parliament: war was declared on China in retaliation for her "arrogance" and "provocations".

In June 1840, the main body of the British "Eastern Expedition"* arrived off Macao, and within a matter of days had sailed northward. Its immediate objective was the island of Chusan at the entrance of Hangchow Bay, just south of the little town which western commercial activity would turn into the great port of Shanghai. The Chinese put up such resistance as was possible, but their antiquated means of defense stood no chance against the concentrated fire of some fifteen British warships.

Lord Jocelyn, "Military Secretary to the China Mission", recorded the fleet's arrival before the town of Ting-hai:

In the afternoon of the 4th of July I accompanied Captain Fletcher, commander of Her Majesty's ship *Wellesley*, on board the Chinese admiral's junk, which we recognized by its more numerous pennons and three tigers' heads painted on the stern. Our orders were to summon the town to surrender within six hours. . . .

In the course of half an hour the Chumpin [Admiral] and suite arrived;† he was an old man, and bore in his face the marks of opium; he wore a red button in his cap, and the other officers mounted blue and white, according to their different grades. . . .

We opened the summons, and they read it in our presence, and indeed before the assembled troop: the deep groans and increasing pressure of the people warned us that we were among a hostile multitude. . . . The summons addressed to the people stated that no injury was intended to them, but it was against their rulers and their servants we had come to make war for their unjust acts. Of this they seemed perfectly aware; but they hated the invading barbarians more bitterly than their Tartar rulers;‡ and their clenched hands and anxious faces proved to us how false was the idea that we were come among a people who only waited for the standard of the foreigner to throw off a detested and tyrant yoke.

After some conversation they agreed to accompany us to the flag-

---

* Under Admiral Bremer, and consisting of a score of warships and transports carrying about 4,000 British and Indian troops.

† They were on shore when the British came on board.

‡ The Manchu dynasty, which had occupied Peking in 1644 and had been ruling over China ever since.

ship, and, upon our proposing to remain as hostages on board their junk, they simultaneously refused, and begged we would take a seat in their boat to the *Wellesley*.

All was there repeated to them to the same end as what they already knew; and the reason and purport of our present hostile movement on the place was explained. They complained of the hardship of being made answerable for wrongs that we had received at Canton, and said, naturally enough, "Those are the people you should make war upon, and not upon us who never injured you; we see your strength, and know that opposition will be madness, but we must perform our duty if we fall in so doing.". . .

During the whole of that night the shore presented a most beautiful spectacle, the hills around and suburbs appearing a moving mass of variegated light. In China no individual ever moves out at night without these painted lanterns, carrying them in their hands, or on short bamboos. By their help we could perceive that crowds were busy throwing up some more of their wretched embankments, and placing jingals* and fresh guns in position.

The merchant junks were faintly seen, through the shades of darkness, heaving up their heavy anchors, and stealing silently through the fleet, laden halfway up their masts with goods and merchandise, and crowded with women and children; these were allowed to pass without molestation. . . .

The dawn of day brought much the same spectacle as the preceding, excepting that a few guns were mounted on the Joss House hill, and the Mandarins were seen actively employed running about along the wharf. Soon afterwards they were remarked to take their different stands with the troops, one among them with his party in the martello tower being particularly conspicuous. The war junks were drawn up and crowded with men.

The British men-of-war were lying in line with their larboard broadsides toward the town, at a distance of two hundred yards from the wharf and foot of the hill. They consisted of the *Wellesley*, 74 [guns]; *Conway* and *Alligator*, 28; *Cruiser* and *Algerine*, 18; and ten gun brigs. At eight o'clock the signal was hoisted to prepare for action; still, however, time was given by the Commodore, hoping to the last they would repent, and it was not until two o'clock that the

* A long musket or cannon, usually fired from a rest—a weapon frequently encountered in Asia during the nineteenth century.

troops left the transports in the boats of the squadron, and took up their position in two lines in rear of the men-of-war, to land under cover of the fire. At half-past two the *Wellesley* fired a gun at the martello tower: this was immediately returned by the whole line of junks, and the guns on the causeway and the hill; then the shipping opened their broadsides upon the town, and the crashing of timber, falling houses, and groans of men resounded from the shore. The firing lasted on our side for nine minutes, but even after it had ceased a few shots were still heard from the unscathed junks.

When the smoke cleared away a mass of ruin presented itself to the eye, and on the place lately alive with men, none but a few wounded were to be seen; but crowds were visible in the distance flying in all directions. A few were distinguished carrying the wounded from the junks into the town, and our friend the Chumpin was seen borne from his vessel by a faithful few, having lost his leg in the action by a round shot. . . .

On the following morning the desertion of the place became visible from the heights; and through the long vistas of the valleys thousands were seen fleeing, carrying their goods and chattels along with them. The bridge across the outer ditch having been demolished the previous evening, the troops were brought to a momentary halt; the great gate of the town, too, was found to be barricaded, and the wall which surrounded the city to be of great strength. It was, however, soon scaled, and in a few minutes the banner of England was floating over the Chinese city of Ting-hai; the ramparts were found strewed with pikes, matchlocks, and a species of fire rocket, arrow-headed; and on the parapets, packets of quicklime were packed up, to blind the eyes of the barbarians had they endeavored to mount the walls. . . . The main street was nearly deserted, except here and there, where the frightened people were performing the kowtow* as we passed. On most of the houses was placarded "Spare our lives"; and on entering the Joss House were seen men, women and children, on their knees, burning incense to the gods; and although protection was promised them, their dread appeared in no manner relieved.[14]

The British Marines landing on Chusan Island in July 1840 were only the first of a long succession of European troops that were to be sent

---

* Act of reverence, performed by knocking the forehead on the ground while kneeling.

ashore in China as conquering invaders. Following the early Chinese reverses (the British also occupied the Canton River forts), Imperial Commissioner Lin was dismissed and recalled to Peking. His successor, Chi-shan,* realizing the folly of military resistance in the face of overwhelming odds, negotiated the Chuan-pi Convention with the enemy (January 1841), by which England was to be indemnified for her loss in opium. The agreement, however, having been authorized by neither government, was soon repudiated by both of them.

Operations were resumed in the vicinity of Canton. Chinese authorities "persuaded" the British not to enter the city, promising them a payment of six million yuans.† The invaders therefore turned north of the harbor, and soon were harassed by large and determined, if ill-armed, bands of irregulars. Lieutenant John Ouchterlony took part in one such encounter, at the end of May:

Before the British troops had evacuated their position on the heights, the inhabitants of the surrounding villages, bearing arms and standards in considerable numbers, began, on the day succeeding the commencement of the armistice, to assemble in heavy and threatening masses, upon a range of low hills to the westward of the city, excited, it is believed, by inflammatory addresses and placards, circulated among them by influential members of the patriotic gentry of the province, and further, it is to be feared, infuriated by some excesses perpetrated by stragglers from the British outposts. Their object soon became evident; and as it was observed that strong bodies were being detached to their front, preparatory to an attack on the British position, some companies of the 49th and 37th Madras native infantry and Bengal volunteers, together with a wing of the Cameronian regiment . . . advanced against the line which these irregulars had formed. A few volleys of musketry dispersed them, and the British troops, contenting themselves with the destruction of a village in which the enemy had taken post, and of some magazines and stores of arms and provisions found in the neighborhood, were about to retire, when a body of 5,000 to 6,000 strong was seen descending the opposite heights, and advancing in a determined manner toward the post from which they had been driven by our attack in the early part of the day.

The weather had up to this time been fearfully oppressive. Major

---

* Who, contrary to Lin, was opposed to the death penalty for opium offences, as many smokers were otherwise highly respectable persons.

† The Chinese monetary unit.

Becher . . . died in a *coup de soleil*,* and many men had fallen from utter exhaustion, when it suddenly changed—the sky became overcast, and a thunderstorm came on. Some rockets were thrown among the advancing masses of the enemy, but their movement was not for a moment checked, and it became necessary to direct a general charge of the whole British line to repel them. This was, of course, successful; and as soon as the enemy had been dispersed and put to flight in all parts, the General, finding the rain descending in torrents, and every appearance of a tempestuous night, directed a retreat toward the heights occupied by the main body of the army. The muskets of the troops being all furnished with flintlocks, had, of course, by this time become utterly useless, and as the various detachments drew off from the scene of the late conflict, without further attempt to molest them, the Chinese, gathering upon the rear and flanks of the column, harassed them in the most resolute and spirited manner, closing upon the bayonets of the men, and engaging them hand to hand whenever an advantageous opportunity presented itself, as in crossing a stream, or defiling through lanes and village streets. [15]

On occasions, the hard-pressed Chinese also resorted to old magic practices in their struggle against the invaders. A young writer and volunteer fighter, Pei Ching-ch'iao, recorded the following two incidents in the army of General I-ching, who was about to counter-attack the British:

On New Year's Day [February 10, 1842], Wang Ch'eng-feng, a skilful painter of landscapes and figures whom the General had with him in his camp, presented him with a picture entitled *All Proceeds According to Plan*. It had taken him several months to do. It was in a style of great refinement, closely akin to that of the best Academy painters of Northern Sung times.† The General regarded it as a great treasure and asked many members of his staff to inscribe poems on it. [16]

Two days later, on February 12, 1842, a contingent of Miao–tze aborigines joined General I-chin's army. They all wore tiger-skin caps, and the general regarded this as an omen of victory because the year 1842 was the "Year of the

* Sunstroke. In French in original text.

† The Sung dynasty (960–1126) was one of the outstanding periods of Chinese literary and artistic achievements.

Tiger" *(traditionally, each Chinese year was placed under the sign of an* *animal):*

Tiger-skin caps now became the rage in the General's army. There were yellow tiger-head caps, black ones, white ones, winged ones and so on. Someone wrote to the General saying that if a tiger's skull-bone was thrown into the Dragon's Pool this would make the dragon come to the surface and attack and sink the foreign ships. This too was tried, but to no effect.

There were a great many literary men on the General's staff, and ten days before the attack began, he ordered them to compose announcements of victory. Thirty of these were sent in, and the General arranged them in order of merit. The first place went to Min Chia-ku who had composed a detailed and vivid account of the exploits of the various heroes. Second on the list was Ho Shih-ch'i (a fairly well-known calligrapher) who sent in a vast composition, full of classical tropes and brilliant felicities. Never had such prose been since the days when Chang Yüeh (667–730) and Su T'ing (670–727) carried all before them in the literary world.[17]

Between August 1841 and August 1842, hostilities were confined almost *exclusively to naval attacks on the cities of the southern and southeastern* *coast. British firepower was uniformly successful, but Peking learned little* *of the actual turn of events, as the Chinese commanders only sent highly* *favorable reports to the imperial court. Lord Jocelyn noted this typically* *Chinese way of presenting the military situation after he had examined some* *of these reports:*

Some of the Emperor's comments on the dispatches of his officers along the coast, who, wherever they had been chastised, sent up the account of a great victory, are worthy of remark. Upon the dispatch of the General of the district of Che-Keang, he writes, "The General was wrong in not having reinforced the garrison of Chusan, and he therefore condemns the said officer to lose his button; but in consideration of his former good conduct, 'and because the shot fell like mountains from the barbarian vessels', he leaves him in his command, to recover by future prowess his lost honour."

When informed by a dispatch from another of the Generals on the shore of the Yangtze-Kiang that the red-bristled barbarians were wildly careering in the Celestial waters, but that the lightnings of the Empire had cleared them from the coast, he remarks upon it, "Most right; let our servants, however, be merciful, and the officers and the families of the men who have fallen be properly rewarded." Many more announcements of the same description were published in the *Peking Gazette*,★ which some of the paid agents used to obtain for our perusal. It appears that on all the public documents from his servants the Emperor makes these notes, which are then published for the benefit of others, to encourage them to do likewise.

This is merely mentioned to show the utter blindness of the Court to the real state of things, and how necessary it is that arrangements, whether hostile or otherwise, should be carried on at a future period, if thought requisite, with the supreme government, at the very foot of the imperial throne.[18]

In spite of their obvious inferiority, the Chinese troops did not always remain on the defensive. In March 1842, in particular, under the leadership of the Emperor's cousin, I-ching, they made a most gallant attempt at recapturing the city of Ningpo, on the southern shore of Hangchow Bay. Lieutenant Ouchterlony witnessed their spectacular if futile charges against withering British fire:

The suburbs instantly appeared alive with enemies, who poured down upon the gates in columns of dense array and prodigious length, headed by men whose gallantry and determination could not have been excelled. . . . The guard . . . poured in upon the dense mass of men below a close and steady fire of musketry, which took deadly effect among their crowded ranks. . . . But the havoc which was thus taking place among them did not for a long time deter them from persevering in their desperate attempt; and while a few bold men endeavoured to scale the wall, by driving nails into the crevices of the masonry, and so ascending, another party having reared a rude sort of ladder against a part of the rampart . . . their leader, a powerful and courageous man, actually gained the summit [where he was killed].

In the meantime, however, success had attended the efforts of the enemy at the south gate . . . from which they now proceeded in a long and dense column towards the marketplace in the centre of the town, and finding no obstacle to their advance, concluded their comrades at

★ Official court publication, and probably the oldest newspaper in the world.

the west gate had been equally successful, and that Ningpo was once more their own. . . . At this juncture, Captain Moore's howitzer came up, and being run to the front, immediately opened upon the living wall before them with case shot, at a distance not exceeding twenty to thirty yards. The effect was terrific, for the street was perfectly straight, and the enemy's rear, not aware of the miserable fate which was being dealt out to their comrades in the front, continued to press the mass forward, so as to force fresh victims upon the mound of dead and dying which already barricaded the street. The head of the column fell literally "like the Moor's swath at the close of day", and the howitzer only discontinued its fire from the impossibility of directing its shot on a living foe, clear of the writhing and shrieking hecatomb which it had already piled up.

It had, however, been only fired three times, and the destruction would have been far greater had not the short distance prevented the grapeshot from spreading. The infantry party had resumed their platoon firing, the front rank, after discharging their pieces, filing off to the right and left to load and form again in the rear, their places being filled by the next rank, and so on; by which means such a storm of balls was kept up upon the enemy, that in a short time the street was chocked up, and when, for want of a living mark, the men were ordered to advance, their steps fell upon a closely packed mass of dead and dying of fully fifteen yards.[19]

A number of Chinese prisoners were made here and there, and on some occasions the roguish victors humiliated them by cutting off their pigtails.* It was another story, however, when the British encountered Manchu garrisons, as was the case near the town of Chapoo at the mouth of the Yangtze. Rather than surrender to the despised invaders, the proud "Tartars" preferred wholesale suicide—after having massacred their own families in their special permanent quarters. A ghastly spectacle thus presented itself to the advancing British, as described by Lieutenant Ouchterlony:

The Tartars in Chapoo occupied the northwest angle of the city, residing with their families in complete seclusion from the Chinese inhabitants of the place, from whose streets and dwellings they were separated by a regular line of rampart, connected with the main walls on

* A badge of disgrace indeed, and one deeply resented by the Chinese. It was a traditional Chinese way of punishing common offenders.

the north and west faces. The residences of the governor and the principal military and civil officers, as also the arsenal, treasury, gaols, and other government buildings, are situated in this Tartar citadel, as it may be called, and as the Tartars may be said generally to have no calling but that of arms, although often connected with traders of all sorts, every male inhabitant is available for its defence, whether against a sudden outbreak amongst the Chinese, or the attack of a common enemy.

As this place afforded the first opportunity which the expedition had enjoyed of examining that remarkable system of living apart from the Chinese, pursued by the Tartars in all towns where they have adopted permanent residences, much interest was excited by the investigation of the buildings included in what was styled the "Tartar city". It was found to contain, besides magazine for arms, powder, saltpetre, and grain, and a foundry upon a small scale, several exceedingly commodious ranges of barracks, consisting of rows of small houses in streets, with cooking houses, and small plots of ground attached to every town, with guardhouses and parade grounds in their vicinity, and the whole united in a manner which proved that the discipline maintained (as the sole foundation of the throne of the Manchu dynasty) would suffer but little by comparison with that of our more refined armies of Europe.

Miserable, however, was the spectacle presented by the interior of most of the better class of houses in the "Tartar city", on the entrance of our troops: strewed on the floors, or suspended from the rafters, were to be seen the bodies of women and young children, bloody from the wounds by which their lives had been cut short, or swollen and blackened by the effects of poison. Impelled by the same feeling of exclusiveness and pride which characterizes their habits of life as well as of government, it seems that the Tartars of Chapoo, even when defeated and driven from their entrenchments on the heights, never for a moment contemplated removing their families from the town and escaping beyond our pursuit, but, with a stern resolution to maintain to the last the inviolability of their homes (which, though we decry it as barbarian, must yet command a share of our respect), preferred staining them with their blood, to surviving to abandon them to the polluting touch and presence of the invader.

Of the females found dead and dying in the "Tartar city", many had evidently not been their own executioners, but the greater number appeared to have destroyed themselves by strangulation or by poison, after hearing of the defeat of their troops outside the city, and impelled, doubtless, by the exhortations and threats of the fugitives from the field, and by the near approach of the frightful foreigners, at whose hands they had been taught to expect the most unheard-of atrocities. Many Tartar soldiers were also found dead within the city, with their throats cut, apparently with their own daggers, who must have thus fearfully ended their career, after consummating the cruel sacrifice of the lives dearest to them.[20]

In another town at the mouth of the Yangtze, Ching-kiang, the Manchu garrison similarly chose collective self-destruction.* In the early summer of 1842, the British troops began advancing along the river, toward Nanking, a former capital of the Celestial Empire.

Outside the walls of Ching-kiang, on the bank of the country's famed Grand Canal,† lived the poet Chu Shih-yün, whose diary enables the reader to look at that summer's events through Chinese eyes:

[July 9]. The foreign ships have entered Fu-shan creek [ninety miles down the Yangtze]. There are a lot of conflicting rumours and the people inside and outside the walls are all in a state of unrest. However, one rumour is that they are only merchant ships, and that has calmed people down a little. But from the first week of the fifth month [about June 14] rich people had already begun to move out of the town, by order of Lieutenant General Hai-lin,‡ and the number of those leaving grew daily. The Lieutenant General was in a very excited state. All over the town he arrested harmless people on the ground that they were in league with the enemy. He handed them over to the Prefect to imprison and flog, allowing no distinction in the treatment of them. Some of the Manchu troops took advantage of this to go about plundering and pillaging. Fortunately the Prefect had sense enough to see that great injustice was being done, and released many of those arrested. . . .

---

* Resistance there was the strongest so far experienced by the British, who sustained some 170 casualties out of a force of 9,000.

† Linking the Yangtze valley to the Peking area. Formed in the seventh century by the toil of over a million laborers. Restored in the thirteenth century by the great Mongol ruler Kublai Khan.

‡ Commanding the Manchu garrison.

The city gates were kept shut except from the Hour of the Dragon to that of the Monkey [7 A.M. to 3 P.M.], and the western small gate was never open at all. Hai-lin explained that this was to prevent traitors from going in and out. This was early in the fifth month when the foreign ships were far away at Shanghai and when there was still no news of their coming up the Yangtze. But these measures naturally alarmed the inhabitants and resulted in a general migration. . . .

[July 10]. The foreign ships have reached Kiangyin [sixty miles away]. The Governor General has issued a proclamation, reassuring the population. . . . The proclamation ran: "Misleading reports have been spread by a certain captain, who has already been cashiered. The ships in question are merchantmen; moreover it is not considered possible that they will venture far up the river. You can go to your beds and sleep in perfect security.". . .

[July 15]. Today, between the Hours of the Snake and the Horse [9 A.M. to 1 P.M.], the gates were temporarily opened and the people streamed out of the city like a swarm of ants. As my house is outside the walls, many friends stopped there for a short rest. Boxes, baskets, bags and sacks covered the floors, so that there was not an inch of free space. They were mostly waiting for missing members of the family to join them, when they would set out upon their flight either on board ship or in carts. But when the city gates were suddenly shut, there were some who were already outside and wanted to get back, others who wanted to get out but could not, others belonging to families of which one or two members had managed to get out while the rest were still shut in. All these gazed at one another in speechless despair. In my house alone there were twenty or thirty of them, so it may be imagined what the total number was. At the Hour of the Dragon [7 A.M.] a boat happened to come from the north side of the river and I hastily embarked more than twenty members of my household, so that they might be taken back in it across the river and take refuge on the other side; I and my younger brother staying to look after the house. . . .

[July 17]. Five foreign ships have reached the riverside, and a thunderous cannonade is going on. Since this started the city gates have been closed for good and all. Hai-lin does nothing except make his Manchu troops search everywhere for traitors; anyone walking in the street at night whom they don't know by sight they kill on the spot. Having said that the town contains nothing but traitors and threatened to exterminate everyone in it, he moved a big gun and mounted it at the Red Flag Creek, apparently meaning to open fire on the city. The people were in terror; but when they tried to escape they found all four gates closed; and against the south and east gates earth had been piled. There was no possibility of escape and they could only fold their hands and await destruction.

[July 20]. From the eighth to the twelfth day [July 15-19] the foreign ships cruising about on the river did not interfere with Chinese boats that were crossing; but now they dare not go across. Early this morning a rice-transport boat tried to cross. It was challenged by the foreigners, but did not reply. They fired, and wounded one of the crew. . . . At the hour of the Monkey I heard the sound of a large force of our troops coming along the road. I hastened to the gate to look at them and saw that they were marching with war banners flying, in excellent formation, creating indeed a most formidable impression. One of them told me that, as the foreign ships had now arrived in force, these troops had been sent on parade, in order to make a demonstration of strength, and also to search for traitors. . . .

[July 21]. Today at the Hour of the Snake the foreigners disembarked. The Assistant Commissioner Chi-shen and the Commander-in-Chief Liu Yün-hsiao hastily marshalled the troops whom they had secluded in a fold of the hills, and directed operations sitting in carrying-chairs. Our troops fired several rounds; but the foreigners continued to advance. The two generals then left their chairs and fled on horseback whereupon all their men broke into a general stampede up hill and down dale, in the direction of the Tan-yang high road, to the great amusement of the foreigners. . . .

I looked toward the northern gate. Under the wall a fierce cross fire of guns and rockets was in progress. . . . My thoughts turned to the hundreds of thousands of souls, shut into this seething cauldron without chance of escape. What was happening at this moment to this or that lifelong friend or near kinsman? I struggled in vain to keep back my tears.

When the fire at the north gate watchtower was still only beginning, the rocket attack spread to the whole line of parapets toward the east, and was replied to by our men. After a while there was an extremely concentrated attack by rockets on the part near the watchtower on the eastern wall, and now when I cast my eye round the whole circuit of the walls I could not see a single defender, except at the point where the foreigners were actually trying to scale them; here twenty or thirty of our men were still crouching between the parapets. . . .

I was sure now that the city would not hold, and hastened to send someone to fetch my brother, while I myself rested for a time in a small grotto at the foot of the hill. But soon the news became more and more desperate, and I hurried toward the southern hills. I was holding an umbrella and making my way through the blazing sun . . . I reached a hilltop and sat down on a rock. Looking around the walls I saw that the men between the parapets on the eastern wall were still firing guns and rockets, and knew that the city had not yet fallen. . . . In a moment I saw the foreigners spread out over the road and march straight through the southern gate. My brother and I then took a track that went down the hill and reached the house of a certain Mr. Chang, who received us very hospitably, giving us millet and meat. After we had eaten, someone came from close outside the walls, saying, "The city has fallen, but I don't know by which gate they got in."[21]

After the fall of Ching-kiang, the road to Nanking lay open before the invaders. Unhindered by the Chinese, the British warships moved up the Yangtze and threatened a massive bombardment of Nanking. Chinese authorities were by now fully aware of the barbarians' devastating firepower, as well as of their utter incapacity to defend their own territory against the invaders' military might.

The unchallenged presence of the British at the gates of Nanking meant that the Celestial Empire was actually cut in two: a major success, moral rather than military, had been achieved by them, since they had proved their irresistible strength and superiority. In August 1842, China acknowledged the foreigners' victory—and her own weakness—by signing the Treaty of Nanking, which ended the old days of restricted trade at Canton and brought China's traditional isolation to an end as well. An enumeration of the treaty's main provisions clearly shows its far-reaching consequences, and the new turn taken by East-West relations:

1. Lasting peace and friendship between the two nations.
2. China to pay $21,000,000 over a period of four years.
3. The ports of CANTON, AMOY, FOOCHOW, NINGPO and SHANGHAI to be opened to British trade. Consular officers to be appointed to reside there, and regular and just tariffs of import and export duties to be established and published.

4. The island of Hong Kong* to be ceded in perpetuity to her Britannic Majesty, her heirs and successors.

5. All British subjects, whether natives of Europe or India, who may be in confinement in any part of the Chinese Empire, to be unconditionally released.

6. Full and entire amnesty to be published by the Emperor to all Chinese subjects, on account of their having held service or intercourse with or resided under the British government or its officers.

7. Correspondence to be conducted on terms of perfect equality amongst the officers of both governments.

8. The British forces to retire from Nanking on payment of the first six million dollars, but some islands [especially Chusan] to be held until final payments are made and arrangements for opening the ports be completed.[22]

No mention was made of opium and its traffic. The smuggling and consumption of the drug even increased toward the middle of the nineteenth century, the more so as Chinese authorities, desirous to avoid difficulties with the "foreign devils", relaxed their efforts to stamp out the illegal trade (though the prohibition was not repealed).

The Treaty of Nanking constitutes a major turning point in the relationship between the Celestial Empire and the aggressive West. Besides revealing the fundamental weakness of that colossal empire, it also manifested the Western powers' growing ambitions and appetites in the Far East, as other nations took advantage of the new situation. In 1844, an American delegation led by Caleb Cushing† signed the Treaty of Wanghsia which placed American (eventually all foreign) residents under extraterritorial criminal and civil jurisdiction of consular and mixed courts. In the same year the French obtained toleration of Roman Catholicism (Treaty of Whampoa), and in 1845 the measure was extended to Protestantism. By the middle of the century, Belgium, Sweden, Norway and Russia (who had ambitions of her own in the Far East, and was worried by England's advance in the Yangtze area) had obtained treaties on the same basis, including the status of "most-favored nation" granted to England in 1843.

These treaties greatly increased European and American interest in China. Growing foreign communities established themselves in special areas assigned

---

* Occupied in January 1841.

† A Congressman, newspaper editor, lawyer, and Harvard graduate.

to them in the five Treaty Ports,* forming the nucleus of those self-governing settlements that were to play a decisive role in the history of the relations between China and the West. An increasing number of Chinese thus became accustomed to the presence of foreigners, and Western ideas began to percolate into Chinese life. But the great problem of the relation between these new communities and Chinese society was in no way solved, for the simple reason that neither officials nor common people were any more desirous than before to have these foreigners in their country. Continued friction was inevitable, and repeated difficulties arose in carrying out the terms of the treaties. There were riots in Canton, where the people were bitterly opposed to the opening of the city to foreign residence, and there was occasional trouble in the other open ports. Yet commerce increased notably, stimulated by greater freedom and by the pulsing new industrial life in the West. Before long, European and American steamboats made their appearance in Chinese waters.

To the representatives of the West, it seemed as though defeated China, awed by the crushing power displayed by a single Western nation, would abide by the clauses of the treaties. For the Chinese, however, the latter were simply bits of paper which served to ward off the barbarians' natural brutality by according them important concessions in a few ports. As Ch'i-ying, the Chinese plenipotentiary, wrote in expressing his proud conviction of the moral superiority of his nation:

The British barbarians having been persuaded by coaxing, the American and French barbarians have also come this year. I have treated them too in such a way as to put them into good spirits. Born and raised in foreign countries, these barbarians are quite unable to understand the affairs of the Empire of the Middle. They like to gather in large numbers to eat and drink together. I have made them the honor of offering meals to them, after which they invited me to their residences. They all vied with one another as to who would have me as a guest at table. These barbarians are very fond of their wives. So much so, in fact, that the American barbarian *Parker*† and the French barbarian *Lagrené* ‡ have brought theirs along. When I went to their

---

* Where they had the right to build houses, wharves and warehouses, churches, schools, hospitals, etc.

† Peter Parker, of Massachusetts, first American medical missionary (Presbyterian) to China, whose able and disinterested work made him a popular figure among the Cantonese. He was of great assistance to Caleb Cushing.

‡ French plenipotentiary.

homes on an official call, suddenly these women appeared and greeted me. I was greatly embarrassed, but they were highly pleased. This shows plainly that it is impossible to obtain anything from these barbarians with regard to ceremonial, and that it would be useless to try to enlighten their stupidity. They also presented me with some small gifts such as wines, perfumes, etc. For my part, I made them large gifts, on the principle that he must give generously who has received little. These barbarians are now adopting for their persons and their countries honorable Chinese attributes to which they are not in the least entitled. But one should not argue with them over such trifling matters. It is wiser to give in to them in all insignificant details, so as to insure the success of important negotiations.[23]

CHAPTER III

THE T'AI P'ING REBELLION, 1851–1864

THE TREATY of Nanking dealt a serious blow to the prestige of the Manchu dynasty, which had ruled over the Celestial Empire since 1644. True, the immense majority of Chinese, constituted by farmers and coolies, remained ignorant of the treaty and its implications. The average Chinese's outlook on life being confined to its immediate necessities and perplexities, he asked nothing of his country's rulers but to be allowed to pursue his vocation and to rear his numerous offspring in peace. He believed in the divine right of the Son of Heaven to rule, so long as he ruled wisely and did not exact too heavy taxes from his subjects.

Among the empire's more educated and better-informed classes, however, anti-dynastic feelings were spreading. The gentry and literati, or scholars, not only were eager to preserve their own opportunities and local autonomy, but they also felt that after a century of expansion* the Manchu dynasty had outlived its value and was approaching dissolution.

They deeply resented its inability to parry foreign aggression, and began talking about the country being sold to the foreigner. These people were most outspoken in the southern provinces of China, which lie farthest from Peking and thus were least controlled by Manchu power.

A series of natural disasters resulted in great loss of life and property for the rural masses, whose rapidly growing numbers† were all too often ill-nourished, since the cultivated areas increased but slowly and could hardly cope with the country's demographic expansion.

After the Treaty of Nanking, therefore, the interior situation of China was far from satisfactory, and it continued to deteriorate year after year. Thomas

* During the eighteenth century, a series of victorious wars had led the Manchu troops into Tibet, Burma, and Annam.

† China's population doubled from the middle of the eighteenth into the middle of the nineteenth century, jumping from about 200 to 400 million.

Meadows, who served as official British interpreter from 1842 until 1854 and was one of the great authorities on China in his period, has aptly described her changing domestic mood:

The British war with China of 1841–42 was most injurious to the peace of the country, because the power of the Government had for long depended greatly on prestige; because large districts had been brought to ruin; and because the calling out of bands of local militia had taught the people their power. It is well known that, previous to that war, the appearance of the insignia of a Mandarin, accompanied by a few lictors armed with whips, could disperse the most turbulent crowd in Canton, the most turbulent city in the empire; and, by a long-established rule, the people were denied the possession of fire-arms. But during the war arms were so generally distributed that loose characters of all kinds got possession of them, while at the same time respect for the Government had been destroyed by the manner in which its immense pretensions had been broken through by the despised Barbarian; and, instead of venturing on a bold course against the local riots, robber bands, and insurrections which then arose, the Administration, conscious of its military weakness, and still stunned by its recent defeat, began to temporize and appeal. In 1845 at Ningpo, and in 1847 at Canton, when serious disturbances arose from trivial causes, the Mandarins quieted matters only by yielding. The associated banditti of the Triad* increased so in many parts of the country that life and property became exceedingly insecure. The indemnity of 21,000,000 dollars exacted by Britain on account of the war brought on a financial crisis, while trade was suffering from the operations which had taken place.

Great inundations of the Yellow River and of the Yangtze occurred inopportunely to increase the distress and decrease the land tax, the only great source of revenue. In these circumstances, the Government fell upon the fatal expedient of commuting punishments for money, and putting civil offices to sale, thereby increasing the number of criminals at large, holding out inducements to crime, and exciting against itself the animosity of the powerful literary and official classes, who thus saw themselves defrauded of their just privileges. Thus robbers began to increase on land, and pirates at sea; the local governments being powerless to protect, the people armed and organized themselves

* Famous secret society, whose activies spread over much of southern China.

against banditti; and everywhere over China, but especially in the
south, troubles had gathered, and dark times seemed at hand, when in
February 1850 the Emperor Tao Kuang "ascended on the dragon throne
to be a guest on high", and his youthful, ill-fated son, Hsien Feng,
reigned in his stead.[1]

At the Court of Peking, meanwhile, the aging Emperor and his advisers
were hardly aware of the approaching "dark times". Slow communications
throughout a vast empire and incomplete or flattering reports sent in by
servile underlings prevented them from getting a true picture of events. This
ignorance of things to come is well illustrated by the following excerpt from
an audience granted in the late forties by Emperor Tao Kuang to one of his
Mandarins:*

Emperor. Do you think from the appearance of things in Kwang-
tung† that the English barbarians or any other people will cause
trouble again?

Answer. No. England itself has got nothing, and when the English
barbarians rebelled in 1841 they depended entirely on the power of the
other nations who, with a view to open trade, supported them with
funds.

E. It is plain from this that these barbarians always look on trade as
their chief occupation; and are wanting in any high purpose of striving for territorial acquisitions.

A. At bottom they belong to the class of dogs and horses; it is
impossible they should have any high purpose.

E. Hence in their country they have now a woman, now a man as
their prince. It is plain they are not worth attending to. Have they got
like us any fixed time for their soldiers' leaders?

A. Some are changed once in two years, some once in three years.
Although it is the prince of these barbarians who sends them, they are,
in reality, recommended by the body of their merchants.

E. What goods do the French trade in?

A. The wares of the barbarians are only camlets, woollen cloth,
clocks, watches, cottons and the like. All the countries have got them,
good or bad.

---

* Tao Kuang (1821–50), mentioned in the preceding passage, and whose
official) name meant "brilliant reason".

† China's southernmost province, whose capital is Canton.

E. What country's goods are dearest?

A. They have all got both dear and cheap. There is no great difference in their prices of similar articles; only, with respect to the camlets, the French are said to be the best.

E. China has no want of silk fabrics and cottons, what necessity is there for using foreign cottons in particular? For instance, garments can be made of yellow, or pale yellow for the palace,* and people outside could use Nanking cloth coloured, or blue ones. This would look simple and unaffected; but lately foreign flowered cottons have come into use which look very odd. Others use foreign cottons for shirts. Now observe me—the highest of men—my shirts and inner garments are all made of Korean cottons. I have never used foreign cottons.

A. Foreign cotton cloth has no substance, it is not good for clothing.

E. And it does not wash well.

A. Yes, Sire.

E. I suppose opium is bought and sold quite openly in Kwangtung.

A. I should not dare to deceive Your Majesty—people do not dare to buy and sell it openly, but there is no small quantity bought and sold secretly.

E. It appears to me that in this matter too, there must be a flourishing period, and a period of decay. Even if I were to inflict severe punishment; I might punish today, and punish again tomorrow, and all without benefit. If we wait for two or three years—for five or six years—it will of course fall into disuse of itself.

A. Certainly, Sire.[2]

After Emperor Tao Kuang had left his earthly abode "to be a guest on high", he was succeeded on the Dragon Throne† by his nineteen-year-old son Hsien Feng who, unlike his father, reigned for only ten years.‡ A typical product of the degenerating Manchu court which indulged in extravagant luxury, Hsien Feng proved to be a weakling incapable of dealing with China's domestic troubles on the one hand, and with increasing foreign pressure on the other.

* Yellow was the imperial color, reserved to the imperial family.

† Traditional name of China's imperial throne, the dragon being the country's ancient symbol of power.

‡ Until 1860, when he fled to the northern province of Jehol before the Anglo-French troops. He died there in 1861.

Internal strife, by no means a new feature of the empire's long history, assumed unprecedented proportions during his reign. For many centuries, widespread peasant risings had often disrupted the domestic peace, and had even placed a number of rebel leaders on the imperial throne. During the last quarter of the eighteenth century, such large-scale risings occurred in the teeming provinces of Shantung, Honan, and Anhwei.* In the third quarter of the nineteenth century, other serious rebellions (which took advantage of the central government's obvious weakness) involved the well-organized Nien Fei in these same and some neighboring provinces; several southern ethnical minorities, such as the Miao tribesmen in Kweichow; and the bloody risings of the Mohammedans in the eastern provinces of Yunnan, Shensi and Sinkiang, or Chinese Turkestan, which were crushed after a ferocious repression of over ten years.

Of all these rebellions, by far the most dangerous was that of the Christian-inspired T'ai P'ing T'ien Kuo—meaning Heavenly Kingdom of Great Peace—which very nearly toppled the Manchu dynasty and was eventually suppressed with foreign help. Its founder and leader, the mystic Hung Hsiu-ch'üan, was a disappointed scholar† who had come into contact with Protestant missionaries in Canton, and borrowed certain forms of their doctrine. The T'ai P'ing movement, as it is called in short, began as a kind of religious crusade in Hung's native Kwangsi—which forms part of the Canton hinterland— but it soon turned into an anti-Manchu drive. Because of their Christian connections Hung's followers, the T'ai P'ings, generally considered Europeans and Americans as "foreign brothers". Before long, however, their fanaticism and growing excesses not only made them many enemies among their countrymen, but also lost them the sympathy and confidence which many a Protestant missionary had at first expressed on their behalf. One such missionary, the American Charles Taylor, summed up the movement's early career and trends in his memoirs:

Hung Hsiu-ch'üan was known to a Protestant missionary in Canton, with whom he sojourned and studied some of the doctrines of the Bible for two months. He took literary examinations in 1835 at Canton, and then and there received Christian pamphlets from Leang-afa, first convert to Protestant Christianity in China, and a street preacher. He took the pamphlets home to his native Kwangsi, studied them there, and in 1837, during a severe illness, he had a vision in which

---

* Between the Huang Ho and the Yangtze.

† He failed the mandarin (literary) examinations three times.

he was taken up to Heaven, where he saw the Lord Jesus. During the next ten years, he preached the Gospel most successfully, and with one of his friends founded the "Society of God-worshipers". In 1847, he went back to Canton, and there was received by Mr. Roberts, an American Baptist missionary, as an inquirer after truth. . . . The missionary describes him as the most earnest and deeply interested student of Christianity he had ever found in China; but at the same time strongly tinctured with fanaticism. Soon after, however, and for unknown causes, he disappeared. . . .

In the autumn of 1852, a person who was probably his friend visited a missionary in Hong Kong, and gave him written accounts of the movement that had been for several years in progress, and known to foreigners as the Kwangsi rebellion. This was the first intimation we had of the religious character of the conflict, and that the chief was the man who had been taught by the missionary. One of these papers stated that "Hung Hsiu-ch'üan studied books from his early youth, was intelligent beyond comparison, and having read all kinds of books, he went to the examinations at fifteen or sixteen years of age". Then follows in substance the foregoing narrative. It further proceeds— "it was not the original design to raise a rebellion, but from the encroachments and injuries inflicted by the officers and soldiers to which we could not submit, there was no alternative left us".

In the official reports of these very officers they were accused of nothing but denouncing idolatry, breaking the idols in the temples, exhorting the people to believe in Jesus and worship the true God. They were for these things bitterly persecuted, prominent men among them were imprisoned, sometimes beaten, and finally two of them were put to death. This seems to have determined them to assume a defensive attitude. Confidence in the justice of their cause and an avowed trust in God inspired them with a degree of ardor and courage which their adversaries could not successfully resist. The latter were consequently repulsed in every assault upon the anti-idolaters.

These occurrences were not far from the mountainous districts inhabited by the hardy and warlike tribes called the *Miao-tze*, who alone of the native Chinese race were never subdued by the Tartars, but have always maintained their independence, and have been thorns in the sides of these invaders, by making frequent incursions upon them and their subjects in the conquered territory. Ever watchful for opportunities to assail the usurpers, it is more than probable that on learning of this new struggle, they made overtures to their persecuted fellow countrymen, to make common cause with themselves against the government. This, the new religionists could not consistently do, unless the Miao-tze would also adopt the faith for which they were contending and suffering. That they did it—from whatever motive in the first place—is certain, for some of the bravest and most zealous of its champions whom I subsequently became acquainted with in the revolutionary army, were of this noble tribe. . . .

Still, there can be no question, that elated by success and fired by enthusiasm for what they believe to be right, they have run into a wild fanaticism, and set up pretensions which all enlightened people must condemn.[3]

What sort of people were the warlike and fiercely independent Miao mountaineers, who joined the T'ai P'ing groups as they crossed their territory on the way north from Kwangtung? Two French travelers and interpreters were given official information on them while they were dinner guests of an "Assistant Imperial Commissioner" residing at Canton, in the early 1850's:

During the dinner, the conversation came to deal about the Miao-tze, and here are the details which our official host gave us:

"The Miao-tze inhabit a mountain range that rises in northern Kwangtung and expands into the central provinces of the Empire. They usually live in very isolated areas, in groups which rarely exceed two thousand individuals. Their houses are built upon posts, like those of the Malaysians, and they keep their domestic animals under the same roof. They are mainly farmers and warriors. Their race is intrepid, immune to fatigue, and shirks no danger. The Tartars have never been able to subject them. These tribes have preserved their ancient national costume: they never shaved their heads;* they have always rejected the authority of the Mandarins, as well as Chinese customs. Today, their independence is a recognized fact, and our maps show their area as a blank space, as though to indicate that it is not subjected to the Emperor.

"Our latest effort to subjugate them was made during the reign of Ch'ien Lung,† but in spite of the many bulletins that were published

---

* As the Chinese used to do from early childhood onward.

† Who reigned from 1736 until 1795, and received the mission of Lord Macartney in Peking (1793).

to relate the victories of the imperial troops, the undertaking had to be given up. For some time, the peace remained unbroken, but in 1832 their warlike spirit erupted once more.

"They chose an emperor from among them, dressed him in a yellow robe, symbol of supreme authority, and invaded the lowlands, laying them waste. Their invasion had us greatly worried; our troops were beaten by these savage tribes. The Miao-tze were such good fighters that it proved impossible to beat them in the field, but we overcame them by negotiations. The Emperor commissioned clever diplomats, who contacted the rebel leaders and persuaded them, by means of certain advantages, to disband their troops and have them return to their homes."

"Do these people ever come down into the plains?" one of us asked. "Haven't they established some sort of relations with the Chinese?"

"The Miao-tze do not ordinarily venture to come into our cities," our host replied. "They have but little trade with us. Their industry is quite embryonic; they cultivate mountain rice and exploit the forests which their independence protects against the clearing work of the Chinese. Traders travel to their villages, and to them they sell timber which is then floated down into the plains on the many rivers flowing toward the sea. Their relations with their neighbors are limited to the exchange of parts of their crops against manufactured goods which they need. The Chinese are terrified by these tribes, and tell each other all kinds of foolish tales about them. . . . Actually, the Miao-tze are a very handsome and bright race, and it seems to me that their customs are becoming gentler. . . . During the last literary examinations at which I presided, three young Miao-tze were among the candidates, which had never been seen before."[4]

After his "vision" in 1837, Hung Hsiu-ch'üan had become a "new" man, a prophet and a leader. He believed that he was the "Son of God", a second Redeemer called to create a kingdom of social justice, and took the title of "Younger Brother of Jesus Christ". In this coming kingdom, the land would be taken away from absentee landlords, and redistributed among all peasants according to their needs and merit.

A Swiss missionary, Theodore Hamberg, has noted Hung's transformation and also his uncompromising way of meting out justice in his native Kwangsi:

With the return of health, his whole person became gradually changed both in character and appearance. He was careful in his conduct, friendly and open in his demeanor, his body increased in height and size, his pace became firm and imposing. His friend* describes him as being .... a rather tall man, with oval face and fair complexion, high nose, small round ears, his eyes large and bright, his look piercing and difficult to endure, his voice clear and sonorous—when laughing, the whole house resounded; his hair black, his beard long and sandy, his strength of body extraordinary, his power of understanding rare.

Persons of vicious habits fled from his presence, but the honest sought his company. He was ... for several years engaged as teacher of a school about eight miles from his native place. As a schoolmaster he was rather severe, and kept his pupils in strict order; he was however very friendly to those whose character he approved of, and in confidential conversation he occasionally disclosed the thoughts of his heart, whereby it was evident that the impression which his former sickness and visions had made upon his mind had not been effaced. . . .

After he began to adore God, he became very strict with himself. His judgments were frequently severe, and he often chided people. He liked to sit down and chat with honest and upright people, even if they were poor and of lower condition, but he could not tolerate people having dissolute habits, even if they were rich and of high extraction. . . . In his native village, two men who were discovered to have committed adultery so much dreaded the severe censure of Hung, that they absented themselves for several years. A man of bad character, named Moo, had been appointed inspector of the land by ten different villages. This man gradually commenced to flatter the rich, oppress the poor, and beat the villagers. Upon Hung's return from Kwangsi, several accusations were made against this man, to which all gave unanimous evidence, desiring to have him punished for his misconduct. The next day Hung ordered the gong to be struck, and assembled from eighty to ninety families. Moo also appeared, made a humble confession of his guilt, and asked forgiveness, which the assembled villagers were willing to grant, believing his repentance to be sincere. But Hung said, "Yesterday I yielded to the wishes of men, but today I follow the rule of Heaven." Hereupon he deposed Moo from his office, and appointed Kiang-a-si to be inspector of the land. Moo

* A close associate of Hung, whom Hamberg knew.

dared not oppose his decision, or think of revenging himself, and he even sent the usual presents of honor and respect to Hung.[5]

Hung's severity and iconoclastic zeal won him admirers and inevitably turned many people against him. Public opinion, as well as hostility on the part of Mandarins, eventually forced him to give up teaching and preaching. He took his followers into the hills, and gave them a military organization. In 1850, he defeated the imperialist troops sent against him, and began attracting followers from all over southern China: disgruntled peasants, members of secret societies,* as well as various kinds of outlaws and bandits. For some time he was able to impose strict discipline among his troops. As the rebellion spread northward, however, and took an increasingly anti-Manchu turn while at the same time losing its more or less original Christian features, it became synonymous with terror and devastation for much of China.

In 1851, Hung assumed the title Tien Wang, or Heavenly Prince, and in a defiant proclamation, recorded by the British interpreter Thomas Meadows, let it be known that he was going to overthrow the reigning dynasty:

Our Heavenly Prince has received the Divine Commission to exterminate the Manchus—to exterminate all idolaters generally, and to possess the Empire as its True Sovereign. It and everything in it is his, its mountains and rivers, its broad lands and public treasuries; you, and all that you have, your family, males and females from yourself to your youngest child, and your property from your patrimonial estates to the bracelet on your infant's arm. We command the services of all, and we take everything. All who resist us are rebels and idolatrous demons, and we kill them without sparing; but whoever acknowledges our Heavenly Prince and exerts himself in our service shall have full reward—due honour and station in the armies and Court of the Heavenly Dynasty.[6]

This communistic and theocratic attitude of the T'ai P'ing rebellion thoroughly frightened the rich, propertied classes. Nor were the Chinese literati sympathetic with the movement, for they found the teachings of its leaders both too radical and too mystical. The country's many "have nots", idealists, and adventurers, on the contrary, flocked to the rebellion in ever increasing numbers.

* Numerous in China for many centuries. The Triad and the Water Lily societies were the best-known at the time, and strongly anti-Manchu.

As for the court at Peking, it tried at first to dismiss the disorders in the distant southern provinces as mere local acts of banditry. After a few months of persistent defeats sustained by their troops, however, the alarmed authorities endeavored to terrorize the T'ai P'ings into submission by means of large-scale executions of prisoners. Four Europeans witnessed the decapitation of fifty-three rebels in the outskirts of Canton, and one of them described the bloody scene in a letter he wrote to French officials there:

On the 1st of May [1851], I attended an execution with three of my friends on "Potter's Field".* . . . We arrived there at ten o'clock in the morning, and took our station in front of a shop belonging to a mender of old shoes. This was an excellent position, affording as it did a view over the whole ceremony. We remained there quietly until noon, at which time some soldiers and officers attached to the service of the Mandarins arrived, to clear the street and thrust back the onlookers. As in Europe, those who came to see the spectacle were the vilest dregs of the populace—dirty, ragged people, with sinister faces, who wandered about this blood-drenched ground, where most likely they had already seen the execution of a number of their companions, and perhaps of their accomplices.

In a short time, the roll of the gong announced the arrival of the whole procession. Mandarins of all ranks, with the red, white, blue or yellow button, riding on horseback or carried in palanquins, and followed by an escort of musicians, armed servants, and standard-bearers, alighted at a short distance from the place of execution. Contrary to their ceremonious habits, they took up their positions silently in the dismal enclosure.

Then came the condemned men. There were fifty-three of them, each locked in a basket, with his hands tied behind his back and his legs chained; from his neck hung a board on which his sentence was written.

You have often seen in Chinese streets a pair of coolies carrying a pig stretched out at full length in a bamboo case: well, just imagine a human being put in the place of the unclean animal, and you have a correct idea of the fifty-three unfortunate creatures in their cages. When the latter were set down, they were opened and emptied, just as when a pig is turned out in a butcher's shop.

I examined these poor wretches carefully: they belonged to the lower

* Official execution ground at the time.

classes, and were worn out with hunger, looking much more like skeletons than living beings. It was obvious that they had suffered the most dreadful privations. They were clothed in loathsome tatters, wore long hair, and the disheveled tail attached to the crown of the head had been reduced to a third of its normal length. They had evidently belonged to the insurgent bands, which had adopted the fashion of the Mings,* and allowed their hair to grow.

Many of these unfortunate fellows were quite young: some were under sixteen years of age, while others had gray hair. Scarcely had they been thrown on the ground, when they were compelled to kneel; but most of them were so weakened by suffering that they were unable to remain in this position, and rolled into the mud. An executioner's assistant then picked them up and lined them up in a row, while three executioners placed themselves behind them, waiting for the fatal moment. You certainly remember those horrible figures whom we have often seen together in the retinue of the criminal judge at Canton —dressed in a red blouse, wearing a copper crown adorned above the ears with two long pheasant's feathers. Well! These were the executioners, who were now waiting for the signal with a heavy cutlass in their hands. These enormous knives are about two feet long, and the back of the blade is two inches thick: altogether it is a ponderous weapon, shaped like a Chinese razor, with a crude handle of wood.

A Mandarin who closed the cortege now entered the enclosure. He wore a white button, and held in his hand a board showing the order of execution. As soon as this man appeared, the frightful task began. The executioner's assistant, dressed in a long black robe . . . grabbed the victims from behind and, passing his arms under the latter's shoulders, gave them a swinging movement which made them stretch out their necks. The executioner, who now stood in front holding his cutlass in both hands, wielded the weapon with all his strength and, dividing the cervical vertebras with incredible skill and speed, severed the head from the body at a single blow. The dreadful executioner never had to strike twice, for even if the flesh was not completely cut through, the weight was sufficient to tear it, and the head rolled on the ground. An assistant then floored the victim with a kick, as the corpse would otherwise have remained in a kneeling position. After three or four decapitations, the executioner changed his weapon: the edge of the

* The Chinese dynasty (1368-1644), which was defeated by the Manchu, or Ch'ing, dynasty.

blade seemed to be wrung, as if buckled. The execution of these fifty-three wretches lasted only a few minutes.

When the last head had fallen, the Mandarins withdrew silently from the scene, just as they had arrived. . . . After their departure, the executioner picked up all the heads, and threw them into a chest brought for that purpose. At the same time, the assistants took the chains off the victims as they lay in a pool of blood. The heads were carried away, but the bodies were left on the execution ground.

A very sad scene then began: a troop of women with disheveled hair approached with loud shrieks, and dashed wildly toward the fatal spot. These unhappy beings were endeavoring to recognize their fathers, husbands, or children among the headless corpses. It was a frightful thing to see them hurrying about, pondering, and constantly mistaken in the midst of the mutilated remains. Their search continued all day, accompanied by a mournful noise, funeral dirges being mingled with loud cries and sobs.[7]

No measure of repression, however, could stop the fanatical T'ai P'ing forces, whose ranks were steadily swelled as Hung Hsiu-ch'üan and his "generals" (some of whom displayed undeniable gifts of military science) led their forces on a great northern expedition into the Yangtze valley. Besides Hung, four "kings" chosen by him stood out as the revolt's driving personalities. The two French interpreters who described the Miao-tze also sketched the particular role played by each of these "kings":

Hung . . . whose face is bronzed by the sun, is a man of bold, confident appearance. He is about forty years old. His beard and his hair are already gray, and he is said to be endowed with great courage. . . .

Hiang Tsiu-tsing,* or Tung Wang, that is to say "King of the East", is a man of thirty-five. He is short, and pitted with the smallpox, and his scanty mustache stands bristling on his upper lip. He speaks with remarkable facility, and is very accessible to all his subordinates. No one knows from what province he comes; it is only known that he is married to the eldest sister of T'ai P'ing Wang.

Siao Tcha-kouei, or Si Wang, "King of the West", is the Achilles of this cluster of kings. In every engagement he shows himself regardless of personal safety, always fighting in the foremost ranks, and directing his troops with a precision that gives evidence of special

* Or Yang Hsiu-ch'ing, leading rebel strategist.

knowledge. His figure is graceful, his countenance lively and gay; his skin is of a deep yellow, and his oblong face has nothing of the Mongol type, except the distention of the nostrils and the obliquity of the eyes. He does not wear mustaches. This man, one of the most gifted among his brothers-in-arms, is not more than thirty years old, and is said to be married to the younger sister of the King of Peace.*

Fung Hien-san, or Nan Wang, "King of the South", is a man of letters of the province of Canton. He has taken several public examinations, and has gained degrees. He is thirty-two years old, and is said to be very popular among his fellow students, who consider him endowed with great gifts. He does not wear mustaches, and his features are still youthful. Even amid the agitated life of the camps, he spends as much time as possible in seclusion, to pursue his literary studies.

Wei Tching, or Pe Wang, "King of the North", is the Ajax of the insurgent army. He is very tall, and has the dark complexion of a Malay, so that his black mustache contrasts but slightly with his brown skin. He is only twenty-five years of age. His physical strength and his intrepidity have given him a high position among the insurgents, and he is said to be a native of Kwangsi.[8]

Under these youthful and dynamic leaders, the T'ai P'ing armies conquered most of southern China in a little over a year's time, and in April 1852 began their advance down the broad and fertile Yangtze valley. In a proclamation to the people, issued at about that time, they announced their intention to break up the Manchu empire:

Know all people that China belongs to the descendants of the ancient dynasty. Do not be frightened, ye students, farmers, craftsmen and merchants, but remain at your daily work. The fortune of the dynasty of Han† is about to flourish once more, and the foreign dynasty of the Manchus is coming to an end; this is a decree of Heaven, about which there can be no doubt. After a long union, division must follow. In order that things may be firmly restored by the publication of laws, our sovereigns have displayed their kindness, and before prostrating themselves before the Supreme Being have always given assistance to

* Or King Pacifier, another of Hung's official titles.

† One of the earliest Chinese dynasties (whose two branches reigned almost without interruption from 206 B.C. until A.D. 220), famous for its many brilliant achievements. The Chinese often called themselves "Sons of Han".

the unfortunate. After having learned to adore God, they have endeavored to save the people from calamities; they have supported the weak, resisted the strong, and protected the villagers from robbers and bandits. They have not acted like the Taï Te-ou chiefs and others,* who stopped the junks on the rivers, pillaged everywhere and massacred people in town and countryside, after which they asked the Mandarins for passports and safe-conducts to bring themselves into safety.

When our Princes, by the power of Heaven, entered Yung-Ngan,† they extended their benevolence upon everyone and, looking upon the people as their own children, ordered the army to abstain from murder and to take nothing without permission. They are just and impartial as a balance, but if any person refuses obedience, he will be handed over to the officers of the army. Our Princes invite the inhabitants of all districts to surrender, so as to deserve the reward given for their voluntary adhesion. They are now waiting the arrival of the leaders of the other provinces, in order to join their forces and attack the capital of Peking; after which they will proceed to a division of the Empire.[9]

The T'ai P'ings kept advancing in a swift and apparently irresistible tide. Their rapid progress was due not only to increasing popular support, but to the mediocrity, lack of initiative and combativeness generally displayed by the government troops sent against the rebels (and from whom the latter took much of their armament on their northward march). The British interpreter Thomas Meadows has aptly described the peculiar features of the military campaign:

The first movements of the T'ai P'ing and the Imperialist armies are typical of the military proceedings and strategy of the whole subsequent war. The T'ai P'ings take up a position and display a great deal of industrial energy in fortifying it, and no little amount of constructive ingenuity in availing themselves of the natural facilities. . . . As they succeed in effecting it, the Imperialist forces begin to approach. At first these latter station themselves in entrenched camps of observation, at such distances as render their presence no very serious inconvenience to the T'ai P'ings. As their numbers increase with the concentration of troops from various quarters, they gradually hem in the T'ai P'ings, with more or less of resistance on the part of the latter,

* Probably some local feudal lords.   † First rebel headquarters, in Kwangsi.

until an effectual blockade is established. Assaults and storms on the part of the Imperialists are occasionally attempted, but always fail; and are productive of so much loss that they give up the idea of conquering in that way, and confine their efforts to cutting off all channels of supply. In this they are eventually successful; and the T'ai P'ings, straitened by want of provisions, are compelled to break out. They cut their way through their enemies, inflicting far greater damage on the latter than they themselves incur, and move to another position. Such of the Imperialists as dog them too closely on the way meet with some severe check from the T'ai P'ings; but the great body of the Imperialists usually spend some time in plundering the original inhabitants of the place of everything the T'ai P'ings did not take with them, and in slaughtering these unfortunate neutrals as "rebels". In the reports of the Imperialist leaders to the Emperor, as published in the *Peking Gazette*, the breaking out of the T'ai P'ings is called an "escape"; and the move to another position a "flight". But even one of these "escapes" has been from a position of lesser importance to one of greater; and even one of these "flights" has been from a spot more remote from the Imperial Capital, Peking, to a spot less remote from it. . . .

The first fortified positions of the T'ai P'ings were villages or country towns; afterwards they were district cities; then departmental cities; the provincial capital of Hunan was next occupied by them for a month.[10]

Ch'angsha, capital of Hunan Province, was the only large city in which the ill-led government troops held out against the rebels. Everywhere else they were defeated or beat strategic retreats, with the result that the "victories" which their commanders were bound to report to the throne occurred closer and closer to Peking.

A private letter from the Governor of Kwangsi to the Governor of Hupeh, written in the early months of the T'ai P'ing rising, reveals some of the main weaknesses of the Imperialists:

On the 19th of March and on the 6th of April, two battles were fought, but on both occasions the rebels experienced no great loss, owing to the cowardice of our troops. On the 11th of April, the rebels attempted to seize the ferry at Kew Heen-heu [old market town] with the intention of proceeding northward with their combined force.

Fortunately the chief commanders of the irregulars,* recently sent hither, fought vigorously. I did not move up one single man; and the Kwei troops looked on from the top of the mountains, while the whole valley was filled with the rebels! . . .

Tae Ping and Nan Ning† have just sent in word that they are hard pressed; Yu Lin and Po Pih‡ are just about to fall; at Ping Lo and Ho‡ the Major General has been defeated; and it is not known what has become of him. In other quarters, the whole country swarms with rebels. Our funds are nearly at an end, and our troops few; our officers disagree, and the power is not concentrated. The Commander of the Forces wants to extinguish a burning wagon load of fagots with a cup full of water. Furthermore, he keeps up an endless moving and dispatching of the troops, who are wearied with marching along the roads. . . .

General Heang Yung,§ though he has abilities, is of an unjust and narrow mind. He keeps other people's good services out of sight, and publishes his own merits. All the forces from Kweichow and Yünnan detest him. . . . As to these rebels, they have five great leaders. Hung Hsiu is the first, Fung Hien-san is the next. . . . Both are skilled in the use of troops. Hung Hsiu at first conceals his strength, then he puts it forth a little, then in a greater degree, and lastly comes out in great force. He constantly has two victories for one defeat; for he practises the tactics of Sun Pin. . . .||

The rebels increase more and more; our troops the more they fight the more they fear. The rebels generally are powerful and fierce; and they cannot by any means be likened to a disorderly crowd; their regulations and laws being rigorous and clear. Our troops have not a tincture of discipline; retreating is easy to them, advancing difficult; and, though again and again exhorted, they always remain as weak and timorous as before. When personally in command of the above battles, I found that the troops—and they were from several different quarters of the country—were all alike useless.[11]

The closer the T'ai P'ings came to Peking, the more it became obvious that the Manchus' hold over the Chinese masses was definitely on the wane.

* Local militia, used against rebels.   † Districts in southwest Kwangsi.
‡ Southern and western districts of Kwangsi.
§ A leading Imperialist commander.
|| A famous ancient general (fourth century B.C.).

The American missionary Charles Taylor stressed this significant develop-ment in an entry in his journal in July 1853:

The insurgents seem to have made no further movement in the direction of Shanghai,* though it is said that not many days ago a strong force captured, without difficulty, some large cities toward the west. It is also confidently asserted that five or six provinces through which the patriots passed in their victorious march northward—but which they did not attempt to retain in possession—have voluntarily declared in favor of the new movement, and sent in their allegiance to *T'ai P'ing Wang.* The whole Empire is in a ferment of excitement. Disaffection to the existing government is spreading rapidly, and signs of it are manifest in the open resistance to the oppressive demands of the Mandarins in every direction. Only four days ago the enraged populace destroyed the furniture and a part of the buildings belonging to the office of the mayor of this district, and burned the houses of two tax collectors, in consequence of their attempts to force the payment of unjust exactions. The feeling is becoming universally prevalent among the people of all classes, that the Empire is destined soon to change hands.[12]

Naturally, Taylor was anxious to become personally acquainted with the rebel movement, in order to check on its Christian tenets and possibly distri-bute Bibles among its troops. He succeeded in "interviewing" one of its leading generals:

Just as the sun was rising we entered the stockade by a large port-hole, and in a moment more I was surrounded by a motley crowd of dark-visaged, "long-haired"† men and boys, armed with swords, matchlocks and long spears, with small, triangular, yellow flags flying from the points. Many of them had their hair fastened on the top of their head by small turbans of red and yellow silk. Their uniform was multiform, apparently from want of a sufficient quantity of cloth or silk of the requisite colors, which appeared to be yellow for their close jackets, and red or blue for their loose pantaloons. As it was, their garments were as diversified in color as were the soldiers themselves in

* Where the author resided at the time.

† The T'ai P'ings' outward symbol of opposition to the Manchus, who had imposed the pigtail.

age, size, cast of countenance and dialect, for they had been gathered from the several provinces through which the patriot army had passed in its victorious march from Kwangsi northward. . . .

I thus found myself a new and unexpected arrival in the midst of these fierce-looking "long-haired men" who crowded about me in great numbers, and with eager curiosity to learn whence I came, who I was, and what brought me. . . .

The narrator is led to the residence of the commander of the area.

There was here, as before, a crowd of curious spectators, who examined my hat and dress, and hands, with much the same interest with which you would look at a strange animal of some heretofore unheard-of species, in a menagerie. . . .* Before many minutes a man of middle stature, apparently about forty-five years of age, came out from an adjoining room and took a seat near me. He was stoutly built, had a well-formed head, and a piercing black eye that looked out from under a pair of prominent, overarching brows. One of the attendants, who afterwards acted the part of interpreter for me, as he was a kind of secretary to the commandant, told me this was Lo Ta-yun. There was no appearance of an officer in his manner or dress. He had on a short blue silk jacket, and dark-brown loose trousers. I had formed such an idea of the princely appearance of Lo, whose reputation for military sagacity and skill had spread his name widely abroad, that when this personage made his appearance, so destitute was he of the pompous display so common to Chinese officials that I did not believe he was the man . . . and frankly expressed my doubts. . . . I could scarcely credit his repeated assurances that he was the man whom I sought to see, and it was not until his attendants attired him in his official uniform, and he took his seat in the large chair at a table in the middle of the hall, and began to issue his orders to the soldiers who placed themselves in array, and received his commands in the most deferential manner, that my doubts were quite removed. . . .

I was struck with the calm and earnest enthusiasm that pervaded the entire body of troops, and the perfect confidence evinced in the justice of their cause and its final success. To my frequent inquiries as to when and in what direction they would next move, and especially on asking

* Most of the soldiers, being from the interior provinces, had never seen a foreigner before.

the officers when they proposed to come toward Shanghai, they replied, that whenever they received an intimation from the Heavenly Father; as they never moved in any quarter without such direction.[13]

Other foreigners also came into direct contact with the T'ai P'ings as they advanced toward the mouth of the Yangtze. The British interpreter Thomas Meadows has recorded the impressions of a group of Europeans who, in the spring of 1853, were able to travel to the city of Wuhu, some seventy miles south of Nanking:

Here the most cordial feeling was manifested [toward Europeans] by the authorities and people. The visit to this place was of great interest, as it afforded an opportunity of learning from personal observation the character of the insurgent rule over the people in districts which are no longer the seat of war. The state of things is entirely different from that at Nanking. The people are engaged in their ordinary avocations; shops are opened, and trade carried on, as under the old régime, though the former prosperity of the place is by no means restored. Here there is no separation of the men and women,* as at Nanking, but the laws prohibiting the use of opium and tobacco are rigidly enforced. The people stand in great awe of their new rulers, and are obviously governed with a strong hand. The city has suffered severely in the war, a large proportion of it having been burned, leaving many acres of land covered with heaps of rubbish and crumbling walls.

Few, if any, of the people had ever seen a foreigner or a foreign vessel before, and their curiosity and wonder were very great. The greatest deference was shown, however, to those who went ashore. In several instances respectable men, original inhabitants, even fell on their knees in the street before the foreigners and their guides, to testify their respect. The place cannot have been more than three or four months under the undisturbed control of the insurgents, as was shown by the short hair of the inhabitants, who are not now permitted to shave the head (after the Manchu fashion).

Of the many T'ai P'ing officials who here visited the steamer, one stated that he was on his way up the river to attend to the collection of the revenue; another was going up for charcoal for the use of the

* As was the case under Manchu rule, which placed the woman under man's domination.

Heavenly Prince; and a third was in charge of a raft of heavy timber, designed for the erection of palaces at Nanking, for the parents of the Five Princes.[14]

Nanking, former capital of the Celestial Empire, fell to the rebels in March 1853, and for eleven years (until the final suppression of the T'ai P'ings) remained their headquarters and capital.

Peking was still over 500 miles away as the crow flies, but the situation now looked desperate enough for the Manchus, since the rebel movement controlled most of southern China. The thoroughly alarmed young Emperor (Hsien Feng) revealed his helplessness in several naïve and humble supplications to heaven, which were published in the official Peking Gazette:

Filled with dread and apprehension, I humbly entreat Heaven to pardon my offenses, and to spare my unhappy people. May all the officers of the Court and the provinces awaken to better feelings in their hearts, and devise ways and means to ward off the calamities which are now afflicting the people. The students and the people of each locality should also unite their efforts to stop the enemy and swiftly destroy these monstrous rebels. They will thus enjoy endless peace and prosperity under the kind protection of Heaven, while we and our officers shall equally be filled with feelings of respect and gratitude. Since this is the time of the year when the great sacrifices accompanied by fitting ceremonies are to be made, we have manifested our views and given our orders in consequence. We desire that the Board of Rites* and the high authorities of each province shall engrave ·this decree and publish it on yellow paper, in order that our intentions may be known throughout the whole world.

Hsien Feng furthermore made a gesture of personal contrition:

On the 7th of the 2nd Moon,† I, the Emperor, shall spend the night at the altar of Heaven, and shall fervently pray for the peace of my subjects who, from the beginning of the rebellion to the present time, have suffered great calamities in the provinces of Kwangsi, Hunan and Hupeh. I, the Emperor, am also deeply afflicted because

---

* One of the main government agencies.

† March 21, the Chinese year beginning in February.

thousands of people perished in the city of Wuch'ang,* and I most bitterly reproach my officers, who, instead of preventing these calamities by effective measures, began to flee as soon as the rebels made their appearance. . . .

Those who follow the rebels do not act from their own free will. If they return to us, we must receive them well, for they are my subjects. Were not the many millions that have been spent intended to protect my people? In a short time, my troops will have surrounded and annihilated the rebels, and then we shall certainly enjoy peace. If anyone among the rebels kills their leader, not only will he be pardoned, but he will also be rewarded with many favors.

I have frequently reproached myself, and I have prayed to Heaven to forgive my sins, to save my people and not to let them suffer any more on my account. May all future calamities fall upon my head alone![15]

Meanwhile, the insurgent tide kept rolling northward. After the capture of Nanking (where the whole Tartar garrison and its families, or about 25,000 persons, were massacred), the best T'ai P'ing commander, the "King of the East", set out for the crowning act of the rebellion, the seizure of Peking.

At that stage, nature itself came to the rescue of the beleaguered Manchus. The Yellow River, which the T'ai P'ings reached in June 1853, was in the process of shifting its course to the sea from the southern to the northern shores of the Shantung promontory, thus compelling the insurgents to detour to the west through Shansi Province. At the end of October 1853, they had come within thirty miles of Tientsin, but the onset of winter and the lack of troops made the final assault against Peking impossible.

Following this unsuccessful march on the capital, which marked the high tide of the rebellion, the T'ai P'ings gradually retreated to their main operational area in the lower Yangtze valley. Whenever news of one of their rampaging expeditions reached an eastern harbor city, the terrorized population would seek its salvation in a massive flight. One such exodus has been described by the English missionary A. E. Moule:

When we returned to Ningpo we found a panic in the strong city itself. T'ai P'ing spies had been discovered and arrested, and some with great shouting were executed on the parade ground in front of our house. It was known that the rebel hosts were on the move, that

* Near Hank'ou, first large city on the Yangtze to fall into rebel hands (1852).

Shaohing* was threatened, and that the avowed intention of the leaders was to attack Ningpo. The city walls looked brave and warlike, with fluttering flags all round the six miles' circuit; but no display of bunting, no amount of cannon or musket practice, not the sight of the familiar river and broad moats washing and protecting the walls, not the farther line of defense, the hundred miles of the embracing hills, could check the panic and arrested the sad and headlong exodus which now commenced, and ceased not till the city fell in December [1853], when, out of the original four hundred thousand inhabitants, there remained scarcely twenty thousand within the walls. Numbers fled by junks and lorchas† to Shanghai, and a large proportion of these fell a prey to the pirate fleets hovering around the Chusan islands. Others fled to the hills and country villages, where many of them met a worse fate than those who stayed in the city. November, generally clear and bright, was wet and cold and gloomy, and it was an inexpressibly melancholy sight to watch the crowds of fugitives hurrying through the dripping streets with despair on their faces. The crowding was so great that on the 2nd of November a woman was crushed to death crossing the old bridge of boats.

We began to lay in stores as for a siege; rice, and all provisions which always follow the lead of rice, rose in price.... On the 3rd of November news arrived of the fall of Shaohing; on the 5th, the gates of Ningpo were shut early, and so every succeeding day until they were opened by the T'ai P'ings themselves. . . . On the 9th Sir Frederick Bruce‡ having sent positive orders not to interfere with the T'ai P'ings, and the French consul having refused help in consequence of a quarrel with the Chinese admiral, the panic and the mad exodus resumed their disastrous course. The unfortunate authorities did their best to put the city in a state of defence, especially by strengthening the innermost bulwark, the solid walls. On the 9th of November, when walking on the broad top of the walls, we observed bamboo cranes, fitted with ropes and pulleys, ready to let down heavy beams of wood, bristling with iron or wooden spikes, on the heads of the assailants.[16]

In their five "Treaty Ports", the foreigners at first assumed the same attitude of nonintervention as that taken by the British and French consuls at Ningpo.

---

* Large city lying some sixty miles west of Ningpo.

† Small vessels of about 100 or 200 tons, used for inshore trade.

‡ British Consul General.

*Theirs was a policy of wait-and-see that remained largely dependent on the
T'ai P'ings' own attitude toward foreign trade.*

*The Chinese merchants, on the contrary, had but little sympathy for the
rebel movement, since it disrupted the flow of trade and brought them serious
losses. Stocks were piling up in the Shanghai warehouses, exchange rates
were falling dangerously, and the T'ai P'ings had openly proclaimed their
strong hostility to the opium trade. What was more, the rebels had begun to
apply in the Nanking area a series of social and economic measures aimed
at bringing about the "brotherly" (or collective) enjoyment of land and goods,
a policy which could only horrify the propertied classes.*

*In many rural areas, too, the population rose against the brutality and
severity which all too often characterized the rule of the T'ai P'ings. A. E.
Moule has recorded some violent reactions that occurred in Chekiang Province,
to the west of Ningpo:*

The people began to writhe and struggle under the incubus of their
oppressive rulers. On the fine plateau of Ta-lan-san, the "Great Mist
Mountain", three or four thousand feet high, native patriotic levies,
the White Caps, were gathering and drilling. . . . The rebels generally
succeeded in breaking up and destroying these combinations, and the
acts of vengeance and bloodshed among the beautiful western hills
no one can fully describe, for very few survived. . . .

But once at least, and that some time before the roar of English guns
was heard, the White Caps triumphed savagely over their hated foes.
There is a pass over which I have often walked in springtime, the still-
ness broken only by the notes of the cuckoo, or the tinkle of the
mountain streams, or the stroke of the woodman's axe on the hillside,
or the creak of the water wheels in the rice flats lower down. This pass
and the great curve of lofty hills which sweep around and prevent the
possibility of turning it, rang once with shouts and groans, and the
stone path was red with blood. "Little Looking Glass"* was advancing with the intention of penetrating into the rich valleys to the east of
this pass. The White Caps assembled in force, and as the T'ai P'ings
wound round the zigzag path which climbs the pass, they rolled down
great rocks, and pelted the soldiers with stones from the summit. The
rebel musketry fire was of little avail, as the White Caps had shelter
behind crags and walls. The battle raged for some time; but at last,
three hundred of their number having been maimed or killed outright

* Well-known rebel leader.

the rest broke and fled, "Little Looking Glass" himself narrowly escaping with his life. He soon returned, however, with a strong body from Ningpo, and his vengeance was savagely complete. A town of ten thousand people, where we have since carried on mission work, was burnt down, and the whole of the long, lovely valley, twelve miles in extent, bowery with mulberry groves, was blasted by fire, and the precious trees were cut down. . . .

On the 26th of March I was deputed to accompany Mr. Burdon (afterwards Bishop of Victoria) with a large cargo of rice sent by friends in Hong Kong for the relief of our Christians in the country. We had a rough time, our boat being stoned twice by the rebels at the inland custom barriers, but we accomplished our object without serious mishap. We found the populous and beautiful Sanpeh plain groaning under the yoke of the oppressor. While I was sketching on a hilltop, some of the people came up to watch and to talk. "The T'ai P'ings," they said, "are taxing us in an exorbitant manner; seven cash a day for a youth, ten cash for an adult; and off with your head and down with your house in flames if you refuse to pay! The T'ai P'ings! they can never pacify the empire or found a dynasty; only you English can do that.". . . This glorious plain was fearfully ravaged later when the rebels were exasperated by their defeats at the hands of foreigners and by the native rising. I have myself seen ponds and pools which had been filled not long before with the bodies of women and girls who had drowned themselves to escape from T'ai P'ing hands.[17]

The "brotherly" feelings displayed toward foreigners by the rebel movement in its early phase did not as a rule include the Catholics. While the Catholic missionaries tried to keep their converts from getting involved with the T'ai P'ings, the latter endeavored to impose their own brand of Christianity on them. A French Jesuit noted how he and his flock nearly became martyrs in Nanking in March 1853, after the "Heavenly Prince" had proclaimed himself Emperor of China in that city:

Several insurgents entered the chapel in the city, where the Christians were assembled for the celebration of Holy Week. They forbade people to pray on their knees, and ordered the Christians to remain seated while reciting the new prayer to the Tien Wang.* The Christians replied that they were Catholics, and knew no other religion, where-

* Heavenly Prince (or King), title assumed by Hung in 1851.

upon they were told that unless they complied with the instructions within three days, they would all be decapitated. . . .

On March 25, the Christians had gathered for the adoration of the Cross, in accordance with the custom followed on Good Friday. Suddenly the insurgents came rushing in, shouting and threatening: they broke the crucifix, overturned the altar, and insisted on having their own prayer recited. They showed the Christians books containing that prayer. One of our catechists took the book that explains the commandments of God, and presented it to one of the rebel leaders. The latter leafed through the book for a moment, then handed it back, saying: "Your religion is good, and ours does not compare with it; but the new Emperor has issued his orders, and you must obey or die."

After repeated but vain injunctions, the soldiers seized the Christians and tied their hands behind their backs. The women and children exhorted the men to suffer willingly for the purity of their faith. They, too, were seized and manhandled. When all of them were tied up, the men were told that they would be sent before the tribunal of the Emperor to hear their last sentence read to them, after which they were marched into the street. The women and children followed them, and they all walked gladly toward the tribunal. When they arrived there, they had to wait in the anterooms until some officers came and announced to them, on behalf of the Emperor, that because they had refused obeisance, they had all been sentenced to death and were about to be executed by the Eastern Gate. The whole group, therefore, resumed its march across the city, in order to go to the execution grounds. Hardly had they left the tribunal, however, when a gentle old man, no longer able to walk, was beheaded. The rest of the group, numbering some hundred and forty persons, reached the designated spot. There, the same injunctions were repeated to them, but the Christians once more replied: "We are Christians." Many threats were made, but nobody was executed. Toward evening, the whole group was led back to the city and locked up in a large store, which had formerly been the church of Nanking. They spent the night there, with their hands still tied, and some of the Christians even tied to columns. Only one of them succeeded in untying himself and escaping. The next day, new threats were made, and some blows were dealt.

On Easter Sunday, everybody expected to die. Soon the soldiery entered the store and asked whether the Christians were ready to recite the prayer. Some soldiers even said. "We ought to kill all of them," but another soldier replied: "No, for they would all go to Heaven and receive their reward there, while we would only have our sin." The Christians, meanwhile, remained steadfast and did not in the least give in. The women, in particular, as well as some children, defied the soldiers and told them: "Kill us all, so that we may become martyrs and go to Heaven."[18]

Shanghai, the prosperous and rapidly growing* harbor at the mouth of the Yangtze, had its share of trouble too, but it came from another (yet not entirely unexpected) quarter: in September 1853, thousands of southern fishermen broke out from their overcrowded and squalid districts and spread throughout the city. This new rising had been engineered by two secret societies, the powerful "Triad" and the "Little Knife", whose purpose was the restoration of the Chinese dynasty of the Mings.

Another French Jesuit, R. P. Lemaître, has recorded the disorders in Shanghai:

After a very quiet night, I went into the city to celebrate Mass with the Se family, and to baptize two adults. When I got near the large Eastern Gate, I met people running as fast as they could, and who shouted to me to take flight, too. Behind them advanced men dressed in red and armed with swords and pikes. I stepped out of my sedan chair, in order to take a look around. Seeing the gate open, I ventured to enter the city, which I did without any interference. Most of the armed men were Cantonese, or from Fukien,† or local people. The plot had been kept entirely secret, and the Mandarins had had no knowledge of it.

On September 7, at three o'clock in the morning, the rebels had reached the various gates and taken them without meeting any resistance. The Chang Hai-hien‡ was killed with one of his officers. The Tao-t'ai§ was spared by the Cantonese, and led into a house from which he sent a messenger to the Americans begging them to come and deliver him. These gentlemen at first considered sending two hundred

---

* It was still a relatively modest city then (population about 300,000), by no means comparable to the huge metropolis of today.

† Province located opposite Formosa, or Taiwan.

‡ Military commander.

§ Official heading a district; intendant.

sailors to the rescue of the poor Tao-t'ai, but on second thought they became afraid of getting involved in an affair that might have embarrassing consequences. They sent two of their men to see the Tao-t'ai and examine with him the most efficient and least dangerous means of getting him out of the city. The two delegates disguised the Tao-t'ai as a shop clerk and, having provided him with an old, broken umbrella, left with him and one of his officers, who was also disguised. When they reached the wall, not without difficulty, they informed the Tao-t'ai that they would attach a rope under his arms and let him down along the wall. The horrified Tao-t'ai shrank back, and refused to be roped in such a manner. But after one of his rescuers had been lowered in the aforesaid manner, the Tao-t'ai and his companion, seeing that there was no danger, agreed to follow suit. Ever since then, he has resided at the American Consulate under the protection of the guns. All the other Mandarins took flight, and were not pursued.

When I arrived at the house of the Ses, they had already received news of the death of the Chang Hai-hien. I ordered each of them to remain quiet until after Mass, and heard a good many confessions. Several persons, I am sure, believed that this was to be their last confession. After Mass, I went into the street to find out what was going on. The people had been told publicly to remain quiet, and had been assured that the Mandarins alone deserved the wrath of the rebels. The shops were actually reopened at once, but people were very much concerned. I thought it my duty to visit the various Christian families throughout the city, in order to comfort them and somehow cheer them up. I had no difficulty whatsoever going around, and I can even add that I was treated with respect everywhere. . . .

The next day was the anniversary of the birth of the Holy Virgin, and I went again to see the families in the cities. I saw a good many rebels in the streets, and talked to some of them, especially at their guardhouse near the Western Gate. The names of Zi-ka-wei* and Tong-ka-tu† were known everywhere, and I was treated as a friend, as a brother. . . . After I had thus been convinced of the friendly feelings of the men in red, I went to see Father Languillat to inform him of all I had seen. We all agreed that we should calmly stay at our respective posts, and wait for whatever Providence had in store for us, while

---

* Catholic missionary center near Shanghai, which in 1873 became the site of a world-famous observatory.

† Suburb of Shanghai.

treating these men with much patience and kindness. During the next few days, I kept visiting the Christians, and I also talked to the new soldiers. The city gates, however, were guarded very closely by well-armed men. Persons could go through, but not crates or parcels. The rebels wanted to keep the city calm in order to avoid any exodus. For people's safety, they put up posters announcing that any thief or corrupter would be decapitated at once if he bore arms, or flogged to death if he were a private individual. Several executions of thieves who were either caught in the act of stealing or sentenced following the testimony of witnesses, stopped the stealing and plundering. The city and its neighborhood have been relatively quiet during these eight days, but people are apprehensive of the future. Zi-ka-wei is altogether safe, and I do not think our establishments are going to run any risk at all.

The leaders of the Shanghai insurrection have told the consuls that they have acted only upon instructions from the new Emperor, the T'ai P'ing Wang, that they want to be friends with all Europeans, that they have not the least desire to see the population suffer, and that they intend to exterminate the Tartars, as well as all those who persist in staying in their service. . . . Our workers' foreman, Wu Se-hu, is the leader of the men stationed near our gate, in the customs office, under our windows, in the pagoda, and across the street. They have promised us that they would defend us against any aggressors. Monsignor was at first alarmed at seeing a post set up in our vicinity, but I believe that no plundering will take place in our establishment as long as the rebels are here. The day before yesterday, they seized in front of our gate two Cantonese who were robbing a merchant. Two hours later, the robbers had been flogged to death, and the stolen objects were sought until they were found. So you see that, in the midst of all this turmoil, our Good Lord has maintained some order, which is a source of hope to all honest families. Some of the people who tried to flee the city have been robbed on the river or on the road. I have advised our Christians to stay in their homes for the time being, but to be ready to leave in case of emergency.

Every night, some three hundred English or American soldiers keep watch over the European quarter and do not let armed Chinese enter the area.[19]

After the missionaries and other individuals, foreign officials, too, began

contacting the T'ai P'ing leaders in order to sound out their intentions and
to make sure that the lives and interests of their nationals would be respected.
Following the British and American consuls, the French representative, M.
de Courcy, traveled to Nanking on board the warship Cassini. *Father*
Clavelin, who acted as the mission's secretary, has described their arrival in
the new capital:

We were slowly steaming up the river, and came within sight of
Nanking on the morning of December 6 [1853]. . . . A meeting was
arranged for the next day. . . . The *Cassini*, meanwhile, received the
visit of a good many rebel soldiers and officers. We were thus able to
have a close look at their winter outfit, which, after all, is practically
the usual Chinese uniform, the only exception being that the red and
yellow colors are more in evidence. The rebels let their hair grow long,
and have rejected the use of skullcaps. Instead, they wear large hoods,
or some sort of turban, or again a headband in the shape of a purse,
which holds their hair together and falls on the neck. All those we saw
were well dressed, woolen cloth, silk, and even satin being quite common.

On the morning of the 7th, M. de Courcy, Secretary to the Legation,
accompanied by two naval officers and his interpreter, left for the
meeting. I was allowed to accompany him, and my catechist followed
us. Horses were waiting for us on the riverbank. Rebel officers marched
in our front and in our rear, and were preceded and followed by
standards and deafening gongs. We soon reached the ramparts and
followed them for an hour and a half. We came to a gate, but
had to wait there for some time, as the guards had not yet received
the orders to let us enter the city. Before long, we were surrounded by
a large crowd of men and women, who all showed much curiosity,
but did not display any sign of hostility. . . .

We were finally allowed to pass the Western Gate, but before
reaching the audience hall, we covered a distance of over a mile in the
city streets, which are broad and paved, at least in the middle. The
houses look far from pretty. They are generally in poor repair, and
some of them have been set afire by their inhabitants, who preferred
suicide to submission to the city's new masters. Not a single shop is
open. The overall impression is one of sadness, as Nanking has become
a camp rather than a city. . . .

We also noticed a great many women carrying the ration of rice
assigned to each of them. Near the city gate we had already seen heaps

of rice placed along the riverbank and surmounted by banners marking them as public property. The aspect of these women did not denote any misery: I saw no beggars among them. Some of them even wore rich garments, while the majority, without indicating any wealth, were nonetheless decent in appearance. Their general countenance expressed a calm and somewhat sad resignation, but by no means as sad as I had expected, considering the many sacrifices which they had been compelled to make: all of them have been deprived of the sweet family atmosphere, being separated from their husbands, brothers, and children.* They have been organized in collective groups of twenty-five, and every day receive the necessary food and clothing. Even those who are unable or unwilling to do any work, are given the strict minimum necessary to survive. . . . We were told that large feet are back in favor, because of the services they render† to the population.[20]

Two T'ai P'ing "Ministers" received the French in audience:

The spectacle we now saw [Father Clavelin wrote] struck us by its sharp contrast to everything we had observed so far. In the light of the torches burning around the hall, we noticed a numerous audience, and in the rear we saw the two Ministers who were about to receive us. Their large robes of blue satin, richly decorated with magnificent embroidery on their chests, their red laced boots, the diadem of chiseled gold on their heads, their grave and dignified bearing, and a numerous retinue forming the background behind them—in short, everything contributed to lending our meeting an air of dignity and grandeur which, as I have just said, contrasted singularly with the original welcome extended to us.

When M. de Courcy appeared, the Ministers stood up, the introduction was made by the interpreter, and we took seats on both sides. After some explanations concerning the purpose of our visit, we asked the two Ministers a few questions about their religious faith. One of them, speaking for some five or six minutes, gave us a short summary of their doctrine, and did so with incomparable calm, assurance, and dignity. He limited his address to the essential principles of natural law,

* The organization of T'ai P'ing society was largely based upon separation of sexes and age groups.

† The T'ai P'ings displayed a Puritanical zeal in fighting such evils as "small feet" (an old Chinese tradition), adultery, prostitution, alcoholism, etc.

then gave us a short explanation of the origin of idolatry in China, and finally summed up the mission which the T'ai P'ing Emperor believes to have received from Heaven to extirpate idolatry from the surface of the earth. Upon our insisting that we had come with no hostile intent, but rather as friends, the Minister replied at once: "Since you worship the same God as ours and we all have but one Creator, you are not only friends, but brothers as well."[21]

The social, political, and religious organization and mood of the T'ai P'ings were also noted by Father Clavelin:

Immediately after the Celestial King, there are five personages acting as prime ministers, and bearing the ancient title of king. One of them, it is said, has a purely honorific title, while the four others have added the distinguishing name of a cardinal point to their kingly title. The Ministers whom we saw belong to the second class. All inhabitants are divided into bodies of ten thousand persons, men and women alike. Groups of three thousand women, for instance, have as their leader a man who is allowed to see the Ministers. While we were being received by one of the latter, one such leader came and submitted the following petition to him: "The sisters of our division request an additional amount of clothes, because of the cold, which has become intense," and the Minister replied at once: "Go, and do whatever you deem necessary."

It is at Nanking that this community life has found its truest and broadest expression, but without any prejudice to public morals. Indecent behavior and plundering are on the contrary liable to capital punishment. In every women's post, the light is kept burning throughout the night, and the woman on guard beats a small drum at regular intervals.

The principal rebel leaders are from all evidence anxious to maintain a definite hierarchy, and to have it respected. Their arrival or departure is invariably announced by the sound of cannon. Music is being played during their meals, yet we have seen not only the secondary leaders, but also people of lower condition approach them quite frequently.

It cannot be denied that the title "brother" with which the rebels address each other is to a large extent justified. A sort of family atmosphere prevails among them. All their dwellings belong to the community. The food and clothes are being kept in public storage rooms, while gold, silver and valuables are stored in the public treasury building. We were quite unable to purchase any of the uniforms now worn by the rebels. Each leader is personally responsible for the various needs of his subordinates. The fact that a population swelled to more than a million persons by the invasion can still be fed and clothed in the regular manner we have witnessed is truly worthy of admiration, and this the more so as it is happening in the midst of civil war, and under the very eyes of the enemy besieging the city. . . .

The food which we received was quite plain, yet abundant, and we were treated as honorable guests. On several occasions the secretaries, our friends, shared our meals. Before and after each meal they said their prayer to the Heavenly Father, while we recited our Benedicite and said grace also.

Twice a day, the insurgents gather in a vestibule or in some other large room, and address their prayer to the Shan-te [God]. Ten discharges of the cannon announce the prayer made by the Heavenly King. As for us, we performed our spiritual exercises quite freely in their midst. My catechist, in particular, recited as many prayers as fifty rebels. . . .

We asked the rebels how they treat people who refuse to pray with them, and this is what they told us: "People who refuse to pray, or to renounce idols, are put to death. Those who do not believe in anything and are not used to saying prayers are left alone, though we might give them a flogging. If they became too numerous, however, we would kill them too."[22]

During the next ten years, the struggle between rebel and imperial forces moved back and forth, mostly in the Yangtze area. From his capital at Nanking, the "Heavenly Emperor" appointed civil officers, collected taxes, destroyed idols, levied troops, and in some areas introduced education on a more or less Christian basis. At the same time, Hung Hsiu-ch'üan gradually abandoned his original austerity as a leader, and surrounded himself with a large court of officials, "princes" (often chosen from among his kinsfolk), sycophants and . . . concubines. As the years passed by, he engrossed himself more and more in mystical and theological pursuits, letting his many "kings" (whom he multiplied) solve the problems of the T'ai P'ings' economic and social equalitarianism. In matters military, too, he displayed an increasing indifference to, and ignorance of, the slowly deteriorating spirit and organization of his heterogeneous armies.

Much more detrimental to the continued success of the rebels than this aloofness of their supreme leader was the jealousy and subsequent feuding between the various "kings". One of them broke away from the movement and continued warring against the Manchus on his own behalf. Another on the contrary went over to the Imperialists, and became one of the most dangerous opponents of his former companions-in-arms. A third king was murdered on orders from Hung for "insubordination", and by 1856 all original co-leaders had been eliminated by the dictatorial Heavenly Emperor.

As for the Manchu court, the successive defeats of its troops made it turn to the forces of effective loyalty that remained among the Chinese people. The famous scholar Tseng Kuo-fan, grand old man of Hunan Province, was called on to save the country. He organized a river fleet to operate on the Yangtze, and raised an army from among his fellow provincials. He suffered many reverses, but refused to be beaten, and his stubborn and sober gallantry heartened and inspired all the foes of the T'ai P'ings.

The long struggle's final phase came in the early sixties, when the Western powers decided that it was to their advantage to maintain the Manchus in power. The decisive intervention of the "Ever Victorious Army", described in the next chapter, in fact prolonged the Manchu hold on the Dragon Throne by half a century.

Before coming to the rescue of the Manchus, however, the Western powers (actually England and France) engaged in a second military conflict with China. The struggle, as in the case of the Opium War, was a short and uneven one, and China saw herself compelled—much against her wishes—to accept the new demands, essentially in the form of a broader intercourse, which the foreigners imposed on her.

CHAPTER IV

THE ANGLO-FRENCH EXPEDITIONS
1856–1864

The treaties signed between China and the Western powers as a result of the Opium War led to a notable increase in the volume of European and American trade with the Celestial Empire. The missionaries too, both Catholic and Protestant, profited greatly from the treaty clauses which allowed foreigners to establish themselves in the five Treaty Ports.

No real progress, however, was made in the relationship between East and West. The Chinese—officials and common people alike—remained staunchly opposed to the presence of "foreign devils", or "barbarians", in their empire. The average Chinese's unchanged attitude was one of hostility, suspicion, and arrogance. In his eyes, the defeats of 1842 represented a mere accident, and this the more so as Chinese officials had euphemistically described the treaties as means of "pacifying" the "rebellious" barbarians or "bringing them under control" through the imperial "compassion" toward strangers lacking "reason" and good manners.

The behavior of many foreigners, it is true, left much to be desired, as they spoke and acted like conquerors rather than people bent on creating an atmosphere of mutual respect and understanding. Lord Palmerston, for instance, strongly urged the British trading companies to keep a close check on their employees' proper conduct.

Under the circumstances, China's officialdom found it easy to stir up and fan popular xenophobia. In Foochow,* foreigners were spat at in the face. In the traditionally turbulent city of Canton, anti-foreign riots increased in numbers, and so did the secret societies' hostile pamphlets. Among the latter, the "Placard of the patriotic people of Kwangtung denouncing the

---

* One of the five Treaty Ports.

English barbarians" was one of the most inflammatory and vulgar ever posted in China:*

The thoroughly loyal and patriotic people of the whole province of Kwangtung instruct the rebellious barbarian dogs and sheep for their information. We note that you English barbarians have formed the habits and developed the nature of wolves, plundering and seizing things by force. . . . In trade relations, you come to our country merely to covet profit. What knowledge do you have? Your seeking profit resembles the animal's greed for food. You are ignorant of our laws and institutions, ignorant of right principles. . . . You have no gratitude for the great favor of our Celestial Court. . . . You use opium to injure our common people, cheating us of silver and cash. . . . Except for your ships being solid, your gunfire fierce, and your rockets powerful, what other abilities have you? . . .

Today, if we do not exterminate you English barbarians, we will not be human beings. You have killed and injured our common people in many villages, and seriously hurt the universal harmony. You also completely destroyed the coffins in several places, and you disastrously damaged the Buddhist statues in several monasteries. This is properly a time when Heaven is angered and mankind is resentful; even the ghosts and spirits will not tolerate you beasts. . . .

Our hatred is already at white heat. If we do not completely exterminate you pigs and dogs, we will not be manly Chinese able to support the sky on our heads and stand firmly on the earth. . . . We are definitely going to kill you, cut your heads off and burn you to death! . . . We must strip off your skins and eat your flesh, and then you will know how tough we are. . . . We ought really to use refined expressions. But since you beasts do not understand written characters, therefore we use rough, vulgar words to instruct you in simple terms.[1]

It was only natural that the "English barbarians" should be vilified much more often than other foreigners. England was in full industrial and commercial expansion in the middle of the nineteenth century, and her presence in China was far more conspicuous than that of any other nation.

Opium remained, as before, the leading article of importation into China,

---

* Posted in 1841 (after the British had withdrawn their forces) by villagers who had suffered economically from the Opium War.

followed far behind by cotton fabrics and small manufactured goods.* China's chief exports were silk, tea, and . . . coolies.

This modern form of slavery constitutes one of the saddest aspects of Sino-Western relations, and seems to have been initiated toward 1850 by the Spaniards looking for cheap labor on the sugar plantations of Cuba (then a Spanish possession). Over a period of a quarter century, about half a million coolies—young farmers from poverty-stricken areas, former T'ai P'ing rebels, or simply riffraff recruited with the complicity of Mandarins eager to get rid of undesirable elements—were shipped to the West Indies or to the mines of Peru and California.†

Hong Kong and Macao were the two main centers of coolie traffic. The British Government soon closed Hong Kong to the illicit trade, but it continued at Macao, which at the time was notorious as one of the most immoral places in the world. A slimy breed of coolie brokers, Portuguese and Chinese for the most part, enticed and trapped their victims into "volunteering" for the long journey across the Pacific under frightful conditions. Mutinies occurred on many a ship, and the transpacific death toll averaged at least 10 percent of the unfortunate and ignorant emigrants.

A French traveler witnessed some of the traffic's most shocking aspects:

Let me now accompany you into this dark dwelling that fairly resembles a heavy Venetian building. Do enter, if you dare, into this humid and obscure cellar, and what do you see behind the bamboo bars of this immense cage? Men, whose only garments are a pair of drawers and a blue, sleeveless cotton jacket. They are lying on gray sand full of earth lice, sea fleas, cockroaches and myriapods of the most dangerous kind. Here they are waiting to be shipped to the tropical countries where the coolie nowadays replaces the African slave. Indeed, this is the latest form of slave trade, in which only the color of the merchandise has changed.

These unfortunate fellows have been picked up in some famine-ridden area, or on the banks of some dried-out river. Lured by the promise of immediate well-being, and of a gay sojourn in Macao or Canton, they have signed a contract which binds them for six years to an unknown plantation owner. When the day of departure arrives, a

---

* Such as clocks, mechanical toys, and other Western gadgets.

† Main reasons for the coolie traffic: the need of labor arising from the discovery of gold in California, the lack of cheap labor in Central and South America, the gradual suppression of slave labor in the United States of America.

consular agent comes and officially checks that the "volunteers" are leaving of their own accord. True, they can refuse to board ship, but ... they are all indebted. .... They have been told that Havana, Callao, or the other colonies toward which they are being shipped are only five or six days away. ... So they go on board, where they are highly surprised to see their tobacco, pipes, and knives taken away from them. ...

In 1858, a large American clipper carrying coolies to Havana anchored at Manila harbor. A few days after his departure from China, the captain had realized that he did not have enough water on board, and for this reason had decided to call at that port in order to add a few more barrels. When they saw that their vessel dropped anchor, the Chinese, who had been told that the trip would be short, believed that they had indeed reached their destination. They could smell the sweet fragrance of land, and became rather excited, but to their dismay they saw the captain go on land without them. After having waited for several hours, they gathered around the first mate and told him that they would throw him into the sea if they were not disembarked at once. The ship's crew thereupon was hastily armed, rescued the first mate, began firing upon the mutineers, threw them back in between decks with their sabers, and nailed planks on the hatchways and portholes. The temperature at the time was forty degrees Centigrade in the shade in the streets of Manila. The prisoners, whose voices were but faintly heard on deck, were probably protesting that they were suffocating. .... But no one took the trouble to check on their condition, and soon a gloomy silence, broken at rare intervals by a piercing cry, had settled on the ship. The captain, unfortunately, spent the whole day and the night on land, where he was the guest of a wealthy Spaniard established there, and watched the dances of the beautiful and nonchalant Creole girls dressed in light attire. Upon boarding his ship the next morning, he was at once struck by the prevailing silence.

"Your Chinese are sulking, or perhaps they are asleep," the second mate told him casually. "Yesterday, they tried to jump off the boat, believing they had arrived; I had them locked up in the hold, where they are well under control. All is well."

The captain, an experienced man, grasped the situation at once. Having seized an ax, he began battering down the planks, and ordered his crew to do likewise. When fresh air entered the clipper's hold and chased its stifling reeks, it was much too late: the three hundred

Chinese were found asphyxiated, and this writer saw them, together with the whole indignant population of Manila, laid down on the beach near a common grave, filled with lime, that was to unite all of them.

After four months of detention awaiting trial, the second mate and part of the crew were sentenced to one year in jail. A few days later, the captain sailed back to Canton with his ship, and there took on another such infamous load.[2]

The scandalous exportation and pitiless exploitation of the coolies excited popular feeling in Western countries and even among Europeans residing in China. Not before 1873, however, did the Chinese government appoint a three-man commission* that was sent to Cuba to find out about the condition of coolies working there.

In October 1874, the commission submitted the results of its inquiry. They circulated its findings widely throughout China in the form of an illustrated pamphlet entitled Pictorial Glimpses into Hell, *and confirmed once more the conviction, all too deeply rooted in the Chinese minds, of the brutality and wickedness of the foreign "barbarians". The commission's report reads:*

It appears from all the declarations and petitions that eight-tenths of the Chinese workers stated that they were either forced or tricked into crossing the ocean—that during the journey the death rate, due to wounds resulting from blows, sickness or suicide, exceeded 10 percent —that upon their arrival in Havana they were sold as slaves, a small minority being sold to families or in shops where they were ill-treated, while a large majority became the property of owners of sugarcane plantations and had to endure the worst acts of cruelty—that their work is too hard and the food insufficient, that the working days are too long and that punishment by rods, whips, chains and other means have caused all sorts of suffering and wounds. During the past few years, many Chinese were beaten to death or died from their wounds, or hanged themselves or cut their own throats, or again poisoned themselves with opium or threw themselves into caldrons filled with boiling sugar. Our own eyes have seen a good many Chinese with broken arms or legs, men who were blind, whose heads were covered

---

* Composed of a Chinese heading a "Mission of Instruction" in the United States, an Englishman, and a Frenchman who held high positions in the Chinese Customs Administration.

with sores, others with broken teeth, mutilated ears, lacerated skin and flesh, all these marks being obvious signs of cruelty and visible to everybody.

Upon expiration of the contracts, owners generally refuse to grant certificates of liberation and insist that new commitments be signed, sometimes for more than ten years, during which time people are ill-treated as before. If they do not accept these contracts, they are sent to the workhouse, where they are being used to repair roads, chained together and closely supervised, without any salary. Such treatment is in no way different from that of criminals in jail. . . .

Not only are they unable ever to go back to China, but they cannot even earn wages and live freely. . . . From the 29th of the first moon (February 17), date of our arrival in Cuba, to the 23rd of the third moon (May 8), when we left again, almost all the Chinese workers whom we saw were being ill-treated, and we heard only complaints. We have seen all this with our own eyes and have heard it with our own ears, all three of us.[3]

In the five Treaty Ports, meanwhile, tension mounted as incidents opposing Chinese and foreigners multiplied. Following the example of their emperor, who had dismissed the signatories of the treaty of Nanking, the higher Chinese officials remained haughty and distant in the rare audiences which they granted to Western traders, diplomats or missionaries. Their policy, as before, was to degrade foreigners in the eyes of the people. More often than not, they openly disregarded the existing treaty provisions, or argued and quibbled without end over minor questions for the sole purpose of annoying the "Fan Kwae".

The latter, on the other hand, kept complaining about Chinese arrogance and disloyalty, about the inadequate housing or trading facilities, and generally about the slow growth of Sino-Western intercourse.

The distinction between the [treaty] "city" (forbidden by the Chinese version of the Treaty of Nanking, but open in the English text!) and the "port" became the source of endless and irritating squabbling.

Over and above all, however, it was the increased commercial pressure, brought by constant industrial growth in the West, that eventually led to a new military conflict. While the impatient and aggressive Europeans endeavored—by a variety of means—to get the most out of the existing concessions, the Chinese did their level best to prevent the despised intruders from gaining any further advantages.

The spark that touched off a new series of armed interventions on the part *of the Western powers was the "Arrow incident". On October 8, 1856, a small vessel, the lorcha* Arrow, *sailing under the British flag (her captain was English, the crew Chinese) and engaged in opium traffic between Hong Kong* and Canton, was boarded in the latter port by order of the Cantonese authorities. The Chinese crew was forcibly carried off on a charge of "being in collusion with barbarians", and the vessel's ensign hauled down with marked official ostentation.*

Despite this insult to the Union Jack, followed by acts of violence (in December 1856, the European factories at Canton were set afire), the British Parliament was at first opposed to armed intervention. Lord Palmerston,† however, dissolved the House of Commons and eventually had an expeditionary force ordered on its way to Canton.

France joined the expedition a few months later, but for another reason. The treaty of Whampoa (1844) had made her the official protector of Roman Catholicism in China, but whereas the Western missionaries and their growing Chinese flocks were protected by edicts of toleration in the few areas having foreign settlements, persecutions occurred frequently throughout the rest of China.‡ The event that brought about France's armed intervention was the gruesome assassination, on February 29, 1856, of Father Chapdeleine in the province of Kwangsi. Mgr. Guillemin, Apostolic Prefect of both Kwangsi and Kwangtung provinces, has described Father Chapdeleine's martyrdom, which was given wide publicity in the French press:

On February 24th of this year, Father Chapdeleine was arrested in his district, where he had been the first missionary to preach the Gospel. He was at once brought before the Mandarin and subjected to tortures whose very memory makes one shudder. To begin with, his cheek was struck one hundred times with the deadly leather sole, a single blow of which is enough to give you a bloody jaw. . . . Having thus been rendered incapable of talking or answering, he was forced to

---

* Where large numbers of Chinese had settled with British approval. The British had permitted them to register vessels of their own, sail them under the British flag, and engage in trade with the five Treaty Ports.

† Prime Minister at the time.

‡ Chinese hostility toward Christianity was essentially a manifestation of xenophobia, and may be summed up by the following questions put by a Shantung magistrate to a native Christian brought before him: "You were born in China, you eat Chinese food, you wear Chinese clothes, you are protected by the Chinese Emperor; whatever makes you learn anything from foreign devils?" (quoted in the memoirs of the Reverend Timothy Richard).

lie on his belly and received one hundred rattan blows on his back. During all these tortures, he neither sighed nor complained even once, so that the Mandarin and his assistants could not hide their admiration and stupefaction.

Believing that such a remarkable silence was due to some magic power, the Mandarin ordered the killing of a dog, whose blood was sprinkled upon the missionary in order to suppress the magic spell. The Mandarin's assistants then continued to strike the missionary, without counting the blows, until their victim was absolutely unable to move. He was carried back into the jail, being quite incapable of walking even one step. Some time later the assistants, still apprehensive of the missionary's magic power, brought him a meal containing meat of all the vilest animals, so that he might lose his "superstitions". Father Chapdeleine knew that members of secret societies abhor such meat, regarding it as an antidote to their mysterious rites, and ate of each kind in order to show that he did not belong to any prohibited society. This was the only food he received from the day he was arrested, February 24, to the day of his death, February 29, since the Mandarin had declared that whoever brought anything to the victim would share his fate.

The Mandarin, meantime, was eager to get rid of his prisoner. On the 27th, he subjected him to the frightful torture of the iron chain, and on the 28th he had him locked up in the cage where dangerous criminals are strangled. On the 29th, seeing that his victim was still breathing despite the incredible tortures to which he had been submitted, the Mandarin ordered one of his fiercest assistants to cut off the missionary's head and to hang it on a tree outside the city. There the children began throwing stones at it, so that it fell down and rolled into the dust and mud, where dogs and pigs fought over it and tore it to shreds before they ate it. Nobody seems to know what happened to the body: some people say that Father Chapdeleine was buried in the plot set aside for criminals, while others, probably closer to the truth, declare that he was chopped to pieces and thrown among the refuse, where he was eaten up by the many foul animals that fill the streets.

And what happened to his heart? This is too horrible a thing to tell, and unbelievable indeed: my tongue cannot say it, and my hand refuses to write it! His heart was torn out of his chest and, still beating, was placed on a plate, where it was closely and joyously examined by his barbarian and bloodthirsty torturers. Then they chopped it into pieces, fried it in a pan with pig's grease and ate it, hardly done, with the ferocity of wild beasts.[4]

In October 1857 the British Commissioner Extraordinary, Lord Elgin, met in Hong Kong (where he had arrived in June) with the French Ambassador Extraordinary, Baron Gros. There they were soon joined by the Anglo-French expeditionary force, and actual operations began in December, after the Chinese—reasserting their virulent hostility and contempt—had repeatedly rejected the two Western powers' demands for reparations.*

Hostilities were at first confined to the southern coast of China, and more particularly to the Canton area. Once more, Western military superiority meant rapid and easy victories for the invaders.

A French officer, Baron de Bazancourt, has described the preliminary bombardment of Canton:

On the evening of December 27 [1857], all clocks were synchronized on board the ships, so that each of them might begin the bombardment at the same moment. Shortly before dawn on the 28th, all crews were at battle station, impatiently awaiting the signal. When the conventional signs were finally hoisted and accompanied by two shots of cannon, the triple shout, "Vive l'Empereur!"† and the hurrahs of the British rippled all along the mooring line like an electric wave. The *Phlégéton* and the *Actéon* had just fired their first shot against the city.

A strange thing then occurred. Hardly had the thundering detonations of the thirty-two vessels broken the silence of the rising day, when the Cantonese population came running out on the shoreline and, more surprised than frightened, watched with great amazement the thick columns of smoke rising to heaven. Before long, however, the heavy smoke hid the ships from sight, so that their presence was marked only by the flaming flashes erupting from their sides at regular intervals.

The more daring among the population along the shoreline squatted calmly on the beach and from there followed the unusual spectacle with impassive countenances. Others, on the contrary, jumped into boats and hurried off toward the island of Honan, against which we had no hostile intention.

* Lord Elgin had come in a very conciliatory mood, believing as he did that the wrongs were by no means all on the Chinese side.

† Meaning Napoleon III, staunch supporter of Catholic interests.

It was an odd spectacle indeed: a throng of men, women and children crowded pell-mell in their boats, rowing toward the allied vessels, crossing their line of mooring and repeating their gestures of respect and submission as they drew closer.

Another strange fact worth relating is that the Chinese supplier responsible for the crews' daily provisions delivered the food as usual during the bombardment.

Our cannonade was kept up at a slow but regular pace during the whole day on the 28th. Already in the morning, several fires broke out in the city, and through our telescopes we could observe the Chinese trying to put them out under the bombardment. They had hardly succeeded in one spot when a fire would break out in some other quarter.[5]

The landing of troops, recorded by the French diplomat Marquis de Moges, was little more than a military promenade:

Our bombardment was concentrated against the eastern side of the city, where the assault was to take place, our aim being the opening of a breach in the wall and putting its defenders to flight. From the maintop of each vessel, a sailor was reporting the points of impact, as well as the effect produced by the shells. Two shots only, fired by the Chinese artillery, fell in the vicinity of our gunboats. . . .

Meanwhile, the sailors and soldiers had begun landing at about one-half mile from the city, halfway between Bartier Fort and French Folly, and were progressing without meeting any difficulty except that presented by the uneven terrain. During the night, the landing spot had been secured by six hundred British marines. Our troops were advancing but slowly along the narrow paths between the rice fields. Before long, they met the Chinese army, or rather groups of the enemy. Hidden among thickets or behind graves, the Chinese opened up a rapid fire upon our surprised men, showering them with a hail of bullets and arrows. Several of our soldiers were wounded, one of them a young sailor of the *Audacieuse*, who was felled by a bullet in his chest.

It must be pointed out here that this was the first time that Chinese soldiers had come out from behind their walls—perhaps as a result of the bombardment—in order to fight European soldiers in the open. Theirs is a strange way of fighting: they wave red or yellow flags to challenge their enemies and provoke them into battle, and also to fill themselves with courage. They are armed with matchlocks and huge jingals seven and a half feet long, which they set up and maneuver in pairs, one of the soldiers supporting the gun on his shoulder while the other does the aiming and firing. They also throw arrows and a kind of rocket arrow whose unusual and swishing sound at first somewhat surprised our men.[6]

Before reaching the walls of Canton, the expeditionary force captured poorly defended Fort Lin. On this occasion Laurence Oliphant, secretary to Lord Elgin, acknowledged the superiority of French élan:

When our fieldpiece came up, and a shell burst near them, these brave defenders unhesitatingly evacuated the fort—a fact as patent to our allies as it was to ourselves. When the banner of the last man had disappeared behind the rising ground beyond, the French rushed in, and it must be admitted that there was no reason why we should not have done the same. It was an operation entirely devoid of risk for either party, but to our allies is due the credit of their superior quickness of perception. Indeed, so little of this quality had some of our own men, that they rushed at the fort with loud shouts, apparently mistaking the *tricouleur* which waved from its walls for a Chinese banner. As the French sailors often carry small *tricouleur* flags in the pockets of their spacious trousers, their conquests are rapidly proclaimed. Upon this occasion the leading marine, having been provident enough to supply himself with a national "pavilion", sprung upon the walls flag in hand, and shouting "Vive l'Amiral! l'Empereur! la France! l'Angleterre!" all in a breath, created an immense amount of enthusiasm, and was embraced by his admiral, and invested with the legion of honour on the spot. . . .

As soon as the Chinese perceived us in position, the guns from the city opened upon us, but without much effect. Meantime the naval brigade and marines had been coming up, and extending far to the right, over undulating ground covered with graves and clumps of wood. From Lin's Fort we had an excellent view of a skirmish in which they engaged with some braves, who now appeared for the first time in some force. These latter were soon driven back to the base of the hill on which Gough's Fort is situated, but only to advance again as our men retired. Indeed, as a considerable distance separated the combatants throughout, the Chinese seemed to gain confidence from this mode of warfare, and began to collect in great numbers behind a small village, from which they made a grand advance, with quantities of banners waving, and great yelling and vaporing, throwing forward skirmishers in pairs carrying jingals, making contemptuous gestures at their enemies, and indulging in diverse antics, for which their leader, a tall man in blue, who carried a huge sword, was especially conspicuous. He was followed by a standard-bearer, capering along ten yards in advance of the crowd. This brave army ultimately succeeded in occupying a straggling wood, and in ensconcing themselves in the horseshoe graves with which the hillside abounded, and which formed natural rifle pits. Above these, with their heads well under cover, they defiantly waved flags, and managed, with their jingals, to wound some of our men as they dodged from one grave to another. The hill presented somewhat the appearance of an animated rabbit warren. Two or three shells, however, judiciously dropped among them from Lin's Fort, soon started them from their hiding places; and the gentleman in blue displayed even more agility in hopping back again at the head of his army than he had in his advance.[7]

Canton itself was assaulted and occupied—after a token resistance that cost the Allies but trifling losses*—on January 2, 1858. As he entered the city with the British troops, Oliphant met with looting parties, scenes of destruction, and a submissive population:

On our way to the city I observed in the suburb large looting parties, composed of Chinese blackguards, ransacking the houses, and looking out for stragglers from our men, with whom they occasionally exchanged shots. They preferred, however, to be left alone, and kept as much out of sight as possible. At one place a pawnbroker's tower was being thoroughly gutted; a party on the top were engaged in overhauling the contents, and throwing over to their comrades below rich furs and brocaded silks; nor had we time, as we passed rapidly on, to interrupt them in their deeds of spoliation. It was already becoming evident that the work of administering the government of a large city containing a million and a half of inhabitants, so ready, upon the first

* Eight killed and seventy-one wounded among the British force of nearly 5,000 men; two killed and thirty wounded out of a force of 900 Frenchmen—according to Oliphant.

opportunity, to prey upon each other, would be by no means an easy task for foreigners totally unused to, and comparatively unacquainted with, the system by which vast urban populations were governed and controlled, and only in one or two instances able to speak their language.

A great part of the suburb had been destroyed, so as not to afford shelter to thieves or assassins upon the immediate line of communication. . . . As we passed along the west wall flanking the Tartar quarter, the people were collected in groups gazing at us with interest, but with an air of profound respect and submission; when we warned them to disperse, they at once obeyed. . . . At the western gate we were informed by the English officer who had been on guard there for some hours, that great crowds had been pouring out of the town, but that, when assured of our pacific intentions, they had ceased to manifest alarm or leave the town. . . . As we turned along the south wall we observed terrible evidence of the destructive effects of the bombardment. The south gate had been totally destroyed by fire, and a broad scar of burnt houses extended toward the centre of the city.[8]

After the fall of Canton, the British captured the local viceroy, Yeh, and deported him to Calcutta, where he eventually died.* His absence made it easier to deal with his successor, the Mandarin Pihkwei. Much to the surprise of the British, Pihkwei soon wrote to Lord Elgin begging him to resume normal intercourse with the Cantonese merchants:

Still it is, without doubt, essential that, so far as trade is concerned, no time should be lost. By every day that the opening of the port is accelerated, by so much is the restoration of public confidence accelerated, not only in the minds of the Chinese, but in the minds of the merchants in every nation as well. The conditions of trade would probably be in accordance with the old regulations under which imports and exports were entered and inspected, and the duties on them paid. Your Excellency is, of course, thoroughly conversant with them. I would add that, from the ninth moon of last year to the present time, a twlevemonth or more, the mercantile communities of both our nations have been subjected to loss. The eagerness with which

* He was the first high Chinese official to be deported by the British, and perhaps the only Chinese official who was ever made personally responsible for attacks on foreigners.

merchants will devote themselves to gain, if the trade be now thrown well open, will increase manifold the good understanding between our nations, and the step will thus, at the same time, enhance your Excellency's reputation.9

Important as it was, the capture of Canton impressed the Court of Peking but little. The Son of Heaven, true to his predecessors' time-honored policy, had not the least intention of entering into direct negotiations with the insubordinate barbarians; that was the exclusive responsibility of the local viceroys. When, therefore, Lord Elgin and Baron Gros, accompanied by the American and the Russian ambassadors, arrived at Shanghai to open talks with the imperial plenipotentiaries, the latter told them that they should go back to Canton and there negotiate with the successor to Yeh (whom the Allies themselves had established as viceroy, and who had been temporarily confirmed as such by an imperial edict)!

There was no way out of the diplomatic impasse. Only a direct military threat to the Chinese capital could bring about a change of mind at the imperial court. The Anglo-French Allies accordingly carried the war to the north: in May 1858, they captured the forts of Taku commanding the entrance to Tientsin, less than a hundred miles east of Peking. The Allies entered Tientsin on the last day of May, and a few days later began negotiating with duly accredited Chinese officials.

The resulting Treaties of Tientsin (June, 1858), concluded separately between China and England, France, the United States and Russia, provided essentially for the residence of Western diplomats at Peking,* the opening of five more ports to foreign trade, toleration of Christian missions throughout the empire, and permission to foreigners to travel in the interior.

In the same year, the Treaty of Aigun gave Russia (who nursed considerable ambitions in the Far East) the north bank of the Amur river.

The Western powers, it seemed, had been given satisfaction, and soon they withdrew their forces from Tientsin. But the Chinese, whose main preoccupation was to gain time, had some surprises in store for them. When the British and French plenipotentiaries returned to Tientsin in June 1859 to exchange ratifications, they found that the mouth of the Pei River leading to that city had been strongly fortified. The Allied gunboats tried to force the passage, only to be severely repulsed. An attempted landing failed, too.

* Diplomatic representation at Peking—a primary object of the expeditions of 1857-8—was to make relations between China and the West easier and more normal, in the minds of the British and French.

Returning to the attack in August, the Anglo-French fleet eventually fought its way through, and toward the end of the month Lord Elgin and Baron Gros were back in Tientsin. A bombastic imperial edict, meanwhile, had called on the local population to resist the invaders by all possible means:

Last year, the barbarians tried to force the entrance of the Peiho, but within a moment's time their boats were sunk, and thousands of enemy corpses were floating on the waters, as far as a mile from the shores.

I had hoped that such a lesson would make the barbarians more circumspect, but this is not so: less than one year after their defeat, they have returned in greater numbers and more insolent. Taking advantage of the low tide, they have landed at P'ei-tang and have attacked the forts of Taku. But, being barbarians, they attacked them from behind. Our soldiers are used to meet the enemy head on, and never expected such cowardice and treachery. The barbarians have occupied Tientsin, and are proud of their success, instead of being filled with shame. My wrath will soon overtake them, and exterminate them without pity.

I hereby command my subjects, Chinese and Manchu alike, to hunt them down like evil animals. Let every village toward which these devils may be nearing, be evacuated. Let all food they might capture be destroyed. Their cursed race will thus be overcome by hunger, and will perish like fish in a dried-out pond.

Given in Yuan-min-yuan, on the 23rd day of the second moon of the ninth year of our reign.[10]

At about the same time (1860), inflammatory proclamations against foreigners were being posted in the streets of newly conquered Canton. The British promptly ordered the Mandarin Pihkwei to put an end to such provocations. Pihkwei complied, and as a result the startled Cantonese were soon reading an entirely novel kind of poster, similar in contents to the following quoted by Lord Elgin's secretary:

Whereas the Canton people have a habit, whenever they see a foreigner, of shouting out "Fan-kwei", and otherwise committing themselves, in utter violation of all rules of proper demeanour, and of the conduct that is due from man to man, you forget that there is no distinction between natives and foreigners; that foreigners are but as the people of other provinces; and that there should be between you courteous intercourse and mutual concession; that you should not intentionally show contempt for them or stand aloof from them. . . .

This is to signify to all you, the people, that henceforth, when you meet foreigners in the streets, you must behave to them civilly; you must neither use the term "Fan-kwei", nor any other opprobrious expression. You are not either to post placards containing anything offensive to foreigners. We, the authorities above mentioned, spare not to reiterate this caution to you. We, at the same time, command all police and constables to keep strict watch, and to seize those who transgress. If you offend, you will be punished with the utmost severity. Do not, therefore, pursue a course which you will repent when it is too late. Do not disobey. A special notification.[11]

Meanwhile, the Anglo-French expeditionary force, some twenty thousand men strong, * *was advancing toward Peking. In the absence of well-organized and efficient armies capable of dealing with the invaders, the Chinese at first tried a variety of delaying tactics, such as sham peace negotiations, or the capture of Western negotiators for subsequent blackmail ("Stop your troops, and we'll return the prisoners; stop advancing, or else!").*

But the Allies were decided to teach the Chinese a lesson. There was no stopping them, and the Chinese knew it. In the campaign's only battle worth that name, their field commander, General Seng-ho-lin-tsin, was defeated by the French under General Cousin de Montauban. The latter's secretary, the youthful Count d'Hérisson, has left a lively description of the victory of Palikao:†

From the reports of our scouting parties and the information gathered among the population, we learned that the Tartar army which we had defeated at Chang-chia-wan had received new reinforcements, and had taken up positions near the bridge of Palikao, a few miles ahead of us. The bridge is a fine example of stone and marble work that links the banks of the imperial canal running from T'ong-cheou to Peking.

The bridge owes its name to the distance separating it from T'ong-cheou: eight *li*, the *li* being a Chinese measure of some 500 yards. Palikao means "bridge of eight *li*". . . .

* Or some 13,000 British troops, including a thousand cavalrymen, and nearly 7,000 French troops.

† The French general subsequently was made "Count of Palikao". The twenty-year-old d'Hérisson spoke and read Chinese.

In the morning of September 21, we drank our coffee at dawn and resumed our forward march. The air was clear, and rather brisk; a light mist lay over the canals and fields, and hid the bright sunshine from our eyes. We had no maps of any kind. All we knew was that the canal led to Peking, and that it was spanned by a bridge. Therefore, we followed the canal. The countryside was lovely: meadows studded with clumps of tall trees, a wonderful battleground.

General de Montauban had 5,000 bayonets under his command, plus a small contingent of artillery. The British had an equal number of troops at their disposal, not quite as many infantry, but some cavalry.

The French had decided to advance on the right, their commander in chief and his staff progressing on the wing. To our left was the brigade of General Jamin. The vanguard was formed by the brigade of General Collineau, advancing between the brigade of General Jamin and the British. The latter were to execute a wheeling movement, cross the canal on a trestle bridge about one mile behind the Chinese, and move into their flank while we attacked them head on.

We were still four kilometers from the bridge when we saw its high, white arches, which stood out in stark contrast to the green countryside. The plain was also dotted with tombs of Mandarins built under the tall trees.

We noticed at once a very large body of Tartar cavalry slowly trotting toward us in good order. It was a rather impressive sight, and kept advancing in several well-organized groups. The horses looked strong and healthy. In the open spaces separating these groups, we could distinguish the infantry lined up in a sort of entrenched camp, and amidst the tree clumps we now discovered a number of rather well concealed batteries of artillery.

The spectacle before our eyes was rendered particularly strange and impressive by the fact that one could not hear a single command, as all the enemy movements were controlled by means of banners waved up or down, or sideways, like navy signals.

The enemy's advanced squadrons trotted to within fifty yards of our skirmishing lines, whose brisk fire knocked down the first row of horses and produced some swaying and a certain amount of disorder among enemy ranks. The banners were waved somewhat faster, the enemy ranks were straightened, and the cavalry wheeled to the right, evidently trying to turn Collineau to the left and to rush into a breach left open between his brigade and the British, who had moved away from us when they began their own maneuver.

Collineau, fortunately, never lost his head, and presently we had the satisfaction of hearing the volcano-like explosion of his brigade. His artillery began firing mercilessly, while his infantry kept up murderous salvos in both front and flanks, in order to break the enemy's encircling masses of men and horses. In this he was successful, at the very moment when we had to stand our ground against a similar attack from the other wing of the Tartar cavalry trying to outflank us on the right.

Our whole army was in danger of being trapped by the enemy's well-executed pincer movement. . . . We were anxiously waiting for the artillery led by Captain Dispot to begin firing at the enemy, whose ranks, depleted by our musketry fire, were constantly being closed and kept advancing in ever denser masses. As the artillery's action was slow in coming, I heard a commandant next to me calmly state to Colonel Schmitz: "Tomorrow, we'll all be tending the flocks of Seng-ho-lin-tsin."

That commandant is now Minister of War, and his name is Campenon. His prediction nearly came true. If the Chinese artillery had been abreast of the cavalry, our fate might well have been sealed on that lovely plain. Fortunately for us, we either attacked the Chinese at closer quarters than they had anticipated, or perhaps their artillery crews were no better than those that defended Taku, and whom we had generously released after their capture. They had evidently hurried back to their commander in chief, and now their shells were flying over our heads. Our situation, therefore, was actually not half as dangerous as it looked.

Presently we heard from Colonel de Bentzmann, commander of the artillery. He began by firing some rocket shells on a reduced trajectory. They flew in very low, and exploded under the horses. Disorder thus set in, and when the Chinese infantry came to the rescue of the cavalry, Dispot's battery poured forth such a barrage of shells that we could see deep furrows opening within the enemy's dense masses of men and horses. The attack gradually turned into retreat, and the cavalry fell back toward the bridge, but not without closing its ranks.

At that very moment, Montauban ordered the sounding of the charge for both brigades, and the whole French army rushed toward the bridge, which was defended by ten cannons manned just as badly

as the rest of the enemy artillery. Their shells, too, flew over our heads.
. . . It was like fighting in a dream: we kept advancing, firing, and
killing the enemy, yet no one, or hardly anyone, was hurt in our own
ranks.

The crews of the ten cannons defending the bridge were all killed
at their posts by the light infantry of the 2nd Battalion.

At the entrance to the bridge stood a gigantic Tartar, flag-bearer
of the commander in chief. He was holding a huge yellow banner with
black inscriptions, and waving it in all directions. All Chinese leaders
kept their eyes on it, as it transmitted the supreme commander's
orders to the entire army.

Already the enemy was in full retreat; the battlefield and the bridge
defended by the Chinese elite were strewn with corpses. However,
this Tartar stood fast at his post, alone and abandoned by all,
probably dispatching the supreme commander's last orders. In spite
of the bullets and shells whistling around him, he remained imperturbable. We all admired his sublime courage, and General Montauban
exclaimed: "Ah! what a gallant man! I hope he won't get killed. But
why the devil doesn't he flee with the rest of them? Save him!"

Some soldiers dashed forward in an effort to capture him. At that
very moment, the storm of fire that had spared him for half an hour,
as if to better imprint his heroic profile upon our minds, finally
crushed him. His huge banner was swept away, carrying with it his
arm still clutching the pole.

The bridge with its ten cannons had been taken at last. We could
see the last disorganized Tartar units disappearing on the horizon. It
was three o'clock in the afternoon, and the battle had lasted since eight
in the morning. . . .

We had sustained only trifling losses. Between the British and the
French, we had no more than 51 men killed and wounded. As for the
Chinese, they had left at least a thousand men on the field.[12]

*Peking fell to the Anglo-French forces almost without a fight. The young
and debauched Emperor fled to the north (Jehol) under pretext of going on a
"hunting trip".*

*Before entering the Chinese capital, the Allies looted and burned the
Emperor's famed (and splendid) Summer Palace, a deed which provoked a
storm of protests in Europe—and of course horrified the Chinese. General
de Montauban gave the following version of the plundering:*

After having visited apartments of indescribable splendor, I had sentries posted everywhere and ordered two captains, MM. Schelcher and Brives, to make sure that no one entered the Palace, and that everything in it be kept intact until the arrival of the British commander in chief, Sir Hope Grant. . . . At eleven o'clock, General Grant arrived at the camp accompanied by Lord Elgin. . . .

Now that the British leaders were present, we discussed how the best use could be made of all the wealth contained in the Summer Palace and decided, in accordance with the instructions we had received, that the spoils should be equally divided between the two armies. To this end, we designated three commissioners for each army, and ordered them to set aside the most precious objects, so that they might be shared in an equal manner. We would have been quite unable to carry all the objects away, because our means of transportation were much too limited. While these objects were being selected by Lord Elgin, I saw to it that the Queen of England had first choice, as this was to be a gesture of courtesy on the part of France.

Lord Elgin chose a baton of commandment belonging to the Emperor of China, made of green jade, which the Chinese value very highly. A little later a similar baton was found, and set aside for His Majesty the Emperor of France. . . .

An orderly handed me a note from General Jamin informing me that a hiding place, said to contain the Emperor's private treasure, had been discovered. The General had placed sentries before the spot until my arrival. . . . The vault was opened in the presence of the same three commissioners who had been appointed in the morning. Behind its door was a tiny courtyard; to its left and right, and locked by a low double door, were two vaults in which we found small gold and silver ingots estimated at about 800,000 francs, plus a number of cases containing, it is said, necklaces made of various sorts of glass beads, jade and pearls. . . .

The money was divided in the same precise manner as all the other objects, and each of the two armies received 400,000 francs, or an amount of about 80 francs for each French soldier. For this latter distribution, we designated a commission composed of an officer, a noncommissioned officer, and one soldier for each corps. It was presided by Generals Jamin and Collineau.

When the money had been distributed, the commission contacted the several corps in order to decide on the fate of the captured objects.

The army's spontaneous reply was that all precious objects found in the Imperial Palace should be sent as a gift to Her Majesty the [French] Empress, who in addition to having patronized the China expedition, had provided it with the first-aid equipment needed for the sick and the wounded.[13]

This official "distribution" of the Emperor's wealth was followed by a lusty free-for-all in which the British and French troops indulged for several days. The British subsequently asserted that the looting was started by the French, and the latter naturally laid the blame on their allies.

The colorful and turbulent, if sad, episode, recorded by Count d'Hérisson, was given an ironic touch by the presence of greedy and irreverent Chinese plunderers:

The commission began its work at once, and in a calm manner. The most striking, if not most precious, objects were removed one after another. . . . It was in the middle of the afternoon, and the armed sentries were still standing watch around the Palace, in which the commission was at work. Every now and then, soldiers on fatigue duty and loaded with trinkets would emerge from the building and excite the admiration of the troops gathered around the sentries. After unloading their spoils, these soldiers would get back into the Palace by showing their special pass.

The troops watching this first phase of the looting were made up of a motley crowd, as French and British infantry, scouts, artillerymen, spahis, the Queen's dragoons, Sikhs, Arabs and Chinese coolies were freely intermingled. A rumor spread in the throng and was repeated in many tongues by all these men packed together with eyes wide open and shining, the greed aroused, their mouths dry. They were saying to one another: "When the main loot is gone, it will be our turn to help ourselves. Darn it, we've deserved our share. We've come far enough. . . ." And they were laughing, and pushing each other around. . . . The beginning of disorder was evident. A worried General de Montauban was pacing back and forth at the other end of the place. . . . The situation did not as yet warrant his intervention.

Suddenly, we heard a trumpet call, and learned that a company in arms was needed. What had happened? A very simple thing. . . . The Chinese farmers of the surrounding area, who had been told about the riches contained in the Palace, had managed to sneak up to the walls of the park, and there began talking to our coolies. The latter were equipped with ladders, which were reared against the walls, and before long the crowd of large, looting and pigtailed sparrows swooped down on the park lanes and rushed toward the Palace. The armed company was called on to disperse them.

Before it was mustered, however, a second trumpet call resounded. This time, soldiers armed with nothing but canteens and pots were needed in order to form a chain and fight several fires that were starting. In China, whenever a fire breaks out, people think first of protecting themselves against thieves, who as a rule appear at the danger spots before the firemen do. As a matter of fact, professional thieves are apt to start fires, considering them very helpful and even indispensable to any well-organized robbery.

Thus it happened that the Chinese and our coolies had brought with them wicks and straw cords, everything in short needed for the burning of a palace, and had begun their nice work at once.

When the soldiers learned of this new development, which rumors had exaggerated, their impatience gave way to indignation. Only a moment ago, they were saying: "Those Chinese are going to filch everything," and now they added: "Those scoundrels will burn everything!" As a result, a rush which could not be stopped took place by the gates. The sentries were swept off their feet, and the crowd of soldiers dashed forward, together with the armed company and the fire fighters. Every man immediately began helping himself and carried his loot away.

I was thus given an excellent opportunity to compare the genius of the two allied nations. While the French played the game straight, and acted individually, the British proved more methodical, and from the very beginning went about the looting in an organized manner. They moved in by squads, as if on fatigue duty, carrying bags, and were commanded by noncommissioned officers who, incredible as it sounds (yet strictly true), had brought touchstones with them. Where the devil had they found them? I don't know, but I can swear that they did possess such tools normally used by jewelers, and by our commissioners at pawnbrokers' stores. . . .

The British and French, officers and soldiers, were thus mingled in the Palace, together with the Chinese and our coolies, whose hatred for their northern countrymen had prompted them to storm the Taku forts on our side. . . . It would have been too much to ask our men to let this human stream, in which all races were represented, rush by without being engulfed by it. Such abnegation would have been beyond human resistance. . . . Our men rushed in with the rest of the crowd, and behaved like all of them. What could the general do? What could his officers do? Nothing, absolutely nothing. If they had tried to stop the looting, they would simply have been swept away by the crowd; they would have compromised, perhaps even lost, their prestige and with it the future of the expedition, as well as their own reputation, the glory and even the lives of their men. On our side, as well as on that of the British, all the commander in chief could do was to close his eyes to the situation. . . . General de Montauban remained in his tent, almost alone, and so did Grant, who had also been abandoned by his officers. . . .

Being a mere spectator, I deeply enjoyed this strange and unforgettable vision: the swarming of men of all types and colors, the overcrowding of representatives of all human races on a heap of spoils, hurrahing in all tongues of the world, hurrying about, bumping into one another, stumbling, falling down and getting up again, swearing and shouting, all the while carrying their loot away as fast as they could. It all looked like a giant ant hill half-crushed under the foot of a passer-by, with its panic-striken black workers fleeing in every direction carrying a grain, a larva, an egg, or a straw between their mandibles. Some soldiers had buried their heads in the red-lacquered chests of the Empress, others were half-hidden among heaps of embroidered fabrics and silkware, still others were filling their pockets, shirts and kepis with rubies, sapphires, pearls, and pieces of crystal, or again were loading their chests with necklaces made of large pearls. Others were leaving the grounds with armfuls of clocks and watches. Sappers had brought their axes and were smashing the furniture in order to collect the jewels which were set in the wood. One of them, looking very earnest, kept striking a lovely Louis XV clock in order to get its dial showing the hours with figures in crystal, which he believed to be diamonds. . . .

One could distinguish two groups among our soldiers: a minority of smart fellows, and a large majority of grown children. The former had laid their hands on the jewels, coins, piasters, candy- or snuff boxes, golden table sets and pearl necklaces. The children, on the other hand, had mainly been tempted, in the midst of all this unbelievable accumulation of wealth, by the many ingenious mechanical toys and clocks of

European origin which had been generously abandoned by the British. For this very reason, the second night we spent in front of the Summer Palace was a mad and giddy one. Every soldier had his mechanical bird, rabbit, or monkey, his music box, or his alarm clock. The whole area was but one continuous symphony: the hours were constantly struck by a multitude of different tones interrupted here and there by the sad snap of an overstrained spring breaking in the hands of an inexperienced owner. Thousands of mechanical rabbits rolling their drums gave the symphony its bass tone, which was accompanied by the monkeys beating their cymbals, and by some four thousand romances simultaneously rising from as many music boxes. Above all these sounds, one could also hear the flourish of birds, the song of flutes, the high pitch of clarinets and the twang of strings, intermingled with tunes from cornets and bagpipes, and all this again was now and then drowned out by our easily amused soldiers roaring with laughter.

It was a virtual nightmare.

Before sunrise, the looting began all over again.[14]

The burning of the Summer Palace was ordered by Lord Elgin—despite the entreaties of Baron Gros to spare it—in retaliation for the killing and mistreatment of some twenty allied prisoners.* The harshness of such retribution struck Chinese authorities with awe and considerably hastened the settlement of the conflict.

In Peking, meanwhile, the population's anxiety grew daily. The Allies' irresistible advance created alarm and confusion in the minds of a people already shocked by the flight of their Emperor. A member of the Hanlin Academy† has described the capital's plight in his diary:

In the 7th moon of the "Keng Shen" year [August 1860], five or six days after my mother fell sick, rumours began to circulate that the barbarians had already reached Taku. . . . So far, however, there had been no fleeing from the city. His Majesty was seriously ill, and it was known that he wished to leave for the north, but the Imperial Concubine Yi and Prince Seng dissuaded him from this and assured him that the barbarians would never enter the city. . . .

---

* Out of a total of thirty-nine hostages held by the Chinese. Seven of the prisoners killed were British, and among them was the correspondent of the London *Times.*

† Or Imperial Academy, which included the country's leading literati.

During the next few days, people began to leave Peking, for the report was spread that our troops had been defeated at Taku, and that a Brigadier General was among the slain; the garrison had fled from Pei-t'ang and the forts were in the hands of the barbarians. . . .

On the 13th of the 7th moon, I noticed a change for the worse in my mother's condition, and straightway applied for ten days' leave of absence from my official duties. I kept her ignorant of the political situation and urged her to abstain from worry of every kind. But every day the news was worse, and people began to leave the city in thousands. . . .

Rumours were now rife that the barbarians had already reached T'ungchow, and were going to bombard Peking on the 27th, so that everyone was escaping who could leave the city. . . . On that day, our troops captured the barbarian leader Pa-hsia-li [Parkes]* together with eight others, who were imprisoned in the Board of Punishments. Thereupon the whole city was in an uproar, and it became known that His Majesty was preparing to leave on a tour northwards. But the Concubine Yi persuaded some of the older officials to memorialize, urging him to remain, none of which Memorials have been published. All the Manchu and Chinese officials were now sending their families away and their valuables, but the large shops outside the main gate were doing business as usual. . . .

On the 4th my mother called me to her bedside and said: "I cannot possibly recover. See that all is prepared for the burial.". . . Meanwhile the confusion in Peking was hourly increasing, and huge crowds were hurrying from the city. Most of the city gates were closed for fear of the barbarians, but the Chang-yi gate in the southern city was still open.

On the 7th, our troops engaged the barbarians outside the Ch'i-hua gate. The van was composed of untrained Mongol cavalry, who had never been in action. No sooner had the barbarians opened fire than they turned as one man, broke their ranks and stampeded upon the infantry in their rear. Many were trampled to death, and a general rout followed, our men fleeing in every direction and the barbarians pressing on to the city walls. . . .

Early next morning we heard the news of another engagement outside the Ch'i-hua gate, upon which news His Sacred Majesty, attended by all his concubines, the Princes, Ministers and Dukes, and

* British truce envoy, subsequently killed by the Chinese.

all the officers of the Household, left the city in a desperate rout and disorder unspeakable, affording a spectacle that gave the impression that hordes of barbarians were already in close pursuit. As a matter of fact, the foreigners were still at a considerable distance, and at the Summer Palace, where the Court lay, there was nothing whatsoever to cause the slightest apprehension. I cannot understand why His Majesty was allowed to leave; up to the very last the Yi Concubine begged him to remain in his Palace, as his presence there could not fail to awe the barbarians, and thus to exercise a protecting influence for the good of the city and people. . . .

Meantime, my mother's condition was becoming critical. . . . On the morning of the 12th, she passed away, abandoning her most undutiful son. . . . Not a friend came near us, and every door in the neighborhood was closed. . . .

On the 19th I conveyed my mother's remains to the temple; I found all quiet there, but my progress through the city gate was very slow because of the crowd. On the 23rd there were but few people abroad, and these clustering together in small groups and speaking in low voices. Suddenly, a little after midday, an immense blaze was seen to the northwest, and speedily it was reported that the barbarians had seized Hai-tien and the Summer Palace. Our army is said to number half a million men, and yet it seems that not one of them dare oppose the barbarians' advance. They have about a thousand of cavalry, yet they move about at will in our midst as if in an uninhabited wilderness! . . .

On the afternoon of the 24th, vast columns of smoke were seen rising to the northwest, and it was ascertained that the barbarians had entered the Summer Palace, and after plundering the three main halls, leaving them absolutely bare, they had set fire to the buildings. Their excuse for this abominable behaviour is that their troops got out of hand, and had committed the incendiarism. After this they issued notices, placarded everywhere, in very bad Chinese, stating that unless terms of peace had been arranged before midday on the 29th, they would bombard Peking, in which case all inhabitants who did not wish to share the fate of the city had better remove themselves to a safe distance.

On this day it was reported that the Sacred Chariot had reached Jehol in safety, but His Majesty had been greatly alarmed, and had issued a Decree expressing regret for his failure to commit suicide on the approach of the invaders. The Emperor is reported to be ill, and it is said that the Princes Tsai Yuan and Tuan Hua are trying to get themselves appointed to the Grand Council. Should the Emperor die, the Yi Concubine will be made Empress Dowager, but at present she is reported to be at variance with the Princes, who are endeavouring to prejudice the Emperor against her. . . .

On the 29th, the barbarians entered the city by the Anting gate, occupying its tower and the wall adjoining. . . . With the exception of the officials entrusted with the duty of negotiating, not one remained in the city.[15]

The capture of the world-famous capital and the ease of the Allied victory had proved the extraordinary weakness of China. Negotiations were opened at once and conducted briskly by Lord Elgin and Baron Gros, whose instructions were to obtain clearly defined commercial and religious privileges. Only one week after the fall of the capital, the Chinese plenipotentiaries signed the Treaties of Peking with England and France (October 1860).*

An amusing "technical" incident, recorded by the British commander in chief, Sir Hope Grant, enlivened the otherwise very formal treaty ceremony exposing the embarrassed Chinese to the overbearing British signatories:

We entered the gates of the Hall of Ceremonies, marched through gardens, up the paved way, and on approaching the grand entrance were met by Prince Kung† and about 500 Mandarins, some of whom were princely looking fellows, dressed in silk robes of state. The Prince came up and closed his hands in front of his face, according to the Chinese salute; but Lord Elgin returned him a proud contemptuous look, and merely bowed slightly, which must have made the blood run cold in poor Kung's veins. He was a delicate, gentleman-like looking man, evidently overpowered with fear. We were placed in chairs of state, in the most honourable position, the left-hand side, and the convention was laid before the Imperial Commissioner, who on this occasion was invested with full powers. After talking over several points, he signed it and ratified the former treaty. . . .‡

---

* On two different days, first with England, and then with France.

† Half brother of the Emperor, and China's leading statesman at the time; he exercised a moderating, rather than a decisive, influence in foreign affairs.

‡ Of Tientsin (1858). The author enumerates the nine clauses of the Treaty of Peking on p. 260 of his Memoirs.

In the midst of the ceremony the indefatigable Signor Beato, who was very anxious to take a good photograph of "the Signing of the Treaty", brought forward his apparatus, placed it at the entrance door, and directed the large lens of the camera full against the breast of the unhappy Prince Kung. The royal brother looked up in a state of terror, pale as death, and with his eyes turned first to Lord Elgin and then to me, expecting every moment to have his head blown off by the infernal machine opposite him—which really looked like a sort of mortar, ready to disgorge its terrible contents into his devoted body. It was explained to him that no such evil design was intended, and his anxious pale face brightened up when he was told that his portrait was being taken. The treaty was signed, and the whole business went off satisfactorily, cxccpt as rcgards Signor Bcato's picture, which was an utter failure, owing to want of proper light.

Refreshments were offered to us, which Lord Elgin declined, and, after a proper amount of bowing, we took our departure. The following day the French treaty was also signed. The war was now at an end, and the good tidings were conveyed home by my aide-de-camp, Anson.[16]

Essentially, the Treaties of Peking confirmed and broadened the "Treaty of Peace, Friendship and Commerce" signed two years earlier at Tientsin. Eleven new ports were opened to foreign trade, among them the all-important harbors of Tientsin, near the capital, and Shanghai, guarding the entrance to China's vital artery, the Yangtze valley. For the first time in Chinese history, and much against China's official wishes, Western ambassadors were permitted to reside in Peking.

Another important clause (and a source of troubles still to come), secured by France, was the right of Catholic missions to hold land. Yet the policy of European powers at the time was not really one of territorial aggression (as was to be the case toward the end of the century): what they wanted mostly was security for trade—and missions.

The one big exception to the rule was Russia, whose land hunger proved considerable. During the negotiations at Peking her minister, posing as a friend of China, offered his offices as mediator. After the signature of the treaties, he naturally suggested a return for his country's services. Russia asked—and was given—a long strip of territory extending south of the Amur river along the Pacific. Near its southern tip she founded Vladivostok; she now had an ice-free seaport in the Far East, which was also to become the terminus of the Trans-Siberian Railroad at the end of the century.*

Before being able to take full advantage of the privileges thus wrested from the Manchu dynasty, England and France had to overcome yet another obstacle, and that was the immensely destructive T'ai P'ing rebellion,†described in the preceding chapter. By 1860, the rebels had lost much of their original dynamism and sense of purpose, but they occupied most of the strategic Yangtze valley (coveted by British interests) and were still too strong for the ill-organized imperial armies.

Western travelers returning from T'ai P'ing territory brought back tales of growing disorder, poverty, and decadence. Among these was Lord Elgin's secretary, Laurence Oliphant, who had accompanied the British Consul Wade on a fact-finding mission in 1858:

A noisy particoloured crowd, jostling each other into the water in their anxiety to inspect us, received us as we stepped on shore. We were surrounded by a mob of these long-haired, long-robed raga-muffins as we walked into the fort through the wretched gateway which served as its principal entrance, and, passing along a narrow, half-ruined street, were ushered into a dilapidated yamun in a state of repair. Strains of a discordant music announced our approach to the high dignitary within, whom we found seated in solemn state behind a high table or altar, upon which stood two open carved jars like wine coolers, of silver or imitation silver, which contained long thin slips of wood covered with Chinese characters. The chamber was a small, square apartment, hung with scrolls of yellow silk, covered with texts and mottoes in Chinese, belonging, apparently, as much to Confucianism as to Christianity; and the presiding genius himself was a stout, sensual-looking man, with a keen eye, and an intelligent but bad cast of countenance. He was dressed in a robe of yellow silk which fell from his neck to his heels, and was devoid of ornament; round his head was wrapped an orange-coloured handkerchief, in the centre of which, above the forehead, was fastened a single piece of jade, mounted in a gold setting. His long hair was collected in a bag, and hung in the

---

* The China of Mao Tse-tung has repeatedly denounced the "unfair" treaties of Aigun and Peking, and claims as her own the territories then ceded to "imperial-istic" Russia. Vladivostok means "Master of the East", in Russian.

† In addition to laying waste vast areas of fertile land, it cost the lives of some twenty million Chinese.

nape of his neck, as though an imitation of the fashion prevalent among English young ladies of the present day.

Bowing to us slightly as we entered, How—for so was this great man called—beckoned us to chairs, the mob by which we had been followed crowding unceremoniously into the small apartment. Not the smallest respect was shown by the insubordinate rabble to their leader, who strove in vain to keep them from pressing round, much to the disparagement of the dignified manner which he evidently desired to maintain in our presence, and by which he hoped to impress us with a due sense of his rank and importance. The odour of garlic which pervaded his undisciplined retainers, their boisterous and noisy manner and filthy aspect, rendered our audience by no means so agreeable as it might otherwise have been. A perfect equality seemed to reign, or rather an absolute confusion of ranks and persons, well dressed and ragged, old and young, thronged impetuously into the little room. It struck me, however, that the young predominated: many of these had been rebels all their lives, and had no tails, but generally the tail was wrapped round the long tangled hair.

How told us that to his functions of commander and judge he united those of high priest. The thin slips of wood in the silver vases were inscribed with various punishments, and the form of sentencing consisted in his selecting and throwing to the criminal the punishment to which he was condemned. . . .

The leaders were Canton men of the worst description. Drunkenness and opium-smoking were prevalent vices, as one of their number, who spoke Cantonese English, and was evidently a blackguard of the first water, unhesitatingly admitted. In the original code promulgated by T'ai P'ing, opium-smoking was punishable by death. One of the first questions we were asked by How was, "What have you got to sell?" They were evidently sceptical when we denied that we were traders, and How recurred to the subject before we left him. He had been a merchant in a small way at Canton.

We now proceeded to the exploration of the surrounding streets, and . . . were accompanied on our rambles by a crowd, with the more intelligent of whom Mr. Wade got into conversation upon religious subjects; but their theology was of the vaguest description, and did not prevent them from using the foulest language to each other. We saw very few women, and they were evidently all from the north, probably captured on some of their raids in that direction.[17]

Naturally, this physical and moral decay of the T'ai P'ings impressed the British—and all other Westerners—very unfavorably. The Protestant missionaries, whose initial reaction toward the rebellion had generally been openly sympathetic, had by now denounced the movement's idolatrous practices* and excesses of many kinds. From a Western standpoint, therefore, the waning revolt was unacceptable both morally and commercially.

The T'ai P'ings themselves provoked Western intervention when they attacked Shanghai in 1860, and again in 1862, uniting against them the city's disparate (and discordant) military outfits: imperial troops, Chinese pirates preying upon friend and foe alike, crews of British or French warships temporarily anchored in the port, and last but not least, the motley crowd of Western adventurers organized by the American F. T. Ward† and soon to become famous under the name "Ever Victorious Army".

In the spring of 1862, Commander de Marolles led a contingent of French marines into battle and made the following entries in his diary:

April 1. Today, the French and British admirals have decided to undertake a series of expeditions against the T'ai P'ings, whose destructive deeds kept increasing as a result of the Chinese authorities' incapacity and cowardice. It was of great importance to the British that the silk- and tea-growing areas continue to ship their products to Shanghai, and that the opium grown in Bengal further poison the Chinese. . . .‡

April 3. Departure of the French and British columns. At about one kilometer beyond Zi-ka-wei, we found but ruins and devastation. The rebels had come that far. As in the neighborhood of Shanghai, a great many coffins had been placed on the ground, along the road....

April 4. We had arrived to within half a mile of the rebel camp. The British were late, so we halted our men, waiting for the British artillery to move up. Presently they arrived, and we advanced in battle formation against the flag-bedecked fort, the British on the right, our men on the left, and the artillery in front of us. It opened fire at 600 meters, while Ward's men deployed a skirmishing line on our right.

---

* In particular, the "Heavenly King's" insistence on being worshiped.

† Who, after having served under his fellow countryman William Walker in Mexico and Nicaragua in the fifties, had come to China, where he adopted Chinese customs and married a Chinese girl.

‡ Additional clauses to the Treaties of Tientsin had legalized the importation of opium, and large quantities kept flowing into China thereafter.

The enemy replied with jingals, and we were glad to discover that his artillery was very poor. At about 150 meters, my men were formed into two assault columns. Suddenly, the enemy fire stopped everywhere. . . . We decided to pursue the T'ai P'ings on the run, but they had a substantial lead on us, having abandoned their arms and all objects liable to hamper their flight. Meanwhile, soldiers of our Chinese battalion, a number of Ward's men and all our coolies rushed into the camp, where they seized large amounts of booty. The camp was afterwards set afire, and burned until the evening. . . .

After an hour's pursuit we gave it up, being quite tired. At 2 P.M. we lunched in a field containing a rather large number of coffins. One of my young surgeons informed me that he had seen a female body in an advanced state of decay in a nearby coffin, and asked me for permission to take one of the feet with him, as he wished to donate it to the Navy hospital at Rochefort,* which did not as yet possess such a rare object! I granted him the permission, for the sake of science. . . .

May 14. Still on the road. We followed several canals; the countryside lay waste, inhabited.

May 15. Marched through Tsong-kao, half burned out. Few inhabitants.

May 16. Still that driving rain. We reached the town of Nan-ch'iao, with a population of 25,000, and which the rebels have made into one of their main strongholds. . . .

May 18. Nan-ch'iao has been set afire by our shells, and has been plundered by the nearby farmers. The place was well fortified. In the middle of the day, when we thought that the T'ai P'ings were on the run, small groups of them attacked us and were killed fighting very gallantly. We seized many horses and mules, great amounts of food. No young women. Made 2,000 prisoners, without knowing what to do with them. Father Lemaître interrogated them, and according to their replies we divided them into two categories: those who looked like fairly good fellows were released and made to promise that they would never serve under the T'ai P'ings again; but those resembling gallows birds were delivered into the hands of the Imperialists following us, and were killed by them. We left a garrison of 100 French infantry and as many British at Nan-ch'iao.[18]

On September 24, Commander de Marolles noted that Ward had just

* Small port (population 30,000) in western France.

been killed while leading an assault against a mud-walled village. He was only thirty-one, and died the way he had lived: recklessly, after having won a score of victories in a matter of seven months.

Another American, Burgevine, replaced Ward at the head of the "Ever Victorious Army", but he lasted little longer, before meeting his own tragic end.★

The rugged outfit of mercenaries was then reorganized and shaped into a coherent and efficient fighting force by the British Major (later General) Charles G. Gordon, better known as "Chinese" Gordon. Its numerical strength varied from 3,000 to 5,000 men; the commissioned officers were all foreigners, mostly American and British. Gordon himself was often in his army's front rank leading the attack and, amazingly, was wounded only once —by a shot through the leg—during the fourteen months of his spectacular campaign.

A hero to his men, Gordon was equally admired by the Chinese, who bestowed their highest military award upon him. One of China's leading statesmen of the time, the Viceroy Li Hung-chang,† had only praise for him:

It is a direct blessing from Heaven, I believe, the coming of this British Gordon. . . . He is superior in manner and bearing to any of the foreigners I have come into contact with, and does not show outwardly that conceit which makes most of them repugnant in my sight. Besides, while he is possessed of a splendid military bearing, he is direct and businesslike. Within two hours after his arrival he was inspecting the troops and giving orders; and I could not but rejoice at the manner in which his commands were obeyed. . . .

What a sight to tired eyes and elixir for a heavy heart it is to see this splendid Englishman fight! I have just returned from nine days and nights with him, and if there is anything I admire nearly as much as the superb scholarship of Tseng Kuo-fan,‡ it is the military qualities of this fine officer. Fight—move—fight again—move again—landing

★ His troops' pay was in arrears, and their morale (and discipline) fell accordingly. A Shanghai banker who refused to advance the necessary amount of money was beaten up by the hot-tempered Burgevine, who eventually went over to the T'ai P'ings. He was later captured—and drowned, accidentally or wilfully, during his transportation in a bamboo cage.

† He came into special prominence toward the end of the century, during China's unhappy war against Japan.

‡ Celebrated contemporary philosopher, chief Chinese architect of victory over the T'ai P'ing rebellion.

his men—planning by night and executing by day—planning by day and executing by night! He is a glorious fellow!

Yesterday when I left him to return for a brief space, I told him he was my brother. . . . Could I have said more in all the words of the world?[19]

Under the relentless pressure of the "Ever Victorious Army" and the renewed attacks of the Imperials led by such able commanders as Tseng Kuo-fan and his two disciples, Li Hung-chang and Tso Tsung-t'ang, the slowly distintegrating T'ai P'ings suffered defeat after defeat in and near the lower Yangtze valley, where their main forces were bottled up in the early sixties.

One of the last rebel strongholds was the city of Soochow, west of Shanghai. It was besieged and starved out by Gordon's troops during the fall of 1863. Its defender, Li Hsiu-ch'eng, the "Faithful King" and one of the rebellion's most remarkable figures, wrote to the "Heavenly King" (entrenched in Nanking) to inform him of the city's desperate straits:

From this beleaguered place, I indite these lines. Our provisions are exhausted; in the camp, the cooking pots are empty. The stove is cold and there is no drug that can allay the pangs of hunger. Corpses are carved in pieces and mothers sell their sons for food. For many days past we have been shouting "Dinner is ready" at mealtimes, so as to deceive the enemy concerning our lack of provisions. Our plight is grievous, resembling that of the turtle in the tureen: our danger is that of the tiger at bay upon the mountain precipice. Your Majesty has founded a new Empire, but if its roots be shaken, the branches are agitated. Soochow is your Majesty's lower jaw: if the lips perish, the teeth must speedily decay. As soon as you have been able to force a way through the beleaguering armies, it behooves you to dispatch troops to our assistance. I send these few lines beseeching you to take care of your health. Interrupting the whetting of my spear, I write this message, earnestly praying for your welfare.[20]

Instead of coming to the help of his most faithful lieutenant, however, the Heavenly King busied himself with irrelevant and visionary matters in the midst of a worshiping society of women. The strange atmosphere surrounding him in the rebellion's closing days has been ably conveyed by Andrew Wilson, editor of the British-sponsored paper China Mail *and a friend of Gordon's:*

While Soochow was in course of being taken in 1863, the Faithful King managed himself to get admission to the Rebel capital, and besought the Tien Wang* to make his escape and give up the city, as it could no longer be held, and was deficient in the necessities of life; but the monarch, according to the Faithful King's Autobiography, was highly displeased at this proposal, and indignantly exclaimed, "I have received the commands of Shangte (God) and of Jesus to come down upon earth and rule the Empire. I am the sole Lord of ten thousand nations, and what should I fear? You are not asked your opinion on anything, and the Government does not require your supervision. You can please yourself as to whether you wish to leave the capital or to remain. I hold the Empire, hills, and streams with an iron grasp. and if you do not support me there are those who will. You say, 'There are no soldiers!' But my troops are more numerous than the streams. What fear have I of the demon Tseng [Kuo-fan]? If you are afraid of death then you will die."

It was in this way only that the Heavenly Monarch would look at practical matters. Burying himself in the depths of his palace, and engrossed with religious exercises and the society of his women, he gave himself no concern about either the approach of his enemies or the terrible state of his people. When anyone memorialized him on internal affairs, or made suggestions pertinent to the preservation of the kingdom, he would invariably silence them with remarks on heaven and earth, which, as the Chung Wang† complains, were "totally irrelevant to the main point of view". When it was mentioned to him that only the very wealthy people in Nanking had any food to eat, he issued a decree that the remainder should support themselves upon "sweet dew", and illustrated his meaning by ordering some herbs from the palace garden to be prepared for his own dinner. His subordinates in the Government were allowed to do as they liked so long as they professed implicit submission to his decrees; but their chief was very particular with them in regard to points of theological phraseology, and threatened to draw any one asunder between five horses who omitted a due use of the term "Heavenly" in all official documents. . . . At no time had he personally interfered much in the detail of government or in the management of fighting.[21]

Soochow fell in December 1863, and a few months later Nanking in turn

* Heavenly Prince.   † Faithful Prince.

was invested by the imperial armies. The Heavenly King committed suicide (by swallowing gold coins) in June 1864, and thus ended the great T'ai P'ing rebellion which had lasted for some fifteen years and came close to toppling the Manchu dynasty.

Nanking surrendered in July 1864, and on that occasion the Imperial armies slaughtered some 100,000 rebels over a period of three days. Those among the T'ai P'ings who were lucky to escape, fled southward into the mountains of the Canton area, where they constituted half-patriotic and half-piratical bands of "White" and "Black" pavilions.*

The end of the T'ai P'ing rebellion opened the Yangtze valley to Western expansion, confirmed the political power of the viceroys who had successfully fought the rebels,† and gave a new lease on life to the tottering Manchu dynasty. On (or behind) its throne now stood the formidable Tzu Hsi, favorite concubine of Emperor Hsien Feng and his widow since 1861.‡

In the name of the boy Emperor, the young§ Empress Dowager issued a special decree expressing official exultation at the crushing of the revolt and rewarding the victorious generals:

This glorious victory is entirely due to the bountiful protection of Heaven, to the ever-present help of our Ancestors, and to the foresight and wisdom of the Empress Regent, who, by employing and promoting efficient leaders for their armies, have thus secured cooperation of all our forces and the accomplishment of this great achievement, whereby the soul of our late father in Heaven must be comforted, and the desire of all people fulfilled. . . . This rebellion has now lasted fifteen years, during twelve of which Nanking has been held by the rebels. They have devastated about a dozen provinces, and have captured some hundreds of cities. Their final defeat we owe to our Generals, who have been combed by the wind and bathed by the rain in bringing about the destruction of these unspeakable traitors. We are therefore bound to recognize their exceptional services by the bestowal of exceptional rewards. Tseng Kuo-fan first contributed to this glorious end by raising a force of militia in Hunan and a fleet of war vessels with

---

* The latter fought the French in Indochina (Tonking).

† By raising local armies with the taxes they collected for the imperial government, much of which they kept for their own purposes. The best-known example is that of Tseng Kuo-fan, who thus organized the "Braves of Hunan", his native province in central China.

‡ He died in Jehol at the age of thirty.

§ She was then thirty years old.

which he won great victories, saving his province from complete ruin. He recaptured Wu-ch'ang, cleared the whole province of Kiangsi, and, advancing eastward, recovered city after city. That glorious success has finally crowned our efforts is due chiefly to his masterly strategy and courage, to his employment of able subordinates and to his remarkable powers of organization. We now confer upon him the title of Senior Guardian of the Throne, a marquisate of the first rank, hereditary in perpetuity, and the decoration of the double-eyed peacock's feather.[22]

CHAPTER V

THE ERA OF VICEROYS, 1860–1894

THE T'AI P'ING rebellion created profound changes in the Manchu government, primarily by shifting the center of gravity from Peking to the provinces in both financial and military matters. Greater freedom of action was yielded to the viceroys, most of whom were Chinese. They now proceeded to take full advantage of their increased status and power, and did so by participating more and more actively in the decisions—and intrigues—of the imperial court.

China's humiliating defeats by small European armies, on the other hand, convinced many a Chinese official that the problems created by Western contact could not be solved by traditional methods alone. New ways of dealing with foreign barbarians were called for, and efforts at modernizing her institutions should be undertaken without delay.

Probably the first man to come forward with practical suggestions was a scholar of Soochow, Feng Kuei-fen, who called for China's "self-strengthening". In a series of forty essays written around 1860,* Feng insisted on the adoption of Western knowledge and on the manufacture of foreign weapons in order to "better control" rebellion from within or aggression from abroad:

The world today is not to be compared with that of the Three Dynasties.†. . . Now the globe is ninety-thousand *li* around, and every spot may be reached by ships or wheeled vehicles. . . . According to what is listed on the maps by Westerners, there are not less than one hundred countries. From these one hundred countries, only the books of Italy at the end of the Ming dynasty, and now those of England have been translated into Chinese, altogether several tens of books. Those

* Feng declined to have them published, but they were widely read—by his friends and government officials—and had far-reaching influence.
† Of ancient China.

which expound the doctrine of Jesus are generally vulgar, not worth mentioning. Apart from these, Western books on mathematics, mechanics, optics, light, chemistry, and other subjects contain the best principles of the natural sciences. In the books on geography, the mountains, rivers, strategic points, customs, and native products of the hundred countries are fully listed. Most of this information is beyond the reach of our people. . . . If today we wish to select and use Western knowledge, we should establish official translation offices at Canton and Shanghai. Brilliant students up to fifteen years of age should be selected from those areas to live and study in these schools on double rations. Westerners should be invited to teach them the spoken and written languages of the various nations, and famous Chinese teachers should also be engaged to teach them classics, history, and other subjects. . . .

If we let Chinese ethics and famous [Confucian] teachings serve as an original foundation, and let them be supplemented by the methods used by the various nations for the attainment of prosperity and strength, would it not be the best of all procedures? . . .

The most unparalleled anger which has ever existed since the creation of heaven and earth is exciting all who are conscious in their minds and have spirit in their blood; their hats are raised by their hair standing on end. This is because the largest country on the globe today, with a vast area of 10,000 *li*, is yet controlled by small barbarians. . . . According to a general geography by an Englishman, the territory of our China is eight times larger than that of Russia, ten times that of America, one hundred times that of France, and two hundred times that of England. . . . Yet now we are shamefully humiliated by those four nations in the recent treaties—not because our climate, soil, or resources are inferior to theirs, but because our people are really inferior. . . . Why are they small and yet strong? Why are we large and yet weak? We must try to discover some means to become their equal, and that also depends upon human effort. . . .

What we have to learn from the barbarians is only the one thing, solid ships and effective guns. . . . Funds should be assigned to establish a shipyard and arsenal in each trading port. Several barbarians should be invited and Chinese who are good in using their minds should be summoned to receive their instructions so that they may in turn teach many artisans. . . . The workers should be double-paid so as to prevent them from quitting. . . .

Peking. Western Gate. *Radio Times Hulton Picture Library.*

Emperor Tao Kuang, entrusted by Heaven with the task of watching over the prosperity of the Empire of the Middle, receives the high dignitaries (civilian and military Mandarins) in the Forbidden City.

Ruinous results of the ever-increasing use of imported opium among the Chinese: pallid and emaciated faces, and cataleptic trances.

Right. This Chinese archer would probably have held his own against Western cavalry of the fourteenth century. In 1860, at the gates of Peking, he stood no chance against Western marines.

Right. A "Tiger" of the Chinese imperial army. In the Opium War, soldiers of this type fought hopeless battles against the guns of the Royal Navy. *Radio Times Hulton Picture Library.*

October 22, 1860. For the first time in history, Western troops enter Peking.
On the ramparts, the Chinese endeavour to frighten the enemy by shaking
paper dragons and tigers.

Left. 1900. In order to drive out the "foreign devils" and massacre the Chinese Christians, this "Boxer" child had armed himself with a "big knife," traditional weapon of Chinese peasant revolts.

Below. Anti-Christian Boxer tract. The representation of Christians as pigs and of Westerners as goats corresponded to a traditional Chinese pun.

THE BOXER REBELLION, 1900

Above. Chinese troops at the Eastern gate of the Forbidden City. The headsman stands in the centre; the guards' uniform is relatively modern.

Below. These "Foreign Devils" are stationed at the back of the American Legation, which was besieged by the Boxers.

Tzu Hsi, Empress Dowager. Her guile and cruelty enabled her to rule over China for half a century. Note the long nails, also worn by the literati as a visible sign that they performed no manual work.

The banderole is dated 1903 and reads:

Maternal, kind, august, protecting, peaceable, fostering, glorious, indulgent, grave, sincere Empress, whose life shall be long, respectable, pious, proud, wise and brilliant—Holy Mother of the Great Ts'ing Empire at the present time.

Two medals, representing two different periods. *Above*, Yuan Shik-k'ai, would-be savior of imperial China. *Below*, Sun Yat-sen envisions a new, republican China.

Eventually we must consider manufacturing, repairing, and using weapons by ourselves. . . . Only thus will we be able to pacify the empire; only thus can we play a leading role on the globe; and only thus shall we restore our original strength, and redeem ourselves from former humiliations.[1]

Feng's bold and novel propositions were well received by the few but influential Chinese officials who, like him, wished to introduce Western technology into their country. Foremost among them were the famed scholar-general Tseng Kuo-fan and his coadjutor, Li Hung-chang.

Until his death in 1872, Tseng shared much of the moral leadership of China, and was instrumental in the creation of arsenals and institutions for linguistic and scientific studies.* In order to get foreign machinery, he used the services of Yung Wing, first Chinese graduate of an American university (Yale 1854).†

From the far more numerous conservative circles, however, came vehement protests against such Westernization. The leader of conservative opposition was Wo-jen, head of the Hanlin Academy and tutor to the boy Emperor. In 1867, he attacked Tseng's innovations in a memorial to the imperial throne:

According to the viewpoint of your slave, astronomy and mathematics are of very little use. If these subjects are going to be taught by Westerners as regular studies, the damage will be great. . . . Your slave has learned that the way to establish a nation is to lay emphasis on propriety and righteousness, not on power and plotting. The fundamental effort lies in the minds of people, not in techniques. . . . The empire is so great that one should not worry lest there be any lack of abilities therein. If astronomy and mathematics have to be taught, an extensive search should find someone who has mastered the technique. Why is it limited to barbarians, and why is it necessary to learn from barbarians?

Moreover, the barbarians are our enemies. In 1860 they took up arms and rebelled against us. Our capital and its suburbs were invaded, our ancestral altar was shaken, our Imperial palace was burned, and

---

* In particular the arsenal of Shanghai, and the interpreters' college at Peking, or T'ung-wen Kuan, whose curriculum soon included astronomy, chemistry, physics, biology, geography, anatomy, mathematics, metallurgy, etc.

† In the seventies, 120 students went to the United States, 30 to England and France.

our officials and people were killed or wounded. There had never been such insults during the last 200 years of our dynasty. All our scholars and officials have been stirred with heart-burning rage, and have retained their hatred until the present. Our court could not help making peace with the barbarians. How can we forget this enmity and this humiliation even for one single day? . . .

Your slave fears that what our scholars are going to learn cannot be learned well and yet will be perplexing, which would just fall in with [the foreigners'] plans. It is earnestly hoped that, in order to maintain the general prestige of the empire and to prevent the development of disaster, the Imperial mind will independently decide to abolish instantly the previous decision to establish such studies in the language school. The whole empire will be fortunate indeed![2]

In more than one way, this letter was typical of Chinese feelings after the signing of the Peking Treaties. The Westerners were, even more than before, the "rebellious" barbarians, the "enemies". As the years went by, hatred of strangers kept increasing at every level of Chinese society, and was generally encouraged by the highest Mandarins.

During the next half century, one person more than any other incarnated China's conservative forces, and that was the Dowager Empress Tzu Hsi, a most remarkable (and sinister) woman, often compared with Elizabeth I of England and Catherine II of Russia. In 1851, she was known as Ye-ho-no-la when, aged seventeen, she was chosen, together with twenty-seven other Manchu beauties of aristocratic descent, as a concubine of young Emperor Hsien Feng. The Emperor at once became very fond of her, and five years later she gave birth to the heir presumptive.

After the death of Hsien Feng, in 1861, she became China's de facto ruler, and remained so with but one brief interval* until her own death in 1908. The nominal emperors were puppets in her iron hand: first her son, a dissolute weakling who died in 1875 (aged nineteen), and then her nephew, Kuang Hsü (1875–1908), who vainly tried to shake off her all too vigorous tutelage.

Intensely fond of power, Tzu Hsi was also a resourceful, courageous, and very crafty woman. For two generations loyalty to her person and admiration for her Machiavellian genius inspired the untiring efforts of China's foremost soldiers and statesmen in upholding the inefficient and corrupt Manchu dynasty, struggling against irresistible forces of aggression from without and incurable disorganization within.

* In 1898, at the time of the famous Hundred Days.

As a pure Manchu, Tzu Hsi never thought of anything but Manchu interests, and in pursuing these she rarely hesitated as to the means to be chosen: she would back her friends and ruthlessly destroy her enemies, and was as consummate an intriguer as any member of the corrupt aristocracy that surrounded her. The people feared and revered her, while her enemies cowered in silent hatred; all they could do was to circulate at the court lampoons denouncing her cruelty and debauchery.

One of these lampoons, signed "An Anhui official", described Tzu Hsi's pitiless intervention in a long-standing feud between her chief eunuch, Li Lien-ying,* and another leading eunuch, Liu:

Li hated Liu (whose influence for a time exceeded his own), and slandered him in every possible way to the Empress, but Liu was very cunning, and managed to anticipate calumny with explanations which always pacified Tzu Hsi.

One day, however, he offended Her Majesty, who reproved him severely; this time, Li's abuse of his rival fell on attentive ears and Tzu Hsi, giving way to a passion of rage, ordered Liu to attend her immediately. When he appeared, she recapitulated the list of his offenses, some thirty in all, and ended by saying: "Do you not think you merit decapitation?" Liu realized that there was no hope, so kowtowed, saying, "Your slave deserves to die a myriad deaths, but I implore the Old Buddha† to remember that I have served her, as her dog or her horse, for thirty years; let her grant me at least the favour of dying with a whole skin."‡ She pondered over this for a minute, and replied: "Very well; you may go now, and await my further commands." She bade her handmaidens conduct him to a small antechamber and lock the door on him. Then she burst out laughing, and called all her eunuchs and women to her side. "I have a new amusement for you today," she said. One of the women was told to bring a small case from her bedroom; Ye-ho-no-la opened it with a tiny key which she wore at her girdle. It contained about twenty phials, one of which she selected and poured out some of the contents, a pink powder, into a wine cup. She mixed some water with this and bade the attendant take it to Liu and say that he was to drink the contents and then lie quietly down. The attendant soon returned and reported

* Whose influence dominated palace politics until Tzu Hsi's death.
† Popular nickname of the aging Empress, stressing her wisdom.
‡ Slicing off the victim's skin was a common form of execution.

that Liu had thanked Her Majesty for her benevolence, and had done as directed.

Tzu Hsi waited about ten minutes and then said: "You may now see the fun I promised you. Open Liu's door and see how he fares." The eunuch was lying aparently asleep; though dead, he showed no trace of suffering.[3]

On another occasion, * *Tzu Hsi had one of her nephew's concubines (who had openly dared contradict her) thrown into a well. Around her, meanwhile, an increasingly degenerate nobility indulged in all sorts of fads and crazes, such as the one recorded by an anonymous Manchu official in his diary:*

I remembered particularly one occasion, during the dog days of 1892. It was a very hot day, and some friends had invited me to join them in an excursion to the Kiosk and Garden known as "Beautiful Autumn Hillock", just outside the southwest gate of the Southern city. . . . This spot is well-shaded and delightfully cool, and visitors can take their tea quietly at the open-air rest, while enjoying the pleasant and busy scene. Pedlars and wine sellers come here to ply their trade, acrobats and conjurors perform to earn a few cash from the idle rich, and there are strolling musicians. There are also sheltered nooks for the comfort of visitors, so that one might fancy oneself in the heart of the country.

At the table next to us sat a young man of about eighteen: his face was as black as soot and he looked thin and ill-nourished. His queue was plaited round his head and he had inserted a bone hairpin in his hair, after the manner of the Peking hooligan class in summertime. He wore no socks and was stripped to the waist. His only garment was a very shabby pair of short trousers, which hardly reached to the knee, all covered with grease and mud, and badly torn: in fact, he was scarcely decent. He wore a pair of dilapidated grass slippers, through which his toes protruded.

Strange to say, this miserable-looking beggar had on his right thumb a large ring of green jade worth at least 1,500 taels, and he carried a beautiful and very costly carved fan with a jade handle. He sat, with legs crossed, on the ground, drinking wine. His conversation was full of vulgar oaths and the lowest Pekingese slang. I noticed, however, that

* In 1900, when the Court was about to flee northward before an international expedition sent out to crush the Boxer rebellion.

the waiters showed him a very particular and eager attention and hardly ever left his side. To their other patrons their behaviour was very different, being somewhat offhand and brusque.

I was lost in bewilderment at this spectacle, wondering what it meant, when the sun began to sink behind the hills and the guests to leave. All of a sudden I observed the arrival of a smart official cart with red wheels set far back,* and a train of some twenty well-groomed attendants. I then realized the truth and awaited developments with some curiosity. Two officials came up the hillock, both wearing the button of the third rank and peacock's feather. They were evidently officers of the bodyguard; one of them carried a hatbox and a bundle of clothes, while the other held a basin and ewer. They approached the young beggar, and reverently addressed him: "Your Highness's carriage is ready. You have an engagement to dine at Prince Kung's palace tonight, and we ought to be starting." So the young blood got up, took a towel and washed his face. We were all astonished at the transformation, and could scarcely suppress an exclamation of surprise. The dirty black of his face had been replaced by a delicate white complexion, and though thin, he had the distinctive features of the Manchu Princes. We perceived that he had daubed his face with charcoal.

He then attired himself in his proper clothes, with the jewelled buttoned hat which princes wear, decorated with the triple-eyed peacock's feather. The two officials humbly escorted him to his carriage; he drove off and was soon lost to view.

The head waiter then whispered to me: "That was the Beileh,† Tsai Lien." I replied in amazement: "What does he mean by such behaviour?" "Oh," said he, "don't you know the latest craze of our young Princes in Peking?" He went on to tell me how Prince Chuang, Prince K'o, Prince Tuan, the Beilehs Lien and Ying, Prince Ch'ing's son Tsai Chen . . . and many others, made a practice of adopting this guise, and were constantly causing disturbances in houses of ill fame, taverns, etc., and street rows, as the police were afraid to interfere with them. The Prince we saw was comparatively well behaved.

I was horrified to hear this, and said: "This surely portends evil to our Empire. Such things occurred just before the Sungs were finally defeated by the Mongols and also at the close of the T'ang dynasty.

* A type of vehicle that could only be used by persons of very high rank.

† Manchu title given to the sons of imperial princes.

History is full of such examples. Mark my words, China will be plunged into dire calamities before ten years have passed."[4]

Along China's extensive coastline, the ports and concessions opened by the final treaty settlement of 1860 constituted as many bridgeheads for Western penetration, and soon bore the unmistakable marks of the foreigners' manifold activities and habits.

Shanghai, in particular, developed into a bustling and modern seaport whose exceptional location at the mouth of the Yangtze made her China's commercial capital before the end of the century. European visitors were amazed, and sometimes disappointed, by the city's extraordinary growth and . . . Westernization. This was the case of the French sinologist Maurice Jametel, watching the scenery from the deck of an incoming ship in 1886:

On our right, the steadily increasing number of houses told us that we were nearing a large city. Soon, however, the Chinese dwellings disappeared, and instead we saw European villas with white façades and elegant verandas. Through our field glasses we could even glance into their interior parts, and to our surprise discovered all the comfort of Western civilization. Even the gardens of these elegant houses, with their well-tended flower beds and carefully mown lawns, reminded us of the most fashionable villas of Kew and Enghien* much more than of the land of bells and bamboo screens.

This first disappointment was followed by even greater ones. The presence of European elegance in all its triteness, when you expect to find purely Asiatic features, was in itself frustrating enough, but worse was yet to come. Behind the villas appeared the storehouses, uniformly covered with galvanized zinc sheets expanding their shiny rooftops as far as the eye could see. Steam launches were plying the river in all directions, constantly tooting their shrill whistles, while powerful cranes were creaking and groaning under the heavy loads they had to carry. So little Chinese was all this that it required a real effort of imagination to convince the visitor that he actually found himself in the "Flowery Kingdom".

Beyond the bend of the river, where a wooden bridge in excellent repair linked the American concession to the English settlement, the scene changed once more, but without becoming more typically Chinese. On the contrary, as we advanced the environment reminded

* Wealthy suburb of Paris.

us more and more of Europe, from which we were then separated by forty-five days of navigation. On the riverside, a garden with green lawns and lovely clusters of lilacs and roses, was hiding the British Consulate, whose flag proudly waved in the wind. In the middle of the garden, a small iron kiosk containing music desks reminded us of Naples' *Villa nazionale.* On the river itself, large English and German steamers were moving up and down.

We kept going upstream. After the English garden, we noticed a broad, macadamized quay bordered by trees. A water carriage was moving along that quay, in the same direction as ours. . . . We came to Shanghai's Lombard Street. . . . The architecture was different. Along the quay stood a long row of buildings looking more wealthy than elegant; its style was bizarre rather than beautiful. These were the palatial buildings of the city's leading banks. We first saw the splendid residence of the Hong Kong and Shanghai Banking Corporation, the only bank having its main office in the Far East—at Hong Kong— where both its board of trustees and stockholders hold their meetings, while its London office is but a branch similar to those the bank has established in Asia. The other banks, on the contrary, are merely branch offices of well-known Western financial institutions, and their lower status is revealed by a different style: whereas the Hong Kong and Shanghai Banking Corporation occupies a palace, its competitors, the Oriental Bank (which no longer exists), the Agra Bank, the Mercantile and the Chartered Bank are merely located in splendid hotels. Our own Comptoir d'Escompte de Paris maintains an agency next to these large British establishments.[5]

At the hotel where he stayed, Jametel found himself surrounded by all the comforts and amenities of Western civilization:

In the city's overcrowded streets, the noise of human voices and wheels was deafening, and painful to our unaccustomed ears. We felt greatly relieved, therefore, when we were able to sit down and relax in the elegant vestibule of the Hotel des Colonies.

Its Swiss owner came forward to greet me at the entrance. From the vestibule I could glance into a comfortable lounge already lit by a gas luster, as the sun had set during our arrival. On the lounge's green-draped table were lying some Europeans papers, such as the *Temps,* the *Figaro,* the *Journal de Genève,* the *Journal Amusant,* and *La*

Vie Parisienne, which had arrived by the boat on which I had traveled. Several Europeans were chatting while sipping a green or brownish apéritif, absinthe or vermouth. Through an open door on the other side of the vestibule I could see a large dining room filled with long tables covered with white tablecloths. . . .

In the evening, at dinner, I found myself among Europeans only. They were discussing the merits of an Italian operetta troupe that had arrived from Yokohama on the previous day. While listening to these music lovers, I enjoyed as refined and delicious a meal as if I had been at Brébant's, in Paris, or at Blanchard's, in Regent Street. Even the most demanding gourmets will agree that they can risk the trip from Paris to Shanghai, after having looked at the menu of my first dinner there, which I quote *in extenso*: Pea soup à la Soubise; caviar and sardines; chicken patties; pheasant and roast beef, English style, with peas; and for dessert: ice pudding, Roquefort cheese, apples and grapes. The wines were equally good: Bordeaux and dry port, plus dry champagne; the British set the fashion here, and since they dislike sweet wines, the latter are usually dry.

After dinner, I accepted an invitation to go to the theatre, in spite of my weariness. The troupe was by no means first rate, but so little had I expected to see *Les Cloches de Corneville* played in China, and this in an elegant, gas-lit hall, that I readily forgave the performers their inexperience, and the female singers their faulty roulades.

The audience was possibly even more Western than the setting. The men wore black suits and white ties, while the women were in gala dress, glittering with jewels and perfumed by lovely bouquets from the gardens and greenhouses of the villas that I had admired while coming up the river. All these handsome foreigners settled in Shanghai seem to enjoy a perfectly happy and secure life, even though the imagination of people back in Europe often fancies them as having to face all sorts of dangers in the midst of cannibals called the Chinese. The current topic of discussion was the latest novel by Zola, which had arrived with the ship that brought me to the city. . . .

After the show, I went to the European Club, where I had been graciously invited to celebrate my happy arrival with champagne. During the excellent supper prepared by the club's Chinese cook, two large screens called pankas, hanging from the ceiling of the dining room and agitated by native servants, filled the room with pleasantly cool air.

After some generous champagne toasts ... I took a closer look at the club's splendid facilities. They included a billiard room, a game room, and a large reading room containing a well-stacked library. On the table in its middle, I found European and American papers and reviews such as the *Times*, the *New York Tribune*, the *Edinburgh Review*, the *Kölnische Zeitung*. The French tongue was well represented too, by the *Journal de Genève*, the *Temps*, the *Revue des Deux Mondes* and the *Bibliothèque Universelle*.

The building also includes a number of private rooms that are held at the disposal of the members of clubs located in other Far Eastern harbor cities, who automatically become members of the Shanghai club when staying in that city.[6]

In stark contrast to the dynamic changes taking place along China's coasts, life in her vast interior went on unchanged. The few foreigners, missionaries and traders for the most part, who ventured far inland met with scenes that could have occurred centuries earlier.

In 1872, the French missionary Abbé Vigneron visited Chungking:

Everything in this large trading center contributes to making its streets filthy and muddy: its enormous population, the constant coming and going of boatmen and travelers, the rainy climate, and the immediate proximity of the big river.*. . . In addition to the scent of musk peculiar to China and the Chinese, and which is quite bearable after one has become accustomed to it, there are many other odors that would put to flight even the least sensitive among my countrymen: smells of filth, of refuse, odors coming from kitchens or butcher shops, and innumerable others.

On the other hand, one can find in Chungking shops of all kinds, and they are all well kept. Some sell remedies, others offer superb palanquins, either for city use or for travel; still others specialize in embroidered silk fabrics adorned with fancy drawings mainly representing colorful birds or flowers. Keep going, and you will see next a merchant exhibiting a remarkable collection of copper vessels such as pans, teapots, washbasins, water tubes and small pipes. In the shop next to his, you will be shown beautiful chinaware, flower pots, plates and saucers, rice cups, tea or wine cups, all of them being

* The Yangtze.

decorated with symbolic or historic figures as well as with maxims written in beautiful characters. . . .

Whatever the merchants may sell—idols, furniture, glasses, precious stones in the shape of globules or rings, oval, square or triangular fans made of silk, fine paper or palm leaves—they are all in their stores, wealthy-looking in their silken dresses, grave and imperturbable, ceremonious in manners and speech alike. They watch you walk by while puffing their water-tube pipes, or computing some figures on their little machines, the s'uan-pans with three bars carrying movable wooden balls. And what a noise, what an animation in the streets, on the large flat stones of the black and slippery pavement. A juggler is performing his tricks near a puppet theatre which shows that this form of entertainment belongs to all countries; close by, a fortune-teller is surrounded by farmers who have come to the market, and are displaying the very same human curiosity shown by people in our own country. Fruit merchants are selling slices of orange and a kind of dried figs for as little as a sapek. A barber has laid his clever hands on the shaven head of a son of Han and is plaiting his pigtail with remarkable dexterity. A whole people of workers, employees, soldiers and carriers is pushing and jostling its way about, while the deafening noise of exploding firecrackers and rockets marking some celebration, is heard all around. . . .

Still elsewhere, the young clerk of a large firm is running toward the harbor to take charge of the goods being delivered to his employers. Wealthy bourgeois are strolling around with their fat bellies and, being very curious persons, inquire about the latest bits of news. Well-to-do ladies toddle along on their small feet, leaning on the shoulders of two maids, while a few dignified Buddhist monks, draped in their large ashen-gray robes, make their way through the crowd. Suddenly, the roll of gongs fills the air, and the throng gives way to the cortège of a Mandarin running through it: palanquin and standard-bearers, carriers of insignia and scrolls, they all arrive and disappear in a moment's time. The poor people have hardly had a chance to take off their straw hats and let down their queues, and I can see some of them rubbing their ribs after having been struck by the palanquin of the great man—who is "the people's father and mother"—or by the rattan of his retinue.[7]

When traveling in the interior, foreigners invariably had to cope with

uncomfortable hotels and an inordinate curiosity on the part of the natives.
In 1877, the French sinologist Jametel was on his way to Peking:

According to the Chinese translation of my Joanne guidebook, Yen-tsuen [a small town located between Tientsin and Peking] has very good hotels, whose names are given in the book. My coachman drove me to one of them. Our coach entered a courtyard more suggestive of a farm than of an inn. The presence of several vehicles similar to mine, however, indicated that we had arrived at a well-known inn indeed. And the innkeeper found enough time to hasten up to my carriage and show me into the building in the back of the courtyard, reserved for persons of distinction. I followed him into a large room which was almost level with the ground. Our arrival routed a swarm of chickens perched on the two rickety armchairs and the bandy-legged table that constituted the room's furniture. The chickens, it seemed to me, had taken the habit of filling the space left empty by travelers, for the room's mud floor left no doubt as to their regular presence. . . .

Three of the room's walls were covered with wallpaper, but through its many holes one could see the building's ugly mud structure. Huge cobwebs hung from the paper-made ceiling. The shrewd insects had set their traps at the right spot: so numerous were the flies on the table, that they actually coated it with a black carpet hiding a thick layer of grease left there by several generations of travelers. . . .

My boy . . . disappeared for a moment, and came back holding in his hand a horsetail fastened to a short wooden handle. It was a flyswatter which he had just bought in a nearby store, for in northern China flies are such a common scourge that you may obtain arms against them even in the smallest village. . . .

Immediately after my arrival at the inn, I became its "great attraction". News of the presence of a "foreign devil" had spread rapidly throughout the little town, and when I sat down for dinner a crowd gathered before the door. My boy closed the door, but the crowd clustered around the window, whose aging paper* was already full of holes. However, as these natural spy holes were less numerous than the onlookers, the latter simply made new holes by sticking their fingers through the fragile paper. There ensued a series of small detonations, after which the window was all but gone. I then ordered my boy to re-open the door, but the yellow gapers interpreted

* Much more commonly used than glass, at the time.

my order as an invitation to enter, and promptly surrounded my table.

I was at first quite upset by such unwanted audience, but after a while the spectators' conversation became so interesting that I prolonged my meal beyond the usual time, in order to enjoy their company. As could be expected, it was my face that intrigued them most, the chief topics of their remarks being my blond hair, my long beard, the shape and more particularly the size of my nose.

Then they had an animated discussion about the purpose of my journey to Peking.

"He is on a business trip," someone remarked. "People like him residing in Tientsin are all traders."

"No," said somebody else, "he must be a gun- and cannon-teacher. I have met many of these devils in Szechuan,* and they all spent their time teaching our soldiers how to use arms for war."

Many equally silly opinions were ventured, and the discussion might have degenerated into actual dispute, had it not been for a deep voice heard over all the others and informing the audience that "nobody here present understands the foreigners' affairs. This fellow is going to Peking to present his tribute to the Son of Heaven."[8]

During the second half of the nineteenth century an increasing number of travelers also arrived from "down under". A Protestant missionary from Australia, George E. Morrison, traversed most of southern China in the nineties and, like all adventurous foreigners, had to put up with the "spontaneous" reactions of people who had never before seen a pale face:

On the rocks at the landing a bevy of women were washing, beating their hardy garments with wooden flappers against the stones; but they ceased their work as the foreign devil, in his uncouth garb, stepped ashore in their midst. Wanhsien† is not friendly to foreigners in foreign garb. I did not know this, and went ashore dressed as a European. Never have I received such a spontaneous welcome as I did in this city; never do I wish to receive such another. I landed at the mouth of the small creek which separates the large walled city to the east from the still larger city beyond the walls to the west. My laoban‡ was with

---

* One of China's western (and innermost) provinces, bordering on Tibet. Its largest city is Chungking.

† In Szechuan Province, and, like Chungking, situated on the Yangtze.

‡ The author's youthful guide.

me. We passed through the washerwomen. Boys and ragamuffins hanging about the shipping saw me, and ran toward me, yelling: "Yang kweitze, Yang kweitze".*

Behind the booths a storyteller had gathered a crowd; in a moment he was alone and the crowd were following me up the hill, yelling and howling with a familiarity most offensive to a sensitive stranger. My sturdy boy wished me to produce my passport which is the size of an admiral's ensign, but I was not such a fool as to do so, for it had to serve me for many months yet. With this taunting noisy crowd I had to walk on as if I enjoyed the demonstration. I stopped once and spoke to the crowd, and, as I knew no Chinese, I told them in gentle English of the very low opinion their conduct led me to form of the moral relations of their mothers, and the resignation with which it induced me to contemplate the hyperpyretic surroundings† of their posthumous existence; and, borrowing the Chinese imprecation, I ventured to express the hope that when their souls return again to earth they may dwell in the bodies of hogs, since they appeared to me the only habitations meet for them.

But my words were useless. With a smiling face, but rage at my heart, I led the procession up the creek to a stone bridge where large numbers left me, only to have their places taken on the other bank by a still more enthusiastic gathering. I stopped here a moment in the jostling crowd to look upstream at that singular natural bridge, which an enormous mass of stone has formed across the creek. . . .

Then we climbed the steep bank into the city and entering by a dirty narrow street we emerged into the main thoroughfare, the crowd still following and the shops emptying into the street to see me. We passed the Mohammedan Mosque, the Roman Catholic Mission, the City Temple, to a Chinese house where I was slipped into the court and the door shut, and then into another to find that I was in the home of the China Inland Mission, and that the pigtailed celestial receiving me at the steps was Mr. Hope Gill. It was my clothes I then learned that had caused the manifestation in my honor. An hour later, when I came out again into the street, the crowd was waiting still to see me, but it was disappointed to see me now dressed like one of themselves. In the meantime I had resumed my Chinese dress. "Look," the people said, "at the foreigner; he had on foreign dress, and now he is dressed in Chinese even to his queue. Look at his queue, it is false." I took off my

* "Foreign devil, foreign devil".   † Theological jargon.

hat to scratch my head. "Look," they shouted again, "at his queue; it is stuck to the inside of his hat." But they ceased to follow me.⁹

These highly curious and taunting Chinese crowds now and then gave vent to their deeply rooted xenophobia. Indeed, they had little or no desire to see foreigners establish themselves—or even travel—in China. The history of the forty years or so following the Peking Treaties is largely made up of underhand attempts on the part of the Chinese court to evade the obligations it had accepted, and to transfer to the "barbarians" the disaffection of its subjects; of the ever-increasing irritation of the powers, exasperated by the murder of imprudent missionaries, and of mutual provocation that led to explosive situations.

The hostility of Chinese crowds toward strangers, more or less openly abetted by Chinese officialdom, was in the first place directed against the missionaries and their native converts, or "secondary devils".* Not that the Chinese government was per se intolerant and persecuting: in matters religious it was on the contrary indifferent and profoundly skeptical. But many a Mandarin believed that under the pretense of religion, the missionaries were actually securing partisans for the invasion of the empire and the overthrow of the dynasty by foreign nations. The privileges enjoyed by the missionaries (extraterritoriality) and to a certain extent by their flocks, irked both the Mandarins and the common people. The latter, on the other hand, believed in rumors accusing the Christians of cannibalism† and other strange practices. Last, but not least, there was the irritating problem of land and buildings claimed by the missionaries, which was summed up in the circular issued in 1871 by the head of the Grand Council,‡ Prince Kung:

During the last few years the restitution of chapels in every province has been insisted upon without any regard for the feeling of the masses, the missionaries obstinately persisting in their claims. They have also pointed out fine handsome houses (belonging to, or occupied by, the gentry or others) as buildings once used as churches, and these they have compelled the people to give up. But what is worse, and

---

* Particularly the Catholics, who were by far the more numerous (hundreds of thousands of converts, probably); Protestant converts numbered about 50,000 toward the end of the century. There are no reliable statistics.

† A wilful distortion of the doctrine of transubstantiation ("Take ye, eat and drink, this is my body . . .").

‡ China's highest government agency at the time.

what wounds the dignity of the people, is that they often claim as their property *yamens*, places of assembly, temples held in high respect by the literates and the inhabitants of the neighborhood. Buildings which were once used as chapels have been in some cases sold years ago by Christians; and, having been sold and resold by one of the people to another, have passed through the hands of several proprietors. There is also a large number of buildings which have been newly repaired at very considerable expense, of which the missionaries have insisted on the restitution, refusing at the same time to pay anything for them. On the other hand, there are some houses which have become dilapidated, and the missionaries put in a claim for the necessary repair. Their conduct excites the indignation of the people whenever they come in contact with each other, and it becomes impossible for them to live quietly together.[10]

Thus the growth of the Christian Church, whether Catholic or Protestant, was achieved at the expense of a great deal of bad feeling. Hardly a year passed without a riot in one province or another, involving destruction of property and sometimes loss of life. *

The year 1868, for instance, was marked by serious anti-foreign outbreaks in widely distant provinces of the empire. The bloodiest rioting of the whole century, however, was the Tientsin massacre of June 1870, in which sixteen French Sisters of Charity, the French Consul and several French subjects lost their lives. The massacre had been planned for several weeks, and was perpetrated by an organized band led by the city's fire brigade.

A French traveler witnessed the outrage:

The situation began to deteriorate toward the middle of May, as alarming rumors spread among the people. Children had disappeared, it was said; they had been stolen by persons in the pay of the missionaries and killed by nuns, who had torn out the children's eyes and hearts in order to prepare drugs and remedies.

It was by no means the first time that such absurdities were circulated, and we hoped that they would fade away, as had been the case

---

* "We do not want these missionaries," was the reaction of the Viceroy of Hangchow upon learning of the assassination of two Swedish missionaries. "We oppose them, we raise riots against them, we destroy their churches, we kill their converts, we murder the foreigners themselves" (quoted in the memoirs of the Rev. Timothy Richard).

previously. Contrary to our expectations, however, these latest rumors became increasingly persistent. A visible change was noticeable, not only in the mood of the ordinarily hostile populace, but in the attitude of respectable persons as well. An undefined and superstitious terror took hold of people's minds. The nuns, though highly considered so far, now only met with cold or hostile glances when going out. No one made way for them any more. One evening, groups gathered in front of their building, and again the evening after. Accusations multiplied, facts were quoted, and people believed them. . . .

Fate itself seemed to conspire with the authors of such sinister rumors. An epidemic broke out in the nuns' orphanage, and several children died. They were buried at the cemetery of the poor, behind the French Consulate. For several days in a row, some hundred people went there in the morning. Many coffins were opened and the bones strewn around, those of the Christians being grossly insulted. Father Chévrier rushed to the spot, seized a man who had been caught in the act of desecrating tombs, and took him to the Consulate. He immediately went to see the Consul, M. Fontanier, and begged him to intercede with the Chinese authorities. The agitation, he insisted, must be calmed; the Mandarins could easily restore peace, if they only wished to; but if the literati were given free rein, there would be a catastrophe; we were alone, and lost in the midst of this vast population; the concessions were far away; besides, they were being threatened, too, and therefore could not come to our assistance, since there was not a single gunboat on the Pai-ho [river]. Thus spoke the mission's superior. His intervention, however, had no effect upon the Consul, who got rid of the importunate missionary by refusing to see him again. Meanwhile, the situation was growing worse every day. . . .

The arrival of General Chen Kuo-chüai in Tientsin was the signal for increased agitation. Incendiary posters appeared in all streets. They demanded extreme penalties for recruiters and bewitchers of children. Passing by a group of common people whispering to one another, the comprador or native agent of a European resident overheard the remark, "Let's kill all foreigners." Other people were heard saying, "Let's hurry and kill them; it's the right moment, since there is no warship on the river."

On June 20, a large number of people gathered on the pier. Some of the most daring among the men began throwing stones and bricks

THE ERA OF VICEROYS, 1860-1894

against the Mission building and the Consulate. The groups dispersed when night fell. . . .

Already at six o'clock in the morning of June 21, when mass was celebrated, the cathedral was overcrowded. Native Christians, believing that their last hour had come, were pressing around the two Fathers' confessionals. After nine o'clock, gatherings far larger than those of the previous evening began forming in front of the Mission building and the Consulate, and soon all kinds of projectiles were hurled at the windows. A massive invasion seemed imminent.[11]

The missionaries vainly besought the Mandarins to disperse the threatening crowds. Vainly also did the French Consul, M. Fontanier, appeal to the local "High Commissioner"—or chief Mandarin—Chong. On his way back from Chong's residence, he was attacked by the mob:

When he returned to the Consulate, he knew that he was going toward certain death. He could probably have saved his life, had he stayed at the residence of the High Commissioner, but he unhesitatingly rejected Chong's suggestion and left the Yamen followed by his Chancellor. A dozen minor Mandarins, charged by Chong to protect him, accompanied him on foot. The Che-yuan* went along too, first in his chair, and then on foot. Hardly had the Consul left the palace when his side was speared by a lance. It was his first wound. He was extremely excited at the time, and was seen gesticulating violently. Perhaps to calm him somewhat and thus prevent him from irritating the crowd, the Che-yuan touched him with his hand. Believing that he was being insulted, the Consul shouted: "Miserable Che-yuan, despicable Mandarin, don't you do anything to hold the populace back?" The magistrate shook his head and replied: "It's no business of mine."

The group had reached the quay, toward which converged several small streets, all of which were full of people armed with pikes. They rushed toward the two Europeans. M. Fontanier discharged his revolver without hitting anyone, and then aimed at very close range at the Che-yuan. When the latter, a short and stout man, saw the revolver pointed at his person, he threw himself behind his servant, who was fatally wounded and died a few days later. The mob shouted: "He is killing us, let us kill him together with all those who dare stop

* Leading city (police) official.

us!" Thereupon the Che-yuan and all the Mandarins of the escort began to flee. It was half past one in the afternoon, and the crowd had arrived at a small pagoda located halfway between the bridge and the church. The two Frenchmen, though thrown to the ground and pierced by many lances, managed to get on their feet, charged the furious mob and, breaking through it, reached the Consulate's main gate, where they expired under the blows of their pursuers.

At the same moment, Fathers Chévrier and Chou, fleeing before a horde of murderers who had cornered them in the sacristy, jumped through a window into the Consulate's courtyard, and tried to hide in a small pavilion sheltered by rocks. But the mob that had just finished off the Consul and his Chancellor rushed upon them and killed them too.[12]

It was now the turn of the Sisters of Charity to fall victims to the blood-thirsty mob:

Toward half past two in the afternoon, amid the clang of gongs and the explosion of firecrackers, hordes of people shouting, "Death to the French! Death to the foreigners!" gathered in front of the nunnery. The building was set afire, and its gate was rapidly battered down. The assailants encountered the sister superior, who was at once pierced by a lance and killed by many saber strikes. The other nuns fled into the church's cellar, into the garden and the pharmacy. Within a matter of minutes, they were seized and massacred. Such was the rage of the mob that the nuns probably died at once. Their bodies were hacked to pieces and thrown into the flames. A few shreds of roast flesh and some calcinated bones heaped together in the hospital's courtyard was all that remained of these saintly women. . . .

Several native Christians lost their lives near the nunnery. The others, hounded by the bloodthirsty mob, fled in all directions and endeavored to hide at the homes of friends or to leave the city. One woman was throw into the river and taken out again after she promised that she would testify against the nuns (who were already dead) and declare that she had been bewitched by them. She was taken to the Yamen for questioning, a curious fact worth mentioning, as it is one of the many proofs that the murderers acted methodically and under the leadership of people who were eager to secure in advance the necessary excuses for their conduct. . . .

A British citizen residing in that same neighborhood owed his life only to the devotion of his comprador. The latter hid his master under the roof of the house, between two chimneys, closed the door and the windows, and, while quietly smoking his pipe, showed the entrance key to the passing mob, saying: "Do come in, the owner has left for the [European] concession."[13]

Naturally, the French ambassador at Peking strongly protested the Tientsin massacre, but Prince Kung, head of the government, replied to his representations with insolent indifference.*

In the seventies, the powerful Mandarins were often as busy appeasing the Chinese crowds as exciting them against foreigners. Between 1876 and 1879, a dreadful famine ravaged ten northern provinces, killing from 15 to 20 million people. Among the Westerners who exerted themselves to give help and relief to the Chinese was the influential Baptist missionary Timothy Richard, of the London Mission Society, whose diary records the suffering of Shansi Province:

On June 30th [1876] two scholars . . . between thirty and forty years of age . . . came to see me, but as I was too busy, they called the next day by appointment. On entering, they prostrated themselves and asked to be accepted as my disciples. After some talk I discovered they were a deputation from a number of people who desired me to head a rebellion as the authorities were not providing food for the perishing people. They had already rented a house, and a large number of men were ready to execute my commands. I told the deputation that I could not dream of any such action, as it would only increase the suffering of the people. Once begun, no one knew where such a revolt would end, but it would certainly entail great bloodshed. I advised them to devise constructive instead of destructive methods for improving the condition of the people. . . .

As the winter drew near, the distress became more acute. Reports came in from villages where previously there had been forty inhabitants reduced to ten survivors. The price of grain rose rapidly to three and four times its usual rate. Many people, hearing that grain was cheap in Manchuria, migrated across the Gulf of Pechihli. Those who could not afford to travel were forced to pull down their houses and sell every inch of woodwork in them, whether doors, windows, frames, or

* In 1873, however, a special mission of apology was sent to France.

rafters, as firewood, and so get money to buy millet chaff to try and keep body and soul together.

In order to keep warm in the depth of winter the poor wretches dug deep pits underground, where twenty, thirty, and even fifty persons would live together. Here the vitiated atmosphere, as well as the lack of food, caused a large number of deaths. At first the survivors could not afford to dig a separate grave for each, so they made two large holes, one for men, the other for women, into which the dead were thrown. Afterwards the dead were left where they fell, sometimes in their homes, sometimes in the villages, sometimes on the roads, there they were devoured by wild dogs, wolves, and vultures. . . .

January 28th, 1878. Started on a journey south through the centre of the province to discover the severity of the famine. I rode on a mule, and had a servant with me, also on a mule. Before leaving the city we could not go straight to the south gate, as there was a man lying in the street about to die of starvation, and a crowd had gathered round.

January 29th. Passed four dead men on the road and another moving on his hands and knees, having no strength to stand up. Met a funeral, consisting of a mother carrying on her shoulder a dead boy ten years old. She was the only bearer, priest, and mourner, and she laid him in the snow outside the city wall. . . .

January 30th. Saw fourteen dead on the roadside. One had only a stocking on. His corpse was being dragged by a dog, so light it was. Two of the dead were women. They had had a burial, but it had consisted only in turning the faces to the ground. The passers-by had dealt more kindly with one, for they had left her her clothes. A third corpse was a feast to a score of screaming crows and magpies. There were fat pheasants, rabbits, foxes, and wolves, but men and women had no means of living. One old man beside whom I slowly climbed a hill said most pathetically: "Our mules and donkeys are all eaten up. Our labourers are dead. What crime have we committed, that God should punish us thus?"

February 1st. Saw six dead bodies in half a day, and four of them were women: one in an open shed, naked but for a string around her waist; another in a stream; one in the water, half exposed above the ice at the mercy of wild dogs; another half clad in rags in one of the open caves at the roadside; another half eaten, torn by birds and beasts of prey. Met two youths of about eighteen years of age, tottering on their feet, and leaning on sticks as if ninety years of age. Met another young man carrying his mother on his shoulders, as her strength had failed. Seeing me looking at them closely, the young man begged for help. This is the only one who has begged since I left T'ai-yuan fu.*

Saw some men grinding soft stones, somewhat like those from which stone pencils are made, into powder which was . . . to be mixed with any grain, or grass seed, or roots and made into cakes. I tried some of these cakes, and they tasted like what most of them were—clay. Many died of constipation in consequence of eating them. . . .

February 2nd. At the next city was the most awful sight I ever saw. It was early in the morning when I approached the city gate. On one side of it was a pile of naked dead men, heaped on top of each other as though they were pigs in a slaughterhouse. On the other side of the gate was a similar heap of dead women, their clothing having been taken away to pawn for food. Carts were there to take the corpses away to two great pits, into one of which they threw the men, and into the other the women. . . . For many miles in this district the trees were all white, stripped clean for ten or twenty feet high of their bark, which was being used for food. We passed many houses without doors and window frames, which had been sold as firewood. Inside were kitchen utensils left untouched only because they could not be turned into money. The owners had gone away and died.

February 3rd. Saw only seven persons today, but no woman among them. This was explained by meeting carts daily full of women being taken away for sale. There were travellers on foot also, all carrying weapons of defence, even children in their teens, some with spears, some with bright, gleaming swords, others with rusty knives, proofs of their terrible plight. We did not feel very safe in their midst. . . .

February 4th. Having gone so far, and seeing such terrible sights, I decided to return to T'ai-yuan fu, as I had sufficient proofs of the horrors of famine to move even hearts of stone.

Even the wolves were becoming fearless. Seeing a wolf by the roadside one day, I yelled at him, expecting him to flee in terror. On the contrary, he stood and stared at me, as if wondering at my boldness in facing him.

Returning along the same road, we had a daily repetition of the same ghastly sights, until I sometimes wondered whether the scenes were not the imagination of a disordered mind.[14]

* Capital city of Shansi Province.

In happier times, when China's traditional scourge (the famine) was not stalking the countryside, the Reverend Richard had ample time to convince himself of the Chinese farmers' stereotyped opinion about foreigners. What struck him most was the ever-recurring accusation of "rebelliousness" obviously stemming from official sources:

The situation was well illustrated by the following incident, which took place near Ch'ing-chow fu, Shantung, in 1875. At dawn of day I was riding out of a Chinese village. The street was empty save for a solitary man who was finishing his dressing by putting on his jacket. As I came up to him, he looked at me with keenest eyes and asked whence I came.

"From Ch'ing-chow fu," I replied.

"But," he said, "you are not a Chinaman; you are a foreigner."

"Yes," I replied, "I am from England."

"England!" he exclaimed. "That is the country that rebelled against us" (referring to England's first war with China in 1837).

"She could never rebel," I said, "because she never belonged to China."

"But she did," he retorted. "Before that time she was one of the nations that paid tribute to China." (The presents brought by Lord Macartney and other embassies to China were recorded by Chinese historians as tribute from England.) "When England revolted, it was the greatest rebellion since the world began."

These words, which he spoke with great indignation, indicated exactly the attitude of the Chinese Government. [15]

Though they remained profoundly convinced of the superiority of their own civilization, the attitude of China's leaders toward the West and Western methods was by no means always negative. Their efforts at national regeneration and modernization, however, lacked continuity and overall planning. The promising innovations championed in the 1860's by Tseng Kuo-fan and his disciple Li Hung-chang were followed by an apparent stagnation and apathy in the 1870's and 1880's. Also, the movement of "self-strengthening" took place in an atmosphere of corruption, as the otherwise progressive viceroys proved as eager to enhance their own power and wealth as that of their country.

Among the major achievements of these decades, and representing concessions to Western organization and inventiveness, were the Tsungli

Yamen, a sort of Foreign Office handling all aspects of relations with Western powers;* the Maritime Customs Service, built up by Sir Robert Hart as a mainstay of government revenue; the sending of hundreds of gifted students to England, France, and the United States; the mission of the American diplomat Anson Burlingame,† accompanied by two Chinese associates, on a goodwill tour to Europe and the United States (1868–70); the establishment of Chinese legations in the leading Western capitals in the 1870's; the training of a Western-styled army and navy, and the building of arsenals, railroads, telegraph lines, factories and technical colleges.

After the death of Tseng Kuo-fan (1872), China's modernization was carried on under the able leadership of Li Hung-chang and his protégés. Li held many high posts from the age of thirty onward, the principal being that of viceroy of the capital province of Chihli (or Hopeh)‡ from 1870 to 1895. As such he was responsible for all "foreign matters", meaning the conduct of diplomatic relations and the introduction of Western technology.

Li's many achievements have been enumerated by John W. Foster, his American assistant during the peace negotiations of 1895 (Shimonoseki), following the war which China lost to Japan:

He has been called the Machiavelli of China and her greatest word-warrior; for his last forty years were largely spent in crossing swords with the representatives of European and American statecraft. His remarkable ability and knowledge of foreign affairs made him indispensable to the Empress Dowager, and to him the liberal terms procured from the victorious allies are largely due. Under difficult conditions he won many a political bargain. Thus he was compelled to follow Sir Thomas Wade to Chefoo and signed the Chefoo Convention (never ratified) in 1876;§ at Tientsin the Li-Fournier Convention of 1884; the treaty with M. Patenotre in 1885;‖ the Li-Ito Convention of Tientsin regarding Korea in 1885.¶ . . .

* It was created in 1861, at Peking, and served as the prototype of a foreign office until the creation of the Wai-wu-pu, or Ministry of Foreign Affairs, in 1901.

† One of the few foreigners ever to enjoy the full confidence of Chinese officials, in particular, that of the redoubtable Tzu Hsi.

‡ Comprising the cities of Peking and Tientsin.

§ Following the assassination of the British interpreter Margary near the Burma border; China was to pay an indemnity, and to open ten new ports. England ratified the Convention in 1885.

‖ After the Franco-Chinese Wars of 1884–5.

¶ By which China granted Japan certain rights in Korean affairs.

Though the Empress Dowager often reprimanded him, and deprived him of the Yellow Jacket* and insignia of office, she recognized his worth, afflicting him in this way less than others of whose power she was jealous, and at his death granted him an honor never before granted to a Chinese subject under the Dynasty, that of having a shrine built to his memory at the capital, in addition to one in each of the five provinces which he had governed. . . .

Li Hung-chang was powerful because of his wealth, his army, and his skill in diplomacy. To increase his wealth or influence, or benefit China, he was willing to be double-faced or even ten-faced. He was wanting in the Christian or Confucian standard of morality, yet he preserved a certain rugged integrity of purpose that makes him a great man and patriot. He served his country and his ruler faithfully—and, it might be added, himself, for during his public career he accumulated great wealth and performed great public industrial service by means of it. He financed the first cotton cloth mill company in Shanghai, was prominent in the Chinese Steam Navigation Company, with its fine fleet, which he practically owned, helped the first steam railroad through. He also introduced the Steam Merchant Marine, opened schools, and employed foreign teachers to teach modern methods and the use of modern machinery. He established a medical college to train doctors for service in the army and navy in Tientsin. He opened the first coal mines and built the first arsenal.

The leader of Chinese progress, advocate of foreign methods, he was opposed to the foreigner. His advice to his own people was, "Let us use the foreigner, but do not let him use us." This trait was manifest in all interviews; though never denied an audience, the foreigner went away with the feeling of having given much information and received none. . . . Whenever the military and naval power was helpless, he would secure a victory by diplomacy. . . .

He was a conservative, and adhered to the customs and superstitions of antiquity; yet a progressive, introducing enlightenment and reform. While he professed to see the danger of the opium curse, he was still one of the greatest poppy growers in the land. He united the traits of cordial philanthropy and heartless cruelty, of truthfulness and mendacity. By his own people he was both loved and hated, despised and feared, degraded and exalted above any other Chinese.[16]

* High—and rare—distinction.

For thirty years or so, Li stood unrivaled (though by no means unassailed at the court), the "word-warrior" par excellence, guardian of the diplomatic approaches to Peking, chief exponent of China's grievances, and mitigator of the penalties periodically exacted from her in defeat. While fully sharing the Chinese officials' dislike and distrust of the foreigner, he constantly kept in mind the latter's military superiority. His attitude was one of temporizing conciliation, as he was determined to oppose the brute force of the Western world by subtleties of superior statecraft.

The innovations sponsored by men like Li Hung-chang were opposed and derided by conservative rivals and their hireling censors at the court. More often than not, they were also hampered by deeply rooted popular superstitions. Railroad tracks, in particular, were likely to disturb the spirits of the earth. Thus the tracks of the first railroad line built by Europeans (some seven miles long, between the center and the harbor of Shanghai) were torn up in 1877 by order of Chinese authorities, and the station was converted into a temple dedicated to a Chinese goddess.

Another well-known pioneer in the adoption of Western technology was Tso Tsung-t'ang, who prompted the building of steamships and railroads. His actual realizations included a shipyard near Foochow, a woolen mill and two arsenals in the northwestern province of Kansu. In a letter to a friend, Tso proudly described the visit paid by a Russian mission to the arsenal of Lanchow, in 1875:

I have established an arsenal in the capital [of Kansu] with Lai Ch'ang in charge. Its aim is the imitation of foreign fire-arms and explosive shells for offensive and defensive purposes. A few years ago when Sosnowsky* came to Lanchow he always boasted in our conversations about the superiority of Russian fire weapons as if they had no equal. When asked about the details of these foreign arms, he intentionally magnified the story to frighten his listeners. When I told him with emphasis that our new arsenal was capable of casting guns measuring up to the Russian and Prussian standards, he only smiled at me without making any reply. Later he was taken to visit Lai's place [the arsenal] where he made a thorough inspection. When he came back from the arsenal, I asked his opinion of it. He and the other Russians were unanimous in their praise. They suspected that the iron, which possessed excellent qualities, must have been imported from Western countries, but were told it was made locally, which greatly surprised

* Head of the Russian mission.

them. While in the arsenal the foreign visitors repeatedly looked at Lai Ch'ang as if they have never before met such an ingenious person. [17]

The Russians were not the only foreigners who inspected China's Western- ized institutions. From England came Lord Beresford, entrusted by the British Chambers of Commerce with a study of China's economic possibilities. In the course of his travels, Lord Beresford made the acquaintance of Yuan Shih-k'ai, famous soldier-politician (and a protégé of Li Hung-chang) who in 1912 became President of China. Yuan's instrument of power was his relatively modern army, the country's best at the end of the century:

On October 27, 1898, I went to Hsiao Chan [in Chihli Province] to visit General Yuan Shih-k'ai, and to attend a review of troops. I stayed two days and one night with the General, and during that time I not only saw all his troops paraded and manoeuvred, but had ample opportunity to examine the equipment of all their arms. I also visited the stores, clothing, and provisions, made myself acquainted with the complement of each regiment, and went carefully through the monthly pay sheets of the whole army. I have every detail connected with the establishment and maintenance of his force.

The strength of the army was 7,400 men—mostly Shantung men. These and the Hunanese are reported to make the best soldiers in China. General Yuan Shih-k'ai is a Chinaman, and his army is composed of Chinese. The infantry were armed with Mauser rifles—German made. He had ten 6-gun batteries of artillery of different calibres, throwing from 1-lb. to 6-lb. projectiles. The cavalry were armed with lances and a Mauser infantry rifle. On parade the whole force appeared an exceptionally smart body of men of extremely fine physique. They were evidently well fed, and their uniforms were very serviceable and well kept. Most other armies are clothed in an ordinary Chinese dress, with a large badge sewn on in front and rear. At my request the General put them through various parade movements, and then carried out manoeuvres in the surrounding country which proved to me that both officers and men were thoroughly conversant with their duties. Their discipline was excellent. With the exception of the artillery and the Maxims, all equipment was serviceable and efficient. . . .

I found the General most energetic and intelligent, and a well- informed and well-educated man. He is also a thoroughly patriotic Chinaman, and most loyal to the dynasty. He expressed genuine anxiety as to the future of his country, and was quite of opinion that unless she undertook some measures for her own preservation nothing could save her falling to pieces. He said, now that China was weak, all Europe, while professing the most sincere goodwill toward her, was seizing portions of the Empire under cover of naval and military demonstrations. I asked the General if he could make any suggestions that would be for the benefit of China, and at the same time one which European countries would assent to. The General answered that no proposal that the Chinese could make would receive the consent of the European Powers; that a Chinese would naturally make a proposition for the maintenance of the Empire, while European countries showed by their actions that they wished to split up the Empire and divide it among themselves.

The General was very sympathetic with regard to the question of reorganizing the Chinese Army as one Imperial Army, but thought that the command and the finance should be entirely in the hands of the Chinese, even if foreign officers were employed.

If all the Chinese generals were like General Yuan Shih-k'ai, the armies and their financial arrangements would not be in the condition they are now. General Yuan Shih-k'ai spends the money he receives for his army as intended. He personally superintends the payment of his men's wages and the distribution of rations and clothing.

This army is the only army complete in all detail, according to European ideas, that I found in China.[18]

Before long, China's revamped army and navy were given a chance to prove their value in the face of renewed Western aggression. With the development of new means of action—the opening of the Suez Canal (1869), improved steamships, use of telegraphic cables—the West steadily increased its economic and military pressure against the clumsy Chinese giant. Three powers—Russia, England, France—were particularly eager to secure substantial spheres of influence, and they were soon joined by a surprisingly successful Asiatic imitator of Western methods and techniques, Japan.

China's northwestern and northern provinces thus became the domain of Russian and Japanese expansion; England strengthened her foothold in the lower Yangtze valley, and occupied Burma (1852–86); France conquered Indo-China (1862–87).

It was against the French that China had to resume military operations. In 1874, a French expedition had occupied Tonkin, and in 1883 France proclaimed her protectorate over the neighboring kingdom of Annam. The latter was nominally under the suzerainty of China, and appealed to her "big brother" for help. Together with regular Chinese troops, bands of "Black Pavilions"—remnants of the defeated T'ai P'ings for the most part—entered Annam with the consent of the local Mandarins. The French repulsed them, and in May 1884 the Convention of Tientsin confirmed France's protectorate over Tonkin.

The Chinese, however, did not withdraw their troops from Tonkin, as promised at Tientsin. A French column, nearly a thousand men strong, which set out from the vicinity of Hanoi in order to occupy the border town of Langson, was ambushed near the village of Bac-le. Captain Lecomte subsequently described the unpleasant affair, which took place in rugged woodland ideally suited for an ambush:

The colonel reviewed the advance guard, and formally ordered the officers to prevent their men from opening fire, whatever attitude the Chinese might assume. . . .

After a few minutes' march, the advance guard came upon a clearing in the forest. The scouts reported the presence of groups of Chinese. The colonel renewed his order not to open fire, but rather to try to motion the Chinese away.

The advance guard, continuing its progress, traversed the clearing. When the cavalry group commanded by Lieutenant Huteau came near a notch in the steep hill, a large body of Chinese entrenched in three field works and probably mistaking these cavalrymen for the column's commander and his staff, opened fire on them. Two horses were killed, two men wounded, and Lieutenant Huteau had his helmet torn off by a bullet. The group turned back.

Despite repeated bugle calls to cease fire, ordered by Colonel Dugenne, the Chinese kept shooting. Our advance guard was now under heavy fire from all sides, and began shooting back as well as it could. There could no longer be any doubt: from the surrounding heights came the shrill sound of Chinese bugles, and almost at once the enemy, whose troops, massed behind the bushes on our right, were waiting for this signal, began attacking us vigorously. . . .

The column was encircled in the clearing, and hastily built an entrenched camp before nightfall.

Our men began digging trenches on all four sides of the camp. The pontoniers had been compelled to leave their tools in order to help their comrades return the fire from the Chinese forts. They were able to carry their dead and wounded back into camp, but the heavy Chinese fire prevented them from recovering their abandoned tools.

One of our marines had been killed at the outset and was lying across the road in front of the forts. Several attempts to recover his body were frustrated by the Chinese, who kept up an intense fire on anyone trying to move. Eventually, we succeeded in bringing him back to camp, but his head had been cut off by the Chinese.

The few tools belonging to the company of Captain Buquet were distributed among all the men, and the terrain was cleared of its bushes over a space of about fifty yards. This task, however, was not finished before two o'clock in the morning. Groups of ten men were posted in the bushes, sixty yards ahead of the camp, while others were ordered into the trenches and kept vigil all night. . . .

The Chinese kept up their fire, and their shooting became lower, more accurate. Lieutenant Delmotte was hit in the kidneys; several men and animals were wounded. Anyone trying to cross the camp with a light at once unloosened heavy enemy fire. In the emergency ward, the doctors were compelled to attend to the wounded behind a screen of boxes. . . .

Rain began falling toward half past two, and brought coolness to our wounded, who stopped complaining. The Chinese ceased fire at that time, also. We lay down in the mud, after having given our coats to the wounded. So exhausted were we that we slept for several hours despite the rain. When dawn broke, we were up again, rested and ready for action. . . .

Toward half past seven in the morning, several Chinese soldiers left their forts and crept behind large rocks halfway up the steep slope, whence they could overlook our camp. They began shooting, adjusting their range as if on target practice, and then, after a quarter hour, opened a steady fire on us. Ten of our men were opposite them and kept firing in volleys, but with little visible effect, as the Chinese were well hidden among the rocks. The sun rose above the trees, and was already very hot.

At eight o'clock came the lugubrious sound of Chinese bugles from the forts. The Chinese on the left bank of the river opened fire again, and little by little shooting resumed all through the forest. The action was on again everywhere, just as it had been on the previous evening. The enemy's fire was directed chiefly at our advance posts. . . .

Toward eleven o'clock, the shooting became much more intense. Our situation looked desperate. . . . On the Chinese side, we could hear repeated appeals. Every now and then, one of our men or mules fell to the ground. Within a matter of minutes, four wounded men were killed in the emergency ward. We were surrounded on all sides, and it had become quite obvious that if we did not move out of that place, our column would be completely wiped out before long. . . .

Eventually, the French broke out of Bac-le, and retreated:

On our way back on the Song-t'uong [River], we passed a number of rafts drifting downstream. On these rafts, the Chinese had attached the bodies of our soldiers killed at Bac-le. All of them had their helmets sewn to their shoulders, but they were empty: their heads had been cut off.[19]

The "ambush of Bac-le" created considerable emotion in France, the more so as it was magnified by the press and the opposition, led by Clemenceau. Revenge for China's "treachery" came swiftly: at the head of two squadrons, Admiral Courbet was instructed to bombard the arsenal at Foochow—the very enterprise which French engineers had helped to establish some twenty years earlier—to land troops, and to destroy the war material and stores.

In Canton, Chinese authorities issued an appeal to all-out resistance by the population:

The French have violated the international laws and the treaty signed at Tienstin. They have attacked Chinese soldiers on the bridges of the Goddess of Mercy, at Langson, in Tonkin, killing many of them. . . .

Consequently, you must consider the French as your enemies, and cooperate wholeheartedly with the Government in the defense of our country. The following rewards will be granted, according to people's merit:

For the killing of a commander in chief, 10,000 taels and an official rank with a kingfisher's feather.

For the killing of an officer with seven stripes,* 3,000 taels and an official rank with a kingfisher's feather.

* An imaginary rank—does not exist in the French army.

For the killing of an officer with five stripes, 1,000 taels and an official rank with a peacock's feather.

For the killing of an officer with three stripes,* 500 taels and an official rank with a peacock's feather.

For every French soldier or sailor killed, 100 taels.

(Great care must be exercised in distinguishing the enemy from other foreigners.)

For the capture of a first-class battleship, 100,000 taels.

For the capture of a second-class battleship, 80,000 taels.

For the capture of a first-class gunboat, 40,000 taels.

For the capture of a second-class gunboat, 20,000 taels.

For the capture of a warship launch, 100 taels.

If the ship is destroyed, only half of the above-mentioned amounts will be paid; if the ship is captured, it will become the property of its captors.

For the guns taken from the enemy, 5,000 taels plus an official rank will be given for guns of more than 10,000 catties,† and for smaller guns, amounts proportionate to their size.

Whoever comes forward with a plan by which the French may be defeated in battle, will receive 30,000 taels.

These rewards will be paid by the Provincial Treasurer.

The 10th day of the 7th moon of the 10th year of the reign of Kuang Hsü.[20]

No plan to defeat the French in the open was devised, but the Chinese gave a better account of themselves than in previous encounters with European troops. In subsequent engagements near Langson, their Yunnan and Kwangsi armies inflicted considerable casualties on the French, producing consternation in Paris—and toppling the government.

French prestige, however, was fully restored by Admiral Courbet's forcible intervention at Foochow. Within half an hour or so, his warships destroyed nearly all of China's fleet, sustaining but little damage themselves. Courbet then sailed through the Formosa Strait, and occupied the island's northern tip, as well as the Pescadores some time later. But his troops were decimated by a mysterious sickness, and Courbet himself died of it in June 1885.

In the meantime, a personal representative of Sir Robert Hart (British

* Five and three stripes indicate the ranks of colonel and captain, respectively.

† In China (and other Eastern countries), the catty is a weight of about 1 1/3 pounds.

Inspector General of China's Maritime Customs) had arrived in Paris, and his good offices led to the conclusion of the Second Treaty of Tientsin (June 1885), by which China recognized France's protectorate over Tonkin and Annam.

These events had conclusively shown the insufficiency of China's "self-strengthening": she still was no match for Western military power. Her predicament only grew worse when, toward the end of the century, Japan joined the rapacious circle that was closing in with the avowed purpose of eating up the "slices of the Chinese melon".

The corrupt Manchu regime had outlived its time, and was unable to reorganize and unite the empire against the foreigners, whom it continued to hoodwink by every possible means. Between 1886 and 1891, Tzu Hsi, whose hold over the Dragon Throne tightened with the passing years, had the Summer Palace (burned by Lord Elgin in 1860) rebuilt with the funds gathered for the reconstruction of the fleet destroyed by Admiral Courbet! At the end of the century another, and powerful, reform movement was in full swing, but it was short-lived: Peking's incurable apathy and traditionalism proved still stronger.

CHAPTER VI

THE PARTITION OF CHINA, 1894-1905

TOWARD THE end of the nineteenth century, the somnolent and ill-governed Chinese empire lay more than ever wide open to foreign encroachments. More and more openly also, the emboldened "barbarians" exhibited their appetite for Chinese territory. Sometimes they presented their demands together in order to impress the weak but proud giant, and sometimes they acted separately to prevent one of their potential rivals from getting too much.

The most pressing danger at that time came not from a European power, but from a small and relatively unknown neighbor, Japan, whose brutally revealed strength and ambition were to astound the world.

In the middle of the seventeenth century, when China opened her doors to the West, Japan had isolated herself from the rest of the world.* During the next two centuries, Japan's feudal society was dominated by the Samurais, professional warriors in the service of the country's leading nobles, the Daimyos, who in turn obeyed the Shogun, holder of the real power in Edo (Tokyo). The Mikado, or Emperor, was then confined to the ambiguous role of religious leader, in the city of Kyoto.

The country's voluntary isolation ended in 1854 when the American Commodore Matthew C. Perry, commissioned by President Franklin Pierce to open relations with Japan, secured the Treaty of Kanagawa, which opened two ports to American trade and included a most-favored-nation clause. Similar treaties were signed by the Shogun with England, Russia, and Holland (1854–5). In 1856, the American Consul General Townsend Harris obtained a formal commercial treaty opening Japan to American trade.†

* Foreigners (mostly Dutch, also Spaniards and Portuguese) were expelled, and the Japanese were forbidden to leave the country.

† Providing for unsupervised trade and permanent residence at five ports, an envoy at Edo, extraterritoriality, a conventional tariff, and prohibition of the import of opium.

A first, and important, step had thus been made toward regular foreign intercourse. Anti-foreign sentiment, though, was strong throughout the country, and became linked with a pro-emperor movement.

In 1868, a vigorous young ruler, Mutsuhito, ascended the imperial throne, shook off the Shogun's tutelage, and assumed direct control of the nation. Under his able leadership, Japan deliberately and rapidly adopted industrialization on Western models and within twenty years became a modern world power. The feudal regime was abolished and replaced by a strong centralized bureaucratic government fashioned along Western lines. Mutsuhito's reign (1868–1912), or Meiji Period,* thus added an Asiatic power to the group of European nations endeavoring to split up China, and at the same time made Japan a mighty rival of these same nations.

The first clash between China and Japan occurred in 1874, when a Japanese expedition sailed toward Formosa to punish the murder (in 1871) of Japanese by natives. The result of the dispute—China paid an indemnity, thus revealing her military weakness—encouraged Japan to undertake the more ambitious project of dislodging China from her position as a suzerain of Korea.†

After a number of years of rivalry and intrigue in Korea, Japan's opportunity came when in 1894 the Korean queen appealed to both China and Japan to help her quell an anti-foreign insurrection. The Japanese troops, who were ready and well-trained, seized the royal palace in Seoul, which led China and Japan to declare war on each other. A series of easy Japanese victories, achieved on both land and sea (September 1894–February 1895), once more proved the helplessness of the Chinese giant, while at the same time revealing to all the efficiency of Japan's modern war machine. Tzu Hsi made a supplicatory appeal to the Great Powers (which had welcomed China's defeat), but was advised first to endeavor to come to terms directly with Japan.

It was the aging Li Hung-chang who was given the humiliating task of going to Japan and there asking for peace terms. The Treaty of Shimonoseki (April 1895), which sealed China's defeat, was harsh indeed: China recognized the independence of Korea, ceded to Japan the Pescadores and Formosa,‡ paid a heavy indemnity and opened four more ports to foreign commerce.

---

* Literally, "enlightened peace".

† The country had been a tributary to the Manchus since 1637. China did not protest a Japanese treaty (1876) recognizing Korean independence, but a convention signed in 1885 provided for the withdrawal of troops of both powers from Korea.

‡ Only in 1945 did these territories become Chinese again.

SPHERES OF INFLUENCE OF THE GREAT POWERS IN CHINA,
c. 1900

* From Merideth E. Cameron, Thomas H. D. Mahoney and George E.
McReynolds: *China, Japan and The Powers*, 2nd. edition. Copyright © The
Ronald Press Co., New York.

Before returning to China (where provincial officials made him responsible for the defeat, calling him a "traitor"), Li endeavored to convince the Japanese Premier, Count Ito Hirobumi, that their two countries ought to unite in a common effort to check their common enemies, the European powers. Part of their conversation ran as follows:

Li: In Asia, our two countries, China and Japan, are the closest neighbors, and moreover have the same language.* How could we be enemies? Now for the time being we are fighting each other, but eventually we should work for permanent friendship. If we are enemies endlessly, then what is harmful to China will not necessarily be beneficial to Japan. Let us look at the various European countries which, even though their military forces are strong, do not lightly start hostilities. Since we Chinese and Japanese are on the same continent, we should also imitate Europe. If the diplomatic ministers of our two countries mutually and deeply understand this idea, we ought vigorously to maintain the general stability of Asia, and establish perpetual peace and harmony between ourselves, so that our Asiatic yellow race will not be encroached upon by the white race of Europe.

Ito: I am very much pleased with the idea of the Grand Secretary [Li]. Ten years ago when I was at Tientsin,† I talked about reform with the Grand Secretary. Why is it that up to now not a single thing has been changed or reformed? This I deeply regret.

Li: At that time when I heard you, sir, talking about that, I was overcome with admiration, and furthermore I deeply admired, sir, your having vigorously changed your customs in Japan so as to reach the present stage. Affairs in my country have been so confined by tradition that I could not accomplish what I desired. . . . In the twinkling of an eye ten years have gone by, and everything is still the same. I am even more regretful. . . . This time, when I went to Peking and talked to scholars and officials, I found that some of them have also thoroughly realized that our country definitely should undergo reform before we can stand on our own feet. . . . Your honorable country, after it has been so reorganized by you,‡ sir, is very admirable.[1]

* Meaning the written language, as the Japanese use Chinese characters.

† When he and Li signed the convention by which both countries were to withdraw their troops from Korea.

‡ Count Ito was his country's leading progressive statesman; unlike Chinese officials, he was widely traveled, having been in Europe and in the United States.

China's officialdom felt deeply humiliated by the country's losses to the Japanese, a nation which, as Chinese historians often remind themselves, took its first lessons in civilization and culture from Chinese scholars and artists.* The defeats sustained during the Sino-Japanese War of 1894–5 were the more galling as they had been inflicted by people whom the Chinese currently indulged in calling "dwarf bandits". In addition to bringing the prestige of the Manchu dynasty to a new low, the entirely unexpected humiliation stirred and awakened the majority of the educated Chinese, and demands for broad reforms grew louder all the time.

The European powers, on the other hand, no longer knew any restraint: their chief object was to carve as large a share as possible from the immense heritage of the "Sick Man", and they now launched upon a brazen scramble for Chinese territory. Before helping themselves, however, three of them— Russia, Germany, and France—intervened and obliged Japan to return the Liaotung Peninsula (southern Manchuria) to China, against an increased indemnity. Naturally, the three expected to be well repaid by the Chinese.

Russia was first to attack the quarry. By a secret treaty concluded at the coronation of Nicholas II in Moscow by Li Hung-chang she obtained the right to build the Trans-Manchurian Railway.† Two years later (1898), she extorted from China a 25-year lease on the Liaotung Peninsula with Port Arthur, and the right to build a railroad leading there.

France had secured extensive territorial and commercial concessions in 1895, in the southern provinces; in 1898, she obtained a 99-year lease on Kwangchow Bay and vicinity, with the right to extend the Tonkin railroads into Yunnan.

Germany, on the pretext of the assassination of two Catholic missionaries in Shantung and determined to use "brutal recklessness",‡ occupied Kiaochow Bay (1897) and subsequently exacted a 99-year lease on the bay, with exclusive rights to build railways and develop mines in Shantung.

England was busy securing her hold over the Yangtze valley, and needed no new territory. In 1898, however, she received a lease of Weihaiwei, near the tip of Shantung Province, to run as long as the Russian occupation of Port Arthur.§

---

* Especially in the seventh and eighth centuries, known as Japan's classic age.

† As a link in the Trans-Siberian line to Vladivostok. It was financed by the newly created Russo-Chinese Bank, whose capital was chiefly of French origin.

‡ Kaiser Wilhelm II's own expression.

§ England was of course carefully watching every Russian move, and was already contemplating using Japan against Russia.

Italy, too, tried to join the rush for the spoils, but her demand for a port concession in Chekiang (1899) was rejected by a show of force on the part of China.

The one notable exception in this open scramble for the "slices of the melon" was the United States, whose policy so far was nonaggressive. American commercial interest in China was indeed insignificant at the time, partly because of the weakness of the American Merchant Marine immediately after the Civil War, and also because of the country's absorption in the development of its own great natural resources in the West. In 1899, John Hay, American Secretary of State, secured the Great Powers' assurances that the "open door" to equal commercial opportunity would be maintained in their respective spheres of influence.

Thus, as the nineteenth century drew to a close, China had become an arena in which the Western powers were jealously competing with one another and maneuvering for increasingly larger gains. The reports which the French ambassador at Peking, M. Pichon, sent to the Quai d'Orsay★ in 1899, clearly reveal the fluctuations of the diplomatic situation:

January 24. The recent manifestations† were due to England's excessive ambitions in the Empire of the Middle and should, in my opinion, call our attention to the consequences of China's possible acceptance of British claims. What exactly are these claims? According to the Shanghai papers, to the speeches of Lord Beresford, to the representatives of the "China Association", and to articles published by London papers and magazines, England should claim the Yangtze *Basin* (and not only the big river's *valley*) as her share in the distribution of spheres of influence among foreign Powers. Now the enclosed map, which I ordered drawn up for this very purpose, shows clearly the extent of such ambitions: the Yangtze Basin covers more than half of the Empire's territory, and from an economic point of view it includes practically all the areas which probably contain most of the country's wealth and prosperity. . . .

We must also take into account the exaggeration of polemics, and the insufficient authority of writers and orators in defining what they call England's rights. The partition of the Empire is by no means an accomplished fact, and it is unlikely that the interested Governments are prepared to agree to the absorption of such a vast domain by one

★ Location of the French Foreign Ministry, on the left bank of the Seine.

† Anti-foreign demonstrations, foreboding the risings of 1900.

of them. There is a long way indeed from the claims conceived by the agents of British imperialism, to its actual realization. . . .

February 25. According to my latest information, the Chinese authorities intend to prevent us from further expanding our Shanghai concession by giving away its hinterland. Shall I protest?*. . .

March 6. The news, spread in Tokyo, about a possible demand for a Japanese foothold in Fukien,† seems to be well founded. I know that the Japanese ambassador at Peking has reacted favorably to Italy's initiative in Chekiang, and it is generally believed that he will soon present similar demands in the name of his Government, which is said to keep an eye on Sansha [north of Foochow]. . . .

June 8. I am told that the Austrians have designs of their own on Sansha Bay, whose hydrography they have recently explored. I do not think they are going to claim or occupy it in the near future, but they might well take advantage of an incident deemed to be favorable.[2]

Also in 1899, the French Apostolic Prefect in Kwangtung, Mgr. Chausse, sent home a letter describing the latest developments in the Canton area:

England has recently annexed a vast territory on the continent, opposite Hong Kong. Being in favor of the Open Door policy, she naturally began by grabbing the largest share.

The [British] seizure of the Kowloon area [near Canton] has caused much glee in Hong Kong's international circles. The Governor of Victoria‡ had asked to be given audience by the Viceroy of Canton, in order to request him to maintain order throughout the newly ceded territory. The Viceroy has promised to do so. The Union Jack was to be hoisted on a Monday: great festivities were to take place, all the city's leading personalities had been invited, and a steamship had been rented to bring them to the appointed spot. On the preceding Saturday, the Secretary, accompanied by twenty policemen, had set out to make the necessary preparations. However, having arrived within two kilometers from the spot, he found 1,500 Chinese soldiers entrenched there, and when the policemen began their work, they were fired upon.

---

* Paris instructed him to "oppose any extension of the international concession that would not be accompanied by a similar extension of the French concession".

† Province opposite Formosa.

‡ Capital of the island of Hong Kong.

News of the incident created a great deal of emotion in Hong Kong. Monday's festivities were put off indefinitely, and a British army replaced the guests. . . . The Chinese were beaten and driven out of the territory.

Revenge came quickly. A large market place that was not included in the area ceded by China was attacked and annexed without the shedding of a single drop of blood, and without any other formalities. Today, people throughout the whole surrounding area talk only about this incident, and Canton is generally considered likely to fall into British hands too!

And what is France doing at Kwangchow Wan, you may ask. Well, she, too, is annexing territory around the Bay. True, she is proceeding more slowly. She has founded her capital near Haitao Fort. The Chinese have already started settling there, and since their population is increasing rapidly, I have decided to send a missionary among them.[3]

At the other end of China, meanwhile, the Russians were busily organizing the newly acquired Liaotung Peninsula. In 1901, a French military mission visiting Manchuria was amazed by the ambitious projects of the Russian ally.* One of its members has described the beginnings of the city of Dalny (Dairen, but now Lüta):

Port Arthur [now Lüshun] is chiefly a military capital. Its main business center and its seaport, of which the Russians expect wonders, will be the newly created city of Dalny, whose completion is being pushed very actively. We could not fail visiting this large and interesting city, which, the Russians hope, will become the queen of Far Eastern trade. . . .

Upon our arrival at the pier, we were welcomed by their chief engineer, Mr. Sakarov, who introduced us to his little kingdom. First, we visited the offices where we saw the plans and projects. We met the architect responsible for the planning of the city and its monuments. He showed us a huge map of Paris hanging in his office, and said, "It is here that I found my inspiration." We walked for miles and miles in order to find out about the application and practical execution of the general plan. . . .

* France and Russia had signed a military convention (directed mainly at Germany) in 1893.

The port, the city and its trade are being created out of nothing; a credit in the amount of 18 million rubles has been allotted to the realization of this project.

An area of several square miles has been bought from its many Chinese owners: terrain, houses and tombs have all been paid for, their total price amounting to half a million rubles. For the time being, the former owners may remain on their property, but they are to be evicted when necessary as the work progresses. . . .

On the space thus bought will rise a large and well-planned city, with a Chinese and a European section separated from one another by a public garden. The European city, in turn, will be subdivided in a logical manner, according to the needs of the city and the limitations imposed by the terrain. The administrative city, on the other hand, will be erected along the seashore, on the present site of the offices and the homes of the engineers.

Between the public garden and the railroad, a perfectly level area will allow a radial arrangement of buildings. In the center, a monumental exhibition pavilion will adorn the future "Nicholas Square"* and from there, radiating like the points of a star, ten broad avenues will originate leading to public buildings such as Orthodox, Catholic or Protestant churches, museums, a theatre, a library, and schools. This will be the city's business and industrial section, and it will contain huge buildings housing the warehouses. In the immediate vicinity of the Chinese quarter, a large bazaar with railroad connections will be the focal point for all traffic, as well as the center of exchange between Europeans and Chinese.

Separated from this latter area by the railroad, and located on a gently sloping terrain divided by broad avenues intersecting each other at right angles, the residential section will be built. The houses to be erected there will contain the city's wealthy inhabitants, who will thus be sheltered from the noise and hustle of the trading area.

Finally, and still farther away from the business center, a hilly area will be covered with villas surrounded by parks and gardens.

The city's streets and avenues have been laid out, but all the public monuments and a number of private homes are still to be built. When these are completed, terrain and existing buildings will be sold to private individuals, probably by auction sale. The engineers and

* Named in honor of Tsar Nicholas II, 1894–1917.

architects have carefully avoided the excessive uniformity which one often observes in such newly created cities; they have endeavored to diversify the architectural styles as much as possible. In particular, they have avoided large, barrack-like apartment houses; all the houses built so far for personnel are small, one-story homes that can accommodate four small households of workers.

Finally, the latest means of comfort and hygiene, such as water canalization, a sewer system leading to the sea, small courtyards and gardens around the houses, etc., are provided throughout the entire city. Even small streets, located behind the houses and intended for rubbish, or garbage, are being built. In short, Dalny is to become a model city equipped with all the amenities and displaying all the progress of our twentieth-century civilization.

The harbor will be vast, and will include three huge piers: one for the unloading of coal and oil, and the two others for commercial activities. It will be twenty-eight feet deep, and therefore accessible to the largest vessels. An arsenal and dry docks will be built nearby. One of the latter, of colossal dimensions, will be able to contain two of the largest ocean liners, or the mightiest ironclad existing today. . . .

A large electric power plant, located in the center of the city, will send forth power and light everywhere.

All aspects of the program have been started and are being pushed most actively; some fifteen engineers and architects are at the head of a personnel of 200 Europeans; as for the Chinese and Korean coolies, they constitute human anthills all over the place, their number varying from 10,000 to 20,000.

Such, then, is the overall plan for the creation of Dalny. The Russians are sparing no expense to make this a splendid city and a first-rate harbor. They even talk of superseding Shanghai, and perhaps Hong Kong too.[4]

The Western enclaves in China were more than operating bases for European and American commercial and religious activities. The contact with Western ideas and methods stirred Chinese minds and led to the formation of a new China, eager to find in the foreigners' outstanding achievements the very means of checking the foreigners' invasion of the country. A young and studious élite thus became increasingly conscious of the fact that behind the technical achievements which made the West so strong there lay a Western culture which was worth knowing well. This in turn created a demand for

*translations of Western books, first technical works, then works on inter-
national law and Western history, and even novels.**

*Naturally, these books became an important factor in China's evolution
toward the end of the nineteenth century. They inspired the advocates of
reform, whose voices became ever louder and bolder, until they reached the
very ear of the Emperor. The rapidly mounting sales of Western books,
noted by the Rev. Timothy Richard,† was indicative of an important
change in the minds of China's educated classes:*

For eighty years public opinion in China had set its face against
Christian literature. Christian tracts were actually made into soles
for Chinese shoes, and the final fate of most of the rest was to be
collected and burned along with other papers containing Chinese
characters, in temple buildings. The booksellers of China refused to
handle, on any account, any Christian books for sale, considering it a
transaction disloyal to their country and unworthy of honourable
men. But in 1895, after the appearance of Mackenzie's *History of the
Nineteenth Century* . . . and other books . . . a great change came over
the Chinese bookseller. In one city alone—Hangchow—there were no
less than six pirated editions of the *Nineteenth Century*, one edition de
luxe for the rich, the others for people of lesser means. Altogether
there must have been a million pirated copies in circulation throughout
China. The *Essays for the Times* were also pirated. In Peking during the
first months of the Reform Movement in the winter of 1895–6, a
paper was started by the Reform Club, not only reprinting the articles
in Dr. Allen's *Wang Kwoh Kung Pao*,‡ but also taking its very name.

By this time, therefore, the barrier that had so long existed between
Christian and non-Christian literature was broken down. Instead of
regarding Western publications as unworthy to be handled by them,
Chinese booksellers were only too glad to sell our books, and small
wonder, for copies of the *Nineteenth Century* sold at two dollars in
Shanghai could be sold at six dollars in Sian fu. We have no means of
knowing what profits were made by those who pirated our books, but

* Most of these translations were the work of English and American Protestant
missionaries assisted by Chinese scholars.

† Probably the most influential missionary who advocated reform; he was at
home in China's official circles, enjoying their esteem and confidence.

‡ Literally, *The Globe Magazine*, Chinese periodical published in Shanghai by
the American missionary Young J. Allen.

those who bought our publications at our own depots secured to the Society* an annual profit of more than the contributions sent us from England and Scotland, and consequently enabled us frequently to make large free grants where we thought they would be useful.[5]

The actual impact of Western culture upon progressive Chinese minds was forcefully revealed in the eighties by the writings of one of the leading scholars of his day, the Cantonese K'ang Yu-wei. The transformation of Japan, where he had studied, had filled K'ang with enthusiasm. After his return to China, he published in rapid succession his Renovation of Japan *(1885), a* Life of Peter the Great, *a study on the* Constitutional Changes in England, *and a* History of the Greatness and Decadence of Turkey. *A later work, entitled* Study of Confucius as a Reformer *(1897), earned him the ironic nickname of "Modern Confucius".*

K'ang and his disciples founded the "Higher Learning Society", or Reform Society, to which belonged some of the most intelligent Hanlins† in Peking, as well as a number of censors and undersecretaries of the Grand Council. His most brilliant disciple, Liang Ch'i-ch'ao,‡ insisted on the inevitability of reform and, like his master, pointed to famous historic examples to rouse and convince his countrymen:

Why is it necessary to reform? In general, there is nothing in the universe which does not change. The change between daytime and evening makes the day; the change from winter to summer makes the year.... When the purple or red blood circulates in the body, when second by second carbon is breathed out and oxygen is breathed in, and a thousand changes take place in a day, thus the living person is formed. . . .

Those who advocate no change frequently claim, "We follow the ancients, follow the ancients." Do they know that from prehistoric, ancient, medieval and modern times down to the present day, there have been many hundreds of thousands and myriads of changes? . . .

Now here is a big mansion which has lasted a thousand years. The tiles and bricks are decayed and the beams and rafters are broken. It is still a magnificent big thing, but when wind and rain suddenly come up, its fall is foredoomed. Yet the people in the house are still happily

* The London Missionary Society, to which Richard belonged.
† Members of the Hanlin Academy.
‡ Who became one of China's leading statesmen in the early twentieth century.

playing or soundly sleeping and as indifferent as if they have seen or heard nothing. Even some who have noted the danger know only how to weep bitterly, folding their arms and waiting for death without thinking of any remedy. Sometimes there are people a little better off who try to repair the cracks, seal up the leaks, and patch up the ant holes in order to be able to go on living there in peace, even temporarily, in the hope that something better may turn up. These three types of people use their minds differently, but when a hurricane comes they will die together. . . . A nation is also like this. . . .

India is one of the oldest countries on the great earth. She followed tradition without change; she has been rendered a colony of England. Turkey's territory occupied three continents and had an established state for a thousand years; yet, because of observing the old ways without change, she has been dominated by six large countries, which have divided her territory. . . . Poland was a famous country in Europe. Her political institutions were not developed, internal struggles arose daily. Russia, Prussia, and Austria made mutual agreements and divided her as their meat. The Moslems in central Asia have usually been well known for their bravery and skill in warfare, and yet they observe the old ways without changing. The Russians are swallowing them like a whale and nibbling them as silkworms eat mulberry leaves. . . .

Among the European countries industry is promoted and commerce is protected, because they fear the sources of profits may be captured by others, and the country on account of that may be impoverished and distressed. Generals must have knowledge, soldiers must be literate and must drill day and night as if approaching a great enemy; their ships and weapons are up to date, and they really compete in maneuvers, because they feel that if they show the slightest military weakness they will be defeated, probably never to rise again. Other administrative measures are all like this. They make comparisons among themselves and every day stimulate each other. . . . But this so-called independent or isolated country, China, has never seen great enemies. Proudly she regards herself as high and mighty, and says no one is her equal.[6]

Another well-known advocate of reform was Chang Chih-tung,* whose ideas were expounded in his widely read Exhortation to Study *(1898).*

* Viceroy of Kwangtung-Kwangsi (1884–9) and of Hunan-Hopei (1889–1907).

Chang made famous the slogan, "Chinese culture for the foundation, Western learning for practical application". Education, industrialization, and the building of a strong army and navy constituted the leading themes of his reform program.

In his Exhortation, *Chang denounced the conservatism and apathy of Chinese officialdom,* and the lack of logical thinking in government circles:*

Those who reject reforms generally belong to three categories. One consists of the narrow-minded scholars who are ultraconservative; the defects of ultraconservatism are easy to understand. Another consists of the vulgar officials who like to take improper ease. For reform we must tax our thinking, must collect funds, must select people, and must do actual work. These are all inconvenient to the selfish plans of those who are confused and lazy, and who like to shirk work, to be influenced by favoritism, or to take the easiest tasks. Therefore, under the cover of bookish and conservative talk, they gloss over the subterfuges of slippery officials who take improper ease. Such are their true feelings. When asked about their academic ideas and the governmental principles of the traditional Chinese system, all is revealed to have been neglect and sham on their part. They have not done a single thing. . . . The third kind consists of the talkative scholars who like to be captious. Actually, in recent years there have been some imitations of Western methods which bore no fruit.

There are, however, four reasons for this. The first is, all people care for their selfish purposes, and so they plan only for themselves and no progress is made—for example, the various officials in charge of factories and the various people who went abroad. This is a defect of the people, not the defect of the reform. The second is the inadequacy of funds. From this comes a deficiency of money on all sides which prevents superior products, such as the shipyards. This is a defect of the times, not the defect of reform. Third, there is no fixed policy at Court. A new thing may be suddenly taken up and then suddenly suspended, with nothing accomplished, such as the sending of students abroad and of officials from the capital to travel in foreign countries. This is the defect of unfounded reports [as to their behavior], not the defect of reform. Fourth, there are instruments but no personnel to handle them. When we had not yet learned mechanical engineering, we bought machines; when we had not yet trained captains or admirals,

* Opposition to reform came mostly from high Manchu officials.

we purchased a fleet—such were our navy and the various factories. This is the defect of having the wrong sequence in what should go first or later, not the defect of reform.[7]

The writings of K'ang Yu-wei eventually attracted the attention of the imperial tutor who, together with a few other liberal-minded court officials, introduced him to Emperor Kuang Hsü. The latter had become of age in 1889, and was chafing under Tzu Hsi's constant and stern control. It was only natural, therefore, that he should prove receptive to K'ang's bold pleas for reform.

In an interview granted in October 1898 to a journalist of the China Mail, *K'ang recalled his reception at the court:*

The Emperor ordered me to hold a conference with the Ministers of the Tsungli Yamen. On January 3rd last the conference took place. All the members of the Yamen were present; I was received with all respect as their guest. The conference lasted about three hours. I had to say that everything in China must be reformed and follow Western civilization. . . .

I could see that the majority of them were against reform. The Viceroy Jung-lu* made the remark, "Why should we change the manners and customs of our ancestors?" To this I replied: "Our ancestors never had a Tsungli Yamen. Is not this a change?" The first thing I suggested was that China should have a properly constituted judicial system—that a foreigner should be engaged to work conjointly with myself and some others to revise the laws and the government administrative departments. That I hold to be the most important change. This must be the basis on which all other changes and reforms must rest. The construction of railways, the creation of a navy, the revision of the educational system, every other reform will follow; but unless we change the laws and administration all other changes will be next to useless. Unfortunately, the Emperor has been pushing on the other reforms before preparing the way for them. That has contributed to bring about the present crisis.

The following morning Prince Kung and Weng Tung-ho† reported the conference to the Emperor. Prince Kung was against me, although I have heard it said that he admired my abilities, and thought me clever

* Trusted adviser of the Empress Dowager.
† Tutor of the Emperor.

and able. But he said of me: "He is talking nonsense; he speaks about changing the ways of our ancestors!" Weng Tung-ho gave my proposals his support.

The outcome of the conference was that I was ordered by the Emperor to submit my proposals to him in the form of a memorial. The gist of my memorial was as follows. I told the Emperor that all the customs and ways and manners of our ancestors must be renewed. Nothing could be usefully followed so far as Chinese history was concerned. I advised the Emperor to follow in the footsteps of Japan, or in the footsteps of Peter the Great. As a preliminary step I advised the Emperor to command all his Ministers of State and all the high officials in Peking to go before the places where they worshipped the gods, and also to the Ancestral Halls, there to make an oath that they were determined to introduce reforms. My second suggestion was to have the laws and administration revised; my third, that he should open a Communication or Despatch Department, through which any one would be able to memorialize the Throne.... I advised the Emperor to select young, intelligent men, well imbued with Western ideas, to assist in the regeneration of the Empire, irrespective of their position, whether they were lowly born or of high degree; that they should confer with the Emperor every day and discuss the measures for reform, first devoting their energies to a revision of the laws and administration. . . .

My memorial also showed how funds were to be raised. I pointed out the enormous loss of revenue that occurred yearly. Taking the magistracy of Nanhai (which is my native district), I informed the Emperor that the total revenue derived from that district was $240,000 per year, but the actual amount going into the Imperial Purse was only something over $20,000. I recommended a complete change of the system, under which the whole of the revenues of the country would go into the Imperial Purse. . . . With this money in hand it would be an easy thing to get a navy to protect our coast and to establish naval colleges for the training of officers. State railways could also be constructed and other necessary reforms effected.

I was told that the Emperor was highly pleased, and said that he had never seen a better memorial nor such a good system as I proposed. He recommended the memorial to the consideration of the Tsungli Yamen for report. . . . All the Ministers would report was that the memorial was so sweeping, that it practically meant the abolition of the present great Ministers, and therefore they did not like to report upon it themselves. . . . I also sent to the Emperor two books written by myself, one entitled *The Reform of Japan*, and the other *The Reform of Russia by Peter the Great.* . . .

On June 16th I was granted an audience with the Emperor. It lasted for two hours. Port Arthur and Dalny had just been taken over by Russia, and the Emperor wore an anxious, careworn expression. . . . He was led in by eunuchs, and took his seat on a dais on a large yellow cushion, with his feet folded beneath him. He sent his attendants away, and we were left alone; but all the time we were conversing his eyes were watching the windows, as if to see that no one was eavesdropping. There was a long table in front of him with two large candlesticks. I knelt at one of the corners of the table, and not on the cushions in front of the table which are reserved for the high officials. I remained kneeling during the whole of the audience. We conversed in the Mandarin dialect.*

The Emperor said to me: "Your books are very useful and very instructive."

I practically repeated what I said in my memorial about the weakness of China being owing to the lack of progress.

The Emperor said: "Yes, all these conservative Ministers have ruined me."

I said to him: "China is very weak now, but it is not yet too late to amend." I gave him the example of France after the Franco-Prussian War. In that case the indemnity was much greater than China has paid to Japan. The territory lost was greater, because France had lost two provinces and China had only lost one [Formosa]. . . .

I asked him to look at the difficulties Japan had to overcome before she could reform on modern lines. There the military or feudal party had more power than our present conservative Ministers, but the Mikado adopted the proper course by selecting young and intelligent men, junior officials, some of whom he set to work out the reforms in the country, while others went abroad to learn foreign methods, and returned to make Japan the powerful country which it is today. I repeated to him what Peter the Great did to make Russia powerful, saying, "You, the Emperor, I would ask you to remove yourself from the seclusion in which you live. Come boldly forward and employ

* China's official tongue (Pekingese), as opposed to the country's many other dialects.

young and intelligent officials. . . . In case China is unable to produce a sufficient number of intelligent men to give effect to the reforms you initiate, I strongly advocate the employment of foreigners, particularly Englishmen and Americans."[8]

"Boldly forward" the Emperor did come: in a series of "Reform Decrees" issued in rapid succession between June 11 and September 16, 1898, or the period known as the Hundred Days of Reform, he announced the modernization of China's traditional examinations,* the creation of a Service of Translations, of naval and agricultural colleges, the promulgation of a public budget, the dismissal of conservative officials, and the abolition of sinecure positions, etc.

The young Emperor meant well, and was sincere in his desire to invigorate his somnolent empire. His last decree frankly (and somewhat pathetically) stated his position as a fatherly ruler:

In promoting reforms, we have adopted certain European methods, because, while China and Europe are both alike in holding that the first object of good government should be the welfare of the people, Europe has travelled further on this road than we have, so that, by the introduction of European methods, we simply make good China's deficiencies. But our statesmen and scholars are so ignorant of what lies beyond our borders that they look upon Europe as possessing no civilization. They are all unaware of these numerous branches of Western knowledge whose object it is to enlighten the minds and increase the material prosperity of the people. Physical well-being and increased longevity of the race are thereby secured for the masses.

Is it possible that I, the Emperor, am to be regarded as a mere follower after new and strange ideas because of my thirst for reform? My love for the people, my children, springs from the feeling that God has confided them to me and that to my care they have been given in trust by my illustrious Ancestors. I shall never feel that my duty as Sovereign is fulfilled until I have raised them all to a condition of peaceful prosperity. Moreover, do not the foreign Powers surround our Empire, committing frequent acts of aggression? Unless we learn and adopt the sources of their strength, our plight cannot be remedied. The cause of my anxiety is not fully appreciated by my people, because the

---

* Calligraphy and the eight-legged essay were to be replaced by a "modern question".

reactionary element deliberately misrepresents my objects, spreading the while baseless rumours so as to disturb the minds of men. When I reflect how deep is the ignorance of the masses of the dwellers in the innermost parts of the Empire on the subject of my proposed reforms, my heart is filled with care and grief. Therefore do I hereby now proclaim my intentions, so that the whole Empire may know and believe that their Sovereign is to be trusted and that the people may cooperate with me in working for reform and the strengthening of our country. I command that the whole of my Reform Decrees be printed on Yellow paper and distributed for the information of all men. The District Magistrates are henceforth privileged to submit Memorials to me through the Provincial Viceroys, so that I may learn the real needs of the people. Let this Decree be exhibited in the front hall of every public office in the Empire so that all men may see it.[9]

Unfortunately for the Emperor, opposition to his enlightened ideas was powerful, and determined as well. Intrigues on the part of dismissed or threatened officials soon became rife, and centered around the semi-retired Empress Dowager. So far, the latter had maintained an attitude of silent watchfulness, but it was obvious enough that the reform effort threatened her directly.

Her reaction was characteristically swift and uncompromising. With the help of her trusted friend Jung-lu, the senior Manchu military commander and leading opponent of the reform movement, and the complicity of Yuan Shih-k'ai (leader of China's only modern army, who had seemed to be favorable to the reformers), she carried out the coup d'état *of September 1898. Most reform leaders were arrested*—six of them being eventually executed—and the Emperor himself was imprisoned, and to his very end† remained a half-forgotten figure confined to the Ying-t'ai pavilion, on the lake lying near the Summer Palace.*

The reformers were courageous men full of new ideas, but destitute of experience and of practical sense. Also, they were but a few, and had no popular support. They had made a beginning, however, and if the reform period was short-lived, the ideas behind it survived (together with some of

* K'ang Yu-wei succeeded in escaping abroad into exile, as well as Liang Ch'i-ch'ao.

† His death was officially announced on November 15, 1908, one day after that of Tzu Hsi.

their authors), and were soon to determine the course of other historic events.

As for the Chinese masses, they remained inert and ignorant, hardly conscious of the fact that they were a nation. To them, the Western world was still an unknown domain, with the result that the few Chinese then traveling abroad were all too often shocked by Western customs. This was the case of the self-exiled scholar Hwuy-Ung, who was living with a cousin in Melbourne:

You, my venerable brother,* know how we measure a woman: that she must neither be seen nor mentioned by strangers. Here the first question asked of a person of repute is, "How are your wife and family?" No special mention is made of the eldest son; none of the mother-in-law, who is often little regarded. No inquiry is made of his happy age, with us a usual complimentary question. They do not congratulate a person looking old, but think it a polite remark to say he looks ten parts young. When people meet in public, notice is first taken of the women—thus making them overestimate themselves— by taking off the hat, a thing we consider uncivil. We think it not proper to fix eyes on a person of distinction; but to contemplate the second button of his jacket, only occasionally to glance at his face. In this land I have seen some women and even small female children— often the boldest—staring at men so that they feel shame. Looking round after passing them in the street. . . .

Women here act as men do with us; the men, as our women. My elder brother would be like lost in a desert. Women are freeing themselves from the rule of men and, like liberated slaves, become tyrants, or like starved wretches who when at table gorge themselves beyond prudence. . . .

Thinking to say something pleasing to my cousin's wife, I asked, "How old are you?"—one of our customary forms of greeting. For unknown reasons her face turned red with anger, and she gave some sharp reply, I could not understand. My cousin laughed long and loudly, adding to my confusion. He spoke to her, but she was not appeased. Then he told me that women in this country do not like their age to be asked or known; and if they must declare it, always took a good many years off. Strange people! Is age honourable or not?[10]

Hwuy-Ung was even more embarrassed by the equality of, and promiscuity

---

* Hwuy-Ung was writing to his elder brother in China.

between, sexes when he was taken to a public ball, and he also felt deeply puzzled on the occasion of his first contact with such typically British games, exported the world over, as cricket and rugby football:

It has been ten parts hot during Polite Worship [Sunday] before. The people do not strike sleep in the heat of the day. Not so; like ants, they are more lively. On Polite Worship day six, my cousin took me with him below noon to see two ten two men* playing game on a grass ground surrounded by buildings with rows of seats; from them one obtains good view. This game is called *Kli-kei*. . . . The players struck fiercely with heavy flat clubs at a hard ball, and sometimes hit. Then ran past each other between sticks stuck in the earth, as if hunted by ox-headed tormentors. . . . The people, usually quiet, had much excitement at times, and ten thousand voices roared like the noise of a thunderclap. I asked my cousin what made them so furious, and he said because one man caught the ball. There was more serious cause, no? For men having reason cannot be stirred by that small thing. . . .

It is top good game, teaching to aim at what is right, and fight against assaults of wrongdoing. No other desire could have urged to endure the prolonged exertion in that great heat. For the men must have suffered torments of the Buddhist hell. In truth, some of them with fiery red faces looked like demons. I had sorrow for them. . . . There was much repetition in the game, so that I had fatigue and struck sleep. But people roared with delight and excitement. . . .

I went a moon before with my [English] instructor to see the game they call *Foo-poh*. This game has even more fame than *Kli-kei*, described in my letter old year. It is played in winter heaven, for it requires top endurance and activity. Before I arrived at the place . . . I heard the roar of voices two three *li* distant. I knew not what to feel. Going near, a deaf man could hear again and one with hearing made deaf. Within the edge were three ten thousand men and women. . . . The game was same as a battle; two groups of men in struggling contention. These young, strong, quick men what do? Men on one side try to kick goose-egg pattern ball between two poles that represent a gate or entrance. They run like hares, charge each other like bulls, knock each other down rushing in pursuit of the ball to send it through the enemy's pole. When the ball is kicked good and caught with quickness, then the voices of the people burst forth like the sound of

* Twenty-two: there are eleven players in each team.

a mountain wave dashing against a cliff. Men and women mad with excitement yell and scream at the players. . . .

It is a violent game, and men are often injured. But to make them bold and hardy it passes ten thousand games, for it is like fighting. Men thus brave will make top good soldiers. We must adopt this game in the eighteen provinces. . . . We sons of T'ang* do not like violent things. But on earth more parts are obtained by force. So we must learn some violence.[11]

The confusion produced in Hwuy-Ung's mind by the strange Western customs was exceeded, however, by his admiration for the Westerners' astounding inventiveness:

The foreigner has ingenious devices that cannot be surpassed. By the aid of these, extraordinary deeds are performed. . . .

If my honourable elder brother read that a man's voice could be heard from Canton to Amoy, he would marvel at the power of his lungs; yet a feeble old man could so be heard with an instrument connected with the iron electric serpent. . . . With the latest telescope the moon can be brought within a hundred *li*. Messages can be sent ten thousand *li* through mountains and across oceans, borne on mysterious airwaves. A man may speak into a trumpet and his voice be preserved for generations, and be made to repeat what he spoke as often as desired. I hear-say that in the near future it will be possible for one man to see another speaking to him, and hear his voice from the opposite side of the earth. A picture can be made, representing a wedding feast, or a procession, or the meeting of great men in public, with all their movements and actions, as really happened. This picture may be made to reappear at any time, ten thousand generations after. . . .

Boats have been constructed to swim as well beneath the waves as on them—full of water-hand-men. A contrivance like a bird, governed by a man, can rise from the earth or the water, and fly more quickly and higher than the eagle. Thus have men acquired the power we attribute to the spirits of the air, the sea, and the earth! For these marvellous powers, who can refuse admiration? . . . You stand before a good big machine, a maze of wheels, large, very small, moving slow, very quickly; a complication of levers, screws, and shifting

* Illustrious Chinese dynasty (618–907) marked by high cultural attainment.

bands—doing all the thinking and dexterous manipulation. At one end is a huge roll of paper, and at the other is a pile of printed, cut, and folded newspapers—thousands within one period bell. At the end of another machine is a great pile of tobacco; at another end, neatly made cigarettes drop out as quickly as the eye can follow. . . . There is no end to these wonders. . . . But the wonders performed by the electric fire are supremely amazing. You press a button and a whole city is illuminated; a mighty soldier-ship slides majestically into the waters; a huge bridge connects the sides of a wide river; a mountain of rock is torn away. . . .

These are doings of men we have in our conceit called *barbarians*, and have pictured in our country as monsters, having ears reaching down to the ground, and with short legs and long arms like monkeys![12]

At the time when Hwuy-Ung wrote, "we must learn some violence", China was seething with discontent. Opposition to the inefficient and corrupt Manchu dynasty was mounting throughout the country. At the Court of Peking, Manchu and Chinese high officials were frequently at loggerheads over the essential aspects of domestic and foreign affairs. A wave of xenophobia, fed by increasing foreign encroachments as a result of the humiliating defeat inflicted by Japan's "pygmy warriors", was sweeping the empire. Hatred of Christians and of all foreigners, and opposition to every kind of innovation, united the most ignorant and fanatical elements among the people, who were, moreover, surreptitiously egged on by the Mandarins. Violence was in the air indeed, and the Chinese crowds were only waiting for a signal to vent their anti-foreign anger upon all the barbarians within reach.

This signal came from the Boxer movement, or I-hc-ch'üan, a secret brotherhood practising the art of self-defense (ch'üan), or "boxing", which had developed into a pro-Manchu and anti-foreign organization.* In 1899, when the Chinese government ordered Shantung province to organize militia forces against German encroachments there, the society changed its name to I-ho-t'uan, or "Righteous and Harmonious Militia", thus adopting the status of a semi-official defense force.

The Boxers appealed to various popular superstitions, and believed themselves immune from death on the battlefield. One of the first reports on their anti-foreign agitation is contained in a letter written in June 1898 by a French Jesuit, Father Gouverneur, from Chihli:

---

* According to Chinese scholars, it existed without interruption since 1727.

On the seventh day of the third moon (April 27, 1898), during the baccalaureate examinations which bring together in the prefectural city thousands of candidates, always very turbulent, a placard was posted at the four corners of Taiming-fu. Our people told us about it and we sent our catechists to take down the placard and bring it to the attention of the proper authorities. Behold the tenor of this bit of Chinese literature, which has at least the merit of being quite clear (which is a rare quality in Chinese):

"*Notice*. The patriots of all the provinces, seeing that men of the West overreach Heaven* in their behavior, have decided to assemble on the 15th day of the fourth moon and to kill the Westerners and burn their houses. Those whose hearts are not in accord with us are scoundrels and women of bad character. Those who read this placard and fail to spread the news deserve the same characterization. Enough! No more words are needed."[13]

Another firsthand testimony, also from Chihli, was that of the French Lazarist missionary M. Planchet, describing the hypnotic spells by which the Boxers impressed their countrymen:

This is what you can see in public squares. They begin by drawing three circles in the sand, and write several Chinese characters in the center of the circles. Then they fold their hands upward on their forehead, close their eyes, and recite a given formula, which is posted in all the marketplaces. After a few minutes of such invocation, if it proves successful (there are many failures), the performer falls backwards. Somebody must raise him to his feet, as he is quite unable to get up by himself. His assistant then asks him who he is. The hypnotized fellow, his eyes still closed, invariably gives the name of well-known Chinese historic figures, either a general or a great emperor. Again he is asked what weapon he would like to receive. He always asks for a knife or a sword. As soon as he is in possession of the desired weapon, he begins making—with closed eyes—all the boxing and fencing motions known in China, and this with a dexterity he did not have before, and which he loses immediately after the performance. In order to come out of his spell, someone must place his hands on his forehead. Only then does he become normal again.[14]

* Or, "transgress all limits".

Chinese officialdom more or less openly tolerated and protected the Boxers' anti-foreign intrigues and demonstrations.* The inevitable result was that they became increasingly bold, as shown by the following passage from the diary of Baron d'Anthouard, Secretary to the French Embassy at Peking:

May 21, 1900. The Boxers are already very numerous in this city, and are said to number several thousand men. They first invaded the suburbs, then the Chinese city, and finally the Tartar city in small groups. You can see them everywhere. The Catholic Mission knows that some of its workers belong to the movement, but does not dare dismiss them, lest there be a retaliation.

The Boxers' posters cover the walls. They distribute handbills, and advocate the massacre of foreigners and the destruction of all religious institutions. They no longer take the trouble to hide, and move about carrying their insignia: a red scarf tied around their heads with the inscription "Fu" (Happiness) on the front of it, a kind of red coat of arms on their chest, and red bands around their wrists and ankles. They also carry flags with the inscription, "We fight by order of the Emperor and for the salvation of the Dynasty". Their handbills announce the forthcoming massacre of the "Western devils". . . .

The Boxers are a secret society whose members are illuminati, convulsionaries, and fanatics . . . driven by a spirit of hatred toward foreigners.

For their initiation ceremony, they work themselves into a state of nervous exaltation that suppresses the sensation of pain and the consciousness of danger. This they achieve by means of deafening shouts, wild contortions, and frenzied antics with lance and sword. The ceremony takes place either in broad daylight or at night, and in the midst of a crowd driven wild by the spectacle. Moreover, the imagination of the crowd is strongly affected by the use of charms, incantations, and superstitious rites. The result is a kind of collective autosuggestion similar to that observed among convulsionaries and illuminati: sensibility disappears, and the candidates hit themselves with swords and also strike other people frantically. Young men and young literates, being more impressionable, are most likely to come under the spell of this type of nervous perturbation. A well-known

* The foreign legations in Peking protested the Boxers' activities and semi-legal status; the Tsungli Yamen replied evasively that orders for their suppression would be sent to the viceroys.

case is that of a Boxer who, having been made a leader at the beginning of April, ordered his daughter hacked to pieces in the course of one such public ceremony. After recovering from his nervous spell, he realized his crime and committed suicide.

In order to impress the crowds, the initiated pretend to be invulnerable, and they demonstrate their contempt for European arms by ordering some of their confederates to fire upon them with blank cartridges; they drop to the ground, as if hit, and immediately rise to their feet again, holding in their hands the projectile they had hidden in their clothes.[15]

Anti-Western tracts distributed by the Boxers spread the weirdest rumors among the gullible crowds. A French military engineer has quoted a Chinese schoolteacher who distributed such tracts:

I have summed up, in chronological sequence, the most important manifestos which Lo Cheng-leang [another Boxer] has given me to be distributed outside the eastern gate:

The 6th day of the 3rd moon of the 26th year of the reign of Kuang Hsü [April 5, 1900]. The scandalous conduct of Christians and barbarians is irritating our Gods and Geniuses, hence the many scourges from which we are now suffering. The dreadful drought afflicting vast areas this year will continue as long as one single Western devil resides between the Four Seas.*

The 10th day of the 3rd moon [April 9]. The iron roads and iron carriages are disturbing the terrestrial dragon and are destroying the earth's beneficial influences. The red liquid which keeps dripping from the iron snake [rust-laden water falling from oxidated telegraphic wires] is nothing but the blood of the outraged spirits of the air. Incurable diseases will strike us if these reddish drops fall near us. . . .

The 10th day of the 4th moon. Festival of the Dragon and of the Spirits of the Earth.

The missionaries extract the eyes, marrow and heart of the dead in order to make medicaments. Whoever drinks a glass of tea at the parsonage is stricken by death: the brains burst out of the skull. The drinks offered by these traitors are but poisons that corrode your stomach. The unfortunate people attending religious services are being

---

* Traditional representation of China, lying in the center of the earth and surrounded by seas inhabited by strange spirits, demons, and barbarians.

bewitched. As for the children received in orphanages, they are killed and their intestines are used to change lead into silver and to make precious remedies.

All these facts were known to us, but it is necessary for ordinary and ignorant people to be informed of them, too.[16]

Another Boxer notice instructed people to get rid of foreigners—and Chinese Christians—by using violence:

Attention: all people in markets and villages of all provinces in China—now, owing to the fact that Catholics and Protestants have vilified our gods and sages, have deceived our emperors and ministers above, and oppressed the Chinese people below, both our gods and our people are angry at them, yet we have to keep silent. This forces us to practise the I-ho magic boxing so as to protect our country, expel the foreign bandits and kill Christian converts, in order to save our people from miserable suffering.

After this notice is issued to instruct you villagers, no matter which village you are living in, if there are Christian converts, you ought to get rid of them quickly. The churches which belong to them should be unreservedly burned down. Everyone who intends to spare someone, or to disobey our order by concealing Christian converts, will be punished according to the regulation when we come to his place, and he will be burned to death to prevent his impeding our program. We especially do not want to punish anyone by death without warning him first. We cannot bear to see you suffer innocently. Don't disobey this special notice![17]

The Boxers, in other words, meant business. Despite repeated warnings of impending danger, however, the foreign legations at Peking remained optimistic and let themselves be deluded, in the spring of 1900, by the Tsungli Yamen's assurances that there was no cause for fear.

The storm burst at the end of May. The railway line and stations between Peking and Tientsin were attacked and destroyed, churches were burned down, Chinese converts and isolated groups of Europeans* fell victims to the Boxers' irrational fury.

* Such as a group of ten Swedish missionaries ruthlessly hunted down and put to death in Shansi Province—on the charge that they were responsible for a severe drought in that area (1900).

During the first few weeks of disorder, the imperial government made only halfhearted attempts to suppress the Boxers, and used persuasion rather than force.* At the court, an anti-foreign Manchu clique hoped to use the Boxers as auxiliaries to expel all foreigners from China, but it was opposed by a moderate party led by Tzu Hsi's intimate adviser, Jung-lu. Between the two groups, the Empress Dowager (who had resumed full control after her nephew's disgrace) at first hesitated.

Meanwhile, an international force of about 2,000 men, under the British Admiral Seymour, failed to make its way through to Peking, being repulsed by imperial troops cooperating with the Boxers (June 10–26), but it seized the Taku forts. This action in turn led to a Chinese declaration of war (June 20). A proclamation issued by Tzu Hsi commanded the enrolment of Boxers, thus officially recognized, the massacre of all Christians, and the general expulsion of foreigners.

Tzu Hsi's decision came at the end of protracted discussions among the divided members of her Grand Council, as shown by the Court Annals:

The Old Buddha† first called on all present to draw near to the Throne; then, speaking with great vehemence, she declared that it was impossible for her to brook these latest indignities put upon her by the foreigners. Her imperial dignity could not suffer it. Until yesterday, until, in fact, she had read the dispatch addressed to the Tsungli Yamen by the Diplomatic Body, it had been her intention to suppress the Boxers; but in the face of their insolent proposal that she should hand over the reins of government to the Emperor, who had already proved himself quite unfitted to rule, she had been brought to the conclusion that no peaceful solution of the situation was possible. The insolence of the French Consul at Tientsin in demanding the surrender of the Taku forts was bad enough, but not so grievous an affront as the Ministers' preposterous proposal to interfere with her personal prerogatives as Sovereign. Her decision was now taken, her mind resolved; not even Jung-lu, to whom she had always looked for wise counsel, could turn her from this purpose. Then, addressing more directly the Chinese present, she bade them all to remember that the rule of her Manchu House had conferred many and great benefits upon the nation

---

* The Chinese general who, with 6,000 troops, was assigned the task of dispersing the Boxer bands obstructing the Peking-Tientsin railroad line, did not use violence against them.

† Popular nickname of Tzu Hsi, then sixty-five.

for the past two hundred and fifty years, and that the Throne had always held the balance fairly in the benevolent consideration for all its subjects, north and south alike. . . . It was therefore now their duty to rally to the support of the Throne, and to assist it in putting an end, once and for all, to foreign aggression. . . .

In matters of vital principle, she said, these foreigners ignore the sacred doctrines of the Sages; in matters of detail, they insult the customs and cherished beliefs of the Chinese people. They have trusted in the strength of their arms, but today China can rely upon millions of her brave and patriotic volunteers. Are not even striplings taking up arms for the defence of their country? . . .

Turning to the Emperor,* she asked for his opinion. His Majesty, after a long pause, and with evident hesitation, urged her to follow Jung-lu's advice, to refrain from attacking the Legations, and to have the foreign Ministers escorted in safety to the coast. But, he added, it must be for her to decide. He could not dare to assume any responsibility in the matter.

The junior Chinese member of the Council, Chao Shu-chi'ial, then spoke. He begged the Old Buddha to issue orders for the immediate extermination of every foreigner in the interior, so as to avoid the danger of spies reporting on the nature and extent of the patriotic movement. Her Majesty commanded the Grand Council to consider this suggestion and to memorialize in due course for an Edict.

After him, however, each in his turn, the Manchu, Li Shan, and the Chinese Hsü Ching-ch'eng and Yüan Ch'ang implored the Empress not to declare war against the whole world. China, they said, could not possibly escape defeat, and, even if the Empire should not be partitioned, there must arise great danger of rebellion and anarchy from within. Yüan Ch'ang even went as far as to say that . . . he did not believe in the authenticity of the despatch demanding the Empress's abdication, which Prince Tuan† professed to have received from the Diplomatic Body; in his opinion, it was impossible that the Ministers should have dared to suggest any such interference with China's internal affairs.

At this Prince Tuan arose and angrily asked the Empress whether she proposed to listen to the words of a Chinese traitor? Her Majesty rebuked him for his loud and violent manner of speaking, but ordered

* Who had retained advisory powers, and was consulted on that occasion.

† Leader of the anti-foreign group.

Yüan Ch'ang to leave the Audience Hall. No one else dared to say anything.

She then ordered the promulgation of the Decree, for immediate communication to all parts of the Empire; at the same time announcing her intention of sacrificing at the ancestral shrines before the commencement of hostilities. Prince Chuang and Duke Lan were appointed joint Commanders in Chief of the Boxers, but Tzu Hsi gave them clearly to understand that if the foreign Ministers would agree to take their departure from Peking this afternoon, Jung-lu was to do his best to protect them as far as Tientsin.[18]

Thus the wily "Old Buddha", in an effort to protect the Manchu dynasty against mounting domestic opposition, temporarily saved her throne by channeling popular unrest against the foreigners. Naturally, her decision to recognize the Boxers gave their movement a tremendous impetus, and the immediate result was a furious general attack upon all foreigners—white and yellow alike—residing in Tientsin and Peking. On June 20, the German Minister, Baron von Ketteler, was assassinated on his way back from the Tsungli Yamen, and some time later the Chancellor of the Japanese Legation was also murdered by a street mob. The Boxers attacked and burned the French cathedral of Peking, and hundreds of native converts perished in the flames.

In Tientsin, the Chinese Christians were massacred—and shops selling foreign goods plundered—as early as June 15. A French naval officer watched the Chinese merchants' massive exodus:

On our way back from the French Consulate, along the Paris and Tientsin streets, we were greatly surprised by the unexpected spectacle unfolding before our eyes. These two leading commercial arteries of the Chinese city, which only two days ago were so full of life and crowded with a teeming mass of busy Chinese, now presented an entirely different and very strange aspect. Without a single exception, all the native proprietors and merchants were hastily packing their goods and furniture into crates and bundles. Several shops had already been completely emptied, and their doors were locked. Only their large golden signs, which still displayed their beautiful characters on the doors and windows, revealed the departed owner's type of trade. All over the place, thousands of coolies, like so many ants, kept loading all sorts of bundles at the ends of their bamboo poles, and then dis-

appeared toward the mysterious and distant walled city. I interrupted
one of these merchants, a grocer, who was feverishly piling Chinese
candies into a huge crate:

"Why are you leaving?"

"I am leaving because everyone else is leaving."

"And why is everybody leaving?"

"The Boxers are coming tonight, and they will kill and burn everything and everybody," and he pointed to a large, red poster which I
had not yet noticed. It had been pasted against his window by some
anonymous bandit during the night before, and announced an imminent attack. Then, seeing that I had no further question to ask, he
resumed his packing with the utmost haste.[19]

*The same witness was equally surprised, toward the end of June, by a
perfectly well-led attack executed by Chinese regulars:*

The Celestial troops kept advancing, but in two groups at present.
The last group remained in reserve, while the first came closer and
spread out while progressing. All their movements were executed in
perfect order; the Chinese officers were leading their men as if on
maneuvers, and without forgetting even one of the articles stressed in
our own manuals. I was absolutely amazed to see them progress with
such remarkable discipline.

Having arrived at a distance of about 400 yards from the mud wall,
the Chinese infantry opened fire, but the Siberian troops,* who were
under cover and had let the enemy come close enough, replied most
energetically. An intense fusillade now broke loose, and some stray
bullets hit the salt heaps near which I stood. Within a few
moments, however, the ill-protected Chinese line sustained heavy
casualties, and yet they showed no sign of discouragement. They
began taking cover, hiding as well as possible in every fold of the
ground. At the same time, the mortar sections of the second battalion
advanced in regular formations across the plain and kept filling the
increasing gaps of the assaulting line. Their steady and precise fire gave
the Russians a great deal of trouble, but while this action was in full
swing the second Chinese group, which so far had remained inactive,
suddenly began advancing and entered the fray in company formations.

* French, German, English, American, Russian, Japanese and Italian units were
then stationed at Tientsin.

At the very moment, however, when the Chinese reinforcements were about to enter into action, the Russian battery opened a devastating fire on them. I could see the Celestials drop like ninepins, as the shells exploded within their dense formations and burst them wide open. In a matter of minutes they sustained terrible, and irreplaceable losses. I could see the reserve troops swaying, slowly at first, and then faster and faster, until the enemy began a general retreat toward the north.[20]

Fortunately for the besieged foreigners, relief came relatively fast: an international expedition, sent from Taku, took Tientsin on July 14 and definitely warded off any offensive return of the Chinese.

The situation was much more serious in Peking, where nearly a thousand Western men, women and children withstood a siege of almost two months in the legation quarter.

In the city proper, the rampaging Boxers (often assisted by regulars) committed innumerable atrocities, mainly against Chinese "secondary devils", or Christians. Heng Yi, a Kiangsi man who had come to the capital to visit a cousin, was a horrified and powerless spectator:

After the murder of the German Minister . . . the ruffian soldiery of Tung Fu-hsiang entered and sacked nearly every house in my neighbourhood. All through the 24th and 25th [June 20–21] I could hear the shrieks of the women and children, whom they were butchering, and their shouts, in the Kansu dialect.* "Bring out the Secondary Devils!" On the 26th, a Manchu Censor impeached them to the Throne, and the Old Buddha sent for their General, Tung Fu-hsiang, and bade him make an example of the culprits. Accordingly, on the evening of that day, twenty soldiers were beheaded just at the entrance to my lane.

Even this exemplary punishment did not abate their fury, for the next day another large contingent started looting again, and in due course approached my house. My cousin ordered the gate man to draw the bars across the main gate, but I begged him to do nothing of the sort. "Our only hope to escape being massacred is to parley with them." My cousin agreed, so we collected the whole of the family in one of the main rooms, and told them not to get excited or scream. I had scarcely mustered them when nineteen of the Kansu

* These were Mohammedan troops from the northwest—fiercely anti-foreign and anti-Christian.

braves came rushing in. Their swords and clothes were still dripping with blood, as if they had come from a shambles. I went forward to meet them, saying politely, "I know what you have come for: you are looking for secondary devils. However, none of us have 'eaten' the foreign religion. You will see that we have an altar to the kitchen god in our back premises. The whole of our family is now here; will you not take a look through the house to see if there are any Christians in hiding?" I meant by this to imply that we should offer no opposition to their looting whatsoever they pleased. I also called a servant to prepare tea. Our guests received these overtures pleasantly enough, and after a few minutes of energetic looting they returned to my guest room, and some of them sat down to take tea.

One of them remarked, "You seem to be thoroughly respectable people; what a pity that you should reside near this nest of foreign converts and spies." After a brief stay they thanked us politely, apologizing for the intrusion, and retired with their booty. It was then about 2 P.M. We lost about $4,000 worth of valuables. Shortly afterwards, flames were bursting from our neighbour's premises, so I made up my mind to remove my family to a friend's house in the north of the city. In spite of these deeds of violence, even intelligent people still believed that the Kansu soldiery were a tower of defence for China, and would be more than able to repel any number of foreign troops. A friend of mine reckoned that 250,000 persons lost their lives in Peking that summer.[21]

The siege of the Peking legations would probably have succeeded, had it not been for the protection of Jung-lu, who never relaxed his efforts to secure peace. The French Minister, M. Pichon, recorded day after day the changing aspects of that memorable siege:

June 24. Towards 11 A.M., the British Legation was attacked by soldiers and a large body of Boxers uttering ferocious shouts. One of the Legation's doors was riddled with bullets, but fortunately it had been buttressed from the inside by means of stones and sandbags. The assault lasted for more than three quarters of an hour. We opened a breach in a nearby wall, and through it a group of sailors made a sally and killed a fair number of soldiers. The latter retreated together with the Boxers, yelling wildly. Fires were raging on all sides, and the Legations were literally surrounded by them. The Russo-Chinese

Bank was burning, and the walls of the French Legation were licked by flames destroying nearby houses. In one of them, our marines killed twenty-one soldiers.

The Germans and Americans occupied the wall and built a barricade on top of it, only to lose it and regain it under the steady fire of a Chinese cannon. They eventually maintained their ground despite repeated enemy attacks. . . .

June 25. The morning began very quietly. Suddenly, at ten o'clock, the Chinese opened fire on all sides . . . and more particularly against the area where over 2,300 Chinese Protestants and Catholics are huddled together. . . . The hellish racket lasted until about five in the afternoon. . . . Our reply was only sporadic, as we are slowly running out of ammunition. Bad news from the American sectors, where the wall is alternately being lost and regained. . . . Our losses are mounting: a French sailor, a Japanese and a German killed, several wounded. . . .

June 28. The fire that started in the French Legation last night has not yet been put out. Climax of the enemy attack at four o'clock. The Chinese were hiding behind the doors and in the ruins of burnt-out houses, and kept shooting away at the walls and barricades. Some of them, perched on the remnants of the Italian Legation, were hurting us badly. Our soldiers eventually succeeded in setting aflame an enemy barricade by throwing against it a bale of straw soaked with petroleum. The Austrian Chargé d'Affaires and his gallant wife, Mrs. von Rosthorn, participated in that action under my very eyes. . . .

July 2. The ladies are busy making sandbags with silk fabrics and tapestry from Ningpo. Each bag is worth about 10 Mexican dollars. . . .*

July 7. We are losing ground every day, and have again been compelled to move our line of defense back. . . . In a nearby storage room, an old-fashioned cannon has been discovered. . . . An American gunsmith has put it back into commission, and is at the same time busy manufacturing suitable projectiles. It has been christened "The Empress Dowager", or "Betsy".

July 8. Our roofs are crumbling, and as a result our ceilings are

---

* In order to alleviate her chronic shortage of currency, China used Western bank notes and coins even after the latter had long been withdrawn from circulation in their country of origin. At the time of the Revolution of 1911, she still possessed 500 million Mexican dollars (or piasters), which were then the most common Western currency.

caving in. Our heroic sailors are still holding out, and so are the defenders of the Fu building. They are surrounded by fire, their barricades are crumbling, and they are retreating before the flames and under the enemy projectiles, but they give up only the ground they cannot possibly hold. They have dug trenches and erected new barricades, and keep protecting the Christians, whom the Chinese pursue with the relentlessness of wild beasts. "Betsy" is making a tremendous noise, but has succeeded in keeping incendiary teams away. Our means are ludicrous, and yet our little troop's desperate efforts are keeping at bay a fully equipped army, whose cowardice and ignorance are only matched by its wickedness.[22]

At the beginning of August, famine threatened the valiant "little troop", but help was close at hand. A month after it had captured Tientsin, the international expedition (under Count von Waldersee, who arrived in China after hostilities were over) finally reached Peking and relieved the sorely pressed legations.

B. L. Putnam Weale, British employee of the Chinese Customs Service, has narrated the exalting hours of liberation:

It was the night of the 13th. Not a word had been heard of the relief columns, not a message, not a courier had come in. But could anything have dared to move to us? Even the Tsungli Yamen, affrighted anew at this storm of fire which it can no longer control, had not dared or attempted to communicate with us. We were abandoned to our own resources. At best we would have to work out our own salvation. Was it to be the last night of this insane Boxerism, or merely the beginning of a still more terrible series of attacks with massed assaults pushed right home on us? In any case, there was but one course—not to cede one inch until the last man had been hit. . . .

By ten o'clock every sleeping man had been pulled up and pushed against the barricades. Privately all the doubtful men were told that if they moved they would be shot as they fell back. Everywhere we had been discovering that in the pitch dark many could hardly be held in place. By eleven o'clock the fire had grown to its maximum pitch. . . . From the great Tartar Wall to the Palace enclosure, and then round in a vast jagged circle, thousands of jets of fire spurted at us; and as these jets pushed closer and closer, we gave orders to reply steadily and slowly. Twice black bunches of men crept quickly in front of me, but were melted to pieces. By twelve o'clock the exhaustion of the attackers became suddenly marked. . . .

But hardly had the fire dropped for ten or fifteen minutes than it broke out again with renewed vigour. Fresh troops lying in reserve had evidently been called up, and by one o'clock the tornado was fiercer than ever. Our men became intoxicated by this terrible clamour, and many of them . . . could no longer be held in check. By two o'clock every rifle that could be brought in line was replying to the enemy's fire. If this continued, in a couple of hours our ammunition would be exhausted, and we would have only our bayonets to rely on. I passed down my line, and furiously attempted to stop this firing, but it was in vain. In two places the Chinese had pushed so close, that hand-to-hand fighting had taken place. This gives a lust that is uncontrollable. . . . Everything was being taken out of our hands. . . .

Suddenly above the clamour of rifle fire a distant boom to the far east broke on my ears, as I was shouting madly at my men. I held my breath and tried to think, but before I could decide, boom! came an answering big gun miles away. I dug my teeth into my lips to keep myself calm, but icy shivers ran down my back. They came faster and faster, those shivers. . . . You will never know that feeling. Then, boom! before I had calmed myself came a third shock; and then ten second afterwards, three booms, one, two, three, properly spaced. I understood, although the sounds only shivered in the air. It was a battery of six guns coming into action somewhere very far off. It must be true! I rose to my feet and shook myself. Then, in answer to the heavy guns, came such an immense rolling of machine-gun fire, that it sounded faintly, but distinctly, above the storm around us. Great forces must be engaged in the open. . . .

I had been so ardently listening to these sounds that the enemy's fire had imperceptibly faded away in front of me unnoticed, until it had become almost completely stilled. Single rifles now alone cracked off; all the other men must be listening too—listening and wondering what this distant rumble meant. Far away the Chinese fire still continued to rage as fiercely—but near us, by some strange chance, these distant echoes had claimed attention.

Again the booming dully shook the air. Again the machine guns beat their replying rataplan. Now every rifle nearby suddenly was stilled, and a Chinese stretcher party behind me murmured, "*Ta ping lai tao liao*" —"The army's arrived." Somebody took this up, and then we began shouting it across in Chinese to our enemy, shouting it louder and louder in a sort of ecstasy, and heaving heavy stones to attract their attention. We must have become quite crazy, for my throat suddenly gave out, and I could only speak in an absurd whisper. . . . Oh, what a night![23]

After having suffered from the fury of the Boxers, Peking was now looted by the vengeful international force. Many Chinese families committed suicide. The court fled to Sian,* Tzu Hsi being disguised as a peasant woman, and did not return to the capital until January 1902.

Throughout the provinces, where foreigners and Chinese Christians were much less numerous than in the Peking-Tientsin area, Boxer outbursts were sporadic and definitely milder, yet several hundred Westerners (mainly missionaries) lost their lives.† To a remarkable extent, the disturbances spread in direct relation to the time needed for the spread of news from Taku, Tientsin and Peking.

In a collective note dated December 22, 1900, the foreign powers indicted China for "crimes against the laws of nations, against the laws of humanity, and against civilization". Being suspicious of one another, these powers also haggled for months over the settlement to be imposed upon China. The French finally produced an acceptable formula, and on September 7, 1901, the Boxer Protocol, signed by twelve powers, provided for expressions of regret, punishment of the principal culprits,‡ payment of a heavy indemnity, maintenance of the current prohibition of the import of arms, establishment of a permanent legation guard at Peking, dismantlement of all forts, and military control of the road from Taku to Tientsin.

While Germany favored extreme severity, Russia and Japan (who were both eying Manchuria) advocated moderation. The United States, in the name of an "Open Door" policy, expressed her opposition to any partition of China, or to any international control disadvantageous to American trade.

China had nothing to oppose to the ever stronger "barbarians," and most of her leaders—including Tzu Hsi—realized that the way back to tradition was closed. Great changes were indeed called for.

* Capital of Shensi Province, on the Yellow River. Also Sianfu, or Hsian.

† 230 in Shansi, which had a strongly anti-foreign Manchu viceroy. Other viceroys (in Yangtze valley) protected the refugees.

‡ Nearly a hundred, designated by the powers; several were executed.

CHAPTER VII

THE END OF THE CHINESE EMPIRE
1906–1916

DURING THE decade which followed the Boxer debacle, decisive events modified the course of Chinese history. Some of them, and not the least, occurred on the domestic scene, while others resulted from foreign intervention. All these events, however, took place against a background of apparently unalterable traditions deeply rooted in China's masses.

Chu Teh, commander in chief of China's Red armies at the time he described his austere childhood to the American journalist Agnes Smedley, grew up in a closely knit—and matriarchal—peasant family whose unchanged ways were typical of millions of other families throughout the empire:

My grandmother organized and directed the entire household economy. She allotted each member his or her task, the heavy field work to the men, the lighter field work and household tasks to the women and children. Each of the four daughters-in-law took their turn, a year at a time, as cook for the entire family, with the younger children as helpers. The other women spun, sewed, washed, cleaned, or worked in the field. At dawn each morning the daughter-in-law who was cook for that year arose, lit the fire, and started breakfast. When we heard my grandfather moving about, all the rest of us also got up and went immediately about our chores, such as carrying water from the well, chopping wood, feeding the ducks, pigs and chickens, or cleaning up.

All the meals were the same the year round. The men ate together, for such was the custom, and after them the women and children. We were too poor to eat rice except on rare occasions. Breakfast was a gruel of kaoliang [sorghum], with perhaps a little rice or some beans mixed in, and with a common bowl of vegetables. We also had tea, but without sugar, of course. Dinner and supper consisted of about the same things. Instead of gruel, the kaoliang mixed with rice was cooked dry and there was a common bowl, or perhaps two, of boiled vegetables. When my brothers and I managed to fish without being caught—we loved to fish—we might have a bowl of rice. Meat or other special food was served only at the lunar New Year celebration, if at all.

Though Szechuan was a salt-producing province, salt was so expensive that poor people bought as little as possible. . . .

My grandmother apportioned not only the work, but she also rationed the food according to age, need, and the work being done. . . . She was an unusually capable woman and a good administrator, and like all the other members of my family she worked according to her strength until she was laid in her coffin. She saw to it that the landlord was paid his annual rent, which was over half the grain crop together with feudal dues such as extra presents—eggs, a chicken here and there, and sometimes a pig. We all hated these ancient feudal dues . . . because the landed gentry imposed all sorts of obligations and duties of a servile character on us and other peasants.[1]

Contrasting with this faithful continuation of century-old customs in the countryside, a wave of "Europeomania" prevailed among the harbor cities' younger generation toward 1910. Jean Rodes, well-known correspondent of the French daily Le Temps, *was an amused witness of the latest Westernizing fads:*

Outwardly, this new mentality was revealed by the suppression of the pigtail and the adoption of European clothes instead of the national dress. For some years, only young men having studied abroad were bold enough to do this, but in 1910 they were imitated by young people of the large seaports, where the Chinese are in daily contact with our civilization. In Hong Kong and Shanghai, a campaign for the suppression of the pigtails was organized. In Canton, students and young employees of the European offices located on the Shameen concession have founded a "Society for European Dresses". Its members were recruited the more easily as they could thus pretend to possess the latest fashion without actually having to prove it.

I must add that when I stayed in Hong Kong and Canton, at the end of the year 1910, such habits made an unpleasant impression upon the traveler. There were many shaven heads whose all too vivid contrast with the traditional dress gave a truly unesthetic appearance to the otherwise elegant Chinese type. Some of these fancy fashions were hybrid to the point of being simply grotesque. I remember having seen one of these strange dandies one day on the new quay of Canton where such fellows usually exhibit themselves. He was wearing trousers, pink braces and a shirt, plus a stovepipe hat, and, thus attired, was strolling along visibly satisfied with himself and his so-called progressive Western fashion. Others again were merely sporting very tight drawers and lightly colored sweaters which they had bought in the British stores of Hong Kong's Queen's Road. [2]

A change at the beginning of the century which struck foreigners favorably was the noticeable decrease in name-calling. The English missionary A. E. Moule, who spent half a century in China, recorded this fact with much satisfaction:

Of one thing I can speak positively, from personal recollection, and it seems to me significant of a true change in the general attitude of China toward her Western guests and visitors and immigrants, and that notwithstanding spasmodic and ominous hints of a desire, not yet extinct, to get rid of us altogether. I refer to the cessation in every district with which I am acquainted of a hateful practice, which during the course of many years had become so common and apparently incurable, that it no longer aroused indignation or caused any serious annoyance. Opprobrious names and epithets, such as "demon", "white demon", "red-haired monster", "ladrones", and the like, were everywhere applied by the Chinese, by grown-up men and children alike, to foreigners. The polite retort that if, in China's noble phrase, "within the Four Seas all are brethren," then it follows that within the Four Sea all are demons, robbers, and red-haired, might turn the edge of the attack for the moment, but still the odious and un-Chinese discourtesy continued. After 1900, however, whether awed by the supernatural and sublime courage of the Christian, Western and Chinese, in the fires of martyrdom, or amazed at the staying and conquering power of the gallant beleaguered band in Peking (where again Chinese Christians bore so much of the brunt of the conflict), or convinced of the futility of either abuse or brutal violence in trying to remove the foreign incubus, the Chinese have ceased to employ these evil epithets, and the salutary silence has rarely been broken since.[3]

It was only natural that the desire "to get rid of us altogether" should linger on. This is illustrated by the following incident, recalled by the same witness, and which also shows that the Chinese were making good progress in learning English:

A few days ago a foreign lady and her husband were sketching near the wall of the enlighted and progressive city of Shanghai—an innocent and lawful diversion here, where kodaks are in full operation. A number of lads and others gathered round; and as one obstructed the view, he was politely asked to move aside. This scion of young China's nobility shouted out in clear English one of the carefully acquired aphorisms of the new learning: "We stand on our sovereign rights. This is China; I am a Chinese, and can stand where I please." But young China and old China (though old China knew better) have yet to learn that there are no sovereign rights which allow the Chinese to be tyrannous, cruel, unjust; and no law, written or unwritten, which permits the Chinese to part with their good manners. This forms, to my mind, the saddest and most ominous feature of China's awakening, of her so-called Renaissance, of her new life and hope and plans for reform and rejuvenescence. She is in danger of losing in part what the T'ai P'ings were charged with losing wholly, the two bright characteristics of Chinese nationality, education and good manners.[4]

Life in the crowded and bustling Chinese cities, meanwhile, went on as usual. The atmosphere of Canton in 1910, described by Jean Rodes, was little different from that of the preceding generations:

The main impression one brings back after having visited that city is of having wandered around in a vast sewer. .... A broad drain runs along every street, but since it is never cleaned out, the dirty water which people pour into it through small holes dug before their doors remains stagnant, and the stench rising from it is even more nauseating because the sticky paving stones covering the drain are ill-joined or shaky and near the point of collapse. Here and there, special jars that are but rarely removed overflow with fermented urine that soaks the ground and poisons the air. All day long, coolies make their way through the crowd, carrying a pole on their shoulders, at each end of which hang wooden vessels filled with feces. Foul stenches rise from aging heaps of refuse piled up on every corner. A filthy canal, full of all sorts of objects stuck in its murky and stinking mud, winds its way through the city. From the shaky houses, dripping with squalor, that are built on the very edges of this canal, thus seeming to squat along a dung pit, comes a steady flow of refuse. I crossed the canal several times, while holding my nose. The bridges spanning it have stairways, whose steps are crowded with hideous beggars harassing the many passers-by with their ceaseless wailing. . . .

Preceded by the warning cries of the carriers and advancing with astounding speed, my chair ran along endless furrows which opened through the seething crowds and, like a ship's prow, ploughed through the throng of pedestrians amidst the rhythmical yelps of the coolies bent under their bamboo poles.

Altars dedicated to the protecting spirits stand at the street entrances. Their double row of black lacquered tablets bearing golden inscriptions give them a singularly exotic yet religious appearance. In small niches near the entrance of shops, sticks of sandalwood burn in order to keep off malignant spirits. In the shops, where both owners and clerks look as impassive and smooth as priests, lights burn in front of the ancestors' altar. Some façades, gilded and wrought like precious jewelry, look like rich sanctuaries. . . .

Going further, one sees dirty butcher's shops, grill rooms with lacquered and shining ducks displayed, and cheap restaurants. The ground is soaked with muddy water, spittle, and blood. When I passed that area, the air was especially heavy with rancid kitchen smells, and odors of incense and opium, because all the people were joyously getting ready for the New Year's festivities. The walls were being covered with the traditional formulas of happiness, and over their doors people were hanging up large new lanterns painted with shining fish paste, and bearing red and black signs of longevity.[5]

The changes which took place in China during the first decade of the twentieth century resulted in part from domestic unrest, and in part from the spectacular success achieved by modernized Japan.

Tzu Hsi had learned a bitter lesson from the horrors of the Boxer crisis and her inglorious flight to Sian. She was now fully convinced of China's inherent weakness, and of the stern necessity for remedial measures. Not the least of her talents was her extraordinary adaptability to change, and after her return to Peking she proved it by a complete about-face from her former policy of reaction to one of sweeping reform.

A series of epoch-making decrees, inspired by her chief advisers Chang Chih-tung and Yuan Shih-k'ai,* aimed at the empire's educational, economic, and military reorganization. Intermarriage between Manchus and Chinese was for the first time sanctioned; the empire's legal code was revised; Chinese and Manchu officials in the service of the state were placed on a footing of absolute equality; the recruiting of 14 divisions, trained under foreign instructors, was begun; and thousands of able students were sent to study abroad (at government expense), mainly to Japan, but also to Europe and the United States. In 1907, one year before her death, the "Old Buddha" crowned her work of reform by issuing an edict promising constitutional government within nine years.

In her personal life, however, Tzu Hsi remained to the very end deeply attached to her ancestral Manchu traditions. This is strikingly illustrated by the following incident, opposing the headstrong Mistress of China to the American painter Miss C. A. Carl, working on her portrait; it was recorded by Princess Der Ling, First Lady in Waiting to the Empress Dowager, and one of the rare Chinese women who had received a Western education:†

During the latter part of the second moon Miss Carl worked very hard to get the portrait finished and Her Majesty again consulted her book in order to select a lucky day on which to put the final touches to the picture. The 19th of April, 1904, was chosen by Her Majesty as the best time, and Miss Carl was duly notified. Miss Carl most emphatically stated that it was quite impossible to finish the portrait properly by the time named, and I told Her Majesty what Miss Carl said, explaining that there were many small finishing touches to be added and I suggested it would be better to give Miss Carl a few days longer if possible. However, Her Majesty said that it must be finished by four o'clock on the 19th day of April, and therefore there was nothing further to be said.

* Li Hung-chang and Jung-lu died in 1901 and 1903, respectively; Yuan Shih-k'ai was the creator of China's most modern army.

† She was the daughter of an enlightened Manchu official, ambassador to Japan and France, and was at home in Paris society. In 1907, she married an American.

About a week before the time fixed for completion Her Majesty paid a visit to the studio to finally inspect the picture. She seemed very much pleased with it, but still objected to her face being painted dark on one side and light on the other. As I have said before, I had explained that this was the shading, but Her Majesty insisted on my telling Miss Carl to make both sides of her face alike. This led to a pretty hot discussion between Miss Carl and myself but she finally saw that it was no use going against Her Majesty's wishes in the matter, so consented to make some slight alteration. Happening to catch sight of some foreign characters at the foot of the painting Her Majesty inquired what they were and on being informed that they were simply the artist's name, said, "Well, I know foreigners do some funny things, but I think this about the funniest I ever heard of. Fancy putting her own name on *my* picture. This will naturally convey the impression that it is a portrait of Miss Carl, and not a portrait of myself at all." I again had to explain the reason for this, saying that it was always customary for foreign artists to write their names at the foot of any picture they painted, whether portrait or otherwise. So Her Majesty said she supposed it was all right, and would have to remain, but she looked anything but satisfied with it.[6]

The finished portrait eventually was shipped across the streets of Peking on a miniature train especially built for that occasion,* and people humbly knelt before the "sacred figure" as if it had been the original herself.

That Tzu Hsi had a supremely high opinion of herself is shown by the following remarks she made one day to Princess Der Ling:

"Do you know, I have often thought that I am the most clever woman that ever lived, and others cannot compare with me. Although I have heard much about Queen Victoria and read a part of her life which someone has translated into Chinese, still I don't think her life was half so interesting and eventful as mine. My life is not finished yet and no one knows what is going to happen in the future. I may surprise the foreigners some day with something extraordinary and do something quite contrary to anything I have yet done. England is one of the great powers of the world, but this has not been brought about by Queen Victoria's absolute rule. She had the able men of Parliament behind her at all times and of course they discussed everything until

* The painting was on its way to the Saint Louis, Missouri, Exposition.

the best result was obtained, then she would sign the necessary documents and really had nothing to say about the policy of the country.

"Now look at me. I have 400,000,000 people, all dependent on my judgment. Although I have the Grand Council to consult with, they only look after the different appointments, but anything of an important nature I must decide myself. What does the Emperor know? I have been very successful so far, but I never dreamt that the Boxer movement would end with such serious results for China. That is the only mistake I have made in my life. I should have issued an Edict at once to stop the Boxers practising their belief, but both Prince Tuan and Duke Lan told me that they firmly believed the Boxers were sent by Heaven to enable China to get rid of all the undesirable and hated foreigners."[7]

Without any doubt, Tzu Hsi's career was "very successful", and remained so till her death. In 1902, she had returned in triumph to the Forbidden City,* and during the last few years of her reign won the respect, and in some cases even the affection, of the European and American community in China.

Even more remarkable than her own, however, was the success which China's latest adversary, Japan, achieved at that time at the expense of Russia. Both powers were determined to annex Manchuria, which made an early clash inevitable. The ambitious and self-confident Japanese, who in 1902 had signed an alliance with England, opened hostilities in February 1904 by attacking Port Arthur (without declaration of war). The ill-led Russians were repeatedly—though not decisively—beaten in Manchuria, and in May 1905, in the Straits of Tsushima, Admiral Togo annihilated a Russian fleet of 37 vessels that had come all the way from the Baltic Sea.

By the Treaty of Portsmouth, signed in September 1905, after mediation efforts by President Theodore Roosevelt, Russia recognized Japan's paramount interest in Korea, transferred to Japan her lease on the Liaotung Peninsula and the railroad to Changchun, and ceded southern Sakhalin. Manchuria was to be evacuated by both Powers, and was returned from Russian to Chinese administration. It was the end of Russia's "thrust to the south," and it was the first time in modern history that a "yellow" nation had beaten a "white" nation.

The rapid and unexpected Japanese victory stunned the world, and once more revealed to China the advantages of learning the lessons of the West.

* Traditionally, that part of Peking reserved to the exclusive use of the imperial family and court.

An immediate result was the creation, upon Chang Chih-tung's recommendation of Japanese education, of a Ministry of Education. Thousands of Chinese students now swarmed to Japan,* but while the official Japanese institutions of learning greatly helped these students, many of them fell victims to educational quacks who made it a business to give them a rapid, makeshift training and then sent them home with graduation certificates and with a proud—but entirely unjustified—feeling of great personal achievement.

Writing in a students' journal on the unsatisfactory overall results of this massive exodus, Ling Chi Hong, Chinese resident in Tokyo, had this to say:

The ease with which a few of the Japanese-returned students obtained their literary degrees and high government appointments caused a great increase of Chinese students pursuing their studies in Japan, so that within a few years their number reached as high as thirteen thousand. Though a few were bent on real education, the majority went to the country merely for the name of being a returned student, and for the prospect that was held out to them of becoming officials. Consequently there was a mad "speculative" rush for Japanese education, but few stayed longer than from three to six months.

There were not a few covetous Japanese who took advantage of this educational speculation, and schools of all sorts and descriptions, from the so-called normal to the collegiate institutions, were started by hundreds of these enterprising people to cater to the wants of our Chinese youths. The prices of food and other commodities, which have been low for centuries, suddenly rose to high figures in Tokyo, in consequence of the lavish and extravagant habits of our Chinese students, many of whom were connected with rich and influential families. Tuitions and diplomas also had their premiums and exorbitant prices were demanded from the Chinese students both as matriculation and graduation fees.

The value or worthlessness of such an education is apparent to right-minded men. In order to get a real education in Japan two years must at least be devoted to the study of the language and five years would be the minimum time before one can get a fair education.

The farce of Japanese education soon came to the knowledge of the Imperial Government, and in 1906 the Board of Education of Tokyo was instructed by our government to enforce strict regulations for the control of Chinese students. As soon as the above-mentioned order

* As many as 15,000 were there at one time.

was reported in the newspapers, the Chinese students held a meeting at the hall of the Chinese Students' Alliance of Tokyo. The members held divided opinions, some proposing to return and others to remain. As a result, more than half left Japan.[8]

One of the most active Chinese then residing in Japan was a handsome forty-year-old Doctor of Medicine hailing from the vicinity of Macao, Sun Yat-sen. As a true representative of the ever-increasing number of liberal-minded and Western-learning malcontents from the traditionally turbulent Canton delta, Sun was the founder of several secret societies with which he tried ten times before 1911 to overthrow the Manchu dynasty. He lacked neither courage nor determination, and had traveled around the world.

Western influence and anti-Manchu sentiment marked his early years: his father was a Christian, and one of his uncles fought with the T'ai P'ings. Having received his secondary education in Honolulu* and his Western medical training at Hong Kong, although he was only semi-trained in the Chinese classics, Sun meant to follow previous reformers in using Western methods for the regeneration of China. In 1894, he had founded the Hsing-Chung-hui, or "Revive China Society", and after his first failure to raise the standard of rebellion (1895),† he organized the Chinese communities in Japan, Hawaii, and America.‡

Sun's political principles crystallized more slowly than his pertinacious plotting against the Manchus. According to his own testimony, it was during his two-year sojourn in Western Europe (1896–8) that his doctrine's threefold principle—"Eliminate the Manchus, eliminate the Monarchy: open the road to Socialism"—took shape in his mind.

At the very beginning of his European sojourn, as he himself wrote, Peking very nearly succeeded in bringing his revolutionary career to an end:

I left Honolulu in June, 1896, for San Francisco, where I remained for a month before proceeding eastward. There I met many of my countrymen and was well received by them. I spent three months in America, and came to Liverpool by the S.S. *Majestic*. In New York I was advised to beware the Chinese Minister to the United States, as he is a Manchurian, and has but little sympathy with Chinese generally and a reformer in particular.

* Where one of his brothers was established, and had invited him.

† Canton was to be captured, and the Kwangtung province declared independent, but the coup was badly planned and clumsily executed.

‡ Many of which were wealthy, and helped finance Sun's campaign.

On October 1st, 1896, I arrived in London and put up at Haxell's Hotel in the Strand. I went next day to Mr. Cantlie's . . . where I received a hearty welcome from my old friend* and his wife. Lodgings were found for me. . . . Henceforth I proceeded to enjoy my stay in London and to become acquainted with the many sights, the museums and the historical relics in this the very centre of the universe. What impressed me, a Chinaman, most was the enormous vehicular traffic, the endless and unceasing stream of omnibuses, cabs, carriages, wagons, and wheeled conveyances of humbler character which held the streets. The wonderful way in which the police controlled and directed the traffic, and the good humour of the people. The foot passengers are, of course, many, but they are not in such crowds as we find in Chinese streets. . . .

I had been frequently at Mr. Cantlie's, almost daily in fact, and spent most of my time in his study. One day at luncheon he alluded to the Chinese Legation being in the neighbourhood, and jokingly suggested that I might go round and call there; whereat his wife remarked, "You had better not. Don't you go near it; they'll catch you and ship you off to China." We all enjoyed a good laugh over the remark, little knowing how true the womanly instinct was, and how soon we were to experience the reality. . . .

On Sunday morning, October 11th, at almost half-past ten, I was walking toward Devonshire Street, hoping to be on time to go to church with the doctor and his family, when a Chinaman approached in a surreptitious manner from behind and asked, in English, whether I was Japanese or Chinese. I replied, "I am Chinese." He then inquired from what province I came, and when I told him I was from Canton he said, "We are countrymen, and speak the same language; I am from Canton." . . .

My would-be Chinese friend, therefore, addressed me in English until he found my dialect. Whilst he was talking we were slowly advancing along the street, and presently a second Chinese joined us, so that I had now one on each side. They pressed me to go into their "lodgings" and enjoy a smoke and chat with them. I gently demurred, and we stopped on the pavement. A third Chinaman now appeared and my first acquaintance left us. The two who remained further pressed me to accompany them, and I was gradually, and in a seemingly friendly manner, led to the upper edge of the pavement, when

* Sun had studied medicine under him at Hong Kong.

the door of an adjacent house suddenly opened and I was half-jokingly and half-persistently compelled to enter by my companions, one on either side, who reinforced their entreaties by a quasi-friendly push. Suspecting nothing, for I knew not what house I was entering, I only hesitated because of my desire to get to Mr. Cantlie's in time for church, and I felt I should be too late did I delay. However, in good faith I entered, and was not a little surprised when the front door was somewhat hurriedly closed and barred behind me. All at once it flashed upon me that the house must be the Chinese Legation. . . .

I was shown into a room and told to remain there. An old gentleman with white hair and beard came into the room in rather a bumptious fashion and said:

"Here is China for you; you are now in China."

Sitting down, he proceeded to interrogate me. Asked what my name was, I replied, "Sun".

"Your name," he replied, "is Sun Wen*; and we have a telegram from the Chinese Minister in America informing us that you were a passenger to this country by the S.S. *Majestic*; and the Minister asks me to arrest you."

"What does that mean?" I enquired.

To which he replied: "You have previously sent in a petition for reform to the Tsungli Yamen in Peking asking that it be presented to the Emperor. That may be considered a very good petition; but now the Tsungli Yamen want you, and therefore you are detained here until we learn what the Emperor wishes us to do with you."[9]

Sun's arrest made headlines in London, and he subsequently learned that he was to be shipped off to China for execution there. Fortunately for him, his British friends moved heaven and earth to get him out of his predicament. Scotland Yard was alerted, the Foreign Office too stepped in, and after a detention of ten days, Sun was a free man again.

Back in Japan, he founded the T'ung Meng Hui, or "Sworn Chinese Brotherhood" (1905), and thus became the official leader of China's revolutionary organizations, whose immediate purpose was to eject the Manchus. A manifesto issued on that occasion laid down Sun's main political and social

* The author's "official" name, Sun Yat-sen being the Cantonese pronunciation.

242 THE AWAKENING OF CHINA

ideas. Republicanism and land redistribution* were the outstanding—and truly revolutionary—features of the new program, to be achieved by force:

Since the beginning of our nation the Chinese have always ruled China; although at times alien peoples have usurped the rule, yet our ancestors were able to drive them out and restore Chinese sovereignty so that they could hand down the nation to posterity. Now the men of Han have raised a righteous [patriotic] army to exterminate the northern barbarians. This is a continuation of heroic deeds bequeathed to us by our predecessors, and a great righteous cause lies behind it; there is none among us Chinese who does not understand this. But the revolutions in former generations, such as the Ming dynasty† and the T'ai P'ing Heavenly Kingdom, were concerned only with the driving out of barbarians and the restoration of Chinese rule. Aside from these they sought no other change.

We today are different from people of former times. Besides the driving out of the barbarian dynasty and the restoration of China, it is necessary also to change the national polity and the people's liveli-hood. . . . In former days there were heroes' revolutions, but today we have a national revolution [*Kuo-min-ko-ming*]. "National revolu-tion" means that all people in the nation will have the spirit of freedom, equality, and fraternity; that is, they will all bear the responsibility of revolution. . . . Therefore we proclaim to the world in utmost sincerity the outline of the present revolution and the fundamental plan for the future administration of the nation.

1. *Drive out the Tartars:* The Manchus of today were originally the eastern barbarians beyond the Great Wall. They frequently caused border trouble during the Ming dynasty; then when China was in a disturbed state they . . . conquered China, and enslaved our Chinese people. Those who opposed them were killed by the hundreds of thousands, and our Chinese have been a people without a nation for

---

* Among social reformers, Sun Yat-sen had read Bakunin and Karl Marx. His agrarian ideas, however, owed as much to Chinese traditions (system of Ching, reforms of Wan An-shih, T'ai P'ing movement) as to Western socialism. Although he never was a Communist in the Western sense of the term, Sun wrote in 1924 that China accomplished a Communistic agrarian revolution before Russia, namely at the time of the T'ai P'ings.

† Established in 1368 by a monk (Ming T'ai Tsu) turned insurgent amidst anarchy. It was replaced by the Ch'ing (Manchu) dynasty in 1644.

two hundred and sixty years. The extreme cruelties and tyrannies of the Manchu government have now reached their limit. . . .

2. *Restore China:* China is the China of the Chinese. The government of China should be in the hands of the Chinese. After driving out the Tartars we must restore our national state. . . .

3. *Establish the Republic:* Now our revolution is based on equality, in order to establish a republican government. All our people are equal and all enjoy political rights. The president will be publicly chosen by the people of the country. The parliament will be made up of members publicly chosen by the people of the country. A constitution of the Chinese Republic will be enacted, and every person must abide by it. Whoever dares to make himself a monarch shall be attacked by the whole country.

4. *Equalize land ownership:* The good fortune of civilization is to be shared equally by all the people of the nation. We should improve our social and economic organization, and assess the value of all the land in the country. Its present price shall be received by the owner, but all increases in value resulting from reform and social improvements after the revolution shall belong to the state, to be shared by all the people, in order to create a socialist state, where each family within the empire can be well supported, each person satisfied, and no one fail to secure employment. Those who dare to control the livelihood of the people through monopoly shall be ostracized.[10]

By a combination of great personal exertion and the constant help of faithful propagandists, Sun Yat-sen steadily increased the number of supporters of the revolution, especially among Chinese overseas communities. One of his most zealous backers was Paul Linebarger, an American judge whose enthusiasm for Sun's cause made him abandon his profession in order to devote his life to the approaching revolution.*

The following two excerpts from Linebarger's addresses before Chinese gatherings are typical of his untiring efforts in support of Sun:

(Tokyo, October 12, 1906—Chinese Students' Club)

Dear Co-Supporters of Dr. Sun:

I am, indeed, very gratified at this surprise meeting which is so

---

* Linebarger was descended from a pre-Revolutionary line of Alsatian frontiersmen. The son of a stern and learned Methodist minister in Illinois, he studied law in Paris and Heidelberg, was a U.S. judge in the Philippines and foreign legal adviser of Sun Yat-sen (1907–25).

much larger than any I believe could be gathered together in Japan. In fact, ever since I left Manila, I have frequently reflected upon the great progress Dr. Sun has already made in his organization work. I had no idea that the communications from one revolutionary center to another were so rapid and exact, for no sooner does my ship arrive in port than a delegation of Dr. Sun's followers comes to meet me. You have some mysterious way of communicating your revolutionary matters from one remote point to another which I do not yet understand. . . .

I shall talk to you freely and at length concerning our program as directed by Dr. Sun Yat-sen, for you are nearly all students who have come here from China for the special purpose of modernization. I am surprised to find so many European languages spoken here. It is remarkable how quickly the Chinese absorb foreign languages when they have an opportunity. There never should have been such a jibber-jabber as pigeon English if foreigners in China had only recognized this great linguistic ability of the Chinese. . . .

(Honolulu, October 23, 1906—Merchants and Labor Associations)
Dear Future Citizens of the Chinese Republic:

. . . Although you are comparatively few in numbers here in Honolulu and in the Hawaiian Islands, generally, that is all the more reason why you should get together and support Dr. Sun. . . . I want to impress on all of the Chinese of the Hawaiian Islands that the great honor in which Dr. Sun's leadership is held, is a great credit to each of them individually. . . . I have already suggested the particular reason why Honolulu should be made a revolutionary center. This reason is the constant passing to and fro to Honolulu of Overseas Chinese going to and from China. When any of these transient Chinese indicate their support of K'ang Yu-wei or Liang Ch'i-ch'ao,* just tell them although these are very illustrious men, great scholars and true patriots from an idealistic, scholarly viewpoint, that nonetheless, they are on the wrong track politically. How can you reform the Manchus? . . .

The Manchu dynasty is supported by all that there is of a cunning and irrevocable desire to continue the old effete customs of the past, customs which are becoming daily and daily more rotten. Tell these Overseas Chinese as they come and go through Honolulu, that there is no other program for the redemption of China save that proposed

* Who advocated a constitutional monarchy.

by Sun Wen. The failure of the 1898 reforms of K'ang Yu-wei plainly proved that fact. . . . It would be easier to change a tiger into a lamb, for the hundreds of thousands of office-holding parasites in China today have a political power over the throne which will never again even allow the beginning of such a reform as that proposed by K'ang Yu-wei. Deceptions and false pretenses will continue to be advanced by Peking.[11]

Though constantly menaced by Peking's agents or its diplomatic pressure (he was expelled from most countries bordering on China), Sun Yat-sen never gave up his fight for a new regime. His thought and action were not always clear and logical, but he never lost faith in the ultimate triumph of his cause. "He may not be a great man," a Western journalist one day said of him, "but he certainly is a great force."

The French journalist Jean Rodes interviewed Sun in Indo-China:

In June 1907, I managed to have a long conversation with Sun Yat-sen. We did not meet in Hong Kong, as I then purposely reported to the *Temps* in order not to reveal his actual residence, but in Hanoi, in a house surrounded by gardens, near the Boulevard Gambetta, where he was hiding. He had been informed of my desire to interview him, and had replied that he would be pleased to receive me. A Chinese friend of his one evening led me to his retreat.

Though forty, he was young in appearance. With his European dress, his closely cropped haircut, and his fairly large head with high cheekbones, he looked much more Japanese than Chinese. I was struck at once by the extraordinary impassiveness of his countenance, indicative as it was of Sun's outstanding tenacity and energy. His is one of those impenetrable and stony faces behind which one feels the presence of an unusually self-possessed mind, as well as of a very strong character steeled against adversity.

We sat down at a very small table in a large room entirely devoid of furniture, but whose walls were covered with maps of China. It actually resembled the dwelling of a nomad not knowing where he would be the next day. A male servant brought us tea, and I began my interview at once. Obviously, I had no hold over his mind, and I began to despair of being at all able to start any kind of conversation. His thought seemed to be absent, but he was in fact observing me very carefully. Only after having convinced himself that I was not an enemy, or one of those international agents working for any political police the world over, did he begin to answer my questions.

This was, according to my notes, the gist of our conversation:

"Do the rebels of Amoy, Swatow, and Pakhoi, who rose recently,* count among your supporters?"

"Most likely."

"Will you go back to China to head the insurrection?"

"Yes, but the moment has not yet arrived. Moreover, the real outbreak will not take place in the South, but in the Center."

"Will there also be a rising in the North?"

"Yes, because I have many supporters in Tientsin, and even in Peking. China has reached the point where a revolt against the Mandarins and the Manchu dynasty is more likely than ever before."

"Is it true, as one hears people say, that you intend to establish a republic, and a socialistic republic at that?"

"Absolutely, but my program does not quite correspond to European ideas of such a government, for the simple reason that Chinese customs and ways of thought are much different from your own."

"It seems to me that in order to achieve such a radical change, you will first have to bring about a moral revolution. Do you intend to attack the traditional principles of Chinese society, that is, the worship of ancestors and the strict family laws which rule a Chinese's life and suppress his individuality?"

"Such is our goal indeed. We wish to suppress all the tyrannical aspects of these customs, while at the same time respecting the positive moral aspects of ancestor worship. In short, we too, like the French Revolution, advocate the rights of man."

"Are you supported by secret societies?"

"Yes. In the past, these societies were anti-foreign, but today they are mainly reform-minded, and anti-dynastic. The Chinese have come to realize that their country's woes stem from the Court and the Mandarins much more than from Europeans. It was always the Mandarins who provoked anti-foreign riots, in order to divert the wrath of a people dissatisfied with the administration.

"Above all, we are anti-Manchu, because this usurping dynasty has brought about our national decline. So long as China remains under its domination she will be weak, and her weakness will endanger world

---

* Several rebellions broke out before the Revolution of 1911, and were either provoked or supported by the T'ung-Meng-Hui.

peace by exciting the greed of other nations. By strengthening our country and giving her a regime adapted to present-day needs, we are furthering the peace of the world. And far from being hostile to Europeans after our victory, we shall welcome mutual intercourse with a view to promoting the modernization of China."

"Do you cooperate with K'ang Yu-wei and his party?"

"K'ang Yu-wei is a reformer indeed, but we cannot work with him because he is a Monarchist and pro-Manchu, and because his society aims at preserving the empire."

"What do you think of the reforms initiated by the Government?"

"The Court is not being sincere. Besides, it is quite unable to keep its promises. There is not one intelligent Chinese, be he from the North or from the South, who does not doubt the Court's duplicity."

While talking, he had become excited, and I had seen the initial expression of mistrust gradually wane from his eyes, which at the end were alive with youthful enthusiasm. When I took my leave, he shook my hand very firmly, and repeatedly begged me to join in the defense of such a righteous cause.[12]

The death of the seventy-three-year-old Empress Dowager (1908) practically meant the end of the Manchu dynasty. A three-year-old boy (P'u-I, proclaimed Emperor under the name Hsuan T'ung) now occupied the Dragon Throne, and the power passed to the Regent, the vacillating and reactionary Prince Ch'un. The latter most unwisely proceeded to restore the former Manchu predominance in the administration's higher echelons.* His shortsighted policy inevitably incurred the hostility of many powerful and able Chinese officials, hitherto loyal to the throne, but who now began to turn toward Sun Yat-sen's revolutionary propaganda.

The government's failure to grasp the rapidly changing situation and to face it with the unhesitating firmness which alone appeals to Oriental minds, led to ever deeper uneasiness and disgruntlement throughout the empire. The Westernized intellectuals and students, or "Young Chinese", wanted to replace the corrupt Manchu dynasty by a truly representative and responsible government and were getting impatient. Together with the powerful merchant class, they demanded the early convocation of a national assembly.

Economic difficulties heightened the tension still further. The wealthier

* He dismissed Yuan Shih-k'ai, and appointed Prince Ching, most reactionary of the imperial princes, to the post of Prime Minister. He also appointed his own brothers to lucrative posts.

classes complained over increased taxes, resulting from the reorganization of the army and the building of railroads. The poorer classes, on the other hand, were hard hit by the catastrophic failure of crops (the worst in forty years) which occurred in the central—or Yangtze—provinces. China, in short, was ripe for revolution.

It came in October 1911, and Sun Yat-sen, who was at the time in Denver, Colorado, learned of it through the American papers.

A popular uprising, caused by discontent with government intervention in the administration of the Hankow–Szechuan railroad, had broken out in the latter province in September.* Sun Yat-sen's agents had fanned the emotions of the people, but the rising had been quelled within weeks.

The actual outbreak of the Revolution took place in Hankow, and was triggered off by the fortuitous discovery of the headquarters of the revolutionary organization in that city.† On October 10, the troops of the "Modern Army", forming the garrison of nearby Wuch'ang, rose in revolt and elected Colonel Li Yuan-hung as their leader. The movement, fed by popular discontent, spread rapidly through the western and southern provinces, without causing much bloodshed. By the end of November, practically all the provinces south of the Yangtze were in open rebellion against Peking.

October 10, or the "Double tenth" (i.e., the tenth day of the tenth month) subsequently became China's national holiday. In the first days of the revolution, according to the testimony of the British Consul Sir Meyrick Hewlett, the number ten had a very peculiar practical application:

When the revolution broke out, few foreigners knew which way it would turn. Naturally, among Americans especially, there was an intense joy at the birth of a new republic and extensive lectures were given in American missions on the benefits of republicanism. Boys, cooks and coolies were indiscriminately urged to join the army, although many of us had doubts as to the wisdom of this policy; for in China it is easier to lose a job than to find a new one; and no one could help viewing with serious misgivings a future with soldiers who had no proper employment and who would in many cases be reduced to banditry for a living. However, at this period all relations were extremely happy.

* The government had decided to buy the railroad, whereupon the stockholders had protested that they were being shortchanged; their protest had been supported by a strike of the merchants.

† Revealed by the accidental explosion of a bomb in a house in the Russian concession.

Seeing the bitter feelings which gave birth to the revolution, for the Manchu was an alien ruler, it cannot be said that there was an excess of bloodshed, though naturally certain brutalities were perpetrated. For example, it was a common thing to make people in the streets count to ten; this was done because in the North the word "ten" is pronounced in a hard manner and in the South the same sound is considerably softened. It was, therefore, known at once by the pronunciation of this word whether the man was from the North or not. I am afraid that only too often Northerners,* discovered in this manner, were killed.[13]

One of the reform decrees issued by the late Tzu Hsi had abrogated the compulsory wearing of pigtails, outward symbol of Manchu customs and domination. Like the T'ai P'ings before them, the revolutionaries now proceeded to hasten the generalization of a more typically Chinese hair style.

The French journalist Edmond Rottach, who traveled widely through China, witnessed many of their interventions to such effect:

So far, it cannot be said that all the pigtails have disappeared. However, if the Cantonese keep repeating the act of *t'i pien tze* [cutting the queues] as I saw it performed in a train by an officer and a soldier, the practice will certainly become general. These two uniformed comptrollers, or executors of a new kind, began at the rear end of the train and, moving all the way through it, chopped off every single queue— even the best hidden—with their small scissors. They made people take of their skullcaps, under which they often found an old man's thin queue plaited around the head, and no one escaped the operation. Some people kept silent, others would laugh; an old man, however, in that train where I saw over twenty queues thus taken off, resisted and created a scandal by gathering all the train's passengers in his car. He defended himself, arguing that in the village where he lived nobody had suffered such mutilation, so much so that the irate officer finally left him alone.

At the smaller stations, I noticed that all the farmers still wore thick queues. In Shanghai, too, I saw that the police agents have kept their long queues. In Nanking, however, soldiers of Cantonese origin have

* That is, Manchus. The seizure of Sian, capital of Shensi (where the court had fled in 1900), by the revolutionaries was followed by a terrible massacre of the Manchus in that city.

been full of zeal for more than two months; one meets there many poor creatures whose hair, falling no lower than their necks, gives a dark frame to their leaden and bony faces. . . . These poor devils looked like phantoms, and would have inspired Gustave Doré.[14]

The revolutionary movement was particularly strong, and understandably so, in large harbor cities like Canton, traditional home of revolutions, and semi-Westernized Shanghai, "Queen of the Far East." A prominent role was also played by Nanking, capital of the empire under Chinese rule; its fall, in November, greatly enhanced the prestige of the Republican party, which decided at once that the city should become capital of that part of the country which had accepted the new regime.

Even the theatre—a favorite entertainment with Chinese—served the revolution. In Shanghai, the French traveler and writer F. Farjenel went to see the latest play, whose heroes were the Republican soldiers:

There were all sorts of people among the spectators. Women and girls were particularly numerous, and one could easily distinguish the various classes of society according to the quality of people's dress. My neighbors in the loge next to mine were two charming young girls, dressed in brocaded silk, and wearing flowers in their hair. They had come with their parents, and were eating cookies and drinking tea. My presence intrigued them, because the program I was holding in my hand showed that I understood the play. They kept giving me sidelong glances, so as not to cause any breach of good manners by displaying an indiscreet curiosity. They were greatly interested by the play.

The story was about a young, Westernized officer who had married a European girl. The actor impersonating the girl† was highly talented. He frequently changed his dress, wore the low-necked fashion most naturally, and managed the skirt in a very successful manner. To prepare himself for this particular role, he had taken lessons from a

* The marching out from Nanking of the imperialist general Chang Hsum, at the head of his old-style braves, symbolized the passing away of picturesque old China, while the occupation of the city by the republican general Hsu Shao-cheng and his following of smart, modern soldiers marked the advent of a new China conscious of its strength.

† There were only male actors in the traditional Chinese theatre. Today, there are actresses as well, and the Communist regime insists on themes serving "China's socialist revolution".

European woman at Shanghai; the Chinese talent for imitation did the rest. The young woman's pregnancy was passed over rapidly and discreetly; soon she presented her husband and parents with a baby, represented by a doll wrapped in swaddling clothes.

The young man's parents, as well as his sisters, were greatly surprised by such new customs. Their attitude constituted the play's comic relief, as its deeper story revolved around the present political conflict between the traditional world of Mandarins and Republicans. Eventually, of course, the latter had the upper hand. The revolutionary soldiers charged a fortress, chasing from it the Manchus dressed in old-fashioned garb. One could hear the fusillade on all sides, and see a fire break out. Surprisingly, the fire did not overtake the new theatre's many settings, although flames did actually invade the stage.

At the end, there was a parade of the victorious revolutionaries, with a large display of flags. I could have believed myself at the Châtelet.* The play ended amidst the crowd's applause and cries of "Hao! Hao! Good, good!" which Chinese spectators invariably utter whenever they can no longer contain their pleasure. Needless to add, cries of "Long live the Chinese Republic!" burst forth when, during the climactic final apotheosis, the soldier-actors swung and waved their flags around the stage.[15]

Shortly after their seizure of the "Southern capital" (Nanking), the revolutionary forces established a provisional government in that city. Their troops, meanwhile, continued to advance beyond the Yangtze, in the general direction of the "Northern capital", or Peking. The imperial government had little with which to oppose them, since most of its generals refused to march against the rebels unless a constitution was granted.

Peking itself was panic-stricken by the tremendous success scored by the revolution within a few weeks. The city's tense atmosphere in early November has been described by the French journalist Edmond Rottach:

There were days on which the stations were overflowing with panicky and half-demented crowds. Even the first-class cars and box-cars were so crowded that there was hardly any standing room left in them. Hundreds of poor people, who had found no room inside the trains, stood precariously between the cars, on the buffers and hooks, where they had attached their bedding and their small pigskin trunks.

* Well-known theatre in Paris.

Rather than remain in Peking, they ran the risk of freezing to death during a trip lasting from several hours to a whole day. Wealthy people rented whole cars and filled them with their families, including their fragile little wives and their restless children eating sweets or fruits. They also took with them all of their possessions, even their carriages with their harnessed mules, which, together with the servants, the poorer fugitives and all kinds of bundles, were jammed into freight cars. The exodus from Peking lasted for several days, and it was estimated that 300,000 persons fled the city;* the trains came back empty. . . .

In the early evening, quiet prevailed everywhere, and by nightfall the center of the city, so very slow in its modernization process, was shrouded in silent darkness. Small and weak electric bulbs shedding a reddish light and lined only along one side of the streets, shone poorly over heaps of dust, piles of mud and snow, and deep ruts. The lower parts of doors, which were rotting behind their sheet-iron plates, had been hastily repaired by means of heavy beams, and a good many sidestreets had been barricaded with large wooden barriers, as if city authorities had meant to limit the expected invasion to some sections only. At night, one could see three or four shivering policemen standing guard before these wooden gates, armed with rifles and bayonets; and now and then, the silence of the night was broken by the passage of a patrol.[16]

In its utter helplessness, the Manchu court recalled Yuan Shih-k'ai to military command. Yuan had been brutally dismissed three years earlier, but behind him stood China's best army. He returned to Peking—on his own terms and protected by his faithful soldiers—in the middle of November.

Among the handful of Europeans who witnessed his entrance into the frightened capital was the French journalist Jean Rodes:

The news of the arrival of Yuan, scheduled for the afternoon, suddenly changed the atmosphere and reassured the Chinese. Far from having diminished, his prestige had increased during his absence from power. Only two days ago, without serious reason, everything seemed to be lost, but now his impending return meant salvation.

The stores had been closed, the schools deserted; the police agents

* Out of a population of about one million at that time.

hailing from other cities had all gone, and the jinrikisha runners themselves, normally so numerous on all crossroads, had disappeared too.
Peking, in short, offered the peculiar aspect of a city struck by terror.
After the headlong flight of the chief Mandarins and Princes, amidst
the complete confusion prevailing at the Court, it seemed as though
the monarchy would collapse at any moment. China's capital could
have been taken over by a single corporal with four men. But as soon
as the arrival of Yuan was announced, this exceptional opportunity,
which the revolutionaries could have grasped, was lost.

True, after his three-year residence on his estate, Yuan had taken
plenty of time before accepting the invitation of his mortal enemy,
the Regent. He had demanded full powers, and thus returned to Peking
as a dictator rather than as a savior. . . .

Having entered the station, I found the platform where Yuan's train
was to arrive crowded with troops. A string of sentries stood on top of
the nearby Tartar wall, whose high mass of stones dominated the
station. All precautions had been taken against attempts of assassination;
the throwing of a bomb, lately the Kemingtang's* favorite weapon,
was particularly feared. All doors had been locked, and in front of the
soldiers there stood only a group of Mandarins, in whose midst a
young man attracted attention. He was the only person present who
was wearing the ceremonial costume, and obviously had some difficulty
preserving the impassiveness prescribed by the ritual. He was Yuan's
eldest son. . . .

Among those waiting, there was not a single Manchu official, not
one member of the imperial family. Their complete absence was fully
indicative of the grave loss of face which Yuan's return, however much
implored, meant for the Court.

The European element was represented by three or four legation
secretaries and myself, standing on a bench. Our eyes were glued to
the track which ran parallel to the enormous Tartar wall, and we
waited impatiently for things to happen. Had the dismissed minister
changed his mind? . . . An endless hour went by in this fashion.

Finally, a locomotive pulling a great many cars entered the station,
but only soldiers got off the train, and immediately took their positions
in front of the soldiers already waiting on the platform. A few minutes
later, a second advanceguard convoy arrived, more soldiers descended
from it, and lined up on the other side of the platform. . . .

* Sun Yat-sen's party, or "party of the revolution".

A third train, carrying Yuan this time, but still full of soldiers of his personal guard, chugged slowly into the station. It had barely stopped when the soldiers, armed with rifles, jumped out of their cars; they dashed forward in a disorderly fashion, yet in a compact mass, and surrounded the car of their leader. After Yuan had in turn left the train and exchanged a few rapid words with his son, the soldiers surrounded and escorted him in such close formation that it looked as though he was being carried in the midst of a hugh bunch of bayonets. . . .

Yuan wore the traditional simple Chinese dress. He looked as vigorous as ever, but his hair had whitened during the four years since I had seen him last. While advancing in the midst of this vast display of brute force, he was beaming with satisfaction, but one could also discern on his face a trace of bewilderment and even some secret apprehension. Passing before our small group, he turned toward us and replied to our greetings with the somewhat theatrical smile of a gladiator entering the arena.[17]

The energetic Yuan Shih-k'ai thus became the arbiter of the situation. Under his able command, the imperial troops crossed the Yangtze and forced the "Republican army"* southward. The population remained passive, and it seemed that Yuan's superior means would soon give him victory. Hankow, starting point of the revolution, fell into his hands.

Yuan, however, had plans of his own. Instead of pursuing his campaign against the Republicans, he signed a truce with their leader Li Yuan-hung and delegated his lieutenant and adviser T'ang Shao-yi to open peace negotiations with them in Shanghai. Yuan meant to get rid of both the Manchus and the revolutionary government.

A race for the leadership of new China now began between Yuan and Sun Yat-sen. From Colorado, the latter had hurried back to his homeland via New York (where he learned that he was the President-designate of the Chinese Republic), London (where he was assured that the British government would not allow Japan to assist the Manchu dynasty), and Paris (where Premier Clemenceau received him very cordially). He arrived in Shanghai on Christmas Eve of 1911, and a week later was installed at Nanking as the first President of the United Provinces of China.

On January 5, 1912, Sun Yat-sen and his Foreign Minister Wu T'ing-

* Recruited mostly among jobless coolies and hungry farmers.

fang* *issued a Republican Manifesto which, in addition to denouncing Manchu "tyranny", pledged the Republic's goodwill and cooperation toward all "friendly" nations:*

Greeting.—The hitherto irremediable suppression of the individual qualities and national aspirations of the people having stifled the intellectual, the moral, and the material development of China, the aid of revolution has been invoked to extirpate the primary cause, and we now proclaim the resultant overthrow of the despotic sway wielded by the Manchu dynasty and the establishment of a Republic. . . .

The policy of the Manchu dynasty has been one of unequivocal seclusion and unyielding tyranny. Beneath it we have bitterly suffered, and we now submit to the free people of the world the reasons justifying the revolution and the inauguration of our present government.

Prior to the usurpation of the Throne by the Manchus the land was open to foreign intercourse and religious toleration existed, as is evidenced by the writings of Marco Polo and the inscription on the Nestorian tablet of Sian-fu.†. . .

They [the Manchus] have levied irregular and unwholesome taxes upon us without our consent, have restricted foreign trade to Treaty Ports. . . . They have retarded the creation of industrial enterprises, rendered impossible the development of natural resources. . . . They have repeatedly rejected our most reasonable demands for better government. . . .

The cultivation of better relations with foreign peoples and governments will ever be before us. It is our earnest hope that foreign nations who have been steadfast in sympathy will bind more firmly the bonds of friendship, that they will bear in patience with us in the period of trial confronting us in our reconstructive work, and that they will aid us in the consummation of the far-reaching plans which we are now about to undertake, and which they have been so long and so vainly urging upon the people of this our country.

With this message of peace and goodwill the Republic of China cherishes the hope of being admitted into the family of nations, not merely to share their rights and privileges but also to cooperate with

* A clever and influential diplomat who at the time lived in affluent retirement in Shanghai.

† Allusion to the existence of "Nestorian" Christians (named after Nestorius, patriarch of Constantinople, 428–31) in Shensi Province.

them in the great and noble task called for in the upbuilding of the civilization of the world.[18]

An altogether different document, inspired by the power-hungry Yuan Shih-k'ai, was the Abdication Edict by which the boy Emperor stepped down from the Manchu throne on February 12. After having pressed the Regent into resigning, Yuan asked one of his Cantonese lieutenants to draft the edict, in which the Dowager was made to say:

Today the people of the whole Empire have their minds bent upon a Republic, the Southern provinces having initiated the movement, and the Northern Generals having subsequently supported it. The will of Providence is clear and the people's wishes are plain. How could I, for the sake of the glory and the honour of one family, oppose the wishes of teeming millions? Wherefore, I, with the Emperor, decide that the form of government in China shall be a constitutional Republic, to comfort the longing of all within the Empire and to act in harmony with the ancient sages, who regarded the throne as a public heritage.[19]

Thus fell—with very little fuss—the last of the twenty-six historic dynasties of China, and thus ended a history more than three thousand years old. The terms granted to the fallen Manchus by the Republicans (among whom the Southerners dominated), were extremely generous,* and proved that their "despotic sway" had not been too cruel after all.

Sun Yat-sen and Yuan Shih-k'ai now stood out as the only two contenders for supreme leadership, and little by little their differing political views brought them into conflict. Sun was the champion of democratic republicanism aiming at a parliamentary regime, and possessed a majority in the Nanking provisional assembly; Yuan, on the other hand, desired a constitution vesting the power in his sole person, and was backed by the country's best divisions. Thanks to this military superiority, Yuan was able to impose himself on the assembly. The latter, in turn, believing that Yuan would be its prisoner, elected him President of the Republic in the place of Sun, who resigned in order to avoid civil war.

Instead of coming to Nanking, however, Yuan remained in Peking, where

---

* Hsuan T'ung was allowed to call himself the Manchu Emperor, and to enjoy the rank and privileges of a foreign sovereign residing on Chinese soil (in the Summer Palace!).

in 1913 the newly arrived American Minister, Paul S. Reinsch, got to know
him and gained an insight into his conception of a republic:

"My opponents are disloyal. They would pull down my government." He who spoke was cordial in his manner as he thus offhandedly
epitomized his theory of government.

Yuan Shih-k'ai, President of the Chinese Republic, was short of
stature and thickset; but his expressive face, his quick gestures, his
powerful neck and bullet head, gave him the appearance of great
energy. His eyes, which were fine and clear, alive with interest and
mobile, were always brightly alert. They fixed themselves on the
visitor with keen penetration, yet never seemed hostile; they were full
always of keen interest. . . . Frenchmen saw in him a resemblance to
Clemenceau; and this is borne out by his portrait which appears on
the Chinese dollar. In stature, facial expression, shape of head, contour
of features as well as in the manner of wearing his mustache, he did
greatly resemble the Tiger.

I had noted these things when I was first presented to the President,
and I had felt also the almost ruthless power of the man. Republican
in title he was, but an autocrat at heart. All the old glittering trappings
of the empire he had preserved. . . . I had passed between files of the
huge guardsmen of Yuan Shih-k'ai, who had Frederick the Great's
fondness for tall men; and I found him in the showy palace of the great
Empress Dowager, standing in the main throne hall to receive me.
He was flanked by thirty generals of his household, extended in wings
at both sides of him, and their uniforms made it a most impressive
scene.

But that was on an occasion of state. Later, at a more informal
interview . . . I observed Yuan's character more fully. He had just
expelled from Parliament the democratic party (Kuo Min Tang);
then he had summarily dismissed the Parliament itself. Feeling, perhaps,
a possible loss of American goodwill, he had sent for me to explain
his action.

"It was not a good parliament, for it was made up largely of inexperienced and young politicians," he began. "They wished to
meddle with the Government as well as to legislate on all matters.
Their real function was to adopt a permanent constitution for the
Republic, but they made no headway with that." And with much
truth he added: "Our traditions are very different from your Western

ones and our affairs are very complex. We cannot safely apply your abstract ideas of policy."

Of his own work of stirring up, through emissaries, internal and partisan controversies which prevented the new parliament from effectively organizing, Yuan of course omitted to speak. Moreover, he said little of the possibility of more closely co-ordinating the executive and the legislative branches; so while he avowed his desire to have a constitution forthwith, and to reconstitute Parliament by more careful selections under a new electoral law, I found myself thinking of his own career. His personal rule, his unscrupulous advancement to power, with the incidental corruption and cold-blooded executions that marked it, and his bitter personal feeling against all political opponents—these were not qualities that make for stable parliamentary government. . . .

"As you see," Yuan beamed eagerly, "the Chinese Republic is a very young baby. It must be nursed and kept from taking strong meat or potent medicines like those prescribed by foreign doctors." This metaphor he repeated with relish, his eyes sparkling as they sought mine and those of the other listeners to get their expressions of assent or reserve.[20]

Yuan's dictatorial manners inevitably brought him into conflict with the national assembly, consisting of three members from each of China's eighteen provinces. Two opposition parties were founded in the spring of 1912: Liang Ch'i-ch'ao's Harmony or Progress party, advocating a strong executive, and Sun Yat-sen's Kuomintang or Nationalist party,* championing the American-inspired system of parliamentary government.

The elected Parliament met in April 1913, and floundered along† until January 1914, when Yuan dissolved it. In July 1913, Sun Yat-sen organized the "Second Revolution" in the southern provinces, but it was brought to an end in August by the bloody capture of Nanking. Once more, Sun took the road into exile and, together with a good many Republican members of Parliament, became a refugee in Japan.‡ In October, Yuan had himself

* Also spelled Kuo Min Tang; literally, the "Party of the People and the Country".

† Two months after its convocation, it had not yet elected its principal officers.

‡ Where he married (in second wedlock) Miss Chung-ling Soong, daughter of a fellow revolutionist, and his junior by thirty-three years.

elected President of the Republic, and diplomatic recognition of the new Peking government was extended within days by all the leading powers.

The Chinese masses had remained indifferent to the changes, and though Republican sentiment was fairly widespread in southern cities, Yuan was for the time being firmly in control of state affairs. His position had been further enhanced in April 1913 by a loan of £25,000,000 which he secured from England, France, Russia, and Japan. In May 1914, a "constitutional compact" gave him a ten-year term of office, with wide powers.

But Yuan had still higher ambitions, and was contemplating the foundation of a new dynasty. With this in mind, he performed the age-old imperial rites of the Winter Solstice, which had been discontinued in 1911. A correspondent of the French quarterly L'Asie Française (organ of French interests in the Far East) witnessed the ceremony's revised version:

The lofty dignity and slow but precise unfolding of the rites, as prescribed by centuries of unviolated tradition, suffered greatly from Yuan's all too obvious fear of being assassinated. . . .

Instead of using a cortege of palanquins and ambling mules, always a picturesque spectacle, he drove to the Temple of Heaven* in an armored car. O shades of Ch'ien Lung† and of the illustrious dead! In the inner precincts and on the sacred ground itself, within sight of the White Altar, whose great simplicity strikingly symbolizes the fundamental dignity of China's old civilization, the head of the Republic behaved as on a battlefield. Protected by two rows of soldiers, he proceeded rapidly and silently along the broad avenue leading from the Imperial Palace to the entrance of the Temple, at the time when dawn broke over the city. His bodyguards galloped in front of him and behind him, and no civilian was allowed even to appear in the streets.

He observed none of the long watches in the Room of Fasts, prescribed by an uninterrupted tradition, nor any of the lengthy and complicated ceremonies which, in days past, preceded the final invocation to Heaven.

The President left his palace shortly after seven, and by half past eight he was back behind its well-guarded walls. The traditional

---

* Where the Emperors worshiped at dawn, sacrificing silk, jade cups, and bullocks to the Supreme Being. Today, the well-preserved Temple is a favorite sightseeing place with Chinese tourists.

† Well-known Manchu Emperor (1736–95).

sacrifice of a black bull had been dispensed with, and a number of ritual formalities had also been shortened. Naturally, the ceremony's solemnity suffered from such haste. The grandiose proceedings were overshadowed by the invisible presence of Young China, always ready to plot and assassinate. The pompous robes of the President, dressed as high priest, and of his retinue glittered brilliantly under the rising sun. The sacrificial music, the ablution ceremonial, and the solemn acts of the symbolic ritual did follow each other in normal succession, but within the time limits set by Yuan.

Meanwhile the armored car, an ominous reminder of the dangers created by Young China, was waiting and ready to take off, while the Imperial Avenue remained empty of people.[21]

Instead of bringing about the Republic dreamed by Sun Yat-sen and the Kuomintang, the Revolution of 1911 thus served the personal ambitions of a general. Yuan's dictatorship was not devoid of merits: by the end of 1914, China was a unified country held firmly in control through Yuan's military "sons".* Another—and significant—achievement for which the name of Yuan will be remembered was his successful campaign against the import and consumption of opium, as well as against poppy growing in China, particularly widespread in Yunnan and Shensi.

Yuan's ostentatious respect for ancestral rites—too lightly dismissed by the Republicans—won him the support of China's traditionalist rural masses and of the still-influential Mandarins. Following a monarchist campaign conducted by the Ch'ou An Hui, or "Society for the Preparation of Peace", then a referendum and an invitation from a hand-picked "National Convention" (December 1915), Yuan accepted the imperial office for the ensuing January 1st. However, growing opposition at home (a successful rising in Yunnan) and abroad made him postpone the coronation.

He died in June 1916—from chagrin according to some sources, poisoned according to others—and was succeeded by Li Yuan-hung, who promptly restored the Constitution of 1912 and convoked the original Parliament of 1913.

* Or disciples, who were bound to him by a strong protégé-patron relationship.

CHAPTER VIII

BETWEEN ANARCHY
AND RECONQUEST, 1917-1928

THE PERIOD of ten years or so which followed the death of Yuan Shih-k'ai was one of progressive collapse of both central and local government, with a concomitant increase in civil strife, banditry and anarchy. There arose no leader popular enough to command the loyalty of all the Chinese. Widespread corruption only hastened the general breakdown of authority. As traditional controls were removed, the selfish use of political power for private profit was accentuated. This in turn fostered rebellion and an increasing lack of confidence in the government.

China was now torn asunder by the ambitions and rivalries of her "war lords", none of whom proved strong or able enough to unite the country under his sway. Essentially, Chinese history during this confused decade is that of the struggle between the Republican party commanding Parliament and supported by the military governors of the South and the league of northern generals backed by the Manchu reactionary party.

Another important factor in the shaping of China's destiny at the time was the Russian Revolution of October 1917. Increasing numbers of Chinese leaders began turning to Soviet Russia for inspiration in solving their country's domestic and external problems. A "Society for the Study of Marxism" was founded in 1918 in Peking, and six years later Stalin's special envoy to China, Abram A. Joffe, officially assured Dr. Sun Yat-sen of the Russian people's "warmest sympathy" for China.

Traditional local feuds also erupted in violence and further increased China's domestic chaos. The British Consul, Sir Meyrick Hewlett, was well acquainted with the military governors or war lords of the central provinces:

Many of the War Lords had received their military training in

Japan. In the majority of cases they were completely indifferent to the misery and suffering they caused, and merely coveted position for the wealth it brought to their private pockets. Some were kept in position by their adherents, who relied on the success of their chiefs for their own prosperity. In a wealthy province like Szechuan, where the Salt Revenue alone produced from £80,000 to £140,000 a month, it was well worth while holding the position of Military Governor for a few months. They usually selected the large official residence of the Viceroys, Governors, Treasurers, Judges and other officials of the Manchu days for their headquarters. These residences comprised a series of spacious courtyards, large attendance halls, numerous private rooms and ample accommodation for the personal bodyguard. The entrance was always imposing with its sweeping curved roofs and huge solid wooden doors, and the wide courtyards, which had to be traversed before access to the reception rooms was attained, all added to the dignity of the habitat of the War Lord.

I am unable to speak for the rest of China, but in Szechuan these residences were well-kept, the guards were smart and discipline good. If you were a personal friend of the War Lord you were courteously received, usually with a guard of honour, but if you were unknown the sentries and attendants had a distinct tendency to be rude. I was always able to secure a private interview, though on certain occasions underlings and secretaries had an irritating way of hanging about.

It is a mistake to think of the War Lords as ill-clad, badly housed brigands. Far from it; practically all they did was on a grand scale, including the levying of taxes. They were delightful to meet, and the soul of generous hospitality. Moreover I found that if they trusted you it was fully and without reservation. If pure patriotism and not personal greed had been the foundation of their actions, I feel that with careful selection China could have easily produced some very great military leaders from among the War Lords, but by those who loved China most it was felt during the darkest hours of chaos between 1915 and 1925 that nothing but some great common national danger could ever weld China together, and even if that occurred the question of a leader who could guide the destinies of united China was still unsolved.[1]

During these "darkest hours of chaos", it was more or less possible to distinguish four different zones of influence, so to speak. In the south, especially in the Canton area, lay the stronghold of Sun Yat-sen; in the north the "Feng-tien clan", under Marshal Chang Tso-lin, held Manchuria from 1911 till 1928; and between Peking and the south, the "Ngan-fu clan", led by General Tuan Ch'i-jui and supported by Japan, was contending with the "Chihli clan" commanded by General Wu Pei-fu and backed by the Anglo-Americans. In addition, two provinces called themselves independent: Szechuan in the west, and Hunan in the country's very heart.

To a certain extent, the struggle between the Ngan-fu and the Chihli clans led to open contest between their respective foreign backers. Japan, in particular, whose aggressive designs grew bolder with each passing year, kept a sharp eye on all aspects of American activities in China. Contrary to other foreign powers, the United States had no territorial claims in China, and for this reason enjoyed a privileged position in the minds of the Chinese. In his memoirs, the American Minister to Peking, Paul S. Reinsch, recalled his country's positive influence—together with Japanese displeasure—on the eve of World War I:

The United States of America enjoys a position of great advantage for assisting the Chinese Government and influencing its development in the direction of free national life. The lack of a desire for political interference, the real sympathy felt in America with the strivings of the Chinese people, and cultural, educational, and charitable work unselfishly performed, have given the United States the undivided confidence of China. It is certainly true that the Chinese people are anxious to follow in the footsteps of the United States if they may only be permitted to do so. . . .

Among the specific American interests already existing in China, that of missionary and educational work had at this time to be given the first rank. . . . It is plainly the result of individual impulse on the part of a great many people animated by friendly motives, and not the result of a concerted plan of propaganda. . . . There is no trace of a desire to establish a permanent tutelage. An institution like the Y.M.C.A. acts with the sole thought of helping the Chinese to a better organization of their own social and educational life. . . . The Chinese have an intense respect for their educators, and it has been the good fortune of many Americans—men like Dr. W. A. P. Martin and Dr. Charles D. Tenney—to win the devoted loyalty of innumerable Chinese through their activity as teachers.

Among commercial enterprises the Standard Oil Company was carrying petroleum to all parts of China. It had introduced the use of the petroleum lamp, had extended the length of the day to the hundreds of millions of Chinese, and even its emptied tin cans had become ubiquitous in town and country, because of the manifold uses to which these receptacles could be put. For efficiency and close contact with the people, the Chinese organization of this great company was indeed admirable. . . .

The Bethlehem Steel Corporation had in 1910 concluded a contract with the Imperial Government for the construction of vessels to the value of $20,000,000. When I came to China, a vice-president of the corporation . . . was in Peking, ready to arrange with the republican government for a continuance of the contract. The American banking group was a partner in the Hukuang Railways, in which it shared with the British, French, and German groups. An American engineer was employed at the time in making a survey of a portion of the proposed line along the Yangtze River. . . . Prof. F. J. Goodnow of Columbia University, a recognized authority on constitutional law, had been retained [as adviser] by the Chinese Government and was at this time in residence at Peking. The Ministry of Communications on its part had sought a man familiar with railway accounting, and had called upon the late Prof. Henry C. Adams, the noted economist and railway expert of Michigan University. . . .

One evening, we were guests of the manager of the Russo-Asiatic Bank. An amateur theatrical performance was in progress. . . . In the intermission between two plays I encountered the Japanese minister, and, finding that he desired to talk, wandered with him to the smoking room. . . . Mr. Yamaza was more talkative than I had ever seen him. As was his custom, he had consumed ardent waters quite freely, but, as always, his mind was clear and alert. "In Shensi and Chihli province," he opened up, "the exertions of Japanese nationals in the matter of the concession to the Standard Oil Company have given them a right to be considered. I have been contending to the Chinese that Japan has a prior interest in the oil field of Shensi Province. Do you not know that Japanese engineers were formerly employed there?"

On my part, I expressed surprise that the Japanese papers should make so much noise about the American oil concession, whereas it was quite natural that Americans, who had done business in China for over a century, should occasionally go into new lines of enterprise.

But it soon became manifest that Mr. Yamaza was thinking of the Bethlehem Steel contract. "I must tell you," he said, "of the strategical importance of Fukien Province to my country." Then followed a long exposition. "China," he concluded, "has promised not to alienate this province to any other power, and Japan has repeatedly asserted an interest in that region. . . . The grant to Americans," the Japanese minister remarked, "seems to indicate that China does not care much about the international friendship of Japan."[2]

The outbreak of World War I gave Japan an ideal and unique opportunity for the execution of some of her ambitious projects on Chinese territory. While China declared herself neutral in the conflict, Japan declared war on Germany (August 23, 1914) and a few weeks later captured the German-held port of Tsingtao, in Shantung. It was only the beginning of a vast design subsequently known as "Greater Asiatic Japan", and which aimed at eliminating the Western powers from China.

The first blow fell on January 18, 1915, when the Japanese Minister, calling privately on Yuan Shih-k'ai, presented him with "21 Demands" amounting to an economic monopoly over China. Japan's unilateral action surprised and shocked the European powers, but they were in no position to stop the Japanese, and the latter knew it. In vain did China turn to President Woodrow Wilson for assistance. He refrained from intervening because of the United States policy of neutrality, and also, as he wrote to Paul S. Reinsch, because "direct intervention . . . would very likely provoke the jealousy and excite the hostility of Japan, which would first be manifested against China herself". Naturally, the Chinese were deeply disappointed by the negative attitude of the United States.

In spite of the bitter resentment caused in China by the brazen Japanese claims, Yuan Shih-k'ai eventually gave way, and in May 1915 bowed to a Japanese ultimatum by accepting a modified version of the original demands.* From that moment Chinese hatred of foreigners was concentrated mainly on the "dwarf bandits", and China looked upon Japan as her most dangerous adversary and the greatest menace to her integrity.

Paul S. Reinsch noted the far-reaching consequences of the twenty-one demands in his memoirs:

Mr. Liang Tun-yen, Minister of Communications, called on me on

---

* In this new version, Japan insisted on succeeding to German rights in Shantung; demanded an extension to ninety-nine years of the leases in southern Manchuria, with commercial freedom; a half interest in Hupeh iron mines and steel mills, and in a Szechuan colliery; and assurance that no part of China's coast should be leased or ceded to any power.

October 1st [1914], expressing deep concern over the action of the Japanese in Shantung. He stated his conviction that, in departing from the necessary military operations around Tsingtao, it was Japan's plan to stir up trouble in the interior of China with a view to more extensive occupation of Chinese territory. From Japanese sources he had information to the effect that the Japanese militarists were not satisfied with the reduction of Tsingtao, but wished to take advantage of this opportunity to secure a solid foothold—political and military—within the interior of China. . . .

President Yuan Shih-k'ai had wished to see me; so I called on him informally on October 2nd. In stronger terms than Minister Liang he set forth his apprehensions. "From information in my possession," he stated, "I am convinced that the Japanese have a definite and far-reaching plan for using the European crisis to further an attempt to lay the foundations of control over China. In this, the control of Shantung through the possession of the port and the railway is to be the foundation stone. Their policy was made quite apparent through the threatened occupation of the entire Shantung Railway, which goes far beyond anything the Germans ever attempted in Shantung Province. It will bring the Japanese military forces to the very heart of China.". . .

The Chinese people were becoming more and more alarmed about Japan in Shantung. The large number of petitions and manifestoes which came to me, as the representative of a friendly nation, from various parts of China, gave me an idea of how widespread was this anxiety. Some of these protests were written with the blood of the petitioner. . . . The Chinese felt that any understanding with Japan would inevitably lead to the total subjection of China to the political dominance of her neighbor. They distrust all professions of Japanese friendship. Whenever I tried to argue that a frank understanding between China and Japan was desirable, I was told that China could not trust Japan; that Japan must not be judged by her professions, but by her past acts, all of which show a determined policy of political advance veiled by reassuring declarations.

Thus the Chinese feared Japanese intrigue at every point. They believed that revolutionary activities, as in the past, were getting encouragement from Japan. The Japanese were ready to take advantage of and aggravate any weakness which might exist in Chinese social and political life. They would fasten like leeches upon any sore spot. . . .

It was plain that the Russians, too, while allied with Japan, were quite aware of the dangers inherent in the Chinese situation. Taken with recent Japanese advances in Inner Mongolia, a situation was created in northern China which would be regarded as dangerous by the Russians. Discussing the unrest in China, the Russian Minister said to me significantly: "The situation itself does not impress me as serious; the only serious thing about it is that the Japanese say it is serious.". . .

It was not until January 22nd [1915] that I learned the astonishing nature of the Japanese proposals. Calling on one of the Chinese ministers on current business, I found him perturbed. He finally confided to me, almost with tears, that Japan had made categorical demands which, if conceded, would destroy the independence of his country and reduce her to a servile state. He then told me in general terms their nature, saying: "Control of natural resources, finances, army! What will be left to China? Our people are being punished for their peacefulness and sense of justice." The blow evidently had come with stunning force, and the counselors of the President had not been able to overcome the first terrified surprise, or to develop any idea as to how the crisis might be met. . . .

The British, who had more extensive interests at stake than any other foreign nation, had shown agitation. British residents and officials expressed deep concern because their government, being necessarily preoccupied with events in Europe, could not give full attention to the Far East. As the action of Japan had been taken under the aegis of the Anglo-Japanese Alliance, it seemed to the British that this was being used to nullify any influence which Great Britain might exercise, as against a plan on the part of Japan to seize control of the immense resources of China and of her military establishment. . . .

This policy of Japan deeply affected American prospects and enterprise in China, as, also, that of the other leading nations.[3]

The post-1911 period of China's history was not only marked by the dominant role of her war lords, and by Japan's growing interference in her domestic affairs. The fall of the empire, and the rejection of age-old traditions which it had symbolized, also led to a deep crisis within Chinese civilization. China's intelligentsia was now faced with one great—and new—problem: how to determine and define the values and goals of the Republican regime. While the political scene was marked by anarchy and violence, remarkable efforts toward the ideological reconstruction of Chinese life were pursued by the country's leading scholars. It was a strange contrast indeed.

Discussions and conflicts of opinion developed over such fundamental problems as the relationship between the material and spiritual aspects of life, the merits of materialism and nationalism, the meaning of the scientific method, the choice between Westernization and national traditions, and—last but not least—the doctrines of socialism, anarchism, and communism.

The leading liberal scholar of early Republican China was Ts'ai Yuan-p'ei, who had received a traditional Chinese education and was at the same time well versed in Western philosophy.* From 1917 till 1927, he was Chancellor of Peking National University, and as such gathered around him a group of intellectuals who awakened the younger generation to its new tasks and duties. Ch'en Tu-hsiu, in particular, who in 1916 became Dean of the School of Letters of Peking University, exercised a tremendous influence over the rising generation of Chinese students. Ch'en himself was deeply influenced by French culture,† and in 1915 had founded the monthly magazine La Jeunesse,‡ in which he denounced Confucian formality and conformism, while at the same time stressing the decisive importance of science and democracy.

There was also Hu Shih, a close associate of Ch'en, and who had spent seven years in the United States, where he had become a disciple of the internationally known philosopher and educator John Dewey. As Professor of Philosophy and Chairman of the Department of English Literature at Peking University, the brilliant and controversial Dr. Hu championed the written vernacular, or pai-hua, as a literary medium.

Lu-hsiun, China's greatest writer in this century, was also living in Peking at the time. Between 1918 and 1925, he published a series of novels accurately describing his country's troubles and travail.

In his popular "Call to Youth" issued in 1915, Ch'en Tu-hsiu proposed six sweeping principles for the guidance of the rising generation:

Youth is like early spring, like the rising sun, like trees and grass in bud, like a newly sharpened blade. It is the most valuable period of

---

* He was a member of the Hanlin Academy, and had studied at the University of Leipzig, Germany.

† He had studied in France from 1907 till 1910, and there became a revolutionary.

‡ French subtitle, the publication's Chinese title being Hsin-ch'ing-nien, or "New Youth".

life. The function of youth in society is the same as that of a fresh and vital cell in a human body. . . .

As for understanding what is right and wrong, in order that you may make your choice, I carefully propose the following six principles, and hope you will give them your calm consideration.

1. *Be independent, not servile*

All men are equal. Each has his right to be independent, but absolutely no right to enslave others nor any obligation to make himself servile. . . . I have hands and feet, and I can earn my own living. I have a mouth and a tongue, and I can voice my own likes and dislikes. I have a mind, and I can determine my own beliefs. I will absolutely not let others do these things on my behalf, nor should I assume an overlordship and enslave others. . . .

2. *Be progressive, not conservative*

"Without progress there will be retrogression" is an old Chinese saying. . . . All our traditional ethics, law, scholarship, rites and customs are survivals of feudalism. When compared with the achievements of the white race, there is a difference of a thousand years in thought, although we live in the same period. . . . I would much rather see the past culture of our nation disappear than see our race die out now because of its unfitness for living in the modern world. Alas, the days of the Babylonians are past. . . .

3. *Be aggressive, not retiring*

. . . If your aim is to influence the people and establish a new tradition, I suggest that you make further progress from your present high position. It is impossible to avoid the struggle for survival, and so long as one draws breath there can be no place where one can retire for a tranquil hermit's life. . . .

4. *Be cosmopolitan, not isolationist*

Any change in the economic or political life of one nation will usually have repercussions over the whole world, just as the whole body is affected when one hair is pulled. . . . Take the recent events of our country as evidence: Japan suddenly rose in power, and stimulated our revolutionary and reform movements; the European War broke out, and then Japan presented her demands to us; is this not clear proof? When a nation is thrown into the currents of the world, traditionalists will certainly hasten the day of its fall, but those capable of change will take this opportunity to compete and progress. . . .

5. Be utilitarian, not formalist

The social system and the thought of Europe have undergone a change since J. S. Mill's advocacy of utilitarianism in England and Comte's advocacy of positivism in France. More recently their system and thought have undergone another change, with the great advancement of science in Germany, where material civilization has reached its pinnacle of achievement. . . . If we do not restring our bow and renew our effort, there will be no way to revive the strength of our nation, and our society will never see a peaceful day. As for praying to gods to relieve flood and famine, or reciting the *Book of Filial Piety* to ward off the Yellow Turbans*—people are not infants or morons, and they see through these absurdities. . . . That which brings no benefit to the practical life of an individual or of society is all empty formalism and the stuff of cheats. And even though it were bequeathed to us by our ancestors, taught by the sages, advocated by the government and worshiped by society, the stuff of cheats is still not worth one cent.

6. Be scientific, not imaginative

. . . There was only imagination and no science in the unenlightened days of old, as well as among the uncivilized peoples of today. . . . Our scholars . . . our farmers . . . our industrialists do not know science. . . . Our merchants . . . our physicians know no science. . . . All these nonsensical ideas and unreasonable beliefs can be cured at the root only by science. For to explain truth by science means proving everything with fact. Although the process is slower than that of imagination and arbitrary decision, yet every step taken is on firm ground; it is different from those imaginative flights which eventually cannot advance even one inch. The amount of truth in the universe is boundless, and the fertile areas in the realm of science awaiting the pioneer are immense! Youth, take up the task![4]

Chinese political life, meanwhile, went on in an atmosphere of growing confusion and anarchy. Two important events—an abortive attempt at restoring the Manchu dynasty, and China's declaration of war against Germany and Austria–Hungary—took place in 1917.

* Current phrase for bandits.

*The unsuccessful restoration of the boy Emperor (who had abdicated in 1912) was conducted by a northern general, Chang Hsün, whose troops still wore the pigtail reminiscent of Manchu domination. The attempt was defeated within less than two weeks (July 1-12), and a protégé of the late Yuan Shih-k'ai, Marshal Feng Kuo-chang, became President of the Republic. At about the same time (September 1917), a secession government under Sun Wen (Sun Yat-sen) was established at Canton.**

Peking declared war on Germany and Austria–Hungary in August, 1917. Chinese labor battalions were sent to France, Mesopotamia, and Africa. Canton, however, refused to follow suit; its reasons for remaining neutral in the world-wide conflict were expounded in a much-publicized telegram which Sun Yat-sen sent to the British Prime Minister, Lloyd George:

Both as a Chinese patriot and as a grateful friend of England, to whom I owe my life, I consider it my duty to point out to you the regrettable consequences to China and to England which will follow the agitation created by certain of your agents with the object of inducing China to enter the European conflict. . . . I have come to the conclusion that a rupture of Chinese neutrality would be disastrous to both our countries. China is still in her infancy, she still needs much care; and if internal discord were to break out, anarchy would quickly break her up.

Up to the present China has had unlimited faith in the strength and in the ultimate triumph of England, but since this agitation, carried on by well-intentioned but shortsighted people, has been started, certain English dailies even desiring the dispatch of several Chinese divisions to Mesopotamia, this confidence has been greatly shaken. The entry of China into the war would be dangerous to her existence as a nation and would lessen the prestige of England in the Far East. The mere wish to induce China to join the Allies appears to Chinese minds as an avowal of the incapacity of the Allies to end matters with Germany. . . . This question has already raised bitter dissensions among our statesmen. Discord may entail anarchy, which in China evokes two formidable elements, hatred of the foreigners and the Muslims. Since our Revolution the feeling of hatred for the foreigner has nearly disappeared, but a spirit of hostility with regard to strangers still

---

* This schism between the governments of Peking and Canton dominated Chinese politics until 1927, when the Kuomintang under General Chiang Kai-shek set up a new government at Nanking.

exists, and might in these critical times give rise to another Boxer movement, and to a general massacre of the Europeans. If war is declared against a particular power, the ignorant masses will not distinguish its nationals from those of the other powers, and the consequences of this confusion would be all the more fatal to England, since she has the largest interests in the Far East.

Neither can one fail to take account of the Muslims, who look upon it as sacrilege to fight against their Holy Land.* But the worst result of the anarchy in China would be, I fear, to provoke dissensions in the group of the Entente which would be a disaster for their cause. Under these conditions it cannot be expected that China will do otherwise than maintain a strict neutrality.[5]

Sun Yat-sen's apprehensions, unfortunately, were largely borne out by the proceedings and results of the Treaty of Versailles. Not only did it fail to return the former German concessions in Shantung to China, but it confirmed Japan's gains in that strategic province. In this the treaty actually sanctioned the previous Lansing-Ishii Agreement†by which the United States had recognized the "special interests" of Japan in China—against empty Japanese pledges of maintaining China's integrity and independence.

As a result, China refused to sign the treaty, and a fairly effective boycott of Japanese goods was organized throughout the country. Chinese resentment was the stronger as the nation felt abandoned by President Wilson himself, in whom its leaders had placed high hopes. An embarrassed and apprehensive American Minister at Peking wrote:

Probably nowhere else in the world had expectations of America's leadership at Paris been raised so high as in China. The Chinese trusted America, they trusted the frequent declarations of principle uttered by President Wilson, whose words had reached China in its remotest parts. The more intense was their disappointment and disillusionment due to the decisions of the old men that controlled the Peace Confer-

* Turkey. Chinese Muslims are a majority in the country's western provinces, where they constitute a "national minority". Groups of Muslims also exist throughout most of China's 18 provinces, and probably number as many as 40 million souls. Communist China, however, denies this fact, as she wishes to recognize only the existence of a western minority race.

† Signed in November 1917, between the U. S. Secretary of State Robert Lansing and Viscount Ishii, of Japan, and often considered as one of the weakest and most mistaken documents of American diplomacy.

ence. It sickened and disheartened me to think how the Chinese people would receive this blow which meant the blasting of their hopes and the destruction of their confidence in the equity of nations.

In the universal despair I feared a revulsion of feeling against America; not because we were more to blame than others for the unjust decision, but because the Chinese had entertained a deeper belief in our power, influence, and loyalty to principle. They would hardly understand so abject and complete a surrender. Foreign papers, also, placed the chief responsibility on the United States. The British in China felt that their government had been forced into the unfortunate secret agreements with Japan when it could not help itself, because of the German danger and the difficulties Japan might raise by going over to the other side. The United States, whose hands were free, could have saved us all, they said, by insisting on the right solution. They had really hoped for this; their saying so now in their editorials and in private conversation was in no spirit of petty hostility, but they had to give vent to their feelings. I feared the Chinese might feel that they had been betrayed in the house of their friends, but they met the blow with sturdy spirit. They never wounded my feelings by anything approaching an upbraiding of the United States for the part that President Wilson played at Paris. They expressed to me their terrible dejection, but said merely that President Wilson must have encountered very great difficulties which they could know nothing about.

They all knew, of course, that the case of China had been weakened by the treaties made through the connivance of Tsao Ju-lin and his associates in the fall of 1918.* Their resentment was turned toward Japan, which had thus taken advantage of the war and the weakness of China, and against the Chinese politicians who had become Japan's tools.

The Americans in China, as well as the British and the Chinese, were deeply dejected during these difficult weeks. From the moment America entered the war there had been a triumphant confidence that all this sacrifice and suffering would establish just principles of world action, under which mankind could live more happily and in greater security. That hope was now all but crushed.[6]

This second blow to Republican China's honor and self-respect was felt even more deeply than the humiliation resulting from Japan's twenty-one

* Tsao Ju-lin, then China's Vice-Foreign Minister, had conducted negotiations with Japan; many Chinese patriots considered him a traitor.

demands. In addition to being infuriated by the unfair treatment given their country at Versailles, the Chinese also realized—for the first time perhaps—that they stood alone in a cynical and profit-seeking world. Their "confidence in the equity of nations" was lost indeed.

A spontaneous wave of indignation, spearheaded and then organized by the students—soon supported by the merchants—swept the country. It was the first time in China's long history that public opinion was aroused and organized on a nationwide basis. The movement started with the "explosion" of May 4, 1919, which, appropriately enough, was initiated by the students of Peking University marking the anniversary of the presentation of Japan's ultimatum of 1915, which they called "National Shame Day".

On that day, some ten thousand boys and girls from primary to university age, carrying banners inscribed with patriotic slogans,* marched in ordered ranks down the broad artery leading to the legation quarter in order to ask sympathy from the plenipotentiaries of the Allies (still gathered at Versailles). They were turned back by the legation police, and subsequently stormed and wrecked the residence of Tsao Ju-lin, Minister of Finance. Some twenty "leaders" were arrested and jailed.

A student of Peking University, who participated in the May 4th demonstration, described his feelings and those of his friends:

I was a student of the National University at this time. I could feel the great unrest among our students. We were greatly discouraged. During the Armistice of 1918 we had been quite hopeful. We thought that now all of the nations had learned a lesson. Accordingly, on November 30, 1918, the students of our university held a great mass meeting at the National Central Park in Peking. The main subject was "Anti-Militarism". And in January, 1919, the students of the University who were publishing *The Renaissance*,† also emphasized this point. "If the world does not want to give up militarism," they said, "China should lead the world, doing so first."

But when the news of the Paris Peace Conference finally reached us we were greatly shocked. We at once awoke to the fact that foreign nations were still selfish and militaristic and that they were all great liars. I remember that in the evening of May 2nd very few of us slept.

* Such as, "We do not recognize the 21 demands", "Give us back Tsingtao", "Please protect our national territory".

† Periodical expounding the ideas of Young China, and insisting upon human brotherhood and peaceful coexistence.

I and a group of my friends talked almost the whole night. We came to the conclusion that a greater world war would be coming sooner or later, and this greater world war would be fought in the East. We had nothing to do with our government, that we knew very well, and at the same time we could no longer depend upon the principle of any so-called great leader like Woodrow Wilson, for example. Looking at our poor people and at the pitiful ignorant masses, we couldn't help but feel that we must struggle.[7]

The May Fourth Movement, or "Student Revolution", as it has also been called, spread across China with remarkable speed. "Students' Unions" sprang up in every large city. The schools were deserted, while the boys and girls went into the streets and village marts to arouse the people. Protest groups were organized in practically every walk of Chinese life, and the masses of the people were marshaled for action. It was, historically speaking, the second great popular Chinese demonstration against foreign interference and oppression, the first being the Boxer uprising.

Throughout the month of May, 1919, student demonstrations, strikes, and a general boycotting of Japanese goods kept Chinese authorities in a constant state of alarm. Hundreds of arrests were made, but in many cases the students converted their jailers. The crowds, too, sided with the students.

One of the most interested foreign spectators witnessing these events was Professor John Dewey, whom many Chinese students knew well. In a letter from Peking, dated June 1, 1919, he wrote:

We have just seen a few hundred girls march away from the American Board Mission School to go to see the President* and to ask him to release the boy students who are in prison for making speeches in the street. To say that life in China is exciting is to put it fairly. We are witnessing the birth of a nation, and birth always comes hard. . . .

Yesterday we went to see the temples of the Western Hills, conducted by one of the members of the Ministry of Education. As we were returning along the big street that passes the city wall we saw students speaking to groups of people. This was the first time the students have appeared for several days. . . . This morning when we got the paper it was full of nothing else. The worst thing is that the

---

* Meaning the President of the Republic, "Old" Hsü Shih-ch'ang, who had been elected in the summer of 1918 by a newly elected Parliament.

University has been turned into a prison with military tents all around it and a notice on the outside that this is a prison for students who disturb the peace by making speeches. As this is all illegal, it amounts to a military seizure of the University and therefore all the faculty will have to resign. . . . The other thing we heard was that in addition to the two hundred students locked up in the Law Building, two students were taken to the police rooms and flogged on the back. These two students were making speeches and were arrested and taken before the officers of the gendarmes. Instead of shutting up as they were expected to do, the boys asked some questions of these officers that were embarrassing to answer. The officers then had them flogged on the back. . . . We saw students making speeches this morning about eleven . . . and heard later that they had been arrested and that . . . there are about ten thousand striking in Peking alone.

The marching out of these girls was evidently a shock to their teachers and many mothers were there to see them off. The girls were going to walk to the palace of the President, which is a long distance from the school. If he does not see them, they will remain standing outside all night and they will stay there until he does see them. I fancy people will take them food.[8]

Eventually, and under growing public pressure, the government had to give way. The jailed students were released with apologies, and the Chinese officials who in 1918 had negotiated a rapprochement with Japan were dismissed with orders to stand trial (after they were safely in Japan!). Also, the government announced that it would support the policy of its delegates in Paris—who refused to sign the peace treaty.

Thus the May Fourth Movement ushered in a new era of Chinese history, and may be regarded as the beginning of actual modern history for China. As Ambassador Reinsch noted in his memoirs, "out of the evil of the Paris decision came an inspiring national awakening of the Chinese people, a welding together for joint thought and joint action".

For the first time in her long history, China had roused herself and wrung from her government a specific surrender. True, that government had little authority over the country at large, being all too often a tool in the hands of war lords; and yet national public opinion had been organized for positive action. In the face of foreign encroachments, too, the China of 1919 presented a united front with a definite purpose. Instead of fanatics exploiting the super-

stitions of ignorant masses, as had been the case during the Boxer rebellion, Chinese anti-foreignism now was led by well-educated young men inspired by truly patriotic and justifiable motives.

The student movement also produced a cultural revolution, a kind of renaissance known as Hsin Ch'ao, or "New Tide". Many schemes for a better educational system, and for improving the condition of the masses* sprang up in the early twenties. Finally, the young energy released by the student movement was partly channeled into a new, and more or less intellectual, form of anti-foreignism sometimes tinged with anti-Christianism (even though students of Christian institutions were foremost in the May Fourth explosion).† This new attitude was defined by a young scholar from Shanghai, where students, merchants and artisans had displayed an impressive unity of purpose in their anti-Japanese campaign:

The term "anti-foreignism" naturally suggests its opposite, "foreignism". The latter has been the order of the day; the former now sets in as its reaction. By "foreignism" is meant the attitude to worship all foreigners, to accept their words blindly; by "anti-foreignism" is meant the negation of "foreignism"—the attempt at self-reliance and freedom from foreign influence. The prevalent feeling in China has been that foreigners as such are superior to the Chinese; it is this feeling which sets China to be a pupil of the West. The result is material improvement, but spiritual degeneration. Man in China begins to lose his self-respect, becomes a mere imitator. Now sets in the opposing movement; man begins to feel that, after all, all men are equal, that foreigners, too, have their imperfections, and that we need not feel humiliated before them. . . .

"Anti-foreignism" has nothing in it which will endanger foreign interests in China. Its main attack is leveled against those of our own brethren who have so lost their self-respect as to acknowledge foreigners their masters in everything. If it attacks foreigners at all, it merely attacks those who have the impudence to assume a superior air and look down upon all Chinese. As foreigners help us, we honor them;

---

* Such as free "people's schools" for illiterate adults and poor children, which students organized in marketplaces, temples, etc; and the "Citizen Education" campaign co-sponsored by the Y.M.C.A., the guilds, and the Kuomintang in the southern provinces.

† There were at the time about half a million Protestants and two million Catholics in China; the Y.M.C.A. was the "civic club" of many towns.

as they love us, we love them in return, but as they despise us, we hate them. Time there has been when foreigners, taking advantage of our ignorance, trampled our rights under foot; but let bygones be bygones. It is hoped that our foreign friends will cease to treat China as a partially civilized nation, or to feel themselves in any way superior to the Chinese. Then and only then the East and West can live harmoniously together and cooperate toward the progress of common humanity.[9]

China's national revulsion of 1919 served as a warning to foreign powers, and was not without influence on the Washington Conference (November 1921 to February 1922) called by President Warren G. Harding to discuss naval limitation, as well as problems affecting the Pacific and the Far East. The ensuing Nine Power Treaty* guaranteed China's sovereignty, independence, and territorial and administrative integrity; maintained the "Open Door"; and secured the evacuation of Japanese troops from Shantung.† For her part, England announced the return of Wei-hai-wei, or Weihai—actually effected in 1930.

During the years immediately following the Washington Conference, Chinese authorities, often backed by popular demonstrations, became increasingly aggressive in their demands for the abolition of "unequal treaties" and the revision of custom tariffs. Anti-foreign strikes became a familiar feature in the life of China's numerous harbor cities. They culminated in the spring of 1925 in a series of anti-Japanese and anti-British outbreaks which had particularly ugly undertones in Shanghai, Canton, and Hong Kong.

Bloodshed occurred on May 30th at Shanghai, in what was to become widely known as the "Shanghai incident" (Western version) or the "Shanghai massacre" (Chinese version). The trouble started in the International Settlement with student demonstrations protesting the death of a Chinese laborer in a Japanese-owned cotton mill.‡ They ended in a clash with the British police, during which nine students were killed. Photographs of the dead bodies were sent all over the country and students were urged to rise against the "British tyrants".

* England, France, Italy and Japan were invited to discuss naval limitation; in addition, Belgium, Holland, Portugal and China discussed Far Eastern affairs.

† Japan, however, remained in Shantung by means of her participation in the province's important mining and industrial enterprises.

‡ China's industrialization began with cotton spinning, which was introduced by the British and developed by Japanese and native capital.

The British Consul Sir Meyrick Hewlett, who had recently been transferred from central China to Amoy, now went through "one of the worst situations" he was ever called upon to face:

I crossed the harbour early on the morning of 6th June, 1925, about an hour before the time I had been told the [student] demonstration was to take place. . . . It was headed by young fellows in firemen's helmets, short-sleeved dark shirts, shorts, black stockings and black shoes. They carried red-and-white pennons on lances and were picturesque enough if one's mind had not been fixed on matters weightier than a pleasing spectacle. The procession proper was composed of scholars, boys and girls, down to tiny mites of very young age. They were accompanied by riff-raff out for mischief. Headed by Shanghai agitators they yelled slogans: "Annihilate the Imperialists",* "Abolish Consuls", "Give us back the Concessions", "Britons have slain our compatriots in Shanghai", "Remember China's shame". These slogans were also written on flags which had been smeared in blood in many cases and with further slogans calling on their compatriots to avenge the martyrs of Shanghai. . . . All the schools were represented in the procession; and as I have said even girls' schools and tiny children. The passionate hatred which the leaders strove to rouse in even the smallest hearts affected me more than any ideas of patriotism which underlay the movement. . . .

As I had to get across the harbor again to return to my office, I could not wait till the demonstrators had all passed. I chose my time, however, and selected a girls' school as the safest contingent to cross in order to get to my gig. One of the principal agitators glowered at me, but I was not molested.

The same afternoon a selected body of students who had organized and led the demonstration called on me and indulged in very wild talk. They had previously been to see the Japanese Consul, who said the matter was no concern of his. . . . I like to recall that this interview ended happily. They returned to a meeting which was awaiting their report and frankly stated they had been shown every courtesy and that they were not prepared to demonstrate further. . . .

During the height of the anti-British demonstrations I went alone

---

* There was at the time considerable talk of "Bolshevist influence," but the strike at the cotton mill was probably due more to tough methods used by Japanese foremen than to Red propaganda.

with my Chinese clerk ... to a school which was holding a meeting to discuss further disturbances. For an hour and a half I answered questions till, when some of the more truculent were getting offensive, one of the leaders said the British Consul came voluntarily, he has shown extreme patience and politeness and also he is our guest, I will not have any more questions asked. . . .

In spite of the apparently peaceful ending of the first demonstration we were by no means out of the wood. Anti-British pamphlets literally poured forth; posters were freely displayed all over the native city, showing students being murdered in the streets of Shanghai, and wild appeals were made to all to rise against the British tyrants. The General in command of the troops in an inland town near by stated that he was ready to declare war on Great Britain and forbade the entry of any British goods into places under his immediate jurisdiction. Students went so far as to examine postal parcels and, if they contained British goods, to throw them into the harbour. Stocks, too, of cigarettes belonging to the British-American Tobacco Company were burnt; for these Captain Lin* ultimately paid compensation.

It was perhaps small wonder that the majority of Britons desired naval protection, but I was so convinced that the presence of one of H.M. ships would cause a wild explosion and further relied so implicitly on Captain Lin that I rigidly adhered to my determination to place the whole responsibility of affording protection on the Chinese authorities. This attitude led to a certain amount of unpleasantness, and on one occasion a leading Briton stormed into my office and accused me of gambling with the lives of their women and children. I told him if he did not feel they were safe to send them to Hong Kong, that he appeared to want brandy, bayonets and blood, and I was determined he should not have them.

As, however, massed meetings were frequently being held by merchants, students, Labor Societies and all sorts of new Societies such as "Root Out the Tyrants" Society, I felt steps must be taken to check the growing discontent, and as I was reliably informed that a Boycott Committee had been formed by the merchants and a Strike Committee by the Labour Guilds, I determined to see the Chairman of the Chamber of Commerce who was a great personal friend of mine.[10]

Thanks to his typically British composure and also to the help of his

* Local commander in chief, and a friend of the British Consul.

Chinese friends, Hewlett succeeded in maintaining peace, and "for a few days all went well". Toward the end of the month of June, however, and under the impulsion of the Shanghai agitators who had so far been "disappointed in their desire to leave their bones in Amoy", new demonstrations broke out. Fortunately for British interests, they too were eventually called off:

The demonstration was followed by a memorial demonstration on 30th June, the first month after the Shanghai Incident. It followed the lines of the first demonstrations, the leaders with their heads swathed in cloths, foaming at the mouth and leaping in mad frenzy; but they received little response, and Chinese marines kept the agitators and their immediate following from the main procession. The boycott was then finally instituted and a general strike was also pending. I redoubled my efforts against the strike, working through every channel I knew, but I could not persuade the peace-loving majority to impose their wills on the noisy minority. I was, however, able to persuade the Labour Guilds that agitators had nothing to lose by creating disturbances, that Labour alone suffered, and it was among the Labour groups that I saw glimmerings of the development of healthy public opinion. In fact the boatmen's guild refused to strike unless they were guaranteed $30 a month instead of the $9 offered them by the student leaders.

I knew that a strike fund had been formed, and I also learned from friendly sources that the Chinese in the Netherlands East Indies were making a collection to send to this fund. I therefore went to the Chairman of the Chamber of Commerce and asked him why he did not send the strike funds to the general fund at Shanghai, pointing out that as no blood had been shed in Amoy and Amoy was consequently known as the city of shame, they might redeem their reputation by such an action. I knew that whereas $10,000 and whatever might come from Batavia* was dangerous in Amoy, it could mean nothing when sunk in the hundreds of thousands, if not millions, collected in Shanghai. Not knowing money was coming from Batavia he took my advice, and when the Batavian subscription came it was useless and was also sent on. The strikers thus had no funds to fall back on.[11]

In Canton and Hong Kong, the anti-foreign strikes (which lasted for

* Former capital of the Dutch East Indies, the Jakarta of today.

several months) were more massive—and therefore effective—as they were
actively supported by both the Kuomintang and the rapidly growing Com-
munist groups organized by the Russian "advisers" Borodin and Galen.

The Hong Kong banks suspended all payments, and the harbor was all
but paralyzed. A French diplomat, Paul Morand, was one of many foreigners
who witnessed the Crown Colony's momentary decline:

Hong Kong is falling asleep. In Shanghai, I have already seen a
greater number of expensive warships than useful steamers plying the
muddy and brownish water of the Yangtze. "The God of war is great,"
says a Chinese proverb, "but a sapek is greater than the God of war."
The port of Hong Kong, which is British crown territory, is all but
deserted. All the cargo boats are immobilized on its quiet waters,
their merchandise being piled up on the piers, or still waiting down
in the hold. Following mysterious orders given by the Chinese labor
unions, a strike of coolies has broken out and was immediately successful in all ports. A quarter hour after our arrival in Yokohama, the
first Japanese port where we anchored on our journey from America,
the thousand Chinese crew members of our proud *Empress*—queen
of the Pacific—dropped their bags on the ground and abandoned the
passengers.

In Hong Kong, even the officers' residences every day receive
anonymous telephone calls whose purpose was to check whether
servants on strike have resumed their work.

The sale or purchase of British goods is being boycotted. Little by
little, revolutionary China endeavors to bring the city to its knees by
commercial ruin, or even by starving it out. The credit of the powerful
British banks in the Far East has already been affected. As a rule,
everything is being paid with a signature in these countries, and even
cocktails can be paid for on credit. Now, however, and this is quite
unprecedented, signs put up in hotels and stores warn people that "You
will greatly help us by paying in cash".[12]

It was natural that China's newly born national consciousness should in
the first place crystallize and bear fruit in her large cities. It was there that the
restless students found ready allies in the ancient (and powerful) merchants'
and artisans' organizations. It was there also that the foreign presence was
most obvious, both in its negative aspects and in its beneficial results. And it

was there, as in all the cities of the world, that life as such was changing most rapidly.

The spirit of new China, on the other hand, brought with it a widening gap between the younger and the older generations. While the latter clung faithfully to their ancestors' traditions and superstitions, especially in the countryside, young people turned increasingly to the more pragmatic and efficient methods of the West.

Nature itself continued, as before, to dispense both its blessings and its curses throughout the vast land of the Chinese. Bumper crops, floods and droughts made life normal or impossible in turn. That perennial scourge of China, famine, ravaged the northern provinces in 1920, killing people by the tens of millions.* A French missionary established south of Peking was a powerless witness to the frightful misery around him:

The poor, especially the women and children, besiege my residence begging for help. I give them whatever I can to alleviate their hunger, but unfortunately I cannot give them very much. Only yesterday, I watched a long line of wheelbarrows stretching from the city's Northern gate to the Sisters' Hospital; they contained all the belongings of these poor people abandoning their homes. Entire villages are thus emigrating.† One sees people of all ages: wretched mothers carrying or pushing their starving children; or very weak old men and women (I saw a woman over eighty years old) huddled in wheelbarrows and pushed by their children.

Day after day, the same procession continues. It is heartbreaking! The misery has become unbearable to the point that many people commit suicide. I was informed that in a certain village, a person I knew well had hanged himself. In another village, a family, after having exhausted all the food that was left, mixed poison with the last meal, and as a result all of its members died. Such and similar scenes are constantly being repeated everywhere.[13]

The country's chaotic situation grew still worse when ancient local feuds

---

* It was caused by vast floods in 1917, followed two years later by an unprecedented drought.

† Between 1923 and 1937, anarchy and famine forced nearly 6 million Chinese to emigrate to the virgin lands of Manchuria; order and a relative prosperity prevailed there under the iron hand of Marshal Chang Tso-lin (1911-1928). This massive Chinese migration eventually outnumbered the Manchurian nomadic tribes, with the result that today the area is called the "Northeastern Province".

broke out with renewed intensity. These provincial wars proved the more costly as the central government was quite unable to stem the mounting tide of anarchy.

In western China, in particular, Szechuan and Yunnanese armies (bearing such colorful names as "Long Legs", "Pumpkin Party", "Will discuss with Anyone"*) fought each other ferociously. In the summer of 1920, Yunnanese forces were operating in the vicinity of Chengtu, capital of Szechuan, where Sir Meyrick Hewlett was then British Consul:

I was right in my surmise as at 5.45 A.M. the opposing forces were attacking outside the North Gate, and at 8:30 they entered the city.

There was a hideous massacre at the city gate which was closed against the retreating troops, who had been sent out of the city on the night of 3rd September. Among these unfortunates was a body of seventy mounted women; only seven escaped and the bodies of the slain were subjected to nameless indignities.

After two days' rest the Szechuan armies pursued the Yunnanese to the Lung Ch'uan Yi heights, about twenty miles from Chengtu, and forming the eastern boundary of the Chengtu plain. As the proportion of men was four to one in their favour they made a frontal attack on the Yunnan position, but after seven days had made no impression on the enemy. And then occurred what must be one of the most dramatic incidents in any war. The story was told me by a special representative of the Szechuanese Commander in Chief. Seven hundred Yunnan men stripped; some were entirely naked, some naked to the waist. Armed with knives and revolvers they rushed the Szechuan camp of 16,000 men at the foot of the hills. The attack was a complete success. Panic seized regiment after regiment and the whole force fled to within the shelter of Chengtu city walls.

About ten of these heroes, for heroes indeed they were, were captured and, naked as they were, kept in the streets on show in cold drenching rain before being murdered. Two were killed and cut up in the streets and I saw the hearts and livers hanging in a cookshop. Two others were wrapped in wadding and burnt alive in the public park before a huge crowd of men, women and children. Two others were taken to a temple; their shoulders were slit and candles put in. They were forced to kneel at the altar when the candles were lit, and

---

* The first, because of its capacity to run away from the enemy, the two others because of their opportunism.

on the flame reaching the bare skin, were hacked to pieces. I called on the Commandant of the City Guards and pleaded for the other prisoners who were incessantly being tortured, making holes in shoulders, back and even head and inserting candles being common. I told him I considered the men were heroes and deserved care; they were under orders, and it was the men who sent them to fight who deserved punishment. He merely laughed and said, "Very well, we all know your love of humanity and I will give orders there are to be no more tortures."

This success, alas, tempted the tough warrior Chao Yu-hsin to attack Chengtu. With his small force it was a fatal move. He had told me he considered one of his men equal to nine Szechuanese, but I had warned him to be careful the day did not come when they were one too many. His chief anxiety was shortage of ammunition. To draw Szechuan fire and make them not only waste ammunition but think he was well supplied, his men used to put firecrackers into kerosene tins and set them off in different places making a sound like rapid rifle fire. He had also found skillful tapping of wood to sound like the rat-tat-tat of a Maxim was very effective. Chao shelled the city and the Canadian Mission Hospital was twice hit, but I managed to get a message to him telling him the location of British premises and the gun was at once trained in a direction which would not affect our properties.

I will never understand what induced a really capable leader like Chao Yu-hsin to descend into the plain. He had only 4,000 against at least 16,000 and he could never have captured the walled city. As it was, the Szechuanese rapidly recovered from the severe shaking they had received at the hands of the seven hundred naked heroes and on the morning of 19th September launched a very successful sortie. I watched the battle, first from the Canadian Mission Hospital and then from the city wall. It was like a sham fight at an Aldershot Tattoo, and the men were at such close quarters the doctors told me many of the wounded had powder marks from the rifles of their enemies. The Yunnanese so vastly outnumbered were simply massacred, and every prisoner was massacred in cold blood, a fact admitted to me by the garrison Commander.[14]

Unorthodox tactics and switches of troops from a vanquished general to his victor were common features of the civil war between local military dictators between 1920 and 1926. Bribery was very frequent too, as many war lords

*relied much more on their war chests or diplomatic abilities than on the
questionable value and fighting spirit of their soldiers. More often than not
the latter were but mercenaries without ideal or cause to defend.*

*A Frenchman residing in Peking watched a typical outfit passing through
his neighborhood:*

Two rows of soldiers were marching down the entire width of the
street. In the streamlets running on both sides of the street, two more
rows were advancing in single file; they were dragging their feet
through the murky water which the inhabitants pour into the street,
and wore a light, very strange and completely worn-out footgear. . . .

The commander looked as tattered as his men, and you could not
distinguish him except for the fact that every now and then he tripped
over his exceedingly long sword; he was marching ahead of his soldiers,
and talking to a ceremonious-looking civilian with unctuous and
kindly manners. The soldiers' rifles swayed back and forth with each
step, and sometimes nearly hit their neighbor in the eye. The men
whistled, coughed, cleared their throats, spit, blew their noses between
the fingers of their one free hand, and called to each other from row
to row with the hoarse and guttural cries so typical of the Chinese.

These soldiers resembled all Chinese soldiers. They were recruited
from among coolies disgusted with life's hazards, adventurers, and
fatalists impressed by the strength, if not by the prestige, of their
army. They knew that their pay was hardly more regular than that of a
coolie, but they also knew that their weapons furnished them with
irresistible arguments. These warriors were extremely picturesque.
Their caps were either too small or too big, and their broad tailored
jackets hung loosely on their bodies or were squeezed within heavy
bandoliers worn after the German fashion. The sack-like bottoms of
their trousers seemed to provide plenty of space for additional supplies,
and they wore a remarkable variety of shoes within the same unit:
Chinese slippers, sneakers, open shoes laced with a large and very
fashionable knot, walking boots that were never polished, and lace
boots whose broken elastics were no longer of any use, and whose
wide-open tops and straps undescribable had well-nigh lost their
shape. . . .

These soldiers were advancing and marching at ease, without in the
least caring about their task. They knew that their prestige was gone,
or, in the words of a Chinese proverb, that "one does not make a

prostitute out of an honest girl, a nail with good iron, or a soldier out of an honorable man". They no longer had any illusions, and this is why they no longer pretended to a smart military bearing, nor did they display any restraint.[15]

It was small wonder that the aimless rabble which all too often constituted the war lords' armies turned to banditry whenever they saw their profit in it. Paul S. Reinsch described the typically Chinese bandit-soldier relationship:

Brigandage is an established institution in China, where it has operated so long that people have become accustomed to it and take it for granted as a natural visitation. At this time there was a vicious circle around which brigands and troops and rich citizens and villagers were traveling, one in pursuit of the other. The brigands were recruited from disbanded soldiers—men who had lost connection with their family and clan. Often their families had been wiped out by famine, flood, or disease, or had been killed in the revolution. At other times the individual may have lost touch through a fault of his own causing him to be cast out. It is very difficult for an isolated person, without family and clan connections, to re-establish himself. The easiest way is to enlist in the army. If that cannot be done, he becomes a brigand. Brigands foregather in provinces where the administration is lax or in remote regions difficult to reach. They lie in ambush and seize wealthy persons, who are carried off to the hills and released only when ransom is paid. In this way, a considerable tax is levied on accumulated wealth. This money the brigands spend among the villagers where they happen to be. Meanwhile, the Provincial Governor bethinks himself that a certain brigade or division has not been paid for a long time and therefore might cause trouble, so he announces what is called a "country cleansing campaign". The situation is so intolerable that the general sees himself forced to go to extremes, and to send his troops with orders to exterminate the brigands. They proceed to the infested regions; the brigands, having meanwhile got wind of these movements, depart for healthier climes, leaving the troops to quarter themselves on the villagers, who are by them relieved of the money which they have made out of the brigands. Some brigands may be unfortunate enough to be caught; some will be shot as an example, and others will be allowed to enlist. When the soldiers have dwelt for a while among the villagers, they report that the bands have now been fully suppressed and that the country is cleaned. They are then recalled to headquarters; their general reports to the governor, and is appropriately rewarded. Meanwhile, the brigands return from their safer haunts and begin again to catch wealthy people, whom they relieve of their surplus liquidable property. And so the circle revolves interminably. . . .

Returning to Peking from a trip to the Philippines I found that Mr. Kyle, an American engineer on the Siems-Carey railway survey, and Mr. Purcell, another employee, had been seized by bandits in a remote part of Honan. The bandits took a large sum of silver these men were carrying to pay off the surveying parties farther up toward Szechuan, then they decided to hold Kyle and Purcell for ransom. . . .

The company was quite ready to pay the ransom, and I could easily have induced the Chinese Government to pay it. I was advised that this would be the only certain way of rescuing the men, but I felt it would be a dangerous precedent; as the bandits would then go on taking and holding foreigners for ransom. . . . One night, Mr. Purcell escaped. . . . I notified the Governor General that he must surround the whole region where the bandits were, telling them emphatically that if anything happened to Mr. Kyle the band would be hunted down and exterminated.

The threat was "got across" to the bandits, and with it a promise that those instrumental in restoring the captive would escape punishment and in some way be rewarded. After a week's further suspense Mr. Kyle was delivered to the pursuing troops and forthwith returned to Peking. The chief of the band was rewarded with a commission in the army; his henchmen were enlisted as soldiers. But those who had no part in the delivery were one by one caught and executed. So, in the end, a salutary example was set to keep bandits from interfering with foreigners.[16]

An attack by bandits on the Tientsin-Pukow express on May 7, 1923, was widely publicized in the West. A sister-in-law of Mr. Rockefeller, Jr., was among the kidnapped. The London Times published the following report from Peking:

The railway outrage on the Shantung border has created a great sensation here. Only the scantiest details are available, but it appears that one British subject was killed, twenty-four foreigners and about two hundred Chinese were kidnapped, while ten foreigners and some Chinese escaped to the nearest station and telegraphed the news.

The bandits, who are variously estimated at between one thousand and five thousand in number, had torn up the line, so that when the express arrived the engine and tender were derailed and turned turtle, bringing the train to a standstill. The hour was 2:30 in the morning, when the three hundred passengers must have been asleep and the foreigners were in their night clothes.

Chinese methods on such occasions are well known. The bandits seek to inspire terror by demoniac yelling and shouting and furious firing of rifles, and the horror of such an experience in the dead of the night for the helpless passengers can well be imagined.

The Tientsin-Pukow railway forms part of the railway connexion between Peking and Shanghai, and carries a heavy passenger traffic, both foreign and Chinese, as well as most of the tourists who visit the Far East. Since its opening in 1912 traffic has frequently been interrupted by military movements, but bandits have never before ventured to attack the line, on which there is so much foreign traffic.

The outrage occurred near the station of Lincheng, in a region with a very bad reputation. Within a radius of fifty miles five Provinces adjoin each other, and the area is a safe refuge for innumerable rascals, who, when hunted by the authorities in one Province, escape into the next and repeat the operation whenever they find it expedient. In the absence of co-ordinated action by the different provinces the criminals generally succeed in evading capture.

There is little doubt that the present outrage was committed by ex-soldiers; in fact, a great part of the Northern armies is recruited in this region, and it is a partial explanation of the difficulty of dealing with bandits in China that the regular forces and the bandits are so akin. The soldiers can seldom be induced to deal faithfully with the bandits. It is a feature of the present situation in this country. Although the regular armies number nearly one and a half millions, brigandage is more widespread than at any time in recent history. The bandits loot, burn, kidnap, and murder right under the noses of the Tuchuns [Military Governors] and are rarely molested.[17]

Amid the growing anarchy prevailing in the early twenties, a few powerful *war lords were able to impose—and maintain for some time—their authority over large areas of China. The duration of their power depended largely on the faithfulness or fickleness of their lieutenants. In the summer of 1920, for instance, General Tuan Ch'i-jui, leader of the Ngan-fu clan and master of Peking since 1916,* was defeated by a coalition formed by Marshal Chang Tso-lin and the Chihli clan because of the defection of one of his divisions. As a result, the capital changed hands.*

The French journalist and writer Abel Bonnard† was then staying with friends not far from Peking:

In the far distance, a few shimmering lights indicated the presence of Peking. We had just begun to enjoy the pleasant sight when someone came to fetch my companion. He was called to the telephone at the nearby dispensary set up by the French physician whose guests we were to be that evening. My companion soon returned with the news that everything had changed: the troops of Tuan Ch'i-jui had been defeated and were most likely to reach the city walls as fugitives and robbers. In order to keep them outside, the city would certainly lock its gates, and we were therefore requested to return at once. . . .

The officer commanding the nearby village introduced himself, and warned us that the road had been barricaded, and that we would not be able to proceed. . . .

The road leading to Peking was usually very crowded, but now it lay deserted under the hot sun. Finally, the top of the ramparts appeared before us. Automobiles driving through the suburbs rounded the last curve and came to a halt before the gate, because it was closed. . . .

Nobody was working in the suburbs, and we found ourselves in the midst of an irresolute crowd standing around idly. One could sense that it would not take much to change people's uneasiness into outright fear. We entered the small military post leaning against the wall, and began our negotiations, but who was going to take it upon himself to let us in? . . .

The arrival of the fugitive soldiers would be very annoying for us because, with the city gates remaining closed, the prevailing anxiety would only be increased. Then, behold, one, two, three of them began to arrive, downcast and exhausted creatures still wearing the badge with their general's colors. They entered the post and exchanged a

* Where he succeeded Yuan Shih-k'ai, being one of his most trusted lieutenants.
† Minister of Public Education under Marshal Pétain.

few words with the soldiers guarding the gate. There was no show of either animosity or friendliness between the two groups. Their contact was as cautious as that of insects touching and feeling each other with their antennas. These soldiers, too, wanted to enter the city where only a few days ago their leaders were the masters, but which refused to receive them at present. As we waited, the heat increased. . . .

A few more stragglers arrived. Were large numbers of them to be expected? Suddenly, we learned that, thanks to our Legation, the gate was to be opened to us. Commands resounded on the other side of the gate, followed by the powerful noise of chains and the creaking of bolts, which would have produced a wonderful effect in a melodrama. Finally, one of the huge portals was opened, and our automobiles entered the bastion's ravelin, while a cordon of soldiers barred the passage behind us. The second gate then opened, and we went into the city through the huge wall.

For weeks, Peking remained shut, for fear of being invaded and plundered. Meantime, we learned how the defection of a division had turned the tide, and how one of the vanquished generals, in order to flee more rapidly, had ordered the train carrying him away launched at full speed against his own troops.

The city had to be nourished; toward evening, some of its gates were half opened, and then the farmers rushed in, loaded with baskets and fresh vegetables. These days of idleness and anxiety were the hottest of the summer, and we were told that the heat was greater than usual. Being walled in only added to our unpleasant feeling of suffocation.[18]

In October 1924, it was the turn of Marshal Wu Pei-fu, head of the Chihli clan, to be betrayed by some of his generals while he was engaged in a campaign against Marshal Chang Tso-lin, master of Manchuria.

Two months later, Wu Pei-fu granted an interview to a French journalist:

Marshal Wu Pei-fu arrived in Hankow on December 31, 1924, and I managed to interview him soon afterwards. He came from Honan and hoped to reach Hunan, but the military governor Siao Yao-ngan would not let him pass through his territory. Wu had with him an escort of two battalions commanded by General Mu. . . .

It would be a mistake to believe that Marshal Wu has been demoralized by his defeat. On the contrary, he is, as ever, full of initiative and energy, and shows not the least sign of being discouraged. He has plenty of stamina, and is without doubt an above-average man.

He received me with a smile in the railroad car where he had established his quarters.

"Many of us," I said, "regret the misfortune that has befallen you after all your efforts toward national unity."

"My personal fate does not really matter. It is the country that must be pitied. As far as I am concerned, my honor is safe, and that is the only thing that really counts. Besides, I have not been vanquished. I have been betrayed."

"You mean that before leaving Peking, you did not know that some units were unreliable?"

"I more or less suspected it, and this was the reason why I sent the 3rd Army (under Feng Yu-hsiang) in the direction of Kai-lo, so as to remove it from Peking. As another precautionary measure, I also ordered all the troops of General Hu moved to that same area, officially to reinforce the 2nd Army, but actually to prevent the 3rd Army from returning to Peking in case it rebelled. I never suspected that General Hu would march with General Feng."

"Why did you have so much confidence in General Hu?"

"For the simple reason that I have done so much for him that I never thought he would prove himself so ungrateful. It is I who helped General Hu organize his army by supplying him with arms and money, so as to enable him to pay his troops. All his junior officers went through a three-month stage in my division. I had even founded a special school to instruct them, as these officers were former brigands without any military knowledge. I did my best to train them. Having treated his troops as I treated my own Third Division, I did not think that they would ever be unfaithful to me."

"Their turnabout must have been very painful to you?"

"No, not really, because in these times no one has any principles any more, and everybody follows his own interests. The troops of Hu behaved like others. If I wanted to get mad at them, I would also have to get mad at everyone else."

"And what about Suen-ye? Didn't you think he might betray you too?"

"Not at all! Suen-ye is the chief commander of the escort of the President. He should have been the last to betray his master! And yet, while I was still in Peking and before leaving for the front, I had contemplated—as a precautionary measure—leaving my Third Brigade behind in order to keep watch over Peking. The very idea of such a measure, however, frightened the President's entourage because it believed that I wanted to change the presidential escort in order to organize a coup d'état.". . .

"What are your present plans? In view of the chaotic situation, why don't you retire to a safe place to rest and wait for a favorable opportunity to make a comeback?"

"There is no safe place for me. I am being attacked from all sides."

"And what about the international concession?"

"I shall never place myself under foreign protection. Besides, as long as the President is not free, I shall not give up my efforts."

"Why do you care so much for the President? People say that he has not always been good to you."

"Good or not good, he is my leader, and it is my duty to stand by his side. Now that misfortune has befallen him, I cannot abandon him."

"Your loyalty is worthy of admiration indeed. But this principle of being faithful to somebody is a very old one; today, China is a Republic."

"Where do you see a Republic? China is, on the contrary, a country without system; anarchy and treason prevail everywhere. Betraying one's leader has become as natural as eating one's breakfast. This is the underlying cause of today's chaos throughout China. Underlings think of nothing but getting rid of their leaders in order to take their place, so disorder keeps spreading without end. I am not like these people, and I show the world that not all Chinese are unprincipled."

Thereupon, I took my leave.[19]

The new ruler of Peking now was General Feng Yu-hsiang, better known as the "Christian Marshal". It is said that his troops were baptized collectively by means of fire hoses, which did not prevent Feng from receiving substantial subsidies from Soviet Russia.

Compared to the nondescript gatherings of soldiers that constituted the armies of most Chinese war lords, Feng's troops, described here by an English missionary, were superiorly organized and well disciplined:

As is usual with well-trained Chinese troops, these movements were very creditably carried out, the handling of the arms, dressings and marchings being extremely smart and soldierlike. The men were very evenly matched as regards height, averaging some 5 ft. 6 in. or 5 ft. 7 in., well-set-up, and sturdy. I saw no immature boys in the ranks— a common phenomenon in the average Chinese division. They were clad in the universal Chinese blue-gray uniform, carried a rolled great-coat over their right shoulder, water bottle, entrenching spade, bayonet and frog, and two linen bandoliers containing 75 rounds of ammunition. Footgear consisted of light canvas boots with leather soles.

Following the dismissal of the parade, we were invited to inspect some of the barrack rooms. Those that we saw were clean, but lacking in all but absolute necessaries. Each room was occupied by a *p'eng*, i.e., a section, which consists of a sergeant, a corporal, and twelve privates.

The rooms were large and could easily have accommodated double the number. Of furniture there was none; the whole section slept together on a raised brick platform, covered with straw and a clean white sheet. There were no blankets, the men making use of their greatcoats, etc. Straw pillows were provided, and each man had a piece of calico in which to wrap his simple belongings. Beyond this the brick-floored rooms were innocent of any adornment if the mural decorations are excepted. These were sufficiently interesting to merit a few words.

Every room had a map of China as she was some one hundred years ago, and before her territory had been encroached on by foreign nations. Those portions of the Empire which had been lost, e.g., Korea, Formosa, French Indo-China, etc.,* were coloured a vivid crimson. In addition there were numerous coloured prints representing Biblical subjects; others consisted of pictures exhorting the men as to the manner of their lives. Thrift was a favorite subject, and exhortations to "Get all you can, save all you can, give all you can," and that "Thrift makes for happiness" were everywhere to be seen.

Attached to the barrack rooms were classrooms where ordinary and military subjects are taught. General Feng insists that every soldier should be able to read his own language, and in the classrooms which I saw, men were being taught to recognize everyday Chinese characters.

* Within less than fifty years before World War I, China lost the following territories: the Liu-ch'iu Islands (1879), Formosa (1895), Port Arthur (1905) and Korea (1910) to Japan, and Indo-China to France (1885). Also, Outer Mongolia, which became "autonomous" in 1913 and passed under Russian influence together with northern Manchuria; and finally Tibet, which also became "autonomous" in 1913 and concluded an agreement with England (securing India's northern border).

Cookhouses were attached to the barrack rooms, each kitchen cooking for a *lien* or company of 125 men. The cookhouses, while extremely primitive, were, like all the buildings I saw, kept extremely clean. The food provided is as simple as it well can be, consisting of rice, millet, and cabbage or other vegetable. Meat is rarely on the menu owing to shortage of funds. . . .

We were next invited to visit the "factories," or workshops, and this proved to be the most interesting event in the day's programme. . . . The scheme is that, as far as possible, each *ying* (battalion) shall be taught a separate craft; thus there is a battalion of bootmakers, a battalion of weavers, and so on. In the workshops we visited I saw men being trained as carpenters, weavers, tailors, boot and shoemakers, and wool carders, and there are other shops where men are taught to be blacksmiths, farriers, etc. . . .

Following our visit to the workshops, we were given a gymnastic display. The gymnasts, to the number of some 200 or 250, were all officers, for it is the rule that all officers of the rank of colonel and under shall take part in gymnastics. Owing to the cold weather the display was only a short one, but we saw some excellent work on the horizontal bar, horse, and parallel bars as well as pole-jumping, etc.

The last item on the programme was a visit to the female schools, and there we saw what must be an extremely rare sight in China, viz., officers' wives and daughters being taught to read and write their own language.[20]

Among the various military dictators who shaped China's destinies during the turbulent twenties, probably the most successful was Marshal Chang Tso-lin, who ruled over Manchuria between 1911 and 1928.* Besides presenting himself as a defender of Confucian traditions, Chang was anti-Communist (in 1927, his troops executed a spectacular raid against the Russian embassy at Peking), and also anti-Japanese (he was killed in 1928, when his armored train was blown up by a Japanese bomb).

Chang's troops occupied Peking in 1926. A few months later the wife of a French diplomat succeeded in interviewing the foxy and almost inaccessible war lord:

I did not want to leave Peking without having met Marshal Chang

* He had about 500,000 men under his command, about twice as many as the other leading war lords.

Tso-lin, the northern dictator, or, as people call him there, "the Marshal.". . .

I contacted the dean of the diplomatic corps, M. Oudendik, Minister of the Netherlands, as I had been told that he was held in high esteem by the Marshal because of his knowledge of China and the Chinese, and because of his wisdom, tact, honesty, and good judgment. When informed of my desire to see the Marshal, however, the kind diplomat frowned, saying:

"Madam, don't think of it! Would you have considered seeing the Emperor of China? The Marshal does not receive journalists, tourists, or least of all, women!"

Nonetheless, I was granted an interview. . . .

The Marshal's residence was surrounded by a long, greyish wall guarded by sentries carrying rifles with fixed bayonets. At one of the huge gates, I handed my card to a long-robed Chinese who went inside without even glancing at it. I was wearing a long dress with long, pagoda-style sleeves covering the wrists and striped with the colors of the Chinese [Republican] flag.* This, I thought, would make a favorable impression on any northern patriot.

The Chinese wearing a black dress came back, accompanied by a small fat man with a jovial and crafty countenance, who shook hands with me and bade me welcome in impeccable French.

"The Marshal will receive you shortly. We are preparing an offensive, and he is still in conference with his generals. But I am going to let him know that you are here. I am M. Wu-ching [Foreign Minister]."

To kill time, we struck up a conversation.

"What do you think of our capital, and of our streets? The Marshal, you know, insists on cleanliness and order."

The city, I must say, was well policed. I remember seeing two heads, still dripping with blood, swaying in a fisherman's net by the door of a theatre: two soldiers had been executed there for having disregarded the law that forbade them to enter the theatre without paying.

M. Wu-ching probably read my thoughts:

"What else could we do? Stern punishments are salutary warnings

* From top to bottom, five horizontal stripes symbolized the union of China's five main populations: red (Chinese), yellow (Manchu), blue (Mongol), white (Muslim), and black (Tibetan).

to any mutineers. Pity is unforgiveable when it comes to setting an example. . . . Do drink your tea, please, and have a cigarette. I am going to fetch the Marshal."

The glass-paneled door finally opened. Next to M. Wu-ching, and advancing with precise steps, there came a small and thin man in a long black robe under the classical silken jacket, and wearing a Chinese skullcap. It was Chang Tso-lin. He bowed with considerable grace and dignity, and clasped my fingers in his delicate hand, while giving me a direct and brief look that was at the same time amused, grave, and curious.

I looked at him closely, too. His gold-crowned upper incisors were slightly protruding under his heavy and bristly mustache. His mouth was firm, and of a dull red color. Was he a tyrant, a bandit, a barbarian? In front of me stood an elderly gentleman with a delicate, aristocratic face. I looked vainly for a cruel quiver at the corner of his mouth, or a hard glimmer in his eyes. I saw no trace of such cruelty or toughness, and yet I knew that not so long ago, Chang Tso-lin had ordered the execution of a traitor who was abjectly prostrated at his feet, in the humble attitude of the kowtow. This, indeed, was against tradition, as one should at least wait until the culprit has stood up again. I had also been told that the Marshal could fly into a rage whenever he lost a Mah-Jongg game, and that he was neither weak, nor sentimental.

While we conversed, M. Wu-ching acted as an interpreter.

"Your Excellency, a moment ago I was telling your Minister that I admire the cleanliness of Peking."

"Have you not seen Mukden? You must go there, because it is in Manchuria that I began the country's reorganization. You will see the arsenals. . . . Here, you may visit the airfield, and fly with our pilots in our own planes. We also have tanks."

"Your Excellency, what are you going to do with the Russian agitators that are being held in your jails? A few days ago, you gave an order to have the Chinese traitors strangled."

Chang winked in the direction of his Minister, and after a moment of silence, answered:

"What shall I do? If I punish them, the Whites will accuse me of violating their rights. If, on the contrary, I let them go unharmed, my own people will reproach me for being unforgivably lenient."

"But, Your Excellency, you are going to defeat the mounting Red tide?"

"We hope so. . . . But we need money, and a great deal of it. We don't have enough money. At any rate, as long as I am the master of Peking, I shall guarantee the safety of the Europeans. But we should cooperate and help each other more. There are too many divisions and too many rival interests. . . . The war is expensive, very expensive."

His hands calmly crossed over his knees, Chang Tso-lin asked me to tell him about my adventures in China. He smiled. Twenty minutes thus went by, an incredibly long time for an interview, I was told. The Marshal lifted his cup to his mouth, and then got up and excused himself. We were both delighted with each other. We shook hands, whereupon I took my leave.[21]

The "Russian agitators" who proved so embarrassing to Chang Tso-lin were part of the increasing number of special agents and propagandists whom the Soviet Union had sent to the Far East in the wake of the Bolshevik Revolution. China's intelligentsia had been greatly impressed by the overthrow of Tsarism, and some of its most respected leaders soon turned to Marxist ideology as they searched for solutions to the woes besetting their own country.

Among the early converts to Marxism, two professors of Peking University played a leading role in the founding of the Chinese Communist Party. One was Ch'en Tu-hsiu, chief editor and regular contributor to the liberal magazine La Jeunesse, *and the other was Li Ta-chao, a returned student from Japan who taught political science and economics. In 1918, Li and his disciple Mao Tse-tung (then assistant librarian at the University) had founded the "Society for the Study of Marxism",* * and in 1921, both Ch'en and Li took part in the five-day secret gathering which actually gave birth to the Chinese Communist Party.*

The gathering (which included the Dutchman Maring, representing the Comintern) took place under trying conditions, later recalled by one of the participants:

In the second half of June, 1921, nine persons took up residence on the upper floor of the girls' school located on Rue Poubalou, in the French concession of Shanghai. The lower floor of the school was completely empty, as the students and teachers were on vacation. The

* Today, Li Ta-chao (who was killed in 1927 by order of Chang Tso-lin) is honored as the principal Party founder, because Ch'en Tu-hsiu, head and general secretary of the party until 1927, was then ostracized and expelled.

only person remaining in the building was the cook, who was also the janitor. An acquaintance of his requested that he prepare the meals of the newly arrived guests every day. He was also instructed to see to it that no stranger ever entered the school. . . . The cook did not understand the dialect of his guests, who in turn did not speak the Shanghai dialects. Some of them spoke Hunanese, while others used the Hupeh or Peking dialects.

The newcomers were the delegates of various Communist organizations existing throughout China. They had gathered in Shanghai for the purpose of officially organizing the Chinese Communist Party. The first congress of that party took place toward the end of July. Chang Kuo-t'ao was elected chairman, and Mao Tse-tung and Cheou Fu-hai were elected secretaries. The first meeting was held in the afore-mentioned school, but the following meetings took place at the home of Li Man-tsin. The congress lasted for four days.

The following four questions were on the agenda: (1) The political situation. (2) The fundamental tasks of the Party. (3) The bylaws of the Party. (4) Problems of organization.

These questions, especially those concerning the fundamental tasks of the Party and the principles of organization, provoked very lively discussions. One body of opinion was that of the "legal Marxists". They were led by Li Man-tsin, who contended that the Chinese proletariat was still too young really to understand Marxism, and that a prolonged campaign of propaganda and education should therefore be undertaken within its ranks. Li did not deem it necessary to found a true proletarian party; he opposed the dictatorship of the proletariat, and advocated bourgeois democracy. He asserted that the proletariat could be organized legally and politically educated within the framework of a bourgeois democracy, and that it was not at all necessary to create labor unions immediately. The party's full attention should rather be given to the students' movement and cultural progress. Li further stated that, in the first place, the intellectuals should be well organized and steeped in Marxist theories. It would then be possible, with the help of the intellectuals, to organize and educate the workers. Li, therefore, opposed the creation of a disciplined and aggressive proletarian party. Instead, he suggested a union of progressive intellectuals, and the legal organization of a large and peaceable party devoted to the study of Marxist principles. His conclusion was that all people who advocated and propagated Marxist principles could become members of the party. These people would not necessarily have to belong to a specific organization within the Party, nor would they have to participate in its daily activities. This point of view was also advocated by Li-ta and Chen Kong-po.

On the other hand, there was a group representing the extreme Left, headed by Luen Jen-ch'ing. He insisted that our immediate goal was the dictatorship of the proletariat, and he was opposed to the use of legal means. In his view, intellectuals were nothing but ideological agents of the bourgeoisie, who should as a rule be prohibited from joining the Party. Pao Huei-cheng was of the same opinion.

Most delegates, however, were vigorously opposed to both of these viewpoints. The resolutions that were finally adopted stressed that the Party's essential task was the establishment of a proletarian dictatorship. With regard to actual tactics which would be most effective during the transition period, it was pointed out that the Party, far from renouncing participation in a democratic movement, should, on the contrary, take the leadership of such a movement and fully commit the proletariat to it. The congress decided on the organization of a well-disciplined and aggressive working-class Party. The development of a strong labor movement was considered to be the fundamental task of the Communist Party. It was further specified that the Party should use legal means to organize itself as long as such means were beneficial to the proletariat. With regard to practical organization and conditions of admission to the Party, it was decided to profit from the experience of the Russian Bolshevik Party. . . .

Hardly ten minutes after we had left the residence of Li Man-tsin, nine spies and policemen broke into it and searched it. With the exception of legal Marxist literature, however, they found nothing and therefore could not arrest anyone. Each of us had to find a separate refuge for that night. We could not return to the girls' school, as we had every reason to believe that our activities there had put the police on our trail.

It had been our original intention to finish the work of the congress in seven days, but this incident forced us to finish it in five days. However, we were unable to find a safe spot in Shanghai, and we decided to go to Nai-hu instead, near Ta-sin, at a distance of nearly two hundred miles from Shanghai . . . where we would not be bothered by too many nature lovers. After we arrived there, we rented a large boat and bought some food and wine. Thus, while pretending to make a boat trip on the lake, we continued the work of the congress.[22]

In terms of traditional foreign encroachments, the Russian Revolution was a happy event for China. It meant a sudden pause in the steady, sinister advance from the north which for generations had come to be almost a normality in Chinese history. In 1919, the Soviet Union had announced that she would return, without compensation, all rights, privileges, and properties extorted from China by the Tsarist regime. This piece of good news was at first received with much skepticism by the Peking Foreign Office, but it soon evoked a favorable response in Canton, whence the rival government established by Sun Yat-sen and his Kuomintang campaigned for the allegiance of the Chinese masses.

Sun Yat-sen had been deeply disappointed by the limited interest which the Western powers had shown toward his country at the time of the Versailles settlement. He had been further disappointed by the fact that these same powers kept backing leading war lords while at the same time refusing to recognize his southern "Republic" as China's legitimate government. Sun therefore turned to Russia and her newly fostered propaganda line of "Asia for Asiatics". Russian support came in August 1922, with the arrival of Abram A. Joffe, who was one of the Soviet's ablest diplomats at the time.*

Joffe presented Russians as Asiatics longing to free their Chinese brothers from the chains of the "imperialist" West. A first result was the Sun–Joffe Declaration of January 26, 1923, staking out the common ground on which Russian Bolshevism and Chinese Nationalism could build their alliance:

Dr. Sun is of opinion that, because of the nonexistence of conditions favorable to their successful application in China, it is not possible to carry out either Communism or even the Soviet system in China. M. Joffe agrees entirely with this view; he is further of the opinion that China's most important and most pressing problems are the completion of national unification and the attainment of full national independence. With regard to these great tasks, M. Joffe has assured Dr. Sun of the Russian people's warmest sympathy for China, and of their willingness to lend support.[23]

After this "statement of principle", there followed a brief but very active

---

* Joffe paid scant attention to the distrustful Chinese Foreign Office and concentrated on lectures in the universities, where he aroused a tremendous response.

period of cooperation between the Kuomintang and the Kungch'antang, or Chinese Communist Party. Sun Yat-sen, whose bid for national leadership was constantly being thwarted by the powerful opposition of northern war lords,* reorganized the Kuomintang on Soviet structural lines. In speeches he made in 1923, he stressed the role of the Party as the foundation of the state, the need for strict discipline within the Party and the subjection of the individual member to the Party. A Russian adviser, Michael Borodin, arrived in Canton in August 1923, and fully approved of Sun's new orientation.

In January 1924, the first Kuomintang national congress admitted Communists to the party, in order to broaden the basis of support for the nationalist revolution. In a series of lectures which Dr. Sun gave that year, he laid final emphasis on the "Three Principles" of his political doctrine (Nationalism, Democracy, Social Progress) which he had already defined in 1905. He died of cancer in March 1925.

Meanwhile, the newly founded Whampoa Military Academy had begun training the officers destined to lead the Kuomintang armies in the large-scale offensive that was to conquer China in the near future. The Academy was headed by an energetic and ambitious young general, Chiang Kai-shek, who had been trained in Japan and had recently come back from a visit to Soviet Russia. Chiang was assisted by Russian and German instructors, and his political adviser was Chou En-lai.

While accepting Russian military advice as a necessity imposed by circumstances,† Chiang had no illusions as to the unselfish purposes of the Communist movement. In March 1924, three months after his return from Moscow, he recorded his innermost feelings about Communism in a letter to his "Elder Brother" (actually his best friend, who was an ardent supporter of cooperation with Russia):

. . . From my observation, the Russian Party is lacking in sincerity. Even when I told you, my Elder Brother, that only 30 percent of what the Russians say was believable, it was said only because you, my Elder Brother, were so enthusiastic in believing the Russians that I had not the heart to disappoint you altogether. Regarding their respect for Mr. Sun personally, they are not Russian Communists but international partisans. As for those of our country who are in Russia, they have nothing except slander and suspicion for Mr. Sun.

* Sun organized several unsuccessful expeditions against them.
† His leading adviser was a Russian, General Blücher, alias Galen.

The sole aim of the Russian Party is to make the Chinese Communist Party its legitimate heir. They do not believe that our Party could co-operate with them in the least, helping each other to achieve success. As regards their policy in China, they want to make Manchuria, Mongolia, the Mohammedan Province and Tibet each a part of their Soviet, and even as to China proper they are not without the wish to put their fingers in. . . . What they call "Internationalism" and "World Revolution" are nothing but Kaiser Imperialism. They have only given it a new name and made it puzzling to distinguish one from the other. Russians, as well as the English, French, Americans and Japanese, it seems to me, all have it in their minds to promote the interest of their own respective countries at the cost of other nations. . . .

Some of our own Chinese Communists who are in Russia always scold other people as slaves of America, of England and of Japan, never realizing that they themselves have already completely become slaves of Russia. . . .[24]

The Communists, for their part, had few illusions about Chiang. In a secret report sent to Moscow, the Russian adviser Stepanov drew the following portrait of the Kuomintang leader:

My views regarding the character of Chiang Kai-shek are shared by the Chinese Communists, including the Chairman of the Central Committee (Ch'en Tou-sieou). We consider him to be an individual with outstanding characteristics, the principal one of which is an inordinate desire for glory and power, and an insatiable urge to become China's hero. He prides himself in promoting not only the Chinese National Revolution, but the World Revolution as well. His actual understanding of the problems of the revolution, however, is quite another story.

In order to attain his goals, he needs power and money. It is true that he does not use this money to enrich himself, but he never hesitates to grant huge sums as gifts and favors. In particular, he consistently subsidizes the papers in order to gain their support. His analyses of China's or the world's problems are very good. He acts according to his personal views only, without the support of the masses, but in order to attain the glory he is seeking, he sometimes endeavors to make use of the masses, the Chinese Communist party, or ourselves. His ambition to be China's great hero and his desire to take advantage of the national revolutionary movement make him sway back and forth between the Right and the Communists. He speaks of the "Red Disaster" in order to please Chinese public opinion, for the phrase "Red Disaster" is very much on the mind of the Chinese today.

Chiang is full of tenancity and determination. Compared to the average Chinese, he is unbelievably outspoken. He often accepts suggestions and advice from trusted subordinates, but he can also be suspicious and jealous. He never agrees to discuss any problem, and allows no one to decide in his stead.

Such is my opinion, which might not be altogether correct, on the personality of Chiang.[25]

The first open rift between the Kuomintang and the Kungch'antang occurred one year after the death of Sun Yat-sen. In March 1926, Chiang Kai-shek, taking advantage of Borodin's absence, expelled the Russian advisers from Canton and "neutralized" that city's Communists. Two months later, the Kuomintang leadership passed a resolution barring Chinese Communists from key posts in the Party.

The Comintern, however, instructed the Chinese Communists to stay on as members of the Kuomintang, so as to maintain at least a semblance of unity. But from that time onward, Communism considered Chiang as its Number One enemy in China.

Chiang himself, who had been appointed Commander in Chief of the Kuomintang forces, was about to plunge into the enormous task of unifying China. In July 1926, he began the "March to the North" at the head of the People's Revolutionary Army and, following the T'ai P'ing route through Hunan, reached the Yangtze in early October. The campaign's remarkably quick success was largely due to the effective use of political warfare, which was applied for the first time in Chinese history.*

In the wake of this spectacular achievement, the Communists regained very strong positions within the Kuomintang government, which was moved from Canton to Wuhan.† By allying themselves with the Kuomintang's left wing, they actually secured a majority.‡ In their jockeying for power,

---

* The troops were preceded by political agitators who won people over to the Nationalist cause, and sometimes fanned popular risings.

† Large urban concentration (over 2 million) comprising the three cities of Hankow, Wuch'ang and Hanyang, straddling the Yangtze.

‡ Membership in the Chinese Communist Party also rose rapidly at the time. From some 340 intellectuals in 1923, it grew to 10,000 in 1925 and 58,000 in 1927—plus 35,000 adherents of the Communist Youth. Communist influence was strong among China's 3 million organized laborers.

the Communists were greatly helped by the resourceful Borodin. An American journalist and writer specializing in the coverage of revolutions, Anna L. Strong,* analyzed the Russian adviser's role:

Michael Borodin, invited four years before by Dr. Sun Yat-sen to come as Adviser to the Kuomintang Party and the Nationalist Government, lived and worked on the floor above *The People's Tribune.†* At the side entrance which led to the door of his apartments, were always standing from one to half a dozen automobiles, belonging to officials of the government who had come to consult him. Inside his various rooms, at all hours, day and night, meetings of the Kuomintang or the Communist Party were going on.

To the English-speaking community in Hankow, Borodin was a force almost superhuman, but he was regarded rather as a devil than an angel. "Have you really seen him? What does he look like?" they would whisper. And when they knew that I had met him several times and expected to meet him again, they hardly knew whether to regard me with unusual respect or unusual suspicion. They looked on him as the sole author of every new decree or document, whether Eugene Chen's notes to foreign governments,‡ or Madame Sun Yat-sen's statement of her reasons for leaving Wuhan. Every move he made was the subject of excited comment. If he even chanced to sleep normally at night, and the light which often burned in his office till three in the morning was darkened, men passing the house after midnight and seeing it in darkness, would spread the word through Hankow that Borodin had "escaped last night in his private airplane," which meant of course that the fall of Wuhan was a matter only of hours. Totally unused to expecting any ability in government from Chinese, and misled by the legend of the "strong man" under which Anglo-Saxon peoples have always envisaged the government of "backward nations," they were unable to see any governmental force anywhere except in Borodin. In this, as far as the actual members of the Wuhan government were concerned, they were not so far

---

* Miss Strong covered the world's revolutions for a period of some thirty years after World War I, and wrote several books about them. She contributed to the *New Statesman and Nation*, *Pacific Affairs*, *Harper's*, the *Atlantic Monthly*, *The New York Times* and the *New York Herald Tribune*.

† Kuomintang paper intended for propaganda abroad, mainly in the United States. It was managed by two American journalists.

‡ Chen was the Kuomintang's Foreign Minister, and a leader of its left wing.

wrong. All of these members were constantly coming to him, not only for the advice which his long experience in many revolutions enabled him to give them,* but even more for the strength of revolutionary purpose which he had and which most of them lacked. Among them all, as they swayed and compromised between the power of the mass movements and the power of the militarists, he alone seemed able to mark out a clear path and give reasons for it. His reasons were so sound and based on such broad experience that, for a long time, they held even those members of the Kuomintang whose natural interests were against the movement of workers and peasants.[26]

While the Kuomintang's military campaign rolled northward, Chinese Communists conducted campaigns of their own among the peasants of the rich and populated central provinces of Hunan and Hupeh.

In Hunan, the Peasant Movement was organized by young Mao Tse-tung. In a report which at the time was judged heretical by orthodox Communists (because it stressed "rural revolution" over and above the revolutionary abilities of the urban proletariat), Mao pointed to the irresistible strength and "historic mission" of China's vast peasant masses:

On a thirty-two-day (January 4–February 5, 1927) inspection tour of five *hsien*† of Hunan . . . I have collected a considerable body of materials by listening carefully to reports made by experienced peasants and comrades in the peasant movement at information meetings held both in county seats and villages. Many aspects of the peasant movement directly contradict what we have learned from the gentry in Hankow and Changsha.‡ Some unique incidents have never been seen or heard of before. These conditions, I think, prevail in other provinces too; thus various arguments against the peasant movement must be controverted immediately and the erroneous decisions of the revolutionary regime [of Wuhan] in regard to the peasant movement must be quickly corrected. Only thus can the revolution benefit in the future. The further development of the peasant movement is a tremendous problem. Within a short time, hundreds of millions of peasants will rise in Central, South and North China, with the fury of a hurricane; no power, however strong, can restrain them. They will break all the

* Especially in Turkey, where Borodin had been adviser to Kemal Atatürk shortly before coming to China.
† Districts, or counties.
‡ Capital of Hunan Province.

shackles that bind them and rush toward the road of liberation. *All imperialists, war lords, corrupt officials, and bad gentry will meet their doom at the hands of the peasants.* All revolutionary parties and comrades will be judged by them. *Are we to get in front of them and lead them or criticize them behind their backs and fight them from the opposite camp?* Among these three alternatives every Chinese can choose freely, but the current situation demands a quick decision. . . .

From October (1926) to January of this year, the membership of the Peasant Associations jumped up to 2,000,000 and the number of people under their direct command increased to 10,000,000 (when joining a Peasant Association, the peasants usually put down one name for the whole family; thus 2,000,000 members means 10,000,000 people). About half of the entire peasantry in Hunan is organized. In some places . . . almost the entire peasantry has been incorporated into the Peasant Associations and takes orders from them. After organizing themselves extensively, the peasants began to take action. Thus, within four months, an unprecedented agrarian revolution broke out.

Down with the Village Bosses and Bad Gentry, All Power Belongs to the Peasant Associations. After the peasants organized themselves, action ensued. The major targets of their attack were the *t'u-hao*,* bad gentry, and illegal landlords, as well as the old patriarchal ideology, corruption of city officials, and undesirable village customs. This attack was like a hurricane: only those could survive who bent to its force. As a result, privileges of the feudal landlord class, thousands of years old, were totally swept away. Their prestige and prerogatives were altogether abolished. After the overthrow of the gentry's power, the Peasant Associations became the only organs of power and the slogan "All Power to the Peasant Associations" became literally true. Even such trifles as quarrels between married couples were referred to the Peasant Associations for settlement. No problem could be solved independently of the Peasant Association membership, whose every word passed for a command. . . .

Outsiders could comment only favorably, not critically, on the Peasant Associations. Bad gentry and illegal landlords were deprived of their right of free speech; nobody dared to voice objections. Under the Peasant Association regime, the top-layer *t'u-hao* and bad gentry fled to Shanghai; the second layer fled to Hankow; the third layer to Changsha; and the fourth layer to the county seats, while the

* Village bosses.

small fry of the fifth layer and below surrendered to the Peasant
Associations in the villages.

"I contribute ten dollars, so please let me join the Peasant Association," pleaded the small fry bad gentry.

"Ha! Who cares about your bloody money?" answered the
peasants.

Many middle and small landlords, as well as rich and middle
peasants who formerly opposed the Peasant Associations, now begged
for admission to them. I met a number of these people in the places
I visited, and they said: "I beg the commissioner from the capital to
endorse me.". . . *Very Bad and Very Good.* The peasant revolution in
the countryside awakened the gentry from their sweet dreams. When
the news reached the cities from the villages, the urban gentry protested
tumultuously. On first arriving in Shanghai, I met people of different
backgrounds and heard a lot of gossip. From the middle social strata
to the Kuomintang right wing the general comment was "very bad".
Even some revolutionary-minded people did not object to this
comment, especially when they used their imagination as to conditions in the countryside. Some progressive elements only remarked
apologetically: "Though this is bad, it is inevitable during the process
of revolution." All in all, nobody entirely denied the epithet "bad".
But as pointed out previously, it is actually the rising up of the vast
peasant masses to accomplish their historic mission; it is the rising up
of the democratic forces in the countryside to overthrow their feudal
forces in the villages, which is the goal of the national revolution.

Sun Yat-sen devoted forty years to the national revolution; what
he wanted but failed to achieve has been accomplished by the peasants
in a few months. The patriarchal, feudal *t'u-hao* and bad gentry,
together with the illegal landlords, were not only the foundation
of the dictatorial regime of the past several thousand years, but also
the tools of the imperialists, war lords, and corrupt officials. This is
a great achievement unprecedented in the past forty years or several
thousand years. This is "very good" and not in the least "bad", and
not at all "very bad".[27]

Naturally, the Communists were equally active organizing the Chinese
workers, particularly in the bustling harbor cities. Yü Mo Hwai, a young
agitator from Shanghai, told Miss Strong of his successful efforts among
various categories of laborers and employees:

"When I came back from the labor Congress in Canton, the troops had grown too strong for me to escape them in the province, so I decided to go to the city of Shanghai and organize municipal workers. I gave a bribe of $50 to the foreman of the Power Works in French town, and for this he gave me a job in the power plant. It was a very good job, for from this point of vantage I organized four unions of city employees—the streetcar men, the street cleaners, the power plant and the waterworks. I had them ready in a few months for the advance of the Nationalists, and it was we who took over power in the city.". . .

He organized the workers on the Nanking railway and got their wages raised from 20 to 25 cents (gold) per day with a rest day every two weeks. Later they got a rest day every Sunday. . . . He organized the Ningpo Railway and got the same terms there. He organized municipal laborers in Shanghai and their wages rose from $7.50 (gold) a month for an eleven-hour day to $8.60 a month.

"All this success," he told me, "influenced other municipal workers, so we were soon able to organize a Federation of Municipal Employees, including telephone, telegraph, electric works, waterworks, and postal. Thus we were ready for the General Strike by which we took power in the native city.

"The labor pickets," he said, relating that stirring event, "seized the police headquarters by surprise and captured eight hundred rifles. With these and with clubs and railway implements we gathered thousands of workers and disarmed the Fengtien guards at the arsenal. It took two and a half days' hard fighting till we captured the arsenal for the Nationalists. All power was now in the hands of the labor unions. Before the army came, we chose a temporary municipal government, a Committee of Nineteen, of which five were chosen by the unions. Five district groups of labor pickets kept order. We sent a telegram of allegiance to the Wuhan Government and were accepted by them."[28]

*The lower Yangtze area, with the two large cities of Nanking and Shanghai, fell to the Nationalists in March 1927. The seizure of Nanking was accompanied by an attack on the city's international concessions which cost the lives of six foreigners.**

* According to many, the attack (conducted by both soldiers and civilians) was engineered by Communist elements eager to embarrass Chiang—but the available evidence is inconclusive.

Chiang Kai-shek and the conservative wing of the Kuomintang now set up a new government at Nanking, which meant an open break with the radical element at Wuhan. The Nationalists launched into a country-wide hunt of Communists and labor leaders throughout southern China. Shanghai was "purged" in April 1927, and a Communist rising was crushed in Canton in December of that year. Having been chased out of the large cities, the Communists retreated to Hunan and Kiangsi provinces, where Mao Tse-tung and Chu Teh began reorganizing them for new and greater tasks.

Surface harmony between the rival governments of Nanking and Wuhan was restored (in August 1927) by the elimination of Russians and Communists from Wuhan in return for the temporary retirement of Chiang Kai-shek. The forty-year-old Chiang took advantage of this lull in his stormy career to get married to Soong (or Sung) Meiling, a Protestant, American-educated, and wealthy young lady of great charm. She was the sister of Sun Yat-sen's widow, of T. V. Soong (Nationalist Minister of Finances), and of the wife of the great banker H. H. K'ung, Minister of Industry, Commerce, and Labor. Chiang, in other words, allied himself with the Chinese "upper" bourgeoisie, which in turn was linked to the Western business world by many solid bonds.

In the struggle for supremacy which henceforth put the Kuomintang and the Kungch'antang in opposition throughout the greater part of China, the Nationalists had won the first round. But the Communists were far from being decisively beaten or eliminated, or even discouraged. Many more rounds were to follow—the struggle was going to be long, bitter, and destructive for both sides.

CHAPTER IX

VICTORIES OF THE KUOMINTANG
1928-1935

THE CENTRAL Executive Committee of the Kuomintang was determined to take full advantage of the remarkably successful "March to the North", and decided on an early resumption of military operations in order to complete the unification of China. In April 1928, Chiang Kai-shek was recalled from his official "retirement", and placed in command of a fresh northern campaign. In this new venture, Chiang was assisted by the magnetic (if erratic) "Christian" Marshal, Feng Yu-hsiang; his principal opponent was the "northern" Marshal, Chang Tso-lin, whose rule over Manchuria had the approval of Japan.

Once more, victory smiled on the Nationalists. After a short conflict (May 3 to 11) with Japanese troops, sent to protect residents of Tsinan (or Chinan, capital of Shantung), Chiang began his drive against Peking. The opportune death of Chang Tso-lin (engineered by the Japanese, whose advice Chang had rejected) made his task easier, and on June 8 the Nationalists entered the northern capital.* In October, the Nationalists transferred the capital to Nanking which, unlike Peking, was not garrisoned by foreign contingents, and had the advantage of lying in the economic heart of China. In November of that year, Chang Tso-lin's son, Chang Hsueh-liang, completed the country's unification by recognizing the Nanking government.

Having thus secured a certain degree of unity at home, the Kuomintang next endeavored to reduce the privileges of Western powers in China. Obviously, the diplomatic approach was the best means of obtaining any result, and within weeks after the military conquest, the new masters of China launched into a peaceful offensive aiming at the abolition of the "unequal treaties".

Sir Meyrick Hewlett, who arrived in Nanking in August 1928 as British Consul General, was the first foreign diplomat to experience the winning charm of the new Chinese attitude:

My first visit was to the Vice-Minister of Foreign Affairs, Y. L.

* It was renamed Peip'ing, while Chihli Province became Hopei.

Tong, who proved a real friend. He was related to Feng Yu-hsiang. He said I was very welcome and all were glad to see me as I was the first Consul General in Nanking, and he hoped the other Powers would follow our example. Nothing now stood in the way of good relations; a new era had begun and there would be no going back. He affirmed there was a distinct desire to draw closer to Great Britain and everyone was pleased to have the representative of Great Britain back again. I told him how glad I was at last to be at my own post, and that I had no intention of harping on bygones. . . .

I knew his wishes were a gradual handling of cases systematically and methodically, working up, rushing nothing, in fact, in the phrase he had used to T. V. Soong,* "taking the small jumps first". Tong said Dr. Wang† was most anxious Sir Miles‡ should visit Nanking and was prepared to give him a rousing reception. He added, as a hint, perhaps a Tariff Autonomy Treaty could be drawn up before he came and the Treaty signed at the same time. Like T. V. Soong he harped on the centralization of finance being the real problem and he said it really looked as if Federated States was the solution. I replied that I knew from experience in Hunan, Szechuan and Fukien that the Federal spirit was very strong, but I feared so much was said of a united China it was not a solution which could be mentioned. China was united in her national government, but provincial feeling was very strong. I did not add what I felt, that it was a regrettable fact that the only thing which really united China was an anti-foreign outburst.[1]

Being an old hand in Chinese affairs, Sir Meyrick knew from personal experience that anti-foreignism was indeed a current feature of China's atmosphere at the time. More specifically, he knew that England shared with Japan the honor of being a prime target of anti-foreign outbursts. From his new and responsible post at Nanking, he endeavored to influence Chinese public opinion favorably, and hit upon the idea of using that typically British sport, football,§ in an effort to gain goodwill:

* Brother-in-law of Sun Yat-sen and of Chiang Kai-shek. Played a leading role in Chinese finances after 1924.

† Wang Ching-wei, favorite disciple of Sun Yat-sen and head of the government. Became head of the puppet government established by the Japanese at Nanking in 1940.

‡ British Ambassador to China.

§ Or association football (soccer), not to be confused with American football.

Universities, especially the University of Nanking, were filled with students whose patriotic zeal led them to be keenly anti-British. I felt the best way to combat this regrettable spirit of hatred would be through football, so I arranged a series of matches between the ships of the Yangtze flotilla* and Gingling College. . . .

The success of these games with Gingling College brought a challenge from the [Nanking] Central University which was *the* hotbed of anti-foreign agitations. I decided to risk it, although I knew some of the students had vowed they would never permit sailors in any uniform to enter their compound.

The police were worried over this venture, and the Chief of the Police was present with a large guard in mufti. The men who came from H.M.S. *Sepoy* were told to pay no attention to any queer things the Chinese might do, such as substituting players while others got their breath, and to take anything that might happen good-naturedly. The ship was asked to supply the referee, and never have I seen a match so skilfully handled. When the *Sepoy* was leading 3–1 he gave a foul against them in front of their goal. The University back took the free kick and missed. The huge crowd roared with delight and there was no danger of any trouble after that. During the game one of their team tripped up one of our team from behind, but our fellow at once presumed it was an accident and on getting up shook hands with the offender, an action spotted by the huge crowd which was watching. A rattling good match was won by the ship 5–3, and the University asked me to arrange at least two matches a month during the following season. I was told that the matches did much to improve the play of the students, especially in headwork, to which they had paid little attention till they saw how effective it was with our men. One of the Chinese teachers said, "In any case your fellows have taught them not to mind making their hair dirty!"[2]

After 1930, "retrocession commissions" were entrusted with the delicate task of negotiating the gradual surrender of extraterritorial rights and concessions. The "small" nations (Italy, Spain, Belgium) complied more readily than the "great" powers which, of course, enjoyed far broader privileges in China, and were little inclined to give them up.†

* Small warships for the protection of British residents.

† The United States, England, and France made their final "retrocessions" (to Chiang Kai-shek) only in the course of World War II.

In the meantime, and thanks to the relative unity and stability achieved by the recent Kuomintang victories, Western business along the Chinese coast experienced a period of remarkable prosperity. Shanghai, in particular, was by far the wealthiest city of China, controlling about half her foreign trade and fully deserving the proud title of "Queen of the Far East". Life in Shanghai was good and glorious in the thirties, especially for the successful Western taïpan, or "big boss". An American journalist who knew the booming city well, E. O. Hauser, has analyzed the peculiar atmosphere surrounding Western businessmen there:

In the well-burnished brass plates with the names of all these firms, big and little, old and new, there was the soul of Shanghai. . . . The gates with those well-burnished brass plates were guarded by Indian Sikhs, ferocious with beards and turbans. Upstairs, behind large windows, were white men in shirt sleeves. They were working a little harder than their forebears, the *taïpans* of the nineteenth century. Their office hours were a little longer, and there were always a few things that had to be taken care of today—not the day after tomorrow. Airmail communications, via Hong Kong, with Britain, France, and America, had begun to interfere with their traditional leisure. But the spirit of Shanghai's early age still lingered on. The White Man, behind his desk, was still king. He had more liberty and more elbow room than his colleague in the city of London, and the big boss would hardly ever talk down to him. The White Man, even in the offices of Standard Oil or Butterswire, was the White Man's equal. And the Chinese staff, shroffs and clerks and bookkeepers, were way below the wildest griffin.

Surely not every white man was a *taïpan*, in the Shanghai of 1936. Most of them had come out here as simple employees, on common contracts. The terms were five years' work and six to ten months' paid furlough in most British houses, a little less in many American firms. After the end of the first term, another equally long term would begin, and so on. Salaries were far higher than those paid for civilian jobs at home, and they were paid in American dollars or in sterling. Anybody who made more than 25,000 Shanghai dollars a year was a *taïpan*. The average *taïpan's* income was 75,000 dollars.

Western firms had their offices all over downtown Shanghai—along the streets with the city names: Nanking Road, Peking Road, Canton Road; and along the streets with the names of provinces: Chekiang

Road, Szechuan Road, Kiangsi Road. (The city streets and the provincial streets crossed each other at right angles, warp and woof fashion.) But the Bund* had remained Shanghai's favored location throughout these ninety years, and the offices in the big white Bund buildings were still superior to all others. Some of them were air-conditioned by now. And out of their windows the Shanghai gentlemen overlooked the shimmering river below, saw the long gray silhouettes of their warships, and the flat Chinese country behind Pootung. They were proud of Shanghai.

At four-thirty in the afternoon, the white man left the office. If he was a *taïpan* with 75,000 dollars a year, his big black automobile was waiting for him. Otherwise, he just took a rickshaw. One did not get much pleasure out of a motorcar, anyway. Only one or two good roads were leading out of Shanghai into the countryside, and those were bandit-infested most of the time. So the white man took a rickshaw: one of those rickshaws that came shooting over from at least five different directions as soon as he emerged from the gate with the well-burnished brass plates. . . .

The white man remembered the first time he had taken a rickshaw, the day he had arrived in Shanghai. The humanitarian misgivings he had about being pulled by a fellow man. It had worried him a good deal, at that time, that his puller would inevitably die from consumption within a few years. It had troubled him to think of the puller's feet. . . .

It was different now. He had forgotten his misgivings and he had come to enjoy his daily rickshaw ride. He knew, now, that the dripping back in front of his feet did not consider his job as humiliating. He knew that his half-naked coolie was a good sport, with his own, highly developed sense of humor; that he soaked his twelve-copper sandals in water to make them softer even at the risk of making them less durable. . . .

The white man enjoyed the soft rhythm that came from the coolie's feet, through the shafts, rocking the rickshaw as it rolled along. No other vehicle was so relaxing. . . .

The white man lived on Avenue Haig, or Hungjao Road, or Bubbling Well, or Great Western. Many of the 75,000-dollar-a-year *taïpans* still had their villas, out there. But the majority of the Shanghai

* Broad embanked quay along the Whangpoo River, a combination of waterfront, business center, and promenade.

gentlemen had moved into those modern, ten- or fifteen-story apartment houses that had been put up, not too far from the offices, and the flats were cheaper, and just as comfortable as the pretentious villas. They had large windows, good ventilation, much air and much light. They had electric refrigerators and electric fans, and there were large bottles with drinking water in every room—Shanghai water had to be boiled before it could be drunk, and the bottles had narrow necks so that the "boys" could not throw pieces of ice into the disinfected water.

There, in his well-furnished apartment, the white man would have dinner with his wife or, if he was a bachelor, with the other bachelors that shared his "mess." And, if he was a bachelor, he would go out shortly after dinner to have his fun. Shanghai was the place to give a bachelor all the fun he could possibly ask for. Throughout those turbulent years, through revolutions and civil wars, through crises and depressions, Shanghai had gone on with the world's most glamorous, most sparkling night life. Beneath a million brilliant lights, the cabarets and gambling houses, the theatres, teahouses, dancing halls, singsong places, were jammed with customers. There was the jai-alai, upon Avenue du Roi Albert, where thousands of white and yellow men were winning slow and losing fast, every night. There was the Canidrome, where they had dog races and where they doped the greyhounds so persistently that one of the poor animals collapsed right on the track one evening. But Shanghai's greatest attraction was still its "cabarets," where the Shanghai gentlemen could dance with the girls for as little as ten cents or as much as one dollar a dance— according to the cabaret's class and reputation.

You drifted into one of those cabarets, an hour or so before midnight, you chose your table not too far from the floor, and you looked them over: the pretty Chinese girls with their slit silk dresses and with too much rouge on their soft cheeks; the glorious Russians with their décolleté evening gowns—Chanel and Molyneux models, if you did not look too closely; the stupid and touchingly attractive Koreans; the slightly simian half-castes; the quick and clever Japanese. They were all sitting there, in a row, smoking their cigarettes, some of them giggling. And you bought your ticket and danced with them, and if you invited one of them to your table, you had to pay something extra and the girl had apple cider that turned into champagne on your chit. But if you wanted to go home with her, she would have to ask the management first. And so you made your rounds through the Ambassador, the Casanova, the Venus Café. . . . You had beer or brandy at one of those cheap places over in Hongkew where you could pet a fourteen-year-old Chinese girl behind a filthy curtain. And you might wind up in "Bloody Alley," where you went to get as much local color as possible, among the drunken soldiers and sailors of the armies and navies of the world.

You could have other, less stormy amusements if you were more discriminating or married. Shanghai did not offer much along the line of sophisticated entertainment. There was still no opera, no lectures to speak of, no Western stage. The first showing of a Hollywood movie, under these circumstances, assumed the proportions of a major event on the social calendar, with all the consuls and *taïpans* attending, in full evening dress. Or you might have ventured to one of those dreadful performances given by the amateur actors and actresses at the Lyceum Theatre. You might, perchance, hear the nephew of the Chairman of the Municipal Council sing.

On those hot summer evenings when Shanghai's asphalt streets were radiating the heat that they had absorbed during the day, Shanghailanders would go out to Jessfield Park to listen to the Municipal Orchestra. All the *taïpans* would be there, and they would bring their wives. They would recline in deck chairs and look up to a dark ultramarine sky where scores of comets drew their gleaming paths. The Municipal Orchestra would play Mozart's *Eine Kleine Nachtmusik* and the faint suggestion of a breeze would comb the lawn. . . .

Some sixty thousand foreigners were living on the twelve square miles of the two foreign municipalities and on the few "outside roads" under their control. Nearly twenty thousand of them were refugee Russians who did not "count." Another twenty thousand were Japanese who kept to themselves. Of the remaining twenty thousand, nine thousand were British, four thousand Americans, two and a half thousand French. The rest were Germans, Scandinavians, South Americans, and half-caste Portuguese. There was, in other words, a white community of less than twenty thousand people which played society. And this limitation gave Shanghai's social life a peculiarly intimate touch. In a metropolis of four million—small-town rivalries and gossip. . . .

Occasionally, an enterprising *tai-tai** would attempt to introduce

* The wife of a *taïpan*.

a new note into Shanghai's social life. Some American ladies pioneered, although not too successfully, in inviting both Chinese and foreigners to their homes. One of them, Mrs. Chester Fritz, who gave parties every Sunday night, prided herself on presiding over Shanghai's only "salon". Foreigners mingled with prominent Chinese—Madame Chiang Kai-shek and the "Young Marshal," Chang Hsueh-liang, were among her guests. But the hostess was too extravagant (she always wore a turban) to be taken seriously. Malicious people insinuated that her personality might have gone far toward stimulating the business of her husband, Chester Fritz, of Swan, Calbertson and Fritz, brokers.

But exceptions like this did not change the picture. The British style of life prevailed. The British had constructed the Shanghai scheme, and it was only fair to let them set the pace for Shanghai's social life. Most of the "do's" and "don'ts" were British, and a good many Americans were ignominiously absorbed by Shanghai's British atmosphere. They were absorbed to the extent of taking their tea with cream, of saying "I cawn't" and "rawther," and waving "Cheerio !" to their friends. They dressed for dinner.[3]

China's countless villages and small towns, meanwhile, were as yet untouched by modern influences. Age-old traditions still governed the daily life of the peasant masses, and parents asserted their authority as firmly as ever in molding the fate of their children. Prearranged marriages and child-hood engagements, in particular, were commonly accepted manifestations of parental power—and filial obedience.

Increasing numbers of country boys and girls, however, rebelled against this old-fashioned custom. They had usually attended secondary school, where they had come into contact with more liberal ideas and had developed minds of their own. One such rebel was a Hunanese girl, Hsieh Pingying, who fought in the revolutionary ranks in the late twenties and thirties, and became one of the half-dozen well-known women writers of China. In her autobiography, Miss Hsieh recorded the incident when she refused to marry Hsiaoming, a well-bred young man to whom her parents had long ago "engaged" her:

"Father, I have come home especially to settle this matter," I began. "You must remember the letter I wrote you. I cannot possibly live with Hsiaoming. We are not even fond of each other; indeed, we feel absolutely nothing toward each other. His ideas, his interests, differ altogether from mine. I cannot understand his character, I just do not understand him. How can I be his wife?"

"You don't want to live with him? Do you mean to say you wish to break the engagement?" Father shouted and banged on the table.

"Yes, I have come back to break it off," I replied calmly.

Mother shouted, angrily, "You can't break the engagement unless you leave this house and never come back. . . . No matter what you do, you can't escape." She raised her hand as if to strike me. Father left the room puffing with anger, and I could not go on, and went to my bedroom and wrote a five-thousand-word letter explaining why I did not want to be married.

The next day, to my surprise, Father did not seem to be a bit touched by my words, but, with a severe countenance, started berating me. [*The author vainly argued that husband and wife should share the same ideas or beliefs.*] . . ."Hunh!" my father exclaimed. "Ideas? What need has a woman of such dangerous revolutionary ideas? Of course, you have had several years of education and you will be allowed to be a primary schoolteacher after marriage. I don't think he will object to that."

"Don't argue with her any more!" Mother burst out. "She is not even human! We are her parents. How dare she oppose us?" Turning to me, she went on, "When we sent you to school, we were hoping that you might learn social manners and a sense of honor. We did not expect you to turn out to be a beast. You don't even care for your parents! This engagement was made when you were still suckling at my breast. Are you so shameless as to break it and ruin your parents' name and disgrace your ancestors?"

She quoted an old verse: " 'A good husband and a good wife are predestined.' No matter what kind of person you are engaged to, you've got to marry him. . . . Marriage is something already settled in your previous incarnation. How can you oppose it?"

I listened without a word, without even a sneer, for I knew before she spoke all that she was going to say. . . . Mother was scolding again, saying that she had not thought that I would disappoint her thus after sending me to school for so many years. She said she was not going to let any of the daughters of Elder Brother and Third Brother go to school any more. . . .

Absorbed in my thoughts, I suddenly heard Father renew his curses.

"What kind of witch house is the school! Every girl comes out of it bewitched and demands the breaking of the engagement her parents have settled! She has to break it, however good it is."

"Of course," I said. "How can parents know what kind of husband or wife their child should have? Marriage is a great part of life. Every one has to choose for herself if marriage is to be successful!". . .

"Outrageous! A young girl picking a husband for herself!" Mother cried. "The Hsiao family has high standing. . . . And I have received so many presents from the family! Last year your fiancé even came to congratulate me on my birthday. Now you are creating this scandal. How can I ever face them? The proverb says, '. . . A good girl will never marry twice.' Do you remember the story in the *Book of Heroines*?"

Father interrupted. "Do you think she reads the *Book of Heroines* any more? She reads only novels of free love, newspaper stories. . . . She is affected by all this and is turning against her parents, against the conventions!"

"The old conventions were set by the sages thousands of years ago." Mother's tone became more and more severe. "And you, a girl, dare to defy them! Don't you know how chastity-monuments were built? Even girls of twelve know the importance of chastity. . . ."

I realized that it was completely useless to argue with her. The only thing was to fight it out, not to give in until I had broken the engagement.

She went on, "The Hsiaos own a lot of property and you can earn money too. . . . You will have a very comfortable life!". . .

"Don't talk of these things," I cried with visible annoyance. "I'd rather marry a poor man I love than a rich man!"

"What do you want then?" Mother banged on the table.

"She wants to break the engagement," Father answered for me.

"What will she do if she can't break it?"

"In her letter she said she would commit suicide!"

"All right! Let her do it! I have brought her up and sent her to school in vain. Perhaps I owed her a debt in the previous incarnation, and I am asked to repay it now!"

Mother burst into tears and struck her head against the wall. Afraid that she might be hurt, Father went to her and held her, and my sister and sister-in-law went to her too, and while they were thus occupied, I slipped away and went outside to walk.

The sun was warm, but my heart was sad and cold.[4]

One of the most urgent tasks confronting the Kuomintang after its more or less complete conquest of China (local war lords and renascent Communism were constant sources of trouble) was the reorganization and modernization of the country's backward economy. Considerable efforts were made in the domain of public works, and resulted in visible improvements in such essential branches as railroad communications, postal service, telecommunications, and naval installations. The Kuomintang leaders, on the other hand, called on powerful foreign firms (Imperial Chemical Industries, I. G. Farben, Standard Oil, etc.) to help develop China's infant industrialization.

One name, or rather nickname, epitomized both the economic and the political methods pursued by the Kuomintang. It was that of the "Soong clan" (meaning Chiang Kai-shek's relatives on the side of his wife, the former Miss Soong), whose members held most of the regime's choice posts and dreamed of building up a powerful capitalistic economy in their country.

The Soong clan's most typical representative was Harvard-educated T. V. Soong, who controlled seven banks, twelve commercial firms, twenty-two factories, and one steamship company. A Swiss journalist who met him in 1933 drew the following sketch of "Tee-Vee's"* personality:

He has the uninhibited, youthful and merry appearance of an American boy, and one rather fancies him playing football at Harvard University than walking in a long robe on the streets of Nanking. Even more striking than his physical resemblance to an American is Soong's ability to make rapid decisions, his taste for action and initiative, as well as all other qualities which Americans, by whom he was trained, call efficiency. . . .

These characteristics would be precious in any statesman of any country. They are doubly precious in China, because they are found there so rarely. At the same time, however, they estrange Soong from the rest of his countrymen, who no longer recognize themselves in him.[5]

Essentially, the leadership of Kuomintang China was assumed by the

* It was fashionable at the time, in Westernized Chinese families, to "Anglosaxonize" one's name by placing the initials of the first and middle names before the family name. As a result of this un-Chinese practice, Soong Tse-wen became known as "T. V." (pronounced "Tee-Vee") Soong.

"returned students". Most of these came from the industrial and trading bourgeois families of China's leading harbor cities or were sons of the landed gentry.

*The peculiar features of these foreign-trained students were portrayed by the French "colonial" physician and writer Marc Chadourne who, by the way, minimized the influence of France:**

What are the distinguishing features of a "returned student"? First of all, the color of his jacket—because they do not revert to Chinese dress until several months after their return home. Iron-gray means back from the United States, navy-blue means back from England (preferably with gold-rimmed glasses), beige or light gray, back from Lyons or Paris's Latin Quarter. Students who have not left their homeland wear purple jackets. Also, each type of dress carries with it a specific type of behavior, accent, and manners.

The American-trained student is definitely the one most strongly marked by his re-education. He is characterized by a strong Yankee accent, horn-rimmed glasses, gold-crowned teeth, the chewing-gum habit, and the very un-Chinese phrase, "Time is money." Moreover, he is precise, dogmatic, resolute, and somewhat stiff in the knowledge of his superiority. He shows no indulgence, at least during the first few months of his return, toward the old country's slow ways, disorder, and lack of hygiene. He drinks only water. He no longer uses the bowl and chopsticks; he forsakes the Mah-Jongg restaurants and opium dens, preferring the modern-style girl students to the small female singers. Eventually, though, he will come back to the latter.

He is fully determined to change China. Together with Professor Hu Shih,† who is also American-educated, he holds that the *spiritual* superiority of the Far East over the West is but an old Mandarin myth for the consumption of Kayserling‡ and of some tired European philosophers of the postwar period; that a country's civilization cannot be founded on smoke of incense, dreams of bonzes and poetic calligraphy, but upon its material progress; that a civilized nation does not use half its children as rickshaw pullers for the enjoyment of the other half; and that there is a deeper spiritual value in a dynamo or in an

---

* Many of Red China's leaders, beginning with Chou En-lai, studied in France and there became revolutionaries.

† Champion of the *pai-hua*, or "plain speech" style of writing.

‡ German world traveler, writer and philosopher.

X-ray machine than in the prayer of an old, vermin-ridden beggar passing away while muttering his *Nama Amita Buddha.** He is healthy, matter-of-fact. He no longer believes in the spirits of the pagoda, nor in the virtue of strength of character. He believes in the Buick, the radio, the Victrola, the vernacular speech. He writes in English, thinks like an American businessman, and reads his newspaper at the Y.M.C.A. Sometimes he may convert himself to Protestantism, just as one takes to playing tennis or cricket. It is fashionable, elegant. Some students have spent long years in the United States, while others were born there in the Chinese communities of New York or San Francisco. They will become China's great men, like her present Foreign Minister, M. C. T. Wang. . . .

In contrast to these students, and perhaps the least changed, are the young men coming back from Boul' Mich' or Place Bellecour.† Their somewhat bohemian appearance is typically "Franco-Chinese". They wear loosely tied bows and crumpled trousers, and display a certain propensity toward idleness; they are, moreover, characterized by their habit of scheming, their sly skepticism, a taste for empty and pompous phrases, or advanced opinions borrowed—without thorough examination—from such famous yet rather "outdated" authors as Proudhon, Auguste Comte, and Emile Zola.[6]

The methods adopted by the Kuomintang authorities in their drive for a new China were often autocratic. Stringent censorship, for instance, was imposed whenever it was deemed necessary (or convenient) by national or local leaders.

The French journalist M. Nachbaur, chief editor of the Journal de Pékin, *denounced this lack of freedom in a letter he wrote in January 1931 to the Belgian periodical* La Nation Belge:

Censorship here is being imposed in all fields, and with a severity unknown in European countries, so that it is very difficult abroad to obtain an accurate picture of the present situation in China.

The Chinese press is absolutely at the mercy of the authorities, including local committees which do not hesitate to prohibit the

* Buddhist ritual prayer for the dying.

† The Boulevard Saint-Michel in Paris ("Boul' Mich'" to Parisians) and Bellecour Square in Lyons are favorite meeting places of the students in these two cities.

publication of certain papers, and even jail journalists who do not comply. Nothing can be published that might cause any prejudice to officialdom and the men in power. Even the foreign press, which is not controlled by Chinese jurisdiction, has lost its independence. Thus the circulation of the *North China Star*, the *North China Daily News*, and the *Journal de Pékin** was interrupted by the Chinese postal authorities, which refused to ship the papers. This embargo lasted for three months, and ended only when the papers implicitly promised to henceforth abstain from publishing information detrimental to Chiang Kai-shek and his ministers. . . .

The Ministry of the Interior has warned that . . . papers publishing "incorrect" news . . . will be liable to pay a minimum fine of $200. It must be added that cablegrams sent out by foreign correspondents are also censored, and that the press card is sometimes refused to certain correspondents because Chinese authorities dislike their faces or their opinions. From such examples, it is easy to realize how little freedom of press and of speech is being tolerated by the regime of the Chinese Republic.[7]

After 1934, the Kuomintang sponsored a kind of moral order, called the "New Life Movement," throughout China. Chiang Kai-shek, whose private life was very austere, followed the progress of the movement personally. His wife—who from the very beginning played a very active role in Nationalist China—explained the new order's principles to a French journalist:

The aim of the "New Life Movement" is to teach the Chinese citizen to appreciate life as it is. Its actual purpose is to revive the four traditional and fundamental virtues of Chinese civilization: *li, yi, lien,* and *ch'e,* or etiquette, justice, integrity, and conscience. The use of these virtues in the humblest domains will enable people to get along with one another, to educate themselves, to help each other and to adapt themselves to their surroundings. The daily practice of these four virtues will show that a healthy people can produce a sound government, which in turn will be able to solve the great problem of our national life. Self-respect will create in each person a feeling of individual responsibility. This feeling again will spread throughout the country and make it strong. Eventually, these four ancient virtues

---

* Leading American, English, and French papers in China, respectively.

will produce in China a change of minds and hearts that will in due time crown both our spiritual and our material revolution.

The "New Life Movement" has spread throughout the country. In the remotest villages, our students are endeavoring to propagate the principles of science, hygiene, and cleanliness. "New Life" is the phrase one hears most often in the mouth of the Chinese. Already at the mouth of the Whangpoo River, the Shanghai-bound traveler who reads Chinese is assailed by the movement's slogans exhorting him to be clean, dignified, simple and honest. If he goes as far as Nanking, he finds these same slogans written on placards mounted on telephone posts, and wherever there is some space—in buses, ships, and other public vehicles. Cleanliness and elegance (the proper use of handkerchiefs) are strictly compulsory. It is not rare to see the highest local authorities clean the streets in order to set an example for the population. In the cities, a health inspector visits each house every week, and posts a sign with the inscription: "clean", "fairly clean", or "dirty", as the case may be.[8]

Another Kuomintang creation was the "Rural Service", an organization sending students to the countryside, where they spent their vacation helping the peasants harvest their crops.

The immense majority of China's hard-working and illiterate peasant masses was quite poor, overburdened with taxes, and debt-ridden.* At least two-thirds of the country's cultivable land was concentrated in the hands of resident or absentee landlords, rich peasants, officials, and usurers making up only ten percent of the total rural population. The Kuomintang did very little to promote rural education, or to reduce the exorbitant land taxes and interest rates overtaking the peasant's limited means. It was little wonder, therefore, that increasing numbers of peasants became receptive to Communist propaganda and its promise of land reform.

China's peasantry invariably suffered more than the rest of the population from such crises as drought, famine and flood. The years 1929 to 1934 were particularly dramatic in that respect. In the northwestern provinces, from three to six million people perished of famine between 1929 and 1932. The young American journalist Edgar Snow visited some of the drought-stricken areas:

* Land taxes, plus various "surtaxes", generally took from forty-five to sixty-five percent of the peasant's modest income. Indebtedness was an ancient Chinese rural problem; local usurers charged interest rates of 100 percent, 200 percent, 300 percent.

This catastrophe passed hardly noticed in the Western world, or even in the coastal cities of China. . . . I was twenty-three. I had come to the East looking for the "glamour of the Orient", I suppose. I believe I fancied myself an adventurer, and this excursion to Suiyuan had begun as something like that. But here for the first time in my life I came abruptly upon men who were dying because they had nothing to eat. In those hours of nightmare I spent in Suiyuan I saw thousands of men, women, and children starving to death before my eyes. . . .

Children are even more pitiable, with their little skeletons bent over and misshapen, their crooked bones, their little arms like twigs, and their purpling bellies, filled with bark and sawdust, protruding like tumors. Women lie slumped in corners, waiting for death, their black bladelike buttocks protruding, their breasts hanging like collapsed sacks. But there are, after all, not many women and girls. Most of them have died or been sold.

I don't mean to dramatize horror. These are things I saw myself and shall never forget. . . . I saw fresh corpses on the streets of Saratsi, and in the villages I saw shallow graves where victims of famine and disease were laid by the dozens. But these were not the most shocking things after all. The shocking thing was that in many of those towns there were still rich men, rice hoarders, wheat hoarders, money-lenders, and landlords, with armed guards to defend them, while they profiteered enormously. The shocking thing was that in the cities— where officials danced or played with singsong girls—there was grain and food, and had been for months; that in Peking and Tientsin and elsewhere were thousands of tons of wheat and millet, collected (mostly by contributions from abroad) by the Famine Commission, but which could not be shipped to the starving. Why not? Because in the north-west there were some militarists who wanted to hold all of their rolling stock and would release none of it toward the east, while in the east there were other Kuomintang generals who would send no rolling stock westward—even to starving people—because they feared it would be seized by their rivals.[9]

Between 1931 and 1934, the main Chinese rivers (Yangtze, Huang-ho, Huai, plus Grand Canal) overflowed their banks, flooding an estimated total area as vast as all of Italy.

A French Jesuit missionary stationed near the Yellow River, or Huang-ho, wrote the following report in April 1934:

The situation began improving at the beginning of the month. The happiest piece of news we received was that all gaps, including that of Chang-yuan which had proved fatal to our area, had been closed. The repair work cost the government no less than half a million dollars. Let us hope that no further damage will occur in August, when the waters will rise again.

For eight months now, the villages and Christian communities of our province have suffered from the floods. According to an official report, 3900 villages were flooded; 529,000 houses collapsed;* 3,199,000 persons have fled; 270,000 of them have lost everything, and 50,000 people have died. During these eight months, the floods have brought about untold misery. In Kai-cheou, our houses, colleges and schools are crowded with refugees, boys and girls for the most part; their parents have returned to their homes to find out whether anything is left of them. The winter was particularly severe for these poor people, because the floods covered most of the countryside. People had erected mud huts on higher ground, but there were bad surprises. When the weather turned cold, masses of ice began accumulating along the widest gap, and at first formed a natural barrier. But soon the river's level rose again, and the ice dam eventually gave way under the pressure of the water masses. The country was flooded once more, and many villages were taken by surprise. Thousands of persons are said to have been drowned in the icy floods.

At the present time, the flood is receding at the rate of one foot per day. People are slowly rebuilding their houses, and wheat is being sown on higher ground. But we cannot as yet communicate with Christians of the southern areas. It is still impossible to travel on foot, and our boats are quite unable to advance through the thick mud.[10]

South of the flooded Yangtze valley, a new type of Chinese society was coming into existence in Kiangsi, Fukien, and Hunan. Communist agitators were hard at work indoctrinating and organizing the rural masses for any early unleashing of the nationwide "hurricane" predicted by Mao Tse-tung.

Following its estrangement from the Kuomintang, Chinese Communism at first persisted in relying almost exclusively on the workers (and students) in its bid for power. China's industrial proletariat, however, was much too weak—both from a numerical and an organizational point of view—to succeed in establishing a "new order". One after another the Communist

* Country dwellings were small and built with light materials.

risings of the late twenties were crushed by the Kuomintang authorities. The "White terror" subsequently imposed by the Kuomintang in the large eastern cities weakened the workers' movement still further. In 1931, the leading exponent of the Moscow-styled "proletarian revolution", Li Li-san, was expelled from the Central Committee of the Chinese Communist Party, which meant that new methods, better adapted to conditions in China, were to be adopted.

By that time, Mao Tse-tung and Chu Teh, who from the very beginning insisted on such "unorthodox" tactics as massive peasant risings and military ventures, had achieved spectacular results of their own, especially in Kiangsi Province. By means of agrarian reforms,* they rallied the peasantry to the Communist cause; their actual instrument of power was the Chinese Red Army, founded in 1928 and trained in hard-hitting and fast-moving guerrilla warfare. In December 1931, the Communists proclaimed a "Chinese Soviet Republic" in their Kiangsi stronghold, with Mao Tse-tung as Chairman of the "Provisional Government".

Mao's initial success, quite naturally, was due in the first place to the loyal support of the peasantry, from whose ranks came the majority of Red soldiers. In their increasingly bitter fight against Chiang Kai-shek's "White" troops, the Communist partisans were repeatedly saved from annihilation by the courage and devotion displayed by the rural masses. This was explained to the American journalist Edgar Snow by General P'eng Teh-huai, Commander of the First Front Red Army:

"It is absolutely necessary for the partisans to win the support and participation of the peasant masses. If there is no movement of the armed peasantry, in fact, there is no partisan base, and the army cannot exist. Only by implanting itself deeply in the hearts of the people, only by fulfilling the demands of the masses, only by consolidating a base in the peasant Soviets, and only by sheltering in the shadow of the masses, can partisan warfare bring revolutionary victory."

P'eng had been pacing up and down the balcony, delivering one of his points each time he returned to the table where I sat writing. Now he suddenly stopped, and stood thoughtfully reflecting.

"But nothing, absolutely nothing," he said, "is more important than this—that the Red Army is a people's army, and has grown because the people helped us.

---

* Such as land redistribution, reduction of taxes, establishment of Peasant Councils, creation of schools.

"I remember the winter of 1928, when my forces in Hunan had dwindled to a little over two thousand men, and we were surrounded. The Kuomintang troops burned down all the houses in a surrounding area of 300 *li*, seized all the food there, and then blockaded us. We had no cloth, we used bark to make short tunics, and we cut up the legs of our trousers to make shoes. Our hair grew long, we had no quarters, no light, no salt. We were sick and half starved. The peasants were no better off, and we would not touch what little they had.

"But the peasants encouraged us. They dug up from the ground the grain which they had hidden from the White troops, and gave it to us, and they ate potatoes and wild roots. They hated the Whites for burning their homes and stealing their food. Even before we arrived they had fought the landlords and tax collectors, so they welcomed us. Many joined us, and nearly all helped us in some way. They wanted us to win! And because of that we fought on and broke the blockade."

He turned to me and ended simply, "Tactics are important, but we could not exist if the majority of the people did not support us. We are nothing but the fist of the people beating their oppressors!"[11]

The Nanking government soon realized that the Kiangsi Soviet Republic constituted a far greater threat to Nationalist hegemony over China than the various war lords still refusing to recognize its authority. Accordingly, a series of "annihilation campaigns" (six in all, between 1930 and 1934) were organized by Chiang Kai-shek in an effort to eliminate what Nanking called the "Red bandits".

Though Chiang had superior material means at his disposal, and was advised by such outstanding German generals as von Seekt and Falkenhausen, his "human material" often proved quite mediocre. The British journalist Peter Fleming, who was one of the few Westerners to be admitted to the Kiangsi front, has described the peculiar atmosphere and organization prevailing among Nationalist troops:

For the last three years there have been permanently garrisoned in Kiangsi between 100,000 and 200,000 Government troops, and the lot of the inhabitants (as they freely admit) could hardly have been worse if the whole province, instead of only half of it, had been in the hands of the Reds. Press gangs, conscript labour, extra taxes, and many forms of indignity and extortion have made their lives a burden to them, and in return they have received only the most inadequate protection. If anything is calculated to make the Chinese peasant turn spontaneously to Communism (or to anything else that presents itself) it is having troops permanently billeted on him. . . .

The thing that struck me most on the front was that every officer to whom I spoke was thinking in terms of defence, not of attack. There is no real "front" in Kiangsi. Fortifications have been erected round the villages and towns, and an uncoordinated system of isolated garrisons has thus been established. Outside these fortifications there are no outposts and few patrols; news of a Communist advance is the signal for the soldiers to withdraw into the villages. When I was in Kiangsi preparations were on foot for Chiang Kai-shek's autumn offensive, and it struck me as significant that—as part of these preparations for a general attack—an order had been issued to all villages of more than two hundred families to build three forts if they had not got them already. Similarly, while work was going forward night and day on a huge military aerodrome at Nanchang, the capital of the province, the defences of that city, more than one hundred miles from the frontiers of the Communist territory, were being strengthened with scarcely less expedition. . . .

The Chinese soldier is commonly regarded as a joke by foreigners, and as a pest by compatriots. He is a mercenary. He often is, and always looks, absurdly young. . . . In billets he very seldom pays for what he eats, and the division to which he belongs was almost certainly created by diverting some part of the national or provincial revenue from more legitimate and needful expenditure. Should his general meet with a reverse, whether military or financial, he will be turned loose on a district, which is probably far from his home, with a rifle, a few rounds of ammunition, and a grievance against society. It is ten to one that his next appearance will be as a bandit.

As things stand, he is a nuisance, unmitigated by his usefulness in a time of national emergency; his only redeeming feature is his cheerfulness, and even that is too often soured by shortage of pay and rations. Small wonder that the people hate him. Take, for instance, the case of a town like Nanchang. Apart from the periodic incursion, during major but invariably unsuccessful campaigns of better-class troops from Nanking, the town had been garrisoned for the past three years by the *n*th division. The *n*th division came from the North. They were strangers, with a different language* and a different diet from the

* There are many local dialects in central, and even more in southern China; outsiders do not understand them.

people on whom they were quartered. Their discipline had never been good, and it must have been hard to maintain even at its normal low level in that labyrinthine town, where billets were inevitably scattered and where there was no place inside the walls which could be used as a parade ground. Once you marched your men in you virtually lost control of them.

Most of the time there was nothing for the troops to do. Their vile marksmanship could not be improved, for lack of ammunition to practice with. Their equipment was ridiculous. In a file of four men you would often see three different makes of rifle (the commonest was Japanese). The homemade stick bombs which dangled by lengths of old string from their belts looked (fortunately for the passer-by's peace of mind) about as likely to explode as the dumbbells which they resembled. Only a crack division can afford leather equipment; these men carried their cartridge clips in cotton bandoliers, and one day I saw half a dozen of these spread out in the sun to dry after being washed with the ammunition inside them. The nth division were, at best, caterpillars of the commonwealth. Those romantically situated forts* were prosaically evacuated at the first serious threat of danger, and expeditions which marched out against the Reds returned minus their rifles and their officers.

There you have a picture of the Chinese soldier at his worst. It is an accurate picture, but it is also unjust. For the curious thing is that the Chinese soldier has it in him to be a very good soldier. He inherits all the advantages of the Japanese soldier except his military traditions. Though you might not think it to look at him, he has great strength and endurance. He can live on next to nothing. He is often a man of courage and resource, and he will be loyal to a good master. On regular pay and full stomach his high spirits combine with his fatalism to keep his morale high, even when things are going badly. . . .

Why, then, is he in practice such a contemptible failure? Why is he a liability all round? . . . Because of his leaders. His leaders have almost never given him a chance. For every one Chinese battle that is won by strategy and tactics, nine are won by a particularly unscrupulous form of commercial diplomacy. Though there have been exceptions, the average Chinese general fights only as a last resort; he makes war by secret negotiations, under cover of a cloud of bombastic and defiant telegrams. Most battles are lost and won before a shot is fired.[12]

* A series of small fortifications located around the city.

The Nationalist leaders, naturally, were confident that the "Red bandits" would be crushed and eliminated before long. They had more men, more money, better weapons and better equipment than the elusive enemy, and Chiang Kai-shek spared none of his superior means in his successive drives toward "final" victory.

In the summer of 1933, Fleming managed to interview the austere, taciturn, and rather "formidable" Chiang, who by that time had risen to the rank of Marshal and was the Kuomintang's leading personality:

He came into the room quietly, and stood quite still, looking at us.* He wore a dark blue gown and carried in his one hand a scroll, evidently part of the agenda of his conference. He was of rather more than average height, and unexpectedly slim. His complexion was dark, his cheekbones high and prominent, and he had a jutting, forceful lower lip like a Habsburg's. His eyes were the most remarkable thing about him. They were large, handsome, and very keen—almost aggressive. His glances had a thrusting and compelling quality which is very rare in China, where eyes are mostly negative and noncommittal, if not actually evasive.

We stood up and bowed. Chiang Kai-shek motioned us to sit down. I was conscious of his eyes. The interview began.

I got through the essential courtesies as quickly as possible. The Marshal replied to them with businesslike and un-Oriental brevity. Then I came to our purpose. I said that China was the only country whose armies were actively and continuously engaging the forces of Bolshevism in the field, and that the world's interest in, and sympathy for, China would be stimulated by firsthand information, hitherto lacking, about what was happening on the spot. Would the Marshal allow my friend and myself to go up into Kiangsi and get that information?

The Marshal, after disconcerting me with a piercing stare, said that he would. He would wire that morning to the Governor of Kiangsi at Nanchang and instruct him to grant us every facility.

This was splendid. This was what we wanted. I thanked him warmly. And how soon did he expect to see the Red areas cleared up and the problem of Communism in China solved? Chiang Kai-shek replied, rather perfunctorily, that the Red armies at present in the field would

* Fleming was accompanied by a Chinese friend and interpreter.

be wiped out by that winter; after that would come the rehabilitation of the Communist areas, for which he had already drafted plans.

It was obvious that Chiang Kai-shek enjoyed the sound of his own voice far less than most politicians, in China and elsewhere. He was not the usual type of glib and rather impressive propaganda-monger; he did not cultivate salesmanship. He was moreover a busy man in the middle of a busy morning. I decided that we should make a better impression if we emulated his laconic methods and anticipated his wishes by cutting our interview as short as possible. I therefore asked him only one more question: When might we expect a *rapprochement* between China and Japan?

"On the Manchurian issue, never," said Chiang Kai-shek firmly.*

We rose and took our leave, with many expressions of gratitude. As we parted I received one more of those formidable glances, of the kind which prompts an involuntary self-accusation of some grave sartorial omission. We trooped down the garden path feeling very small. . . .

I retired abashed. Here was a man with a presence, with that something incalculable about him to which the herd instinctively defers. He was strong and silent by nature, not by artifice. . . . He may not be a great statesman, or a very great soldier . . . but he has something to him. He is a personality in his own right.[13]

Chiang Kai-shek was not far from the truth when he told Fleming that the Red armies would be "wiped out" within a matter of months. After four unsuccessful attempts to invade the Red areas and take them by storm of superior force, he now adopted a new strategy—the systematic surrounding of the numerically inferior enemy,† plus a strict economic blockade. About half a million men and nearly 400 modern aeroplanes were engaged in this fifth and largest military campaign, which got under way in the fall of 1933.

Losses were heavy on both sides, as both knew that a decisive struggle had begun. Day after day, the Nationalist Air Force bombed and machine-gunned soldiers and civilians alike in its efforts at annihilation. The peasant population suffered enormously: according to Kuomintang sources, about one million people were killed or starved to death in the process of recovering Soviet Kiangsi.

* In 1931–2, Japan occupied Manchuria, and subsequently established a puppet state, Manchukuo.

† The Reds could muster a total firing power of about 100,000 rifles, but had neither heavy artillery nor planes.

Less than a year after the beginning of Chiang Kai-shek's powerful drive, victory seemed to be close at hand: the Reds were all but caged, and their resistance grew weaker. Once more, however, they succeeded in out-maneuvering and outsmarting the "Whites". On October 16, 1934, they began a dramatic and year-long retreat, known as the "Long March" and famous ever since in the annals of Red China, which over a distance of ten thousand miles took them from Kiangsi to Shensi—where a "secondary" Soviet base had existed since 1933.

Besides the main strength of the Red Army (about 90,000 men, subsequently joined by nearly as many partisans from Hunan and Szechuan), thousands of Kiangsi peasants—old and young, men, women, and children—started out on the long and murderous trek.* Fatigue, sickness, famine, and almost constant enemy attacks killed the majority of the Red marchers, whose survivors surmounted scores of natural obstacles before reaching the Shensi haven.

Among the brighter episodes of the Long March, the daredevil crossing of the deep and swift Tatu River was probably the most spectacular. The bridge spanning the gorges of the river was the last possible passage east of Tibet; its capture meant another breakout from imminent encirclement, and relative freedom of movement through central Szechuan. The wooden flooring of the bridge had been partly removed by the Whites, whose machine guns and troops were poised for action.

Edgar Snow, who at the time spent many months among China's Communists, has described the exploit in some detail:

No time was to be lost. The bridge must be captured before enemy reinforcements arrived. Once more volunteers were called for. One by one Red soldiers stepped forward to risk their lives, and, of those who offered themselves, thirty were chosen. Hand grenades and Mausers were strapped to their backs, and soon they were swinging out above the boiling river, moving hand over hand, clinging to the iron chains. Red machine guns barked at the enemy redoubts and spattered the bridgehead with bullets. The enemy replied with machine guns of its own, and snipers shot at the Reds tossing high above the water, working very slowly toward them. The first warrior was hit, and dropped into the current below; a second fell, and then a third. But, as they drew

---

* The peasants believed that the return of the Kuomintang meant the return of the landlords. Factories were dismantled, and machinery loaded on mules and donkeys. Much equipment was abandoned during the march.

nearer the chains, the bridge flooring somewhat protected these dare-to-dies, and most of the enemy bullets glanced off, or ended in the cliffs on the opposite bank.

Never before had the Szechuanese seen Chinese fighters like these —men for whom soldiering was not just a rice bowl, but youths ready to commit suicide to win! Were they human beings or madmen or gods? wondered the superstitious Szechuanese. Their own morale was affected; perhaps they did not shoot to kill; perhaps some of them secretly prayed that they would succeed in their attempt! At last one Red crawled up over the bridge flooring, uncapped a grenade, and tossed it with perfect aim into the enemy redoubt. Desperate, the officers ordered the rest of the planking to be torn up. It was already too late. More Reds were crawling into sight. Paraffin was thrown on the planking, and it began to burn. But then about twenty Reds were moving forward on their hands and knees, tossing grenade after grenade into the enemy machine-gun nest.

Suddenly, on the southern shore, their comrades began to scream with joy. "Long live the Red Army! Long live the Revolution! Long live the thirty heroes of Tatu Ho!" For the Whites were withdrawing, were in pell-mell flight! Running full speed over the remaining planks of the bridge, right through the flames licking toward them, the assailants nimbly hopped into the enemy's redoubt and turned the abandoned machine gun against the shore.

More Reds now swarmed over the chains, and arrived to help put out the fire and replace the boards. And soon afterward the Red division that had crossed at An Jen Ch'ang came into sight, opening a flank attack on the remaining enemy positions, so that in a little while the White troops were wholly in flight. . . . In an hour or two the whole army was joyously tramping and singing* its way across the River Tatu into Szechuan. Far overhead angrily and impotently roared the planes of Chiang Kai-shek, and the Reds cried out in delirious challenge to them. As the Communist troops poured over the river, these planes tried to hit the bridge, but their torpedoes only made pretty splashes in the river.

For their distinguished bravery the heroes of An Jen Ch'ang and Liu Ting Chiao† were awarded the Gold Star, highest decoration in

---

* For the sake of morale, Red troops sang frequently. Mao Tse-tung, a poet in his own right, wrote several of their marching songs.

† Meaning, the Bridge built by Liu.

the Red Army of China. Later on I was to meet some of them in Ninghsia, and to be amazed by their youth, for they were all under twenty-five.[14]

In order to prevent the enemy from living on the lands through which they fought each other, both the Reds and the Nationalists practiced a scorched-earth policy. Near Chengtu, in central Szechuan, a French missionary, Father Eymard, returned to his stations after the passage of the Reds:

I left Pao-ning in the early morning of December 2nd [1935]. After we had crossed the Chia Lin-chiang [River], it began to rain. As we progressed, the roads became increasingly bad. Because we were wading through ankle-deep mud, we advanced with great difficulty. The first leg of our journey brought us to Miao Ko-leou, some sixty *li* distant from Pao-ning. We had all the trouble in the world finding a dwelling place, because that village, like all those we had passed through during the day, had been more or less burned down. The few houses that had been spared were left without doors, windows, frontage, or partitions. All faces expressed sadness and anxiety. When I inquired who the authors of this destruction were, I was told, "On the right bank, it was the Government troops who burned the houses; on the left bank, the Reds."

On December 3rd at dawn, we resumed our slow progress through the mud, and breakfasted after a march of some twenty *li*. The two inns that used to stand on that spot had been burned by the Reds; we ate our rice in a wretched straw hut open to all winds. Near Leang-chuei-tsin, the hills had been completely stripped of their fine and very old spruces, as the Reds had cut them down at a man's height to serve in the building of fortifications.

In the afternoon, the road became so bad that after an advance of fifty-five *li*, we despaired of ever reaching our destination for the night. We decided to stop, being quite exhausted, and were lucky enough to find lodgings of sorts in a straw hovel standing near the road.

December 4th. Still the same troubles and difficulties on our muddy trip. The village of Yun-chia-p'ai, where we intended to spend the night, had been leveled to the ground by the Reds. This compelled us to keep going, through the pitch-dark night, as far as the village of Houa-t'ong-ch'ang.

December 5th. We departed early in the morning. The road was better than during the preceding days, and we reached Kuen-yang-ho toward three in the afternoon. All the inns which used to stand along this road had been burned. Of the chapel, only the shell remained: the door, the floor, the ceiling, as well as all the furniture had disappeared. . . .

January 2nd, 1936. Today, I left for T'ong-chiang. I noticed but little damage in the two first marketplaces I passed. Farther up, however, the town of Tsin-chiang-tu had been partly destroyed by fire, our small residence having been miraculously preserved. We proceeded on our way, and discovered that the inns of Chen-tsiang-ya and of Tai-lo-t'ung had been completely destroyed. In the large town of Yang-pei-ho, traces of fire were visible too: this fire had not been started by the Reds, however, but by the troops of the 29th Army during their headlong flight before the Reds.

After having passed through a few more villages destroyed by fire, we came within sight of T'ong-chiang, which had for some time been the capital of the Soviet Republic of Szechuan.

Having learned that the Catholic Residence no longer existed, I went to the inn, left my luggage there, and went to see the chapel in order to ascertain the damage. The parsonage had been completely burned down; only the shell of the church survived; no Christians were left in the city. Their houses had been burned too, and they had left for better climes. . . .

The foregoing account gives only an incomplete idea of the present situation of the areas I have visited. What shall I add concerning the cruelty of the Communists during their three years of occupation? I do not think it exaggerated to state that at least 300,000 persons were killed or disappeared in the districts of Pa-cheou, T'ong-chiang and Lan-chiang. The arrival of the Red troops was greeted joyfully by the common people, who had suffered so much from the Government soldiery. Little by little, however, massive executions of the wealthy, and then of the proletarians suspected of being lukewarm toward the new regime, damped people's enthusiasm. The initial joy was succeeded by a general uneasiness. Finally, the population greeted the departure of the Red Army with the same feeling of relief as it had welcomed its arrival.

Even though the Red Army is gone, however, the Communist doctrine has left deep imprints on people's minds. It has opened new horizons to the proletarian class, which is now endeavoring to

preserve the newly won advantages. The farmers refuse to pay their
annual rent to the landowners, tenants reject the idea of paying their
rent, debtors no longer acknowledge their debts, etc.[15]

*Following its crossing of the Tatu River, the half-starved and steadily
dwindling Red Army had to negotiate two other, and even more formidable,
natural obstacles before entering the less rugged provinces of Kansu and Shensi.
One was a series of high snow-capped mountain ranges inhabited by
ferociously hostile tribes, and the other was a vast expanse of "Grasslands"
which, too, took a heavy toll of human lives.*

*Edgar Snow has summarized the final tribulations of the survivors of the
Long March:*

The most dangerous and exciting travel lay before them, for the
route they chose led through wild country inhabited by the independent
Mantzu tribesmen, and the nomadic Hsifan, a warring people of eastern
Tibet. Passing into the Mantzu and Tibetan territories, the Reds for
the first time faced a populace united in its hostility to them, and their
sufferings on this part of the trek exceeded anything in the past. They
had money, but could buy no food. They had guns, but their enemies
were invisible. As they marched into the thick forests and jungles and
across the headwaters of a dozen great rivers, the tribesmen withdrew
from the vicinity of the march. They stripped their houses bare,
carried off all edibles, drove their cattle and fowl to the plateaus, and
simply disinhabited the whole area.

A few hundred yards on either side of the road, however, it was
quite unsafe. Many a Red who ventured to forage for a sheep never
returned. The mountaineers hid in the thick bush and sniped at the
marching "invaders." They climbed the mountains, and when the
Reds filed through the deep, narrow, rock passes, where sometimes
only one or two could pass abreast, the Mantzu rolled huge boulders
down to crush them and their animals. Here were no chances to
explain "Red policy toward national minorities," no opportunities for
friendly alliance! The Mantzu Queen had an implacable traditional
hatred for Chinese of any variety, and recognized no distinction
between Red and White. She threatened to boil alive anyone who
helped the travelers.

Unable to get food except by capturing it, the Reds were obliged

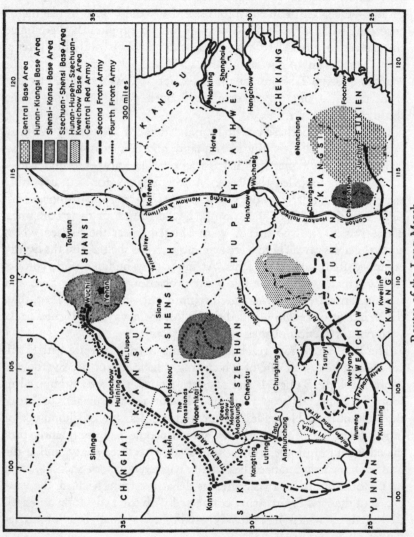

Routes of the Long March

Legend:
- Central Base Area
- Hunan-Kiangsi Base Area
- Shensi-Kansu Base Area
- Szechuan-Shensi Base Area
- Hunan-Hupeh-Szechuan-Kweichow Base Area
- Central Red Army
- Second Front Army
- Fourth Front Army

300 miles

Provinces and places (as labeled on map): NINGSIA, CHINGHAI, Sining, Lanchow, Huining, SHANSI, Taiyuan, Wuchi, Yenan, KANSU, Mt. Liupan, Latsekou, The Grasslands, Maoerhkai, TIBETAN AREA, SIKANG, Kantse, Kangting, Mt. Min, Great Snow Mountains, Mookung, Luting, Tatu R., Anshunchang, Chengtu, Chungking, SZECHUAN, Siang, SHENSI, Yellow River, Kaifeng, HONAN, Hofei, ANHWEI, Wuchang, HUPEH, Yangtse River, Hankow, Wuchang, Peking–Hankow Railway, KIANGSU, Nanking, Shanghai, Hangchow, CHEKIANG, Nanchang, Changsha, KIANGSI, Chingkanshan, Juichin, FUKIEN, Foochow, Canton, Peking–Hankow Railway, KWANGSI, Kweilin, Kweiyang, Wumeng, KWEICHOW, Tsunyi, Fenpan River, I AREA, Golden Sand River, YUNNAN, Kunming, HUNAN to make war for a few cattle. They had a saying then that "to buy one sheep costs the life of one man." But from the Mantzu fields they harvested green Tibetan wheat, and vegetables such as beets and turnips—the latter of an enormous size that would "feed fifteen men," according to Mao Tse-tung. On such meager supplies they equipped themselves to cross the Great Grasslands. "This is our only foreign debt," Mao said to me humorously, "some day we must pay the Mantzu and the Tibetans for the provisions we were obliged to take from them." Only by capturing tribesmen could they find guides through the country. . . .

In the Grasslands there was no human habitation for ten days. Almost perpetual rain fell over this swampland, and it is possible to cross its center only by a maze of narrow footholds known to the native mountaineers who led the Reds. More animals were lost, and more men. Many foundered in the weird sea of wet grass, and dropped from sight into the depth of the swamp, beyond reach of their comrades. There was no firewood; they were obliged to eat their green wheat and vegetables raw. There were even no trees for shelter, and the lightly equipped Reds carried no tents. At night they huddled under bushes tied together, which gave but scant protection against the rain. But from this trial, too, they emerged triumphant—more so, at least, than the White troops, who pursued them, lost their way, and turned back, with only a fraction of their number intact.

The Red Army now reached the Kansu border. Several battles still lay ahead, the loss of one of which might have meant decisive defeat. More Nanking, Tungpei, and Moslem troops had been mobilized in southern Kansu to stop their march, but they managed to break through all these blockades, and in the process annexed hundreds of horses from the Moslem cavalry which people had confidently predicted would finish them once and for all. Footsore, weary, and at the limit of human endurance, they finally entered northern Shensi . . . and on October 20, 1935, a year after its departure from Kiangsi, the vanguard of the First Front Army connected with the 25th, 26th, and 27th Red Armies, which had already established a small base of Soviet power on Shensi in 1933.[16]

Less than twenty thousand survivors of the Long March reached the Shensi base, just south of the Great Wall. They had passed through a dozen provinces, and had broken through ten enveloping armies. Chinese Com-

munism had suffered a severe, but by no means decisive, defeat at the hands of the Nationalists.

As for the latter, their success since the launching of the 1928 northern campaign had been remarkable, if not continuous. The years 1928 through 1935 were, in fact, happy years for the Kuomintang in more than one way, because its victories were many-sided. Most countries had recognized the Kuomintang as China's only legitimate government. The Red peril had been largely eliminated. On the economic front, too, real progress had been made in several important fields. Chiang Kai-shek and his fellow Nationalists had good reasons for believing that their revolution was the right solution for China's many problems.

Perhaps the Kuomintang could have succeeded in firmly uniting the country under its banner, if it had seriously tried to improve the condition of China's vast rural masses, thereby depriving Communism of its essential raison d'être. But a new, and increasingly acute, danger was looming at the horizon: Japan had resumed her conquering advance into the heart of China. Once more, and increasingly so in the future, China's vital energies were devoted to fighting the foreigner.

CHAPTER X

FROM MANCHUKUO TO THE "UNITED FRONT", 1931-1937

THE WASHINGTON Conference of 1922* had only temporarily slowed down the expansion of Japan on Chinese territory. Narrowly confined in their picturesque but mountainous and relatively poor islands, and enjoying a remarkable economic boom after World War I, the ambitious and hard-working Japanese were fully determined to carve out an economic empire within China's vast and underdeveloped lands. Essential raw materials such as coal and iron, scarce in Japan, were abundant in China. Also, the latter's teeming millions constituted a potentially unlimited market for the consumption of Japanese goods, and in Manchuria there was still plenty of room for Japan's rapidly increasing population.

What Japan wanted, in short, was a vast foothold on Asia's mainland, control of China's trade (and more particularly control of the all-important Yangtze valley) and, possibly, the cooperation of large numbers of natives. During the twenties, it became increasingly obvious that in order to achieve her goal, Japan meant to grab for herself the commercial monopoly so far enjoyed by the Western powers.

While thousands of Japanese crowded into Shanghai's International Settlement and soon formed the largest foreign group there, increasing numbers of Koreans—subjects of the Mikado since 1910†—settled in Manchuria, where they became competitors of the recently emigrated Chinese peasants. Frequent incidents, centering mainly around questions of irrigation, pitted the two groups in opposition.

One such incident, which occurred in July 1931, received headline treatment

* See page 278.

† When Korea was formally annexed to Japan, and renamed Chosen. There were about 800,000 Koreans in Manchuria in the early thirties.

in the Japanese press and provoked serious anti-Chinese riots throughout Korea. At the same time, Japanese public opinion was being prepared for possible armed intervention in Manchuria. In a like manner, anti-Japanese feeling ran high throughout China. Finally, news of the killing of Captain Nakamura* in western Manchuria inflamed Japanese opinion, and precipitated the now inevitable conflict.

In the night of September 18–19, 1931, the Japanese troops stationed in Manchuria for the protection of the South Manchuria Railway line occupied Mukden, whereupon China appealed to the League of Nations. The latter appointed a Commission of Inquiry under the chairmanship of Lord Lytton. The commission traveled to Japan, China and Manchuria, interviewed the leading protagonists of the dispute, and upon its return to Geneva presented a lengthy report—known as the Lytton Report—describing Manchurian developments in detail:

As September wore on, the growing tension between Japanese and Chinese interests in Manchuria reached such a point that it was apparent to all careful observers that a breaking point must soon be reached. The public press of both countries tended rather to inflame than to calm public opinion. Vigorous speeches of the Japanese War Minister in Tokyo, counselling direct action by their army in Manchuria, were reported. Protracted delay by the Chinese authorities in making satisfactory investigation of and redress for the murder of Captain Nakamura had particularly incensed the young officers of the Japanese Army in Manchuria, who clearly showed their sensitiveness to irresponsible remarks and slurs made by equally irresponsible Chinese officers on the streets or in restaurants and other places of close contact. And so the stage was set for the events which followed.

On the morning of Saturday, September 19th, the population of Mukden woke to find their city in the hands of Japanese troops. During the night sounds of firing had been heard, but there was nothing unusual in this; it had been a nightly experience throughout the week, as the Japanese had been carrying out night manoeuvres involving vigorous rifle and machine-gun firing. True that, on the night of September 18th, the booming of guns and the sound of shells caused some alarm to the few that distinguished them, but the majority of the

---

* Captain Nakamura had been sent on a special mission into interior Manchuria, and represented himself as an agricultural expert. At the end of June 1931, he was arrested and subsequently shot as a spy by Chinese military authorities.

population considered the firing to be merely another repetition of Japanese manoeuvres, perhaps rather noisier than usual.[1]

The Japanese version of events was presented to the Lytton Commission by Lieutenant Kawamoto:

According to the Japanese versions, Lieutenant Kawamoto, with six men under his command, was on patrol duty on the night of September 18th, practising defence exercises along the track of the South Manchuria Railway to the north of Mukden. They were proceeding southwards in the direction of Mukden. The night was dark but clear and the field of vision was not wide. When they reached a point at which a small road crosses the line, they heard the noise of a loud explosion a little way behind them. They turned and ran back, and after going about 200 yards they discovered that a portion of one of the rails on the down track had been blown out. The explosion took place at the point of junction of two rails; the end of each rail had been cleanly severed, creating a gap in the line of thirty-one inches. On arrival at the site of the explosion, the patrol was fired upon from the fields on the east side of the line. Lieutenant Kawamoto immediately ordered his men to deploy and return the fire. The attacking body, estimated at about five or six, then stopped firing and retreated northward. The Japanese patrol at once started in pursuit and, having gone about 200 yards, they were again fired upon by a larger body, estimated at between three and four hundred. Finding himself in danger of being surrounded by this large force, Lieutenant Kawamoto then ordered one of his men to report to the Commander of No. 3 Company, who was also engaged in night manoeuvres some 1,500 yards to the north; at the same time, he ordered another of his men to telephone (by means of a box telephone near the spot) to Battalion Headquarters at Mukden for reinforcements.

At this moment the southbound train from Changchun was heard approaching. Fearing that the train might be wrecked when it reached the damaged line, the Japanese patrol interrupted their engagement and placed detonators on the line in the hope of warning the train in time. The train, however, proceeded at full speed. When it reached the site of the explosion it was seen to sway and heel over to one side, but it recovered and passed on without stopping. As the train was due at Mukden at 10:30 P.M., where it arrived punctually, it must have been about 10 o'clock P.M., according to Lieutenant Kawamoto, when he first heard the explosion.[2]

Still according to the Japanese version, fighting was then resumed. Lieutenant Colonel Shimamoto, who had received Kawamoto's telephone request for reinforcements, decided to attack the Chinese barracks:

Although his force was then only 500, and he believed the Chinese army in the North Barracks numbered 10,000, Lieutenant Colonel Shimamoto at once ordered an attack on the barracks, believing, as he told us, that "offence is the best defence". The ground between the railway and the North Barracks—a distance of about 250 yards—was difficult to cross in mass formation because of patches of water, and, while the Chinese troops were being driven back over this ground, Lieutenant Noda was sent up the railway with a section of the 3rd Company to intercept their retreat. When the Japanese reached the North Barracks, which were described as glittering with electric light, an attack was made by the 3rd Company, which succeeded in occupying a corner of the left wing. The attack was vigorously contested by the Chinese troops within, and there was fierce fighting for some hours. . . . By 6 o'clock A.M. the entire barracks were captured at the cost of two Japanese privates killed and twenty-two wounded. Some of the barracks caught fire during the fighting; the remainder were burned out by the Japanese on the morning of the 19th. The Japanese stated that they had buried 320 Chinese, but only found about twenty wounded.

In the meantime, operations in other places were being carried out with equal rapidity and thoroughness. Colonel Hirata received a telephone message from Lieutenant Colonel Shimamoto about 10:40 P.M. to the effect that the South Manchuria Railway track had been destroyed by Chinese troops and that he was about to start to attack the enemy. Colonel Hirata approved his action and himself decided to attack the walled city. The concentration of his troops was complete by 11:30 P.M. and his attack commenced. No resistance was offered, only occasional fighting on the streets, mostly with the Chinese police, of whom seventy-five were killed. At 2:15 A.M. the wall of the city was scaled. . . . At 6 A.M. the occupation of the eastern wall was completed; the arsenal and aerodrome were captured at 7:30 A.M.

. . . The total casualties in these operations were seven Japanese wounded and thirty Chinese killed.[3]

The Chinese version of these same events stressed that the sudden and un-provoked Japanese attack had not been anticipated, and found the Chinese troops quite unprepared:

According to the Chinese version, the Japanese attacks on the barracks was entirely unprovoked and came as a complete surprise. On the night of September 18th, all the soldiers of the 7th Brigade, numbering about 10,000, were in the North Barracks. As instructions had been received from Marshal Chang Hsueh-liang on September 6th that special care was to be taken to avoid any clash with the Japanese troops in the tense state of feeling existing at the time, the sentries at the walls of the barracks were only armed with dummy rifles. For the same reason, the west gate in the mud wall surrounding the camp which gave access to the railway had been closed. The Japanese had been carrying out night manoeuvres around the barracks on the nights of September 14th, 15th, 16th and 17th. At 7 P.M. on the evening of September 18th, they were manoeuvring at a village called Wenkuantun. At 9 P.M., Officer Liu reported that a train composed of three or four coaches, but without the usual type of locomotive, had stopped there. At 10 P.M. the sound of a loud explosion was heard, immediately followed by rifle fire. This was reported over the telephone by the Chief of Staff to the Commanding Officer, General Wang I-Cheh, who was at his private house situated near the railway, about six or seven miles from the barracks, to the south. While the Chief of Staff was still at the telephone, news was brought to him that the Japanese were attacking the barracks and that two sentries had been wounded. At about 11 o'clock P.M., a general attack on the southwest corner of the barracks began, and at 11:30 P.M. the Japanese had effected an entry through a hole in the wall. As soon as the attack began, the Chief of Staff gave orders for the lights to be extinguished, and again reported to General Wang I-Cheh by telephone. The latter replied that no resistance was to be offered. Distant artillery fire was heard at 10:30 o'clock P.M. from the southwest and northwest. At midnight, live shells began to fall inside the barracks. On reaching the south gates, the retreating troops of the 621st Regiment found that the Japanese were attacking that gate and that the guard was withdrawing. They accordingly took shelter in some trenches and earthworks until after the

Japanese soldiers had passed through into the interior, when they were able to make their escape through the south gate and reached the village of Erhtaitze, to the northeast of the barracks, about 2 A.M. Other troops made their escape through the east gate and the empty barracks just outside the east wall, finally reaching the same village between 3 and 4 A.M.

The only resistance was offered by the 620th Regiment, quartered in the northeast corner building and the second building south of it. The commander of this regiment stated that, when the Japanese troops entered through the south gate at 1 A.M., the Chinese troops withdrew from one building to another, leaving the Japanese to attack empty buildings. After the main body of the Chinese troops had withdrawn, the Japanese turned eastwards and occupied the eastern exit. The 620th Regiment thus found themselves cut off, and had no option but to fight their way through. They started to break through at 5 A.M., but did not get completely clear until 7 A.M. This was the only actual fighting that took place in the barracks and was responsible for most of the casualties. This regiment was the last to reach the village of Erhtaitze.[4]

From these contradictory reports, the Lytton Commission concluded that the Chinese "had no plan of attacking the Japanese troops", and that the latter's operations during the night of September 18, 1931, "cannot be regarded as measures of legitimate self-defense".*

The Japanese, meanwhile, proceeded rapidly with the execution of pre-arranged plans, and seized the whole of Manchuria's three "Eastern Provinces". In February 1932, they proclaimed the independence of Manchukuo, or "Manchu Land", amid general hostility and indifference of its predominantly Chinese population. A few weeks later, young Henry P'u-I (who abdicated the Dragon Throne in 1912 at the age of three) was installed as regent. In March 1934, P'u-I was promoted Emperor of the puppet state, where Japanese advisers and secretaries controlled all important activities.

The Lytton Commission spent some six weeks in Manchuria (April 20 to June 4, 1932) in order to ascertain the attitude of its inhabitants toward the new "State". Japanese authorities were hardly cooperative, but the commission succeeded nevertheless in interviewing representatives of practically all walks of life:

* It added, however, that "the officers on the spot may have thought they were acting in self-defense".

There were no doubt occasional real dangers in the unsettled conditions of the country, and we are grateful for the efficient protection with which we were provided throughout our tour. But the effect of the police measures adopted was to keep away witnesses; and many Chinese were frankly afraid of even meeting members of our staff. We were informed at one place that, before our arrival, it had been announced that no one would be allowed to see the Commission without official permission. Interviews were therefore usually arranged with considerable difficulty and in secrecy, and many informed us that it was too dangerous for them to meet us even in this way.

In spite of these difficulties, we were able to arrange private interviews with businessmen, bankers, teachers, doctors, police, tradesmen and others, in addition to our public interviews with "Manchukuo" officials, Japanese consuls and military officers. We also received over 1,500 written communications, some delivered by hand, the majority sent by post to different addresses. The information so received was checked as far as possible from neutral sources.

Many delegations representing public bodies and associations were received, and usually presented to us written statements. Most of the delegations were introduced by the Japanese or "Manchukuo" authorities, and we had strong grounds for believing that the statements left with us had previously obtained Japanese approval. In fact, in some cases persons who had presented them informed us afterwards that they had been written or substantially revised by the Japanese and were not to be taken as the expression of their real feelings. These documents were remarkable for the studied neglect to comment either favourably or otherwise upon Japanese participation in the establishment or maintenance of the "Manchukuo" administration. In the main, these statements were concerned with the relation of grievances against the former Chinese administration and contained expressions of hope and confidence in the future of the new "State".

The letters received came from farmers, small tradesmen, town workers and students, and related the feelings and experiences of the writers. After the return of the Commission to Peiping* in June, this mass of correspondence was translated, analysed and arranged by an expert staff specially selected for the purpose. All these, 1500 letters,

* Name of Peking before it became China's capital. The actual Chinese name, Pei-ching, means "Capital of the North", in opposition to Nanking (Nan-ching), "Capital of the South".

except two, were bitterly hostile to the new "Manchukuo Government" and to the Japanese. They appeared to be sincere and spontaneous expressions of opinion.

The higher Chinese officials of the "Manchukuo Government" are in office for various reasons. Many of them were previously in the former regime and have been retained either by inducements or by intimidation of one kind or another. Some of them conveyed messages to the Commission to the effect that they had been forced to remain in office under duress, that all power was in Japanese hands, that they were loyal to China, and that what they had said at their interviews with the Commission in the presence of the Japanese was not necessarily to be believed. Some officials have remained in office to prevent their property from being confiscated, as has happened in the case of some of those who have fled to China. Others, men of good repute, joined in the hope that they would have power to improve the administration, and under promise of the Japanese that they would have a free hand. . . .

The minor and local officials have in the main retained their offices under the new regime, partly because of the necessity for earning a living and supporting their families and partly because they feel that if they go worse men might be put in their place. . . .

The "Manchukuo" Army . . . consists in the main of the former Manchurian soldiers reorganized under Japanese supervision. Such troops were at first content to take service under the new regime provided they were merely required to maintain local order. But, since they have on occasions been called upon to engage in serious warfare against Chinese forces and to fight under Japanese orders side by side with Japanese troops, the "Manchukuo" Army has become increasingly unreliable. Japanese sources report the frequent defection of "Manchukuo" forces to the Chinese side, while the Chinese claim that one of their most reliable and fruitful sources of warlike supplies is the "Manchukuo" Army.

The Chinese businessmen and bankers who were interviewed by us were hostile to "Manchukuo". They disliked the Japanese; they feared for their lives and property, and frequently remarked: "We do not want to become like the Koreans." After September 18th, there was a large exodus of businessmen to China, but some of the less rich ones are now returning. Generally speaking, the smaller shopkeepers expect to suffer less from Japanese competition than do the larger merchants and manufacturers, who often had profitable relations with the former

officials. Many shops were still closed at the time of our visit. The increase in banditry adversely affected business in the countryside, and the
machinery of credit has largely broken down. . . .

The professional classes, teachers and doctors, are hostile to "Manchukuo". They allege that they are spied upon and intimidated. The
interference with education, the closing of universities and some
schools, and the alterations in the school textbooks, have added to their
hostility, already great on patriotic grounds. The censorship of the
press, post and opinion is resented, as is also the prohibition of the entry
into "Manchukuo" of newspapers published in China. There are, of
course, Chinese who have been educated in Japan who are not included
in this generalization. Many letters were received from students and
young people directed against "Manchukuo".

Evidence regarding the attitude of farmers and town workers is
divergent and naturally difficult to obtain. Opinion among foreigners
and educated Chinese was to the effect that they were either hostile or
indifferent to "Manchukuo". The farmer and worker is politically
uneducated, usually illiterate, and normally takes little interest in the
Government. . . . The farmers have good grounds for believing that
the new regime will lead to an increased immigration of Koreans, and
possibly of Japanese. The Korean immigrants do not assimilate with the
Chinese, and their methods of agriculture are different. While the
Chinese farmer mainly grows beans, kaoliang [grain-bearing sorghums]
and wheat, the Korean farmer cultivates rice. This means digging
canals and dykes and flooding the fields. If there are heavy rains, the
dykes built by the Koreans are liable to burst and flood neighbouring
Chinese land, ruining the crops. There have also been constant quarrels
in the past with Koreans over land ownership and rents. . . .

It was, we were told, impossible to stimulate in the towns a show
of popular enthusiasm for the inauguration ceremonies of "Manchukuo". Generally speaking, the attitude of the town population is a
mixture of passive acquiescence and hostility.

While we found the Chinese majority either hostile or indifferent
to the "Manchukuo", the new Government receives some support
from among various minority racial groups in Manchuria, such as the
Mongols, Koreans, White Russians* and Manchus. They have in varying degrees suffered oppression from the former administration, or

* Refugees from the Bolshevik Revolution, for the most part. They numbered
about 100,000—mainly in and near Harbin.

economic disadvantage from the large immigration of Chinese in the last few decades, and, while no section is entirely enthusiastic, they hope for better treatment from the new regime, whose policy in turn is to encourage these minority groups.[5]

The conclusion of the Lytton Commission was that the creation of Manchukuo did not flow from a "genuine and spontaneous independence movement," and recommended the establishment of an autonomous Manchurian administration under Chinese sovereignty. Approving the Commission's report in its General Assembly of February 1933, the League of Nations adopted the Stimson formula★ of nonrecognition, and indicated that Japanese military pressure should cease. As a result, Japan officially quit the League in March of that year, and tightened her grip over Manchukuo. One of the first Westerners to be admitted to the puppet state was the British journalist Peter Fleming, who arrived there via Moscow:

At the time of my second visit [in 1933], Hsingking† had hardly adapted itself to the greatness so suddenly thrust upon it. It is a small town, of which the central part, focused round the railway station, has that symmetrical, sanitary, and entirely characterless appearance imposed by Japanese influence on all towns in the Railway Zone. The outskirts are more haphazard and Chinese. A sparse traffic of droshkies, rickshaws, and government officials' cars raises dense clouds of dust in streets which belong neither to the East nor to the West. There is a small hotel, run by the South Manchuria Railway and, like everything Japanese, admirably clean and tidy. I was lucky to get a room there, for the place is full of homeless officials, and most visitors are exiled to the Railway Hotel. The Railway Hotel is so-called for the best of reasons. It consists of a string of sleepers in a siding.

Hsingking was used to Special Correspondents. Members of that overrated profession had been indeed almost its only foreign visitors. Firmly but courteously I was launched upon a round of interviews. For three days I interviewed people without stopping.

The procedure was monotonous and unreal. You picked up an

★ Named after the U. S. Secretary of State, who had notified the signatories of the Washington Treaty that his country would recognize no gains achieved through armed force.

† It had been promoted capital of Manchukuo, instead of Mukden. Its present name is Changchun.

interpreter from the Foreign Office and drove round to keep your appointment. The Government departments were poorly housed as yet, and your Chinese Minister would be found lurking in the recesses of a former school or office building. He received you with the utmost courtesy, bowing ceremoniously in his long silk robe. Tea was produced, and cigarettes. In blackwood chairs you sat and smiled at each other.

He was the Minister of State for this or that. But in one corner of the room sat a clerk who took down a verbatim report of the interview, for submission presumably to the powers behind that throne of which the Minister was, on paper, the representative. So it behoved the Minister to be guarded in his speech. And even if he was not— even if he forgot (or should it be "remembered"?) himself and was prompted by a lucky shot to indiscretion—it did not help you much. For there at your side was the interpreter, and he could ensure that whatever information reached you consisted only of the official facts, garnished with the right official flavour. Quite soon I decided that interviews were a waste of time. . . .

Every time you visit an official he gives you, on parting, a small-ass load of pamphlets, tracts and proclamations. Propaganda Elbow is contracted from carrying this vast and unwieldy bundle back to your hotel. You cannot leave it in a taxi, for there are no taxis in Hsingking. You cannot drop it, unnoticed, in the street. You must lug it dutifully home.

It proves to be heavy stuff in more senses than one. The Japanese are not very good at propaganda, and they go in for it far too much. . . . After reading a few kilograms of the publications of the Ministry of Publicity I lost patience with the stuff. The Japanese, I reflected, are doing what is, taken by and large, good work in Manchuria. They have, for instance, stabilized the currency: an inestimable blessing in a country formerly flooded with worthless paper money by the war lords. And even if it was not good work, no one is going to stop them from doing it. This being so, why this perpetual gilding of the lily? Why these everlasting and redundant attempts to pass off a policy of enlightened exploitation as a piece of disinterested rescue work? This parading of nonexistent virtues, this interminable process of self-vindication, breeds doubt and scepticism in the foreign observer.[6]

Among the negative impressions which the Lytton Commission brought back from Manchukuo, one of the most striking was the "unparalleled growth" of banditry and lawlessness in the new state. As in China, banditry had always existed in Manchuria, and the Japanese at first viewed it as being due exclusively to the inefficiency of the Chinese government.

Before long, however, the Japanese had to admit that they, too, found it difficult to rid the country of this perennial and irritating nuisance. In the summer of 1933, Peter Fleming left Mukden with a flying column of Japanese troops engaged in bandit suppression:

Banditry is the biggest problem which the Japanese are facing in Manchukuo. . . . Pacification of the country—which covers an area greater than that of Germany and France combined, and is mostly mountainous, thickly wooded, and inadequately served by communications—is far from complete. . . . Until the Japanese came in in 1931, Manchurian banditry differed in kind from most of the banditry of China proper, which was in great part a phenomenon of despair, the by-product of civil wars, famines, floods, and plague. . . .

The typical Manchurian bandit was a racketeer, an enterprising and old-established parasite; he operated in small groups, stuck to a certain district, and worked in strict accordance with ancient and universally recognized conventions. Under normal conditions he was not so much a threat to the peace of the community as a permanent and carefully regulated drain on its finances. He probably bulked in the eyes of the British *rentier*—as an iniquitous but inevitable consequence of the way his country's affairs have been mismanaged. He kept the peace in return for a form of bribe, paid partly in cash and partly in kind. To travellers and merchandise passing through his territory he issued an expensive but usually inviolable safe-conduct. His relations with the local defence force were friendly. He was rarely suppressed, but could sometimes be "reclaimed" by a punitive expedition, whose ranks he was probably glad to join under favourable conditions. He was, in fine, a scandal rather than a peril.

His numbers were however augmented and his irresponsibility increased by the Japanese occupation of Manchuria.* The bandit problem changed its complexion. Large bodies of soldiers, without leaders and

* According to Japanese military authorities, quoted by the author, the total number of bandits active in Manchukuo at the time was 212,000, of whom only 65,000 were "old-style" bandits; the others were mostly remnants of regular armies, and peasants "forced into crime".

without pay—the rabble of the broken [Chinese] armies which had attempted resistance—increased the feeling of insecurity and alarm in the country which, while they plundered, they say they meant—one day—to save. Lawlessness in Manchuria reached a pitch unparalleled before. Travel, hitherto safer than in any other part of post-revolutionary China, became an impossibility, and no railway, with the exception of the main line of the South Manchuria Railway, dared to run night trains. For the foreign community the year 1932 was darkened by such outrages as the murder of Mrs. Woodruff and the kidnapping of Mrs. Pawley and Mr. Corkran. For all their good intentions, the Japanese forces in Manchuria were powerless to prevent the establishment of a reign of terror.[7]

In China proper, the creation of Manchukuo brought sharp reactions from all classes of the population. In booming Shanghai in particular (which after the turn of the century had replaced traditionally turbulent Canton in the domain of anti-government and anti-foreign manifestations), anti-Japanese feeling reached a climax in the fall of 1931. An intense Chinese boycott cut Japanese exports to one-sixth of their usual figure.

The American reporter E. O. Hauser, who was well acquainted with life in Shanghai, has described the extent and effects of the boycott:

One hundred twenty-four thousand bales of cotton yarn were shipped from Japan to Shanghai in 1931. This was but one of the items on the list of Japanese exports to China, which had assumed fantastic proportions. Besides the yarn, Japanese textiles and Japanese coal, Japanese paper and Japanese chemicals, an ever-increasing variety of Japanese "sundry" goods were carried by Japanese ships and were dumped into the Shanghai market. It was a twenty-four-hour journey across the Yellow Sea, freights were low and Japanese manufacturers and merchants were satisfied with small profits. Japanese goods were cheap; the Chinese bought them. Japan's trade with China accounted for nearly one-third of her total foreign commerce. And most of it was passing through Shanghai.

Japan's investment in Shanghai had reached a billion yen. There were thirty Japanese cotton mills in the metropolis; they had been financed out of the wartime profits of the Japanese industry at home, they were superior in efficiency and equipment to the Chinese mills, their capitalization was sounder. A fleet of twenty-seven Japanese ships was plying between Shanghai and the Yangtze ports, and the shipping firms had their head offices at Shanghai. All the important Japanese houses had established Shanghai branches by now. And above Shanghai, in the Yangtze valley, Japan held ironworks, railways, a land investment company, a machine plant, a paper mill, and the power plants of twenty-four cities.

In the International Settlement, the Japanese population formed by far the largest foreign group. It had grown from 800 in 1890 to 10,000 in 1920, and it had trebled during the next decade. There were thirty thousand Japanese in Shanghai—more than three times the number of British. . . . The vast majority of the Japanese remained in Hongkew. There, north of Soochow Creek, they had formed a community of their own—"Little Tokyo." . . .

An anti-Japanese boycott of unprecedented stringency was instituted. No longer did the Chinese buy Japanese toys and bicycles and phonograph records. No longer did Chinese firms handle Japanese merchandise. Those who had ordered Japanese goods a few weeks ago now declined to accept them. Chinese banks refused to honor Japanese bills of lading even when the necessary funds had been deposited before. Japanese commodities piled up on Shanghai's piers, clogged the godowns. More than 700,000 tons of cargo had been rejected and could not be disposed of. Japanese shipping went dead. . . . When a Japanese ship was in port, Chinese pickets would prevent Chinese passengers from boarding it or would go after them and throw them overboard. Whoever was caught buying anything "made in Japan" was summarily dealt with. The "Anti-Japanese and National Salvation Association" saw to that.

Commercial relations with Japan were completely broken. Japanese shops and stores had to be boarded up. Japanese bankers and underwriters suffered heavy losses. Vicious posters appeared in the streets—they said, "Down with Japanese Imperialism," and they said, "Kill the Japanese." The Japanese community was running out of food; Japanese freighters did not arrive with shrimps and vegetables any more, and the Chinese grocers did not like to serve Japanese customers, did not like to see a stone smash their windows. Some Japanese residents packed up and left for Japan. Those who remained were fidgety. . . . Japanese tanks and marines patrolled the streets of "Little Tokyo." Excited meetings were held by both the Japanese and the Chinese. Both groups paraded through the streets, shouting insults.[8]

In this tense atmosphere, an untoward incident brought matters to the breaking point. On January 18, 1932, five Japanese Buddhist priests were attacked by Chinese workers in the outskirts of Shanghai. One of the priests died a few days later. A Japanese mob retaliated by burning a Chinese-owned towel factory, and killed two Chinese policemen.

On January 21, the Japanese Consul General presented an ultimatum to General Wu Te-chen, Mayor of Greater Shanghai, demanding that he suppress the anti-Japanese boycott, silence the anti-Japanese propaganda campaign,* and punish the culprits of the January 18th incident.

Andrée Viollis, the special correspondent of a leading French daily, Le Petit Parisien, was on her way to Nanking at the time:

I spent seven hours in the train that took me to Nanking. With the exception of four Britons wearing shorts, who played cards and roared with laughter every now and then, my carriage was filled with Chinese sitting opposite one another in leather-covered armchairs separated by a small table. These Chinese came from all walks of life, from the cosmopolitan businessman wearing a European suit, to the old classic scholar with gray and shiny temples, long, curved nails, and round glasses. All of them were silent and looked worried. Boys in blue cotton robes and carrying kettles kept moving through the car; they poured hot water into people's cups, in which green tea leaves were floating like algae, or into red-painted spittoons placed on the floor, which the travelers made frequent use of.

Our tickets were checked several times by a conductor wearing a uniform with silver designs. He was accompanied by two other conductors wearing similar uniforms, and by three chubby soldiers. Quite a procession!

Every station was guarded by soldiers with rifles over their shoulders. At each stop, our train was invaded by merchants selling fruits, multicolored sweets or colored plaster toys, and even more so by newsboys selling freshly printed Chinese papers whose huge, fat and broad characters left ink on their yellow hands. People bought these papers most eagerly, and read them closely.

Sitting opposite me was a young, blue-robed Chinese wearing horn-rimmed glasses. He read the papers voraciously, all the while affecting to ignore me and looking away from me; at the same time,

---

* Chinese papers were clamoring for war, and some of them even attacked the sacred person of Japan's Emperor.

however, he cast ironic glances and made disdainful movements with his lips in the direction of the cheerfully noisy, redfaced Britons.

At the station preceding Nanking, his hands clenched the paper he had just bought, and his face suddenly grew very irritated. Goaded by curiosity, I risked a question in English, asking him how the news was. He appeared surprised and hostile, and first gave me a long, silent look; then he replied with a marked American accent:

"The news? A most insolent ultimatum issued by the Japanese Admiral Shiozawa, who has just arrived in Shanghai with several warships. This fellow not only demands excuses for the attack against Japanese priests and the articles in some Chinese papers which allegedly insulted the sacred person of the Mikado; he also demands the suppression of the anti-Japanese leagues and an end to the boycotting of Japanese goods, or else Japanese forces will occupy strategic points in Shanghai, including the Chinese city. Five hundred helmeted and armed marines have already entered the city and are assuming airs of conquerors!

"This is an open provocation," exclaimed the young Chinese, "an intolerable insult, or rather a prearranged plan of aggression taking advantage of every possible pretext. As for Europe, she watches this violation of our territory, this gross injustice, with an indifference that is just as intolerable." Whereupon, and without any transition, he launched into a passionate diatribe against the League of Nations.[9]

In Shanghai, the situation was indeed rapidly becoming explosive. When Madame Viollis arrived there, she found hapless Mayor Wu in a dire predicament—and all but abandoned to fate:

The various politicians who were offered government posts, and more particularly that of Foreign Minister, hastily declined the responsibility. Only an unfortunate Vice-Minister remained at the Foreign Office. He, too, would have liked to resign, but being a career man, he was compelled to stay in office. Most likely, he will be forced to sign the future agreements with Japan, after which the terrified and irresponsible fellow will have to face his country's wrath.

Upon my arrival, I found a tense and feverish atmosphere prevailing in Shanghai. The Japanese Consul, Muraï, had set 6 P.M. as the extreme limit for the Chinese answer to the Japanese ultimatum. In the morning of January 28th, at half past eight, a small bomb, made with a tin can containing scraps of metal, exploded against the wall of the Japanese Consulate General. Damage was insignificant, but the cap of the unknown bomb thrower is said to have been found on the spot. The cap, it was also reported, bore the insignia of the *League of the Anti-Japanese Youth*. . . .

Poor General Wu, Mayor of Shanghai, bore the full weight of all responsibilities. At two o'clock in the afternoon, hours before the expiration of the Japanese ultimatum, he gave in and accepted all of its demands. He explained his compliance by a rather poignant declaration: "It is my duty to save the city, and in doing so I must disregard my personal feelings. My honor or dishonor, as well as subsequent praises or blame cannot be taken into account.". . .

Toward evening, the streets became increasingly animated. Newspaper boys were running to and fro, brandishing their Chinese papers. A short while ago, turbulent demonstrations had been staged by the students, who accused Mayor Wu of having yielded too soon, thus losing face.

At half past eleven the poor fellow, who so far had succeeded in remaining brave and composed through many unforeseen and confusing events, was instructed by Admiral Shiozawa to withdraw immediately the Chinese troops stationed near Cha-p'ei. Restless crowds began to gather on large intersections. In the far distance, the Japanese quarter alone remained deserted, its shops being closed, and its lights out. Only one building was brightly shining in the night: the Japanese barracks.[10]

Even before Mayor Wu delivered his meek and submissive reply to the Japanese ultimatum, the Japanese Navy had moved to take matters into its own hands. Toward midnight of January 28th, 400 Japanese marines climbed aboard eighteen military trucks and roared off into Shanghai, flanked by armored cars. After several hours of intense fighting, they occupied the city's Cha-p'ei section. Subsequent Japanese attacks included naval and aerial bombardments. Urgent intervention by the League of Nations and England prevented the "Shanghai War", as it was called, from expanding into a more serious conflict. A truce of sorts was signed in early May.

At that time, the Kuomintang leaders still considered the Communists their chief enemy. Chiang Kai-shek, in particular, insisted that before turning against the Japanese invaders, national unity should be achieved once and *for all. Yet Japan kept up her steady southward push, the more so as a durable pacification of Manchukuo was made impossible by continuous attacks of bandits and irregular guerrillas. In 1935, five northern provinces of China (Shantung, Hopei, Shansi, Chahar, Suiyuan) were granted an autonomous status by Nanking, and became a zone of Japanese influence.**

Chinese public opinion became increasingly vocal in demanding war against Japan. The same demand was constantly voiced by the Chinese Communists, who in 1935 had set up an orderly government in Shensi, and whose main slogan at the time was that "Chinese do not fight against other Chinese". Chiang Kai-shek, however, turned a deaf ear to all of these voices, despite repeated Communist offers of cooperation against the common foe.

A dramatic incident, which occurred in December 1936, eventually led the headstrong Marshal to change his mind. Chiang flew to the capital of Shensi, Sian, in order to inspect the Manchurian troops of "Young Marshal" Chang Hsueh-liang, who of late had displayed an obvious lack of conviction in their struggle against Communist troops.† Shortly after his arrival in Sian, Chiang found himself the prisoner of Chang, who vainly endeavored to force him to declare war on Japan.

Throughout China, news of Chiang's disappearance—and even death—caused widespread dismay. A young free-lance writer from New Zealand, James Bertram, was at the time working at Peking University:

Nobody knew. Rumours of the death of Chiang Kai-shek used to be common in China. In later years they had been less common. But this was something more than a rumour.

What had happened on December 12th in Sian, the City of Western Peace, capital of China's most ancient dynasties? There had been a rebellion and Chang Hsueh-liang and Yang Hu-cheng (the local Shensi commander) had been the leaders of it. So much seemed clear. Between them they had captured the Generalissimo. They had sent a telegram to the Central Government at Nanking announcing this fact and making certain demands for a change of national policy. The versions of these demands differed; interpretations of them were as

---

* Japanese goods were openly smuggled wholesale through this area, and narcotics were poured from it upon the world market.

† This was not surprising. The Manchurian, or "Northeastern", troops under Chang Hsueh-liang (son of Marshal Chang Tso-lin, who ruled over Manchuria until 1928), would much rather have fought the Japanese, who occupied their country. They were irritated by Nanking's passive attitude toward the Japanese invaders, and favored a compromise policy with regard to Communism.

far apart as Moscow and Tokyo. One question came up again and again in these first few days—had Chiang Kai-shek been killed?

The Young Marshal, it was learned, had sent a personal telegram to Madame Chiang, assuring her of her husband's safety. Those who knew Chang Hsueh-liang were confident that this must be true. Others, who knew only his "shifty and treacherous" past, were more sceptical and believed it a ruse. But anyone who knew Chang's troops, the old Northeastern Army from Manchuria, said that whatever the Young Marshal might have wished to do, his troops would have settled the matter by now. Chiang's life was not worth a copper cash.[11]

In the best of journalistic traditions of on-the-spot reporting, Bertram hurried to Sian and was the first foreign writer to get the whole story of the mutiny. He arrived there two weeks after the kidnapping of Chiang Kai-shek,* and reconstructed the event as follows:

All the elements of crisis were there in the Shensi capital. And once more—as so often in China in these last years—the precipitating factor was a student demonstration. Wednesday, December 9th, was the anniversary of the Student Movement in Peking the year before, that had been so effective a protest against Japan's carefully laid "Autonomy Movement" for the five northern provinces. On this day, in Sian, thousands of students from the Tungpei university and the various middle schools of the city paraded through the streets from early morning, demanding reinforcements for Suiyuan.†. . .

Feeling ran high, especially among the younger Tungpei officers. On the next day—Thursday—there was a joint conference of the military commanders of the Northwest and Chiang Kai-shek's staff. The war with the Communists must go on, the Nanking men insisted. If Marshal Chang and his army refused to cooperate, they would be transferred to the South; the "Bandit Suppressor"‡ who had been so friendly with the bandits had already been officially replaced in that office by General Chiang Ting-wen, one of the Generalissimo's most trusted supporters. On December 12th, it was announced, the new order for the resumption of the Anti-Red Campaign would be published in Sian. A deadlock had been reached.

* But two days after Chiang's release.
† That is, against the Japanese.
‡ Current "title" of Marshal Chang Hsueh-liang.

This was the eve of mutiny, as even Chiang Kai-shek seems at last to have realized. On the Friday he ordered a special train to be prepared for his departure the next day, when the new military orders would come into force. But he never caught the train.

Late on that Friday night, an emergency meeting was called by Chang Hsueh-liang and Yang Hu-cheng; this meeting included a number of senior commanders, and the young "radical" group of officers and officials. There were thirteen members present at this midnight conclave, that took the decision to forestall the new campaign by the arrest of Chiang Kai-shek and all his staff.

The Young Marshal gave strict orders that Chiang was to be captured alive: this delicate task was entrusted to the young captain of his bodyguard, Sun Ming-chiu. Sun had command of the Tungpei Special Service Regiment, which included a number of the Peking students who had recently gone to Sian. A similar regiment of Yang Hu-cheng's was detailed to surround the Sian Guest House and other important centres in the city. The whole coup was planned in a couple of hours, with an efficiency that suggests considerable forethought—in point of fact, the young officer group had been living for a moment like this. Zero hour was set for 6 A.M. on the following morning.

Before dawn on that morning of Saturday, December 12th, many people in Sian were awakened by the sound of a gong furiously beaten, followed by the sound of firing from various parts of the city. The Guest House, which stood back in its own grounds and could be easily isolated, had been surrounded in the small hours. At six o'clock Yang Hu-cheng's troops—who have the local reputation, like their leader, of being little more than bandits—broke in to arrest the Generalissimo's staff. Foreigners staying in the hotel were alarmed by the shooting down of doors and the sudden incursion of wild-looking soldiery; there were shots on the landing, and the stairs ran with blood. All rooms were forced open, and there seems to have been a certain amount of looting; Yang's troops got out of hand pretty easily. But the surprise was complete—there was no organized resistance, and the whole staff was captured with only minor casualties. Tales are told of the postures in which some of Chiang's leading generals were discovered, which do more credit to their discretion than to their valour. Fortunately, in China these things are by common consent forgotten as soon as may be.[12]

In addition to occupying the city's "strategic points" (railway station, post office, police barracks) and arresting Governor Chao Li-tze, the disgruntled "rebels" (as Chiang called them) seized all Nanking bombers on the nearby airfield.

The Generalissimo himself, however, was not captured immediately. He subsequently described his short-lived flight:

December 12th. At 5:30 A.M., when I was dressing after my exercise, I heard gun firing just in front of the gate of my headquarters. I sent one of my bodyguards to see what was the matter, but as he did not come back to report, I sent two others out and then heard gun firing again, which then continued incessantly. Thereupon I felt that the Northeastern troops had revolted. On this visit to Shensi I had only my personal bodyguard and twenty uniformed soldiers. Presently Lieutenant Mao sent a messenger to report that a mutiny had broken out and that they had already reached the second gate. . . .

I asked what the mutinous troops looked like and was told that they had on fur caps* and belonged to the Northeastern troops.

Accompanied by Tso Pei-chi, one of my guard officers, and Chiang Hsiao-chung, an A.D.C., I started for the mountain at the back of the house. After crossing the Fei Hung Bridge we found the eastern side door securely locked, and the key could nowhere be found. We then scaled the wall, which was only about ten feet high and not difficult to get over. But just outside the wall there was a deep moat, the bottom of which was about thirty feet below the top of the wall. As it was still dark, I missed my footing and fell into the moat. I felt a bad pain and was unable to rise. About three minutes later I managed to stand up and walked with difficulty. After having walked several tens of paces we reached a small temple, where some of my bodyguards were on duty. They helped me to climb the mountain. . . .

After about half an hour we reached the mountaintop and sat down on a piece of level ground for a short rest. I sent a bodyguard to a cliff before us to reconnoiter. Presently gun firing was heard on all sides. Bullets whizzed by quite close to my body. Some of the bodyguards were hit and dropped dead. I then realized that I was surrounded, that the mutiny was not local and that the whole of the Northeastern troops took part in it. So I decided not to take shelter but to go back to my headquarters and see what could be done. I walked

* Current headgear of the Northeastern, or Manchurian, troops.

down the mountain as quickly as I could. Halfway down the mountain I fell into a cave which was overgrown with thorny shrubs and in which there was barely enough space to admit me. I felt exhausted. Twice I struggled to my feet but fell down again. I was compelled to remain there for a rest and to wait for further developments.[13]

Chiang's predicament did not last long, as he was soon discovered by Sun Ming-chiu (commander of rebellious Chang's bodyguard) and his men, who were anxiously looking for him. James Bertram described the event:

Meantime Sun and his men combed the mountainside in the gray light of dawn, working upward over the snow-covered rocks. The Lishan hills are covered with a network of paths: all of these were searched without result. It was obvious that Chiang could not have gone far in such difficult country. . . . Before long, shouts from the mountainside announced a discovery. Chiang's personal servant had been found, making his way down to the foot of the slope. His master could not be far away.

Halfway up this valley there is a great stone outcrop overhung by a jutting shelf of rock. The place has its history, like every other spot on these ancient hills; it is known as the Hu P'an Shih, or Tiger Rock. And here, hiding in the cleft between rock and mountain, Chiang Kai-shek[*] was at last discovered. He had only a light Chinese gown above his nightclothes, and his bare feet and hands had been torn in his flight through the darkness. Trembling with cold and exhaustion he crouched against the wet rock. In his ears, perhaps, rang still the sound of shots.

Sun hailed him as "Wei Yuan Chang",[†] using the title of his official rank. There was no irony in the words, though there was irony enough in the situation. But Chiang's response was that of a man who had lost all hope.

"If you are my comrades," he said hoarsely, "shoot me now and finish it all."

"We will not shoot!" said the young captain, with some aplomb. "We only ask you to lead our country against Japan. Then we shall be the first to cheer our Generalissimo." The Tungpei men shouted their agreement.

[*] *Chieh-shih* (or "Kai-shek"), the given name of the Generalissimo, means "Between Two Stones" (author's note).

[†] Meaning "Chairman of the Committee", in Chinese.

But Chiang remained on his rock and said with difficulty, "Call Marshal Chang here, and I will come down."

"Marshal Chang is not here," Sun replied. "The troops are rising in the city; we came here to protect you."

This was not precisely accurate, but it seemed to relieve the Generalissimo considerably. He called for a horse to carry him down the mountain, for his feet were bleeding and blue with cold.

"There is no horse here," said Sun. "But I will carry you down the mountain on my back." And he knelt in the snow at Chiang's feet.

It was a curious situation, of the kind that rapidly passes into legend in China. After some hesitation the Generalissimo accepted the offer, and climbed painfully onto the broad back of the young officer. Like a modern Saint Christopher, the latter proceeded solemnly down the slope until a servant arrived with Chiang's shoes. The rest of the return was covered on foot. . . .

The little group descended the hill and got into cars at the highway. Chiang was very reserved and refused even the offer of a greatcoat. He did not seem in a mood for conversation. But Sun Ming-chiu wanted very much to talk.

"The past is the past," he remarked. "From now on there must be a new policy for China."

"I am sure," the Generalissimo answered dryly, "that Marshal Chang has an excellent policy for China."

"This is a time of national crisis," Sun countered. "We hope the Generalissimo will receive the demands of the people."

"I am always ready to consider the demands of Marshal Chang."

"The one urgent task for China," Sun insisted, "is to resist Japan. This is the united demand of the men of the Northwest. Why do you not fight Japan, but instead give the order to fight the Red Army?"

"I never said I would not fight Japan," said Chiang indignantly.

"But the Tungpei army demands that you fight Japan as soon as possible, for their homes have been seized by the enemy, and all China suffers because of their loss."

"I am the leader of the Chinese people," Chiang said firmly, "I represent the nation. I think that my policy is right, not wrong."

"If you represent the Chinese people, why do you not resist Japan? This is the demand of the whole Chinese nation. How can you claim to represent them when you do not carry out their demands?". . .

"I am a revolutionary," Chiang announced. "I am always ready to sacrifice myself. I have never changed my views; and even though you hold me prisoner, my spirit will never submit to another's."

Beyond this he would not speak.[14]

Shortly after his arrival and installation at his "new quarters" inside the walls of Sian, the proud—and highly vexed—Chiang Kai-shek received the visit of his apologetic, low-bowing, and ceremonious captor, "Young Marshal" Chang Hsueh-liang.

Their first interview, described by Chiang, proved fruitless:

Sun told me that Chang Hsueh-liang said he wished me to rest for a while and that he would soon come. I ordered him to send for Chang, who appeared half an hour later. He was very respectful to me, but I did not return his courtesies. Chang stood with his hands at his sides.

I asked him: "Did you know beforehand about today's revolt?"

He answered in the negative.

I continued: "If you have no previous knowledge of the affair you should see that I return immediately to Nanking or Loyang.* Then it may not be difficult to settle this affair."

Chang answered: "I did not know anything of the actual developments, but I wish to lay my views before Your Excellency the Generalissimo."

I retorted: "Do you still call me the Generalissimo? If you still recognize me as your superior you should send me to Loyang; otherwise you are a rebel. Since I am in the hands of a rebel you had better shoot me. There is nothing else to say."

Chang replied: "If Your Excellency accepts my suggestions I shall obey your orders."

I rebuked him by saying: "Which are you, my subordinate or my enemy? If my subordinate, you should obey my orders. If you are my enemy you should kill me without delay. You should choose either of these two steps, but say nothing more, for I will not listen to you."

Chang then explained that in taking this action his motive was revolutionary but not mutinous. . . . "I am not alone responsible for this affair. There are many other people who are in the movement, which should be referred to the people for their verdict. Should the people be in sympathy with this movement, then it will prove that I

———————

* City located in Honan, some 250 miles east of Sian.

am representing the common will of the people, and Your Excellency will realize that my action is not wrong. If the people are not in sympathy with this movement, then I shall admit my own fault, and Your Excellency may resume your work. I believe I have not in any way disobeyed your teachings. Please don't be angry, and consider the matter carefully."

When I heard "the people's verdict" I realized that it was a malicious plot to kill me by using the mob as their excuse. I shouted: "You are crazy. Do you think that the people are in sympathy with your mutiny? Even the so-called 'Popular Front' will not give you their support. You claim that your motives are revolutionary. Can a mutiny be called a revolution?"[15]

Chiang was released on December 25, 1936, after a series of complicated (and typically Chinese) negotiations that included Mme. Chiang Kai-shek, T. V. Soong, and Chou En-lai (former associate of Chiang at the Whampoa Military Academy, and a clever diplomat), whom the Communists had entrusted with the delicate task of reconciliation with the Kuomintang.

Upon his return to Nanking, the Generalissimo was warmly welcomed by the capital's population. During his "captivity", demonstrations of loyalty to Chiang had taken place throughout China, testifying to the country's moral unity. Chiang now reconsidered his former standard reply to restless generals eager to fight the Japanese, that China was not yet strong enough, and that his first duty was to destroy the Reds. Negotiations with the latter led to the end of the long and costly anti-Communist campaign (January 1937), and brought the Shensi government into harmony with Nanking. A few months later (June 1937), Szechuan too was brought into the new national union.

Japan decided to act before China became too strong, and in July 1937 resumed military operations without declaration of war (for technical reasons of international law). Chiang Kai-shek was named Commander in Chief of all Chinese forces, and in September 1937, the "United Front" Kuomintang–Kungch'antang was officially proclaimed. The Chinese Red Army became the "8th Route Army", and the Shensi Soviet Republic was declared an "Autonomous Border Area".

For the first time in ten years, a truce had been achieved between the Reds and the Whites, but no real peace was in sight: the decisive struggle was still to come.

CHAPTER XI

THE SINO-JAPANESE WAR, 1937–1945

THE "SIAN INCIDENT", or Event of the "Double Twelfth", as the Chinese also called it,* had two immediate and far-reaching results: it postponed by nearly ten years the final stage of the struggle between Reds and Whites, and it crystallized the Chinese nation's will to resist any further Japanese encroachments.

A Western observer, who in 1937 traveled widely through China, noted the frame of mind of the Chinese people:

In May and June of last year, I traveled through China from Szechuan to Canton. I also visited Shanghai, Nanking, Kuling† and Hankow in the Yangtze valley, after which I traveled north to Peking, where I arrived on July 5, two days before the outbreak of the conflict.

In the course of my journey, I talked to soldiers, civilians, students, bankers and peasants. All of them expressed one and the same deep desire to see their country achieve its unification and reconstruction in an atmosphere of peace. Everywhere I found people willing to forget Manchuria (at least for twenty years), and to exercise the greatest restraint with regard to the situation in northern China. Naturally, the Chinese agreed that Japan's policy in these northern provinces was quite unacceptable. They deeply resented the establishment of an East Hopei autonomous regime under Yin Ju-keng, the wholesale smuggling of goods through that area, the ravages caused by the illegal traffic in opium and other narcotics which originated in the Japanese concession at Tientsin, and finally, the arrogant manners of many young Japanese officers garrisoned there.

In short, China's general attitude at the time could be summed up

---

* Because Chiang Kai-shek was kidnapped on the 12th day of the 12th month.
† Or Lushang, today a resort town in northern Kiangsi.

in these words: "We do not wish to provoke any incident; we prefer not to use armed force to drive the Japanese out of northern China; but if Japan demands another inch of our national territory, we shall resist her demand with all our power, even though we are not in a position to wage war. We must keep in mind, indeed, that although our Army is seven times the size of the Japanese Army, the latter's ammunition and equipment are ten times better than ours, and the Japanese Navy a thousand times better than ours. We shall try our very best to avoid a conflict in the northern provinces despite frequent Japanese provocation, and yet we are deeply convinced that our national survival depends on our capacity to resist any new aggression."[1]

Naturally, Japan was not unaware of the existence of a "United Front" in China. A new incident gave the Japanese the occasion to strike what they believed would be a decisive blow: on July 7, 1937, Japanese troops on "night maneuvers" at Lukouchiao, near Peking, clashed with Chinese troops. The fighting spread rapidly, and the well-prepared Japanese almost at once launched a large-scale offensive in northern China. Peking and Tientsin fell into enemy hands at the end of July.

Jacques Guillermaz, then a French military representative in China, followed events as closely as he could:

July 30, 1937. I was gazing at the celebrated Marco Polo Bridge, or Lukouchiao, with its double row of three hundred marble lions seated on short columns. . . . "Believe me," the Venetian explorer had written seven centuries ago, "few bridges are as handsome as this one. It is very well conceived and well-built, and is entirely made of grayish marble."

Before me lay the old city of Wanping, built astride the imperial road leading from nearby Peking to the central and southern provinces thousands of *li* distant. The city wall, which the last of the Mings had hastily ordered built against the bandit Li Tzu-ch'eng,* bears the marks of recent fighting. This time, however, the enemy came from the north, from the very capital.

Lukouchiao. For three weeks now, that three syllabled Chinese word has appeared in the papers of the world, and each day it evoked greater anxiety. It was there that in the night of the "double

* Who in 1644 seized Peking from the last Ming Emperor.

seven", the seventh day of the seventh month, a minor incident took place between the small Japanese garrison of Feng-tai and the local Chinese authorities. As a result, the Japanese troops had briefly bombarded and machine-gunned the city, but it was well sheltered behind its massive ramparts. Then negotiations had once more been opened. On July 28, however, the Japanese army and air force had unleashed a sudden and violent attack. Part of the 29th Chinese Army entrusted with the defense of Peking had been surprised and massacred in its Nan-yuan and Si-yuan camps. During the night of July 29th, the few remaining troops had silently withdrawn from Peking, to the other side of the Yong-ting River.

On the morning of July 30th, I went to see who was master of Wanping. I crossed long columns of Japanese infantry wearing short khaki tunics and light caps marked with a yellow star; I also passed groups of small tanks similar to our World War I Renaults, and requisitioned Chinese chariots pulled by small, shaggy horses. Finally, I reached the vaulted gate of the East Wall. It had been opened wide by the combined power of shells and mines; there were no guards left, so I simply walked into the city.

Along the main street, which is also the imperial road, shopkeepers had—either by order or mere prudence—hoisted the victors' white flags with red disk.* Columns of prisoners, chained around their waists and ankles, were advancing slowly, carrying boxes of ammunition. In an angle of the wall sat a group of convicts, their hands and feet bound, seemingly waiting for the end of their sad fate without needless revolt. A little farther, an old woman with a tragic face threw herself on the ground and, after having hit the dust three times with her forehead, implored passers-by to save her son, badly wounded in the chest. Dr. B. had him brought to the French hospital in fact, and there saved his life.

By a most singular coincidence, I met Colonel M., former Japanese trainee in France, at the Western Gate. Thanks to him, I was able to pass the line of sentries armed with automatic weapons, who stood along the river; thus I arrived in the middle of the bridge I had been admiring not so long ago. All was quiet. Abandoned equipment and ammunition testified to the recent passage of a retreating army. I was not interested by them, but instead picked up the paw of a stone lion, which had been broken off by a bullet.

* The national flag of Japan, the flag of "the rising sun".

Suddenly, I discovered a lone and strange corpse. It was not that of a soldier, but of an old, white-haired man with a thin gray beard, who was still carrying a small canvas bag on his back. He had collapsed against one of the marble plates which, together with the lions and their columns, formed the parapet of the bridge. He was leaning forward rather than crumpled, and his face had an expression both surprised and serene. But his chest was smeared with black, coagulated blood, and his naked shoulder was deeply slashed, as from a saber strike.

This pathetic corpse troubled me much more than those of the hundreds and hundreds of soldiers whom I had seen the day before, killed by the scores by enemy shells and bombs as they were marching down the Nan-yuan road. Here indeed was a humble Chinese farmer who probably had left his village at dawn, as he did every day, in order to go to the market, without worrying about events around him, which after all are the business of governments.

The poor, stupefied fellow symbolized the fate of millions of farmers who, after centuries of political indifference, had for the first time been thrown into the horrors of a national war from which such prodigious changes eventually arose.[2]

A small cause—the minor clash near the Marco Polo Bridge—led to momentous events and changes indeed. During the next eight years, China experienced on a vast scale all the horrors of modern warfare, which spared neither her city dwellers nor her peasantry. Though vastly inferior to the Japanese invaders in equipment, the Chinese surprised the world by their dogged and increasingly effective resistance. In his historic appeal to the nation of July 17, 1937, Chiang Kai-shek (henceforth the symbol of China's indomitable will to fight to the end) stressed that there would be no going back, no compromise and no surrender.

The Japanese campaign in northern China—chiefly in Hopei—was followed shortly by the "Shanghai Campaign". In August 1937, the killing of two Japanese marines near Shanghai led to the landing of a Japanese naval force which, however, found itself endangered by vastly superior Chinese forces. A Japanese army was sent in, but even so it took the invaders three months of severe fighting (and heavy bombing) to drive the Chinese out of their "economic" capital.

After the battle, once-prosperous Shanghai was but the shadow of its former self. The silence of death, described by the American journalist E. O. Hauser, now reigned over much of the city:

In November, the Chinese forces abandoned Shanghai. An army of ninety thousand Japanese pursued them up the Yangtze, forging ahead into a crucified land. The war moved on and Shanghai was left behind.

Shanghai was left behind. Silence fell upon the city. It was a strange silence after the infernal din of war; a heavy, stifling kind of silence: the silence of death. Vast sections of the city had been laid waste. Thousands of houses and factories had been bombed to pieces. This time death had done a thorough job. It was final. The big white office buildings, banks and hotels were still there, along the Bund, overlooking the muddy stream below. No one had bothered to destroy them. But behind their windows, life had stopped; and in their forgotten splendor they looked more formidable than ever. They made a front, just as great and as impressive as yesterday, for the gigantic carcass that was Shanghai, the city by the Yangtze mouth. . . .

In the center of Garden Bridge which led into the area under Japanese control, Japanese sentries were stationed. They wore dark uniforms and antiseptic masks, and an order of the Japanese garrison commander requested foreigners and Chinese to respect them "by giving a gentle bow and wishing them Good Morning." And there were people who felt that the gentle bow was not without significance; and that the polite Good Morning opened the funeral rites for the great white city of the East. The four million metropolis, crouching monster-like near the mouth of China's mightiest river, sucking in half of China's trade and guarding China's silver, had given up its ghost.

And there were some who thought that it had been a great and beautiful city for all its avarice. . . . The city that had eaten the lives of a million coolies . . . that had eaten the lives of thirty villages and towns as it grew. . . . The city that had a street where they sold nothing but pink baby bonnets. . . . The city where they heaved four billion cubic yards of mud from the river every year. . . . The city of the muddy flat. There were some who thought it was a pity, after all.

Pestilence crept into the [International] Settlement from the devastated quarters across the Creek, where thousands of Chinese peasant sons were rotting away, where rats and dogs were feasting as they had never feasted before.

And Kuan Ti, the god of war and peace, looked down upon his work. He was a red-faced and rather tallish chap, and he always carried his broad sword; for seventeen hundred years ago, in the time of the Three Kingdoms, he had been a mighty general.[3]

On December 3, 1937, six thousand Japanese soldiers took part in a victory parade in Shanghai. They marched past stolid Chinese onlookers, curious Westerners whom they occasionally roughed up, and thousands of wildly cheering Japanese settlers.

The parade was briefly interrupted by the throwing of a small bomb, and was marked by a series of minor brushes between the touchy Japanese and Western spectators. These incidents were described in some detail by the North China Daily News:

Since early morning Japanese civilians of both sexes ... had streamed into the central part of the Settlement, all carrying Rising Sun flags. They took up positions along the route of the procession and accorded the soldiers continuous "banzais"* as they filed by. In typical fashion they raised flags with both hands over their heads as they cheered. When a general or other high-ranking officer passed, the shouts became particularly loud and enthusiastic. At some points along the route uniformed Japanese stood beating metal discs on which the Rising Sun emblem was traced.

The Japanese banks and commercial houses downtown were all gaily decorated and their doors were thrown open for the first time since the beginning of the hostilities. The Yokohama Specie Bank on the Bund was particularly brightly dressed, and from in front of the building a large number of Japanese citizens greeted the parade. This group included many young women in brilliantly colored kimonos, and small boys and girls in their "Sunday best". All carried Japanese flags and waved them constantly during the march past. One Japanese had a microphone, which he held close to those cheering, and through which the "banzais" were sent to Tokyo and other cities in Japan. ...

The bombing incident developed with extreme swiftness. Chinese crowds were being kept well back from Nanking Road on both sides of the military route. Suddenly in Kwangse Road, south of Nanking Road, a man dressed in a "Sun Yat-sen suit" stepped forward from the mass of onlookers and walked a few steps in the direction of Nanking Road. As a Chinese constable attempted to push him back into the

* *Banzai*: the traditional Japanese patriotic shout, meaning "long life", or "forward!".

crowd he produced something wrapped in a Chinese newspaper and threw it at the column of marching soldiers. It landed near the footpath on the opposite side—and exploded. It was a crudely made hand grenade of the Mills type and it wounded three of the Japanese soldiers, a Japanese civilian, a Sikh constable, a Chinese constable, and Detective Sub-Insp. J. McPhee of Louza Station, who was also on duty at the corner. . . .

Before the bomb had even exploded, a Chinese constable, acting clearly in accordance with instructions, promptly drew his revolver and shot the assailant—a disciplined alertness which was most impressive. Four shots were fired, each making a hit.*

Consternation was caused in the ranks of the Japanese soldiers and the "banzais" of the Japanese spectators stopped suddenly. Commands were shouted and the district was quickly surrounded. Sentries were posted in all the side streets, while groups of soldiers began to search alleyways and buildings. A Japanese soldier fired a rifle shot at a window in the Sun Sun Building at about 1 o'clock, but hit the wall instead. The shot added to the confusion and sent many civilians scurrying for shelter. Ten minutes later the parade was resumed.

It was noticeable both before and after the incident how the men in the moving columns looked up at the buildings between which they were passing as if they expected trouble. . . .

Shortly before 3:30 o'clock in the afternoon Mr. Vaughan Reid, American, was hit about the face by two Japanese officers, wearing white gloves, and by a Japanese soldier who hit him with the butt of his rifle. . . . An unidentified Austrian gentleman managed to pacify them, and escorted Mr. Reid from the scene with the assistance of a foreign police officer from Louza Station.

Several foreign cameramen, who were attempting to get photographs of the Japanese soldiers, were also manhandled by the soldiers, but none were seriously injured.

There was a minor "incident" on the Bund, at the foot of Peking Road, shortly before 2 o'clock when the last sections of the procession were passing. A young foreigner tried to cross the column of marching men but was seized by a Japanese constable . . . and some Japanese reservists. He was roughly handled before a tall Sikh from the Police Reserve Unit got to his side and by his presence alone halted the

* The bomb thrower was left to die on the spot, as the Japanese forbade his transportation to a hospital.

mauling. A foreign police officer came up immediately afterward and settled the difficulty, telling the foreigner he must wait till the parade had passed.[4]

Many, and much more serious, incidents occurred in occupied Shanghai, where looting, rape and murder became common deeds of the Japanese soldiery. Meantime, merciless bombing of Chinese cities by the Japanese outraged world opinion. The League of Nations and the United States condemned the action of Japan, but the latter was not to be stopped by mere rhetorical interventions.*

Following the seizure of Shanghai, the Japanese launched a furious drive up the Yangtze River, where their next big objective was Nanking. All through the fall of 1937, they were engaged in heavy fighting with the Chinese, who kept falling back while denying the invaders a decision. Nanking was captured on December 13.

As the Japanese approached Nanking, Western residents there set up an "International Committee for Nanking Safety Zone" which, in agreement with Chinese and Japanese authorities, established a demilitarized zone of refuge that was soon overcrowded with destitute Chinese fleeing the horrors of war.

In a letter to friends, and then in his diary, an American professor teaching at Nanking University, Dr. M. Searle Bates, described the tragic events which marked that month of December in the "southern" capital:

On December 10, the refugees were streaming into the Zone. We had already filled most of the institutional buildings—Ginling College, the War College and other schools, and now had to requisition the Supreme Court, the Law College and the Overseas buildings, forcing doors where they were locked and appointing our own caretakers. Two Japanese blimps were visible just beyond Purple Mountain, probably to direct artillery fire. Heavy guns were pounding the south gate, and shells were dropping into the city. . . . We were now a community of 27—18 Americans, five Germans, one Englishman, one Austrian and two Russians. . . .

On Sunday the 12th I was busy at my desk in the Safety Zone all

---

* In November 1937, at Brussels, a conference of the powers connected with the Washington Nine Power Pact (1922), boycotted by Japan, also failed to end hostilities in China.

day long. We were using the former residence of Gen. Chang Chun, recently Minister of Foreign Affairs, as headquarters, so were very comfortably fixed, and incidentally had one of the best bombproof dugouts in all Nanking.

Airplanes had been over us almost constantly for the past two days, but no one heeded them now, and the shellfire had been terrific. The wall had been breached and the damage in the southern part of the city was tremendous. No one will ever know what the Chinese casualties were but they must have been enormous. The Japanese say they themselves lost forty thousand men taking Nanking.

The general rout must have started early that afternoon. Soldiers streamed through the city from the south, many of them passing through the Zone, but they were well-behaved and orderly. Gen. Tang* asked our assistance in arranging a truce with the Japanese and Mr. Sperling† agreed to take a flag and message—but it was already too late. Tang fled that evening, and as soon as the news got out, disorganization became general. There was panic as they made for the gate to Hsiakwan and the river. The road for miles was strewn with the equipment they cast away—rifles, ammunition, belts, uniforms, cars, trucks—everything in the way of army impediments. Trucks and cars jammed, were overturned, caught fire; at the gate more cars jammed and were burned—a terrible holocaust—and the dead lay feet deep. The gate blocked, terror-mad soldiers scaled the wall and let themselves down on the other side with ropes, puttees and belts tied together, clothing torn to strips. Many fell and were killed. But at the river was perhaps the most appalling scene of all. A fleet of junks was there. It was totally inadequate for the horde that was now in a frenzy to cross to the north side. The overcrowded junks capsized, then sank; thousands drowned. Other thousands tried to make rafts of the lumber on the river front, only to suffer the same fate. Other thousands must have succeeded in getting away, but many of these were probably bombed by Japanese planes a day or two later. . . .

So ended the happy, peaceful, well-ordered, progressive regime which we had been enjoying here in Nanking and on which we had built our hopes for still better days. For the Japanese were already in the city and with them came terror and destruction and death. They were first reported in the Zone at 11 o'clock that morning, the 13th.

* Chinese Commander in Chief at Nanking.
† German, representative of the Shanghai Insurance Co.

I drove down with two of our committee members to meet them, just a small detachment at the southern entrance to the Zone. They showed no hostility, though a few moments later they killed twenty refugees who were frightened by their presence and ran from them. For it seems to be the rule here, as it was in Shanghai in 1932, that anyone who runs must be shot or bayoneted.

Meanwhile we were busy at headquarters disarming soldiers who had been unable to escape and had come into the Zone for protection. We assured them that if they gave up their equipment, their lives would be spared by the Japanese. But it was a vain promise. All would have preferred to die fighting to being taken out and shot or sabered or used for bayonet practice, as they all were later on. . . .

On Tuesday the 14th the Japanese were pouring into the city— tanks, artillery, infantry, trucks. The reign of terror commenced, and it was to increase in severity and horror with each of the succeeding ten days. . . . The proclamation on the handbills which airplanes scattered over the city saying that the Japanese were the only real friends of the Chinese and would protect the good, of course meant no more than most of their statements. . . .

The problem of transportation became acute on the 16th, with the Japanese still stealing our trucks and cars. I went over to the American Embassy where the Chinese staff was still standing by, and borrowed Mr. Atcheson's car for Mills* to deliver coal. For our big concentrations of refugees and our three big rice kitchens had to have fuel as well as rice. We now had twenty-five camps, ranging from 200 to 12,000 people in them. In the University buildings alone there were nearly 30,000 and in Ginling College, which was reserved for women and children, the 3,000 were rapidly increased to over 9,000. In the latter place even the covered passageways between buildings were crowded, while within every foot of space was taken. . . .

That morning the cases of rape began to be reported. Over a hundred women that we knew of were taken away by soldiers, seven of them from the University library; but there must have been many times that number who were raped in their homes. Hundreds were on the streets trying to find a place of safety. . . . Refugees were searched for money and anything they had on them was taken away, often to their last bit of bedding. At our staff conference at four we could hear the shots of

* Second Secretary of the U. S. Embassy, and American Presbyterian missionary, respectively.

the execution squad nearby. It was a day of unspeakable terror for the poor refugees and horror for us. . . .

Saturday, December 18. A day of complete anarchy. Several big fires raging today, started by the soldiers, and more are promised. The American flag was torn down in a number of places. At the American School it was trampled on and the caretaker told he would be killed if he put it up again. The proclamations placed on all American and other foreign properties by the Japanese Embassy are flouted by their soldiers, sometimes deliberately torn off. Some houses are entered from five to ten times in one day and the poor people looted and robbed and the women raped. Several were killed in cold blood, for no apparent reason whatever. Six out of seven of our sanitation squad in one district were slaughtered; the seventh escaped, wounded, to tell the tale. . . . There are still many corpses on the streets. All of them civilians as far as we can see. The Red Swastika Society* would bury them, but their trucks had been stolen, their coffins used for bonfires, and several of their workers bearing their insignia have been marched away.

Smythe† and I called again at the Japanese Embassy with a list of 55 additional cases of violence, all authenticated, and told Messrs. Tanaka and Fukui‡ that today was the worst so far. We were assured that they would "do their best" and hoped that things would be better "soon," but it is quite obvious that they have little or no influence with the military whatever, and the military have no control over the soldiers. We were also told that seventeen military police had recently arrived who would help in restoring order. Seventeen for an army of perhaps fifty thousand! Yet we rather like the three men of the Embassy. They are probably doing their best. But I had to smile when they asked my help in getting cars and a mechanic for them after so many of ours had been stolen. I felt like referring them to their own military—but instead I took them around to the American Embassy and borrowed our Ambassador's and two others for them and later sent them our Russian repair man.

Monday, December 20. Vandalism and violence continue absolutely unchecked. Whole sections of the city are being systematically burned. At 5 P.M. Smythe and I went for a drive. All Taiping Road, the most important shopping street in the city, was in flames. We drove through

* Name of the Chinese Red Cross.
† Dr. Lewis S. C. Smythe, American, University of Nanking.
‡ Japanese Consul and Consul General, respectively.

showers of sparks and over burning embers. Farther south we could see the soldiers inside the shops setting fire to them and still farther they were loading the loot into army trucks. . . .

Our group here at the house drafted a message to the American Consulate General in Shanghai asking that diplomatic representatives be sent here immediately as the situation was urgent, then asked the Japanese Embassy to send it via navy radio. Needless to say it was never sent. . . .

Thursday, December 23. Seventy men were taken from our camp at the Rural Leaders' Training School and shot. No system—soldiers seize anyone they suspect. Callouses on hands are proof that the man was a soldier, a sure death warrant. Rickshaw coolies, carpenters and other laborers are frequently taken. At noon a man was led to headquarters with head burned cinder black—eyes and ears gone, nose partly, a ghastly sight. I took him to the hospital in my car where he died a few hours later. His story was that he was one of a gang of some hundred who had been tied together, then gasoline thrown over them and set afire. He happened to be on the outer edge so got the gas only over his head. . . .

Christmas Day. The American flag was taken from the Rural Leaders' Training School; seven soldiers spent the night and the night before in the Bible Teachers' Training School and raped the women, a girl of twelve was raped by three soldiers almost next door to us and another of thirteen, before we could send relief. There were also more bayonet cases; Wilson* reports that of the 240 cases in the hospital, three-quarters are due to Japanese violence since the occupation. At the University, registration commenced. The people were told that if any ex-soldiers were there and would step out, they would be used in the labor camps and their lives would be saved. About 240 stepped out. They were herded together and taken away. Two or three lived to tell the tale and, by feigning death after they were wounded, escaped and came to the hospital. One group was machine-gunned, another was surrounded by soldiers and used for bayonet practice. We have had quite a number of cases where men have faced the execution squad, escaped with only a wound or two, perhaps lying all day and into the night covered by the corpses of their comrades to escape detection, and then getting to the hospital or to friends. . . .

Wednesday, December 29. Registration continues, most inefficiently,

* Dr. Robert O. Wilson, American, University of Nanking Hospital.

and the people are given no information as to where and when to appear. More taken as ex-soldiers. Women and old men come kneeling and crying, begging our help in getting back their husbands and sons. In a few cases we have been successful, but the military resent any interference from us. Word comes through from Hsiakwan by a representative of the Chinese Red Cross Society that there are approximately twenty thousand refugees along the river front. The supply of rice we let them have before the Japanese arrived is nearly exhausted and there is great suffering. They ask to come into the Safety Zone, but we are already too crowded. Anyway, the Japanese wouldn't permit it, nor will they permit us to go out there and render help. For the time being they will have to get along as best they can.

Guards are at last posted at the various foreign embassies. But why wasn't it done two weeks ago? Our homes are still left unprotected; and the few guards posted at some of our camps are often more of a nuisance than a help. They demand fire and food, beds and often other things of the people.[5]

The sack of Nanking was not the only feat accomplished by the Japanese soldiery. Similar tales of brutality, sadism, and wanton destruction came from practically all areas occupied by the invader. Not even small hamlets or isolated farms were spared by the fury of the Japanese. Relentless and indiscriminate aerial attacks only added to the horrors of ground operations. Millions of Chinese fled the advancing armies of the dreaded "dwarf bandits".

Foreign property and rights in China, including American and British ships plying the Yangtze, were no longer safe either. This was strikingly illustrated when Japanese bombers attacked the U. S. gunboat Panay *and four British vessels anchored near Nanking.* The rapidly increasing tension in Europe enabled the Japanese to pursue their high-handed policy without running serious risk of intervention.*

By the end of the year 1937, the Japanese were in firm possession of the main cities and lines of communication of the lower Yangtze area, which is normally one of China's most fertile and most densely populated districts. In the wake of the Japanese Army's ruthless advance, however, death and desolation prevailed everywhere. A British correspondent who visited

---

* The attack took place on December 12, 1937, and created acute tension between the powers. The U. S. Government ultimately accepted Japanese explanations, but Japan subsequently evaded all foreign protests.

Sungkiang, a city thirty miles south of Shanghai, telegraphed the following graphic account to London:

Sungkiang, which was the original headquarters of General Gordon's "Ever Victorious Army", and a thriving city on the Shanghai–Hangchow Railway, presented a scene of indescribable desolation and destruction. Acres of houses have been laid waste as a result of aerial bombing, and there is hardly a building standing which has not been gutted by fire. Smouldering ruins and deserted streets presented an eerie spectacle, the only living creatures being dogs unnaturally fattened by feasting on corpses. In the whole of Sungkiang, which should contain a densely packed population of approximately 100,000, I saw only five Chinese, who were old men, hiding in a French Mission compound in tears. They were short of food and begged to be taken to Shanghai.

The condition of Sungkiang is typical of the state of affairs throughout this densely populated delta between Shanghai and Nanking, and testifies to what may have been one of the greatest mass migrations of population in history. No one is able to answer the question of what has happened to the hundreds of thousands, or rather millions, of Chinese who have literally disappeared from this area. The whole thirty-mile route between Shanghai and Sungkiang is like a desert, with rice crops ungathered and left rotting in the fields as far as I could see. The traveller passes a continuous vista of blackened ruins and burnt-out farms guarded over by gruesomely fattened dogs.

Considerable bodies of Japanese troops returning to Shanghai were passed on the road. They represented a strange appearance, being loaded up with piles of loot from the countryside. In many cases rickshaws containing trunks and suitcases were hitched behind cavalry horses and Japanese soldiers were riding donkeys, cows, and even buffaloes, collected from the countryside. Live pigs were tied to artillery limbers, and chickens were carried which had been taken from farms miles from the route that had been visited by foraging parties. At one point on the road was a huge concentration of Japanese supply wagons, and several batteries of field artillery. My attention was caught by thousands of cases of Japanese beer which had been consumed by the Japanese troops.[6]

In northern China, where winters are rugged and natural fuel rare, the

Japanese ransacked the countryside and carried away all wooden objects they could lay their hands on. From the Paoting district, a European missionary described this particular kind of foraging in a letter to friends:

The common people around us ordinary depend largely on leaves, grasses and grain stalks for winter fuel—affording little wood. But the Japanese search for wood everywhere, that they use in prodigal fashion for quick fires. As a result, loose wood now being exhausted, doors, window frames, furniture, farm tools, even the frames of houses that they are pulling down are rapidly being used for fuel. One of our refugee women was telling today with tears in her eyes of losing a weaving loom for fuel. "It is my one means of livelihood," she said. Just across the street from us is a yard that belongs to our native church. In it is one house built some thirty years ago semi-foreign style, with well carpentered panel doors. Day before yesterday two of these were wrenched off for fuel, and the others being strongly held by rusty screws, the soldiers just splintered out the panels from several of them. Yesterday we took off the remaining ones and stored them in our compound. Yesterday several of the soldiers scaled a back wall into a little side court off our main compound and before we knew it had sawed down a tree of 5-inch diameter. When my American colleague accosted them just after the deed was done, they did seem a bit shame-faced.[7]

Japanese plans for the conquest of China envisaged a quick victory and a favorable peace with China, as Japan was then getting ready for still greater conquests in the Pacific area. In particular, Japan's military leaders had hoped that the capture of Nanking—psychologically important as the capital of both ancient and modern China—would mean the end of organized Chinese resistance. Even before they captured the city, peace feelers were put out through the intermediary of the German Ambassador at Nanking, Dr. Trautemann. Generalissimo Chiang Kai-shek, however, made it clear that a united China was going to fight to the bitter end.*

Nanking fell, Chungking (in Szechuan) became China's wartime capital, and hostilities continued unabated. A war of attrition, that was to last for eight years, now began over vast areas of China. The Japanese Navy

---

* When he received the ambassador (who acted on orders from Hitler), Chiang is said to have replied very simply that he would discuss peace only after every single Japanese soldier was removed from China.

blockaded China's coast, but Chiang Kai-shek received increasing numbers of military aircraft and ammunition from Soviet Russia, with whom a nonaggression treaty had been signed in August 1937. The United States and England, on the other hand, made substantial loans to the Nationalist government.

Being unable to force a decision, the Japanese resorted more and more to spreading terror from the air. Scores of large Chinese cities were bombed on a scale unprecedented so far, and world opinion was shocked by this relatively novel and particularly reprehensible form of warfare.*

Soochow, known as the "Venice of China", a picturesque city of 350,000 lying fifty miles west of Shanghai, was crushed under high explosives in November 1937. An American missionary who survived the "Soochow Nightmare" gave an account of the event:

It was a frightening thing to see; a horrible, maddening thing under which to dwell—tons of explosives hurtling down from the skies, exploding in a cascade of bits of human flesh, dirt, stone and mortar. Both night and day death rained upon the city from the circling, droning Japanese planes.

At the early stages of the bombings, the majority of the fear-crazed residents of Soochow sought sanctuary in dugouts. Finally, air raids became so incessant that we debated whether to remain in the dugouts or return to our work and take our chances on missing death. We decided on work. . . .

I cannot pass on to you the feelings that came over me as I saw hundreds of thousands of men, women and children leaving their homes, carrying with them their pitifully small belongings.

By this time, however, boats, rickshaws and other vehicles could not be obtained at any price, and most of the refugees had to flee by foot. My companions and I had previously secured two boats from Chinese soldiers, and it fell to my lot on the night of November 12th to tow these boats by motor launch to Kwangfu with our first contingent of refugees. I immediately returned to Soochow for another load where Chinese soldiers commandeered the two boats, but left me the motor launch. I turned the launch over to my companion and he, with other friends, started off again for Kwangfu.

* To a certain extent, the Japanese were preceded by the Germans, whose bombers crushed the Spanish town of Guernica (April 26, 1937) as part of Hitler's support of General Franco.

It was now too late to enter the city gate so, with a friend, I spent the night in a deserted hospital. It was the night of the big air raid. And only God and the people left in the doomed city of Soochow knew, or ever will know, the horrors of that night. The most dreadful nightmare could not compare with it. The entire city and its environs were lighted with flares dropped from planes. And then death started on its speedy flight from the skies. No human being could have counted the number of bombs released upon this defenseless city. . . . My friend lay flat upon the floor. At times, I got under the bed. Strangely enough, I felt safer there.

At daybreak, we arose and went into the city. The death and destruction we witnessed defies all description. We felt nauseated, sick. The only cheering sight we saw was a Chinese pastor leading a thousand refugees toward Kwangfu. What a picture! Behind him trailed small children, old men and women, the lame and those disabled by bombs and shells—I thought of the Good Shepherd leading His flock. In two days, 5,000 refugees from Soochow had been removed to Kwangfu.[8]

To the nearly one million men thrown into China by Japan,[*] Chiang Kai-shek could oppose only ill-equipped and ill-organized divisions for the most part. Yet the Chinese resisted fiercely, and it became increasingly evident that while the Japanese could capture large cities and important communication points, the countryside would remain in the hands of the Chinese. During the spring of 1938, the invader suffered several reverses, particularly in Shantung Province.

Before the important industrial center of Wuhan (commonly known as the "Chicago of the Orient", and composed of the three cities of Hankow, Wuchang, and Hanyang), stubborn Chinese resistance lasted four months. A French newspaper correspondent, Jean Raynaud, visited the battlefield in that area:

We drove at full speed along roads heavily damaged by the coming and going of trucks, troops, guns, and, most of all, by the rainy season. Our blue headlights gave us barely enough light. We had to grip the truck with both hands, to avoid being thrown overboard. Now and then, our driver swerved smartly to avoid the tank traps built in the

[*] Representing a total of sixteen divisions, out of the twenty-four which were in a state of readiness at the time.

road in anticipation of the next Japanese advance. A railway line which we followed for some time had already been cut in several spots.

Heavy rains had flooded the plains, making the Chinese defense easier but slowing the Japanese offensive. The area had been all but abandoned by its civilian population. Here and there, however, a small light flickered in a house standing beside the road. A few old men and women had refused to leave their homes, and they would stay there until panic-striken by the ever-louder booming of the guns.

One hour after our departure from Hankow, we began passing long columns of soldiers marching along both sides of the road. They were on their way to the front. All through the night, we drove between these almost uninterrupted columns of diversely armed soldiers advancing toward the enemy. Every now and then, we passed a company which had stopped for its hourly rest.

The exhausted men had fallen asleep almost at once. The driver of our truck really needed all of his skill to avoid hitting some of them; in their deep sleep, they stretched either a leg or an arm across the road, quite unconscious of any danger. Each time we stopped, we inquired about the origin of these soldiers. They came from Szechuan, Kwangsi, Kwantung, Hunan, Ngan-huei, and even from the distant province of Yunan. Most of them had come on foot, and some had walked over a thousand kilometers!

These were most unusual soldiers. Many of them carried a bamboo pole across their shoulders; on trays hanging at either end of each pole, the men had heaped equipment, provisions, kitchen utensils, and their entire kit as well. Every soldier carried a fan tucked into his cartridge-filled belt. Some of them marched with slung rifles. Still others carried long poles around which were wrapped pieces of green canvas that helped camouflage the column when it was surprised by daylight attacks from Japanese planes. Finally, one could also see a few stretchers for the wounded, as well as an occasional first-aid kit.

Only rarely did we pass artillery batteries or companies equipped with mules. A few days later, when the troops were falling back, we saw groups of 77mm. Krupp guns retreating in an orderly fashion, also a unit of antitank guns. Coming the other way, there was a battery of mountain guns carried by mules. As far as we knew, the column of trucks carrying the ammunition boxes on which we sat was the only one to have advanced toward the front that day. Along this front, fifty thousand men were thinly spread, which meant that only one

Sun Yat-sen, "Father of the Country," has been claimed both by the Nationalists and the Communists as precursor and guide. He was the living synthesis
of Chinese and Western civilization. His second wife, Soong Ching-Ling,
with him in this photograph, is a sister of T. V. Soong (Finance Minister and
then Foreign Minister in the Nationalist Government) and of the future Madame
Chiang Kai-Shek. She is now a vice-Chairman of the People's Republic of
China.

Red Chinese guerrilla artillery (the People's Militia). Hollow tree trunks bound with telephone wire taken from the enemy, and packed with powder and gravel, "welcomed" the Japanese entering the villages of Northern China.

Peasants carrying a wounded Red soldier. "The Red Army lives among the people as the fish dwells in the water" (Chou En-lai). *Fox Photos Ltd.*

List of official posts occupied by Mao
Tse-tung since 1931:

1931–34: Chairman of the Chinese
Soviet Republic (until the
"Long March").

1934–49: Chairman of the Central
Committee of the Chinese
Communist Party.

1949–59: Chairman of the People's
Republic of China, succeeded
in that capacity by Liu Chao-
tchi.

1959– : President of the Central
Executive Committee of the
Chinese Communist Party.

Below. Mao Tse-tung addressing a group
of country people in 1944, when he was
leader of the guerrilla forces.

Chou En-Lai. In charge of liaison with the Kuomintang, 1937–46. Now President of the State Council (government).

Leading Generals of the Red Army. From left to right, Peng Teh-Huai (Vice C-in-C, Minister of Defence until 1959, Vice-Premier of State Council), Chu Teh (Commander-in-Chief, Chairman of National People's Congress), Yeh Chien-Ying (Chief of Staff until 1959), Nieh Jung-Chen (Commander of Forces in North China until 1959, Vice-Premier of State Council), Chen Yi (Commander of Forces in Central China until 1959, Commander of Red Armies in great Suchow battle, Foreign Minister and Vice-Premier of State Council).

gun and a few rifles could be fired every hour. The Japanese armies, on the contrary, whose objective was Hankow, were equipped with modern weapons: motorized columns, tanks, field artillery and heavy artillery, plus the guns of warships which little by little were moving up the Yangtze, and auxiliary boats which brought ammunition and food, and carried the wounded away.[9]

The contrast between the Chinese and the Japanese armies was striking indeed. This was still true in 1941, when a total of two million invaders or twenty-seven divisions out of fifty-one which Japan fielded at the time were operating in China. A French missionary stationed in Kwangsi was impressed by the strength of the Japanese:

Without going into any details, the Japanese occupation army gives an impression of strong self-confidence and of meticulous organization. Its means of transportation are both numerous and varied. Its automobiles, in particular, are powerful and fast, and the drivers avoid hurting one's ears by excessive honking. The horses are very large and well-fed.

Food seems to be abundant enough, judging by the considerable stock accumulated in our city, or by the quantity of leftovers from meals given to soldiers, or by the time required for the removal of the supplies.

The weapons are in excellent condition, and so is the rest of the equipment; as for the men, they are strong, well-fed, and rather well disciplined.

Even though the river is nearly four hundred yards wide, the Japanese engineers managed to build a pontoon bridge that had withstood two floods. All the Japanese are extremely discreet with regard to any kind of military operation.

Their air force is formidable, and very much feared.

In short, the Chinese army looks rather modest compared to this powerful machine: only the unlimited numbers and the stubborn optimism of the Celestials will eventually defeat it.[10]

After one and a half years of almost uninterrupted fighting (and bombing), the Japanese were in possession of most of northern China and of the Yangtze valley. These were in fact the country's richest and most densely populated *areas. Practically all the large Chinese cities were under Japanese control: Hankow and Canton fell in October 1938, the latter after months of merciless bombing.**

Little by little, as part of their projected "new order" in the Far East, the Japanese transformed China into a Japanese protectorate. They made less and less of a secret of their intention eventually to overthrow the Nationalist regime of Chiang Kai-shek. Repeating the technique employed earlier in Manchukuo, they established their dominion over the conquered territories by means of "autonomous" Chinese local governments. In March 1940, they supported the establishment of a puppet government under Wang Ching-wei (favorite disciple of Sun Yat-sen) at Nanking.

In order to exercise full control over the areas wrung from the Nationalists, the Japanese and their Chinese collaborators used all sorts of bribery, accusations, and terror. The opposition was crushed by "strong" methods, and opponents were occasionally hunted down even on neutral ground represented by foreign institutions.

Dr. Leighton Stuart,† President of the American-sponsored Yenching University at Peking, recorded the many worries he had on his Japanese-surrounded "Island of Freedom":

We had incidents almost daily, usually minor ones but always with the possibility of becoming serious. This was especially true because of linguistic limitations on both sides and the natural suspicions of an occupying army in unfriendly territory. It was not long before I called to my assistance one of our graduates whose family circumstances in childhood and later on his graduate study in Japan enabled him to speak the language as fluently as a native. He was invaluable in all our constant dealings with Japanese military officers and others. . . .

Whenever he proposed it, I would entertain Japanese civil or military officials as part of the price paid for better relations in so delicate a situation. The Japanese High Command arranged from time to time for delegations of their fellow countrymen to visit north China in order to promote their cultural control and perhaps to impress the people "back home" with their own success. They invariably included

* Most of the Cantonese had fled. Capture of the city enabled the Japanese to cut the important Canton–Hankow Railway, chief line for transportation of foreign supplies to the Nationalist forces in the south.

† Born in China of missionary parents, Dr. Stuart was educated in the United States, and in 1904 returned to China as Presbyterian missionary. He was U.S. ambassador to China from 1946 until 1952.

Yenching in such an itinerary, and I had to impress my Western colleagues into helping me entertain the visitors. A few Chinese were occasionally also asked and consented as a supreme evidence of a goodwill that rose above nationalistic pride. . . .

With the protection the students enjoyed on an American-owned campus, it was well understood that they should not take advantage of this to carry on anti-Japanese activities. More than once I had to remind certain patriotic individuals among them that they should either leave our campus and do whatever they had in mind or desist entirely and thus avoid endangering their comrades as well as themselves. The Japanese were constantly on the watch for underground hostility and had a horde of secret police and spies whose reports led to numerous cases of arrest and torture. Our own students were under especial suspicion. The usual procedure was to pull them out of the University buses when they were making weekend trips to the city. My resourceful secretary was remarkably fortunate in getting them released without too much delay or hardship.

One boy was, however, so horribly treated that when he was finally set free he lived for months in abject terror even of his mother, and when I was permitted to call at the home he was still in this state of pathological dread. When I last saw him several years after this experience he was still unable to resume any normal activity. His case made graphic my fears over continuing university work in occupied territory. Another boy confessed to me with an obvious sense of shame that when under interrogation by the dreaded secret police he was given the alternative of prison and torture or acting as a spy on the Yenching campus he had agreed to the latter. He was to report to them weekly what went on. I told him that I had no condemnation of him nor any objection to his reporting whatever he observed on the campus, but asked him to inform me occasionally of their reaction. Before long he told me that they had dismissed him because there was no interest for them in his reports.[11]

Yenching University remained an oasis of freedom until December 1941, when the Japanese attacked Pearl Harbor. At that time, Dr. Stuart and his fellow Americans were arrested and interned until the end of World War II. Long before the outbreak of that war, however, the Japanese had indirectly attacked the position of foreign powers in China, demanding a larger share in the Shanghai international concession and challenging foreign rights everywhere.* *Protests on the part of the Western powers made little impression in Tokyo, the more so as the dangerous situation in Europe was rapidly getting worse.*

The Chinese, in other words, were more and more left to themselves in their struggle for survival. Their Generalissimo, fortunately, could rely on the country's moral unity as well as on its fighting spirit undaunted by the initial disasters.

Not the least determined to resist the invader were China's woman; to begin with, the first lady. In May 1938, Mme. Chiang Kai-shek convoked a National Woman's Conference at the lovely mountain resort of Kuling, southeast of Hankow. One of the participants wrote the following account of that meeting:

In addition to the regular delegates from each province, all the prominent feminine leaders of the country were invited—writers, heads of organizations, professional women, Government officials, and student leaders. I had long been used to large official gatherings and political conventions, but there was something about this meeting which was uniquely impressive.

After the opening ceremonies, Mme. Chiang addressed us. She began by saying that we, the women of China, had always worked and worked hard, but now we would have to work with greater effort in a new direction; we must keep at it day and night if we were to win.

She said: "We, who are gathered here today, are the so-called intellectual leaders of Chinese womanhood. Each one of us has been invited to attend this meeting because we have a definite contribution to make to the ultimate goal. Upon us, therefore, rests a gigantic responsibility—the responsibility of leading our fellow women in every stratum of society."

She went on: "The world admires the courage of our troops and our newly forged unity, but the world is looking at us in wonder; will this unity, achieved in adversity, continue in peace? If it does not continue and grow, we shall have failed and will be doomed.

* In June 1938, for instance, they blockaded the British and French concessions at Tientsin because British authorities refused to surrender four Chinese accused of terrorism. Japanese spokesmen announced that England must give up supporting the Nationalist regime, and instead cooperate with Japan in establishing the "New Order" in Asia.

"One of our first tasks lies within each one of us. We must develop our capacity for personal understanding as a necessary prelude to mass understanding and cooperation. We must realize that it is essential for us to strive and work for unity and cooperation; now, China in war must prepare for peace; and in war or peace, the women of China must lead the way."

Then the meeting was open for discussion of our problems. As things progressed, I was speechless with astonishment. The delegates —some from the Government, some from the provinces, and some from the working classes—gave their reports and presented their problems with such intelligence and facility that I was amazed. Having been an ardent feminist ever since I had started working for the Revolution in those early days in Peking when I was hardly more than a child, I realized now that my dream of the day when women would have a vital part in the destiny of the country was coming true at last, right before my eyes. Listening to them, I realized how much China had changed. They were well informed, poised, and mature; at the same time, they were humane and courageous. It was as if two centuries of social development had been covered in two decades.[12]

After the fall of Nanking and Hankow, the name Chungking symbolized China's all-out resistance to the Japanese. The Chinese victory of Tsaoyang, in northern Hupeh (May 1939), checked the Japanese advance toward Chiang Kai-shek's wartime capital, but the Chinese remained on the defensive. Their inadequate equipment was somewhat compensated for by central China's rugged topography.

Having failed to penetrate farther inland, the Japanese concentrated on systematic and massive bombing of Chungking which was calculated to destroy the city and the morale of the people as well. Thus Chungking became the "most bombarded city in the world". Eventually, bombproof shelters capable of holding four hundred thousand people were bored into the surrounding hills, but not before most of the city had been destroyed and thousands of its inhabitants killed.

The Japanese air raids of early May, 1939, were particularly murderous. A "live" account of the attack which took place in the late afternoon of May 4th was given by a French missionary:

Here they come, 27 heavy bombers flying in from the northeast and advancing in double-row formation. Now they hover over the city, and the first explosions of bombs are heard. In the fading daylight, antiaircraft shells burst below the planes. People have hardly had time to cower against strong walls or weaker columns that will at least protect them from flying splinters. The explosions succeed each other in very steady rhythm. They are getting closer and closer. . . . The houses tremble, and windows burst into pieces whenever some bombs fall into our neighborhood. The infernal dance continues, moving away. A few more explosions, and then one hears only the fading drone of the planes behind which the last few shells are bursting. . . .

The attack is over now, it has lasted for less than a quarter hour. We move up to the second floor, to make sure that the planes are gone. They are, but now a sinister gleam and clouds of smoke rise in the air. Fires have broken out in front of us, on our right, close by, everywhere. The enemy planes have flown over the city only once, but they have followed its longest diagonal, from the northeast to the southwest. As on the previous day, they have showered it with both incendiary bombs and torpedoes, in a pattern of perfect precision. Every fifty yards or so a group of incendiary bombs and two torpedoes have crashed down through the commercial and most populous sections of this overcrowded city. And they have chosen the moment of the day when streets are most crowded, the moment also when people fleeing daytime attacks have returned to the city in the hope that the night would protect them.

After nightfall, Chungking is one vast blazing mass. Quicker than it takes to tell, beams crack, walls crumble, telephone poles collapse amidst showers of sparks and tangled wires. People run about without knowing where to go, stumbling and floundering, trying to escape the flames that close in from every side. . . . The wounded are screaming, as they realize they are about to be burned alive. The municipal hospital with its 250 beds must be evacuated because it is full of sick and injured people from the previous day, and because it is being threatened by a nearby fire. Poor people are endeavoring to pull a few indispensable objects from the flames. Cries and appeals fill the air, and the acrid odor of sulfur and pitch gets caught in people's throats and enters their lungs. Walls are crumbling, and the fires keep spreading. The water tower has been severely damaged, and as a result most water pumps cannot even be used. Small fires converge into one vast blaze, and all quarters of the city's north-central and southwestern parts,

several kilometers long and a few hundred yards wide, are eventually
ablaze. . . .

Three o'clock in the morning. The sirens are heard once more. It
is really terrible, this alert in the middle of the night in the blazing city.
The horrified people dash toward the shelters in an indescribable rush,
trampling upon one another, shouting and crying. Like all the rest of
them, we enter the shelter. Half an hour later, the all-clear signal is
sounded.

Soon daybreak comes; a day of horror follows a night of terror.
The bright May morning sun rises above the smoke, the ruins and the
corpses, many of them calcinated, that litter the streets. There are
corpses everywhere. Loose limbs are scattered about amid smoldering
heaps of furniture and beams, and survivors roam through the burning
ruins, searching feverishly for traces of some relative. There is a woman
bent and crying over half a corpse. I ask myself whether such horrors
are possible at all, or whether I am the victim of ghastly hallucinations.
Yes, it is possible, it is really true, Chungking has become one vast
cemetery.[13]

*Thus it was the Chinese who for the first time in human history experienced
on a massive scale that particularly barbarous form of modern warfare, aerial
bombardment. But it did not destroy their morale, as the Japanese had anticipated it would. The Chungkingese, in fact, reacted much as Londoners did a
few months later under the Blitz: they were even more determined to hold out
and fight on, as were the rest of the Chinese people.*

*In their bombed-out capital, the Kuomintang leaders organized government
services as well as they could. Hollington K. Tong, wartime Vice-Minister
of Information of the Republic of China, has described how he and his
colleagues adapted themselves to the situation:*

We carefully worked out a plan under which we could resume work
immediately, in the event of destruction of our office building. . . .
Our plan was simple. Boxes were provided in every office in which
books and important papers could be regularly kept. Every office boy
attached to our office and homes was responsible for removing to the
scattered mat sheds, or the dugout, certain things as soon as the first
air raid signal was sounded. Typewriters, important papers, and other
irreplaceable pieces of equipment and information were carried out
first—on the usual bamboo poles. By the time the second air raid

alarm was sounded, everything of value would have been in the dugout. After the all clear, the process would be reversed and the things returned to their proper places. It was an exacting task for the office boys but it was always done cheerfully and speedily, and after we adopted the system, we suffered little loss from the air raids. . . .

The 1940 raids were particularly severe. . . . Our good luck ran out on June 28. On that day, we had the fifth of six consecutive days of air raids and the nineteenth of twenty days of raids within a month. One bomb made a twenty-foot hole in front of our office building and another started a fire in a mat shed behind the office. The fire burned for half an hour and we lost our library, one of the rooms housing our business section and twelve rooms in a row of cottages occupied by staff members. . . .

The next morning, before the daily raid, we held a meeting at which Tseng* and I urged courage and preparedness for worse times to come. We improved upon our plan of the previous summer to keep all office equipment not in constant use in places of safety and to send personal belongings away. It was becoming more and more difficult to buy anything except the handicraft products of the farm areas surrounding Chungking, and we all needed to preserve even the most insignificant of our possessions.

After this meeting, we had our daily raid and almost daily ration of half a dozen bombs. It became harder for us to carry on our work. We spent a great deal of our time in dugouts and when in our offices or homes, with roofs or walls blown off or burned away, we were constantly in the way of masons and carpenters who were trying desperately to keep the buildings from crumbling. We were without telephone service for more than a month that summer, and without electric light for weeks. The water supply was inadequate and irregular and this, combined with the 100-degree summer temperature, caused acute discomfort. But our work went on unabated; and our daily releases, and newscasts, as well as feature articles for our own monthly magazine, *China at War*, which was printed in Hong Kong, were written up and transmitted to America regularly.[14]

In January 1941, at a crucial moment of the Sino-Japanese War, the Chinese Central Government was beset by a new, and unexpected, difficulty. It arose from the so-called Anhwei Incident, in which Nationalist troops

---

* Director of the Tong's staff.

attacked the Red "New Fourth Army" operating in the lower Yangtze area. Some ten thousand New Fourthers were either killed or captured and the army's commander in chief was taken prisoner.

*What actually happened is not entirely clear. The New Fourth Army (or NFA, in short) was created in 1938 with Red partisan detachments from the civil war period. In agreement with the Kuomintang High Command, the NFA began anti-Japanese guerrilla operations in southern Anhwei Province and, like the Red Eighth Route Army operating in northern China, succeeded in steadily expanding the territory under its control, despite increasingly ruthless mopping-up campaigns on the part of the Japanese.**

All Red troops were nominally under Chiang Kai-shek's supreme command, although their leaders did not always see eye to eye with the Generalissimo in matters political and strategic. It was probably in the course of a disagreement over ways and means of fighting the Japanese that Chiang decided to act once and for all. He gave his version of the incident in a speech delivered on January 27, 1941:

The behavior of the New Fourth Army, its disregard for orders, attacks on comrades-in-arms, and even acts of mutiny and sabotage had necessarily to be put an end to; it was purely a matter of the assertion of military law. There was not the minutest admixture of issues belonging to the sphere of politics and party relationships. . . .

In November [1940] the New Fourth Army was ordered by the High Command to move northward to engage the enemy in a certain appointed area. It elected not to respond, but waited until after the expiration of the period of time allowed, then to make an arbitrary move southward, executing a premeditated maneuver leading to an attack in broad daylight upon the headquarters of the 40th Division. This plainly mutinous proceeding caused its disbandment as a disciplinary necessity. . . .

The Government had limited itself last year to adjurations, calling upon the New Fourth Army to have done with its constant failure to comply with orders. It obstinately persisted, however, in its evil

* Until the fall of Canton and Hankow (October 1938), the Japanese more or less ignored the Communist forces and concentrated their attacks upon the Kuomintang troops. Red guerrillas, meanwhile, liberated increasingly large areas behind Japanese lines (mostly with arms taken from the invader), and compelled the Japanese to turn powerful forces against the annoying Reds in their rear. The Japanese anti-guerrilla campaigns reached their peak (both in number and ferocity) in the years 1941 and 1942.

courses and at last went beyond all bounds. The situation developed in a way imperatively demanding the most rigorous action.[15]

Two American journalists, Theodore H. White and Annalee Jacoby,* who investigated the Anhwei Incident on the spot, called it "one of the major turning points in China's wartime politics". They gave the following account of the dispute:

The best impartial summation that can be made after consulting all available sources is this: The bulk of the New Fourth Army had moved north across the Yangtze by the end of December. There remained a headquarters detachment, including most of the staff, the high command, and some combat troops totaling something more than 5,000 men. They had been ordered to move north, and the government fixed their route; the Communists claim to this day that it would have taken them directly into Japanese garrisons along the riverbank. They pleaded for a change in route, and their delegate in Chungking, General Chou En-lai, saw the Generalissimo. The Generalissimo, after approving a change, invited Chou to a Christmas dinner, and the two of them drank the cup of peace and friendship; all was settled. Then suddenly Communist headquarters in Yenan† snapped a radio to their Chungking office; the New Fourth Army was trapped and surrounded by government troops, and the headquarters detachment was being massacred. Chou rushed to the Generalissimo. He was unable to see him but was assured that all was going smoothly and that orders were being issued to government units not to impede the march of the New Fourth.

Who was lying? The Communists claim that the Generalissimo's henchmen launched the attack without his knowledge and that when the attack became known, the Generalissimo lied to cover it up and later condoned the action. The Kuomintang claims that the New Fourth Army had attacked government troops, who disciplined the insurgents. This claim blandly overlooks the fact that the Communist unit was heavily outnumbered and consisted mostly of noncombat staff and headquarters personnel.

Chungking buzzed with rumors of an open breach, of an all-out

* Members of the China Bureau of *Time*, White serving as its director from 1939 until 1945.

† In northern Shensi: main Communist base since the end of the Long March.

civil war. . . . The incident itself was bad enough, but the victorious government troops treated their captured Communist compatriots with Japanese ruthlessness. Years later a university professor, not a Communist, who had been captured while traveling with the group, told a gruesome tale of the captivity. He said the Communists had had both men and women on their staff, the women serving as political workers, nurses, and staff members. According to him, government troops raped their Communist captives; the girls contracted venereal disease, and some committed suicide. The captives were held near the scene of battle for a year and a half and were then marched 400 miles overland to a new concentration camp. Both men and women were forced to haul the baggage of government troops; when they sickened, they were beaten; some were shot, and others were buried alive. By the time the professor who told me the tale was released, only 300 prisoners of the several thousand captured were still alive.

The New Fourth Army incident drew a line of emotional hysteria across all future relations of government and Communists. All negotiations ceased. Supplies were cut off from Communist armies everywhere. A blockade of picked government troops was thrown about the Communist civilian base in northern Shensi and sealed airtight. In the beginning it had been a war of all China against the Japanese; now it was a war of two Chinas—a Communist China and a Kuomintang China against the Japanese; and there was a subsidiary war smoldering simultaneously with these two great wars—a war between Communist China and Kuomintang China.[16]

The war of the "two Chinas" against Japan went on unabated until August 1945, at the time of the Japanese surrender to the Allies. As for the rift created by the Anhwei Incident, it became ever wider, but the "subsidiary war" turned into an open—and decisive—struggle only after the end of World War II.

In December 1941, two events contributed greatly to improve the difficult situation confronting the Chungking (or Central) government. One was the American declaration of war against Japan after Pearl Harbor, and the other was the victory obtained over the Japanese in the bloody ten-day battle of Changsha, in central Hunan.*

The correspondent Robert Payne, visiting the Changsha battlefield on

---

* Of which province the city is the capital. The Japanese were opposed by regular troops and at the same time harassed by guerrillas.

January 5, 1942, was struck by the youthfulness and unflinching determination of the victorious Chinese soldiers:

And now from everywhere there appeared blue-helmeted soldiers in light blue padded cotton uniforms. They were all young. They walked in the sunlight out of the shelter of bomb holes with an unexpected swagger, their bayonets gleaming. We photographed them. They smiled. They were very eager to talk about the battle, and they mentioned Colonel Li, who had defended the city from within, with extraordinary respect and affection. "A general or an officer who obtains the respect of his soldiers in China can work miracles," someone said, and it was easy to believe him, for these youths, fingering their bayonets and gazing dreamily at the passing coffins, are soldiers of whom any country could be proud. They were nearly all Hunanese, fighting for their homes—farmers' lads, mostly, with faces like ripe apples and a gay swing in their movements. All winter they had been waiting. To while the time away, they had planted vegetables on their blockhouses, and it was curious to turn into a side street and see, through a curtain of bayonets, lettuces sprouting above corrugated iron houses.

We followed the soldiers along a broken street, where the charred buildings were still smoking. Occasionally only a single wooden post would remain standing. A tree stump or a lamppost with bullet holes was like a wound still bleeding, but those bullet marks on wooden posts were so fresh that they seemed to have been made only a few moments before. Here the nakedness of war appeared in all its violence, for bodies still lay in the houses, and the sound of pickaxes echoed in the still wintry morning. It was strangely quiet. . . . High above the city aeroplanes flew and fought in the cold winter sun. . . . When they had gone, the city was more silent than ever, until suddenly we heard the sound of squealing pigs and turning a corner we watched three Hunanese peasants wheeling their barrows—with immense centre wheels and curved flanks, which were so delicately carved that they would grace a museum of modern industrial art. The barrows contained children in bright red leggings and woollen mufflers, and their expressions were oddly at variance with the expressions of the peasants, who looked grimed and sad with too much wandering. Behind the peasants came the squealing pigs. The peasants told us that they were going back to their homes on the west bank of the river, and their faces under their black turbans lit with relief when the soldiers gave them a right of way. . . .

The Japanese had attempted to gain possession of the burial mound which overlooked the city. From there, with their heavy guns, they could dominate the fortress. And everything in their plans they achieved except that they had failed to bring up any heavy guns at all, for the roads were cut by the partisans. They had obeyed the pure theory, and failed to make it a reality. They fought a battle of the imagination, and inevitably they failed.

Bergery* said: "They are young, but the Chinese were younger. This is what I find extraordinary in the fighting here. The older and more experienced must have been sent down to fight against Malaya and the Philippines. They were superbly confident that they could capture Changsha without trained men."[17]

An almost immediate result of America's entrance into World War II was the arrival of American supplies via the Burma Road.† This was the main route by which Chiang Kai-shek's armies could obtain foreign war material. Tens of thousands of Chinese coolies lost their lives during its construction, which was terminated in January 1939. Naturally, the elimination of the famed Burma Road became a major objective of Japanese military strategy at the beginning of 1942.

For American strategy, on the other hand, it was vital that China be kept an active fighting power on Japan's western flank. It was essential, therefore, to keep Burma inviolate. The U. S. Army entrusted outspoken General ("Vinegar Joe") Stilwell with the momentous task. General Stilwell, who knew China well,‡ demanded that he be given full command power over the Chinese troops on the Burma front, and Chiang Kai-shek promised these powers.

Stilwell arrived in Chungking on March 4, 1942, and almost at once discovered that in addition to fighting the Japanese, he would also have to spend much time arguing with Chiang or the "yes men" surrounding him, and put up with the many irritating aspects of China's inefficient conduct of war. On March 9, he made the following entry in his Papers:

* British war correspondent, and Robert Payne's traveling companion.

† Which the British government had closed in July 1940, and reopened in October of that same year, after the signature of the German-Italian-Japanese Tripartite pact.

‡ He had ten years of prewar service in Asia, spoke Chinese, and was regarded by the U. S. Army as an accomplished student of Oriental affairs.

The outlook is obscure, but if the Japs push, we can't do anything. Rangoon is the vital point. Without it, supply stops. If the Japs go to Mandalay, we'll have to build up in India. Chinese munitions are running short (3 months' activity or 6 months if we piddle). Although I imagine there is a lot of stuff squirreled away. Chinese divisional and army commanders are prone to hang on to weapons and ammunition, and not acknowledge how much they have. If we could get everything together, it might be a respectable total. . . . The Japanese have been strangely quiet. They may be building up for an offensive, or they may be too weak to make one. Nobody knows. The British* haven't taken a single prisoner as yet, and estimates of Jap strength are mere guesses. . . .

When Chiang Kai-shek told me I was to take command of the Chinese Army in Burma I found that he expected to give me the benefit of his advice and experiences. At the time, the 200th Division was at Toungoo, and the 22nd going into Mandalay and the 96th near Lashio.†

He asked me what my plan was and I told him I wanted to concentrate the three divisions near Toungoo. This was not the approved solution: Mandalay, he insisted, was the key to the situation, and he preferred to put both the 22nd and the 96th there, so as to have a strong garrison. We were told to hold Mandalay at all costs. I told him that this would mean that the 200th Division would be beaten‡ and the Japs could then march to Mandalay unopposed. I wanted to fight as far forward as possible, after concentrating all available force. If we could get three divisions concentrated, we would have some chance of holding the Japs, whereas leaving the 200th Division unsupported would mean losing it and having to oppose the Japs later with only the other two. No, that was not the way it would work. He could give me an instance in his own experience. He had just such a case at Chengchow,§ which the Japs were approaching from the east. There were three divisions available, but he was too crafty to put them all out there at once. He put one of them in Chengchow, with orders to defend to the last, and drew the other two back to the west about fifty

---

* Who, together with the Chinese—if not always in full agreement—were holding the Burma front against the Japanese.
† Burmese city, and starting point of the Burma Road.
‡ Which it was.
§ Town in northern China (Honan), near the Yellow River.

miles. The Japs attacked and destroyed the division in Chengchow. But they went no farther. And do you know why? This, he announced, was a matter of psychology—the Japs were so impressed with the determined defense put up by one division that they simply did not have the heart to go and attack the other two. So really he had stopped the Jap attack with the sacrifice of only one-third of his force.

This dazzling victory left me cold. . . . Actually, Mandalay had no military significance and offered no advantages as a position for defense. . . . I ventured to say that if we had all three divisions at Toungoo, maybe we would beat the Japs, but this horrified him because it would leave Mandalay (200 miles in the rear) temporarily unoccupied. In this connection, there was an important thing he wanted me to remember, and that was that because of their deficiencies in armament, equipment and transport, it took three Chinese divisions to hold off one Japanese division, and an attack on this basis was out of the question. Five Chinese divisions were necessary before an attack could have any hope of success. This was the doctrine that the Chinese Army was saturated with. . . .

The G-mo* gave me further instructions in psychology and tactics, and told me if I would observe him and listen for only six months, I could myself learn something of both arts. I emerged from this conference with permission to move one division up behind the 200th in case I felt it desirable on my arrival at the front. Considering his feeling on the matter, this was a handsome concession to make. And in all fairness, it must have been a severe strain on him to put a foreigner in command of regular Chinese troops in action at all. It had never been done before, and he was trying it on short acquaintance with a man he knew little about. . . .

I left, feeling that maybe some real executive authority might be ultimately forthcoming, as agreed, in spite of the cockeyed conception of warfare I had been listening to: it was lucky I did not know then what a long and bitter struggle was going to be necessary.[18]

General Stilwell's passion for what he considered logical and positive action was indeed put to a severe test in the peculiar atmosphere surrounding the Burma campaign. His energies were drained by long conferences with the staff of Chiang Kai-shek, and later by equally long meetings with the British allies under Field Marshal A. P. Wavell.

* Generalissimo.

Within weeks after Stilwell's arrival in Southeast Asia, the entire Allied front in that area collapsed, and the Burma Road was severed by the Japanese.* Until 1945, the only link between China and the outside world was the airlift over the "Hump", or Himalayas, between the towns of Ledo, in North Assam, and Kunming in China.

A picturesque assortment of Chinese and Americans, civilian and military, crowded into Kunming. The American journalists Theodore H. White and Annalee Jacoby pictured their countrymen's life in that town:

The average G.I. in China knew little about the struggle in the stratosphere of Army policy and cared less. He lived on bad food, in stinking, rat-infested Chinese hostels; he had to fight off heat, mud, and disease. No one bothered to explain to him what the war was about. All he knew was what lay within the routine of his daily life— and he hated it. The United States government was Uncle Chump from over the Hump; Chiang Kai-shek was Chancre Jack; Sun Yat-sen was Sunset Sam; all Chinese were "slope-headed bastards," shortened in general conversation to the simple term "slopy."

The main port of entry for all Americans into China was Kunming, capital of Yunnan. Before the war Kunming had been even more backward than Chungking. Its streets were narrow, its alleyways filthy; it was one of the national strongholds of the opium merchants. Almost up to the outbreak of war its prostitutes were penned in a street chained off at both ends; rich families bought girl slaves to serve in the household. The province was ruled by a curious character called Lung Yun, one of the most devious and shaky supports of the national government. Lung disliked Chiang Kai-shek, but his power in the province was so strong that not until after V-J Day did Chiang dare attack him. Within two months of victory, however, the Generalissimo moved against the governor, occupied his capital in a daring coup, and brought Lung in disgrace to Chungking.

The war had dumped into this medieval cesspool two elements out of the twentieth century in the shape of the finest refugee universities in China and the shrewdest banking and commercial speculators in the land. . . . Americans usually arrived at the big airport south of the city. For two or three years this airport was one of the busiest on the globe.

---

* Who had occupied Indo-China after the collapse of France (June 1940), and subsequently concluded an agreement with Thailand whereby Japanese troops were allowed to cross that country in order to enter Burma.

It handled most of the Hump traffic, all Chinese civilian traffic, the Chinese National Airlines' commercial carriers, the courier and mail services, and the combat missions of the Fourteenth Air Force.* . . . The field was never silent for a moment from the roar of plane motors except when a monsoon shut it down completely.

Within a few miles of the airport were scattered fifteen hostels for American personnel, each with five to ten buildings. Of the 70,000 Americans in China probably half were stationed for a longer or shorter period in the Kunming hostels. These were run by the Chinese government, which established a special branch of supply specifically for the care and feeding of Americans. By Chinese standards the hostels were models of elegance. They were warm, they were dry, and the Chinese thought the food was excellent. The Chinese did their best to feed the Americans what they thought the Americans liked—eggs, chicken, pork, vegetables. To most of the Chinese mess attendants and the Chinese soldiers who guarded the buildings even the slops of the American tables were fit for kings. But the average American looked on his accommodations with a jaundiced eye. Six to eight men, crammed into one room, slept on double-tiered bunks; helmets, gas masks, foot lockers, barracks bags, tumbled about in the dust and confusion of the little cubicles. The Americans were nauseated by the filth, grease, and general putrefaction of the messes, which, however, were cleaner than anything the Chinese army had for itself; almost every American who ate at them came down with some variety of dysentery or diarrhea during his stay in China. In the barracks Americans, yelling and cursing, vented their wrath on Chinese serving boys, until finally one American headquarters solemnly posted a general order: "U. S. personnel will not beat, kick, or maltreat Chinese personnel under any circumstances. Such is not the policy of this headquarters."

Before the war Kunming had been a resort town. It was 6,000 feet high; the climate was delightfully clear through most of the year, and the intoxicating sun and sky seemed always to evoke a gay lightheadedness. The American soldiers worked during daylight hours and saw the city usually after dark. Once or twice a week, or as often as they could get a pass, enlisted men would pour into town in search of wine, women, and entertainment, and Chinese touts and racketeers would

* Under General Claire Chennault, aeronautical adviser to the Chinese government.

pluck them clean. Restaurants served buffalo steak at $5.00 a head; whisky was black-marketed at $100 a bottle and up. Fortunate officers made alliances with English-speaking Chinese college students, with nurses, with Red Cross girls. The enlisted men, all of whom seemed bent on finding out personally whether it was true what they said about Chinese women, had to be satisfied with commercialized sex or do without. Venereal disease rates soared. Entertainment for Americans in Kunming consisted of going to the movies, which were always old and usually bad, or playing poker for stakes that sometimes ran into thousands of dollars, or getting drunk. Some of the air-force squadrons could get enough machinery together to make small distilleries and produce a bad potage out of brown sugar, but most of the men stuck to the tried-and-tested Chinese *chin pao* juices—*mao tai, pai kar,* yellow wine, potato alcohol. The army could not spare its precious Hump tonnage to haul beer, liquor, or normal PX supplies over the mountains. . . .

If life was rugged in Kunming, it was worse in the dozens of outposts that were gradually set down all through the land. The Y and Z forces★ split up their men and officers into teams of four or five who were scattered over all the southern fronts. The men lived with Chinese regimental, divisional, army headquarters in the field. Each American team consisted of a radio set, a jeep, a few enlisted men, one or two officers, and a few cases of dehydrated rations; each team had a Chinese interpreter and usually a Chinese cook. They lived in deserted farmhouses, temples, paddy fields, jungle hammocks. They trudged through the dust with the Chinese, crawled over mud-slick mountain trails, slapped at mosquitoes, learned to eat rice and like it, grew either to hate or to love one another. Some of these men came to know the Chinese to whom they were assigned and to cherish a real affection for them; most of them did not.[19]

One of the most remarkable features of wartime China, and one which invariably struck foreigners, was the Chinese people's nonchalance and apparent unconcern amid distressing conditions. The Chinese essayist Lin Yutang, who came to the United States before the war, spent the fall and winter of 1943–4 traveling through his native country. In bomb-scarred

★ "Yoke" and "Zebra" task forces, or Chinese divisions reorganized by the Americans, and engaged in Burma and southeast China, respectively.

Chungking, in particular, he admired the "basic racial qualities" displayed in the daily routine of the overcrowded capital:

The gaiety and unconcern and the stolid endurance of what to Western eyes were really deplorable conditions were outstanding and mystifying. . . . The weakness of China is also her strength. The Chinese people might fight better if they were a little less nonchalant and better disciplined, but also they might endure less well. If the Chinese people were psychologically like the Germans or the Japanese . . . they would also crack quicker. . . .

From their past of grim economic struggles, the Chinese people have developed certain basic racial qualities, not the least of which is nonchalance. A British journalist who had just arrived, a very intelligent man, made a remark that would surprise the Chinese public. He had been through the streets and watched the people strolling placidly along, refusing to give others the right of way. "The Chinese people are great democratic individuals," he said to me. "They don't give a damn for anybody." In a way that is true; but the Chinese, taught by tradition that it is the civilized thing to be polite, not only would be surprised if they heard that remark, but I doubt if they would understand it. Placid and unconcerned, talkative and ready to laugh at others' mishaps as well as their own, they went their way. The faces of the passengers on the bus, whatever else they might be, were certainly not gloomy, and least of all obsequious. They crowded each other, they yielded, they rolled and rocked in their seats, but they did not "give a damn for anybody". If the weather did not behave, they would criticize God himself. Order was very well preserved at the bus stations. But I maintain that public courtesy with strangers, submission to discipline and regimentation are not racial characteristics of the Chinese people.

That was how China carried on the war, each man fending for himself, each family fending for itself and for its friends. That was how the Chinese solved the vast problem of the migration of millions. That was how they had been carrying on for the last seven years. And that was how they were facing the inflation.* Chinese good cheer and unconcern under distressing conditions must now be admitted as one of China's greatest assets in the war.[20]

* Which was very severe. The author quotes a list of prices showing that since 1937, they had risen two hundred times!

Definitely not an asset in the war was the "fending-for-itself" policy adopted by the "Soong clan", which practically controlled the entire political, administrative and military machinery of the Kuomintang during the war years. In the atmosphere of corrupted autocracy which the regime imposed upon "Free" (or unoccupied) China, three members of the clan deserve special mention here.

Chen Li-fu, the party's fanatical and, surprisingly, incorruptible theoretician, headed both the secret police and the "Blue Shirts", or youthful propaganda corps of the Kuomintang, which was especially active on the university campuses. Both organizations were dreaded for their brutality in dealing with the enemies of the regime.

Ho Ying-chin, Nationalist Chief of Staff, made a scandalous fortune and let graft and corruption prevail at every level of the military hierarchy.

The Minister of Finance, H. H. K'ung (who claimed that he could trace his descent back to Confucius through seventy-five generations), was gentle but irresolute, and hardly fit for his responsible post. Public funds were squandered on a grand scale all around him, and his own wife was often the main villain in the story.

General Stilwell's wrathful comments were explicit enough:

March 4 [*1943*]. Chungking. ———* in. He confirms all my most pessimistic opinions. Peanut† is really no dictator. He issues an order. Everybody bows and says "sure". But nobody does anything. He knows all about the smuggling and rottenness, but he hasn't the power to cure it. Ho Ying-chin proposed Liu Ch'ih‡ for Yoke [task force] and the Peanut bawled him out. "What! Would you make a joke out of a serious situation? Would you play politics in such a crisis?"

He knows about the rotten conditions, too, but he can't do anything. Lung Yun [Governor of Yunnan] is not so bad; he just wants to be let alone in Yunnan. His Sixtieth Army can't be moved—they would refuse to obey the order. Opium traffic in Yunnan still enormous. Guarded by soldiers. Big stocks of hoarded gas, cloth, and other commodities. Gang of rascals around Lung Yun. They are loyal because of the money hookup and he trusts them rather than the Central Government which wants to get his graft away from him. The

* A Chinese cabinet member.

† Derisive title which Stilwell currently used in his notes to designate Chiang Kai-shek.

‡ Garrison commander at Chungking.

Yunnan people are suspicious not only of us, but of outside Chinese as well. What saved China was not the fighting of the Army, but the size of the country and lack of communications. We can get our way in Yunnan, but only by going slow. The Chinese Red Cross is a racket. Stealing and sale of medicines is rampant. The Army gets nothing. Malnutrition and sickness is ruining the Army; the higher-ups steal the soldiers' food. A pretty picture.[21]

Madame Chiang Kai-shek, too, was critically appraised by General Stilwell, but in a much more complimentary tone:

Madamissima. A clever, brainy woman. Sees the Western point. (By this I mean she can appreciate the mental reactions of a foreigner to the twisting, indirect and undercover methods of Chinese politics and warmaking.) Direct, forceful, energetic, loves power, eats up publicity and flattery, pretty weak on her history. No concessions to the Western viewpoint in all China's foreign relations. The Chinese were always right: the foreigners were always wrong. Writes entertainingly but superficially, with plenty of sarcasm for Western failings but without mention of any of China's little faults. Great influence on Chiang Kai-shek mostly along the right lines, too. A great help on several occasions.[22]

As the war dragged on, the quality of most of Chiang's troops kept deteriorating. The average Kuomintang soldier was underfed, underpaid, and often ill-treated by his superiors. Desertion and sickness (especially skin disease and trachoma) depleted the Nationalist ranks at an alarming rate. The army's overall situation in 1944, summed up by General Stilwell, was far from reassuring:

In 1944, on paper, the Chinese Army consisted of 324 divisions, 60-odd brigades and 89 so-called guerrilla units of about 2,000 men each. This looks formidable on paper, till you go into it closely. Then you find:

1. That the average strength per division instead of 10,000 is not more than 5,000.

2. That the troops are unpaid, unfed, shot with sickness and malnutrition.

3. That equipment is old, inadequate, and unserviceable.

4. That training is unexistent.

5. That the officers are jobholders.

6. That there is no artillery, transport, medical service, etc., etc.

7. That conscription is so-and-so.

8. That business is the principal occupation. How else live?

How would you start to make such an army effective?[23]

In the spring of 1944, disaster overtook the demoralized Kuomintang armies in Honan province, which in 1943 had been ravaged by the war's worst famine.* An estimated 60,000 Japanese routed the Nationalist Twelfth and Thirteenth Armies totaling some 300,000 men. Even worse than military defeat, however, was the fact that the peasants of the normally rich province turned against the Army. They had suffered bitterly through months of famine and merciless military extortion, and now, armed with bird guns, pitchforks and knives, they began disarming their countrymen by the thousands.† It was the first time in the war that the Nationalist cause was rebuffed by a popular rising.

A still greater disaster was in store for Chiang Kai-shek. Within two weeks of their victorious Honan campaign, the Japanese began a powerful 500-mile drive from Hankow down the railway and valley of the Hsiang River to Kweilin and Liuchow (Kwangsi), their main targets. This new and particularly determined campaign—Japan's last great offensive—was aimed at conquering the many American airfields strung along the main line of the Japanese southward thrust, from which the bombers and fighter planes of the Fourteenth U. S. Air Force were wrecking Japan's sea commerce.‡

As the Japanese offensive unfolded through the hot and humid summer months, it cut across all of eastern China and practically severed Chiang Kai-shek's China in two, threatening to bring about the collapse of the Chungking government. The Changsha Line was broken at the end of May, and Hengyang fell in August. Bickering and internal contention among the Chinese commanders, Cantonese for the most part and generally distrustful of the Central Government, only added to the chaotic situation.

An American reporter followed the Chinese Sixty-second Army whose task was to relieve the Tenth Army trapped in the "gray, uninspiring rice

---

* Out of a normal population of 30 million, 2 or 3 million had fled the province, and about as many had died of hunger and disease.

† Probably as many as 50,000 soldiers were disarmed by the peasants.

‡ The American sea sweeps had so far destroyed or damaged about one million tons of enemy shipping—one-fifth of Japan's prewar merchant marine.

town" of Hengyang around which the green fields shimmered with heat waves:

Panic had struck all eastern China. . . . Refugees poured down the railway line and stuffed themselves into cars with their babies, bedrolls, and luggage. They clung to train roofs, clustered on the cowcatchers, spread boards over brake rods and slept on them. American officers and men mingled in the trek. . . .

Miraculously, at Hengyang, the Tenth Army held. It was cornered, its position hopeless, but it fought with a desperate courage that harked back to the days of Shanghai. Chungking's mercurial mood soared again; the military spokesman claimed the Japanese had been stopped; the press reveled in the glorious stand of the 15,000 embattled men of the Tenth Army. The Chinese staff interpreted the lull in the campaign as the end of Japanese ambition. A huge counteroffensive was announced to drive the Japanese back to their starting line. The Sixty-second Army was ordered back into battle at Hengyang, where Hsueh Yueh had originally wanted it.* This was the moment for which Chungking had been waiting, the final summoning of energies. It made good reading in the press: hamlets were recaptured each day; generals declared that contact with the besieged garrison had already been made. In the field, far from Chungking, the counterattack had a different countenance. The high command had millions of troops on its books, but less than a hundred thousand were within range of action. Of these one army, the Sixty-second, moved toward assault position; it pushed one of its divisions to the point where the enemy held; the divisional commander sent forth two of his three regiments —and these constituted the Chinese drive.

I marched up with the Sixty-second Army as it moved on the Japanese siege ring. With me was Graham Barrow of Reuters. The distance from the railhead to the front was a matter of thirty miles. It was dawn when we fell into the troop column, but the cloudless skies were already scorching. As far as we could see ahead into the hills and beyond were marching men. They crawled on foot over every footpath through the rice paddies; they snaked along over every ditch and

* Hsueh Yueh, the general responsible for the defence of East China, who delighted in the nickname "Tiger of Changsha" (because he had so far frustrated three Japanese attacks against that city), was a good fighter, but he disliked and distrusted the Central Government (whose orders he had to execute).

broken bridge in parallel rivulets of sweating humanity. One man in three had a rifle; the rest carried supplies, telephone wire, rice sacks, machine-gun parts. Between the unsmiling soldiers plodded blue-gowned peasant coolies who had been impressed for supplementary carrier duty. There was not a single motor, not a truck anywhere in the entire column. There was not a piece of artillery. At rarest intervals pack animals bore part of the burden. Now and then during the day a little Chinese pony showed above the heads of the marching troops; ponies were reserved for officers of regimental rank or higher. The men walked quietly, with the curious bitterness of Chinese soldiers who expect nothing but disaster at the end of a trip, none suffering acutely, each bearing the bitterness of decades one day farther along the road. They were wiry and brown but thin; their guns were old, their yellow-and-brown uniforms threadbare. Each carried two grenades tucked in his belt; about the neck of each was a long blue stocking inflated like a roll of bologna with dry rice kernels, the only field rations. Their feet were broken and puffed above their straw sandals; their heads were covered with birds' nests of leaves woven together to give shade from the sun and supposedly to supply camouflage. The sweat rolled from them; dust rose about them; the heat clutched the entire country, and giddy, glistening waves rose from the rice paddies.

Along the way we came on knots of peasants who had been rounded up by the civilian officials for the service of the army. The unit commanders stopped at these stations to pick up baggage bearers, just as a truck in any other army would stop to pick up gasoline at a filling station. The peasants marched with the troops until they were exhausted, then fell out, were fed rice, and were sent back to the service stations again. At night the army holed up for a short rest in the deserted villages a few miles back from the front. The soldiers seized for food what pigs or vegetables the peasants had left in their flight; they tore boards, doors, and wall planking from peasant homes to make beds; they chopped up staves, fence posts, and rafters to make fire for boiling their water and rice.

At three-thirty the next morning the attack was launched. The Japanese held the high hills south of Hengyang; the Sixty-second held a lower ridge facing them. The attacking division had two French seventy-fives, from the First World War, and a few trench mortars. It had 200 shells for the seventy-fives, and it expended them as a miser counts out gold coins. From three-thirty till midmorning the Chinese crawled up the slopes to the Japanese positions. Their rifles and bayonets tried to shoot or dig the enemy out, but at midmorning the Japanese were still there. Graham Barrow and I clambered up to the highest Chinese position in the afternoon to watch the fight. The Chinese mortars whistled fitfully over the crest where the Japanese were dug in; machine guns and rifles rattled at long intervals in the summer heat; not a man was moving along the entire line.

We waited for three days to see the counteroffensive get under way; then we set our faces homeward. We realized that what we had seen had been the counteroffensive, and nothing more would come of the campaign. All that flesh and blood could do the Chinese soldiers were doing. They were walking up hills and dying in the sun, but they had no support, no guns, no directions. They were doomed.[24]

After having rested and regrouped their forces at Hengyang, the Japanese resumed their southward drive at the end of August 1944. Though numerically superior, the tired, ill-organized, ill-fed and ill-led Chinese armies were unable to check the enemy's advance. The Sixty-second Army disappeared completely in five days of fighting. The Ninety-third relief army, which was half-starved before reaching the front, disintegrated without firing a shot. Chiang Kai-shek vainly ordered several general officers shot: morale among his troops was too far gone to be restored by drumhead executions.

By the end of 1944, which was a year of unmitigated disaster for the Kuomintang armies, southern China was cut in two.* Fortunately for Chiang Kai-shek, the Japanese were rapidly losing ground, both in the Pacific (where U. S. forces captured or recaptured the Marshall, Mariana and Philippine islands and began raiding Japan with Saipan-based B-29 bombers), and in Burma (where Admiral Lord Louis Mountbatten's Indo-British forces, supported by U. S. troops and Stilwell-trained Chinese forces, defeated three Japanese armies).

As a result of the overall situation in the Far Eastern theatre of operations, the Japanese invasion of China reached its high-water mark in December 1944, and then receded. A new defense plan, prepared by General Wedemeyer (who replaced General Stilwell in October of that year, and accomplished more by tact and patience than Stilwell did by his dictatorial attitude), enabled

---

* Nearly 500,000 Chinese soldiers had been lost, the entire coast was cut off from the Nationalist government, and eight provinces with a population of more than 100 million had been ripped from the control of Chungking, which was seized by panic.

*the Chinese to check a tentative Japanese offensive in the direction of Chung-king.**

General Wedemeyer's first few months in China, like those of his predecessor, proved dismal and disappointing. Among the senior officers he contacted, there were few whom he deemed "efficient or professionally well trained". Like Stilwell, however, he had confidence in the Chinese soldier,† and successfully continued the work of military reorganization begun by the impatient yet very able "Vinegar Joe":

When I first arrived I noted many objectives that I wanted to accomplish. After carefully weighing the advantages and disadvantages I would submit proposals to the Generalissimo at my daily meetings with him. Although he apparently was in complete accord and expressed approval, action was not always taken.

By this time I had become convinced of the Generalissimo's sincerity of purpose, and my admiration and respect were unequivocal. However, in the interest of following through on proposed action, I discontinued making oral recommendations. Instead, I substituted carefully prepared memoranda embodying each problem requiring action. I submitted two copies: one in English which I signed and the other in Chinese which was sealed with my chop [Chinese seal]. I retained copies of these memoranda in my headquarters and from time to time, if the contemplated action had not been taken, I invited the Generalissimo's attention to them.

I had gradually succeeded in effecting changes which, although not very far-reaching, had contributed toward creating confidence and mutual respect. I had put a stop to the all too frequent expression of derogatory remarks about the Chinese by American officers who had taken their tone from Vinegar Joe. And as soon as I felt sure that Chiang Kai-shek recognized I was a friend who was sincerely striving to help China defeat Japan, I began to make suggestions for reforms, which he received and acted on without offense. For instance, it had worried me that on many occasions I was invited to banquets given by Chinese officials at which some twenty courses were served. Having seen so

* They flew into the battle zone two divisions from northern Burma, where Stilwell had trained them in victory; Chiang Kai-shek also flew in several elite divisions from the Communist blockade in northern China. The Japanese lines of communications, on the other hand, were by now overextended and the Japanese soldiers suffered from the severe cold.

† Provided he was well-trained, well-fed and well-treated.

many half-starved or emaciated Chinese, I felt this was fundamentally wrong, and I recommended that such banquets should be discontinued for the duration of the war. I suggested that he could set an example by restricting the number of courses at his dinners to four. He enthusiastically agreed and the word got around in a tactful manner.

I expressed my concern for the health and feeding of Chinese soldiers. The conditions were terrible and I said, "Generalissimo, if I were a Chinese officer, I believe I would be tempted to 'squeeze' or take money in order that my family could live properly and I could provide food and shelter for them." Chiang responded by doubling the pay of every member of the armed forces. I asked General Marshall to send a food expert to China to study the situation on the ground and make recommendations to alleviate the inadequate and improper diet the Chinese troops were receiving.

Of course, I realized such success as I had in gradually overcoming Chinese distrust and inducing the Generalissimo and his associates to accept recommendations was also, I think, due to never promising them anything without actually doing it. They came to realize that I expected them likewise not to break their pledges. The trouble was that all too frequently Chiang was unable even though willing to carry out my recommendations.[25]

Events moved faster and faster in 1945. The capture of the islands of Iwo Jima and Okinawa provided the American Army with advanced bases for the final assault against Japan—which the dropping of the atomic bomb made unnecessary.

In Burma, on the other hand, final victory was achieved in May; a new road, called the Ledo★ (or Stilwell) Road and built through the jungle and over hills, had reopened the passage to China in January. Spectacular parachute drops executed by the U. S. Tenth Air Force greatly helped the Allied advance through rugged terrain. On that front, two American units astounded friend and foe alike by their daring exploits; they were the famed "Flying Tigers" of General Claire Chennault,† and the commando groups of Major General Frank Merrill, better known as "Merrill's Marauders".

In China proper, the turn of the tide came in the spring months, when the tired Japanese began withdrawing toward the northern provinces in order

★ Town in northeastern Assam, where the road started.

† Airman extraordinary and passionate advocate of air power, which often brought him into open conflict with "ground-minded" General Stilwell.

to regroup their forces. They were relentlessly pursued by the reorganized and reinvigorated Nationalist armies, which by this time had substantially profited from the teaching of their American advisers.

The powerful Russian invasion of Manchuria, begun on August 8, all but sealed the fate of the Japanese armies on China's mainland. Six days later, Japan accepted the Allied terms of capitulation, and American forces of occupation landed in Japan on August 26. Capitulation terms for Japanese forces in China, estimated at one million men, were signed on September 9 in Nanking between Japanese commanders and representatives of Generalissimo Chiang Kai-shek.

After a bloody struggle of eight years, the more or less "united" effort of Nationalist and Communist China had defeated the overambitious "dwarf bandits". An equally bitter struggle now placed the "two Chinas" in opposition. Peace, which the Chinese needed so much, was once more denied them.

CHAPTER XII

RED CHINA, 1935–1945

NONE IN the Red Army feared the distresses of the Long March.
We looked lightly on the thousand peaks and the ten thousand
   rivers,
The Five Mountains rose and fell like rippling waves,
The Wuliang mountains were no more than small green pebbles.
Warm were the sheer precipices when Gold Sand river dashed
   into them,
Cold were the iron-chained bridges over the Tatu river.
Delighting in the thousand snowy folds of the Min Mountain,
The last pass vanquished, the Three Armies smiled. [1]

*Thus wrote Mao Tse-tung, poet, scholar, specialist of guerrilla warfare
and undisputed leader of the Chinese Communist Party. In retrospect, and
with a great deal of poetic imagination, Mao could indeed pass lightly over
the many obstacles and distresses of the Long March, in the course of which he
lost his first wife and nearly died himself. He had every reason for looking
back with pride, and facing the future with confidence.*

*When, in April 1945, Chairman Mao presented his political report to the
Seventh National Congress of the Chinese Communist Party,* he had even
more reasons for smiling as he summed up the party's spectacular progress and
achievements under most trying circumstances. The Red armies had played a
decisive role in anti-Japanese resistance, and had steadily increased their
strength. Membership in the Party was constantly rising, too, and the Communists could rely upon loyal popular support in vast areas of China. The
future looked bright indeed. Said Mao:*

* Held (as the previous congresses) in Yenan, northern Shensi, and grouping
752 delegates representing 1,210,000 Party members.

While I am making this report, our regular forces have been expanded to the strength of 910,000 men, while the people's militia have increased to over 2,200,000.* Our regular forces are still numerically smaller than the existing Kuomintang army (including Central and provincial troops)† by hundreds of thousands, but considering the number of Japanese and puppet troops they are engaging, the vast battlefields they have to cover, their fighting power, their support from the people, the people's militia, and the self-defence corps, their political quality, and their internal unity and solidarity, our regular forces have become the mainstay of the anti-Japanese war. . . .

In recent years practically no serious fighting has occurred on the Kuomintang front, the sword of the Japanese aggressors being chiefly pointed at the Liberated Areas front.‡ By 1943, sixty-four percent of the Japanese forces invading China and ninety-five percent of the puppet forces were contained on the Liberated Areas front only; thirty-six percent of the Japanese forces and five percent of the puppet troops were contained on the Kuomintang front.

In 1944, when the Japanese aggressors launched an operation for the possession of a transcontinental [i.e., Hankow–Canton] communication line, the Kuomintang's chaos and weakness were at once revealed and vast territories in Honan, Hunan, Kwangsi and Kwantung provinces were lost to the enemy within a few months. It was only then that some changes in the proportion of the enemy forces on the two battlefronts took place. But even as I am making this report, out of 40 divisions of 580,000 enemy troops in China (not counting those in Manchuria), $22\frac{1}{2}$ divisions of 320,000 men, or about fifty-six percent, are being used on the Liberated Areas front; only $17\frac{1}{2}$ divisions of 260,000 men, or about forty-four percent, are used on the Kuomintang front. The distribution of the burden against the puppet troops remains entirely unchanged. . . .

The Chinese Liberated Areas, with a total population of 95,000,000, are placed as far north as Inner Mongolia and as far south as Hainan Island. . . . The vast Chinese liberated areas include nineteen large

* These militia groups, usually composed of peasants and artisans, and armed with lances, swords and occasional rifles, were used in secondary military tasks (such as guarding supply lines, reporting on Japanese movements, etc.).

† Placed at the disposal of Chungking by local war lords.

‡ The statement "no serious fighting" is untrue, though Mao was correct in stressing the predominant role of the Red forces.

Liberated Areas, extending over the provinces of . . . Shensi, Kansu, Shansi, Hopei, Honan, Shantung, Kiangsu, Chekiang, Anhwei, Kiangsi, Hupei, Hunan, Kwantung and Fukien.* . . .

The leading ruling clique in the Kuomintang has persisted in maintaining a dictatorial rule and carried out a passive policy against Japan while it has upheld a policy of opposing the people within the country. In this way the Kuomintang armies have shrunk to half their former size, and the major part of them has almost lost its combat ability; in this way, a deep chasm exists between the Kuomintang government and the people, and a serious crisis of poverty, discontent, and revolts among the people is engendered; thus the ruling clique of the Kuomintang has not only greatly reduced its role in the war against Japan, but, moreover, has become an obstacle to the mobilization and unification of all the anti-Japanese forces in the country.[2]

In Chinese Communist annals, the Sino-Japanese war practically corresponds to the "Yenan Period", or period during which the town of Yenan, deeply embedded along yellowish loess cliffs at the junction of two rivers in northern Shensi, was the general headquarters of Communist activities in China.†

A reporter from New Zealand, James Bertram, arrived in Yenan shortly after the Communists took possession of it. He was impressed by the unusual site and aspect of the town, which then contained a population of about 30,000:

I had never seen a more picturesque Chinese city. Yenan at first sight is as fantastic as a Sung painting. It lies in a pass where two rivers meet, at the base of precipitous cliffs. On the west side, battlemented walls climb steeply to a jutting crest, with a watch tower that dominates the sea of hills beyond. The town itself is compactly built across the valley floor, the eastern walls rising directly from the water's edge. And across the river the cliffs rise again, crowned with ruined temples and a lone pagoda.[3]

The "sea of hills" expanding around Yenan is typical of much of northern China. Most of that area, indeed, is covered with thick layers of loess, i.e., pale,

* That is, most of northern and eastern China.

† Communist troops occupied the city in December 1936.

yellowish silt or clay through which the Yellow River and its tributaries have carved deep winding gorges.

Being both fertile and very friable, the loess constitutes a blessing as well as a constant peril for the northern Chinese. The "loess country" was described by the American reporter Agnes Smedley, who went to Yenan in 1937:

All the streams in this part of the country pour into the Yellow River, which is rightly called "China's Sorrow". This almost treeless land is the rich yellow earth, or loess, which washes away easily with the slightest rains. The swollen rivers are thick and yellow and this rich soil is ceaselessly carried to the Yellow River and into the sea; or the river overflows and drowns millions of people.

I could write a volume on this loess country! To understand it one must see it. It is a fine porous earth, without a stone or a bone or a shell in it. Scientists have various theories about it, but the generally accepted idea is that the soil came from Central Asia, from what is now the Gobi Desert. Thousands of years ago Central Asia and the Gobi dried up. The wind carried the dried vegetation and the soil throughout Northwest China. . . .

Scientifically the study of loess is interesting. But during the rains it is not at all interesting to live in such a region. The rain percolates through the earth until whole mountainsides collapse and pour down into the valleys, over the roads and houses, burying everything in rivers and mud. Whole roadbeds slip away, whole hills fall with dull roars. I live in a cave in a mountain of loess and the rain seeps through and permeates everything. Little by little the cave falls in and I have often got a good mouthful of nice, rich yellow earth. Lying here now I listen to the ceaseless drum of the rain outside, and to the roar of the swollen river in the valley below.[4]

It was from their dugouts in the loess of Yenan that the Communists conducted the war against the Japanese. From the outset Mao Tse-tung's "Peasants and Workers' Army" relied heavily on the support of the rural masses, from which most of its recruits were taken. Land reform, low taxes and local self-government were the means by which the Communists

* Mao Tse-tung always insisted on the irresistible strength of China's rural masses. In the anti-Japanese resistance, however, the Reds were joined by thousands of intellectuals and students, who became organizers, teachers, and bureaucratic cadres.

won these masses to their cause. Perhaps even more than by their reforms, however, the Reds gained their popularity by their relentless—and increasingly successful—struggle against the Japanese invader. By a significant shift of emphasis, the Red Army became as early as 1936 the "People's Anti-Japanese Army".

The Chinese peasants, in turn, helped and sheltered the Reds in many ways. James Bertram, investigating Communism in 1936, vainly tried to locate the Red troops in the Shensi countryside. "What soldiers? Red Army?" was the same answer he got everywhere. Luckily, a youthful "student propagandist" eventually led him to the object of his quest:

A little village of clay huts huddled against the loess cliffs. It was guarded by a wall, outside of which children were playing, while old men smoked their evening pipes in the open. The scene was peaceful enough; our guides, as we crossed to the wall, exchanged greetings with the villagers.

"Are you afraid of the Red Army?" our student propagandist asked one group of children. The answer was a peal of laughter; the old men chuckled and wagged their heads. "The Red Army is the army of the peasants. It is the army of the Chinese people." The propaganda party had not wasted its time.

Inside the wall, a troop of some forty soldiers were quartered in two small houses. We were welcomed by their commander—a youthful commissioner in a black uniform who might have been a few years over thirty. He was the oldest man in the party; the average age of the rest, I calculated, was about seventeen.

They clustered around us like schoolboys—these youths who were more heavily armed than any Government troops I had ever seen. The cleanest thing about most of them was their revolvers, but all had the glow of health, and a steady look about the eyes that would have marked them out from any other group of Chinese of their age. A boy of thirteen, with an enormous hand grenade bumping from his belt, brought us tea, laughing all the time at the strange appearance of the first foreigner he had seen.

There is something the Red Army does to its young recruits. All who have come in contact with the Chinese "Reds" (and this includes, in recent years, a number of American journalists) have noticed at once the change of personality they put on with the red star. There is gaiety, comradeship, a touch of recklessness—for the average age in the Red Army is probably under twenty; but there is also a strength and self-reliance which is not common among Chinese brought up in the old family tradition. With this goes an openness of manner that is curiously Western; the whole personality seems to come to the surface.

This group belonged to the Fourth Front Army, under Hsu Hai-tung; they were comparatively "raw", as compared with the veteran troops of Pen Teh-huai of the First Red Army. But most of these youngsters had been with the Reds for five or six years, many having begun as *Hsiao hung kweitze*—"Little Red Devils". They were very representative of the rank and file of these peasant armies, for there were no students or intellectuals among them. Only the leader had been a city worker; and this again was characteristic of the way the cadres of industrial workers had been given the leadership among these slow-witted farmers' sons.[5]

Emphasis on youth and on changed personality was indeed an essential feature of Communist indoctrination. This was particularly striking in the case of the "Little Red Devils", or Red Army Children, mentioned above. James Bertram visited one of their training centers:

The Red Army Children . . . are famous in China. They are the messengers of the peasant armies, entrusted with the gathering of information, and often with secret missives of considerable importance. For a child can get through where a man or woman might be suspect.

Drilling in a sunless courtyard we found a group of some forty youngsters, still in their black prison uniforms, with black peaked caps. All of them had been released from the prisons of Sian after the "Double Twelfth", where they had been held as "dangerous and subversive elements". They were all ages between ten and sixteen.

"You see what Nanking makes war on!" said our guide, the student commander of the youthful company. With a smile he presented us to the "shock-brigader" of this Children's Vanguard. This was a solemn-faced youngster of eleven, who thrust out his chest valiantly and tried to look like a hero. "He worked in the Intelligence Service, and brought over two Government regiments to the Reds." It sounded fantastic, but was by no means impossible.

Most of the group were from Szechuan, and had been attached to the 4th Red Army Corps under the command of Hsu Hsiang-chien. Some of them had no families; many were the sons of landless labourers or poor peasants who had followed the Red Army from their native villages. Two or three came from Kiangsi and Hunan, and had made the long march across seven provinces to the Northwest. Although they were so young, they carried themselves and spoke like men: there was a steady look about their eyes that told its own tale of a childhood that had looked clear-eyed on suffering. They were an amazing little group, and of course, they won Agnes Smedley's heart. The exploits of these "little devils" were meat and drink to her.*

"Where do you come from?" she asked one boy, whose cool eyes stared straight back under his peaked cap.

"From Szechuan."

"What did your father and mother do?"

"They are labourers. They are still in Szechuan. I have no brother or sister."

"Can you read and write?"

"Of course. I learnt in the Red Army."

"What did you do in the Red Army?"

"I worked in the Intelligence Service."

"Why did you leave your home, and join the Reds?"

"To fight for our national liberation."

He had learnt his lesson; the last answer was much more than a phrase. At an age when most children are still running the streets, or (in China) riding the water buffalo, these youngsters had shouldered the responsibilities of men.[6]

*The Eighth Route Army, which was built up around the survivors of the Long March, represented the hard core of Red military power in China.†
In 1939, Mao Tse-tung explained to Bertram that the actual strength and efficiency of that army—which fought the Japanese in northern China—was due essentially to its faithful adherence to three "fundamental" political principles of action:*

* Agnes Smedley: American writer and reporter who traveled widely and championed the rights of oppressed people. A convinced supporter of Hindu nationalists in the twenties, she went to China in 1929 as a reporter for the *Frankfurter Zeitung* and the *Manchester Guardian*. She openly allied herself with the cause of the Chinese Revolution since 1927, and became one of the most widely read foreign authors among China's younger generation. She died in 1950.

† By agreement with the Chungking government, its strength was to be limited to 45,000 men, but as the Sino-Japanese war dragged on (and the breach between Communists and Nationalists widened), it reached the half-million mark.

"Another very important and significant feature of the Eighth Route Army," Mao went on, "is its political work. There are three fundamental principles underlying this.

"First, *unity of the officers and soldiers.* This implies the liquidation of any remaining traces of feudalism, the abolition of the old 'flogging and cursing system',* the establishment of conscious discipline, and the realization of a manner of life in the army whereby all share alike together both bitter and sweet. In this way, our army has achieved a unique degree of solidarity.

"Second, *unity of the army and the people.* This is an unfailing principle with our army. We must keep the closest possible relation with the common people, and never in any way violate their interests. Then the people will support us, work with us, take messages, keep military secrets. Cooperation with the people is an important factor in our military success. Moreover, we must carry on propaganda work, organize and arm the people; we must lighten the economic burden of the masses, and suppress severely those traitors who are endangering the armies of the people. Thus the army and the people can work together, and everywhere our army is welcomed by the people as their friend.

"The Eighth Route Army gets new recruits, not by compulsory draft, but by agitation among and political organization of the people. This method is much more efficient for mass mobilization.

Third, *propaganda among the enemy armies, and special treatment of prisoners of war.* In this work, victory does not depend entirely upon the fighting quality of our armies: it depends also on the deterioration of the armies of the enemy. Though this effect is perhaps not yet significant, in the future it will assume ever greater proportions."[7]

Mao's explanations were no mere propaganda talk. As a rule, the Communist troops followed a clearly defined line of conduct in their relations with people of areas under their control, and abstained from preying upon the country. Bertram, who was one of the first foreign reporters admitted to "Red" China, found little evidence of the fear and suspicion that all too often marked the peasants' attitude toward the military in Kuomintang areas.

He was, on the contrary, impressed by the constructive spirit of cooperation prevailing in Red territories, and admired the strict discipline displayed by units of the Eighth Route Army in the North Shensi villages that quartered them:

* Still existing among Nationalist units in the forties.

The first night out we spent in such a village, and I had a chance to see what the Communists meant by their slogan of "nonviolation of the interests of the people". Though this was within the Special District, where a military party might easily have demanded a billet, rooms (or rather caves*) were rented with the consent of their owners, and paid for in national currency. That evening scene was typical. Though they had covered a day's march that would have prostrated regular troops of most countries, with no food since early morning, as soon as our quarters were decided upon it was the soldiers themselves who set to work, sweeping out the rooms, cooking the evening meal, cutting chaff for the horses—all with invincible good humour. As soon as the word of their arrival got around, half the village gathered in the courtyard—some of them come to gaze with unconcealed dismay at the first foreigner they had ever seen; but more to mingle with the soldiers, talk with them about the war, and pass the time of day. Girls and young women were there, whom any other troops would have sent scurrying to the innermost recess. And always someone came with gifts. Old men would bring tobacco, and offer a communal pipe; or small boys would shyly offer fruit. In the morning cave and court were scrupulously swept out, and the reckoning—not without traditional bargaining—paid in full.

What it means from a purely military point of view to have a countryside solidly behind your armies, only those who have learnt to depend upon the support of the masses really know. I had seen the fatal effects of a lack of cooperation between the peasants and the Chinese armies in Hopei, when the Japanese in their first occupation of the north ran open lines of communication across a densely populated country without the slightest interference. They would have met with a different reception here.[8]

Soon after their arrival and installation in Shensi Province, the Communists applied the same measures that had won them the peasant support in their former Kiangsi stronghold, and began implementing a vast agrarian reform. Edgar Snow, another among the first Western journalists to visit Soviet China, explained the reform's initial stage:

Redistribution of land was a fundamental of Red policy. How was it

* Cave dwellers were traditionally numerous in Shensi's soft loess hills and cliffs; even today, caves shelter a good many Shensi peasants.

carried out? Later on, for reasons of national political maneuver, there was to be a drastic retreat in the Soviet land policy, but when I traveled in the Northwest the land laws in force (promulgated by the Northwest Soviet Government in December, 1935) provided for the confiscation of all landlords' land and the confiscation of all land of rich peasants that was not cultivated by the owners themselves. However, both the landlord and the rich peasant were allowed as much land as they could till with their own labor. . . .

What was a landlord? According to the Communists' definition (greatly simplified), any farmer who collected the greater part of his income from land rented out to others, and not from his own labor, was a landlord. By this definition the usurers and *t'u-hao*★ were put in about the same category as landlords, and similarly treated. . . .

Classes other than those mentioned above were not subject to confiscatory action, so a big percentage of the farmers stood to benefit immediately by the redistribution. The poorest farmers, tenants, and farm laborers were all provided with land enough for a livelihood. . . .

The land problem—confiscation and redistribution—was greatly simplified in the Northwest by the fact that big estates were formerly owned by officials, tax collectors, and absentee landlords. With the confiscation of these, in many cases the immediate demands of the poor peasantry were satisfied, without much interference with either the resident small landlords or the rich peasants. Thus the Reds not only created the economic base for support in the poor and landless peasantry by giving them farms, but in some cases won the gratitude of middle peasants by abolishing tax exploitation, and in a few instances enlisted the aid of small landlords on the same basis or on the patriotic appeals of the anti-Japanese movement. There were several prominent Shensi Communists from landlord families.

Additional help was given to the poor farmers in the form of loans at very low rates of interest or no interest at all. Usury was entirely abolished, but private lending, at rates fixed at a maximum of 10 percent annually, was permitted. The ordinary Government lending rate was 5 percent. Several thousand agricultural implements made in the Red arsenals, and thousands of pounds of seed grain, were supplied to landless peasants breaking wasteland. A primitive agricultural school

★ *T'u-hao*, which actually means "local rascals", is the Reds' term for landowners who also derive a big part of their income from lending money and buying mortgages (author's note).

had been established, and I was told it was planned to open an animal husbandry school as soon as an expert in this field, expected from Shanghai, had arrived.

The cooperative movement was being vigorously pushed. These activities extended beyond production and distribution cooperatives, branching out to include cooperation in such (for China) novel forms as the collective use of farm animals and implements—especially in tilling public lands and Red Army lands—and in the organization of labor mutual-aid societies. By the latter device great areas could be quickly planted and harvested collectively, and periods of idleness by individual farmers eliminated. The Reds saw to it that a man earned his new land! In busy periods the system of "Saturday Brigades" was used, when not only all the children's organizations, but every Soviet official, Red partisan, Red guard, women's organization, and any Red Army detachment that happened to be nearby, were mobilized to work at least one day a week at farming tasks. Even Mao Tse-tung took part in this work.[9]

In their sweeping confiscation measures, the Reds also included the property of foreign missions, and in so doing often took advantage of anti-foreign feelings still existing among the Chinese.

Inevitably, missionary comments on Communist land reform were less detached than those of visiting journalists. Father De Jaegher, who was stationed near the town of Ankuo (about 100 miles south of Peking), saw the Red troops drive out the Japanese and then turn to the task of establishing their own new order:

The Communists divided the peasants into five categories which were to become, according to plan, five different classes. These classes were, first, the rich; second, those in easy circumstances; third, the moderately comfortable; fourth, the poor; and fifth, the hired laborer. There was no fixed rule for determining a man's class, but in each village those with the most land were labeled "the rich", and the rest were classed in proportion. The scale was, therefore, altogether relative to place, because the "rich" of one village could be the "moderately comfortable" of another.

The "poor" and the "hired laborers" were chosen as the basis of the organization, the point from which the attack was to be launched against the other classes. This attack would follow the Communist theory that riches come only from personal labor, and the wealth acquired by "exploiting" the worker—i.e., the poor and the hired laborers—must be taken by force of the party. The seizure and transfer must be accomplished even if violence and bloodshed ensue. Four great means were to be employed to this end.

The first of these was *Fan Shen Hui*, or the reversing of the poor and the rich. The workers and the hired farm laborers banded together to become the masters of their erstwhile masters. The second means was *Fu Ch'ou Hui*, or vengeance, which allowed the poor to revenge themselves on the rich. The third method was *Ch'ing Suan Hui*. Through this device, "the paying of scores", the Communists found a really excellent pretext for despoiling the rich. Every "injustice" committed by a living person or by any one of his ancestors had to be atoned for, with accumulated interest. And of course an injustice, real or imagined, could always be found. And last, *P'in Ku Nung T'uan*, or the organization of the hired and poor, took precedence over all the others and was itself under the immediate direction of the political administration of the central Communist government. . . .

The first stage of the class struggle, then, results in the confiscation of real property—a house, or a farm, or mission building, or just land. In the second phase, in what the Chinese call a "new examination", the Communists take over what they didn't seize the first time— personal possessions, clothing, bedding, furniture, etc. If this "new examination", which is also a confiscation of property, doesn't bring the subject around to an acceptance of communism, his "examiners" go on to the third phase, which they call *ch'ing hsün*, or "counting the money to the last cent". In this phase the Communists scrutinize not only one's personal account but also the accounts of his immediate and distant forebears, as far back as they care to go, which means, of course, as far back as they have to go to make some kind of case against a man so that they can squeeze something else out of him in the name of "justice".

The ridiculous lengths to which the Communists carry this are best illustrated by the experiences of some French missionaries whose fine, improved property the Communists coveted. They charged that the missionaries had failed to pay proper wages to their employees.

"What employees?" the head of the mission asked.

"The Chinese workers who were employed by you during the Boxer Rebellion," he was told.

"In 1900?" he asked incredulously.

"That's correct," the examiner replied.

The head of the mission protested the ridiculousness and injustice of such a charge, but to no avail. The Communists confiscated the mission itself, the buildings, printing press, the hospital, everything. . . .

Sometimes it is a chicken for which they say they must have proper legal compensation for "the people". They will start with the modest enough cost of the chicken and then go on to add to that figure the market price of all the eggs the hen might have produced over a period of years, and the cost of the hens from those eggs, and the price for the hens from the eggs from the hens from the eggs of the first chicken, and on and on and on until the senses reel.

The Boxer Rebellion in 1900 was fixed on as a favorite point from which to begin this weird system of financial calculation. The Communists could make useful propaganda from the fact that it was a rebellion against foreigners in China. They told the people that the Boxers were patriotic Chinese who had tried to rid China of "foreign imperialists".[10]

Many of the social changes introduced by Communism were definitely beneficial, and eliminated some outstanding evils afflicting Chinese society. From the Soviet Republic of Shensi, Edgar Snow reported that unemployment, beggary, and opium smoking had disappeared; child slavery and prostitution had, according to the Reds, been "liquidated". Foot binding and infanticide were criminal offenses, and polyandry and polygamy were prohibited.

In the realm of family life, the Red regime greatly enhanced and normalized the traditionally low status of China's women, and subjected the man-and-wife relationship to a series of new rules that contrasted strikingly with the ancient customs. These new rules were summed up by Edgar Snow:

The myths of "communized wives" or "nationalization of women" are too patently absurd to be denied, but changes in marriage, divorce, and inheritance were in themselves extremely radical against the background of semi-feudal law and practice elsewhere in China. Marriage regulations included interesting provisions against mother-in-law tyranny, the buying and selling of women as wives and concubines, and the custom of "arranged matches". Marriage was by mutual consent, the legal age had been moved up sharply to twenty for men and eighteen for women; dowries were prohibited, and any couple registering as man and wife before a county, municipal, or village Soviet was given a marriage certificate without cost. Men and women actually cohabiting were considered legally married, whether registered or not—which seems to rule out "free love"—and their offspring were legitimate. No illegitimacy of children was recognized.

Divorce could also be secured from the registration bureau of the Soviet, free of charge, on the "insistent demand" of either party to the marriage contract, but wives of Red Army men were required to have their husband's consent before a divorce was granted. Property was divided equally between the divorcees, and both were legally obliged to care for their children, but responsibility for debts was shouldered by the man alone (!), who was also obliged to supply two-thirds of the children's living expenses.[11]

In the field of education, too, vigorous efforts were made by the Reds in their endeavor to "raise the cultural level" of the backward Chinese rural masses.* Progress was slow during the first few years, partly because competent teachers were few, and partly because Communist energies were increasingly channeled toward the anti-Japanese struggle.

Speeded-up courses were the rule, and priority was given to political, military, and technical subjects. Edgar Snow witnessed the beginnings of Soviet education in Shensi, which was divided into an institutional, a military, and a social branch:

Under institutional education the Reds already claimed [in 1937] to have established about 200 primary schools, and they had one normal school for primary teachers, one agricultural school, a textile school, a trade-union school of five grades, and a Party school, with some 400 students. Courses in all these lasted only about six months.

Greatest emphasis naturally was on military education, and here very much had been achieved in two years, despite all the handicaps of the little beleaguered State. There were the Red Army Academy,

---

* In northern Shensi, which is one of the remotest areas of China, the illiteracy rate was about 95 percent at the time, as compared to 80 percent in the average rural area of China. In a conversation with Edgar Snow, the Communist Commissioner of Education (Paris-educated Hsu Teh-lih) called Shensi "one of the culturally darkest places on earth".

and the cavalry and infantry schools. . . . There was a radio school, and a medical school, which was really for training nurses. There was an engineering school, where the students actually got the rudimentary training of apprentices. . . .

Even in social education the Soviet aims were primarily political. There was no time or occasion to be teaching farmers literature or flower arrangement. The Reds were practical people. To the Lenin Clubs, the Young Communist Leagues, the Partisans, and the village Soviets they sent simple, crudely illustrated *Shih-tzu*, or "Know Characters", texts, and helped mass organizations form self-study groups of their own, with some Communist or literate among them as a leader. When the youths, or sometimes even aged peasants, began droning off the short sentences, they found themselves absorbing ideas along with their ideographs. Thus, entering one of these little "social education centers" in the mountains, you might hear these people catechizing themselves aloud:

"What is this?"

"This is the Red Flag."

"What is this?"

"This is a poor man."

"What is the Red Flag?"

"The Red Flag is the flag of the Red Army."

"What is the Red Army?"

"The Red Army is the Army of the poor men!"

And so on, right up to the point where, if he knew the whole 500 or 600 characters before anyone else, the youth could collect the red tassel or pencil or whatever was promised. Crude propaganda, of course. But when the farmers and farmers' sons and daughters finished the book they could not only read for the first time in their lives, but they knew who had taught them, and why. They had grasped the basic fighting ideas of Chinese Communism.

And, anyway, I should think it was a lot more amusing than teaching people to read via the this-is-a-cat, that-is-a-mouse, and the what-is-the-cat-doing, the-cat-is-eating-the-mouse method. Why teach to realists in allegories?[12]

The Communists also promoted "mass education" by means of political and anti-Japanese plays. The theatre had always been a favorite form of entertainment with Chinese crowds, and the Reds used it generously in towns

*and villages, and among civilians and military alike. Edgar Snow attended
a number of such theatrical performances:*

People were already moving down toward the open-air stage,
improvised from an old temple, when I set out with the young official
who had invited me to the Red Theatre. It was Saturday, two or three
hours before sunset, and all Pao An* seemed to be going.

Cadets, muleteers, women and girl workers from the uniform and
shoe factory, clerks from the cooperatives and from the Soviet Post
Office, soldiers, carpenters, villagers followed by their infants, all
began streaming toward the big grassy plain beside the river, where the
players were performing. It would be hard to imagine a more democratic gathering. Even some goats were grazing on the tennis court not
far beyond.

No tickets were sold, there was no "dress circle", and there were
no preferred seats. I noticed Lo Fu, secretary of the Central Committee,
Lin Piao, president of the Red Academy, Lin Pai-chu, the commissioner
of finance, Mao Tse-tung, chairman of the Government, and other
officials and their wives, scattered through the crowd, seated on the
springy turf, like the rest. No one paid much attention to them, once
the performance had begun.

Across the stage was a big pink curtain of silk, with the words,
"People's Anti-Japanese Dramatic Society", in Chinese characters, as
well as Latinized Chinese, which the Reds were promoting to hasten
mass education.† The program was to last three hours. It proved to be
a combination of playlets, dancing, singing, and pantomime—a kind
of variety show, or vaudeville, given unity chiefly by two central
themes: anti-Nipponism and the revolution. It was full of overt
propaganda, wholly unsophisticated, and the "props" were primitive.
But it had the advantage of being emancipated from cymbal crashing
and falsetto singing, and of dealing with living material rather than
with meaningless historical intrigues that are the concern of the
decadent Chinese opera.

Finally, what it lacked in subtlety and refinement it partly made

* Capital of the Chinese Soviet Republic (Shensi) until the end of 1936, when
Red headquarters were transferred to Yenan.

† Communist educators had worked out an alphabet of twenty-eight Latinized
letters by which they claimed to be able to reproduce nearly all Chinese phonetics,
and had also published a little pocket dictionary containing the commonest
phrases in "Latinized Chinese".

up by its robust vitality, its sparkling humor, and a sort of participation between actors and audience. Guests at the Red Theatre seemed actually to *listen* to what was said: a really astonishing thing in contrast with the bored opera audience, for in China opera-goers chiefly spend their time eating fruit and melon seeds, gossiping, tossing hot towels back and forth, visiting from one box to another, and only occasionally looking at the stage.

The first playlet here was called *Invasion*. It opens in a Manchurian village, in 1931, with the Japanese arriving and driving out the "non-resisting" Chinese soldiers.* In the second scene, Japanese officers banquet in a peasant's home, using Chinese men for chairs, and drunkenly making love to their wives. Another scene shows Japanese dope peddlers selling morphine and heroin and forcing every peasant to buy a quantity. A youth who refuses to buy is singled out for questioning.

"You don't buy morphine, you don't obey Manchukuo health rules, you don't love your 'divine' Emperor P'u-I," charge his tormentors. "You are no good, you are an *anti-Japanese* bandit!" And the youth is promptly executed.

A scene in the village marketplace shows small merchants peacefully selling their wares. Suddenly Japanese soldiers arrive, searching for more "anti-Japanese bandits". Instantly they demand passports, and those who have forgotten them are shot. Then two Japanese officers gorge themselves on a peddler's pork. When he asks for payment they look at him in astonishment. "*You* ask for payment? Why, Chiang Kai-shek gave us Manchuria, Jehol, Chahar, the Tangku Truce, the Ho-Umetsu Agreement, and the Hopei-Chahar Council,† without asking a single copper! And *you* want us to pay for a little pork!" Whereupon, they impale him as a "bandit".

In the end, of course, all this proves too much for the villagers. Merchants turn over their stands and umbrellas, farmers rush forth with their spears, women and children come with their knives, and all swear to "fight to the death" against the *Erh-pen-kuei*—the "Japanese devils".

* The Communists currently claimed—not without reason—that Kuomintang troops fought poorly.

† Territories and agreements, ceded and signed between 1933 and 1935, by which Nationalist China surrendered the country's northern provinces to Japanese control. The Communists frequently reproached the Kuomintang leaders with having yielded too easily to Japanese demands, and denounced some of these leaders as traitors.

The little play was sprinkled with humor and local idiom. Bursts of laughter alternated with oaths of disgust and hatred for the Japanese. The audience got quite agitated. It was not just political propaganda to them, nor slapstick melodrama, but the poignant truth itself. The fact that the players were mostly youths in their teens and natives of Shensi and Shansi seemed entirely forgotten in the onlookers' absorption with the *ideas* presented.

The substratum of bitter reality behind this portrayal, done as a sort of farce, was not obscured by its wit and humor for at least one young soldier there. He stood up, at the end, and in a voice shaking with emotion cried out: "Death to the Japanese bandits! Down with the murderers of our Chinese people! Fight back to our homes!" The whole assembly echoed his slogans mightily. I learned that this lad was a Manchurian whose parents had been killed by the Japanese. . . .

Second number on the program was a harvest dance, exquisitely done by a dozen girls of the Dramatic Society. . . . They had genuine talent.

Another unique and amusing number was called the "United Front Dance", which interpreted the mobilization of China to resist Japan. . . . Then there was something called the "Dance of the Red Machines". By sound and gesture, by an interplay and interlocking of arms, legs and heads, the little dancers ingeniously imitated the thrust and drive of pistons, the turn of cogs and wheels, the hum of dynamos—and visions of a machine-age China of the future.[13]

Despite untiring Communist efforts toward enlightening and modernizing the rural masses of Soviet China, most Red peasants and soldiers had little or no idea of the enormous material and technical progress going on outside their own limited sphere of life. Whenever they came into contact with the marvels of modern civilization (usually in larger cities), they were speechless —or flustered—with astonishment.

The American traveler and writer Agnes Smedley, who followed the advance of the Eighth Route Army in 1937 and 1938, vividly described the naïve reactions of some of her youthful companions as they entered the city of Sian, capital of Shensi:

In addition to my little *hsiao kwey** and my Szechuan guard, there
* Little [Red] devil.

was a Kiangsi lad of about twenty-five years, the bodyguard of a foreign woman friend of mine who had recently arrived in Sian; and there was another Szechuan youth, the guard of a Chinese woman of our group. These peasants had traveled hundreds and hundreds of miles on the long march with the Red Army. They could ford rivers, push around and over landslides, march through the swampy "Grass Lands" of Sikong where, it seems, no man had ever been before. These four veterans took for granted what was to me most unusual. But they were bewildered and amazed and often delighted as we approached Sian and met real evidences of the modern world.

First came the trucks. Of course they had seen trucks come to Yenan, but they had never been in one. But once on our long and wearisome journey from Yenan, a group of trucks carried our party about thirty miles. My guards took up their positions on one side of the machine, holding on like grim death. Grinning at each other and at the landscape speeding by at fully ten miles an hour, they got their first thrill of an automobile ride. When we halted at a village they all took turns sitting behind the wheel of the truck to see how it felt.

Well, they quickly got used to trucks. They were later to stop gasping at motorcycles, or to wonder at private cars even when they rode in the front seat beside the driver. It was only when we reached Sian that they really began to be astonished at everything. This is not much of a city, and the one-, two- and three-story shops are filled with piles of trashy, expensive things. . . . A city of a quarter of a million, with trashy shops, was to these lads, however, a great city filled with wonders.

When we went to the local headquarters of the Eighth Route Army in Sian, I was so tired I went to my room at once and lay down. The door was at once blocked with people—but not to look at me. They were clustered like bees around the electric light switch near the door. They began taking turns switching it on and off. Each one tried this a number of times, his face turned upward to watch the light bulb on the ceiling. His hand would be pushed aside and another would take his turn. . . .

What many of their experiences in the city were I do not know. In the first days there, they would disappear for hours at a time, walking through the city from one end to the other. I do know that my guard came home triumphantly with a leather case for which he had paid twice as much as he should have, while the next day my *hsiao kwey* went out and bought the same kind of case, in a larger size, for half the price my guard had paid. This made my guard lose face so badly that they had a quarrel. He got the upper hand two days later when he saw a train before the "little devil" saw one. This led to another quarrel, and the *hsiao kwey* dashed off to the railway station. But he did not know that he had to buy a platform ticket. They would not let him through the gates to see the train. His defeat was sad to contemplate, and it was several days later before he could really see a train. . . .

At one time we all went to the modern hotel in Sian to visit my foreign woman friend. This is a fine hotel with polished floors, upholstered furniture in the lobby, electric lights, curtains, white tablecloths in the dining room and goodness knows what. My friend had a room with a private bath. So the boys all poured into the bathroom to see the white tile and nickel, glass and mirrors. They turned on the hot and cold water, tested the washbasin, flushed the toilet repeatedly, and turned around and around admiringly as they looked at themselves in the big mirror.

They visited the hotel to see the bathroom a number of times until they were veterans in that line also. But one wonder of wonders they could never get over—the moving pictures! Coming down from Yenan, I tried to explain what a moving picture was. They did not know what I was talking about. So, on the night of our arrival, they went to the movies. Such was their wonder that they waited impatiently the next morning for the theatre to open. They saw a jungle film, returned with wonder still in their eyes, and told me they had seen lions, tigers, elephants, and a huge hairy animal that looked something like a man. . . . They became movie fans.[14]

These were the men with whom the Communists built up their main fighting force, the Eighth Route Army. In their immense majority, they were young and relatively naïve, and therefore easy to indoctrinate. But they were also brave, loyal and patriotic, and very eager for action.

Edgar Snow, who spent many months with them, has well portrayed the First Front Red Army (which, together with the Second and Fourth Front armies of the civil war period, constituted the Eighth Route Army):

The great mass of the Red soldiery was made up of young peasants and workers who believed themselves to be fighting for their homes, their land, and their country.

According to Yang [Political Commissioner], the average age of the rank and file was nineteen. This was easily believable. Although many men with the Reds had fought for seven or eight or even ten years, they were balanced by a vast number of youths still in their middle teens. And even most of the "old Bolsheviks", veterans of many battles, were only now in their early twenties, the majority having joined the Reds as Young Vanguards, or enlisted at the age of fifteen or sixteen.

In the First Front Army, a total of 38 percent of the men came either from the agrarian working class (including craftsmen, muleteers, apprentices, farm laborers, etc.) or from the industrial working class, while 58 percent came from the peasantry. Only 4 percent were from the petty bourgeoisie—sons of merchants, intellectuals, small landlords, and such. In this army over 50 percent of the troops, including commanders, were members of the Communist Party or the Communist Youth League.

Between 60 and 70 percent of the soldiers were literate—that is, they could write simple letters and texts, posters, handbills, etc. This was much higher than the average among ordinary troops in the White* districts, and it was very much higher than the average in the peasantry of the Northwest. Red soldiers began to study characters from Red texts, specially prepared for them, from the day of their enlistment. Prizes were offered (cheap notebooks, pencils, tassels, etc. but much valued by the soldiers) for rapid advancement, and a great effort was made to stimulate the spirit of ambition and competition.

Red soldiers, like their commanders, received no regular salaries. But every enlisted man was entitled to his portion of land, and some income from it. This is tilled in his absence, either by his family or his local Soviet. If he was not a native of the Soviet districts, however, his remuneration came from a share in the proceeds of crops from "public lands" (confiscated from the great landlords), which also helped provision the Red Army. Public lands were tilled by villagers in the local Soviets. Such free labor was obligatory, but the majority of the peasants, having benefited in the land redistribution, cooperated willingly enough to defend a system that had bettered their livelihood.

The average age of the officers in the Red Army was twenty-four.

* Or Kuomintang.

This included squad leaders and all officers up to army commanders but despite their youth these men had behind them an average of eight years' fighting experience each. All company commanders or higher were literate, though I met several who had not learned to read and write till after they had entered the Red Army. About a third of the Red commanders were former Kuomintang soldiers. Among Red commanders were many graduates of Whampoa Academy (Chiang Kai-shek's officers' training school), graduates of the Red Academy in Moscow, former officers of Chang Hsueh-liang's "Northeastern Army", cadets of the Paoting Military Academy, former Kuominchun ("Christian General" Feng Yu-hsiang's army) men, and a number of returned students from France, Soviet Russia, Germany and Italy. The Reds don't call themselves *ping*, or "soldiers"—a word to which there is attached much odium in China—but *chan-shih*, which means "fighters" or "warriors".

The majority of the soldiers as well as officers of the Red Army were unmarried. Many of them were "divorced"—that is, they had left their wives and families behind them. In several cases I had serious suspicions that the desire for this kind of divorce, in fact, may have something to do with their joining the army, but this may be a cynical opinion.

My impression, from scores of conversations on the road and at the front, was that over half of these "Red fighters" were still virgins. There were few Communist women at the front with the army, and they are nearly all Soviet functionaries in their own right or married to Soviet officials.

So far as I could see or learn, the Reds treated the peasant women and girls with respect, and the peasantry seemed to have a good opinion of Red Army morality. I heard of no cases of rape or abuse of the peasant women, though I heard from some of the southern soldiers of "sweethearts" left behind them. Very few of the Reds smoked or drank: abstention was one of the "eight disciplines" of the Red Army, and, although no special punishment was provided for either vice, I read in the "black column" of wall newspapers several grave criticisms of habitual smokers. Drinking was not forbidden, but discouraged. Drunkenness, as nearly as I could see or learn, was utterly unheard of.

Commander P'eng Teh-huai,* who used to be a Kuomintang

* One of the most experienced and belligerent Red generals.

general, told me that the extreme youth of the Red Army explained much of its capacity for withstanding hardship, and that was quite believable. It also made the problem of feminine companionship less poignant. P'eng himself had not seen his own wife since 1928, when he led an uprising of Kuomintang troops and joined the Reds.

Casualties among the Red Army commanders were very high. They customarily went into battle side by side with their men, from regimental commanders down. A foreign military attaché has said that one thing alone might explain the fighting power of the Reds against an enemy with vastly superior resources. That is the Red officers' habit of saying, "Come on, boys!" instead of, "Go on, boys!" During Nanking's First and Second "final annihilation" Campaigns,* casualties among Red officers were often as high as 50 percent. But the Red Army could not stand these sacrifices, and later adopted tactics tending somewhat to reduce the risk of life by experienced commanders. . . .

Nearly every province in China was represented in the various Red armies. In this sense it was probably the only really *national* army in China. . . . From the highest commander down to the rank and file these men ate and dressed alike. Battalion commanders and higher, however, were entitled to the use of a horse or a mule. I noticed there was even an equal sharing of the delicacies available—expressed, while I was with the Red Army, chiefly in terms of watermelons and plums! There was very little difference in living quarters of commanders and men, and they passed freely back and forth without any formality.

One thing had puzzled me. How did the Reds manage to feed, clothe and equip their armies? Like many others, I had assumed that they must live entirely on loot. This I discovered to be wrong . . . for they start to construct a self-supplying economy of their own as soon as they occupy a district, and this single fact makes it possible for them to hold a base despite enemy blockade. I had also failed to realize on what almost unbelievably modest sums it is possible for a Chinese proletarian army to exist.

To begin with, the Reds had practically no output for armaments; their enemy was really their main source of supply; for years the Reds have called the Kuomintang troops their "ammunition-carriers". From enemy troops the Reds claimed to capture more than 80 percent of their

* In the early thirties.

guns and more than 70 percent of their ammunition.* If this is hard to believe, I can bear witness to the fact that the regular troops I saw were equipped with the latest-type British, Czechoslovakian, German and American machine guns, rifles, automatic rifles, Mausers, and mountain cannon, such as have been sold in large quantities to the Nanking Government.[15]

Students, too, flocked to the Red Armies in increasing numbers. They were either Red sympathizers, or else had been disappointed by the Kuomintang's failure to organize the anti-Japanese resistance in an effective and convincing manner.

In 1938, reporter James Bertram met a group of student "pilgrims" on their way to Yenan:

The roads of China are seldom deserted. Carriers, muleteers, peddlers, itinerant tinkers and knife grinders form one part of a constant stream: to these must be added commonly priests, bandits, vagabonds, and mere peaceful travellers. But the road to Yenan, in these days, was a kind of pilgrimage, with its own special company of wayfarers. We fell in with a group of students who had walked all the way from Sian to attend the new Shenpei University. Girls in flannel slacks and blue denims strode along manfully, with all their baggage in a single bundle; one sunburnt youth who accompanied them told me that this was part of the process of "hardening themselves" for the "anti-Japanese struggle". They were counting (accurately enough) on few comforts in Yenan, once they had arrived.

"Are you a Communist?" I asked this young student, who had introduced himself as a graduate from a Christian college in the north.

"No," he said frankly. "Before, I belonged to no political organization. But now that we wage the sacred war of national liberation, many of us feel that we can learn best from the Eighth Route Army. The leaders in Yenan have great political experience, and they know especially about partisan tactics and mass mobilization. We come to learn these things in the Northwest."

"Where were you at the time of Lukouchiao?"

* Chiang Kai-shek was reported to have remarked, "My military supply services are the best in the world. In addition to supplying my own troops, they also furnish the enemy with supplies." From the Japanese, too, the Reds took much equipment.

"I was in Shanghai; and at once I went to Nanking to volunteer my services. But in Nanking there was nothing—only the old officials, the old bureaucrats. Always we were told to wait in an office, then come back the next day. Many were turned away like this. Such methods cannot help China: we all wanted to have practical training, to work among the people. Then my friend who is in the Party School in Yenan wrote to me and told me of the new *Shenpei Kunghsueh*,* where many students have come since the United Front. I did not tell my family where I was going, but took the train for Sian."

There was a desperate earnestness about this brief narrative, and the tone in which it was delivered. And there was good human material among these young political pilgrims. It was not because they were afraid to take a rifle and go into the front lines that they were here; they could not get the rifles anywhere else. And most of them were only too painfully aware of the shortcomings in their training.

"Before, our lives were much too sheltered," my young informant continued. "We trained our minds, but not our bodies. Now in Yenan we will get another kind of training, and find some work that will be really useful for the war."

It was certainly one of the weaknesses of the Chinese Nationalist Government in the first months after Lukouchiao, that it took so long to adopt a realistic approach to the problem of war mobilization. One result had been that many volunteers, especially those with radical sympathies, had turned naturally to the Northwest when they had met discouragement in other places. Paradoxically enough, in the big cities and in the "revolutionary" South the mass movement lagged. It was in the more primitive, politically backward northern provinces, that were the first affected by the war, and where the Communists had the chance to work most freely, that a genuine popular resistance to the invaders first developed.[16]

Among the few Western journalists who at the time covered life in Soviet China, Edgar Snow probably was the most familiar with conditions there. He described the busy daily routine of the Red soldiers behind the front:

The Red troops I saw in Ninghsia and Kansu were quartered in caves, former stables of wealthy landlords, hastily erected barracks of

* "North Shensi (anti-Japanese) Academy."

clay and wood, and in compounds and houses abandoned by former officials or garrison troops. They slept on hard *k'angs*,* without even straw mattresses, and with only a cotton blanket each—yet these rooms were fairly neat, clean and orderly, although their floors, walls and ceilings were of whitewashed clay. They seldom had tables or desks, and piles of bricks or rocks served as chairs, most of the furniture having been destroyed or carted off by the enemy before his retreat.

Every company had its own cook and commissariat. The Reds' diet was extremely simple; millet and cabbage, with a little mutton and sometimes pork, were an average meal, but they seemed to thrive on it. Coffee, tea, cake, sweets of any kind, or fresh vegetables were almost unknown, but also unmissed. Coffee tins were more valued than their contents, for nobody liked coffee, it tasted like medicine, but a good tin could be made into a serviceable canteen! Hot water was almost the only beverage consumed, and the drinking of cold water was specifically forbidden.

The Red soldier, when not fighting, had a full and busy day.... [He] observed a six-day week. He arose at five, and retired to a "Taps" sounded at nine. The schedule of the day included: an hour's exercise immediately after rising; breakfast; two hours of military drill; two hours of political lectures and discussion; lunch; an hour of rest; two hours of character study; two hours of games and sports; dinner; songs and group meetings; and "Taps".

Keen competition was encouraged in broad jumping, high jumping, running, wall scaling, rope climbing, rope skipping, grenade throwing, and marksmanship. Watching the leaps of the Reds over walls, bars, and ropes, you could easily understand why the Chinese press had nicknamed them "human monkeys", for their agile feats at mountain climbing and swift movement. Pennants were given in group competitions, from the squad up to the regiment, in sports, military drill, political knowledge, literacy, and public health. I saw these banners displayed in the Lenin Clubs of units that had won such distinctions.

There was a Lenin Club for every company and for every regiment, and here all social and "cultural" life had its center. The regimental Lenin rooms were the best in the unit's quarters, but that says little; such as I saw were always crude, makeshift affairs, and what interest

* Large, brick-built stoves heating the houses of northern China.

they aroused derived from the human activity in them, rather than from their furnishings. They all had pictures of Marx and Lenin, drawn by company or regimental talent. Like some of the Chinese pictures of Christ, they generally bore a distinctly Oriental appearance, with eyes like stitches, and either bulbous foreheads like an image of Confucius, or no foreheads at all. Marx, whose Chinese moniker is Ma K'e-ssu, was nicknamed by the Red soldiers "Ma Ta Hu-tzu", or "Ma the Big Beard". They seemed to have an affectionate awe for him. That was especially true of the Mohammedans,* who appear to be the only people in China capable of growing luxuriant beards as well as appreciating them.

Another feature of the Lenin Club was a corner devoted to the study of military tactics, in models of clay. The Chinese are very good at this sort of thing. Miniature towns, mountains, forts, rivers, lakes, and bridges were constructed in these corners, and toy armies battled back and forth, while the class studied some tactical problem given to it. Thus in some places you saw the Sino-Japanese battles of Shanghai refought, in another the battles on the Great Wall, but most of the models were, of course, devoted to past battles between the Reds and the Kuomintang. They were also used to explain the geographical features of the district in which the army was stationed, to dramatize the tactics of a hypothetical campaign, or merely to animate the geography and political lessons which Red soldiers got as part of their military training. In a hospital company's Lenin room I saw displays of clay models of various parts of the anatomy, showing the effects of certain diseases, illustrating body hygiene, and so on.

Another corner of the club was devoted to character study, and here you could see the notebook of each warrior hanging on its appointed peg on the wall. There were three character-study groups: those who knew less than 100 characters; those who knew from 100 to 300; and those who could read and write more than 300 characters. The Reds had printed their own textbooks (using political propaganda as materials of study) for each of these groups. The political department of each company, battalion, regiment and army was responsible for mass education, as well as political training. Only about 20 percent of the First Army Corps, I was told, was still in the *hsia-tzu* class, or "blind men", as the Chinese call total illiterates.

There was also a wall newspaper in every club, and a committee of

* *Ma* is a very common last name among Chinese Muslims.

soldiers was responsible for keeping it up to date. . . . The wall news-papers of a Lenin Club gave you a real insight into the soldier's prob-lems and a measure of his development. I took down full notes, in translation, of many of these papers. A typical one was in the Lenin Club, Second Company, Third Regiment, Second Division, in Yu Wang Pao, for September first. Its contents included daily and weekly notices of the Communist Party and the Communist Youth League; a couple of columns of crude contributions by the newly literate, mostly revolutionary exhortations and slogans; radio bulletins of Red Army victories in south Kansu; new songs to be learned; political news from the White areas; and, perhaps most interesting of all, two sections called the red and black columns, devoted respectively to praise and criticism.

"Praises" consisted of tributes to the courage, bravery, unselfishness, diligence or other virtues of individuals or groups. In the black column comrades lashed into each other and their officers (by name) for such things as failure to keep a rifle clean, slackness in study, losing a hand grenade or bayonet, smoking on duty, "political backwardness", "individualism", "reactionary habits", etc. On one black column I saw a cook denounced for his "half-done" millet; in another a cook denounced a man for "always complaining" about his productions. . . .

Some of the Reds' ideas have now been copied—with much better facilities for realizing them—by Chiang Kai-shek's crack "new army" and his New Life movement. But one thing the White armies cannot copy, the Reds claimed, was their "revolutionary consciousness", on which stood their main fortress of morale. What this was like could best be seen at a political session of Red troops—where you could hear the simple but firmly implanted credos that these youths fought and died for.[17]

Unchallenged on top of the Red hierarchy, and greatly admired by his fellow Reds, stood hard-working, well-read and chain-smoking Chairman Mao Tse-tung, who had the reputation of a charmed life. ★

Edgar Snow was the first foreign writer to interview Mao, in 1937, and subsequently got to know him very well. At forty-four, Mao was a "gaunt,

★ In scores of battles, he was never wounded once. On the eve of the Sino-Japanese war, Nanking had placed $250,000 on his head. Mao's wives were less lucky: the first died during the Long March, and the second (whom he subse-quently divorced), was wounded by splinters from an exploding aerial bomb.

rather Lincolnesque figure, above average height for a Chinese," who gave the impression of a strong and very shrewd personality:

The influence of Mao Tse-tung throughout the Communist world of China today is probably greater than that of anyone else. He is a member of nearly everything. . . . Mao seemed to me a very interesting and complex man. He had the simplicity and naturalness of the Chinese peasant,* with a lively sense of humor and a love of rustic laughter. His laughter was even active on the subject of himself and the short-comings of the Soviets—a boyish sort of laughter which never in the least shook his inner faith in his purpose. He is plain-speaking and plain-living, and some people might think him rather coarse and vulgar. Yet he combines curious qualities of naïveté with the most incisive wit and worldly sophistication.

I think my first impression—dominantly one of native shrewdness—was probably correct. And yet Mao is an accomplished scholar of Classical Chinese, an omnivorous reader,† a deep student of philosophy and history, a good speaker, a man with an unusual memory and extraordinary powers of concentration, an able writer, careless in his personal habits and appearance but astonishingly meticulous about details of duty, a man of tireless energy, and a military and political strategist of considerable genius. It is an interesting fact that many Japanese regard him as the ablest Chinese strategist alive. . . .

Mao lived very much like the rank and file of the Red Army. After ten years of leadership of the Reds, after hundreds of confiscations of property of landlords, officials and tax collectors, he owned only his blankets, and a few personal belongings, including two cotton uniforms. Although he is a Red Army commander as well as chairman, he wore on his coat collar only the two Red bars that are the insignia of the ordinary Red soldier.

I went with Mao several times to mass meetings of the villagers and the Red cadets, and to the Red theatre. He sat inconspicuously in the midst of the crowd and enjoyed himself hugely. . . . Mao's food was the same as everybody's, but being a Hunanese he had the southerner's *ai-la*, or "love of pepper". He even had pepper cooked into his bread. Except for this passion, he scarcely seemed to notice what he ate. . . .

* He was the son of a rather prosperous Hunanese farmer.
† In addition to Marxist and ancient Greek philosophers, Mao's long "reading list" includes Spinoza, Kant, Goethe, Hegel, Rousseau, and scores of other writers.

He appears to be quite free from symptoms of megalomania, but he has a deep sense of personal dignity, and something about him suggests a power of ruthless decision when he deems it necessary. I never saw him angry, but I heard from others that on occasions he has been roused to an intense and withering fury. At such times his command of irony and invective is said to be classic and lethal.

I found him surprisingly well-informed on current world politics. . . . He was very interested in the Labour Party of England, and questioned me intensely about its present policies, soon exhausting all my information. . . . His opinion of President Roosevelt was rather interesting. He believed him to be anti-Fascist, and thought China could cooperate with such a man. He asked innumerable questions about the New Deal, and Roosevelt's foreign policy. The questioning showed a remarkably clear conception of the objectives of both. He regarded Mussolini and Hitler as mountebanks, but considered Mussolini a much abler man, a real Machiavellian, with a knowledge of history, while Hitler was a mere will-less puppet of the capitalists.[18]

This portrayal of Chairman Mao was supplemented by the analysis of his personality given by James Bertram:

Mao struck me as having incomparably the coolest and most balanced mind I had encountered in China. Talking to him, one is immediately aware of an immense intellectual force, a brain moving easily and surely along orderly lines of thought. This penetrating intelligence is combined with an essentially practical approach to any problem, and with a deep understanding of his own countrymen. Mao Tse-tung is thoroughly Chinese; he has never been out of China,* and has lived always in the closest possible contact with his own people, especially with Chinese workers. His command of political theory is something he owes, no doubt, to natural gifts, a well-trained mind, and an amazingly retentive memory.

He is an omnivorous reader, and a man of many interests. But what is un-Chinese about him (or at least, untypical of the Chinese intellectual) is his extraordinary grasp of detail, his capacity for sustained mental effort, and his obvious power of concentration on the task in hand without losing sight of ultimate objectives.

I would say that Mao Tse-tung has in an unusual degree the subtlety

* Since this was written, Mao has left China twice in order to go to Moscow.

and flexibility characteristic of the Chinese mind at its best: this is what makes him a successful political strategist in a country that has never been lacking in agile political acrobats. But dominating and controlling this—and it is a much rarer phenomenon in China—is a disciplined, relentlessly driving human will. It is a formidable combination, so formidable that the comparison with Lenin does not seem entirely out of place.[19]

Chou En-lai was, and apparently still is, the Number Two man of the "Chinese People's Soviet Republic". During the civil war, he was Political Commissioner of the First Front Army, and during the Sino-Japanese war he became the Communist chief observer and liaison man in Chungking.

In the following sketch, James Bertram stressed Chou's engaging liveliness and diplomatic charm. Such talents, undoubtedly, help explain the fact that Chou remains Red China's leading "salesman" and troubleshooter abroad:

I had never met "The Insurrectionist", as Edgar Snow had called him, though we had once been together in Sian for a month, at a time when Chou En-lai's eloquence, backed up by the new "line" of the Communist Party, had been chiefly responsible for saving the life of Chiang Kai-shek. Chou was usually to be found at a focus of political tension, and I knew that in the past weeks he had been active in mass organization in Shansi.

The man who came briskly into the room, dressed in a plain "Sun Yat-sen" uniform, was certainly a compelling personality . . . an impression which was heightened by Chou's intense nervous vitality. This was a man who would have been an artist, if he had not been a revolutionary.

His manner was lively, almost gay; and he moved his hands in deft, sudden gestures. He spoke current English with perfect ease, but with an occasional French turn of phrase or a French word to help out a sentence.* Dark eyes were youthful and animated, and lit up as soon as he began to talk. He had an unaffected charm, and the power to convince of the born orator.[20]

On the morrow of the Lukouchiao incident, which started the Sino-Japanese war, the Chinese Red leaders turned more and more exclusively to the task of defeating the invader. In so doing, they were at once more

* Chou had studied in Paris, where he became one of the founders of the Chinese Communist Party in 1921, a few months before its founding in China.

*determined and more realistic than the Kuomingtang leaders. Also, they
remained true to the spirit of the "United Front" and cooperated with the
Chungking government, at least until the beginning of 1941, when the unhappy
affair of the New Fourth Army definitely split the Reds and the Whites.*

*In the fall of 1937, a confident Mao Tse-tung told James Bertram that the
war would be a long one, but that the Chinese people would win it:*

What was most impressive to me about Mao's whole analysis of the
war was his supreme confidence in the Chinese people, and in the future
of the Chinese revolution. And there could be no question of the loyalty
of the Chinese Communists to the leadership of Chiang Kai-shek; it
was a loyalty that had already been sealed in blood along the northern
battlefronts. Mao, and every other Communist leader I talked to, had
this same conception of a United Front that was no mere war impro-
visation, but was destined to carry the Chinese people successfully
through the war to the establishment of the "democratic republic"
that had been Sun Yat-sen's most cherished dream.

And they were not looking for any shortcuts, as I found when I
asked Mao Tse-tung how long he thought the war might last.

"We believe the war will be prolonged," he said, "because it will
take time to mobilize the Japanese people against their own fascist
cliques; it will take time for the international situation to be changed in
favour of China's success; above all, it will take time to change the
internal political situation in China itself.

"This last is part of a long process, in which the Chinese people
will learn the lessons of their first defeats, will modify obsolete military
and political systems, and organize on a mass basis for the victorious
war. And while this process is going on, the Japanese fascists and militarists will be preparing the way for their own overthrow.

"So we do not despair after losing battles in this first period; we
will never allow an atmosphere of pessimism or defeatism to grow up
in China. We will accept the fact of a prolonged war, and steadily and
fearlessly prepare the conditions for final victory. We are confident
that, within two years or more, the conditions of Chinese success will
be established, and we will reach a point where Japanese imperialism
must be defeated."[21]

*Despite their optimism concerning the outcome of the conflict, the Red
leaders did not underestimate the Japanese. Occasionally, they even paid*

tribute to the enemy's fighting qualities. This was the case of the Red com-
mander in chief, General Chu Teh, when he explained to James Bertram*
both the strong and the weak points of the invader:

"What is your opinion of the fighting quality of the Japanese army?" I asked. Chu nodded pleasantly.

"Very good," he said. "They are well-trained, and very much better armed than our troops. They use their mechanical arms—tanks, armoured cars, and planes—to great advantage when they get the opportunity. They are good at taking cover, shoot well, and keep their arms in good condition." This frank tribute to enemy efficiency rather surprised me.

"But"—Chu went on—"they have very definite weaknesses. One weak point is their infantry. The Japanese infantry, we have found, is not very good at independent action. They depend entirely on mechanical means of transport for communications and supply. If these are cut off, they are at a real disadvantage. They cannot use animal transport, or human labour, as our armies can. They cannot take advantage of the hill country, but must follow the easiest and most level route.

"When we fight the Japanese, we try to avoid their strong points, and select their weak points for attack. So we always fight in the hills, not in open country. And we have the assistance of the people, whom we organize and train into partisan units, to harass the enemy lines of communication."

Chu went on to show me the position of the scattered Chinese forces . . . in Shansi, Hopei, and Chahar. "You see," he chuckled, as his finger moved from one district city to another, "outside their main lines of advance, the Japanese hold nothing. Our troops are deep in their rear, and—in cooperation with the volunteer mobile units in Hopei, and the partisans—occupy practically the whole of the territory through which they have advanced. *We* have no rear to worry about, for we are fighting in our own country, and everywhere the people support us, give us food and assistance. If necessary, we can rely on the Japanese themselves for ammunition, for their cartridges fit our rifles. So you see there are very good prospects for continuing the war in North China."[22]

* One of Mao Tse-tung's earliest fellow revolutionists. Often nicknamed the "Red Napoleon".

In addition to their intimate knowledge of the country and to the loyal support of the people, the Red commanders also relied on the determination and mobility of their troops. The latter usually operated in bands of several hundred men each, which were linked to one another and to regional headquarters either by telephone or by radio. Naturally, they excelled at hit-and-run tactics, and during the war's first three years concentrated mostly on destroying Japanese communication lines and supply columns. Major attacks, in which some twenty or thirty thousand swiftly gathered Red troops (often assisted by an equal or greater number of min ping, or peasant militia) were coordinated to resist a Japanese drive, were undertaken only under special circumstances.*

Agnes Smedley crossed the Pacific to see the Red troops in action, and shared the rugged life of the Eighth Route Army for several months:

We are moving through a region where not even ordinary rough paper can be bought. There are no nails, no oil or fat, no salt, no fuel for fire. I shall be writing in the dead of winter without a blaze to warm me. And (need I tell you?) without sufficient food. Our food even now in the autumn is rice, or millet, as a base, with one vegetable. Today it was turnips, and yesterday it was turnips. Sometimes we have no vegetables at all. There are big armies here and there will be little even of the essentials. Sugar is simply unheard of.

You there† can never conceive of the difficulties under which our army and other Chinese armies operate. The Japanese have trucks, airplanes and other efficient means of transport. We have donkeys, horses, a few mules, and men. Almost all of our army walks. No motorized units here! . . . Twice a week my party tries to buy a chicken to enrich our diet. My companions‡ have not a cent of money. I am the richest person in the army, with money I have borrowed. And this money I must use to feed my two precious animals so they can carry our baggage, typewriting paper, films, typewriter ribbons. I have one uniform and one winter coat and set of winter underwear. I have two pairs of shoes. The others in my party have

---

* Especially during the harvest season (favorite raiding season of the Japanese), or when an important administrative center was threatened; also, when a surprise attack might yield rifles and ammunition from the enemy.

† This first part of the quotation is taken from a letter the author wrote to a friend.

‡ Two newspapermen and three guards.

only the shoes on their feet and they are wearing out. I don't know where we can get new shoes for them. Most of our armies have no stockings at all. . . .

November 6, 1937. We are going with the Enemy Department* to Lin Piao's field headquarters.† The place is secret, and we can find it only with peasant guides. A regimental representative in the village gave us a note to a village beyond, where a young peasant came out to guide us. On the walls of the village were slogans, proclamations of various kinds, and manifestoes of the Eighth Route Army. . . . We go up and around, over, down and around again, these cone-shaped mountains. We are constantly seeing airplanes. By the end of the day we have met thirteen in all. Once we saw three flying in formation, and later, five. They flew lower than usual, looking for our army. We crouched by the side of cliffs and waited for them to pass. . . .

After what seemed endless hours of walking, climbing and riding, we reached Lin Piao's field headquarters. He had been up all night and he and some of his staff were now asleep on their one *k'ang* in a little room hung with military maps. I was in such pain that I lay down when they got up and from the *k'ang* watched them at work. There are telephone lines stretched across this country, and one of them ended in Lin Piao's headquarters. Hsu Hsiang-ch'ien‡ called from Kwangyang village to report that the Japanese were attacking in large forces. Lin ordered the Eighth Route forces there to retreat a little. Later he ordered another retreat, carefully tracing the route of retreat on the map before him. The Eighth Route is waiting for a big battle. But the Japanese have brought in reinforcements, so now they have not just nine thousand men but perhaps two or three times that. Lin Piao and his staff are perfectly calm about it. "We cannot fight them openly," he told us. "There are too many of them. We will employ Partisan warfare. We will select the places where we wish to fight." And so they were retreating and watching and waiting. When the big battle will come is not certain—tonight, tomorrow, tomorrow night. We do not know.

I asked to go to Liu Po-cheng's§ field headquarters. Lin Piao said

---

* Gathering intelligence concerning the enemy.

† Lin Piao: head of the Red Military Academy, and one of the ablest Red tacticians. Divisional Commander at the time.

‡ Veteran Red general.

§ Veteran Red Commander from Szechuan.

no. It was too dangerous. The Japanese are too numerous. If I go with our men, I would have to go with small Partisan groups that move very rapidly. I am not able to walk very far. So I lie on his *k'ang* and listen to the occasional bombardment. "What does it mean?" I ask. "Nothing," Lin says. "The Japanese fire without an objective. We have no 'positions,' so they can do nothing. So they just fire for the psychological effect." He smiled his dry little smile. The airplanes drone over our headquarters, and, seeing nothing, are gone.

The place is jammed. Sardines have an easy time compared to us. There are about eight houses. Our group gets one of the "houses"— caves dug in the loess cliffs. On the *k'ang* sleep my two guards, my two newspaper companions, and, at the end, myself. At the foot of the *k'ang*, on a door, sleeps Tsai Chen of the Enemy Department. Farther back in the cave sleep eight or ten men, or more, on the floor, with some straw beneath them. We all take this for granted, and I suppose that I alone find it unusual.[23]

Until the beginning of the forties, the Reds had neither artillery nor airplanes. Time and again, their fast-moving columns fell into the rear and flanks of the surprised Japanese, coming out of nowhere and vanishing with equal swiftness. Speed and stamina were indeed basic qualities of all Communist fighters, regulars and partisans alike. Moving under cover of darkness to avoid punishment from the air, and following the shortest possible route throughout the countryside, the Reds often outwalked and outmaneuvered the motorized Japanese.

Agnes Smedley watched one such "iron-legged" column file by silently and disappear into the night:

Field Headquarters of Lin Piao. November 7, 1937. This evening, as the shadows began to turn the deep ravines into black pits, I stood on the summit of a terraced mountain. A narrow path strewn with sharp stones led up out of a long dark ravine, around the terraces of stone, steadily upward, until it reached a point where I stood; then it dropped quickly downward into another ravine leading to the north, where it emptied into a valley running east and west through which twenty thousand Japanese troops were moving westward toward the city of Taiyuan.

Up this narrow, stony path came long lines of Chinese soldiers, marching with astounding swiftness. Their clothing was the blue-gray cotton which they always wear, their shoes were cotton cloth slippers with soft soles. Many wore string or rope sandals, and almost all had no stockings. Above their heads extended the ends of their rifles, with bayonets fixed. Some carried machine guns, and behind them toiled mules, heaving under heavy loads of ammunition. In pockets about the waist of each man were many hand grenades, and on their backs were small square packs with gray cotton blankets around them. Two battalions of the old Red Army from Kiangsi were marching to battle, marching with their two-hundred-*li*-a-day stride that has no equal on earth. They were outflanking the oncoming Japanese.

The shadows of the night deepened and the coiling line of men merged with the darkness of the ravines below. One by one the men stepped up out of the darkness and passed along the path, then plunged down into darkness again. For three or four seconds each man passed before me, and as he passed, turned his face toward me. He spoke no word, but passed like a shadow. His soft-soled shoes made no sound. Sometimes a rifle clanked against a shovel on a man's back. Some of the shadowy figures were heaving, and their faces gleamed with perspiration. But no one slackened that steady, swift pace that can cover twice or three times the marching distance of ordinary soldiers.

As each figure stepped up out of the shadows, the faces and figures of the Chinese people passed before me. . . . Some were men as tall and broad as the strongest Western soldier, some shorter and heavy-set, as strong as some of the animals carrying their ammunition, and some thin and wiry. Some were middle-aged men who looked like fathers of families and some were in their early twenties with the light of youth and great vision in their gleaming eyes.

One column passed. There was no one on the path before me; then out of the darkness stepped a peasant, clad as all peasants are, in blue denim, his head wrapped in a short face towel knotted above the forehead so that the two ends spread out like little wings. Such peasants marched before each column, guiding it over the paths, and so intimately linked with the people is this Eighth Route Army that the men follow them, never doubting, never questioning. The peasants also turned their faces toward me, turned to look back without slackening their swift march, and plunged into the darkness beyond.[24]

The peasant guides marching before the unquestioning columns were indeed symbolic of the spirit of cooperation uniting the Red troops and the Chinese

peasants in their fight against their common enemy. Peng Teh-huai, com-
mander of the First Front Army, explained the strength of this wartime bond
to Agnes Smedley:

The Eighth Route Army, Peng said, would organize and arm the people of Shansi and Hopei provinces and all of North China. Whatever happens, this army will not leave the people of North China, will not cross the Yellow River,* but will fight to the end. Even if the Japanese occupy and hold all the big cities and the railways, still the Eighth Route Army, with the armed people, will destroy all railways and roads, will harass and tire the enemy, will wage relentless Partisan warfare upon them so that wherever they step, whether on hill or in valley, they will meet some man or woman, or some groups to attack them. The organization and arming of the people are proceeding with amazing speed, Peng said. The Eighth Route Army has organized twenty thousand men into Partisan units connected with the army in the past six weeks. Only about half of them have arms at present. In Western Hopei and in Chahar, the Eighth Route Army units have already met and united with two Volunteer groups. These Volunteers are workers, peasants, students, who have arisen and captured arms. They are the core of new armies of the Chinese people, and they are of an entirely different character from the regular Chinese armies. They are Volunteers, coming from the heart of the people. . . .

As Peng Teh-hwei said yesterday, "The Eighth Route Army is like the fish, and the people like the water. We move among the people, and the Japanese learn nothing about us. We have no traitors in our ranks."

It is astounding, this instinctive honesty of the Chinese people.† Thousands upon thousands of our troops move here and there, calling mass meetings, posting a thousand proclamations and posters, leaving the hillside and walls of towns covered with countless slogans.‡ Along the route of our march are little bits of white paper with signs which we can follow if we lag behind or are in doubt about the route. One would think an enemy could find us any day. But the enemy never

---

* *i.e.*, retreat into central China, abandoning the North to the invader.

† There was, however, a Chinese "Fifth Column" helping the Japanese for a variety of motives. James Bertram documents this fact in one of his books (*Unconquered*, pp. 289–91).

‡ Stressing hatred of the invader as well as need for national unity.

does. Even its myriad airplanes do not know where to look, and even if they do they see nothing.[25]

The struggle between Red China and Japan may roughly be divided into three different periods. From 1937 to 1940, Communist guerrillas expanded their activities from their north Shensi base across the hills of Shansi and the plains of Hopei to the Pacific and into Shantung Province. In the summer of 1940, the Reds launched a general offensive (called the Hundred Regiments' Battle) against Japanese railway communications in northern China, which paralyzed Japanese traffic for several weeks. Heavy Japanese counterstrokes, however, forced the Reds back toward their solid bases.

Between 1941 and 1943, the Communists desperately resisted a series of Japanese "mopping-up" campaigns, and their control of northern China weakened considerably during that period of struggle for survival.

By 1943, the Japanese were much too busy resisting the great American offensive in the Pacific to divert more strength to China. Their pressure against the Communists decreased as they withdrew to their walled cities and supply lines and dug in. Once more, the Red tide rolled east and south. The Eighth Route Army in northern China, and the reorganized New Fourth Army in the lower Yangtze area, were chiefly responsible for the spectacular Red gains. In the summer of 1944, eighteen "liberated areas"— sweeping in a vast arc from Manchuria to the Yangtze valley and beyond— were under Communist control.

Throughout the entire conflict, the Communist drives were coordinated from Yenan. The Red leadership had never despaired of victory, but it was in the first place the dauntless and enduring courage of the Chinese peasants that defeated the Japanese invaders.

Both conventional and unconventional methods of warfare were used by both sides during the prolonged and increasingly bitter struggle. The Japanese relied heavily on their superior mechanical means, and, like their German allies in Europe, multiplied small and large fortifications throughout the occupied areas. As the war dragged on, they also resorted to a variety of propaganda tricks and to psychological warfare, alternatively using flattery, terror, bribery and alluring promises in order to subdue or convince the Chinese.

The use of hand grenades, mines and tunnels, on the other hand, became the favorite (and most efficient) technique of the Red fighters. In 1944 the American newspaperman Harrison Forman visited central Hopei, where the

Reds had developed a near-perfect combination of mines and underground warfare:

In some districts mine warfare has developed to a fine art. Mine fields are laid at strategic points along the highway. From each mine in the field a string runs through an underground system of brick tubes to a primitive "switchboard" in a farmhouse or other observation post nearby. As an enemy column moves into the mine field the operator calmly pulls this or that string on the "switchboard". The mines explode like lights in a pinball machine as the bewildered enemy dashes back and forth in an effort to extricate himself from the field.

Innumerable booby traps litter the countryside: leaping mines, delayed mines, upside-down mines. . . . With time and success the villagers have grown bolder. Today they provoke and insult the Japanese with slogans painted on flags or hung on scarecrows in the fields. When many of these exploded as the enemy tried to pull them down, he swallowed his pride and decided to ignore them. Whereupon, such slogans multiplied by the thousands—few of them actually mined, of course.

Anything within sight is likely to be mined. And in some districts almost everything is. A basket left in the middle of the road, a plow-share in the field, a paper-wrapped parcel by the wayside—all these things may be mined. A road rut is dug out, a mine is carefully buried, and an old auto tire is rolled lightly over the dusty surface. After a few Jap trucks are blown up in this way, Jap drivers will bump along the surfaces between the ruts—which are also mined. . . .

Periodically, the Japs drove cattle or captive villagers through mine fields to detonate mines. The villagers prepared for such contingencies with string-pull mines. Wang* told me that it was the villagers' practice to wait until the cattle or the captives had passed safely through the field, and then to explode the mines under the Japs who were following.

"When the Japs are determined to crash through the mine fields at all costs, they are often—very often—met at the village gates by blasts from our wooden cannon," Chao Fang† began.

I held up a hand. I wasn't quite sure I had heard him aright.

"Now wait a minute. . . . Wooden cannon, did you say?"

---

* A leader of the local peasant militia, or *min ping*.
† Member of the (Red) Youth Vanguards.

"Why, yes." Young Chao paused a moment. "Oh, of course—the wooden cannon is something new to you. *We* take it for granted, you know."

So Chao described this weapon. A hardwood log, usually about ten feet long, is bored to make a barrel, which is sometimes lined with metal. The outside is tightly wound with stolen Japanese telephone wire to keep it from blowing apart. The charge, weighing anything from five pounds up, is made of broken posts and pans, glass, stones—any tough and sharp scrap material at hand. A hole is cut into the side of a house with the camouflaged muzzle opening flush with the outside wall facing the village gate. An officer watches from a peephole or the rooftop and, when the enemy reaches a given point such as the village gate, orders the crew to fire. The Japs have a superstitious fear of these wooden cannon, since the unorthodox charge, even when it does not kill, makes ugly wounds.

When the Japs carried their attack past the cannon and drove into the village, they would stumble over innumerable booby traps in the streets, in the alleyways, in the houses they tried to enter. They would be grenaded from every rooftop and shot at from every doorway or window. Then there would suddenly come a mysterious lull, and the villagers would seem to disappear completely.

"Then began a new type of warfare—tunnel warfare." And old Wang rolled up his sleeves, took a sip of hot tea, and motioned young Chao to silence. Wang was a specialist in subterranean warfare.

In the early days of the war the villagers dug cellars under their houses, in which to hide from the enemy. The Japs easily found these and rooted out the people, raping, torturing, murdering at will. The villagers then connected their cellars, until a whole village would become a veritable warren of tunnels. But when the Jap came again he would surround the village and make a careful search for every tunnel entrance, driving the people to the surface with fire, smoke, and water. Some of the villages then held council and decided to connect each village's tunnel system with that of the next. It was a staggering undertaking; but if it would save them from slaughter by the Japanese it would be well worth while.

So there exists in Central Hopei today an amazing system of tunnels linking hundreds of villages for miles and miles around, built on a scale that makes New York's subway system seem a child's toy railway by comparison. The tunnels are big enough to house the people together with their livestock and their possessions and are equipped with sufficient food and water for an extended siege.*[26]

Whether or not the New York subway system is a "child's toy" compared to the extraordinary underground system built by the Hopei peasants, the fact remains that the peasants' achievement was truly amazing. Probably no other peasantry in the world ever worked so hard, and displayed such patience and fortitude, in endeavoring to foil the enterprises of a foreign invader and to make life impossible for him wherever he went.

The following explanations, given by a Red colonel to reporter Robert Payne at the end of the Sino-Japanese war, constitute a fitting complement to the preceding description, and possibly stress even more the effectiveness of land mines and "tunnel warfare"† against the Japanese:

Land mines were the easiest things to make. You could make them out of anything. We had the nitre and saltpetre, and we had stones in abundance. In the end half of our land mines were simply stones, bored out, with a cardboard or glass tube like a cartridge inserted in them, and connected by a lanyard or a trip wire to some hiding place where a soldier was watching, or just simply left there to explode when anything touched it. . . . We made their lives miserable with land mines. We were very successful with them, and when we captured their reports, we found that they were frightened to the marrow by every stone and every blade of grass in north China. . . . But still they were powerful, they could build blockhouses and try to narrow us down.

This is where the tunnels came in. They came in gradually, and we learned how to make them and use them only after bitter experience. Generally speaking, there were two kinds of tunnel—a tunnel built from village to village underneath the fields for the purpose of saving the lives of the villagers when the Japanese attacked, and a tunnel built deliberately for fighting in. . . . Some of the most bitter fighting in the war in north China took place six or seven feet underneath the earth.

We had to excavate the tunnels secretly: we would take the earth away to the foot of a mountain and bury it again. When it was raining,

* The firm soil of Hopei allowed such an intricate and vast underground system; it would not have been possible in the friable loess hills of Shensi.

† Today, not surprisingly, this same method is being applied by the Vietcongs.

we would take it to the fields and sprinkle it there. We had to be careful
—there must be no telltale marks of earth, and they must never know
whether we had tunnels or not. It was a game of nerves—we wanted
them to believe that there were tunnels everywhere. It was true in the
later stages of the war, but not in the beginning.

There were all kinds of problems, and we solved them very, very
gradually. The entrance to a tunnel might be anywhere—under a bed,
behind a false wall, anywhere, and always it was carefully concealed,
so that if you went into the room you wouldn't find it in less than
ten minutes. . . . We had trouble with ventilation of course. . . .

There are a lot of dead Japanese in these tunnels still—it saves the
trouble of burying them. But mostly they did not get into the tunnels
—if they tried to, they were blown up with land mines the moment
they dropped into the tunnel entrance. Sometimes they used poison
gas. It was very effective at first, until we learned to put up cotton
quilted blankets soaked with water inside the tunnels—it kept the gas
out. We were fighting on our own middens, and against all tricks, but
the tunnel was the best trick we had; the Japanese would come and
occupy a village, but the villagers had fled. The Three Alls—Burn All,
Kill All, Loot All*—were excellent in theory, but we hid the grain and
we hid ourselves, and we could always rebuild our houses afterwards.[27]

*During the last few months of the Sino-Japanese war, the Japanese with-
drew into Manchuria. In the wake of the rapidly retreating enemy, both the
Communist and the Kuomintang troops endeavored to recover as much
national territory as their means permitted, and did their best to outrace each
other. In this struggle for physical possession of the body of China, both forces
were equally determined to reap vast advantages and to maintain them.
Moreover, both sides claimed and proclaimed that their cause was the cause
of China.*

*The Communists meant to keep North China, which had for years been
their citadel. From there they intended to expand into Manchuria on the
heels of the Japanese. The Nationalists, on the other hand, aimed at re-
establishing the old order throughout the areas they had controlled in 1937,
and then push into the northeastern territories which the Japanese had dominated for fifteen years.*

Thus a nationwide civil strife was sealed within the maturing victory. In his

* Japanese slogan summing up the invader's ruthless policy of repression in the
years 1941–3.

capacity of Supreme Commander of all Chinese forces, Chiang Kai-shek in the summer of 1945 ordered the Reds to follow his directives for final military operations. The Reds countered that their sacrifices and victories against the Japanese gave them the right to disregard Chiang's order—and to occupy the areas of their own choice. As a result, civil war was raging across China within forty-eight hours of victory over the Japanese.

CHAPTER XIII

THE COLLAPSE OF THE KUOMINTANG
1945–1949

PERHAPS MORE than any other nation, the long-suffering Chinese needed peace and normality in the summer of 1945. Both, however, were denied them, and they had hardly time to rejoice over the liberation of their national territory.

The new calamity—the clash between Red and White China—which now befell the country had more or less been anticipated by both camps. Ever since the first split in 1927, and much more so after the massacre of the New Fourth Army in 1941, a backlog of distrust, deceit and extermination* had been piling up. Chiang Kai-shek hated the Reds, and wished to remain the sole master of China. The Communists, for their part, denounced in ever stronger terms the corrupt, inefficient and autocratic rule of the Kuomintang "clique" and, as the Sino-Japanese war drew to a close, loudly demanded the establishment of a "democratic" coalition government in which they would share the power with the country's bourgeois elements.

Many, and deep-seated, differences separated the Kuomintang and the Kungch'antang, and made a reconciliation very difficult. The Communist attitude toward the Kuomintang was clearly summed up by Chou En-lai in a statement he issued on behalf of his Party on October 10, 1944, which was the 33rd anniversary of the founding of the Republic of China:

The Kuomintang Government persists in its abnormal policy of combining halfhearted effort in the war with ative opposition to the Communist Party. And so, when we fight vigorously behind the enemy lines, we are abused as a "traitor party" and a "traitor army", and encounter sabotage and continued attacks from the Kuomintang. . . .

* Mostly among Communists. Dozens of Red dignitaries had lost relatives killed by Kuomintang police. Mao Tse-tung's younger brother was strangled in 1942.

Politically, the Kuomintang authorities cling like death to one-party despotism and personal dictatorship. They forbid existence alike to other parties and to a people's democracy. . . . In the areas controlled by Chungking there is only party rule and no popular election. The various ranks of the People's Political Council, from county to province and the entire country, are all appointed by the Government. All officials, from the head of the smallest village up to the Chairman of the National Government, are appointed by the Government. And these appointments are made exclusively by a small ruling clique in the Kuomintang, the rest of the Kuomintang members and the democratic leaders having no share in them. It is therefore less appropriate to call this "party rule" than to call it an oligarchy.

Moreover, the Kuomintang authorities have set their minds on establishing fascism and so refuse to put into practice the Three People's Principles.* . . . In areas controlled by Chungking, they rob the people of their freedom, bureaucratically dominate the so-called self-government, control public opinion, trample on culture, practice monopoly in industry and commerce, levy extortionate taxes and duties, let loose the Kuomintang Gestapo to tread down rights, and allow bureaucratic capitalists to undermine the people's industrial enterprises. Through all these measures they have brought about an extremely serious political and economic crisis. . . . In order to save China in this crisis, to cooperate with our allies in the war, and to prepare effectively for the counteroffensive, we Communists advocate that the National Government convene an emergency National Council by calling together representatives of the entire country. We propose that the Government abolish one-party dictatorship and set up a coalition government. . . .

The National Government should call this national emergency meeting in the near future, so that further delay may not plunge the Chungking areas into irredeemable disaster. . . . This meeting should take Dr. Sun Yat-sen's revolutionary Three People's Principles as its basis and should pass a program that will meet the requirements of the situation and save China from her crisis. This program must thoroughly change the erroneous military, political, economic, and cultural policies at present pursued by the Kuomintang Government.[1]

* As stated by Sun Yat-sen, who was and still is claimed by both Reds and Whites.

An undeclared civil war had been smoldering during the greater part of the Sino-Japanese war. It was symbolized by the tight military blockade which Chiang Kai-shek had thrown around the Soviet Republic of Shensi, in order to prevent the Reds from expanding into central China. Several hundred thousand of the best Nationalist troops* faced some fifty thousand picked Red troops in that area. It was the largest single concentration of Kuomintang and Communist forces anywhere in China, and also a tremendous waste of manpower at a time of national emergency.

In principle, there were no or few contacts between the two forces. In actual fact, however, Kuomintang soldiers (and to a lesser extent officers) were definitely more amenable to Communist propaganda than Red troops would be to Kuomintang promises. Not surprisingly, the Red Theatre played an active role in enticing Kuomintang soldiers into going over to the Reds.

The following short anecdote, related by Edgar Snow, illustrates the theatre's power of attraction across the White border line:

I met several Young Vanguards, veterans of the Long March, still in their early teens, who had charge of organizing and training children's dramatic societies in various villages.

"Peasants come from long distances to our Red dramatics," Miss Wei proudly informed me. "Sometimes, when we are near the White borders, Kuomintang soldiers secretly send messages to ask our players to come to some market town in the border districts. When we do this, both Red soldiers and White leave their arms behind and go to this marketplace to watch our performance. But the higher officers of the Kuomintang never permit this, if they know about it, because once they have seen our players many of the Kuomintang soldiers will no longer fight our Red Army!"[2]

Negotiations for solving the differences between the Kuomintang and the Communists, conducted by representatives of the two camps during the spring and summer of 1944, failed to achieve positive results. The idea of a coalition government was highly distasteful to Chiang Kai-shek.† His demand that the Communists disband their armed forces (with the exception of ten divisions) was equally unacceptable to the Red leaders, who remembered the

---

* Figures vary from about 200,000 to half a million men.

† Who contended that his control of China was a sacred trust from Sun Yat-sen, and this trust was a responsibility he could not share.

tragedy of the New Fourth Army and saw their army as their sole guarantee of safety.* Neither side really trusted the other.

President Roosevelt, too, stepped into the dispute and endeavored to bring the two parties together. In the fall of 1944, he sent a buoyant and gregarious Oklahoman, General Patrick J. Hurley, as his personal envoy extraordinary to Chungking. Though he was not exactly a student of China, Ambassador Hurley approached his delicate task with typical American optimism and goodwill. Shortly after his arrival in China, he paid a surprise visit to the Red leaders. An American journalist described the amusing scene:

Hurley flew to Yenan on November 7, 1944, to meet the Communist leaders. He landed unannounced and unexpected on the cold, bleak valley airfield, his uniform dazzling, his chest covered with gay ribbons. Mao Tse-tung and the other Communist leaders had been telephoned after Hurley's plane landed. The Communist high command gathered hastily, piled into the war-scarred ambulance Mao used, and raced over the rocky roads to the runway. They piled out pell-mell and ran across the field to meet Hurley. The envoy greeted them affably, gave an Indian war whoop,† and climbed into the ambulance. It was a joyful ride, and everyone became friendly at once as they jounced over the ruts in a welter of dust. When they passed a shepherd prodding some animals, Mao announced that he had been a shepherd boy himself; then Hurley told how he had been a cowboy in his youth. As they passed the shallow Yen River, Mao explained how the water rose in winter and dried up in the dry months; this reminded Hurley of the rivers in Oklahoma—so dry in summer that you could tell when a school of fish went swimming past by the cloud of dust they raised. Colonel David Barrett‡ translated Hurley's jokes into Chinese, and when the ambulance arrived at the American military outpost in the suburbs, it disgorged a gay crowd. That evening the Communists gave an enormous banquet in honor of the November Revolution in Russia, and Hurley was the star guest, though he baffled the Communists with an occasional bellowed "Yahoo!" [3]

Congenial and sincere as he was, Ambassador Hurley failed in his attempt

* "We will offer him [Chiang] one hand in friendship," a Red general remarked, "but our other hand we will hold on our gun."

† Hurley prided himself in his knowledge of the language of the Choctaw Indians.

‡ U. S. military observer in Yenan, and a top American specialist on China.

to break the deadlock between the Kuomintang and the Communists. During the spring and summer of 1945, Yenan Radio grew increasingly vituperative in its denunciation of Chiang Kai-shek, calling him a lunatic and his associates gangsters. Chiang in turn became more stiff-necked, less and less willing to have anything to do with the hated Reds.

Thus armed conflict was the only solution to China's great domestic political struggle. And yet, it seems as though the Communists entered that conflict somewhat reluctantly after the long years of fighting sustained against the Japanese. A leading Red general stressed this fact in an interview granted to the reporter Robert Payne shortly after the outbreak of civil war:

I asked him whether there was any real hope that the war might be stopped. He grinned and poured another glass of beer. "We are doing our best," he said. "No one wants this war. . . . We're all so desperately tired of war, but we'll fight for democracy against dictatorship. There are good people in the Kuomintang, but they don't want democracy apparently. We fought against the dictatorship of the Japanese under conditions of blockade from the Kuomintang. We were surrounded with 'ramparts of copper and iron'. We are bound to be bitter against them, and they are bound to want to conserve their power. Best of all would be to go back to the agreements already made, call a National Assembly and have a real democratic China—as democratic as America or England."

But he could see little hope for the moment. The balance was weighed for war. American intervention was probably insufficient: the issues at stake were so great that it needed the intervention of Soviet Russia and Britain, yet they had kept silent and aloof. . . . The Americans were mediators, but they were also technically and factually at the service of the National Government, and the National Government was no longer representative of the people. "It's all dictatorship—a one-man government—and we are sick and tired of it." He was violent about the corruption in the south and asked whether I had seen any in the north. I said I had been there too little a time to be sure, but it seemed in the highest degree unlikely that anyone on the Communist side was corrupt. There were no advantages that money could bring in the northern areas.[4]

In the race for control of formerly occupied China which now developed between Communists and Nationalists, the rich province of Manchuria naturally became a prime target. The Reds had the immense initial advantage of being much closer to the goal than their rivals. Indeed, at the time of Japan's surrender, the best Kuomintang troops were still hundreds of miles from the coastal lowlands of central and northern China, where troop movements were much easier than through the inland provinces.

The Red commander in chief, Chu Teh, ordered his guerrilla armies to drive north across the dunes and grasslands of Mongolia, in order to join the Russians in Manchuria and cooperate with them in the task of rounding up the Japanese forces.* Chiang Kai-shek tried to counter the move by ordering the Eighth Route and New Fourth armies to remain at their posts and await his instructions. Instead, Radio Yenan snapped back:

We consider that you have given us a mistaken order. Such a mistake is grave. Thus we are compelled to express ourselves to you that we firmly refuse the order.[5]

In his predicament, Chiang was rescued by the U. S. Air Force and Navy, which marshaled all their available resources in the Chinese theatre of war. Over the frantic objections of the Communists and their sympathizers around the world, General Wedemeyer organized a massive airlift in which the giant C-54's flew some 80,000 crack Nationalist troops into Nanking, Shanghai, and Peking. At the same time, the U. S. 7th Fleet landed 50,000 American marines in the ports of Tsingtao and Tientsin.

Negotiations between Chungking and Marshal Malinovsky (Russian commander in Manchuria), on the other hand, had led to an agreement whereby the Nationalist troops were to replace the Russian forces upon the latter's withdrawal. Thus the better part of Manchuria was recovered by the forces loyal to the Generalissimo.

In Manchuria, meanwhile, the Russians had lost no time dismantling the modern industrial equipment installed by the Japanese. A party of American newspapermen on their way to Mukden found evidence of systematic looting all along the road:

As we rolled across the fertile plains of South Manchuria, which normally rank among the world's great bread baskets, producing wheat, maize, kaoliang, soybean, we were struck both by the evidence of very extensive Japanese building and by the dismal scenes of destruction. Even the little hamlets, such as Kaopantze, which in China

---

* The Russians had entered Manchuria on August 9, 1945, three days after the first atomic bomb devastated Hiroshima.

proper would have been a collection of crazy mud and straw shacks, had their modern little railway station, water tower, grain elevators, a few concrete buildings, and prosperous-looking farmhouses. But all along the line, great concrete spans were buckled in the middle; a section of a long steel bridge was out; and burned-out locomotives and charred passenger cars were strewn along the sidings.

There had been no fighting, no air attacks in this area, for the Russians occupied it weeks after the Japanese surrender, and Bill Gray and I began a warm argument about who was responsible for this wanton sabotage. Bill insisted it was the fault of the Chinese bandits, and I said, with just as little evidence, that the Russians had performed it. It seemed to me that the scale of destruction suggested some well-organized force and no casual groups of bandits. I was thinking also of the railway town of Chinchow we had just left, newly laid out and built to a sweeping master plan, and now destroyed by perhaps 30 percent. Some of the state buildings were burned out from inside, and others crumpled and sagged as if a land mine had exploded from inside. China was occupied first by Russians and later for a short period by Chinese Communists. . . .

Mukden was mile after mile of skeletons and emptiness, shells of buildings, frameworks of factories, in which great holes had been gouged to permit the exit of machinery. Mukden in its heyday, when the Russians entered, might have compared favorably with Gary, Indiana; or perhaps Cincinnati. It represented 40 percent of the industry of Manchuria, which in turn was 70 percent of all industry in China. It produced or handled 4 million tons of steel and iron annually, as well as $3\frac{1}{2}$ million tons of synthetic petroleum, handled 15 million tons of coal from the nearby Fushun mines, manufactured 100 planes a month, had automobile plants, textile and rubber and aluminum mills, breweries, and the largest tobacco factories in Asia. In its giant warehouses, the Japanese said, 2 million tons of grain had been stored. Now Mukden looked as if a horde of steel- and concrete-eating termites had passed through.

Nearly all of industrial Manchuria, with the exception of Dairen, had been built from the ground up during the fourteen years of Japanese occupation. Into Mukden the Imperial government and the Japanese monopolies poured billions of yen, building a series of model communities, each devoted to special industries, around the core of the old city.

Mukden had some 5,000 factories when the Russians entered, of which there were 900 plants employing more than 200 workers. Now, the Chinese in our party estimated, two thirds of the smaller industrial plants had been stripped clean, and 90 percent of the larger ones were damaged or completely destroyed. Most of the big factories were, of course, exclusively Japanese. Some of the smaller firms making consumer goods were financed by Chinese capital.[6]

In the early stage of the civil war, Chinese public opinion—to the extent that it existed—regarded Chiang Kai-shek as the rightful leader of China, and generally expected him to remain at the helm of affairs. Chiang's popularity, however, was no longer comparable to that which he enjoyed on the eve of the Sino-Japanese war. He had promised much, but done little to improve the condition of China's teeming masses.

During the years 1945 and 1946, disgruntlement with and sometimes open opposition to Chiang's autocratic regime increased sharply throughout the country. Lack of freedom, police brutalities, heavy taxes, harsh recruiting drives, unfulfilled promises of political and social reform, corruption and inefficiency of the Kuomintang bureaucracy had been long-standing complaints. To these were now added the grumblings and indignation resulting from unchecked inflation, growing economic chaos and plain hunger.

One of the most outspoken and bitter opponents of the Kuomintang methods was Chiang's own sister-in-law, Madame Sun Yat-sen,* widow of the "Father of the country". A British war correspondent, Stuart Gelder, was curious to know how she felt about the Kuomintang's claim to be the sole trustee of Dr. Sun's wishes and guardian of his principles:

Early in 1944 I went to her Chungking home and asked Madame Sun Yat-sen whether she considered Chiang Kai-shek, her sister's husband, was governing according to those wishes. I think if this cultured and most courageous lady had been given to such habits she would have spat on her carpet as she replied. I knew that she was a critic of Kuomintang Party policy and that she had protested vigorously against the blockade of the Communist armies and denial of supplies to them. I had not realized the bitterness of her attitude to her brother-in-law. "He has not even attempted to put one of my husband's principles into operation for twenty-four hours," she said.

* Who subsequently became a Vice-President in Red China.

She spoke in contemptuous terms of the inefficiency of Government services and the corruption with which they were riddled.

"You will discover this for yourself, and then when you write it they will accuse you of being a Communist," she continued.* "They even call me a Communist, so there is no length to which they will not go to prove that anyone opposed to them is not what they call a 'red bandit'."

She went on to this effect:

There is only one hope for China, and that is a coalition government of all parties on a democratic basis. This is not a government. It is a dictatorial tyranny which makes the war an excuse for its repressions. But do not imagine that all members of the Kuomintang are responsible for it. That is not so. All members are not reactionaries, but all reactionaries are members. Some of them feel they may be an influence for good by remaining inside. The outside world must know that there are many Chinese in Kuomintang China who are truly Liberal and Progressive, but have no voice in affairs. We cannot say so, because we are not allowed. I am not allowed to leave Chungking without permission, and they will not allow me to leave China to tell the truth in America and England. Therefore it is important that you should do it. There is a great danger that when the truth does become known, the world will hold the Chinese people responsible for the actions of this Government. But they are not, because they have no voice. There is no freedom here, and some of those in power are no better than gangsters. But we must go on fighting for the truth to be known because this may force them out of power. . . .

I asked Madame Sun if she had expressed these opinions to Chiang Kai-shek. She answered:

"Yes, I have, whenever I have met him, but he doesn't like it, and so he doesn't speak with me any more. I suppose he has given me up as a red bandit, and that's the end of it. I have never hidden my views —that is why I no longer take part in Kuomintang Party affairs, because I will not allow my name to be identified with their actions."[7]

Opinions regarding the duration of the civil war were almost unanimous in insisting that it would not last very long. The disproportion of forces was striking indeed, and seemed to justify such predictions. Chiang Kai-shek had immense military advantages over his foes. He had more manpower, greater

* Government censors later did accuse him of being a Communist.

*firepower, more money and much better means of transportation; he held all the big cities, the most powerful arsenals, and the country's richest provinces, and controlled almost the entire seacoast, giving him access to foreign trade Still more, he was recognized by foreign powers, including the Soviet Union, as head of the legitimate government of China. His largely American-trained war machine, in short, appeared all but irresistible, and it was little wonder that top-ranking Kuomintang generals announced victory within three months.**

The Communists, on the other hand, were more or less isolated in one of the poorer sections of China. They had no air force, few railways, no gunboats, no city of any size, and their industry and trade were primitive compared to those of the enemy. They were generally looked upon as rebels by the outside world, and they were almost the only people who believed that victory would be theirs.

Military operations opened very auspiciously for the Kuomintang, whose forces cleared most Communist-dominated areas with great ease and drove the vaunted troops of the Eighth Route Army north of the Yellow River. Within months, however, the Nationalists found themselves in much the same situation as the Japanese before them: the Reds refused to give battle and, repeating their fire-tested infiltration tactics, maintained and expanded their guerrilla bases all over the countryside between the Yellow River and the Yangtze, in the rear of Chiang's armies.

Once more, the Reds found many ready allies among the Chinese peasantry, and began by making capital of the latter's "antitraitor" drive after the departure of the Japanese troops. Typical instances of this patriotic surge were quoted by the American reporter Jack Belden:†

Though fertilized by ideas and methods of struggle jumping over from Communist areas, this uprising was more or less spontaneous. It had few political aims. The peasants did not think of taking power in the villages. They did not even think of overthrowing the landlord system. All they thought to do was to settle with their traitors who, it just so happened, were most often big landlords.

* An American businessman in Shanghai was even more optimistic. "The Commies don't have a chance," he wrote. "The war will be over in a few weeks." Foreign military observers generally believed that Chiang would not be able to eliminate the Communists altogether, but that he would rapidly succeed in driving them back into the hills, after which he would once more hold most of the country under his sway.

† Who taught at the University of Peking (1938) and during the Sino-Japanese war became a correspondent for several leading American and British papers.

Not only the tenants and the rural workers, but the rich peasants and even small landlords joined the antitraitor movement. But it was the poor peasant's need for relief that gave the movement its eventual characteristic of a demand for land. The tenants, especially, were nursing bottomless reservoirs of bitterness against the landlords. Not only their grain had been uncovered by the landlords and turned over to the Japanese, but even their seed. Pots, pans, even metal farm tools had been taken to meet the Japanese levies, but half the levy had gone into the landlords' storerooms. "Dog legs"* had come into their homes and taken the very cotton out of their quilts to meet fictitious Japanese demands. A peasant in Honan tells how a puppet commander, a landlord's bailiff, threw him in jail and would not let him out until he had given him his daughter.† The wife of a middle farmer tells how a landlord forcibly took ten mow of her husband's land and then shot him and threw him in a coal pit outside of town so that no one would be left to take revenge. One hundred and forty peasants tell how a landlord in western Shantung made them roll stones up the side of a mountain for the Japanese while his dog legs walked behind with clubs, and how their legs, arms and backs were broken in the labor.

The war had made the poor even poorer. The lack of land and hunger made the neighboring landlords' opulence and luxury especially intolerable. The more destitute of the villagers moved into the front of the ranks of the fight. It was they who organized Settlement Meetings and thus gave to the Communists another form of struggle. As impromptu wartime trials got under way in many villages, the peasants' pent-up anger suddenly burst forth in a violent demand for the lands and goods of the traitors in settlement for their suffering. Everything must be paid back, not one robbed cent must be kept. On a cool October morning, the peasants of the village of Likwantun in western Shantung, going from door to door, armed with clubs and pitchforks, called out everybody, small and great, to a meeting against the landlord Maosunpang. "On February 3, you robbed me of three hundred dollars," says one angry peasant. "At that time we had no power. We dared not speak. Your bad behavior is known by everybody.

* A stooge. Common peasant term for a landlord's agent (author's note).

† In China's traditionally agricultural society, the landlord was a powerful and inevitable figure. The abuse of peasants' wives by landlords was a common evil, against which the husbands could do little or nothing.

You helped the Japanese rob us of cotton. Now you must pay it back." The crowd shouts: "You must pay! You must pay!" Another tenant struggles up to the front of the meeting. "You killed several members of my family. We are starving. You must give back what you robbed from us." To meet his debt, the landlord has to sell his grove of a hundred oak trees, his furniture, ninety acres of land and seven of his eight houses. The poor leave the landlord only five acres of land and one house.

That particular traitor was lucky. The people at least left him his head. Such was not the case everywhere. In the mountainous part of Shansi that had been occupied by the Japanese, the people settled with their landlords in a particularly violent way. In these mountains, and the adjoining plains where the 8th Route Army had not penetrated during the war, the relics of serfdom had deep roots; the landlords' hold on the land was particularly parasitic; and the poverty of the village most nakedly revealed. Bursting out after the retreat of the Japanese, the movement immediately became adorned with acts of terror—the more barbarous because the people were more backward.

In a certain district of Tzehisen County in Shansi, three landlord brothers, who had been responsible for the deaths of eighteen farmers during the war, were hauled before a Speak Bitterness Meeting, during which the passions of the crowd mounted to such heights that cadres who had come to watch the meeting were brushed aside and the landlords strung up to trees. In the Taihang Mountains, the village of Toumachuang seized a dog leg and beat him to death with stones. In another nearby village, peasants took a landlord who had been a puppet commander of the Japanese, hitched him up to a plow, cracked a whip across his back and drove him around the fields. "You treated us like beasts," shouted the peasants, "and now you can be our animal."[8]

Tyrannical husbands and despotic fathers-in-law similarly came to feel the vengeful wrath of former "slaves", the maltreated wives, in the Communist-dominated area. The emancipation of women, which was begun in the Soviet Republic of Shensi, was promoted the more actively by the Reds as women played an increasingly significant role both at the front and in the rear.*

* Particularly as nurses, spies, theatrical performers, organizers and agents of various kinds.

"Women's Associations" sprang up all over the Red-held territories and energetically undertook to free the Chinese woman from the bonds that all too often made her a virtual slave within the essential and strongest social unit of old China, the family.

The following incident, which took place in a small village of Hopei Province and was described by Jack Belden, illustrates the rebellion of a young woman in the Red society. Before the local Women's Association headed by Dark Jade, Gold Flower watched her Red sisters administer a severe correction to her brutal husband, Chang:

Fifteen women started for Gold Flower's home, led by Dark Jade. Gold Flower's husband met them in the courtyard. "Why are you here, comrades cadres?" he asked. His tone was polite.

"This is a new society," Dark Jade greeted him abruptly and without any preliminaries. "You must tell the truth of how you have treated our sister. If you do not, you may taste our fists."

Chang smiled. His face and manner were courteous and serene. "Has my wife said something about me?" he asked. What he said was perfectly smooth and friendly, but Gold Flower could see his eyes flickering with animosity.

"It is true, your wife has spoken of you," said Dark Jade. "But your evil doings have also been uncovered by our special investigators. The past was the day of man. But now we have our day given us by Comrade Mao and the Communist party. Speak out or we will bind you up."

A slow color rose in Chang's cheeks. He stood there with his lips tight and eyes black with contempt. "Do what you like," he shrugged. "I don't care. What can a Women's Association do?"

Dark Jade turned to the other women. "Get a rope," she said.

The women stirred. One of them brought a grass rope. She moved to bind up Chang. He drew back. "Get away!" he said. Dark Jade and another girl rushed at him and slapped his face.

Dark Jade's voice had a hard edge. "If you dare move, we shall beat you to death on the spot."

Gold Flower's husband stiffened in surprise. Swiftly the women bound him. Jerking him with unnecessary roughness, they pulled him down the street and then threw him in a room of the Women's Association. Dark Jade slammed and bolted the door.

"Let him starve there for three days, the pig!" she said.

The next day the women gathered in a solemn conclave in the meeting hall.

"Our comrade, Gold Flower, still suffers the evil treatment of her husband," said Dark Jade. "Comrade Gold Flower's personal affairs should be taken as the affairs of all of us. Alone, she cannot fight. But with us she can fight all bad husbands. Now, are you ready to struggle?"

"Ready," answered the crowd.

"All right," said Dark Jade, "we shall first try to treat this bad husband by reasoning with him.* If this does not succeed, we shall no longer be polite."

The women drew up in ranks like soldiers. Gold Flower went to a nearby room. As her husband was led in, various shouts burst from the crowd.

"We have turned over. . . . You cannot treat us badly or we will beat you to death. . . . Tell us the truth. . . . No arguments. . . . If you are frank, you will be treated better; if not, there will be no mercy."

Chang stood before the women listening to their unfriendly greetings with a strained air. "Comrade sisters," he said, "there has been some mistake. Do you know why I married that woman? It was so she could serve us and so she could keep alive. Do you know how badly she has treated our family?"

He looked about with an air of injured innocence.

"All right," said a girl, "tell us what she did to your family."

Chang looked from one face to another, and they were all closed against him. He dropped his eyes in embarrassment. "I am not acquainted with women turning over."

A hiss went up from the crowd.

"Resolutely oppose that bad husband," shouted a girl.

Amid all the shouting, a cadre said: "Now is the time to bring on Gold Flower."

Gold Flower brushed her way through the women until she stood face to face with her husband.

"Do you know why we have brought you here?" Her voice was harsh. "Do you recall how you said you would beat me to death? Well, know that all these women are ready to beat you to death. Now I have nothing more to do with you. I leave all my problems with my sisters to settle."

* "Let us be reasonable" (or "talk reasonably") is a traditional Chinese way of trying to prevent disputes from taking a violent turn.

A voice said: "Are you ready to bow to women?"

Chang bowed low. "I bend my head," he said.

"Your bending head is artificial," said Gold Flower. "Therefore you must take an oath and make a resolution."

Chang was silent.

"What are you thinking?" several women shouted at once.

Chang said nothing.

"Well, what shall we do?" Dark Jade asked the crowd.

"Nothing. Just beat him," said a woman. "Hit him, hit him," shrieked another voice.

As if by a signal, all the women pushed forward at once. Gold Flower quickly went in back of her husband. The crowd fell on him, howling, knocked him to the ground, then jumped on him with their feet. Several women fell with him, their hands thrashing wildly. Those in the rear leaped in, tore at his clothing, then seized his bare flesh in their hands and began twisting and squeezing till his blood flowed from many scratches. Those who could not get close, dove under the rest and seized Chang's legs, sinking their teeth in his flesh.

Chang let out an anguished howl. "Don't beat me! Don't beat me," he bleated in terror. "I'll reform. Don't hurt me any more."

Under the blows of the women, his cries were soon stilled. The women backed off. Gold Flower peered down at her husband. He lay there motionless on the ground, like a dead dog, his mouth full of mud, his clothes in tatters and blood coming in a slow trickle from his nose. "That's how it was with me in the past," Gold Flower thought. Unable to restrain a feeling of happiness, she turned to the other women. "Many thanks, comrade sisters, for your kindness. If it had not been for you, I would not have been able to get my revenge."9

Chang was a tough character and, what was more, a "reactionary". Not only did he refuse to reform and "bow to women", but he subsequently told his wife that if he were younger, he would join the Nationalist Army, take another wife and dismiss Gold Flower. In the course of the heated argument which followed his remarks, Chang tried to beat up his wife, but she succeeded in escaping his fury and, naturally, ran as fast as she could toward the Women's Association Building:

Finding the chairwoman, she yelled at her: "My husband is not yet reformed."

The chairwoman went up to the roof of her house and called

through a megaphone. "Comrade women! Come at once! Something of importance!"

Out from nearly every clay hut in the village tumbled a woman. Rushing toward the Women's Association Building, they heard the chairwoman explain: "Gold Flower's husband is bad again! Get ropes and catch him!"

With Gold Flower in the lead, forty howling women ran through the village. But her husband had already fled. The women chased him for three miles through the fields, but in the dark he escaped. Disconsolately Gold Flower returned home. She thanked everyone for helping her.

"Do not be afraid," several women told her. "Someday we shall catch your husband and bite him to death."

The next day Gold Flower reported her husband's flight to the district magistrate. He told her that the government would be responsible for her safety. Then he said: "Comrade Gold Flower, your husband is only one person. You must think of society as a whole. You must go back to your village and unite the women as a piece of iron."

Gold Flower took his words seriously. She had made up her mind that the old society would never come back again. She, personally, would not let it. Shortly afterward, she called the village women together and made a speech.

"Comrade sisters," she said, "we have been released by the Communist party and the 8th Route Army. This is our day! We must produce grain for the armies to fight Chiang Kai-shek and the Nationalist troops. We must oppose America which is helping Chiang to fight the Liberated Areas."

Then she clenched her fist and shouted slogans she had been taught: "Oppose America! Oppose Chiang Kai-shek! Oppose those fighting the Liberated Areas! Go home and make your husbands participate in the 8th Route Army!"[10]

While in northern China the Reds instituted their new, classless society with varying degrees of success and shook their fists at greedy landlords and recalcitrant husbands, the southern Chinese provinces were ravaged by famine and cholera.

An American journalist, George Moorad, visited the stricken areas:

Kwantung province was ravaged by drought. Under the scorching heat even the hardy bamboo was flowering for the first time in sixty years, and the rice paddies were baked into concrete. Added to famine, the worst cholera epidemic since 1932 had struck, finding Southern China utterly unprepared. Since only two hospitals in Canton were operating—more than one year after war had ended—it was impossible to faintly measure the true number of cholera deaths, but in ten days the two had admitted a hundred . . . cholera sufferers, of whom forty-three had died. Another partial estimate came from the number of abandoned bodies in the Canton streets. In January and February [1947], the abandoned bodies averaged between five and six hundred per month, but when cholera struck, the numbers rose above one thousand monthly. In a brief walk down the Bund one early morning, I counted twenty-three, but a Chinese reporter said I hadn't walked far enough. He had counted ninety bodies the previous morning.

A handful of people, Dr. Frank Herrington of UNRRA,* Ronald Hall, the British Consul, and a skeleton group of Chinese doctors and officers worked against hopeless odds. The National government had allotted only $2,000 to cope with the annual problem of summer diseases, and even this amount was unpaid. Canton had exactly ten syringes, forty-eight needles, and fifteen medical personnel to give inoculations to a population of two millions. There was a famine of vaccines and serums. On nearby Hainan Island, the Japanese had developed an institute for tropical diseases with a laboratory capable of supplying vaccines for all Southeast Asia, but upon the surrender, Chinese forces uprooted the laboratory equipment, imprisoned the Japanese technicians, and turned the precious installations into a concentration camp. American and British authorities had provided some serums from their own supplies, but when the call went to Shanghai for syringes and needles, profiteers quickly cornered the market and held out for fancy prices. Finally the British offered to send some Royal Air Force planes from Hong Kong to spray Canton with DDT, but Kwantung's anti-foreign General Wa-kwei argued that President Chiang Kai-shek was expected to visit the city and would be highly offended by seeing British planes overhead. Chiang canceled his visit to the pestilent city, and British planes were eventually allowed to perform their mission of mercy.[11]

* United Nations Relief and Rehabilitation Administration: much of its aid to China (food and medicines, mainly) went into the black market, and 98 percent of the supplies went to Nationalist areas (details in J. Belden, *China Shakes the World*).

In typical Chinese fashion, the civil war was fought simultaneously in the field and around the conference table. American diplomacy, in particular, was actively (though unsuccessfully) involved in arbitration efforts. After a year of fruitless endeavor, Ambassador Hurley resigned his post in November 1945, whereupon President Truman appointed General George C. Marshall —whom the Chinese knew and respected—as his personal envoy to China.

General Marshall's task was both complex and delicate. It was aptly summed up by two American journalists who were well acquainted with the situation facing him:

The unexampled complexity of Marshall's task stemmed partly from the nature of America's blundering role in the postwar Pacific, partly from the nature of Chinese politics. Marshall's first task was to re-

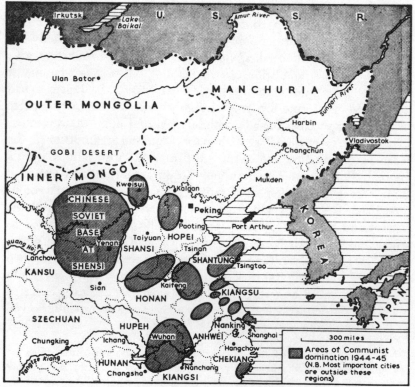

AREAS OF COMMUNIST DOMINATION, 1944–45

establish the integrity of American diplomacy and secure acceptance for himself as high judge in a dispute already mottled with ineradicable malevolence. But he had to project this concept of American state-craft across a situation where, militarily, America stood unclean as partisan in the very dispute he was judging. His predecessor had left him as legacy a policy of armed American intervention and a commit-ment of support to the Kuomintang* which he could not dishonor although this policy cut directly across the diplomacy of peace he was trying to make effective. His second task was to bring together at a single council table a vigorous, dynamic, cocksure Communist Party† and a decadent, unprincipled, corrupt governing party and persuade the two to discuss once more a subject they had been discus-sing for eight years without the slightest approach to solution. . . .

By January [1946], Marshall had succeeded in drawing together both parties in two simultaneous accords: one political, the other military. A Political Consultation Conference, called together at Marshall's urging and including Kuomintang, Communists, members of the Democratic League, and nonpartisans, agreed on a program for the abolition of the Kuomintang dictatorship and the establishment of a multi-party interim government to prepare the nation for a stable postwar regime. Militarily, the Communists and government agreed to a general cease-fire order throughout the land and the incorporation of Communist units in a one-to-five ratio in a new national army.

The agreements were no sooner confirmed than both parties set out to strain at the rules and see how much pressure they would bear. The Kuomintang Central Executive Committee met in March at a session where the new reactionary majority ran a steamroller over the moderates who wished to abide by the accord.‡ . . . The Com-munists . . . countered the Kuomintang's rupture of the Chungking accord by an all-out storm assault on the Manchurian railways which was capped by their seizure of the Manchurian capital, Changchun, and their occupation of the entire railway system from Changchun north to the Russian border.

* Because the United States held that North China, the homeland of the Communists, was a legal vacuum in 1945, and the only legitimate entity qualified to fill it was Chiang.

† Which controlled nearly one-third of China at the time.

‡ Clinging to the old principle that the Kuomintang alone had the right to guide the destinies of China, the reactionaries repudiated the principle of parlia-mentary government, and cut Communist and minority participation.

Marshall, who had flown to America in triumph after his first truce, returned in late April to find his work undone. The prestige of the Kuomintang had been shattered by the Communist victories in Manchuria; Chiang was adamant on the point that before conversations could begin a second time he must re-establish his power at Changchun either by force of arms or by Communist submission. The Communists, more confident than ever, were now convinced that America was in active league with the Kuomintang. Despite Marshall's personal integrity, American ships continued to move government troops north to the battle zone of Manchuria; American experts and technicians arrived at Shanghai with every boat from the Pacific to strengthen the government's administration; American relief supplies, wretchedly maladministered by the government, created wealth for profiteers at the coast, while peasants starved in Communist territory.

Again, Marshall brought his personal prestige to bear. The Communists evacuated Changchun and the government armies entered almost without bloodshed. Chiang flew north immediately to inspect his victorious troops and the Kuomintang press burst into paeans of enthusiasm for the all-out mopping-up drive they felt sure would follow. Kuomintang armies pressed on for several days toward the Sungari River and Harbin. Then, having satisfied his prestige and vanity, Chiang returned, permitted a truce to begin, and negotiations resumed. The armies in the north waited on decision at the capital, gathering strength for whatever future task might be given them.[12]

The second truce, like the first, was short-lived. Both sides were now determined to force a decision in the field, and both were confident of victory. During the summer months of 1946, the Kuomintang censorship and police stepped up their campaign of intimidation and terrorism against all those who dared oppose the Chungking government.* Between Tientsin and Peking, on the other hand, trigger-happy Red guerrillas began ambushing American marines, while the Communists unloosed a barrage of anti-American propaganda.

Thus the mission of General Marshall had failed, too. In the report which he submitted to the White House, the General stressed that bitter mutual suspicion and the prevailing role of extremists on both sides were not only

---

* Scores of newspapers and magazines were suspended; liberals were silenced by fear, jailed, or killed; "thinkers" were registered by police, and in Shanghai were given identification cards of varied colors.

responsible for the failure of negotiations, but made a peaceful settlement of the Kuomintang–Kungch'antang struggle all but impossible.

The conflict now burst wide open. In June 1946, the Nationalist armies launched a massive offensive (involving nearly one million men) against the Communist bases of the great northern Chinese plain, and soon succeeded in surrounding and seriously compressing most of them.

In the reconquered areas, however, the Kuomintang troops adopted a wanton policy of repression which at once antagonized the population and— inevitably—made Communism appear more desirable by comparison. The American reporter Jack Belden visited historic Anyang County,* in northern Honan, in the spring of 1947:

It is a curious and important fact that when the civil war started and the 8th Route Army retreated and gave up nearly all the county to the Kuomintang, almost none of the people went with the Communists, but remained behind to welcome the Kuomintang. Not only did the majority of the farmers remain at home, but also many local cadres, the militiamen and the heads of the women's associations. From what the people in Anyang told me, they did not flee from the Kuomintang because they believed that the reforms the 8th Route Army introduced were merely the reforms that any Chinese government, taking over from the Japanese, would bring.† Not wishing to be involved in any further war, they stayed at home.

But when the Kuomintang armies entered the villages, very often there entered with them the former bandits and landlords who had been puppets and sometimes robbers under the Japanese. These men soon became district heads while their bailiffs became village chiefs. Immediately they began a "countersettlement" against the people of their own villages. They either did this directly or "put the finger" on certain men and women who were dealt with summarily by the army or the Special Service Section of the Kuomintang. It was this counter-settlement that had fanned into being a people's war that was now raging with undiminished violence throughout the whole country.

The landlords were cruelly subtle. On taking over villages from the

---

* Anyang was the seat of an imperial court some 3,000 years ago, and in the course of China's many civil wars, the nearby Chang River (separating Honan from Hopei) had blocked the advance of troops coming from the south.

† In particular, it had recently begun to teach the villagers how to vote, a thing they had never done before.

Reds, either they or the Kuomintang officers would call a public meeting and declare a general amnesty.

"The Communist policy about the land here was very good," the Kuomintang would say. "We don't want to change anything. We can forgive everyone but the village chief, the head of the militia and the chief of the Communist Party in this village. Nobody has anything to fear from us. However, some of you have been led astray by Communist propaganda. If you will just come to the village office and sign a repentance slip, everything will be all right."

And the peasants came. Not knowing any better, they went to the village office and admitted they had joined the women's association or the militia. Seeing nothing wrong in such actions, the gullible peasants fell into a trap. Wives persuaded their husbands to come back from hiding places in the hills. Then, when it seemed as if all the active peasants were once more in the folds of the village, the Kuomintang rounded up all the self-repenters and publicly executed them.

More brutal than the Kuomintang were the landlords. Very often they buried alive men who had engaged in the struggle for reduction of rents. If they could not find these men, they buried their families. And sometimes they threw living women and children who had no connection at all with the Communists into ditches, pits and wells and covered them with earth.

According to the Anyang County government, up to the time of my arrival, four hundred men, women and children had been killed and buried alive in the 423 villages that had fallen into Kuomintang hands.

I have no way of checking these figures, but I have every reason to believe they are not exaggerated. In one village, while I was there, twenty-four bodies, including women and children, were exhumed from a common pit where they had been buried alive and then been partially uncovered and eaten by dogs. In wandering from village to village, I came across numerous people whose relatives had been buried alive.

The worst case of this kind that I saw was in Chintekou, a village of 130 people, on the edge of no man's land. Here, out of twenty-eight families, members from each of twenty-four families had been buried alive or shot by a landlord bandit, named Li Chin-tsang.

When the Japanese evacuated the mountains, Li and the other land-lords went with them. The people then got together and divided Li's land. When the Kuomintang returned to the region, Li came back with fifteen armed men. Just before his arrival, all the men in the village fled away.

Seeing the remaining women and children were frightened, Li tried to calm them. "Don't be afraid," he said, "we are all from the same family." Late that night, however, when the village was asleep, Li and his men went around to all but four houses in the village and took the people out. Ten people he threw down a dry well and buried alive. Fourteen others he forced to lie down in a ditch, then he covered them with earth. Among those buried were a two-month-old baby, a boy of ten and a woman of eighty.[13]

Following their early victories in the plains of northern China, the Nationalist armies carried the war into the very valleys, hills and plateaus of the Communist stronghold, the "Autonomous Border Area".* Yenan fell in March 1947, and for a moment it seemed as though the capture of the Red capital symbolized the collapse of Soviet China.

At the end of June 1947, however, the Communists began the counter-offensive that was to sweep the Nationalists out of continental China within less than two years. Chiang Kai-shek did not believe that the Reds could launch an offensive, nor did his American advisers. During his all-out drive against the Autonomous Border Area, Chiang had denuded his center in Honan, and it was through that province that the Communists advanced toward the Yangtze valley, stronghold of the Nationalists.

The Communist counterdrive had for several months been prepared and concealed by incessant night raids carried on by Red militiamen and guerrillas, with the result that Kuomintang units found themselves isolated both physically and morally. Jack Belden witnessed the Communist infiltration of Honan:

Since they could not fall upon the larger garrisons Chiang maintained at the front, their only recourse was to operate in his rear, to pick off an isolated outpost one night, to disperse a Home Returning Corps on another night and to free a village on a third night. . . .

As soon as they saw that militiamen were operating behind their lines at night, the soldiers of Chiang, who had little belief in the war, took to their pillboxes and would not come out. Thus, further raids became easier. At the same time, various landlords afraid to sleep in

* Extending along the border of Inner Mongolia, and centering around northern Shensi.

local Home Returning Corps barracks, began to collect in a central location for safety. That left further villages free. Then poor tenants realizing they had allies just across the way began to stand up to the landlords who were scared to be too severe.

Now, on my arrival in Anyang, the raids were spreading ever deeper and wider into Kuomintang territory. Every night small groups of three, five, ten and fifteen men were going behind the lines to gather information, to do propaganda work, to fight with the Home Returning Corps and with stray Kuomintang soldiers.

Very often the militiamen who led the raids were refugees from Chiang's areas. Sometimes they went on the raids to get revenge for relatives who had been killed. Most often, however, the raids were intimately connected with the land reform. Their purpose was to protect the results of the land division, to force the landlords to return what they had taken from the people and generally to encourage the poor. Such operations went under the sinister-sounding name of Counter-Counter Settlement. Although there was often much shooting, the raids did not seem to me to be essentially military. Rather did this kind of warfare seem to be a political and a social combat carried on by armed means. The targets of the raids were not so often strong-points or even lines of communications, as they were social institutions, government organs and private individuals. Thus, raiding militiamen would free a girl who had been forced into marriage, depose a hated village chief or kidnap a landlord. In brief, this war aimed at people's emotions and sought to conquer hearts and not territories.

I do not mean that propaganda replaced combat, but rather that the guerrilla war was carried on in an entirely different emotional environment than regular war. An example of this is furnished by the way the guerrillas and the militiamen gathered intelligence. Militiamen, crossing the lines at night, would climb over a house wall, knock on a woman's door and ask: "How are you being treated? How much have you been taxed? What are you getting to eat?" Farmers sneaking over for a day or so to the 8th Route Army side would bring not so much information about Kuomintang dispositions as they would bring the names of peasants who had been conscripted for labor, of women who were being beaten or of children who had lost their fathers.

Time after time I have sat in various villages in no man's land and seen farmers come up to guerrillas and give them information that any regular army officer would have scorned. But such information was extremely useful in this type of warfare. The local guerrillas in learning who was suffering would also learn the name of someone who would probably help them. On the other hand all this information was sent back to the rear where it was collated so that the 8th Route Army could make an effective political and social policy.

While uncovering the suffering of the villagers, the militiamen also uncovered the names of landlords, dog legs and bandits who were treating the people badly. If a landlord took things from the people, the militiamen would send him a letter warning him to return what he had taken. If he did not, they would send him a more peremptory note. If nothing happened, they very often kidnapped him and brought him across the lines in the night.

During a two-month period in Anyang, eighty landlords and members of the Home Returning Corps were brought across the lines in this way. Generally, the subdistrict commissar or the district government head would give them a lecture and then let them go. I don't exactly approve of kidnapping, yet I was sometimes amazed by the patience and forbearance county officials showed toward landlords who had carried arms and fought them.

The operations of militiamen in Kuomintang territory often had a Robin Hood character about them. Since the militiamen were poor men themselves, whenever they found a man or woman in distress they would try to help them out. Undoubtedly the roving farmers in redressing wrongs often committed brutal deeds and to many men they must have appeared as nothing but barbaric murderers. But I have very good reason to know that many poor peasants in Chiang Kai-shek's areas looked on these men who came to them in the night as virtuous outlaws and sometimes as shining Sir Galahads.[14]

Thus, little by little, the Communists were winning the fight for the hearts of the peasants, on which, as Mao Tse-tung had stated, depended final victory or defeat. As a result of the increasingly mobile warfare which the Reds imposed upon the Kuomintang forces,* the "front line" as such slowly disintegrated—as did the morale of Chiang Kai-shek's troops. Red troops reached the Yangtze River in September 1947, and began amalgamating

* In accordance with Mao's well-known formula: "When the enemy advances we retreat, when the enemy escapes we harass, when he retreats we pursue, and when he gets tired we attack."

into ever larger units which were soon to engage in broad-scale mobile maneuvers against Chiang.

As the year 1947 drew to a close, the Red tide had engulfed much of northern and central China, and forced the Kuomintang into the defensive. In a speech delivered on Christmas Day, Mao Tse-tung proudly described the current offensive as "a turning point in history. It signals the end of the counter-revolutionary role of Chiang Kai-shek and the end of more than a hundred years of rule of imperialism in China." At the same time, he outlined the Communist tactics for the year 1948:

1. First strike isolated enemies; later strike concentrated enemies.
2. First take small towns, later cities.
3. Destruction of the enemy's forces and not the capture of cities is the most important objective.
4. In every battle concentrate absolutely superior forces: double, quadruple and sometimes even five or six times those of the enemy.
5. Fight only when there is assurance of victory.
6. Fight several engagements in succession without respite.
7. Destroy the enemy while in movement.
8. Wrest all weakly defended cities from the enemy. Wait until conditions mature and then capture powerfully defended cities.
9. Replenish ourselves by the capture of all enemy arms and most of his personnel. Sources of the men and matériel for our army are mainly at the front.
10. Utilize intervals between campaigns in resting, grouping and training troops, but don't let intervals be long or allow the enemy a breathing spell.[15]

The decisive battles of the civil war were fought in the year 1948, and the Communists won almost all of them. Throughout that year, superior morale was a decisive factor in the chain of victories achieved by the Reds. With few exceptions, the Red troops were well-clad, well-fed and well-led. Discipline was strict, but not brutal, and the relationship between soldiers and officers was marked by mutual trust and esteem. More important still, the Communist forces knew why they were fighting; they had faith in themselves, in their leadership, and in the justice of their cause. Finally, the popular support behind them grew with each passing month.

All too often, and increasingly so as the war expanded across the country, the opposite (or almost) was true of the Kuomintang armies, whose early confidence in a smashing victory was all but shattered in the later part of 1947. The following severe picture of Chiang Kai-shek's army was drawn by Jack Belden:

It is no accident that neither the Japanese war nor the civil war produced a single distinguished name among Chiang's officers. Chiang, himself, as commander in chief, was noteworthy only for his stubbornness, his shrill fits of temper and his military errors, as numerous as they were catastrophic. General Ho Ying-chin* achieved his high position through intrigue and attention to administrative detail. General Chen Cheng, chief of staff and a half-pint counterpart of the generalissimo, lost nearly every battle he directed in the Japanese and the civil wars. General Li Tsung-jen,† more democratic than most, was hamstrung by the generalissimo's distrust of him. . . .

The whole Chinese army, from top to bottom, was riven with inhumanity, double-crossing and terror. Officers without influence were always in danger of execution for some minor error in the performance of duty. Ask some of the American officers who were in Burma how Chinese regiment commanders came crawling to them on hands and knees begging that no reports be made about their military mistakes because they would be sent back to China and shot. . . . Every army headquarters was a nest of spies. The party secret service, the Bureau of Investigation and Statistics, and the Special Service Section surrounded even war zone commanders with a web of intrigue and jealousy, terrorizing the staff one by one until they had isolated the commander. Staff officers were seized from army headquarters by the SSS without the army commander being able to do anything about it. . . .

The attitude of the officer toward the soldier was that of landlord toward peasant—that is, the officer, while sometimes paternal, thought the men under him were ignorant villeins who had few human rights. This relationship dominated in the army. It was, however, much more sharply defined in the army than in the villages, and the soldier was undeniably the lowest scum in Chinese society. "You do not make good iron into a nail; you do not make a good man into a soldier." Such was the national tradition of the old Chinese army. This tradition

* Former Minister of War, acting commander in chief in the field, and an old-time Kuomintang veteran.

† Vice-President of the Kuomintang.

still applied to the army of Chiang Kai-shek because the abortive 1927 Revolution did not change Chinese society as a whole and hence did not change the army.

The fear with which the people looked on the army and the contempt in which the army held the soldier can readily be seen by the way in which the peasant was conscripted for service. The basis of all conscription was graft, bribery and influence. Sons of the rich never entered the army; sons of the poor could never escape. An impoverished widow's only son was always drafted; the numerous offspring of the landlord, never. Since the draftees were the poorest men, they were often the most unhealthy, and it was very common for one-half of the contingent of soldiers to die before they reached the front.

Officers considered it their privilege and right to beat soldiers.* During both the Japanese war and the civil war, I saw soldiers beaten on station platforms with bamboo rods, on highways with automobile crank handles, in rooms with iron bars. I once saw a colonel who had been a former consular official in New York City slap a soldier several times across the face because he couldn't find a pack of cards. When I protested, the colonel said: "That's all these dumb beasts understand."

There were some kindly officers who called their troops "my younger brothers" and who adopted a fatherly attitude to the men under them. But on the whole, the life of the ordinary soldier was but one cut above a pig and a cut below a mule. As a matter of fact, mules, on the whole, were better fed and better cared for than men. . . .

Such was the army of Chiang Kai-shek, based on agrarian gangsterism, semi-serfdom and "loyalty to the leader". Throughout the Japanese war and the civil war that followed, this army was continually beaten because it had no soul. Its commanding staff was distinguished by a scorn of the common soldier, by internal jealousy and fear of the secret service, by ignorance of its own trade, by an insidious self-loathing and by an uncontrollable habit of squeeze. The rank and file, submitting to corruption, tyranny and death, was characterized by a philosophy of despair, by a necessity to loot and by a hatred of their own officers and of the common people who pitied, but despised them. [16]

* Brutalities from higher to lower officers were not uncommon either. A captain who had been slapped and kicked in front of his soldiers by a colonel complained: "The American General Patton is criticized by the American Congress for slapping a soldier. But to what Congress can I turn for help?"

Chiang Kai-shek lost many of his best troops during the campaigns of 1946 and 1947, and, contrary to his Communist foes, was faced by an increasing shortage of manpower. A series of harsh recruiting drives, conducted in the autumn of 1947, failed to give satisfactory results.

Desertions, on the other hand, became ever more frequent, as whole regiments (and even divisions) went over to the Reds or surrendered without a fight.* And while the Red generals grew increasingly bold and confident, Chiang's commanders developed a "defense complex", or "wall psychology"† in the vain hope that they would eventually wear out the enemy. Many of the Kuomintang generals, in fact, no longer sure of victory, were covertly trying to halt the war because they believed that a solution agreeable to both parties could be achieved only by political means.

A Communist winter offensive isolated most Kuomintang garrisons in Manchuria, and on February 27, 1948, the columns of General Lin Piao reached the port of Yingkow, severing all of Manchuria from China. Henceforth, Chiang's northeastern front could be supplied from the air only.

General Barr, head of the Joint U. S. Military Advisory Group, vainly endeavored to convince Chiang that in order to avoid a major defeat in Manchuria, he should evacuate his untenable positions there and regroup his forces south of the Great Wall:

At the beginning of March, 1948, after the Communists had withdrawn their large forces stationed in the vicinity of Changchun and Mukden, following their winter offensive, I strongly urged the generalissimo to take advantage of the circumstances and gradually withdraw from Manchuria. This proposal stupefied him, and he declared that nothing could ever bring him to give serious consideration to such a project. Hoping to arrive at a compromise, I advanced the idea that the garrisons of Changchun, Chilin and Ssup'ing-chi might be withdrawn and brought back into Mukden. The generalissimo replied that political considerations prevented the withdrawal from Changchun, ancient capital of Manchuria, but that he was going to consider a plan to evacuate the garrison of Chilin and bring it to Changchun. The garrison of Chilin was subsequently withdrawn as agreed.

In the next talk with the generalissimo, and after he had again

---

* For example, in January 1947, the whole American-equipped 26th Division surrendered with its commander.

† They dug in behind lines of trenches, or remained behind fortifications and city walls, waiting for relief that almost never came.

expressed his determination not to consider the evacuation of Manchuria, I suggested the launching of an early offensive to open railroad communications between Chinchou and Mukden. The generalissimo agreed enthusiastically and instructed his staff to draw up a plan in cooperation with my assistants.

At a meeting which took place on March 8, 1948, in the War Room of the Ministry of National Defense, General Lo declared that a plan for the opening of a corridor leading to Mukden had been drawn up, and that the plan had been approved by the generalissimo. . . . On May 5, 1948, a combined attack starting from Mukden and Chinchou would be launched in order to open a passage along the railway linking these two cities. A broader strategic plan of operations was obviously lacking, and therefore I inquired about the existence of such a plan. I was told that the Chinese armies were in the process of executing a "Six-Month Plan", and that a "Two-Year Plan" had also been prepared, but that it had not yet been approved by the generalissimo.

A meeting took place on March 17, 1948, in the War Room of the Ministry of National Defense. When discussing the projected offensive that was to open the passage to Mukden, the Chinese declared that it would take six months to repair the railroad line linking Chinchou to Hsinmin.

To the question concerning the extent of the destruction which the Nationalists could achieve before evacuating Chilin, the Chinese replied in a vague manner. I made the remark that a large quantity of arms and ammunition used by the Communists represented Nationalist equipment that had fallen into their hands, and that the method by which such matériel went to the Communists resulted in a prolongation of the war. I insisted repeatedly on this point on later occasions also, but it was to no avail. The Chinese seemed by nature to be quite incapable of destroying any object of value.[17]

With the turning of the tide, the discipline and loyalty of Chiang Kai-shek's field commanders began to ebb away. Well-known officers either opposed their leader more or less overtly, or simply surrendered to the Reds without a fight.* The desire for peace at any cost spread among officers as it did among soldiers in the course of the year 1948.

The Communists were fully aware of the changing mood in enemy ranks,

* This was the case of the commander of the 94th Army, of the governor of Shentung Province, and of three division commanders in Shansi.

and stepped up their efforts at "revolutionary disintegration". In Manchuria, their propaganda campaign among trapped Kuomintang troops, described by Jack Belden, was particularly effective:

During the latter half of 1948, Kuomintang commanders in Manchuria drew back into the cities, with orders, it was said, to hold on until Dewey was elected President of the United States and America poured forth her might in aid of Chiang Kai-shek.* Some weeks before the presidential election, the 60th and the 7th Kuomintang armies retired on the city of Changchun with their heavy American equipment while a small force of the People's Liberation Army of General Lin Piao took up positions of siege around the city. Here the Communists had an extraordinary opportunity to apply their methods of disintegrating Chiang's army by revolutionary propaganda.

Every squad in Lin Piao's forces organized an "enemy work group". They discussed the misconceptions of the Kuomintang troops facing them. Then a program of propaganda was decided upon and a "shouting war" began.

"Brothers!" the voices called across no man's land. "Lay down your arms which you never wanted to take up. Did you join the Kuomintang army? No, you were dragged into it at the end of a rope. Come over to us. If you want, we will send you home. Better still, you can join us and fight to free your homes as we have ours."

A barrage of fire greeted these words. But the words themselves were a red-hot revolutionary medium, a high conductor of ideas, that the rifles could not still. Pretty soon, at scattered places along the front, the rifles ceased firing. At last a squad of seven men led by a soldier named Tang Kuo-hua crossed the lines. The Kuomintang commanders were frightened. They told their troops that the deserters had been disarmed by the Communists and buried alive. This lie was short-lived. For Squad Commander Tang, himself, soon called across the seventy-five yards separating the two forces, and begged his old comrades to follow him into the New China. From a handful, the number of desertions grew to a steady stream.

The Kuomintang tried countermeasures. It scoured Changchun for prostitutes and officers' wives and sent them into the front lines to sing obscene songs and invited the soldiers of the People's Liberation Army to cross over to them. "Brother," called back Lin Piao's soldiers,

* Belden insists that the Republican Party was definitely behind Chiang.

"how can your officers deceive us, when they can't even deceive you?"

Soon letters were exchanged between the opposing forces. One Kuomintang squad wrote saying its commander was sick and resting inside Changchun, but as soon as he came back, they would come over. Another wrote: "Thanks for the cakes, but we are southerners and would like rice. We also can't understand your dialect, find a southerner to shout to us."

Propaganda bombs with leaflets inside them were thrown across the lines. Even small propaganda boats were set loose on the river and floated down into the city. Inside the city itself, posters and whitewashed slogans appeared on the walls and even on the pillboxes of the Kuomintang soldiers. The Manchurian people were joining in the struggle and showing where their hearts lay.

Within a few weeks thirteen thousand officers and men—over one-tenth of Chiang's forces in the encircled city—crept over to the Communist side. Among them were sixteen colonels and 282 officers of the rank of lieutenant or above. All brought rifles and some even brought radio sets. Most of them turned around to fight against their former comrades. . . .

Everywhere the story was the same. Even the commanders no longer wanted to fight. In September and October 1948, the provincial cities of Kaifeng, Tsinan,* Chefoo and Linyi fell to the Communists almost without a struggle. Overnight Chiang lost three hundred thousand troops, including the 93rd Army, the 60th Army and the 70th Army. Not a single one of these commanders fought to the death as the generalissimo had ordered. Some fifty generals preserved their lives by mutinying, surrendering or allowing themselves to be captured. Eighteen full divisions, nine brigades and fifteen regiments within the space of two months were wiped out. Casualties were few. Everywhere white flags were hoisted.[18]

In November 1948, all of Manchuria was in Communist hands. South of the Yellow River, too, the Kuomintang leadership gradually lost control of military operations. Orders and counterorders from above created confusion and despair in the minds of Chiang's generals.

Typical of this chaotic state of affairs was the case of General Chiu Chingchuan, commander of the American-trained and -equipped Second Army

* Capital of Shantung Province.

concentrated northwest of the strategic city of Suchow,* where Chiang Kai-shek expected Communist General Chen-Yi† to attack:

In March, 1948 [General Chiu stated], Cheu-Yi moved north of the Yellow River in order to regroup his forces. Three months later, we were informed that he was preparing an offensive. We were stationed south of the Yellow River, and were facing the 1st, 4th, 6th, and 11th columns, the "Column of the Two Kwangs"‡ and the "Rapid Column". Two of Chen-Yi's columns stationed below Lunghai, the 3rd and the 8th, began a westward movement in the direction of Chengchou. The inept and poorly organized Ministry of National Defense ordered me to move south in order to intercept these columns. I telegraphed that if we did move, the Communists would send the main body of their troops south of the Yellow River. The Ministry replied that if the Communists made this movement, I would still have time to fall back. I obeyed the order and began moving south. We walked fifty kilometers a day, sleeping only two hours out of twenty-four, but Chen-Yi began crossing the Yellow River even before we were able to meet the 3rd and 8th columns. The Ministry thereupon ordered me to fall back to my former position. My soldiers were very angry, but we did retrace our steps.

On June 26, I was ready to enter K'aifeng. From Sian, the Generalissimo cabled me, "Enter the city." But the Ministry of National Defense suddenly panicked. Before I received the Generalissimo's message ordering me to occupy K'aifeng, the Ministry had instructed me to move immediately to Ch'ihsien, and ordered [General] Wou Chao-nien to move from Chengchou to Suihsien.

On June 30, the Ministry instructed me to go to the support of General Chen, commander of the 75th infantry division stationed at Suihsien. . . . I began my eastward movement on July 1st, but my division sustained heavy losses. On July 2, a plane dropped a letter containing the latest bit of information from the Ministry: five new Communist columns, under Liu Po-cheng, were about to attack me! I turned about, but found no Communists. This false piece of news

---

* Or Hsuchou, today. Located on the Peking–Nanking railroad line, and covering Nanking and Shanghai against the southward-moving Red columns. Chiang Kai-shek had concentrated nearly half a million men in that vital area.

† Acting commander in chief of the New Fourth Army.

‡ Made up of soldiers from the two neighboring southern provinces of Kwangtung and Kwangsi.

must have been launched by the Communists themselves, and our Ministry keeps falling into such traps![19]

An even more striking instance of the confusion and helplessness prevailing within the Nationalist leadership during the closing months of the civil war was the following conversation, overheard by Jack Belden in a train between Mukden and Peking:

At a stop along the way, a Chinese cavalry general entered my compartment and seated himself opposite me. I nodded to him, but gave no indication I spoke Chinese. In a short while, an infantry colonel entered the compartment and engaged the general, who was unknown to him, in conversation. By many subtle remarks, the two officers began feeling out each other's sentiments toward the war. The general would make a slight criticism, the colonel would cap it with a stronger one, and the general would follow with a still more bitter comment. Soon both were denouncing the conduct of the war.

"I am a cavalry commander," said the general. "You can use cavalry for reconnaissance, patrol or a charge, but I'm just guarding a railroad. But how can I guard it? The peasants come and take up the tracks. What can I do about that? I am a Northeasterner; shall I shoot my own Northeastern farmers? I ask for orders. But I don't get orders. Nobody has any idea how we should fight. I often wonder why we are fighting. Fourteen years, the Japanese occupied our woods and rivers and hills, and now here we are killing each other again."

The colonel nodded. The conversation lapsed for a moment. We were drawing near to Shanhaikuan where the Great Wall comes down to meet the sea. The colonel looked out the window, then turned back. "You know," he said, "I don't think the 8th Route needs to take Changchun and Mukden. They'll just take the countryside all around, organize the militia, then they'll come down here by the Great Wall and cut us all off. I don't know what the higher authorities are thinking of. We ought to get out of here or stop fighting."

The colonel sounded so lugubrious and the general looked so sad that I could not help but burst into laughter. They both looked at me. "You understand Chinese then?" said the general. I nodded.

"There's no way," he said. "No way. Useless."

Indeed this general was right. There was no way. The soldiers of Chiang Kai-shek on Manchurian soil did not wish any longer to fight.

They began to fraternize with the Manchurian people and then with the 8th Route Army. It was this fraternization that broke up Chiang Kai-shek's vain hopes to hold on to Manchuria. Slowly his hold on the territory beyond the Great Wall weakened and crumbled away.[20]

The Generalissimo was not only losing control over the military situation. Behind the sagging front line, civilian morale and support were also rapidly "crumbling away" during the latter part of 1948. The Chinese intellectuals, in particular, turned their backs on Chiang in ever-increasing numbers. Thousands of them, terrorized and disgusted by the Kuomintang's increasingly harsh police control and repression,* migrated into the "Liberated Areas" and furnished much-needed brains to the still-slender ranks of the Communist Party.

Most intellectuals were politically aloof, though by no means indifferent, when civil war broke out. With few exceptions, they were not Communists, or even sympathizers. It was the government's constant spying on them and gradual suppression of liberty that roused their anger and all but forced them into the anti-Kuomintang (and also anti-American) camp. This was explained to Derk Bodde, a Sinologist who was the first American Fulbright Fellow to be sent to China,† by a well-known liberal professor:

Ten days ago [in September 1948], three or four of us Americans rode out to Tsinghua University, the famous government institution which lies six miles northwest of Peking. There we had a long and frank conversation with a distinguished group of Chinese liberal professors. In the course of it one of my companions said in essence:

"Many Americans, including government officials, wonder why Chinese intellectuals are anti-American and pro-Russian. How would you explain this situation?"

There was a moment of silence, during which the Chinese looked expectantly at one of their number, a distinguished-looking man with graying hair and short-clipped mustache—a former member of the Kuomintang, long noted as one of China's outstanding liberal thinkers. His reply, in carefully phrased English, ran something like this:

---

* Criticism of the regime was currently labeled "Communist-inspired" treason. Freedom of speech practically vanished, especially after the summer of 1948, when Kuomintang authorities drew up "black lists". Universities were raided by police, students were arrested, beaten, killed.

† Though not a newcomer to the country. He and his wife had spent several years in China before World War II.

"Most Chinese intellectuals would prefer not to bother about politics. But while they have heard the government repeatedly proclaim its intention of bringing democracy and honest administration to China, they have seen these protestations repeatedly flouted in actual fact. Indeed, far from improving, the government becomes steadily worse, so that today few thinking people hold much hope for its reform. Then we became increasingly discouraged with reform prospects, but saw no feasible alternative. Though the present government, we felt, was bad, what might take its place would be even worse. During this second phase, intellectuals were uncertain and bewildered. Then came the present, third phase. We have become so completely convinced of the hopelessness of the existing government that we feel the sooner it is removed the better. Since the Chinese Communists are obviously the only force capable of making this change, we are now willing to support them as the lesser of two evils. We ourselves would prefer a middle course, but this is no longer possible.

"But while we Chinese have thus been forced more and more toward the left, we have seen a countermovement at work in America. At one time it apparently wanted a genuinely progressive government in China. During the past two or three years, however, it has seemed to be interested less and less in liberalism and more and more in anything, no matter how reactionary, that might be a bulwark between it and Communism. This change has coincided with growing reaction within the Chinese government itself. The result is an American government which talks constantly about democratic rights yet continues to aid a Chinese government increasingly mindless of these rights. That is why we Chinese have become anti-American—we are not against the American people but against the American government.

"That we are anti-American, however, doesn't mean we are pro-Russian. The very fact that Americans automatically regard anyone who opposes their policies as pro-Russian in itself indicates the prejudice with which they view the whole Chinese situation. Normally we would prefer America to Russia. But today the Communists are China's only hope. Besides, we are not convinced, as are Americans, that they are merely tools of Russian Communism. After all, the Chinese Communists are Chinese as well as Communist, and conditions in China are different from those in Russia. Therefore it is doubtful if Communism of the Russian type can be successfully transplanted to China."[21]

Anti-Americanism, not surprisingly, became a current feature of the atmosphere in Liberated Areas. The Communist propaganda lost no time in denouncing America as the enemy of the Chinese people because she supported the "rebel" Chiang Kai-shek. Jack Belden experienced this anti-American sentiment in the very first Red-held town he visited:

Taking a turn down the street, I was immediately joined by a small boy who ran alongside of me shouting words that sounded like, "*Mei Kuo fan tung.*" Now, *Mei Kuo* means America, but *fan tung*, as far as I had ever heard it, means rice bucket, and to call someone a rice bucket is the same as saying he is good for nothing but eating; or another way of saying a man is fat. Since I wore a fur-lined pilot's suit and since I must have looked well-padded, I was not inclined to take offense at being called an American rice bucket. However, on walking a few steps further, a group of militiamen who were standing before a wall practising songs* suddenly turned toward me, grinned and began singing: "First we had the Japanese Devils and now we have the *Mei Kuo fan tung.*" I could not exactly understand it, but the general sense was quite clearly uncomplimentary and it was not long before I realized that I was being called a "*fan tung pai*"; that is, a reactionary. Being the only foreigner in town, I felt rather blue at being publicly ridiculed, but solaced myself with the idea that now I knew how a Chinese laundryman in America feels when children run after him shouting "Chinkee, Chinkee, Chinaman."

As a matter of fact, the treatment I received on my first morning in Communist territory was extremely mild to the receptions that other foreigners sometimes met in Chinese villages. Later as the war became more bitter, as President Truman evolved his anti-Communist policy, and as American-made planes bombed Communist villages, many Chinese peasants crudely insulted all foreigners in their areas.[22]

By the end of 1948, economic distress and chaos prevailed throughout most of Kuomintang China, and hastened people's estrangement from the regime. Throughout that year, inflation had been skyrocketing. The government vainly issued a new gold yuan currency and proclaimed "permanent" price

---

* These included anti-American slogans, such as the following, quoted by Belden: "Chiang Kai-shek has a stubborn heart—America is his father and mother—He undermines peace and democracy." Slogans to the effect that "We don't want to be American slaves" were current too.

ceilings on all important commodities. Production came to a standstill as factory workers and rickshaw coolies lost their taste for labor and took to robbery. People rushed in mobs to buy whatever the embattled shopkeepers put on sale.* Anarchy set in everywhere, riots broke out and hungry crowds began storming rice shops, grocery stores and coal shops while the police more often than not looked the other way.†

In large cities like Shanghai and Peking, which were overcrowded with half-starving refugee peasants, the country's economic and social disintegration was particularly dramatic. On November 2, 1948, Derk Bodde, who witnessed the collapse of the Nationalist regime in besieged Peking, entered the following "top" news in his diary:

It was an unpleasant surprise to learn yesterday that the new monthly subscription to the *Ta Kung Pao*‡ will cost GY$21 (US $5.25), as compared with last month's rate of about GY$3 (US $0.75). However, even this sum will seem well spent if it brings us many more headlines like yesterday's, which reads (in Chinese):

GETTING FOOD TO EAT IS NOT EASY
BUT GOING TO THE TOILET IS ALSO DIFFICULT

The story that follows vividly describes the troubles of people trying to buy everyday necessities in Shanghai. Barter is widespread, and one must wait in line even to buy toilet paper, sales of which are limited to ten sheets per customer.

Another potpourri of economic items from Kwantung and Kwiechow is headlined:

WHEN BUYING OIL TODAY, HOW DARE ONE ASK THE PRICE?
WHEN MONTHLY WAGES ARE $2, HOW CAN ONE FOSTER HONESTY?

This story describes how at a town near the Canton–Hong Kong Railroad, people no longer dare ask the price of peanut oil, since they know full well that no merchant will sell it at the August 19 price ceiling. All they can do is to hold out a dollar and a bottle, and ask the clerk to pour as much oil into the bottle as the dollar will buy. In

---

* Including diamonds, expensive watches, jade, French pastry and penicillin.
† "Why should I arrest them?" a policeman asked a Western reporter. "I may join them myself tomorrow."
‡ Title of a leading Chinese daily belonging to a newspaper chain selling in several major cities. It may be translated, *Great Public Gazette*.

Kweichow, the story continues, county magistrates now receive less than $10 per month. How, it concludes bitterly, is honesty to be expected under such circumstances?

Other items from the same paper: Tientsin telegraph operators go on hunger strike; employees of the Hopei Medical College in Tientsin "request leave of absence"; during a brief stopover of his plane in Tsingtao, Premier Wong Wen-hao listens to tales of people in distress; professors at Peita and other Peking universities resume classes, but middle and primary schoolteachers continue their strike;* a three-day strike of Yunnan University professors begins today; rice famine continues unabated at Hankow, where teachers have appealed in vain for help.

In other words, the economic distress is not restricted merely to North China where the "Communist bandits" might be held directly responsible. A primary factor is the government's admission, made around mid-October, that the original note issue of GY$2,000,000,000 has already been increased to over GY$9,000,000,000. The resulting pressure on the August 19 price ceilings has proved irresistible. Now, as of November 1, the government has officially removed these ceilings and approved other measures which mean the tacit abandonment of its promised August 19 objectives.[23]

Another, and much-saddened, American observer of China's domestic woes was the wise and dignified missionary and university president John L. Stuart, U.S. Ambassador at Nanking since 1946.† He was fully aware of the Kuomintang's glaring shortcomings, and could not help comparing them to Communist efficiency and discipline:

Meanwhile an internal conflict of which I had long been conscious was becoming more acute. This was in my personal sentiments regarding the two parties. In the Kuomintang were many friends of long standing, for not a few of whom as individuals I had hearty admiration. I knew them to be men of integrity and public spirit as well as with trained intelligence. And yet this party almost from the time it came

* Teachers' strikes, due mainly to poor salaries, were widespread in the fall of 1948. Students queued up for poor professors in the rice lines. A number of teachers and professors committed suicide.

† The Kuomintang government had returned to Nanking a few months after the end of World War II.

into power had tolerated among its officials of all grades graft and greed, idleness and inefficiency, nepotism and factional rivalries—all the evils in short of the corrupt bureaucracy it had overthrown. These evils had become more pronounced after V-J Day in the attempts to crush Communism by a combination of military strength and secret police. The government had been steadily losing popular support and even respect. As the Communist forces advanced in a victorious march toward the Yangtze River, the grandiose plans for defense crumbled amid political bickering, desertions or betrayals, disorderly retreats. Yet this was the government which had been benefiting from substantial American aid in many forms, and in whose principles and aims, as sincerely formulated and as expressed in numerous individual lives, we thoroughly believed.

In painful contrast the Communist Party was free from private graft, officers and men lived very much together, simply and industriously, severely disciplined, thoroughly indoctrinated. All of this was evident as they came into Nanking.* There was almost no mistreatment of the populace. They borrowed extensively but generally returned these articles or made restitution. Their broadcasts boasted of the smooth efficiency of their long southward march, the supplies and attendants sent long in advance by stages, the arrangement for transport and shelter, etc. They had in short perfected their own logistics. Their morale was excellent. The daily drills and lectures went on all around our Embassy property so we had visual and almost too much audible proof of it. The Communist Party was thus giving the appearance of being a dynamic movement fostering among millions those qualities of which China had stood so palpably in need, qualities which Christian missions and other cultural forces had been slowly inculcating among so pitifully few. These gains included capacity for organization, strict but largely voluntary discipline, putting the cause above all personal or family considerations, unselfish service to the underprivileged, the enthusiastic loyalty of idealistic youth. This was no mean achievement, especially in the perspective of Kuomintang shortcomings.[24]

During the winter months of 1948-9, the Kuomintang resistance to the

* On April 24, 1949. At 6.45 A.M. the next day, seventy-two-year-old Ambassador Stuart was rudely awakened by the intrusion of a dozen Red soldiers into his bedroom, who told him that various articles therein would soon belong "to the people".

southward-moving Red tide waned rapidly amid complex intrigues by which some of Chiang Kai-shek's close associates tried to get rid of him while at the same time holding out the olive branch to the Communists. On Christmas Day, 1948, the Communist radio broadcast a list of forty-three "war criminals".* In his New Year's message, the Generalissimo broadcast his own "appeal for peace", which in essence was a sort of no-peace-no-war formula designed to gain time. Two weeks later, Mao Tse-tung came forward with a set of demands amounting to unconditional surrender, and declared that the People's Liberation Army had the power to crush the whole Kuomintang machinery of rule "into dust and extinction".

Events moved swiftly, and by late January, 1949, Kuomintang hopes for improving the military situation were practically gone. Peking, Tientsin and North China had surrendered almost bloodlessly, and the victorious Red columns were within easy shelling distance of Nanking.

Chiang himself, who for years remained blind to the deeper needs of his people, at last saw the writing on the wall. On January 21, 1949, he changed his khaki uniform for the long blue gown and black jacket of the Chinese gentleman, turned his office over to Vice-President Li Tsung-jen, and took off in a two-engined American plane that flew him to his ancestral home in Chekiang Province, some 200 miles south of Nanking. To his frightened Cabinet he had announced that he was retiring in order to make peace with the Communists more possible. The fact that his departure from power was greeted with indifference by the common people proved that his prestige and popularity had fallen to an all-time low.

In his interesting and highly informative Peking Diary, *Derk Bodde depicted life in the northern capital during the "dark days" of December 1948 and January 1949:*

December 21. . . . The aspect of the city as one goes out on the streets these days is pretty grim. Shops close up fairly early in the afternoon, and the lack of electricity makes a place like the Tung An market particularly depressing on these short winter afternoons. We have definitely entered a siege economy. . . .

December 24. . . . The prevailing mood is one of dullness and boredom. We have passed through the first stage of siege, that in which everything

---

* In addition to Chiang Kai-shek, his wife, his in-laws (of the Soong "clan") and top government officials and diplomats accredited in the United States, the list also included various provincial politicians and generals who were conducting their own maneuvers for peace and power.

happened at once, and have reached the second, that of patiently waiting for something conclusive to happen. The curfew, the billeting of soldiers in almost all of Peking's parks and beauty spots, the exodus of so many friends for the south, the cessation of letters from the outside world, the scantiness of news in our single-sheet newspapers, the lack of water and electricity, the desperate struggle for existence of so many poor people, the hectic military movement on the streets which makes one want to stay at home as much as possible, and the almost complete curtailment of social activities—all these make of this once lovely city a place unrecognizably drab and dreary. . . .

On the streets, long lines of civilians, equipped with shovels, being marched off for forced labor on fortifications and the like, are a common sight these days. . . . In the city streets, pillboxes, barbed wire barricades, and the like, become more prevalent; but most work, aside from that on the emergency airfields, seems to be concentrated upon clearing away the thousands of houses that line the outside perimeter of the city wall. . . .

New Year's Day. As if to celebrate the New Year, the electricity unexpectedly came on about an hour ago. And what electricity! Brighter than it has been on many occasions in the past. How and where it comes from we can't imagine, for the main plant, at Shih-ching-shan, has long been in Communist hands. One of the jokes going the rounds the past week is that the Communists phoned several times from Shih-ching-shan, politely offering electricity to the citizens of Peking, but that these offers were all sternly rejected by Fu Tso-yi* for reasons of face. . . .

January 7. Ever since Chiang Kai-shek's "peace" statement of New Year's Day, the war has been in a state of suspended animation. Neither in North nor Central China does there appear to have been much military activity. Chiang's statement has been the signal for a continuing "peace offensive" from the Nationalist side. A few days ago, Nationalist planes dropped thousands of "peace bombs" on the Communists north of Nanking—leaflets urging Chinese not to kill Chinese,† the need for peace, and so forth. Similar appeals, couched in highly flowery and literary language, have been issued the past few days by chambers of commerce, groups of leading Chinese citizens, and other organs in Shanghai, Peking, and elsewhere. They consist

---

* Kuomintang commander in North China.
† Actually a Communist slogan.

of telegrams jointly addressed to the National government and to "Mr. Mao Tse-tung and other Communist leaders." Most striking change of the times, however, is the terminology employed in the paper I now read, the *World Daily News*. In most of its dispatches the contemptuous word *fei* "bandits" has given way to the more respectful *kung* "Communists". . . .

January 15. Today marks the beginning of the second month of siege, and with it the period of inaction seems to have come to an end. . . . Here in Peking a disturbing development has been the sporadic Communist shelling of the center of the city—aimed, it is rumored, at a munition dump in Central Park. . . .

Construction of defense works continues, especially south of the city. On Wednesday afternoon I made a trip to the extreme southern gate and on my way saw thousands upon thousands of laborers plodding southward in stolid lines with picks and shovels. The majority seemed the poorest of the poor. Many of them were either old men, some obviously in frail health, or young boys. The reason is simple: since persons with money can "hire" other workers in their place, the latter are almost invariably recruited from the poorest families. Moreover, since these families are dependent upon the able-bodied wage earners among them, they try to shelter these, if possible, and send the old or young in their place. . . .

January 23. The momentous news of the week, of course, is that the siege of Peking is now officially over. Fu Tso-yi has surrendered. At six o'clock yesterday evening he issued a thirteen-point statement, the gist of which is that his troops are to be gradually moved into the suburbs; order is to be maintained by the existing police force; administrative organs, banks, industries, schools, etc., are to continue as usual under existing personnel; aliens and alien property are to be protected, as is freedom of religion; newspapers are to continue publication; in short, life is to go on as much as possible as before. Nothing is said of Fu's future position or of when the Communists will take over. . . .

Now, with the surrender, in the twinkling of an eye the aspect of the city has been changed from that of impending attack to a semblance of peace. Yesterday the glacis was still covered with thousands of men working like ants to extend its air strip. Today it is absolutely deserted. Unfortunately the armistice comes too late to save the many trees that have been hacked down around its border during the past week. Nor will it restore the many private houses that have been razed around the city walls—amounting, according to the newspapers, to over 16,000 *chien* (room sections).

The futility of these and similar defense activities has been demonstrated the past few days by the way in which Communist fire has reduced the use of the emergency airfields to almost nothing. Virtually the only air activity has been that of trying to drop food into the city. Day after day, for hours at a time, the sky has been noisy with planes circling above the frozen lake of the Pei Hai and dropping bags of rice or flour upon the ice. The first attempts were far from successful. Some bags missed the lake entirely; others broke open, spilling their precious contents over the surface; at least two incautious spectators were hit and injured. After the first day, however, parachutes were used, with much better results, and it was a beautiful sight to see these planes circle the city and suddenly discharge their cargo, leaving a trail of parachutes fluttering gently down to earth. . . .

January 26. Liberation! This is now the great slogan of the day. Everyone talks and writes happily of the "liberation" of Peking by the great "People's Army". So far as the physical appearance of the city is concerned, little has happened as yet. Fu Tso-yi's soldiers are still much in evidence, though said to be gradually moving out, and I have yet to catch my first glimpse of the Communist "Eighth Route Army". During the last two days, however, walls and telephone poles have been plastered with multigraphed posters, exhorting the population to conduct itself peacefully and work for the building of a new China. Most spectacular of all has been the arrival of the long-promised "great illumination". Tonight as I write these words, street lights are burning all over the city for the first time in six weeks.

The absence of greater change, of course, is due to the peacefulness of the turnover and the fact that the old guard still remains in power— an old guard, however, using a vocabulary amazingly different from what it was mouthing only a few days ago. The formerly reactionary *World Daily News* is a typical example. A fair part of today's issue consists of transcripts from the Communist radio, put out, however, under the date line of the Kuomintang Central News Agency's Peking office.

Much of the new talk, of course, stems from deliberate opportunism or plain ignorance of the significance of what is taking place. . . . Yet despite the opportunism, hypocrisy, and lack of comprehension from many sides, there is no doubt in my mind that the Communists come here with the bulk of the people on their side. As one walks the streets, the new feeling of relief and relaxation can definitely be sensed, even though it is hard to describe it in tangible terms.[25]

After a few days of suspense and plenty of fancy "new talk", the first units of the Eighth Route Army finally entered Peking on January 31. Derk Bodde's wife Galia saw them arrive:

Today, less than twenty-four hours after last night's dire predictions,* the "People's Liberation Army" has finally marched into Peking! At 4 P.M., while riding up Morrison Street, Galia saw the first arrivals. At their head moved a sound truck (apparently supplied by the municipality), from which blared the continuous refrain, "Welcome to the Liberation Army on its arrival in Peiping! Congratulations to the people of Peiping on their liberation!" Beside and behind, six abreast, marched some two or three hundred Communist soldiers in full battle equipment. They moved briskly and seemed hot, as if they had been marching a long distance. All had a red-cheeked, healthy look and seemed in high spirits. As they marched up the street, the crowds lining the sidewalks, including our Chin,† burst into applause. Near their head walked a rather nondescript, shabbily dressed civilian —apparently some kind of official.

Behind the soldiers marched students carrying two large portraits: one of Mao Tse-tung, the other presumably of Chu Teh, commander in chief of the People's Army. A military band came next, and finally a long line of trucks carrying more soldiers, students, and civilian employees of the telephone company, railroad administration, and other semi-official organizations. In about ten minutes the parade was over.[26]

An impressive victory parade followed three days later, and Derk Bodde was not a little surprised to recognize in it large quantities of familiar equipment:

February 3. The People's Liberation Army is in complete control, and only occasional groups of "enemy" soldiers are still to be seen. . . . Yesterday Chin reported that he had seen long lines of carts bringing food into the city. Prices have dropped slightly, but it is obvious that

* Of riots and looting, if the stalemate was not settled before long.
† Bodde's Chinese cook.

few serious steps in this direction can be taken before the process of converting gold yuan into the new regime's "people's notes" has been completed. . . .

Today's big event has been the grand victory parade signalizing the formal take-over of the city. It unfortunately coincided with the first real dust storm of the winter. A fierce wind moaned through the scaffolding still enveloping the partially dismantled tiled archway at the south end of Morrison Street. It raised such dust from the nearby glacis that during the biggest gusts it was literally impossible to see across the field. My face was black with grime by the time I returned home.

Prominent in the parade were thousands of students and workers from schools and organizations throughout the city. Many of their colored paper banners and Mao Tse-tung portraits were torn to tatters by the wind. Among the students also marched some well-known university professors. Some groups danced to the rhythmic drum-and-gong beat of the *yang ko* or "planting song"—a simple traditional peasant dance performed in unison by large groups, which is already becoming enormously popular here as the result of the general Communist emphasis upon folk art. More familiar to me was a band of stilt walkers, cavorting merrily in colorful costumes above the heads of the crowds. Other groups, directed by "cheer leaders", chanted, as they marched, the famous "eight points" of Mao Tse-tung.*

Of chief interest was, of course, the Liberation Army itself. I missed the first contingents of infantry and cavalry, as well as part of the motorized units. But in what I did see, lasting about an hour, I counted over 250 heavy motor vehicles of all kinds—tanks, armored cars, truckloads of soldiers, trucks mounted with machine guns, trucks towing heavy artillery. Behind them followed innumerable ambulances, jeeps, and other smaller vehicles. As probably the greatest demonstration of Chinese military might in history, the spectacle was enormously impressive. But what made it especially memorable to Americans was the fact that it was primarily a display of *American* military equipment, virtually all of it captured or obtained by bribe from Kuomintang forces in the short space of two and one half years.

---

* Statement by which Mao rejected Chiang's New Year "peace" offer and substituted eight points of his own. Essentially, they called for: punishment of war criminals, abolition of Kuomintang rule, reorganization of China's armies and government along "democratic" lines, land reform, abrogation of "unequal" treaties.

And what about the reactions of the civilian participants and spectators? Granted that some of the former paraded only because they had been told to do so, and that many were schoolchildren too young to realize the full significance of what was happening, the fact remains that the enthusiasm of most was too obvious to have been feigned, and this notwithstanding that many had been exposed to wind and dust for some four hours before I saw them. I have no doubt that not a few on this day felt a keen sense of personal participation in an event symbolizing the beginning of a new era in Chinese history. . . . As the stream of trucks continued, I heard several exclaim with wonder: "Still more! Still more!"[27]

Less than three months after the Red victory parade in Peking, Nanking in turn fell into Communist hands, and with equal ease. The fall of China's "southern" capital was not of decisive military importance, but its political significance was tremendous. For three decades, the ancient capital of China had indeed been the symbol of the Chinese Republic. It was there that Dr. Sun Yat-sen took the oath as President of the newly born Republic, and it was there, in 1929, that Chiang Kai-shek had set up his capital and headquarters for the war against the Communist guerrilla bands of Hunan and Kiangsi. Now, twenty years later, these guerrillas had grown into an army of nearly three million men. They had taken his proud capital, and Chiang had been quite unable to defend it, let alone hold it, against the Red avalanche.

Nearly half a million Kuomintang troops, including some crack divisions,* were deployed along the southern bank of the middle and lower Yangtze when the Reds announced their intention of crossing its formidable barrier in order to "liberate all of China".† To the still-powerful Kuomintang navy and air force, the Reds had little or nothing to oppose. Behind the two-mile-wide muddy Yangtze, the Nationalists had a definite chance of halting the Communist southward drive—if they had really tried to. But they were no longer in any mood to fight their fellow Chinese, and it was almost unopposed that the Red troops negotiated the stream on wooden boats, junks, and rafts. During the first week after the spectacular crossing, the Reds captured an average of three cities a day, and in October 1949 their vanguards reached the vicinity of Hong Kong. By that time, the civil war as such was all but over.

* Such as the 88th division, which was one of three units originally known as "Chiang's own".

† Joint order (April 20, 1949) of Mao Tse-tung and General Chu Teh to the Red forces.

China had entered the Communist era, and the following conversation between Derk Bodde and a Chinese liberal showed that in 1949, the country's intellectuals generally welcomed the change of regime:

Today I had a talk with Fu, a young and politically minded Peita professor formerly connected with the now defunct liberal *China Reconstruction*. "How do you like our bloodless revolution?" he began. "Much better than the French and Russian revolutions, eh?"

I agreed, but then went on to remark that its most distasteful features, from a foreign point of view, were the control and distortion of news, and absence of publicly expressed divergence of opinion. "What do you propose to write about if you get *China Reconstruction* going again?" I asked.

"Oh, probably such things as industry and economic reconstruction."

"Fine, but what about politics?"

"We shall treat this differently from before." Then he went on, "At first I was as impatient about these things as you are. But now I have come to see them in a different light."

He went on to say that everyone expected the peace agreement to be signed within a day. . . . Then there would speedily be peace in China. A consultative conference would be held in July by the latest, at which a coalition government would be established. The emergency military restrictions would be relaxed and a new intellectual climate emerge. At the moment, however, restrictions were necessary because a state of war still existed and reactionary elements remained active.

"And what about foreign policy? What about the treatment of foreign correspondents?" I asked.

"I am sorry for my personal friends," he replied.[28]

Thus the ancient land of China "turned over", as the Communists put it at the time. Mao Tse-tung's prediction that the country would conquer the city had become true: in its essence, the civil war had been a struggle for the affections of the rural masses, and the Reds emerged victorious mainly because they won the hearts of the peasants. More precisely, because they made a reality out of Dr. Sun Yat-sen's popular slogan granting the land "to the tiller". Six hundred million Chinese (now more than seven hundred million, or nearly a quarter of the world's population) thus passed under the control of the Chinese Communist Party.

SOURCES

CHAPTER I: THE WESTERN "BARBARIANS" AT THE DOORS OF CHINA

1. John Barrow, *Travels in China, containing descriptions, observations, and comparisons, made and collected in the course of a short residence at the imperial palace of Yuen-min-Yuen, and on a subsequent journey through the country from Pekin to Canton* (London: T. Cadell and W. Davies, 1804), pp. 196–9.
2. *Ibid.*, pp. 14–17.
3. Charles Taylor, *Five Years in China, With Some Account of the Great Rebellion* (New York: Derby and Jackson, 1860), pp. 212–13.
4. Henry Ellis, *Journal of the Proceedings of the Late Embassy to China, comprising a correct narrative of the public transactions of the embassy, of the voyage to and from China, and of the journey from the mouth of the Pei-Ho to the return to Canton* (London: John Murray, 1817), pp. 176–83.
5. John Francis Davis, *The Chinese: a General Description of the Empire of China and Its Inhabitants*, 2 vols. (London: Charles Knight, 1836), II, 24–26.
6. *Ibid.*, II, 26.
7. William C. Hunter, *The "Fan Kwae" at Canton Before Treaty Days, 1825–1844, by an Old Resident* (London: Kegan Paul, Trench & Co., 1882), pp. 28–30.
8. Adolphe Barrot, *Un voyage en Chine*, in *Revue des Deux Mondes* of November 1, 1839.
9. M. Huc (Father), *L'Empire chinois, faisant suite à l'ouvrage intitulé Souvenirs d'un voyage dans la Tartarie et le Thibet*, 2 vols. (Paris: Librairie de Gaume, 1857), II, 158–9.
10. Charles Taylor, *op. cit.*, pp. 207–8.
11. C. Toogood Downing, *The Stranger in China—or, The Fan-Qui's Visit to the Celestial Empire in 1836–7*, 2 vols. (London: H. Colburn, 1838), I, 57–59, 77–78 and 122.

12. M. Huc, *op. cit.*, II, 120–1.
13. Hwuy-Ung, *A Chinaman's Opinion of Us and of His Own Country*, translated from the Chinese by J. A. Makepeace (London: Chatto & Windus, 1927), pp. 9 and 23–25.
14. J. Macgowan (Reverend), *Sidelights on Chinese Life* (London: Kegan Paul, Trench, Trübner & Co., 1907), pp. 184-6.
15. *Ibid.*, pp. 186–8.
16. M. Huc, *op. cit.*, I, 3–5.
17. Quoted in William C. Hunter, *Bits of Old China* (London: Kegan Paul, Trench & Co., 1885), pp. 81–82.

CHAPTER II: THE OPIUM WAR, 1839–1842

1. Georges Maspero, *La Chine*, 2 vols. (Paris: Librairie Delagrave, 1925), I, 122–23.
2. William C. Hunter, *The "Fan Kwae" at Canton . . .*, *op. cit.*, p. 65.
3. *Ibid.*, pp. 66–69.
4. J. Macgowan, *op. cit.*, pp. 195–8.
5. William C. Hunter, *The "Fan Kwae" at Canton . . .*, *op. cit.*, pp. 73–77.
6. *Ibid.*, p. 77.
7. *Ibid.*, pp. 136–7.
8. *Ibid.*, pp. 141–2.
9. *Ibid.*, p. 143.
10. Arthur Waley, *The Opium War Through Chinese Eyes* (London: Allen & Unwin, and New York: Macmillan, 1958), pp. 38–39.
11. *Ibid.*, pp. 68–69.
12. Sir George Thomas Staunton, *Observations on Our China Policy* (London: John Murray, 1850), pp. 32–34.
13. *Ibid.*, pp. 36–37.
14. Lord Jocelyn, *Six Months with the Chinese Expedition, or, Leaves from a Soldier's Note-Book* (London: John Murray, 1841), pp. 49–59.
15. Lieutenant John Ouchterlony, *The Chinese War: An Account of All the Operations of the British Forces, from the Commencement to the Treaty of Nanking* (London: Saunders and Otley, 1884), pp. 151–3.
16. Quoted in Arthur Waley, *op. cit.*, p. 164.
17. *Ibid.*, p. 165.
18. Lord Jocelyn, *op. cit.*, pp. 134–5.

19. Lieutenant John Ouchterlony, *op. cit.*, pp. 232–40.
20. *Ibid.*, pp. 269–88.
21. Arthur Waley, *op. cit.*, pp. 197–208.
22. Quoted in Ouchterlony, *op. cit.*, p. 451.
23. Georges Maspero, *op. cit.*, I, 128.

CHAPTER III: THE T'AI P'ING REBELLION
1851–1864

1. Thomas T. Meadows, *The Chinese and Their Rebellions* (London: Smith, Elder & Co., 1856), p. 112.
2. Quoted in *ibid.*, pp. 132–3.
3. Charles Taylor, *op. cit.*, pp. 362–9.
4. Callery et Yvan, *L'insurrection en Chine depuis son origine jusqu'à la prise de Nankin* (Paris: Librairie nouvelle, 1853), pp. 50–53. M. Callery, a former missionary, and M. Yvan, a physician, were attached to the French Embassy as interpreters.
5. Theodore Hamberg, *The Visions of Hung Siu-Tschuen, and the Origin of the Kwang-Si Insurrection* (Hong Kong: China Mail Office, 1854), pp. 14 and 41.
6. Thomas Meadows, *op. cit.*, pp. 149–50.
7. Quoted in Callery et Yvan, *op. cit.*, pp. 100–5.
8. *Ibid.*, pp. 193–4.
9. *Ibid.*, pp. 110–11.
10. Thomas Meadows, *op. cit.*, pp. 147–9.
11. Quoted in *ibid.*, pp. 155–7.
12. Charles Taylor, *op. cit.*, p. 360.
13. *Ibid.*, pp. 343–4 and 349, 352–3.
14. Thomas Meadows, *op. cit.*, pp. 314–15.
15. The two proclamations are quoted in Callery et Yvan, *op. cit.*, pp. 230–3.
16. Arthur Evans Moule, *Half a Century in China, Recollections and Observations* (London: Hodder & Stoughton, 1911), pp. 35–37.
17. *Ibid.*, pp. 55–57 and 59.
18. Rev. Père Brouillon, S. J., *Mémoire sur l'état actuel de la mission du Kiang-nan, 1842–1855 & Lettres relatives à l'insurrection, 1851–1855* (Paris: Julien et Lanier, 1855), pp. 404–8.
19. *Ibid.*, pp. 276–8.

20. Rev. Père Mercier, *Campagne du Cassini dans les mers de Chine, 1851–1854, d'après les rapports, lettres et notes du Commandant de Plas* (Paris: Retaux-Bray, 1889), pp. 294–5.
21. Rev. Père Brouillon, *op. cit.*, pp. 343–50.
22. *Ibid.*, pp. 370–3.

CHAPTER IV: THE ANGLO-FRENCH EXPEDITIONS
1856–1864

1. Ssu-yü Teng and John K. Fairbank, *China's Response to the West, a Documentary Survey, 1839–1923* (Cambridge, Mass.: Harvard University Press, 1954), p. 36.
2. Edmond Plauchut, *Le Tour du monde en cent vingt jours*, article in *La Revue des Deux Mondes*, September 15, 1871.
3. Georges Maspero, *op. cit.*, I, 168–9.
4. Letter of Mgr. Guillemin, quoted by Henri Cordier, *L'Expédition de Chine de 1857–58* (Paris: Alcan, 1905), p. 20.
5. Baron de Bazancourt, *Les expéditions de Chine et de Cochinchine* (Paris: Amyot, 1861), 1st Part, p. 137.
6. Marquis de Moges, *Souvenirs d'une ambassade en Chine et au Japon en 1857 et 1858* (Paris: Hachette, 1860), p. 92.
7. Laurence Oliphant, *Narrative of the Earl of Elgin's Mission to China and Japan in the years 1857, '58, '59* (Edinburgh: W. Blackwood & Sons, 1860), pp. 93–94.
8. *Ibid.*, p. 101.
9. Quoted in *ibid.*, p. 123.
10. Quoted in Georges Maspero, *op. cit.*, I, 134–5.
11. Quoted in Laurence Oliphant, *op. cit.*, pp. 147–8.
12. Comte d'Hérisson, *Journal d'un interprète en Chine*, 25th ed. (Paris: Paul Ollendorff, 1886), pp. 277–85.
13. Cousin de Montauban, *L'expédition de Chine de 1860. Souvenirs du général Cousin de Montauban, comte de Palikao* (Paris: Plon, 1932), pp. 310–17.
14. Comte d'Hérisson, *op. cit.*, pp. 327–50.
15. J. O. P. Bland and E. Backhouse, *China under the Empress Dowager, Being the History of the Life and Times of Tz'u Hsi, Compiled from State Papers and the Private Diary of the Comptroller of Her Household*

(London: Wm. Heinemann, and Boston: Houghton Mifflin, 1910), pp. 12–19.

16. Henry Knollys, *Incidents in the China War of 1860, Compiled from the Private Journal of Sir Hope Grant* (Edinburgh: W. Blackwood & Sons, 1875), pp. 208–10. The author was a Captain in the Royal Artillery.

17. Laurence Oliphant, *op. cit.*, pp. 514–16.

18. Commandant de Marolles, *Souvenirs de la révolte des T'ai P'ing (1862–63)*, in T'ung-pao, 1903: III, 201–22; IV, 1–18.

19. Quoted in J. O. P. Bland, *Li Hung-Chang* (London: Constable & Co., 1917), p. 48.

20. Quoted in E. Backhouse and J. O. P. Bland, *Annals and Memoirs of the Court of Peking* (London: Wm. Heinemann, and Boston: Houghton Mifflin, 1914), pp. 424–5.

21. Andrew Wilson, *The "Ever-Victorious Army". A History of the Chinese Campaign under Lt. Col. C. G. Gordon, and of the Suppression of the Tai-Ping Rebellion* (Edinburgh: W. Blackwood & Sons, 1868), pp. 318–20.

22. J. O. P. Bland and E. Backhouse, *op. cit.*, pp. 61–62.

CHAPTER V: THE ERA OF VICEROYS, 1860–1894

1. Ssu-yü Teng and John K. Fairbank, *op. cit.*, pp. 51–54.

2. *Ibid.*, pp. 76–77.

3. E. Backhouse and J. O. P. Bland, *op. cit.*, pp. 484–5.

4. *Ibid.*, pp. 444–6.

5. Maurice Jametel, *Pékin. Souvenirs de l'Empire du Milieu* (Paris: Plon-Nourrit, 1887), pp. 16–19.

6. *Ibid.*, pp. 30–32.

7. Lucien Vigneron (Abbé), *Deux ans au Se-Tchouan* (Paris: Bray et Retaux, 1881), pp. 72–73.

8. Maurice Jametel, *op. cit.*, pp. 135–9.

9. George Ernest Morrison, *An Australian in China* (London: Horace Cox, 1895), pp. 25–27.

10. Quoted in Alexander Michie, *The Englishman in China during the Victorian Era*, 2 vols. (Edinburgh: W. Blackwood & Sons, 1900), II, 231.

11. Baron de Huebner, *Promenade autour du monde*, 2 vols. (Paris: Hachette, 1873), pp. 392-5.

12. *Ibid.*, pp. 411-12.

13. *Ibid.*, pp. 425-7.

14. Timothy Richard, *Forty-five Years in China. Reminiscences by T. Richard* (London: T. Fisher Unwin, 1916), pp. 100, 117-18, 129-33.

15. *Ibid.*, pp. 156-7.

16. John W. Foster, *Memoirs of the Viceroy Li Hung-chang* (London: Constable & Co., 1913), pp. 4-7.

17. Gideon Chen, *Tso Tsung T'ang, Pioneer of the Modern Dockyard and the Woollen Mill in China* (Peking: Yenching University Press, 1938), p. 54.

18. Lord Charles Beresford, *The Break-up of China* (London: Harper & Brothers, 1899), pp. 270-3.

19. Capitaine Lecomte, *Guet-apens de Bac-Lé* (Paris: Berger-Levrault, 1890), pp. 107ff.

20. A. Pellier, *L'Europe et la Chine* (Limoges: Imprimerie Marc Barbou, 1904), pp. 250-1.

CHAPTER VI: THE PARTITION OF CHINA
1894-1905

1. Ssu-yü Teng and John K. Fairbank, *op. cit.*, pp. 126-7.

2. France. Foreign Ministry, *Documents diplomatiques français (1871-1914)*. 1re série (1871-1900). Tome XV (2 janvier-14 novembre 1899). (Paris: Imprimerie Nationale, 1959) (Textes No. 44, 91, 105, 207).

3. Mgr. Chausse, *Nouvelles de la mission*, in *Les Missions Catholiques*, No. 1582 of September 29, 1899, p. 460.

4. H. Enselme, *A travers la Mandchourie. Le chemin de fer de l'Est chinois, d'après la mission du Capitaine H. de Bouillanc de Lacoste et du Capitaine Enselme* (Paris: J. Rueff, 1903), pp. 45-50.

5. Timothy Richard, *op. cit.*, pp. 231-2.

6. Ssu-yü Teng and John K. Fairbank, *op. cit.*, pp. 154-7.

7. *Ibid.*, pp. 172-3.

8. Mrs. Archibald Little, *Intimate China. The Chinese as I Have Seen Them* (London: Hutchinson, 1899), pp. 576-83.

9. Quoted in J. O. P. Bland and E. Backhouse, *op. cit.*, pp. 175-6.

10. Hwuy-Ung, *op. cit.*, pp. 59–60.

11. *Ibid.*, pp. 67–69 and 91–92.

12. *Ibid.*, pp. 42–45.

13. *Chine et Ceylan. Lettres des missionaires de la Compagnie de Jésus* (little known magazine published irregularly at Abbeville, France), Vol. I, pp. 54–55, n.d.

14. Letter of Father M. Planchet to Mgr. Geurts, Apostolic Vicar in Chihli, quoted in *Les Missions Catholiques*, No. 1647 of December 28, 1900, p. 614.

15. Baron d'Anthouard, *Les Boxeurs* (Paris: Plon-Nourrit, 1902), pp. 17–22.

16. Commandant Harfeld, *Opinions chinoises sur les barbares d'Occident* (Paris: Plon-Nourrit, 1909), pp. 234–6.

17. Ssu-yü Teng and John K. Fairbank, *op. cit.*, p. 190.

18. Quoted in J. O. P. Bland and E. Backhouse, *op. cit.*, pp. 235–8.

19. A. Douglas, *Le Siège de Tien-tsin: 15 juin–15 juillet 1900* (Paris: Berger-Levrault, 1903), p. 80.

20. *Ibid.*, pp. 207–8.

21. Quoted in E. Backhouse and J. O. P. Bland, *op. cit.*, pp. 453–4.

22. France. Foreign Ministry, *Documents diplomatiques. Chine, 1899–1900.* Annexe au rapport de M. Pichon, du 28 août 1900. Notes prises chaque jour par M. Pichon sur les faits qui se sont passés à Pékin du 19 juin au 15 août (Siège des Légations par les troupes chinoises). (Paris: Imprimerie Nationale, 1900), pp. 201–4 and 209.

23. B. L. Putnam Weale (pseudonym of B. L. Simpson), *Indiscreet Letters from Peking, Being the Notes of an Eye-Witness Which Set Forth, in Some Detail, from Day to Day, the Real Story of the Siege and Sack of a Distressed Capital in 1900* (London: Hurst & Blackett, 1907), pp. 190–2.

CHAPTER VII: THE END OF THE CHINESE EMPIRE
1906–1916

1. Agnes Smedley, *The Great Road. The Life and Times of Chu Teh* (New York: Monthly Review Press, 1956), pp. 15–16.

2. Jean Rodes, *La Chine et le mouvement constitutionnel, 1910–1911* (Paris: Alcan, 1913), pp. 209–10.

3. Arthur Evans Moule, *op. cit.*, pp. 264–5.

4. *Ibid.*, pp. 221–2.
5. Jean Rodes, *Le Céleste Empire avant la Révolution* (Paris: Alcan, 1914), pp. 42–45.
6. Princess Der Ling, *Two Years in the Forbidden City* (Shanghai: Thomas F. Millard, 1911), pp. 351–2.
7. *Ibid.*, pp. 356–7.
8. Quoted in J. O. P. Bland, *Recent Events and Present Policies in China* (London: Wm. Heinemann, and Boston: Houghton Mifflin, 1912), pp. 84–85.
9. Sun Yat-sen, *Kidnapped in London. Being the Story of my Capture by, Detention at, and Release from the Chinese Legation, London* (Bristol: J. W. Arrowsmith, 1897), pp. 29–37.
10. Ssu-yü Teng and John K. Fairbank, *op. cit.*, pp. 227–8.
11. Paul Linebarger, *The Gospel of Chung Shan* (Paris: Comité Général Exécutif du Kouomintang en Europe, 1932), pp. 39–40 and 51–52.
12. Jean Rodes, *La Chine nouvelle* (Paris: Alcan, 1910), pp. 291–4.
13. Sir Meyrick Hewlett, *Forty Years in China* (London: Macmillan & Co., 1943), pp. 73–74.
14. Edmond Rottach, *La Chine en révolution* (Paris: Perrin, 1914), pp. 113–14.
15. F. Farjenel, *A travers la révolution chinoise* (Paris: Plon-Nourrit, 1914), pp. 83–85.
16. Edmond Rottach, *op. cit.*, pp. 30–32.
17. Jean Rodes, *Scènes de la vie révolutionnaire en Chine, 1911–1914* (Paris: Plon-Nourrit, 1917), pp. 10–19.
18. J. O. P. Bland, *Recent Events . . .*, *op. cit.*, pp. 53–54.
19. *Ibid.*, p. 170.
20. Paul S. Reinsch, *An American Diplomat in China* (New York: Doubleday, Page & Co., 1922), pp. 1–3.
21. *L'Asie Française*, No. 162 (issue of April–July, 1915), p. 76.

CHAPTER VIII: BETWEEN ANARCHY AND RECONQUEST, 1917–1928

1. Sir Meyrick Hewlett, *op. cit.*, pp. 188–9.
2. Paul S. Reinsch, *op. cit.*, pp. 106, 66–68, 83–84 and 87.
3. *Ibid.*, pp. 124–8 and 131.

4. Ssu-yü Teng and John K. Fairbank, *op. cit.*, pp. 240–5.

5. Georges Maspero, *op. cit.*, II, 133.

6. Paul S. Reinsch, *op. cit.*, pp. 361–2.

7. Tsi C. Wang, *The Youth Movement in China* (New York: New Republic, Inc., 1928), pp. 161–2.

8. John Dewey and Alice Chipman Dewey, *Letters from China and Japan* (New York: E. P. Dutton & Co., 1920), pp. 209–12.

9. Letter quoted in the *Weekly Review* (Shanghai) of November 1, 1924.

10. Sir Meyrick Hewlett, *op. cit.*, pp. 155–9.

11. *Ibid.*, pp. 163–4.

12. Paul Morand, article in *L'Intransigeant* of September 22, 1925.

13. *L'Asie Française*, No. 187, December 1920, p. 421.

14. Sir Meyrick Hewlett, *op. cit.*, pp. 125–7.

15. Jean Bouchot, *Scènes de la vie des Hutungs. Croquis des moeurs pékinoises* (Peking: Presses A. Nachbaur, 1922), pp. 95–99.

16. Paul S. Reinsch, *op. cit.*, pp. 347–9.

17. *The Times*, London, May 8, 1923.

18. Abel Bonnard, *En Chine (1920–1921)* (Paris: Arthème Fayard, 1924), pp. 28–32.

19. *La Politique de Pékin* (French weekly published in Peking), 12e année. No. 3, January 18, 1925, pp. 32–33.

20. Marshal Broomhall, *General Feng, "A Good Soldier of Jesus Christ"* (London: The China Inland Mission, 1923), pp. 66–68.

21. *Interview de Tchang Tso-lin*, article in *L'Illustration* (Paris) of December 31, 1927, p. 794.

22. Pan-tsui Tchen, *Souvenirs sur le Congrès du Parti communiste de Chine*, in *L'Internationale communiste*, 18e année, No. 9, September 1936, pp. 1192–7.

23. Conrad Brandt, Benjamin Schwartz and John K. Fairbank, *A Documentary History of Chinese Communism* (London: Allen & Unwin, and Cambridge, Mass: Harvard University Press, 1959), p. 70.

24. S. I. Hsiung, *The Life of Chiang Kai-shek* (London: Peter Davies, 1948), pp. 210–12.

25. Su-lien yin-mou wen sheng hui-pien (Documents concerning the Soviet Conspiration), Peking, Police Headquarters, 1928—Vol. III, pp. 14–21.

26. Anna Louise Strong, *China's Millions. The Revolutionary Struggles*

from 1927 to 1935 (New York: Knight Publishing Co., and London: Victor Gollancz, 1935), pp. 34–36.

27. Conrad Brandt, Benjamin Schwartz and John K. Fairbank, *op. cit.*, pp. 80–83.

28. Anna Louise Strong, *op. cit.*, pp. 92–94.

CHAPTER IX: VICTORIES OF THE KUOMINTANG
1928–1935

1. Sir Meyrick Hewlett, *op. cit.*, pp. 204–5.
2. *Ibid.*, pp. 222–3.
3. Ernest O. Hauser, *Shanghai: City for Sale* (New York: Harcourt, Brace and Company, 1940), pp. 257–66.
4. Hsieh Pingying, *Girl Rebel. The Autobiography of Hsieh Pingying*, translated by Adet and Anor Lin (New York: The John Day Co., 1940), pp. 115–20.
5. F. Leger, *Les influences occidentales dans la révolution de l'Orient*, 2 vols. (Paris: Plon, 1935), quoting William Martin in II, pp. 112–13.
6. Marc Chadourne, *La Chine* (Paris: Plon, 1931), pp. 159–63.
7. Emile Vandervelde, *A travers la révolution chinoise. Soviets et Kuomintang* (Paris: Alcan, 1931), quoting the letter of M. Nachbaur, pp. 199–200.
8. Article in *Revue Franco-Chinoise*, Paris, 1938 (1er et 2e trimestres).
9. Edgar Snow, *Red Star Over China* (New York: Random House, and London: Victor Gollancz, 1938), pp. 205–7.
10. G. Lischerong, S. J., *Les inondations du Fleuve Jaune*, article in *Chine, Ceylan, Madagascar. Missions des Jésuites français du Nord et de l'Est*, No. 106, June 1934, p. 34.
11. Edgar Snow, *op. cit.*, pp. 278–9.
12. Peter Fleming, *One's Company. A Journey to China* (London: Jonathan Cape, and New York: Charles Scribner's Sons, 1934), pp. 35–36 and 39.
13. *Ibid.*, pp. 225–7.
14. Edgar Snow, *op. cit.*, pp. 187–8.
15. Maurice Eymard (Father), *Les Communistes dans la mission de Chengtu*, article in *Bulletin de la Société des Missions Etrangères de Paris*, No. 173, May 1936, pp. 341–5.
16. Edgar Snow, *op. cit.*, pp. 192–4.

CHAPTER X: FROM MANCHUKUO TO THE "UNITED FRONT", 1931–1937

1. *Series of League of Nations Publications*, Geneva, VII. *Political*, 1932, VII, 12. *Appeal by the Chinese Government—Report of the Commission of Enquiry*, Chapter IV, p. 67.
2. *Ibid.*, pp. 67–8.
3. *Ibid.*, pp. 68–69.
4. *Ibid.*, pp. 69–70.
5. *Ibid.*, Chapter VI, Part III, pp. 107–10.
6. Peter Fleming, *op. cit.*, pp. 72–74.
7. *Ibid.*, pp. 129–31.
8. Ernest O. Hauser, *op. cit.*, pp. 191–6.
9. Andrée Viollis, articles cabled from China to *Le Petit Parisien* (December 23, 1931—March 13, 1932).
10. Same source.
11. James M. Bertram, *Crisis in China. The Story of the Sian Mutiny* (London: Macmillan and Co., 1937), pp. 14–15.
12. *Ibid.*, pp. 128–131.
13. General and Madame Chiang Kai-shek, *General Chiang Kai-Shek* (New York: Doubleday, Doran & Co., 1937), pp. 123–5.
14. James M. Bertram, *op. cit.*, pp. 133–7.
15. General and Madame Chiang Kai-shek, *op. cit.*, pp. 138–31.

CHAPTER XI: THE SINO-JAPANESE WAR, 1937–1945

1. Edward Carter, *Attitude des Chinois à la veille de la Guerre sino-japonaise*, article in *L'Asie Française*, No. 355, December 1937, pp. 324–5.
2. Jacques Guillermaz, *Unpublished Manuscript*.
3. Ernest O. Hauser, *op. cit.*, pp. 316–18.
4. *North China Daily News*, issue of December 4, 1937. Also quoted in Shuhsi Hsu, *Japan and Shanghai* (Shanghai: Kelly & Walsh, 1938), pp. 76–77, 73 and 78.
5. Quoted in Harold John Timperley, *What War Means* (London: Victor Gollancz, 1938), pp. 25–29 and 47.

6. *Ibid.*, pp. 85–86.

7. *Ibid.*, p. 78.

8. *Ibid.*, pp. 87–88. H. J. Timperley, British correspondent in China, published eyewitness accounts in his aforementioned book.

9. Jean Raynaud, *Guerre en Asie* (Dinard, France: Editions Braun et Loirit, 1939).

10. Article entitled, *Onze mois d'occupation japonaise*, in *Bulletin de la Société des Missions Etrangères de Paris*, No. 232, April 1941, p. 228.

11. John Leighton Stuart, *Fifty Years in China. The Memoirs of John Leighton Stuart, Missionary and Ambassador* (New York: Random House, 1954), pp. 126–8.

12. Wei Tao-Ming (Mme.), *My Revolutionary Years. The Autobiography of Madame Wei Tao-Ming* (New York: Charles Scribner's Sons, 1943), pp. 213–15.

13. Testis, *Chungking sous le bombardement, les 3 et 4 mai 1939*, in *Bulletin de la Société des Missions Etrangères de Paris*, No. 211, July 1939, pp. 453–9.

14. Hollington K. Tong, *Dateline: China. The Beginning of China's Press Relations with the World* (New York: Rockport Press, 1950), pp. 113–14.

15. Quoted in Harrison Forman, *Report from Red China* (New York: Henry Holt & Co., 1945), pp. 161–2.

16. Theodore H. White and Annalee Jacoby, *Thunder Out of China* (New York: William Sloane Associates, 1946), pp. 75–76.

17. Robert Payne, *Chungking Diary* (London: Wm. Heinemann, 1945), pp. 44–47.

18. Joseph W. Stilwell, *The Stilwell Papers*, arranged and edited by Theodore H. White (New York: William Sloane Associates, and London: Macdonald & Co., 1948), pp. 52 and 65–69.

19. Theodore H. White and Annalee Jacoby, *op. cit.*, pp. 159–63.

20. Lin Yutang, *The Vigil of a Nation* (New York: The John Day Co., 1945), pp. 40–41.

21. *The Stilwell Papers*, *op. cit.*, p. 197.

22. *Ibid.*, p. 80.

23. *Ibid.*, p. 316.

24. Theodore H. White and Annalee Jacoby, *op. cit.*, pp. 186–8.

25. General Albert C. Wedemeyer, *Wedemeyer Reports!* (New York: Henry Holt & Co., 1958), pp. 321–3.

CHAPTER XII: RED CHINA, 1935–1945

1. Quoted in Robert Payne, *Journey to Red China* (London: Wm. Heinemann, 1947), pp. 90–91.
2. Conrad Brandt, Benjamin Schwartz and John K. Fairbank, *op. cit.*, pp. 297–9.
3. James Bertram, *North China Front* (London: Macmillan & Co., 1939), p. 145.
4. Agnes Smedley, *China Fights Back. An American Woman With the Eighth Route Army* (New York: The Vanguard Press, 1938), p. 8.
5. James Bertram, *op. cit.*, pp. 274–6.
6. James Bertram, *Crisis in China*, *op. cit.*, pp. 193–5.
7. James Bertram, *North China Front*, *op. cit.*, pp. 187–9.
8. *Ibid.*, pp. 215–16.
9. Edgar Snow, *op. cit.*, pp. 216–18.
10. Raymond J. De Jaegher and Irene Corbally Kuhn, *The Enemy Within* (New York: Doubleday & Co., 1952), pp. 87–91.
11. Edgar Snow, *op. cit.*, p. 219.
12. *Ibid.*, pp. 231–2.
13. *Ibid.*, pp. 100–3.
14. Agnes Smedley, *op. cit.*, pp. 27–30.
15. Edgar Snow, *op. cit.*, pp. 256–60.
16. James Bertram, *Unconquered. Journal of a Year's Adventures Among the Fighting Peasants of North China* (New York: The John Day Co., 1939), pp. 95–96.
17. Edgar Snow, *op. cit.*, pp. 281–6.
18. *Ibid.*, pp. 68–71.
19. James Bertram, *North China Front*, *op. cit.*, pp. 180–1.
20. *Ibid.*, pp. 239–40.
21. James Bertram, *Unconquered*, *op. cit.*, pp. 118–19.
22. *Ibid.*, pp. 163–4.
23. Agnes Smedley, *op. cit.*, pp. xv–xvi (Foreword) and 123–6.
24. *Ibid.*, pp. 129–30.
25. *Ibid.*, pp. 164–7.
26. Harrison Forman, *op. cit.*, pp. 139–42.
27. Robert Payne, *Journey to Red China*, *op. cit.*, pp. 183–6.

CHAPTER XIII: THE COLLAPSE OF THE KUOMINTANG, 1945–1949

1. Quoted in Harrison Forman, *op. cit.*, pp. 182–5.
2. Edgar Snow, *op. cit.*, p. 104.
3. Theodore H. White and Annalee Jacoby, *op. cit.*, p. 253
4. Robert Payne, *Journey to Red China*, *op. cit.*, pp. 173–4.
5. Theodore H. White and Annalee Jacoby, *op. cit.*, p. 279.
6. George Moorad, *Lost Peace in China* (New York: E. P. Dutton & Co., 1949), pp. 158–62.
7. Stuart Gelder, *The Chinese Communists* (London: Victor Gollancz, 1946), pp. xx–xxi.
8. Jack Belden, *China Shakes the World* (New York: Harper & Bros., 1949), pp. 164–6.
9. *Ibid.*, pp. 300–2.
10. *Ibid.*, p. 307.
11. George Moorad, *op. cit.*, pp. 221–2.
12. Theodore H. White and Annalee Jacoby, *op. cit.*, pp. 293–5.
13. Jack Belden, *op. cit.*, pp. 223–5.
14. *Ibid.*, pp. 233–5.
15. Quoted in *ibid.*, p. 322.
16. *Ibid.*, pp. 335–8.
17. *Rapport du Général Barr*, article in *Notes et Etudes documentaires*, No. 1,227 (Paris: Secrétariat général du Gouvernement, Direction de la Documentation), pp. 10 ff.
18. Jack Belden, *op. cit.*, pp. 415–17.
19. Quoted in L. M. Chassin (Général), *La Conquête de la Chine par Mao tse-tong* (Paris: Payot, 1952), pp. 170–1.
20. Jack Belden, *op. cit.*, pp. 383–4.
21. Derk Bodde, *Peking Diary. A Year of Revolution* (New York: Henry Schuman, 1950), pp. 23–24.
22. Jack Belden, *op. cit.*, p. 20.
23. Derk Bodde, *op. cit.*, pp. 42–43.
24. John Leighton Stuart, *op. cit*, pp. 242–3.
25. Derk Bodde, *op. cit.*, pp. 78–80, 85, 87, 91–92 and 96–99.
26. *Ibid.*, pp. 100–1.
27. *Ibid.*, pp. 102–4.
28. *Ibid.*, pp. 157–8.

ACKNOWLEDGMENTS

THE PUBLISHERS would like to thank the following authors, publishers and agents for permission to reprint copyright material in this book:

Abelard-Schuman Ltd. for *Peking Diary: A Year of Revolution* by Derk Bodde, copyright 1950.

Félix Alcan for *L'Expédition de Chine de 1857-8* by Henri Cordier, 1905; *La Chine Nouvelle, La Chine et le Mouvement Constitutionnel*, and *Le Céleste Empire avant la Révolution* by Jean Rodes, 1910, 1913 and 1914 respectively; *A travers la Révolution Chinoise, Soviets et Kuomintang* by Emile Vandervelde, 1931.

George Allen & Unwin Ltd. for *The Opium War through Chinese Eyes* by Arthur Waley, 1958.

L'Asie Française for extracts from issues of April-July 1915, December 1920 and December 1937.

Librairie Berger-Levrault for *Le Siège de Tien-tsin: 15 Juin-15 Juillet, 1900*, by A. Doualas, 1903.

Mr. James Bertram for *Crisis in China: The Story of Sian Mutiny*, 1937, and *North China Front*, 1939; Mr. James Bertram and The John Day Company, Inc., for *Unconquered*, copyright 1939 by James Bertram.

William Blackwood & Sons Ltd. for *The Englishman in China During the Victorian Era*, Vol. II, by Alexander Michie, 1900.

Jonathan Cape Ltd. and Charles Scribner's Sons for *One's Company* by Peter Fleming, copyright 1934 by Peter Fleming.

Chatto & Windus Ltd. for *A Chinaman's Opinion of Us and of His Own Country* by Hwuy-Ung, translated by J. A. Makepeace, 1927.

Constable & Co. Ltd. for *Memoirs of the Viceroy Li Hung-Chang* by John W. Foster, 1913; *Li Hung-Chang* by J. O. P. Bland, 1917.

Curtis Brown Ltd. for *China's Millions* by Anna Louise Strong, 1935.

The John Day Company, Inc. for *Girl Rebel: The Autobiography of Hsieh Pingying* by Adet and Anor Lin, copyright 1940 by The John Day Company.

The New Republic, Washington, D.C., for *The Youth Movement in China* by Tsi C. Wang, copyright 1928.

Mr. Robert Payne and William Heinemann Ltd. for *Chungking Diary*, copyright 1945 by Robert Payne, and *Journey to Red China*, copyright 1947 by Robert Payne.

Editions Payot for *La Conquête de la Chine par Mao tse-tong* by Général L. M. Chassin, 1952.

Olivier Perrin & Cie. for *La Chine en Révolution* by Edmond Rottach, 1914.

Librairie Plon for *La Chine* by Marc Chadourne, 1931; *Les Influences Occidentales dans la Révolution de l'Orient* by F. Leger, 1935; *L'Expédition de Chine de 1860, Souvenirs du Général Cousin de Montauban, Comte de Palikao*, by Cousin de Montauban, 1932.

Editions Plon-Nourrit for *A travers la Révolution Chinoise* by F. Farjenal, 1914; *Opinions Chinoises sur les Barbares d'Occident* by Commandant Harfeld, 1909; *Scènes de la Vie Révolutionnaire en Chine, 1911–14* by Jean Rodes, 1917.

Random House, Inc. for *Fifty Years in China* by John Leighton Stuart, copyright 1954, by John Leighton Stuart.

Routledge & Kegan Paul Ltd. for *Sidelights on Chinese Life* by the Rev. J. Macgowan, 1907.

John Schaffner for *The Enemy Within* by Raymond De Jaegher and Irene Kuhn, copyright 1950.

William Sloane Associates for *Thunder out of China* by Theodore H. White and Annalee Jacoby, copyright 1946 by William Sloane Associates, Inc.; William Sloane Associates and Laurence Pollinger Ltd. for *The Stilwell Papers* by Joseph W. Stilwell, copyright 1948 by Winifred A. Stilwell.

La Société des Missions Etrangères de Paris for extracts from their *Bulletin*, 1936, 1939, 1941.

The Times Publishing Co. Ltd. for an article from *The Times*, May 8, 1923.

The Executors of H. J. Timperley, and Victor Gollancz Ltd., for *What War Means* by Harold John Timperley, 1938.

The Vanguard Press, Inc. for *China Fights Back* by Agnes Smedley, copyright 1938 by The Vanguard Press, Inc.

Willis Kingsley Wing for *Report from Red China* by Harrison Forman, copyright 1945 by Henry Holt & Company, Inc.

The Publishers were unable to contact the copyright owners in the following works for permission to use extracts from them, but they would like to acknowledge these works, as follows:

J. O. P. Bland: *Annals and Memoirs of the Court of Peking*, published 1914 by William Heinemann Ltd., London, and Houghton Mifflin Company, Boston, Mass.

J. O. P. Bland: *Recent Events and Present Policies in China*, published 1912 by William Heinemann Ltd., London, and Houghton Mifflin Company, Boston, Mass.

J. O. P. Bland and E. Backhouse: *China under the Empress Dowager*, published 1910 by William Heinemann Ltd., London, and Houghton Mifflin Company, Boston, Mass.

Marshal Broomhall: *General Feng, "A Good Soldier of the Lord"*, published 1923 by the China Inland Mission, London.

Hollington Kong Tong: *Dateline: China*, published 1950 by Rockport Press, N.Y.

George Moorad: *Lost Peace in China*, published 1949 by E. P. Dutton & Co., Inc.

George Ernest Morrison: *An Australian in China*, published 1895 by Horace Cox, London.

Timothy Richard: *Forty-Five Years in China*, published 1916 by T. Fisher Unwin, London.

Wei Tao-Ming: *My Revolutionary Years*, published 1943 by Charles Scribner's Sons, New York.

INDEX OF SOURCES

(Book titles are here given in shortened form. Full references will be found in the Notes on pp. 505–18.)

Anthouard, Baron d': *Les Boxeurs*, 217
Asie Française, L', 259, 283, 367

Backhouse, E. and Bland, J. O. P.: *Annals and Memoirs*, 155, 163, 224; *Recent Events in China*, 238, 255
Barrow, John: *Travels in China*, 28
Bazancourt, Baron de: *Les expéditions de Chine*, 130
Belden, Jack: *China Shakes the World*, 466, 473n, 477, 487, 490, 493
Beresford, Lord Charles: *The Break-up of China*, 186
Bertram, James: *Crisis in China*, 359, 363, 418; *North China Front*, 415, 417, 420, 442; *Unconquered*, 436, 444, 450n
Bland, J. O. P.: *Li-Hung Chang*, 154
Bland, J. O. P. and Backhouse, E.: *China under the Empress Dowager*, 145, 157, 210, 220
Bodde, Derk: *Peking Diary*, 491, 494, 497
Bonnard, Abel: *En Chine*, 290
Bouchot, Jean: *Scénes de la vie des Hutungs*, 286
Brandt, Conrad, Schwartz, Benjamin and Fairbank, J. K.: *Documentary History of Chinese Communism*, 301, 306
Broomhall, Marshal: *General Feng*, 293
Brouillon, Rev. Père: *Mémoire sur l'état actuel de la mission*, 112
Bulletin de la Société des Missions Etrangères de Paris, 336, 385, 389

Callery et Yvan: *L'insurrection en Chine*, 94, 98, 108
Chadbourne, Marc: *La Chine*, 322
Chassin, Général L. M.: *La Conquête de la Chine*, 489
Chen, Gideon: *Tso Tsung T'ang*, 185
Chiang Kai-shek, General and Madame: *General Chiang Kai-shek*, 362, 365

Chine et Ceylan, 216
Cordier, Henri: *L'expédition de Chine*, 128

Davis, John Francis: *The Chinese*, 35
De Jaegher, R. J. and Kuhn, Irene: *The Enemy Within*, 423
Der Ling, Princess: *Two Years in the Forbidden City*, 235
Dewey, John and Alice: *Letters from China and Japan*, 275
Douglas, A.: *Le Siège de Tien-tsin*, 222
Downing, Dr. C. Toogood: *The Stranger in China*, 41, 52n

Ellis, Henry: *Journal of the Proceedings of the Late Embassy*, 32
Enselme, H.: *A travers la Mandchourie*, 200

Farjenel, F.: *A travers la révolution chinoise*, 250
Fleming, Peter: *One's Company*, 329, 351
Forman, Harrison: *Report from Red China*, 393, 451, 457
Foster, John W.: *Memoirs of Li Hung-chang*, 183
France: Foreign Ministry: *Documents diplomatiques*, 198

Gelder, Stuart: *The Chinese Communists*, 464
Guillermaz, Jacques: *Unpublished MS*, 368

Hamberg, Thedore: *The Visions of Hung Siu-Tschuen*, 95
Harfeld, Commandant: *Opinions chinoises*, 218
Hauser, E. O.: *Shanghai: City for Sale*, 314, 370
Hérisson, Comte d': *Journal d'un interprète*, 137, 142
Hewlett, Sir Meyrick: *Forty Years in China*, 248, 261, 279, 284, 311
Hsiung, S. I.: *Life of Chiang Kai-shek*, 303
Hsu, Shuhsi: *Japan and Shanghai*, 372
Huc, Father M.: *L'empire chinois*, 40, 43, 49
Huebner, Baron de: *Promenade autour du monde*, 175
Hunter, William C.: *Bits of Old China*, 50; *The "Fan Kwae" at Canton*, 37, 55, 62
Hwuy-Ung: *A Chinaman's Opinion*, 44, 212

Illustration, L', 295
Intransigeant, L', 282

Jametel, Maurice: *Pékin*, 166, 171

Jocelyn, Lord: *Six Months with the Chinese Expedition*, 72, 77

Knollys, Henry: *Incidents in the China War*, 148

League of Nations Publications (Lytton Report), 343
Lecomte, Capitaine: *Guet-apens de Bac-Lé*, 188
Leger, F.: *Les influences occidentales*, 321
Linebarger, Paul: *The Gospel of Chung Shan*, 243
Little, Mrs. Archibald: *Intimate China*, 207

Macgowan, Rev. J.: *Sidelights on Chinese Life*, 46, 59
Marolles, Commandant de: *Souvenirs de la révolte des T'ai P'ing*, 152
Maspero, Georges: *La Chine*, 54, 86, 126, 136
Meadows, Thomas: *The Chinese and their Rebellions*, 88, 97, 102
Mercier, Rev. Père: *Campagne du Cassini*, 117
Michie, Alexander: *The Englishman in China*, 174
Missions Catholiques, Les, 199, 216
Moges, Marquis de: *Souvenirs d'une ambassade*, 131
Montauban, Général Cousin de: *L'expédition de Chine*, 140
Moorad, George: *Lost Peace in China*, 462, 472
Morrison, George Ernest: *An Australian in China*, 172
Moule, Arthur Evans: *Half a Century in China*, 109, 232

Notes et Etudes documentaires, 485

Oliphant, Laurence: *Narrative of the Earl of Elgin's Mission*, 132, 136, 150
Ouchterlony, Lieut. John: *The Chinese War*, 75, 78, 84

Pan-tsui Chen: *Souvenirs sur le Congrès*, 298
Payne, Robert: *Chungking Diary*, 395; *Journey to Red China*, 454, 461
Peking: Police H.Q.: *Documents*, 303
Pellier, A.: *L'Europe et la Chine*, 190
Petit Parisien, Le, 356
Pingying, Hsieh: *Girl Rebel*, 318
Plauchut, Edmond: *Le Tour du monde*, 124
Politique de Pékin, La, 291

Raynaud, Jean: *Guerre en Asie*, 383

Reinsch, Paul S.: *An American Diplomat in China*, 257, 263, 272, 276, 287

Revue des Deux Mondes, 39

Revue Franco-Chinoise, 324

Richard, Rev. Timothy: *Forty-five Years in China*, 128n, 175n, 179, 203

Rodes, Jean: *La Chine et le mouvement constitutionnel*, 231; *La Chine nouvelle*, 245; *Le Céleste Empire*, 233; *Scènes de la vie révolutionnaire*, 252

Rottach, Edmond: *La Chine en révolution*, 249, 251

Smedley, Agnes: *China Fights Back*, 416, 430, 446; *The Great Road*, 230

Snow, Edgar: *Red Star over China*, 325, 328, 334, 338, 421, 425, 432, 437, 459

Ssu-yü Teng and Fairbank, J. K.: *China's Response to the West*, 123, 159, 196, 204, 219, 242, 268

Staunton, Sir George: *Observations on our China Policy*, 70

Stilwell, General J. W.: *The Stilwell Papers*, 397, 404

Strong, Anna L.: *China's Millions*, 305, 308

Stuart, John Leighton: *Fifty Years in China*, 386, 495

Sun Yat-sen: *Kidnapped in London*, 239

Taylor, Charles: *Five Years in China*, 31, 41, 92, 105

Times, The, 288

Timperley, Harold John: *What War Means*, 374

Tong, Hollington K.: *Dateline: China*, 391

Vandervelde, Emile: *A travers la révolution chinoise*, 323

Vigneron, Abbé L.: *Deux ans au Se-Tchouan*, 169

Waley, Arthur: *The Opium War*, 67, 76, 81

Wang, Tsi C.: *The Youth Movement in China*, 274

Weale, B. L. Putnam: *Indiscreet Letters from Peking*, 227

Wedemeyer, General Albert C.: *Wedemeyer Reports!*, 410

Weekly Review (Shanghai), The, 277

Wei Tao-Ming, Madame: *My Revolutionary Years*, 388

White, Theodore H. and Jacoby, Annalee: *Thunder Out of China*, 394, 400, 407, 460, 462

Wilson, Andrew: *The "Ever-Victorious Army"*, 155

Yutang, Lin: *The Vigil of a Nation*, 402

GENERAL INDEX

Aigun, Treaty of, 135, 150n
American attitude to, and action in, China, 34–35, 85–86, 114–16, 135, 198, 229, 263–5, 272–3, 313n, 374, 382, 397, 400–2, 411, 461–2, 474–6, 479, 491–3; relations with Japan, 193, 379, 395, 409, 411–12
Amherst, Lord, 32–34, 52, 70
Amoy, 84, 86, 279–81; see also Treaty Ports
Anhwei Incident (1941), 392–5
Anhwei province, 92, 393
Annam, 188, 192
Anti-Opium League, British, 70
Anyang County (Honan), 477–81
"Arrow" Incident (1856), 128

Bac-le, 188–90
Barr, General, 485
Bates, Dr. M. Searle, 374
Belgium, 85, 313
Beresford, Lord Charles, 186, 198
Borodin, Michael, 282, 302, 304–6
Boxer movement, 215–29 passim, 230, 237, 272, 275, 277, 424–5
British attitude to, and action in, China, 28, 32, 34, 52–53, Chap. II passim, 110, 121, Chap. IV passim, 186–7, 198–200, 220, 259, 263, 267, 271, 273, 278–82, 294n, 312, 313n, 382, 461, 473–4; relations with Japan, 193, 358, 379, 388n.
British East India Company, 28, 52, 58, 63, 71
Burlingame, Anson, 183
Burma, 187, 397–400, 409–11
Burma Road, 397, 400

Canton, 27, 28, 34–43, 50–51, 75, 86, 89, 92, 98–100, 110, 122, 127, 190, 199–200, 231–2, 233–4, 250, 262, 278, 281, 302, 304, 310, 354, 393n, 473; and opium trade, 55–66; and Treaty of Nanking, 84; and "Arrow" Incident, 128; occupied by British (1858), 130–6; secedes from Peking under Sun Yat-sen, 271; falls to Japanese, 386
Carl, Miss C. A., 235–6
Chahar province, 359
Chang Chih-tung, 205–7, 235, 238
Changchun, 351, 475–6, 485, 487–8
Chang Hsueh-liang, 311, 318, 346, 434; captures Chiang Kai-shek, 359–65
Chang Hsün, 271
Changsha, 103, 306–7; defeat of Japanese at, 395–7
Chang Tso-lin, 263, 283n, 290–1, 311, 359n; occupies Peking (1926), 295–8
Chapdeleine, Father, 128–30
Chapoo, 79–81
Chekiang province, 497
Chengtu, 284–5
Chen Li-fu, 404
Chennault, General Claire, 401n, 411
Ch'en Tu-hsiu, 268–70, 298
Chiang Kai-shek, 271n, 302–4, 309n, 311, 313n, 321, 324, 328–35, 341, 358, 367n, 370, 381–3, 388–9, 397–400, 404–6, 409–12, 429, 436n, 440, 443, 444, 456–98 passim, 502n, 503; becomes C.-in-C. Kuomintang forces, 304; sets up government at Nanking, 310; captured by "Young

Chiang Kai-shek—*contd.*
Marshal", 359; released, 366; and Anhwei Incident, 393–4; retires (1949), 497
Chiang Kai-shek, Madame, 310, 318, 321, 324–5, 360, 366, 388–9, 405, 497*n*
Ch'ien Lung, Emperor, 28–31, 94–95
Chihli clan, 263, 290–1
Ching-kiang, 81–84
Chi-shan, 75
Chi'i-ying, 86–87
Chou En-lai, 302, 322*n*, 306, 394, 443, 457
Chuan-pi Convention (1841), 75
Chuen-pi, "battle" of, 69
Ch'un, Prince, 247
Chungking, 169–70, 389–92, 397, 403, 464–5; becomes wartime capital, 381
Chusan island, 72, 74, 77
Chu Shih-yün, 81–84
Chu Teh, 230–1, 328, 445, 462, 501, 503*n*
Clemenceau, Georges, 190, 254, 257
Communists, Chinese, 282, 298–310, 321, 327–41, 358–60, 366, 392–5, 412, Chaps. XII and XIII *passim*
Coolie traffic, 124–7
Courbet, Admiral, 190–2
Cuba, 124, 126–7
Cushing, Caleb, 85, 86*n*

Dairen (Dalny), 200–2, 209, 463
Dewey, John, 268, 275–6
Dutch East Indies, 27–28, 281
Dutch East Indies Company, 30
Dutch trade with China, 27–28, 37*n*; treaty with Japan, 193

Elgin, Lord, 130, 134–6, 148–9; and the burning of the Summer Palace, 141, 145, 192
Elliot, Captain Charles, 66–68
"Ever Victorious Army", The, 152, 154–5, 380

Feng Kuei-fen, 159–61
Feng Kuo-chang, 271
Feng-tien clan, 263
Feng Yu-hsiang, 292–4, 311–12, 434
Fontanier, M., 176–8
Foochow, 84, 86, 122, 190–1; *see also* Treaty Ports
Formosa, *see* Taiwan
French attitude to, and action in, China, 85, 117–18, 121, Chap. IV *passim*, 175–9, 187–92, 197, 259, 313*n*
Fukien province, 327
Fung Hien-san, 101, 104

Galen (General Blücher), 282, 302*n*
Germany, 197, 229, 265–6, 270–1, 381
Gladstone, W. E., 70
Gordon, General Charles G., 154–5, 380
Grant, General Sir Hope, 141, 144, 148–9
Gros, Baron, 130, 135–6, 145, 148

Hainan island, 414, 473
Han dynasty, 101
Hankow, 304*n*, 305–7, 383–4, 386, 389, 393*n*; and revolution of 1911, 248, 254
Hanoi, 245–7
Harding, President, 278
Hart, Sir Robert, 183, 191–2
Hay, John, 198
Hengyang, 406–9
Hiang Tsiu-tsing, 100, 109
Hirobumi, Count Ito, 196
Honan province, 92, 406, 414, 477–81
Hong Kong, 41, 68, 124, 130, 167, 199–200, 231–2, 278, 281–2, 503; ceded to Britain, 85
Hong merchants, Canton, 35–36, 38, 50–51, 58, 66–67
Hopei province, 359, 370, 451–4, 469–72
Houqua, 50, 63–64, 67
Ho Ying-chin, 404, 483

Hsien Feng, Emperor, 90, 91, 108–9, 135–6, 140, 145–8, 157, 162
Hsin Ch'ao movement, 277
Hsingking, see Changchun
Hsuan T'ung, Emperor ("Henry P'u-I"), 247, 256, 271, 347, 429
Hsueh Yueh, 407
Hsü Shih-ch'ang, 275–6, 292–3
Huai, River, 326
Huang Ho, see Yellow River
Huc, Father M., 40
Hunan province, 263, 306–8, 310, 327, 329, 414
Hung Hsiu-ch'üan, 92–97, 100, 104, 107–8, 112–13, 116, 119–21, 152n, 155–7; founds T'ai P'ing movement, 92; proclaims himself Emperor, 112; commits suicide, 157
Hurley, General Patrick J., 460–1, 474
Hu Shih, 268, 322

I-ching, 76–78
I-ho-ch'üan, see Boxer movement
India, 28, 52, 71–72, 294n
Indo-China, 187, 294, 400n
Italy, 198–9, 313

Japan, 183, 187, 193–7, 199, 209, 229, 237–9, 258–9, 263–7, 269, 272–9, 295, 311–12, 333, 341, Chaps. X and XI passim, 414–17, 421, 444–56, 461–4, 466–8, 473, 477; 1895 war with China, 194; defeat of Russia (1905), 237; 1915 ultimatum to China, 267; occupation of Manchuria, 343; withdrawal from League of Nations, 351; general offensive of 1937, 368; capture of Nanking, 381; attack on Pearl Harbor, 387; surrender to China and Allies, 412
Jeunesse, La, 268, 298
Joffe, Abram A., 261, 301
Jung-lu, 207, 211, 220–2, 225, 235n

Kanagawa, Treaty of, 193
K'ang Yu-wei, 204, 207–10, 211n, 244–5, 247

Kansu province, 338–40
Kiangsi province, 310, 327–34, 340; Chinese Soviet Republic proclaimed, 328
Kiaochow, 197
Korea, 183, 194, 237, 294, 342n, 343, 349–50
Kowloon, 199
Kuang Hsü, Emperor, 162, 207–11, 220–1
K'ung, H. H., 310, 404
Kung, Prince, 148–9, 165, 174, 179, 207–8
Kunming, 400–2
Kwangchow, 197, 200
Kwangsi province, 92–3, 95, 106, 385, 414
Kwangtung province, 64, 90–91, 94, 414, 473; see also Canton
Kungch'antang, 302, 304, 310, 366, 457, 477; see also Communists
Kuomintang (Nationalists), 257, 258, 260, 271n, 277n, 282, 301–10, 311, 314, 321–33, 334n, 336, 341, 358, 366, 386, 388n, 391, 393–5, 404–6, 409, 412, 414–15, 419n, 420, 429n, 433–7, 444, 455, Chap. XIII passim

Lanchow, 185–6
Langson, 188, 190–1
Lansing-Ishii Agreement (1917), 272
League of Nations, 343, 351, 358, 374
Ledo, 400, 411
Liang Ch'i-ch'ao, 204–5, 211n, 244, 258
Liaotung Peninsula, 197, 200, 237
Li Hsiu-ch'eng, 155
Li Hung-chang, 154–5, 182–6, 194, 196–7, 235n
Li Lien-ying, 163
Li Li-san, 328
Li Man-tsin, 299–300
Linebarger, Paul, 243–5
Lin Piao, 428, 447–8, 485, 487
Lin Tse-hsü, 55, 64–69, 75
Li Ta-chao, 298
Li Tsung-jen, 483, 497

"Little Knife" society, 114
Li Yuan-hung, 248, 254, 260
Lloyd George, David, 271
"Long March, The", 334–6, 338–40, 394n, 413, 419, 440n, 459
Lu-hsiun, 268
Lukouchiao, 368, 370, 436–7, 443
Lytton, Lord, 343
Lytton Report, 342–52

Macao, 27, 38–40, 43, 56, 58, 62, 66, 68–69, 72, 124
Macartney, Lord, 28–30, 32, 94n, 182
Malinovsky, Marshal, 462
Manchu dynasty, 72n, 80, 88, 90–92, 97, 101, 108, 109, 121, 150, 157, 162–5, 192, 197, 215, 222, 239, 242–3, 244, 246–7, 254–6, 270
Manchuria (Manchukuo), 200, 229, 237, 263, 283n, 295, 297, 311, 333, 342–60, 367, 386, 412, 414, 455, 461–4, 475–6, 485–8, 490–1
Mandarins, 47–50, 51, 56–58, 62–65, 73, 89, 97–100, 105, 114–15, 124, 162, 174, 176–9, 215, 246, 260
Mao Tse-tung, 298–9, 306–8, 335n, 340, 413–16, 419–20, 423, 428, 440–4, 445n, 460, 481–2, 497, 499, 501–2, 503n, 504; appointed Chairman of Provisional Government in Kiangsi, 328; Chairman of Chinese Communist Party, 413
Marshall, General G. C., 474–7
May Fourth movement, 274–7
Merrill, Major General Frank, 411
Miao-tze aborigines, 76–77, 92–95, 100
Ming dynasty, 99, 114, 242, 368
Mongolia, 267, 294n, 414
Montauban, Général Cousin de, 137–44
Mountbatten, Admiral Lord Louis, 409
Mukden, 297, 343–7, 351n, 353, 462–4, 485–6
Mutsuhito, Emperor, 194

Nakamura, Captain, 343
Nanchang, 330–2

Nanking, 85, 107, 109, 112–14, 117–20, 127, 155–7, 250–1, 254, 256, 271n, 309–10, 311–13, 348n, 374–9, 381, 389, 412, 462, 495–6; besieged by British, 84; captured by T'ai P'ings, 108; by imperial armies, 157; falls to revolutionaries, 250; captured by Yuan Shih-k'ai, 258; by Nationalists, 309; by Japanese, 374; by Communists, 503
Nanking, Treaty of (1842), 84–85, 88, 127
Napier, Lord, 58, 61
Nationalists, see Kuomintang
Ngan-fu clan, 263, 290
Ningpo, 78–79, 84, 86, 89, 109–10, 112; see also Treaty Ports

Opium trade, 51–53, 54–68 passim, 70–71, 85, 123, 151, 260
Opium War, 53, 54, 69–84, 89, 121, 123n

Palikao, battle of, 137–40
Palmerston, Lord, 69–72, 122, 128
Pearl Harbor, 387, 395
Peking (Peiping), 28–34, 102–4, 108–9, 135, 137, 215, 217–22, 251–4, 256–60, 271, 274–6, 286–7, 290–1, 295–8, 311, 348, 368–70, 462, 494, 497–503; falls to Anglo-French force, 140; sack of Summer Palace, 140–9; Boxer atrocities in, 224–9; May Fourth demonstration, 274; captured by Japanese, 368; by Communists, 501
Peking Gazette, 78, 103, 108
Peking, Treaties of (1860), 148–9, 150n, 162, 174
P'eng Teh-huai, 328–9, 434–5, 450–1
Perry, Commodore Matthew C., 193
Pescadores, 27, 191, 194
Pichon, M., 198–9, 225–7
"Pidgin English", 41
Pihkwei, 134–5, 136
Port Arthur, 197, 209, 237, 294n
Portsmouth, Treaty of (1905), 237

Portuguese, 27–28, 34, 68, 124

P'u-I, Henry, see Hsuan T'ung

Roosevelt, President Franklin, 442, 460

Roosevelt, President Theodore, 237

Russian attitude, and action in China, 85, 135, 149–50, 185–7, 197, 200–2, 229, 259, 261, 267, 282, 293, 295, 298–305, 382, 412, 461–4, 466, 491–2; relations with Japan, 193, 237

Seymour, Admiral, 220

Shanghai, 72, 84, 86, 105, 107, 110, 111, 114–16, 122, 127, 128n, 135, 149, 152, 161n, 166–9, 185, 231, 233, 250–1, 254, 277–82, 298–301, 307–10, 314–18, 342, 354–8, 462; "incident" of 1925, 278; captured by Nationalists, 309; "war" of 1932, 358; captured by Japanese, 370–4

Shansi province, 179–81, 359, 468

Shantung province, 92, 265–6, 278, 359, 383, 467–8

Shensi province, 334, 338–40, 359–66, 394n, 413n, 415–23, 425–32, 459, 468, 479n

Shimonoseki, Peace of, 183, 194

Shiozawa, Admiral, 357–8

Sian, 229, 234, 249n, 359–62, 365, 367, 430–2

Sino-Japanese War of 1894–5, 183, 194, 196–7

Sino-Japanese War of 1937–45, Chap. XI passim, 415, 419n, 440n, 443–56, 457, 459, 462–3

Smedley, Agnes, 419n, 430

Snow, Edgar, 443

Soochow, 155–6, 159, 382–3

Soong, Chung-ling, see Sun Yat-sen, Madame

Soong Meiling, see Chiang Kai-shek, Madame

Soong, T. V., 310, 312, 321, 366

Spain, 27, 124, 313

Staunton, Sir George, 29, 70

Stilwell, General Joseph W., 397–400, 409–11

Suiyuan province, 326, 359, 360

Summer Palace, Peking, 140–7, 161, 192, 211

Sungkiang, 380

Sun Ming-Chin, 361, 363–5

Sun Yat-sen, 239–48, 260, 261–2, 271–2, 301–2, 305, 312n, 386, 444, 458, 459n, 464, 503–4; kidnapped in London, 240–1; becomes President of United Provinces, 254; forced into exile, 258; dies, 302

Sun Yat-sen, Madame, 258n, 305, 310, 464–5

Sweden, 85, 175n

Szechuan province, 262–3, 284–5, 334–8, 366, 381

T'ai P'ing rebellion, 92–121 passim, 124, 150–7, 159, 233, 242, 249

Taiwan, 27, 191, 194, 294

Taku, 220, 224, 229

Tao Kuang, 57, 90–91

Tibet, 294n

Tientsin, 135–6, 149, 222–4, 229, 388n, 462; massacre of 1870, 175–9

Tientsin, Treaties of (1858), 135, 149; Convention of (1884), 188; Second Treaty of (1885), 192, 196

Togo, Admiral, 237

Tonkin, 187–8, 192

Treaty Ports, 84, 86, 110, 122, 127, 128n

"Triad" society, 89, 97, 114

Truman, President, 474, 493

Ts'ai Yuan-p'ei, 268

Tsao Ju-lin, 273–4

Tseng Kuo-fan, 121, 154–8, 161, 182–3

Tsinan, 311

Tsingtao, 265–6, 462

Tso Tsung-t'ang, 155, 185–6

Tuan Ch'i-jui, 263, 290

Tucker, Henry St. George, 71

Tzu Hsi, Empress Dowager, 157–8, 162–4, 183–4, 192, 194, 207, 211, 220–2, 224, 229, 234–7, 247, 249

Versailles, Treaty of, 272, 274, 301
Vladivostok, 149, 150n, 197n

Wang Ching-wei, 312, 386
Wanghsia, Treaty of (1844), 85
Ward, F. T., 152-4
Washington Conference, 278, 342
Wavell, Field-Marshal Lord, 399
Wedemeyer, General A. C., 409, 462
Weihaiwei, 197
Whampoa, 38, 57, 63
Whampoa, Treaty of (1844), 85, 128
Wilson, President, 265, 272-3, 275
Wo-jen, 161-2
World War I, 264, 269, 342
World War II, 313n, 387, 395, 397
Wuhan, 304-5, 310, 383
Wuhu, 107-8
Wu Pei-fu, 263, 291-3

Wu Te-chen, 356-8
Wu T'ing-fang, 254-5

Yang Hu-cheng, 359, 361
Yangtze river and valley, 101, 107, 109, 120-1, 149, 150, 155, 157, 187, 197, 198, 254, 304, 355, 374, 379, 385, 393, 466, 481, 503; in flood, 89, 326-7
Yeh, 134-5
Yellow River, 109, 416, 466, 488-9; in flood, 89, 326-7
Yenan, 394, 413n, 415-16, 431, 436-7, 451, 460-2, 479
Yuan Shih-k'ai, 186-7, 211, 235, 252-4, 256-60, 261, 265-7, 290n
Yung Wing, 161
Yunnan province, 260, 284-5, 400